Cryptography, Biometrics, and Anonymity in Cybersecurity Management

Mohammed Amin Almaiah
Department of Computer Science, The University of Jordan, Jordan

Said Salloum
School of Science, Engineering, and Environment, University of Salford, UK

IGI Global
Scientific Publishing
Publishing Tomorrow's Research Today

Vice President of Editorial	Melissa Wagner
Managing Editor of Acquisitions	Mikaela Felty
Managing Editor of Book Development	Jocelynn Hessler
Production Manager	Mike Brehm
Cover Design	Phillip Shickler

Published in the United States of America by
IGI Global Scientific Publishing
701 East Chocolate Avenue
Hershey, PA, 17033, USA
Tel: 717-533-8845
Fax: 717-533-7115
Website: https://www.igi-global.com E-mail: cust@igi-global.com

Library of Congress Cataloging-in-Publication Data

Names: Almaiah, Mohammed Amin, 1986- editor | Salloum, Said Abdelrahim, 1978- editor
Title: Cryptography, biometrics, and anonymity in cybersecurity management / edited by Mohammed Almaiah, Said Salloum.
Description: Hershey, PA : IGI Global, [2025] | Includes bibliographical references and index. | Summary: "The book aims to systematically cover all essential aspects of cybersecurity, with a focus on reporting on cybersecurity security issues and cybersecurity risk management as well as the latest research results, and real-world deployment of security countermeasures"-- Provided by publisher.
Identifiers: LCCN 2024048571 (print) | LCCN 2024048572 (ebook) | ISBN 9798369380147 h/c | ISBN 9798369380154 s/c | ISBN 9798369380161 ebook
Subjects: LCSH: Computer security--Management | Computer networks--Security measures--Management | Cryptography--Data processing | Biometry--Data processing | Data encryption (Computer science) | Data privacy
Classification: LCC QA76.9.A25 C847 2025 (print) | LCC QA76.9.A25 (ebook)
LC record available at https://lccn.loc.gov/2024048571
LC ebook record available at https://lccn.loc.gov/2024048572

British Cataloguing in Publication Data
A Cataloguing in Publication record for this book is available from the British Library.

Table of Contents

Detailed Table of Contents

The most widely used routing protocol for Internet of Things (IoT) networks with limited resources is the (RPL). Network security is a significant issue because of the exponential growth of Internet of Things (IoT) devices and their growing ubiquity in safety-critical settings like healthcare and industry. One possible remedy for threat identification in these networks is using intrusion detection systems (IDS) based on machine learning. To achieve this, a machine learning approach that uses Random Forest (RF), k-nearest Neighbor (KNN), Decision Tree (DT), XGBoost, and Support Vector Machine (SVM) models is presented. The proposed machine learning-based detection approach conducts mitigate feature and classification using the Sine Cosine Algorithm (SCA) with XGBoost to select the smallest number of relevant features, leading to the best solution with the highest accuracy. The proposed model achieves a high accuracy of 97% on the Decrease Rank and Version Number. Also, a high accuracy of 99% on the Hello Flooding.

The Dark Web, a hidden corner of the internet, poses a significant challenge to Law Enforcement Agencies (LEAs) due to its anonymous nature and encrypted networks. While it provides a secure platform for legitimate users, it also enables illicit activities such as cybercrime, drug trade, and terrorism. One major obstacle for LEAs is the practice of URL hopping, where Dark Web sites frequently change their URLs to evade detection. To address this issue, the authors propose a novel ensemble model that leverages machine learning techniques to analyze the content of Dark Web sites and correlate it with existing intelligence. Their system aims to improve the accuracy of tracing URL hopping on the Dark Web, ultimately enhancing the ability of LEAs to track and disrupt illicit activities. By bridging the gap between the Dark Web's anonymity and LEA's monitoring capabilities, their research contributes to a safer and more secure online environment.

Tuqa Al-Makkawi, Hashemite University, Jordan
Ayoub Alsarhan, Hashemite University, Jordan
Qais Al-Na'amneh, Applied Science Private University, Jordan
Mohammad Aljaidi, Zarqa University, Jordan
Mohammed Almaiah, University of Jordan, Jordan
Mahmoud AlJamal, Hashemite University, Jordan
Rabee Alqura'n, Hashemite University, Jordan
Mahmoud Aljawarneh, Applied Science Private University, Jordan

Nowadays, technology is propagation rapidly that it is virtually completely replacing the real world with a "virtual world." Electronic forensics important as medical forensics to investigate electronic crime" which increases with time", to prevent unwanted file recovery, many computer users choose to overwrite files instead of deleting them to collect evidence and analysis by several methods and tools to present in front of the law. This paper studies the collection and analysis of files with an emphasis on deleted files from different resources and evaluates the performance of open-source programs for recovering deleted data using unconventional ways. It discusses some forensics tools, including FTK, and Encase, and the ability to extract the deleted file, showing a general comparison between forensics tools.

domain. By outlining these areas, we pave the way for the development of more secure and robust RGB image encryption schemes utilizing DNA cryptography.

This technique for identifying malicious nodes is known by the inventor as the "KK approach." We compare the throughput and delay of the system with the proposed KK Approach, and the results are superior compared to the earlier techniques. Its abilities to learn, adapt, collaborate, and act independently make it a potent weapon in fighting against cyber threats. It is also capable of learning. However, additional research and development are required to overcome the limitations and challenges associated with its deployment. It is essential to continue investigating and financing state-of-the-art solutions in order to guarantee the security and privacy of these networks. This is because we rely more and more on gadgets connected to the IoT for our everyday needs.

This chapter aims to enhance the security of textual passwords by adding a new layer that involves an individual's typing rhythm without requiring additional devices. It discusses authentication methods and develops a textual password authentication system, which takes advantage of the fact that every user has a distinct way of typing. Twenty participants, including novice and expert users, assessed the proposed system. The measuring metrics used were the False Acceptance Rate (FAR) and False Rejection Rate (FRR). The flight time and typing rhythm were the biometric identification template. The results indicated low false rejection and acceptance rates, with the initial session registering 0.0 FRR and 0.1 FAR. Two weeks later, the second session recorded 0.25 FRR and 0.0 FAR. Using this model, users do not need to select a complex password they might forget. Instead, they can utilize a good rhythm different from their natural typing rhythm, making it challenging to guess.

This system represents a decentralized tweeting social media platform with the objective of furnishing users a communication environment that's both secure and characterized by transparency. Through the integration of smart contracts, users can transact directly and securely without the need for intermediaries. This initiative demonstrates the potential of integrating Blockchain and ReactJS to create a decentralized social media platform, enhancing security and transparency to unprecedented levels. This article aims to create a decentralized social media platform using Block chain which confirms that data is securely stored, immutable and transparent. Proposed system enables users to post tweets, follow other users, like and comment on posts and engage in real-time messaging. In this system a step-by-step approach to implement this secured Tweeting application is presented.

Nowadays, most Java- based applications use the log4j framework because it is a quick and framework which is dependable that is entirely written in programming language Java to have a log of all the information that takes place in the application. The Apache Software License, governs the log4j package, making it widely available for use and modification to suit individual needs. Due to wide usage of API, this particular utility of Java was exploited to malignantly initiate RCE that executes set of commands that puts data of the user at danger of getting it stolen and malignant intent. The IoT devices are at danger since the Log4j vulnerability is so simple to attack. The proposed system with honeypot requires little input and, in addition to alerting the relevant team, contains an internal scanner that can determine whether a specific website is susceptible to the log4jshell vulnerability. It also recognizes

Autonomous vehicles (AVs) play a significant role in intelligent transportation systems (ITS), which handle vehicles without human interference. The AVs are integrated with the Internet of Vehicles (IoV) to connect with more vehicles, sensors, and fog servers and share data. This makes the vehicles vulnerable to attacks and leads to unauthorized access. To overcome this drawback, we introduced biometric authentication for secure communication of vehicles, roadside units (RSUs), and fog servers. In this protocol, we generated two session keys between entities. The communication cost, computation cost, and security parameters are compared with existing methods to show that the proposed protocol is more efficient than others. Finally, the formal and informal security analysis ensures the proposed protocol is more secure.

Preface

Welcome to Cryptography, Biometrics, and Anonymity in Cybersecurity Management, a comprehensive compilation edited by Mohammed Amin Almaiah and Said Salloum. In this volume, our aim is to provide a systematic exploration of essential cryptography, biometrics, and anonymity in cybersecurity Management concepts, methodologies, and technologies.

Our primary objective is to serve as a catalyst for advancing knowledge in cybersecurity. We invite scientists, researchers, academics, developers, policymakers, and cybersecurity practitioners to delve into the wealth of insights presented within these pages.

From academia to industry, from theoretical frameworks to real-world applications, this book offers valuable resources for anyone engaged in the pursuit of securing digital assets and infrastructure.

The topics covered in this book span various domains including machine learning, artificial intelligence, big data, cloud computing, digital forensics, cryptography, and more. Each chapter is crafted to provide both theoretical foundations and practical insights, making it accessible to a diverse audience.

Whether you are a seasoned cybersecurity analyst, a postgraduate student exploring emerging trends, or a policymaker shaping the future of digital governance, we believe you will find this book to be a valuable resource in your endeavors.

We extend our gratitude to all the contributors who have shared their expertise and insights, helping to enrich the discourse surrounding cybersecurity. It is our sincere hope that this book will foster further collaboration and innovation in the ongoing quest to secure our digital landscape.

ORGANIZATION OF THE BOOK

In "**Enhancing IoT Security RPL Attack Detection Using Sine Cosine Algorithm with XGBoost**" by *Qais Al-Na'amneh, Rahaf Hazaymih, Tasnim Al-Harasis, Mohammed Almaiah, Mahmoud Aljawarneh, Braa Qadoumi*. The cahpter employs the machine learning approaches such as Random Forest (RF), K Nearest Neighbor (KNN), Decision Tree (DT), XGBoost, and Support vector machine (SVM) to detect threats. The proposed machine learning-based detection approach conducts mitigate feature and classification using the Sine Cosine Algorithm with XGBoost to select the smallest number of relevant features, leading to the best solution with the highest accuracy. The proposed model achieves a high accuracy of 97% on the Decrease Rank and Version Number. Also, a high accuracy of 99% on the Hello Flooding.

In "**Shedding Light on the Dark Web A Novel Approach to Detect and Track URL Hopping"** by *Anilkumar K.G., Muhammad Noorul Mubarak*. This chapter provides a secure platform for legitimate users, it also enables illicit activities such as cybercrime, drug trade, and terrorism. One major obstacle for LEAs is the practice of URL hopping, where Dark Web sites frequently change their URLs to evade detection. To address this issue, we propose a novel ensemble model that leverages machine learning techniques to analyze the content of Dark Web sites and correlate it with existing intelligence. Our system aims to improve the accuracy of tracing URL hopping on the Dark Web, ultimately enhancing the ability of LEAs to track and disrupt illicit activities. By bridging the gap between the Dark Web's anonymity and LEA's monitoring capabilities, our research contributes to a safer and more secure online environment.

In **"Open-Source Forensics Tools for Recovery of Deleted Data in Unconventional Ways"** by *Tuqa Al-Makkawi, Ayoub Alsarhan, Qais Al-Na'amneh, Mohammad Aljaidi, Mohammed Almaiah, Mahmoud AlJamal, Rabee Alqura'n, Mahmoud Aljawarneh*. This chapter studies the collection and analysis of files with an emphasis on deleted files from different resources and evaluates the performance of open-source programs for recovering deleted data using unconventional ways. It discusses some forensics tools, including FTK, and Encase, and the ability to extract the deleted file, showing a general comparison between forensics tools.

In "**Impact of Decreased Rank Attack on Network Topology of RPL Using Contiki-NG**" by *Qais Al-Na'amneh, Walid Dhifallah, Rahaf Hazaymih, Tasnim Al-Harasis, Mohammed Almaiah. Braa Qadoumi Ayoub Alsarhan*. The chapter emphasizes the necessity of addressing these attacks concerning different scenarios preserving topology, avoiding communication delays, and reducing throughput. The proposed solution significantly decreases the impact of a decreased rank attack on network performance.

In "**Face Recognition: Unveiling Identity through Machine Learning**" by *Brijesh Yadav and Vishal Jain*. In this chapter, face recognition is a type of biometric system that scans and analyses the face of an individual and identifies the individual. It is part of biometrics, which includes fingerprint, eye scanning, palm print, voice, and signature recognition. It increases system security by recognizing the individual who is accessing the system. Face recognition plays a crucial role in crime investigation by identifying and locating criminals. It is essential because it has an enhanced security system, no need for memorization, live detection, scalability, and reduced human error. The first step is locating and scanning the face. It uses artificial intelligence, machine learning, and deep learning. Face recognition and images may also use convolutional neural networks. A convolutional neural network is a type of deep learning that extracts identifying features from data, lacking pre-programmed understanding. It is specialized in image and object detection and analysis.

In "**Protecting Data in the 5G Era a Critical Review of Cryptographic Techniques for Mobile Cloud Computing**" by *Malak AL-Majali, Mohammad Aljaidi, Qais Al-Na'amneh, Ghassan Samara, Ayoub Alsarhan, Braa Qadoumi*. This chapter delves into user privacy concerns in 5G MCC environments. The convergence of mobile computing, wireless networks, and cloud computing has fostered the rapidly evolving field of MCC. Advancements in 5G mobile networks are expected to propel MCC services even further, making them a focal point in the mobile service landscape. However, 5G MCC also presents significant user privacy challenges, including network latency and data security. This paper investigates various cryptographic techniques employed to safeguard user privacy in 5G MCC systems. We compare and analyze encryption techniques, zero-knowledge proofs, MFA, and blockchain, and the inherent challenges associated with each approach.

In "**A Case Study on Cyber Attack Detection using Machine Learning: IDS For Detecting Cyber Attacks Using Machine Learning**" by *Indra Priyadharshini S., Padmavathy T. V. and Shiny Irene D.* This chapter focusses on leveraging machine learning (ML) for cyber-attack prevention, addressing a range of threats and assaults. Machine learning is a crucial component of modern cybersecurity, offering a flexible approach to defend information systems against the constantly evolving tactics of malicious actors.

In "**Advanced Encryption Based Keylogger for System Security**" by *V.R. Balasaraswathi, Ashiq Noor Sudheer, Gautham Vidyashankar, Kevin Sebastian and Priyanshu Pattanaik*. This chapter presents a paradigm shift in network security, combining advanced technology to transcend conventional keyloggers. This software aims to revolutionize monitoring capabilities, specifically targeting keystrokes, while concurrently implementing text encryption mechanisms for log files. Our primary objective is to transform the traditionally perceived risks associated with keyloggers into practical benefits. This keylogger, designed to capture keystrokes, extends its functionality to collect crucial system data, screenshots, and audio recordings—all meticulously recorded in their respective log files which are then encrypted for security purposes.

In "**Survey and Analysis of RGB Image Encryption using DNA Cryptography-Exploring Novel Approaches for Enhanced Security**" by *Karthika Veeramani, Shalini Gupta and Anuj Dhar*. This chapter provides a comprehensive analysis of the state-of-the-art in RGB image encryption leveraging DNA cryptography. We delve into existing techniques, exploring how they utilize DNA encoding, chaotic maps, and other cryptographic primitives to achieve image encryption. We critically evaluate the security strengths and weaknesses of these approaches.

In "**KK Approach to Increase Resilience in Internet of Things: A T-Cell Security Concept**" by *Kutubuddin Sayyad Liyakat Kazi*. This chapter proposes a technique for identifying malicious nodes is known by the inventor as the "KK approach." We compare the throughput and delay of the system with the proposed KK Approach, and the results are superior compared to the earlier techniques.

In "**Enhancing Textual Password Authentication Using Typing Rhythm**" by *Ferdinand Apietu Katsriku, Samuel Darko Abankwah and Winfred Yaokumah*. This chapter aims to enhance the security of textual passwords by adding a new layer that involves an individual's typing rhythm without requiring additional devices. It discusses authentication methods and develops a textual password authentication system, which takes advantage of the fact that every user has a distinct way of typing.

In "**A Survey on Cryptographic Algorithms and Information Security Practices**" by *Jay Kumar Jain, Dipti Chauhan and Anuthi Singh*. In this chapter, the authors studies the cryptography technique. The art of cryptography is considered to be born along with the art of writing. As civilizations advanced, humans organized into tribes, groups, and kingdoms, leading to concepts like power, battles, supremacy, and politics. These concepts created a natural need for secret communication among select recipients, driving the continuous evolution of cryptography. The importance of information and communication systems for society and the global economy is growing with the in-creasing volume and value of data being transmitted and stored.

In "**Lightweight Cryptographic Algorithms for IoT Devices**" by **Yash Rawat and Vishal Jain**. This chapter explains the implementation of 4 main well-known cryptographic algorithms on a stimulated IoT environment using an online software. PRESENT SIMON PRINCE and LEA are implemented on Wokwi and tested for their efficiency and effectiveness. Keywords: IoT, Encryption, Lightweight Cryptography, PRINCE, SIMON, PRESENT, LEA.

In "**H0NEY4LOG: A Comprehensive Tool For SSH Honeypot and Log4j Vulnerability Scanner**" by *Sujatha Gurunathan*. The proposed system with honeypot requires little input and, in addition to alerting the relevant team, contains an internal scanner that can determine whether a specific website is susceptible to the log4jshell vulnerability. It also recognizes and warns of SSH-based threats. On top of a secure system, this scanner and the honeypot add another degree of security.

In "**Augmented Ebola Optimization Algorithm for Anomaly-Based Intrusion Detection System**" by *Mohammad Alshinwan, Abdallah Ehab Awad, Ali Ghassan Mohammad, Yousef Salah Alnajjar, Ahmed Ali Otoom, Radwan Batyha, Mohammad Hijjawi, Saad Said Alqahtany, Omar husain Tarawneh, Laith Abualigah*. This chapter presents a novel anomaly-based intrusion detection system (IDS) model that utilizes the Ebola Optimization Algorithm (EOA) technique for increased performance. The EOA algorithm is hybridized with the Prairie Dog Algorithm (PD) to enhance the performance of the EOA algorithm, called EOA-PD. The EOA-PD technique is used as a feature selection mechanism to determine the most pertinent elements from the dataset that lead to a high level of classification accuracy. In addition, a support vector machine is utilized to assess the effectiveness of the chosen features in correctly forecasting the attacks. Furthermore, The NSL-KDD dataset is used to showcase the efficacy of the suggested methodology across several attack scenarios.

In "**Cyber Attacks through the Ages: Impact Assessment and Defense Strategies**" by *Raman R., Hakam Singh, Nilamadhab Mishra, Abhishek Thakur, Ramamani Tripathy, Rudra Kalyan Nayak, Amit Thakur*. In this research chapter, we will dive into multiple factors of cyber-attacks and explore their types, perpetrators, impacts, and motivations in depth. We will dissect the different methodologies employed by cyber adversaries and their vulnerabilities through different case studies of significant incidents that exploit their role in politics, pursuit of financial gain, and ideological agendas.

In "**Comparative Analysis of Biometric Approaches in Continuous Authentication**" by *Ayeswarya S. and John Singh*. This chapter aims to provide a comprehensive comparison of various biometric methods used for continuous user authentication. Biometric authentication techniques offer unique advantages in terms of security, usability, and continuous monitoring capabilities.

IN CONCLUSION

In the ever-evolving landscape of cybersecurity and risk management, our edited reference book, "Cryptography, Biometrics, and Anonymity in Cybersecurity Management," seeks to provide a comprehensive resource for practitioners, researchers, and academics alike. Throughout the chapters, our esteemed contributors have delved into various facets of cryptography, biometrics, and anonymity, cybersecurity, ranging from risk management methodologies to innovative countermeasures against emerging threats.

From the exploration of cybersecurity risks in online social networks to the development of novel encryption techniques for network image communication, each chapter offers valuable insights and practical solutions to address the complex challenges facing cybersecurity professionals today. By leveraging advanced technologies such as deep learning and chaos theory, our contributors have demonstrated the potential for innovation in safeguarding digital assets and infrastructure.

Moreover, our book underscores the interdisciplinary nature of cybersecurity, bringing together expertise from fields such as machine learning, cryptography, and network security. By fostering collaboration and knowledge exchange among diverse stakeholders, we aim to advance the collective understanding and capabilities in cybersecurity research and practice.

As we conclude this preface, we extend our sincere appreciation to all the authors who have contributed their expertise and insights to this volume. It is our hope that "Cryptography, Biometrics, and Anonymity in Cybersecurity Management " will serve as a valuable resource for years to come, inspiring further exploration and innovation in the ongoing mission to secure our digital future.

Dr. Mohammed Amin Almaiah

Dr. Said Salloum

Chapter 1
Enhancing IoT Security RPL Attack Detection Using Sine Cosine Algorithm With XGBoost

Qais Al-Na'amneh
Applied Science Private University, Jordan

Mahmoud Aljawarneh
Applied Science Private University, Jordan

Rahaf Hazaymih
Jordan University of Science and Technology, Jordan

Braa Qadoumi
Applied Science Private University, Jordan

Tasnim Al-Harasis
Al Hussein Technical University, Jordan

Shahid Munir Shah
Hamdard University, Pakistan

Mohammed Almaiah
University of Jordan, Jordan

ABSTRACT

The most widely used routing protocol for Internet of Things (IoT) networks with limited resources is the (RPL). Network security is a significant issue because of the exponential growth of Internet of Things (IoT) devices and their growing ubiquity in safety-critical settings like healthcare and industry. One possible remedy for threat identification in these networks is using intrusion detection systems (IDS) based on machine learning. To achieve this, a machine learning approach that uses Random Forest (RF), k-nearest Neighbor (KNN), Decision Tree (DT), XGBoost, and Support Vector Machine (SVM) models is presented. The proposed machine learning-based

DOI: 10.4018/979-8-3693-8014-7.ch001

detection approach conducts mitigate feature and classification using the Sine Cosine Algorithm (SCA) with XGBoost to select the smallest number of relevant features, leading to the best solution with the highest accuracy. The proposed model achieves a high accuracy of 97% on the Decrease Rank and Version Number. Also, a high accuracy of 99% on the Hello Flooding.

I. INTRODUCTION

Security risks abound in the networking and communications industry, gravely endangering availability, stability, and security. One common type of attack in wireless sensor networks (WSNs) is the RPL routing attack (Bokka, 2024). RPL attacks are often unnoticed and can continue for a long time without being noticed, which can lead to significant energy degradation and malfunction of devices. Sophisticated methods are needed to detect these assaults because the attackers usually pass for normal network traffic (Laila, 2024). They may cause the network's performance to noticeably deteriorate, showing up as increased latency, dropped packets, and decreased delivery rates. Some attacks, like the Wormhole Attack, can adapt to modifications in the network and carry on operating even after the network's configuration has altered. A comprehensive understanding of the types and aspects of RPL assaults is necessary to detect and prevent them, as well as to preserve network security and integrity.

We have developed a paradigm that emphasizes the many vulnerabilities and vulnerabilities of the RPL protocol to assess RPL protocol assaults in Contiki. We reorganized the project to put security front and center instead of creating a WSN application (Paganraj, 2024).

Figure 1. The network architecture of Contiki

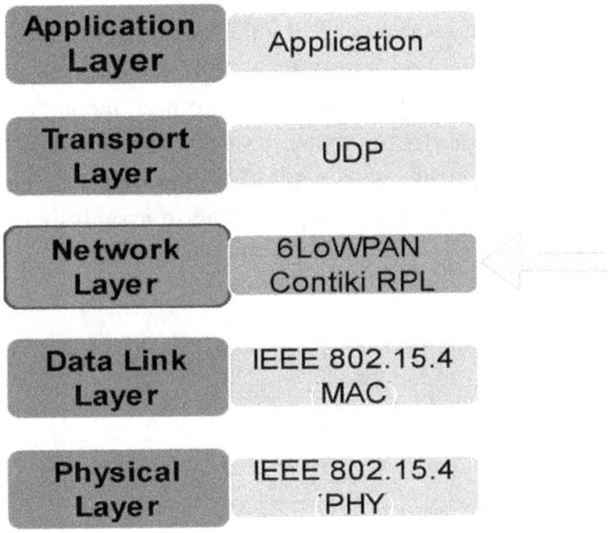

Figure 1 The objective is to create a user-friendly framework for testing malicious nodes in Cooja simulations and to demonstrate the effects of attacks. The theory behind RPL attacks is presented in this publication along with the testing framework, and results from RPL attacks (Rouissat, 2024). In this document, the green nodes indicate the root of DODAG, the red nodes with 'A' labels denote attackers, and the yellow nodes with numbers represent ordinary nodes (Hkiri, 2024).

Although remote procedure call (RPC) is a potent tool for distributed systems, there are security issues associated with it. RPL attacks use design defect exploitation, parameter manipulation, and buffer overflow to target RPC systems. Regular updates, secure coding, and input validation are all components of mitigation (Omar, 2024).

Large amounts of data are produced by information and communication technology (ICT), and machine learning (ML) techniques are employed for analysis and decision-making. Nonetheless, non-discriminative data privacy leaks are a possibility [9]. Both are hosted by the Internet of Things (IoT), and the goal of this study is to examine how IoT and machine learning privacy relate to one another. Targeting network resources like energy and bandwidth, flood assaults can serve a variety of purposes, such as routing overhead, historical denial-of-service attacks, congestion attacks, and the exploitation of network resources for the attackers' benefit. One suggested strategy to mitigate sinkhole and wormhole attacks is the concept of "crowd's forces" (Al-Na'amneh, 2024). The scientific categorization of organisms according to common traits and evolutionary connections is known as taxonomy, and it facilitates comprehension and dissemination of the enormous diversity of life on Earth.

This section covers the taxonomy of RPL attacks, with a focus on the attack that is being studied. When the network's resources run low, malicious nodes in the first category attempt to consume excessive amounts of power, memory, or energy. This might lead to legitimate nodes taking unnecessary actions, which could reduce the network's lifespan by interfering with network availability, node incapacitation, or link congestion. Blue frames designate the precise assault that is being tested (Nejad, 2024).

Figure 2. RPL attack classification

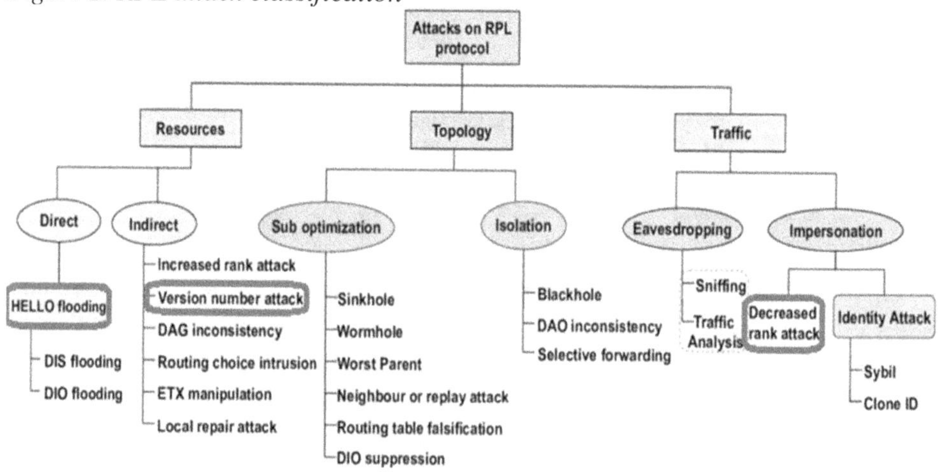

The RPL network architecture is depicted in Figure 2 and is the subject of both direct and indirect network attacks that aim to disrupt regular network operations and isolate certain nodes. This can be separated into two categories: suboptimization, which causes the network to converge to a nuptial structure, and node isolation. The third category includes attacks on network traffic, which aim to infiltrate hostile nodes into the network without affecting routine operations (Al-Na'amneh Q. N., 2024) . Snooping on traffic or posing as original nodes can lead to information leaking. This includes hijacking individual nodes or groups of nodes to obstruct legally transmitted data as well as passive eavesdropping (Mohajerani, 2024) .

IDS are defensive strategies for monitoring and detecting malicious nodes. This paper proposes a new Intrusion Detection System (IDS) (Alfriehat, 2024) using machine learning to detect RPL attacks. Malicious nodes attempt to lower their rank value by sending a DIO message to become a parent or root node. To safeguard against these threats, the RPL network requires a defensive strategy.

We initially classify the attacks using the same taxonomy as indicated in Figure 2; we provide a brief description of each type of attack used in this paper:

- **Hello Flooding (HF):** The goal of the attack is to render network resources or services unavailable. To alert their one-hop neighbors to their presence, the HF assault is executed by repeatedly bombarding the network with numerous "Hello" packets. The malicious nodes' strong transmission power will convince every other node in the network that it is a neighbor (Remya, 2024). The neighboring nodes will reply to those messages in the interim. Massive network traffic will be produced as a result, leading to instability, control overhead, and node resource depletion (Gupta, 2024).
- **Decreased Rank (DRA):** This attack occurs when a rogue node chooses to select the fraudulent node as its parent by broadcasting its bogus rank to nearby nodes. Consequently, other nodes use a fake node to relay their communications. In addition, the fake node misleads neighboring nodes by broadcasting the rank of its predecessor as its own. Although this attack mostly results in increased network traffic (Zilberman, 2024)
- **Version Number (VN)**: attackers alter the version number of an existing DODAG to target RPL's global repair capability. During regular functioning, the root node changes the version number. However, suppose the rogue node sends a DIO message with a higher version number. In that situation, it triggers the global repair process to start and rebuild the DODAG, resulting in increased overhead and draining the nodes' power resources (Rajasekar, 2024).

In this paper, we propose a machine learning-based Intrusion Detection System to safeguard against network attacks Using the Sine Cosine Algorithm with XGBoost to pick the fewest number of relevant features, resulting in the optimal solution with the maximum accuracy and demonstrate the effectiveness of our approach in precisely discriminating between benign and hazardous IoT attacks

The main contributions of this paper are the following:

- RPL attacks are being implemented in Contiki-NG.
- A COOJA-based simulation framework for combining attacks on several nodes for a configurable amount of time.
- propose a machine learning-based Intrusion Detection System to safeguard against network attacks Using the Sine Cosine Algorithm with XGBoost.

The rest of the paper is structured as follows. Section 2 of this paper gives the related works, section 3 displays the machine learning-based Intrusion Detection System to safeguard against network attacks Using the Sine Cosine Algorithm with XGBoost, section 4 provides the results and discussion, and section 5 summarizes the conclusion and future work.

II. RELATED WORK

For IoT routing, particularly in Wireless Sensor Networks, the Routing Protocol for Low-Power and Lossy Networks (RPL) is essential. However, vulnerable to security risks like RPL attacks. These assaults deteriorate performance, interfere with network functions, and jeopardize data integrity. Numerous studies have been conducted on RPL attacks, with an emphasis on finding vulnerabilities, comprehending their methods, and assessing how they affect network security and performance. Investigations conducted early on found protocol flaws (Jaradat, 2023).

Many related works are available in the literature that discuss RPL attacks as shown in Table 1, and their defenses are reviewed in this article. Based on the attack vector and mitigation techniques—such as authenticating, updating, discarding, encrypting, and isolating attacking nodes—it suggests a classification. To evaluate the efficacy of these solutions, the review also provides efficiency criteria and evaluation measures. Finding novel ways to defend networks from routing attacks is the goal (Tahar, 2024).

The increasing use of IoT devices has raised questions about network security, particularly regarding the Routing Protocol for Low-Power and Lossy Networks (RPL). Present-day intrusion detection systems have rather high false alert rates. This study presents the Ensemble Learning-based Intrusion Detection System (ELG-IDS). Through extensive parameter optimization and stacking, it can identify three RPL internal attacks. It is highly accurate, according to experimental results (Albinali, 2024).

(Thamilarasu & Chawla, 2019) developed an intrusion detection model utilizing deep learning to detect malicious traffic in IoT networks. This technique, which divides network data into sessions and examines the characteristics of network activity, detects five different types of RPL attacks: BH, Opportunistic Service, DDoS, SH, and WH. The detection process consists of three steps: mitigation, anomaly detection, and network connection. In the first step, the network channel that is required to capture network traffic is set up and made available. The trial's results show a high degree of success in identifying all forms of attacks, with 96% precision in identifying a DDoS attack scenario.

(Kamel & Elhamayed. 2020) suggested a based mitigate method to decrease the impact of IoT routing attacks on PRC in the context of healthcare. Their architecture consists of three layers: medical data collecting, network routing, and medical application. They used the Synthetic Minority Oversampling Technique (SMOTE) to correct unbalanced data using a real-time dataset generated by the Cooja simulator. For HF attacks, their approach yielded results including a 0.325 logistic loss, 96.87% accuracy, 94.85% precision, 3.13% error rate, 99.65% recall, 93.8% correlation, and 97.19% (Thamilarasu & Chawla, 2019). presented a deep-learning approach to detect Rank assaults in RPL. To evaluate and classify both typical and unusual network traffic behavior, it uses an MLP classifier. They created their dataset by altering the DAG RPL file and icmpv6 parameters in the Cooja simulator to simulate an RPL attack. The experimental data showed a true positive rate (TPR) of 100% and a false positive rate (FPR) of 24%. 96% accuracy was achieved. Additionally, by combining many DL methods to capture the temporal and spatial properties of IoT-LNNs, such as the Long Short-Term Memory (LSTM) models and the Graph Convolution Neural Network (GsCNN),

Furthermore, A comprehensive approach for forecasting routing attacks in IoT-LLNs was created by (Sahay, Geethakumari, & Mitra, 2020). When there is suspicious activity, such as a change in node rank or an unusually high volume of DIS messages, the smart contract sends out a warning impulse. The FNN model combined with LSTM and GCN outputs was utilized to forecast attacks using this impulse. In normal conditions, the framework's accuracy was 94.50%; in topological attacks, it was 86.13%.

To simulate attacks in the RPL network, (Sharma & Verma, 2021)developed a multi-class dataset for a supervised machine-learning model. Fifty-eight features total, acquired from network packets gathered during the simulation, are included in the proposed dataset. The dataset also contains other RPL assaults, including DIS Flooding, Version Number (VN), HF, and Decreased Rank (DRA), in addition to a typical network traffic pattern. Pairwise correlation is a dimensionality reduction technique used by the authors to remove variables that have more than a particular correlation among themselves. In addition, the authors used a correlation ranking filter to weed out features that were not relevant and could potentially confuse the detection algorithm in the feature ranking and selection phases. Additionally, the experimental findings demonstrate that the RF classifier achieves the highest Precision (99.4%), Recall (99.3%), and AC (99.33%) than other classifiers, while the J48 classifier obtained the worst results in all evaluation metrics compared to other classifiers. An analytical examination of IDS performance in RPL-based IoT networks is suggested by (Osman, 2024).RPL-NIDDS17 is statistically analyzed in the proposed investigation. The five machine learning classifiers used in correlation analysis are Artificial Neural Networks (ANN), NB, DT, Logistic Regression

(LR), and Expectation-Maximization (EM) Analysis Clustering. Next, they used AC and FAR measurements to evaluate the classifiers' performance. Additionally, the RPL-NIDDS17 dataset's results are contrasted with several datasets that are frequently utilized in traditional networks, including KDD-99, UNSW-NB15, and WSN-DS. The authors state that the DT has the lowest FAR (3.57%) and the highest AC (93%) of any type. The EM clustering, on the other hand, has the lowest FAR (5.59%) and AC (89.63%).

Three different kinds of RPL attacks—HF, VN, and BH—were the focus of (Kannan, 2024) with a distributed anomaly detection technique for a single mote assault in RPL networks. The recommended approach installs a pre-trained model in network nodes to reduce pointless processes like data collection and model training. To lower communication overheads, the authors also used a distributed architecture. Additionally, they created 20 test groups at first, each with 80 different datasets that were divided into two subsets: a malicious scenario and a regular scenario. Regarding the suggested method, the authors stated that the system had a 0.5% False Positive Rate and can identify VN, HF, and BH assaults with TPRs of 96.1%, 90.2%, and 68.52 percent, respectively.

For RPL-based IoTs, (Qureshi, Rana, Ahmed, & Jeon, 2020) showed a cross-layer IDS. The suggested technique employed a neural network in binary and multiclass classification settings to identify VN, WP, and HF attacks. Regarding the binary classification model's experimental outcomes, the 10-fold cross-validation methods yielded 97.11% DR and 0.34% FPR. Comparatively, the DR and FPR achieved by the 60% split techniques were 96.88% and 0.13%, respectively. Furthermore, the suggested method achieved a high DR of 97.52% in the multi-class model. The outcomes also showed that adding link-layer features improved VN attack detection while lowering the FPR. An efficient method for identifying VN assaults in IoTs that can be implemented at the cloud and IoT-LLN edge was proposed by (Sahay R., Geethakumari, Mitra, & Sahoo, 2020). Moreover, the proposed methodology aims to identify these attacks. Furthermore, several parameters, such as the variation in VN and the amount of VN changes, affect the network's ability to identify VN assaults. Moreover, an alarm will be sent to the root node, which will ban malicious nodes, as soon as they are found within the network. The simulation results show that the proposed framework achieves AC, Precision, and Specificity of 0.98, 1.00, and 1.00, respectively. Nevertheless, the DT, Bernoulli RBM, and LR obtain 95% recall, while the SVM achieves 94 s of PRC.

Also, a Multi-Layer (MLRPL) model that employs an ANN approach to identify DRA attacks in RPL was proposed by (Osman, He, Mahiuob, Mokbal, & Zhu, 2021). The training and testing AC for the binary class were 97.14% and 97.01%, respectively, based on the experimental data. By contrast, the testing and training accuracy of a multi-class model are 96.39% and 96.59%, respectively. All things considered, the proposed model yielded noteworthy outcomes in AC and Precision (97.14%, 97.03%, 0.36%, and 98%).

Table 1. Studies close to the proposed study.

Authors	Approach	Attacks Detected	Dataset	Model	Accuracy
(Yavuz, Ünal, & Gül, 2018)	DL with 3 phases	HF, VN, DRA	generated (IRAD, Cooja)	Multi-Layer Perceptron (MLP)	Accuracy: 99.5%,
(Thamilarasu & Chawla, 2019)	Novel IDS	BH, Opportunistic Service, DDoS, SH, WH	generated from simulation (Cooja)	(DBN and DNN)	Accuracy: 96% (DDoS), Recall: 98.7% (DDoS), F1-score: 0.973; Precision: 98.47%, Recall: 97% (IoT testbed)
(Kamel & Elhamayed, 2020)	Mitigation with CNN	HF, SF, SH, WH, VN	Real-time (Cooja)	(CNN)	Accuracy: 96.87%
(Thamilarasu & Chawla, 2019)	DL for Detect attack	Rank attack	generated from simulation (Cooja)	Multi-Layer Perceptron (MLP)	TPR: 100%, FPR: 24%, Precision: 98%, Recall: 88%, F1-score: 92%, AC: 96%
(Sahay, Geethakumari, & Mitra, 2020)	Holistic framework with GCNN and LSTM	routing attacks	Real-time (Cooja)	GCNN, LSTM, FNN	AC: 94.50% (normal), 86.13% (topological), 82.46% (resource), 91.88% (traffic)
(Verma, 2019)	ML for detecting attacks	HF, DIS Flooding, VN, DRA	Self-generated (Cooja)	RF, NB, J48	99.33% (RF)
(Osman M. H., 2024)	ML for detecting attacks	HF, VN, BH	RPL-NIDDS17, KDD-99, UNSW-NB15, WSN-DS	NB, DT, LR, ANN, EM	93% (DT)
(Kannan, 2024)	ML for detecting attacks	HF, VN, BH	Realtime (Cooja)	Semi-supervised ML (KDE)	96.1% (VN)

continued on following page

Table 1. Continued

Authors	Approach	Attacks Detected	Dataset	Model	Accuracy
(Qureshi, Rana, Ahmed, & Jeon, 2020)	Neural Network for detecting attacks	VN, WP, HF	KDD-99	Neural network	97.52% (multi-class DR)
(Sahay, Geethakumari, & Mitra, 2020)	ML for detecting attacks	VN	IoT-LLN	DT, SVM, Bernoulli RBM, LR	98% (VN)
(Osman, He, Mahiuob, Mokbal, & Zhu, 2021)	ANN for detecting RPL attacks	VN, DRA, HF	IRAD dataset	ANN	97.14%

III. METHODOLOGY

The purpose of IDS is to determine whether an RPL node is normal or malicious. IDS is implemented using ML classifiers. In this section, we discuss our proposed machine learning-based detection approach to conduct mitigate features and classification using the Sine Cosine Algorithm with XGBoost to select the smallest number of relevant features that lead to finding the best solution with the highest accuracy Decreased Rank Dataset, Version Number and Hello Flooding Dataset. This indicates the effectiveness of our approach in accurately distinguishing between benign and harmful attacks in IoT as shown in Figure 3.

Figure 3. Proposed methodology

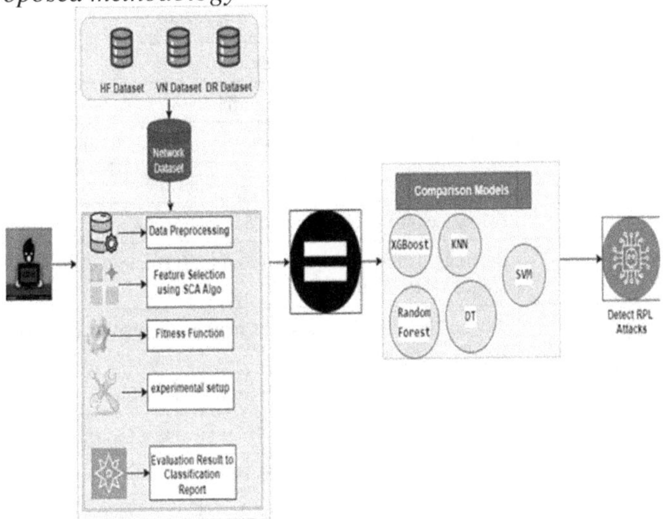

A. Dataset Description and Collection

This section describes how to build a dataset, follow these steps: install the Contiki Cooja IoT simulator; use RPL Attacks to create normal and vulnerable nodes; simulate using the Contiki Cooja IoT devices simulator with the created vulnerable and normal nodes; obtain raw data; and convert the raw data into a CVS file.

It was found during the simulation that by the 30th second, a system of 12 nodes fully formed the DODAG structure. Devices send DIO, DAO, and DAO-ACK messages to one another during DODAG due to the nature of RPL, which produces packet traffic that is distinct from traffic that occurs after DODAG. The data after the 60th second of the original data set is extracted and a new data set is constructed, to stop the machine from learning this difference. It is now possible to compare the data sets produced for each attack and categorize them as vulnerable-normal using a variety of machine learning techniques. Three data sets were created as a result. The features of datasets as shown in the Table 2 for flooding attacks, version number attacks, and reduced rank assaults (Laila D. A.-N., 2024).

Table 2. Description of features:

features	Description
Source Mote	A distinct number for every mote
Destination Mote	identical to the source mote's number
Packet Count:	the total number of source motes in the frame lasting one second.
Source Mote Ratio	(Source: Packet/Mote Count). -second-time interval.
Destination Mote Ratio	(Mote Count/Packet Count at Destination)
Source Mote Duration	the total of all packet durations sent inside a frame of one second, from source to destination.
Destination Mote Duration	the total of all packet durations that the destination received inside the frame of one second.
Total Packet Duration	It is the total of every packet's time within a frame of one second.
Total Packet Length	It is the total of each packet's length inside a frame of one second.
Source Packet Ratio	(Total Packet Length / Sum of Source Packet Length).
Destination Packet Ratio	(Total Packet Length / Sum of Dest. Packet lengths).
DIO Message Count	DIO message counts in the frame of one second.
DIS Message Count	number of DIS messages within a one-second time frame.
DAO Message Count	DAO message count in the one-second frame
Other Message Count	all the messages—aside from DIO, DIS, and DAO—count.

B. Data Preprocessing

All rows with missing values and NANs have been eliminated. Also, due to the disagreement in the numbers in the data, we choose to employ MinMax, which helps to scale the data. Before entering data into a convolutional neural network or standard machine learning models, all data and values should be in the same range with the least degree of variance, as MinMax scaling was utilized, and all associated values were bound to [0,1].

C. Machine Learning Algorithms

Five different machine learning models were used in our study to predict the RPL attack in IoT: Decision Tree (DT), k-nearest Neighbors (KNN), Random Forest (RF), Support Vector Machine (SVM), and XGBoost. We can identify attack patterns and associations in the network traffic since each model contributes special strengths and traits to the predicting task. Our study aims to develop a strong and diverse predictive framework by utilizing the strengths of the SCA algorithm with XGBoost, (RF) for robust ensemble learning and reducing overfitting, KNN for local pattern recognition, XGBoost for powerful gradient boosting and handling large datasets, SVM for effective classification boundaries, and DT for effective hierarchical decision-making. By comparing different models, we can get important insights into how well they each work independently and as a group, improving the precision and dependability of our forecasts, which advances our knowledge of RPL attacks in IoT (Laila D. A.-N., 2024).

- Decision Tree

A powerful and straightforward machine-learning method that may be applied to regression and classification. It works by dividing the dataset into subgroups recursively according to the supplied feature values. Every leaf node denotes the conclusion or classification, every branch shows the decision's result, and every internal node represents a feature-specific decision point. Because it makes interpretation and visualization easier, the tree structure is a common option for understanding the underlying decision-making process. Decision trees are resistant to outliers and missing values, and they can handle both numerical and categorical data (Mahesh, 2020).

- k-nearest Neighbors

A comparatively easy regression or classification algorithm. When a new data point is introduced, the method is to find the k closest data points from the training dataset, and then use each point's class to get the unknown data point's class. One can compute the distance between these points using a variety of distance measures. The Euclidean distance is the distance metric employed in this analysis, and the unknown class is predicted using a weighted version of majority voting (Singh, 2016).

- Random Forest

A robust, adaptable machine learning technique that is excellent at group learning. It creates many decision trees during training and outputs the mean prediction (regression) or mode (classification). By averaging the outputs of numerous trees, this method reduces the risk of overfitting and becomes less susceptible to variations in the training dataset. Moreover, Random Forests are excellent at handling large, highly dimensional datasets; they offer insights into the importance of features, which help identify the variables in the dataset that are most important (Liu, 2021).

- Support Vector Machine

Since vector machines are under the category of supervised learning techniques, they require labeled, known data to categorize newly discovered data. The fundamental method for classifying the data begins with attempting to develop a function that divides the data points into the corresponding labels with either (a) the greatest margin or (b) the fewest errors.

This is because there are fewer errors in larger vacant spaces adjacent to the splitting function since the labels are more easily separated from one another (Fatima, 2017).

- XGBoost

A method centered around decision trees. Gradient tree boosting, for example, uses decision trees as base learners to approximate the underlying prediction function. Boosting is a generic technique. The residual prediction error of the additive model constructed with the current set of base learners is fitted by the next base learner at each iteration. The set of base learners is then expanded to include this new student (Enders, 2021) .

D. Sine Cosine Algorithm (SCA) with XGBoost

The SCA algorithm (Mirjalili S, 2017), a population-based meta-heuristic for problem optimization, was proposed by (Mirjalili S, 2017)in 2016. The trigonometric sine and cosine functions are used by this optimization process to update individual positions in the direction of the optimal solution. The following equations are updated for SCA solutions.

$$\boldsymbol{X}_{ij}^{t+1} = \boldsymbol{x}_{ij}^{t} + \boldsymbol{r}_1 * \sin(\boldsymbol{r}_2) * |\boldsymbol{r}_3 \boldsymbol{P}_{ij}^{t} - \boldsymbol{x}_{ij}^{t}|$$

$$X_{ij}^{t+1} = x_{ij}^{t} + r_1 * \cos(r_2) * |r_3 P_{ij}^{t} - x_{ij}^{t}|$$

Figure 4 shows the effects of sine and cosine functions on equations (1) and (2). In general, the equations are combined and employed as follows:

$$X_{ij}^{t+1} = \begin{cases} x_{ij}^{t} + r_1 * \sin(r_2) * |r_3 P_{ij}^{t} - x_{ij}^{t}| r \geq 0.5 \\ x_{ij}^{t} + r_1 * \cos(r_2) * |r_3 P_{ij}^{t} - x_{ij}^{t}| r < 0.5 \end{cases}$$

In the above equation, x_{ij}^{t} presents the current person at iteration t in the d dimension, P_{ij}^{t} represents the best individual's position at iteration t in the d dimension, and r_1, r_2, r_3 and $r_4$are random parameters. These parameters balance exploratory and exploitative search behaviors, preventing local optima.

Figure 4. The effects of sine cosine functions in Eqs. (1) and (2) on the next position [11]

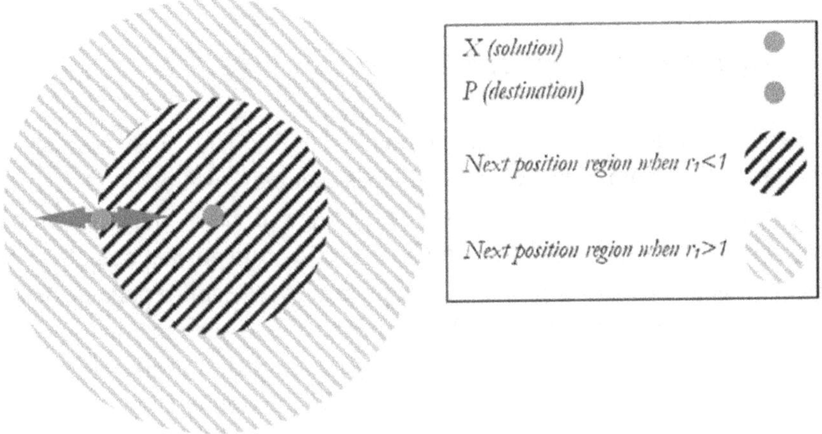

The parameter r_1 determines whether a solution updates its location towards the optimal solution ($r_1 < 1$) or away from it ($r_1 > 1$) r_1 falls linearly from a preset constant (a) to 0 [10], balancing exploratory and exploitative search patterns. It's updated using the following equation:

$$r_1 = a - t\frac{a}{\boldsymbol{T}_{max}}$$

where a is a constant, t is the current iteration, and $\boldsymbol{T}_{max}$ represents the maximum iterations allowed.

Algorithm 1 shows the pseudo-code for the conventional Sine Cosine Algorithm. As shown the related flowchart SCA algorithm in Figure 5.

```
Algorithm 1: The pseudo-code of the sine cosine algo-
rithm
Begin
Iintialize a set of solutions
Initialize a set of solutionsX_i (i = 1,2,...n) randomly
          While tless thanT_max do
Calculate the objective value for each solution
   Update the destination(P = X)
Update the random parameterr_1, r_2, r_3,r_4
Update the solution using the equation(3)
```

```
End while
            Return the destination
End
```

E. Performance Assessment

In this study, various measures were employed to evaluate our suggested model and other models, the most important of which is accuracy, as illustrated in equation (5). This is a measure that represents the percentage of cases that were predicted correctly. The ratio of all cases. Precision is defined as true positives relative to true positives and false positives, as shown in equation (6). Recall represents the ratio of positive cases to false positives and false negatives, as seen in equation (7) and F1-Score Refers to a measure of precision and memory that results in a balanced scale of rating, as shown in equation (8) and last equation calculates the Fitness Function maps the solution to an actual number, with larger numbers suggesting better solutions as shown in equation (9).

$$Accuracy = \frac{T_p + T_N}{T_p + T_N + F_p + F_N}$$

$$Precision = \frac{T_p}{T_p + F_p}$$

$$Recall = \frac{T_p}{T_P + F_N}$$

$$F_1 - Score = 2 \times \frac{precision \times Recall}{Precision + Rrecall}$$

$$F = h1\frac{|S|}{|f|} + h2Error(D)$$

Where $|f|$ represents the total number of the features and $|S|$ reflect the number of selected features, while the weight of the features that are chosen is determined by the parameters $h1$ *and* $h2$, where $h1$€ [0,1]

Table 3 displays the confusion matrix, which is responsible for evaluating the model's performance by presenting the actual and expected categories of the data set (Vabalas, 2019), where TP are the positive cases that were predicted correctly, TN is the positive cases that were predicted incorrectly, FP is the negative cases that were predicted as positive, and FN are the negative cases that were also predicted to be negative.

Table 3. Confusion matrix

Actual	Positive attack	TP	FN
	Negative attack	**FP**	**TN**
		Positive attack	Negative attack
		Prediction	

IV. RESULTS ANALYSIS AND DISCUSSION

This section explains our results obtained from the Cooja simulation, which consists of a malicious Hello Flooding attack, a Decrease Rank attack, a Version Number attack, and a benign attack, which were evaluated based on five machine learning algorithms and the proposed SCA algorithm with the XGBoost Also, the proposed model was evaluated based on five other machine learning algorithms.

A. Experiments

Table 4 displays the parameters used for our SCA algorithm with the XGBoost model, which serves as the foundation for the suggested model. The suggested model was also assessed using four alternative machine learning algorithms: Support Vector Machine, XGBoost, Random Forest, KNN, and Decision tree, where the data was divided into 80% for training and 20% for testing, and the code was written in Python.

Table 4. Parameters for training model

Parameters	Function /Value Used
Population size (Search agents)	200
Number of Iterations	30
Dimension	50
α in the fitness function	1-β
β	0.01

Based on Table 5 and Figure 5 which summarizes the results of the models used in the evaluation, it was found that our proposed model (SCA) algorithm with XGBoost has outperformed all other models, now we explain Decreased Rank attack as the accuracy reached 97%, Precision 96%, Recall 97% and F1-Score 96%. XGBoost acquired result (accuracy 95% Precision 94%, Recall 96% and F1-Score

95%), Random Forest acquired result (accuracy 94% Precision 92%, Recall 94% and F1-Score 93%). And Decision Tree result was (an accuracy of 93% Precision of 91%, Recall of 94%, and F1-Score of 92%). Two algorithms, KNN and SVM had the lowest results and equal in (accuracy, reaching 82%, Precision 81%, Recall 85%), and (F1-Score 81% for KNN), and finally SVM was (accuracy, reaching 81%Precision 79%, Recall 80%, and F1-Score 79%), and we find that our proposed model (SCA)algorithm with XGboost enhanced the result.

Table 5. Classification models evaluation Decreased Rank Attack

Model	*Accuracy (%)*	*Precision (%)*	*Recall (%)*	*F1-Score (%)*
XGBoost	95	94	96	95
KNN: DR	82	81	85	81
Random Forest	94	92	94	93
SVM	81	79	80	79
Decision Tree	93	91	94	92
SCA_XGBoost	**97**	**96**	**97**	**96**

Figure 5. Decreased rank attack models performance

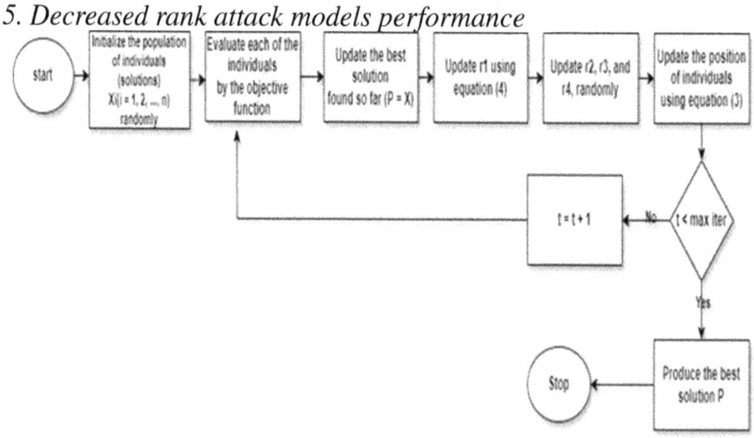

Also, based on Table 6 and Figure 6 which summarizes the results of the models used in the evaluation, it was found that our proposed model (SCA) algorithm with XGboost has outperformed all other models, now we explain the Hello Flooding attack as the accuracy reached 99%, Precision 97%, Recall 99% and F1-Score 98%. XGBoost acquired result (accuracy 98% Precision 94%, Recall 96% and F1-Score 95%), Random Forest acquired result (accuracy 98% Precision 95%, Recall 95%

and F1-Score 95%). And Decision Tree result was (an accuracy of 97% Precision of 93%, Recall of 92%, and F1-Score of 93%). Two algorithms, KNN and SVM had the lowest results and equal in (accuracy, reaching 95%, Precision 86%, Recall 92%), and (F1-Score 98% for KNN), and finally SVM (accuracy, reaching 95%Precision 86%, Recall 91%, and F1-Score 88%), and we find that our proposed model (SCA) algorithm with XGboost enhanced the result.

Table 6. Classification models evaluation Hello Flooding Attack

Model	*Accuracy (%)*	*Precision (%)*	*Recall (%)*	*F1-Score (%)*
XGBoost	98	94	96	95
KNN	95	86	92	98
Random Forest	98	95	95	95
SVM	95	86	91	88
Decision Tree	97	93	92	93
SCA_XGBoost	**99**	**97**	**99**	**98**

Figure 6. Hello flooding attack models performance

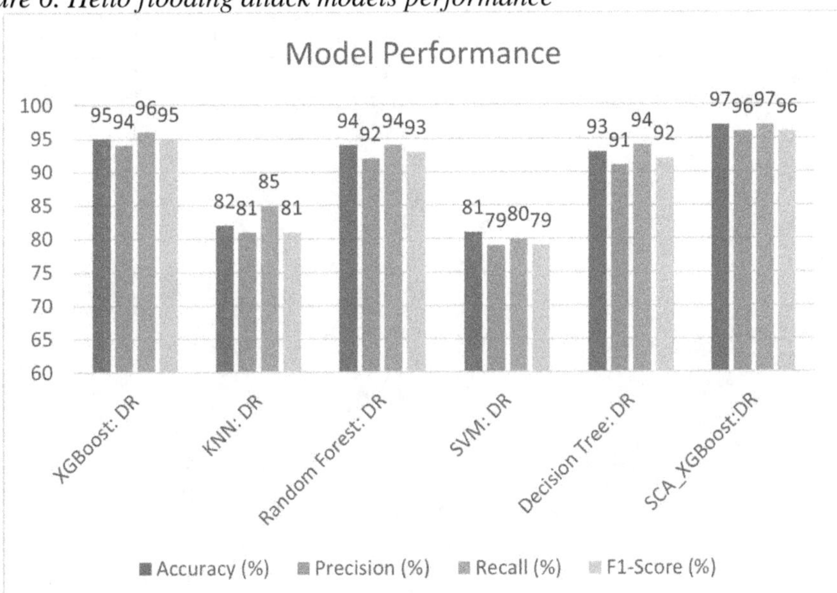

Moreover, based on Table 7 and Figure 7 which summarizes the results of the models used in the evaluation, it was found that our proposed model (SCA) algorithm with XGboost has outperformed all other models, now we explain the Version Number attack as the accuracy reached 97%, Precision 97%, Recall 98% and F1-Score 97%. XGBoost acquired result (accuracy 95% Precision 95%, Recall 96% and F1-Score 95%), Random Forest acquired result (accuracy 96% Precision 95%, Recall 96% and F1-Score 96%). And Decision Tree result was (an accuracy of 94% Precision of 94%, Recall of 95%, and F1-Score of 94%). Two algorithms, KNN and SVM had the lowest results and equal in (accuracy, reaching 89%, Precision 90%, Recall 90%), and (F1-Score 89% for KNN), and finally SVM (accuracy, reaching 76%Precision 75%, Recall 76%, and F1-Score 76%), and we find that our proposed model (SCA)algorithm with XGboost enhanced the result.

Table 7. Classification models evaluation version number attack

Model	*Accuracy (%)*	*Precision (%)*	*Recall (%)*	*F1-Score (%)*
XGBoost	95	95	96	95
KNN	89	90	90	89
Random Forest	96	95	96	96
SVM	76	75	76	76
Decision Tree	94	94	95	94
SCA_XGBoost	**97**	**97**	**98**	**97**

Figure 7. Version number attack models performance

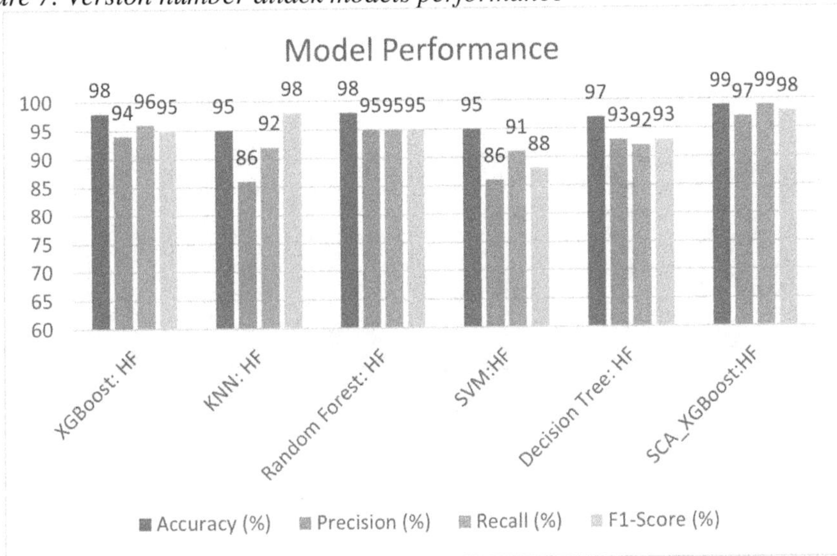

Now, Figure (8) shows the Decrease Rank Attack confusion matrix of the SCA with the XGBoost model, where the matrix shows the relationship between class (0) and class (1), where 0 indicates Benign and 1 indicates the Attack of RPL. FP shows that the true value of non-attack was incorrectly predicted in 4 cases as an attack. In the case that FN shows that the true value is attack, it is predicted 20 times incorrectly as non-attack. This indicates the strength of the proposed model in predicting the Attacks of RPL.

Figure 8. Decreased rank attack confusion matrix

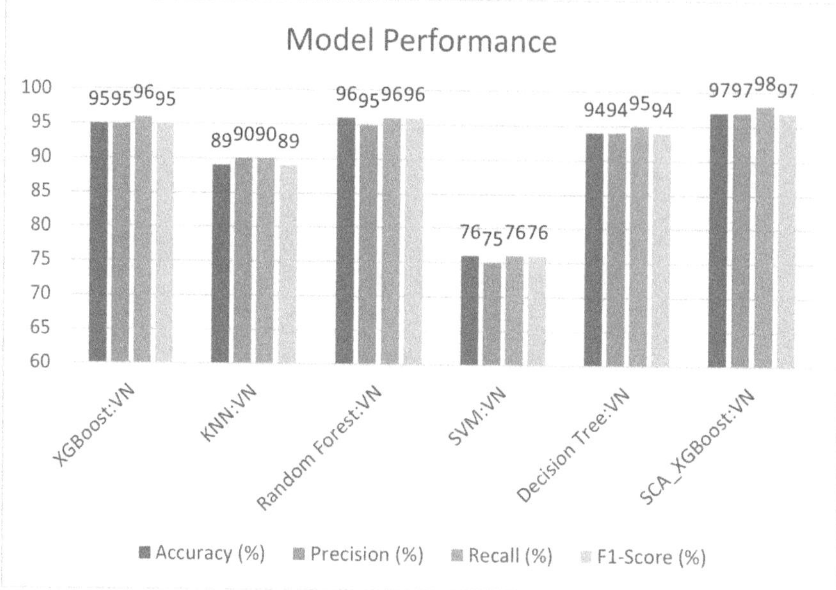

As well as Figure (9) shows the Hello Flooding Attack confusion matrix of the SCA with the XGBoost model, where the matrix shows the relationship between class (0) and class (1), where 0 indicates Benign and 1 indicates the Attack of RPL. FP shows that the true value of non-attack was incorrectly predicted in 0 cases as an attack. In the case that FN shows that the true value is attack, it is predicted 2 times incorrectly as non-attack. This indicates the strength of the proposed model in predicting the Attacks of RPL.

Figure 9. Hello flooding attack confusion matrix

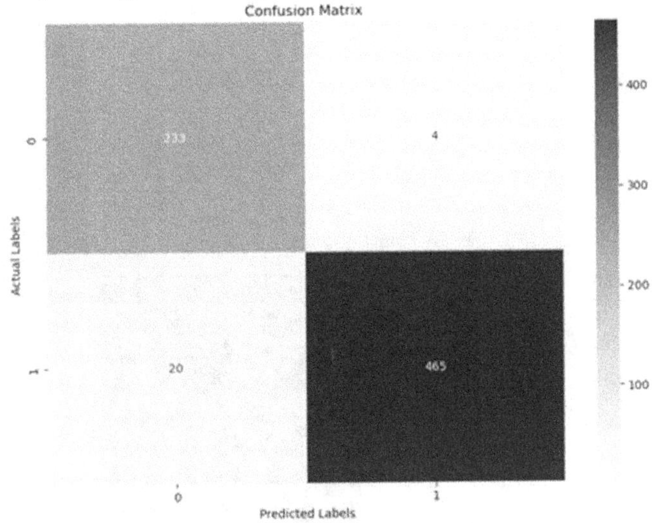

Furthermore, Figure (10) shows the Version Number Attack confusion matrix of the SCA with the XGBoost model, where the matrix shows the relationship between class (0) and class (1), where 0 indicates Benign and 1 indicates the Attack of RPL. FP shows that the true value of non-attack was incorrectly predicted in 0 cases as an attack. In the case that FN shows that the true value is attack, it is predicted 11 times incorrectly as non-attack. This indicates the strength of the proposed model in predicting the Attacks of RPL.

Figure 10. Version number attack confusion matrix

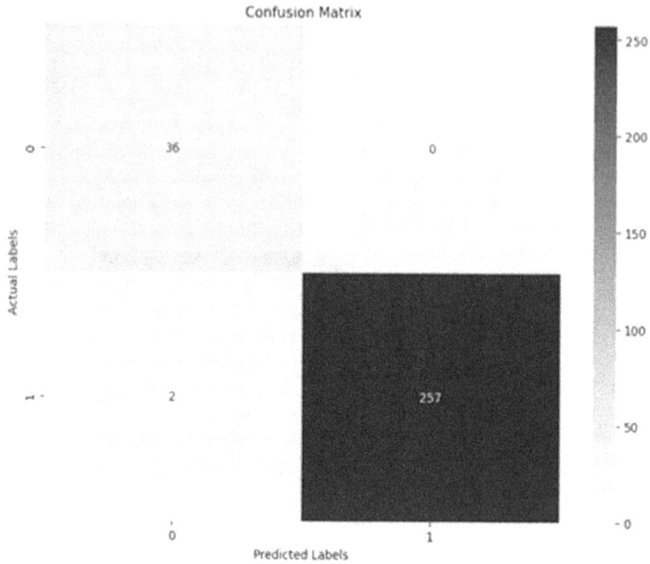

B. Comparison With the Related Studies

Many related studies on the topic of detecting malicious or benign attacks and classifying them used machine learning and deep learning models, but our proposed model outperformed all studies shown in the table Table (9), where our model (SCA+XGBoost for Decrease Rank Attack) achieved accuracy reached 97%, Precision 96%, Recall 97% and F1-Score 96%, Also (SCA+XGBoost for Hello Flooding Attack) achieved accuracy reached 99%, Precision 97%, Recall 99% and F1-Score 98% and (SCA+XGBoost for Version Number Attack) achieved accuracy reached 97%, Precision 97%, Recall 98% and F1-Score 97% compared to the studies described, as there is Study No. 1, they used the DNN and DBN model, and their results were 96%, as well as Study No. 2, they used SVM, RF, NB, and DT, and they got an accuracy of 96.1%, and Study No. 3 used more than one model Machine learning NB, DT, LR, ANN, and EM achieved an accuracy of DT: 93%. but Study No. 4, used the CNN model, and their results were 96.1%, and the last study used GCNN, LSTM, and FNN with an accuracy of 94%, Table (8) shows a comparison between most studies on IoT attack prediction with our proposed study,

REFERENCES

Al-Na'amneh, Q. A. (2024). Next Generation Image Watermarking via Combined DWT-SVD Technique. *International Conference on Cyber Resilience (ICCC)*. IEEE ACCESS. DOI: 10.1109/ICCR61006.2024.10532782

Al-Na'amneh, Q. N. (2024). Improving Memory Malware Detection in Machine Learning With Random Forest-Based Feature Selection. In *Risk Assessment and Countermeasures for Cybersecurity*. IGI Global. DOI: 10.4018/979-8-3693-2691-6.ch006

Albinali, H., & Azzedin, F. (2024). Towards RPL Attacks and Mitigation Taxonomy: Systematic Literature Review Approach. *IEEE Transactions on Network and Service Management*, *21*(5), 5215–5238. DOI: 10.1109/TNSM.2024.3386468

Alfriehat, N. A. (2024). Detecting Version Number Attacks in Low Power and Lossy Networks for Internet of Things Routing. *IEEE AccessReview and Taxonomy*. 65985.

Bokka, R., & Sadasivam, T. (2024). Simulation-based Analysis of RPL Routing Attacks and Their Impact on IoT Network Performance. *Journal of Electronic Testing*, *40*(2), 1–15. DOI: 10.1007/s10836-024-06106-w

Enders, C. K. (2021). A primer on maximum likelihood algorithms available for use with missing data. *Structural Equation Modeling*, *8*(1), 128–141. DOI: 10.1207/S15328007SEM0801_7

Fatima, M., & Pasha, M. (2017). Survey of machine learning algorithms for disease diagnostic. *Journal of Intelligent Learning Systems and Applications*, *9*(01), 1–16. DOI: 10.4236/jilsa.2017.91001

Gupta, H. B. (2024). Security Analysis of RPL-Based IoT Networks: Evaluating the Impact of Attacks on Performance Parameters. *International Conference on Advancements in Smart, Secure and Intelligent Computing*. DOI: 10.1109/ASSIC60049.2024.10508014

Hkiri, A. A., Alqurashi, S., Ben Bahri, O., Karmani, M., Faraj, H., & Machhout, M. (2024). Performance Evaluation of Mobile RPL-Based IoT Networks under Hello Flood Attack. *Electronics (Basel)*, *13*(11), 2226. DOI: 10.3390/electronics13112226

Jaradat, A. S.-N. (2023). *Genetic optimization techniques for enhancing web attacks classification in machine learning*. IEEE Intl Conf on Dependable, Autonomic and Secure Co. DOI: 10.1109/DASC/PiCom/CBDCom/Cy59711.2023.10361399

Kamel, S., & Elhamayed, S. (2020). Mitigating the impact of IoT routing attacks on power consumption in IoT healthcare environment using convolutional neural network. *Int. J. Comput. Netw. Inf. Secur.*, *12*, 11–29. DOI: 10.5815/ijcnis.2020.04.02

Laila, D. A.-N. (2024). Enhancing 2D Logistic Chaotic Map for Gray Image Encryption. In *Risk Assessment and Countermeasures for Cybersecurity* (pp. 170-188). IGI Global.

Laila, D. A.-N. (2024). Simulation of Routing Protocols for Jamming Attacks in Mobile Ad-Hoc Network. In *Risk Assessment and Countermeasures for Cybersecurity*. "ML Estimation of the Multivariate Distribution and the EM Algorithm.". *Journal of Multivariate Analysis*, *63*(2).

Mahesh, B. (2020). Machine learning algorithms-a review. *International Journal of Science and Research (IJSR).[Internet],*, *9*(1), 381-386.

Mirjalili, S. G. A., Gandomi, A. H., Mirjalili, S. Z., Saremi, S., Faris, H., & Mirjalili, S. M. (2017). SALP swarm algorithm: A bio-inspired optimizer for engineering design problems. *Nature-inspired optimizers. Springer,m. Advances in Engineering Software*, *114*, 163–191. DOI: 10.1016/j.advengsoft.2017.07.002

Mohajerani, J. G., Mohammadi Ghanatghestani, M., & Hashemipour, M. (2024). MCTE-RPL: A Multi-Context Trust-based Efficient RPL for IoT. *Journal of Network and Computer Applications*, *229*. DOI: 10.1016/j.jnca.2024.103937

Nejad, F. V. (2024). Analysis of Decreased Rank Attack on RPL-Based IoT Networks. *10th International Conference on Web Research (ICWR)*, (pp. 40-45). IEEE 2024. DOI: 10.1109/ICWR61162.2024.10533332

Omar, A. A. (2024). A Comprehensive Network Traffic Dataset for Sinkhole Attacks in Diverse RPL IoT Networks. *UOS_IOTSH_2024:*, 110650.

Osman, M., He, J., Mahiuob, F., Mokbal, M., & Zhu, N. (2021). Artificial Neural Network Model for Decreased Rank Attack Detection in RPL Based on IoT Networks. *International Journal of Network Security*, *23*, 496–503.

Osman, M. H., He, J., Zhu, N., & Mokbal, F. M. M. (2024). An ensemble learning framework for the detection of RPL attacks in IoT networks based on the genetic feature selection approach. *Ad Hoc Networks*, *152*, 103331. DOI: 10.1016/j.adhoc.2023.103331

Paganraj, D., & Chelliah, M. (2024). RPL: Detection and elimination of resource-related attacks in IoT RPL-based protocol. *The Journal of Supercomputing*, *80*(15), 1–31. DOI: 10.1007/s11227-024-06256-w

Qureshi, K., Rana, S., Ahmed, A., & Jeon, G. A. (2020). Novel and secure attacks detection framework for smart cities industrial internet of things. *Sustainable Cities and Society*, *61*, 102343. DOI: 10.1016/j.scs.2020.102343

Rajasekar, V. R., & Rajkumar, S. (2024). DSAT-IDS: Dissimilarity and Adaptive Threshold-based Intrusion Detection system to mitigate selective forwarding attack in the RPL-based 6LoWPAN. *Cluster Computing*, *27*(9), 1–40. DOI: 10.1007/s10586-024-04564-7

Remya, S. P., Pillai, M. J., Arjun, C., Ramasubbareddy, S., & Cho, Y. (2024). Enhancing Security in LLNs using a Hybrid Trust-Based Intrusion Detection System for RPL. *IEEE Access: Practical Innovations, Open Solutions*, *12*, 58836–58850. DOI: 10.1109/ACCESS.2024.3391918

Rouissat, M. B., Belkehir, M., Mokaddem, A., Bouziani, M., & Alsukayti, I. S. (2024). Exploring and mitigating hybrid rank attack in RPL-based IoT networks. *Journal of Electrical Engineering*, *75*(3), 204–213. DOI: 10.2478/jee-2024-0025

Sahay, R., Geethakumari, G., Mitra, B., & Sahoo, I. (2020). Efficient Framework for Detection of Version Number Attack in Internet of Things. In *Advances in Intelligent Systems and Computing*. Springer International Publishing.

Sahay, R., Geethakumari, G., & Mitra, B. J. (2020). A holistic framework for prediction of routing attacks in IoT-LLNs.

Sharma, S., & Verma, V. A. (2021). Artificial intelligence enabled machine learning approach for routing attacks on internet of things. *The Journal of Supercomputing*, *77*(12), 13757–13787. DOI: 10.1007/s11227-021-03833-1

Singh, A. T. (2016). A review of supervised machine learning algorithms. *n 2016 3rd international conference on computing for sustainable global development (INDIACom)*, (pp. 1310-1315). IEEE.

Tahar, G. E. (2024). Lightweight Mitigation Against DIO Suppression Attack In RPL-Based IoT Networks. *In 2024 6th International Conference on Pattern Analysis and Intelligent Systems (PAIS)*, (pp. 1-6). IEEE.).

Thamilarasu, G., & Chawla, S. (2019). Towards deep-learning-driven intrusion detection for the internet of things. *Sensors (Basel)*, *19*(9), 1977. DOI: 10.3390/s19091977 PMID: 31035611

Thamilarasu, G., & Chawla, S. (2019). Towards deep-learning-driven intrusion detection for the internet of things. *Sensors (Basel)*, *19*(9), 1977. DOI: 10.3390/s19091977 PMID: 31035611

Thamilarasu, G., & Chawla, S. (2019). Towards deep-learning-driven intrusion detection for the internet of things. .

Thamilarasu, G., & Chawla, S. T. (2019). owards deep-learning-driven intrusion detection for the internet of things. *Sensors (Basel), 19*(9), 1977. DOI: 10.3390/s19091977 PMID: 31035611

Vabalas, A. G., Gowen, E., Poliakoff, E., & Casson, A. J. (2019). Machine learning algorithm validation with a limited sample size. *PLoS One, 14*(11), e0224365. DOI: 10.1371/journal.pone.0224365 PMID: 31697686

Verma, A. V.-M., Verma, S. K., Pandey, A. C., Grover, J., & Sharma, G. (2019). A lightweight mitigation solution for DAO insider attack in RPL-based IoT. *Future Generation Computer Systems, 159*, 327–339. DOI: 10.1016/j.future.2024.05.032

Yavuz, F., Ünal, D., & Gül, E. (2018). Deep Learning for Detection of Routing Attacks in the Internet of Things. *Int. J. Comput. Intell. Syst., 12*(1), 39. DOI: 10.2991/ijcis.2018.25905181

Zilberman, A. D., Dvir, A., & Stulman, A. (2024). SPRINKLER: A Multi-RPL Man-in-the-Middle Identification Scheme in IoT Networks. *IEEE Transactions on Mobile Computing, 23*(10), 9971–9988. DOI: 10.1109/TMC.2024.3370894

Chapter 2
Shedding Light on the Dark Web
A Novel Approach to Detect and Track URL Hopping

K. G. Anilkumar
University of Kerala, India

D. Muhammad Noorul Mubarak
University of Kerala, India

ABSTRACT

The Dark Web, a hidden corner of the internet, poses a significant challenge to Law Enforcement Agencies (LEAs) due to its anonymous nature and encrypted networks. While it provides a secure platform for legitimate users, it also enables illicit activities such as cybercrime, drug trade, and terrorism. One major obstacle for LEAs is the practice of URL hopping, where Dark Web sites frequently change their URLs to evade detection. To address this issue, the authors propose a novel ensemble model that leverages machine learning techniques to analyze the content of Dark Web sites and correlate it with existing intelligence. Their system aims to improve the accuracy of tracing URL hopping on the Dark Web, ultimately enhancing the ability of LEAs to track and disrupt illicit activities. By bridging the gap between the Dark Web's anonymity and LEA's monitoring capabilities, their research contributes to a safer and more secure online environment.

DOI: 10.4018/979-8-3693-8014-7.ch002

1. INTRODUCTION

The internet, once hailed as a democratizing force for information and connection, has evolved into a multifaceted reality. Alongside the surface layer of readily accessible websites lies a hidden underbelly, the dark web. The Dark Web refers to a portion of the internet not indexed by traditional search engines and is intentionally hidden from view. This clandestine sector, shrouded in anonymity and inaccessible to conventional search engines, has become a breeding ground for innovation and illicit activity. Although the volunteers of the dark web, as well as other interested parties, often portray hidden services as a beacon of privacy and anonymity for political activists, scholarly research and Law Enforcement Agencies (LEAs) portray a starkly different reality where most hidden services enable illicit activities (Jin, Kim, Lee, & Jeong, 2023).

The dark web's hidden layers harbor significant potential for privacy, communication, and information retrieval advancements. However, they also obscure illicit activities that harm society and present critical threats to the nation. Certain dark webs are more frequently utilized than others, including the Onion Router (TOR), Invisible Internet Project (I2P), and Freenet. These platforms anonymize users' online actions and permit them to access the dark web contents with .onion or .i2p domain extensions or via specific key-based systems (Figueras-Martín, Magán-Carrión, & Boubeta-Puig, 2022). This infrastructure guarantees the anonymity of the user's identity and safeguards their activities from being observed or traced by any third party or LEAs (Manolache, Brad, Barbalau, Ionescu, & Popescu, 2022). These websites are called Hidden Services within the dark web community. They can only be accessed through particular browsers, software, or peer-to-peer systems to facilitate access to this dark web content (Alaidi, Alairaji, Alrikabi, Aljazaery, & Abbood, 2022). Considering the widespread use of TOR in the dark net landscape, our focus is primarily on TOR networks and onion websites in the context of this research paper. For the time being, we have furthermore limited our scope to those onion sites that predominantly offer content in English.

2. RELATED WORKS

The dark web is a hub for illegal activities, including drug trafficking, money laundering, and human trafficking, among others (Munksgaard & Demant, 2016; Biryukov, Pustogarov, Thill, & Weinmann, 2014; Fidalgo, Alegre, Fernández-Robles, & González-Castro, 2019). These illicit goods and services are traded on dark web marketplaces, primarily comprised of sellers and buyers with varying technical expertise. Law enforcement agencies (LEAs) face significant challenges in monitoring and tracing these illegal activities, as dark web marketplaces often switch URLs to evade detection (An ikevičs, 2021).

LEAs employ various strategies to tackle this problem, including charting the directory of hidden services, monitoring dark websites, social sites, and customer data, conducting semantic analysis, and profiling marketplaces (Ciancaglini, Balduzzi, Goncharov, & McArdle, 2013). They also use automated tools such as crawlers, spiders, scrapers, and bots for data collection from the dark web and occasionally conduct manual patrols (Nazah, Huda, Abawajy, & Hassan, 2020). Machine learning algorithms, including deep neural network models, have been utilized for detecting activities based on images and texts found on dark web websites, achieving high accuracy in various scenarios (Fayzi, Fayzi, & Ahmadi, 2023).

However, the rapid shift of dark marketplaces to new URLs remains a significant challenge for LEAs. It requires significant time and effort to manually sift through countless domains to gather information and align it with existing artifacts to identify similarities. Therefore, there is an urgent need for more advanced models and methods to generate insights and carry out forensic investigations to support the LEA community.

3. METHODOLOGY

To address the complexities of the dark web, our study proposes using ensemble models as a viable solution. Combining the predictions of multiple machine learning algorithms, ensemble models can produce more accurate forecasts than any single model. This is achieved through a divide-and-conquer approach, where individual models are aggregated to enhance overall performance. The underlying principle of ensemble modeling is that a collection of weak learners can be transformed into a strong learner, thereby improving the model's accuracy. Our study investigates the potential of a basic ensemble model, leveraging its ability to effectively combine the strengths of multiple base models, which can lead to improved stability and predictive power.

Ensemble methods are a powerful approach to improving predictive performance by combining the strengths of multiple learning algorithms. By lever- aging the diversity of multiple models, ensemble methods can produce more accurate predictions than any single model. This is achieved by combining the predictions of individual base models to generate a final prediction. The fundamental principle behind ensemble modeling is to aggregate the predictions of base models to produce a more accurate outcome. If we denote the base models as bm1, bm2, ..., bmk, and the ensemble model as EM, the general formula for ensemble learning can be expressed as 1

$$EM = fn(bm_1(x), bm_2(x), \ldots, bm_k(x)) \quad (1)$$

Here, x represents the input, $bm_i(x)$ is the prediction of the ith base model, and fn is a function that integrates the predictions of the base models to yield the final prediction. The function fn is determined by the specific ensemble method employed. For instance, in bagging, fn might be a simple majority vote for classification or averaging for regression. In boosting, fn could be a weighted majority vote, where the weights reflect the performance of the base models. In stacking, f might be another machine learning model trained to combine the base model predictions optimally. The choice of fn is critical in determining the overall performance of the ensemble model.

A key factor contributing to the success of ensemble learning is the diversity among the base models. When individual models are distinct and varied, the ensemble can capture a broader range of patterns and relationships in the data, leading to improved predictive performance. Moreover, this diversity makes the ensemble more resilient to errors or biases in any single base model, as the collective predictions can help to mitigate these issues. By combining multiple models, ensemble learning can effectively reduce the risk of overfitting, where a single model becomes overly specialized to the training data and fails to gen- eralize well to new, unseen data. In our approach, we utilize a Random For- est algorithm, a popular ensemble learning technique that leverages the power of multiple decision trees to enhance predictive accuracy. During the training phase, the Random Forest constructs multiple decision trees on different dataset sub-samples, which helps reduce overfitting and improve the model's ability to generalize. By averaging the predictions of these individual trees, the Random Forest produces a more robust and accurate output. For classification tasks, the final output is determined by a majority vote among the trees, ensuring that the most likely class is selected.

Figure 1. Architecture of the proposed methodology

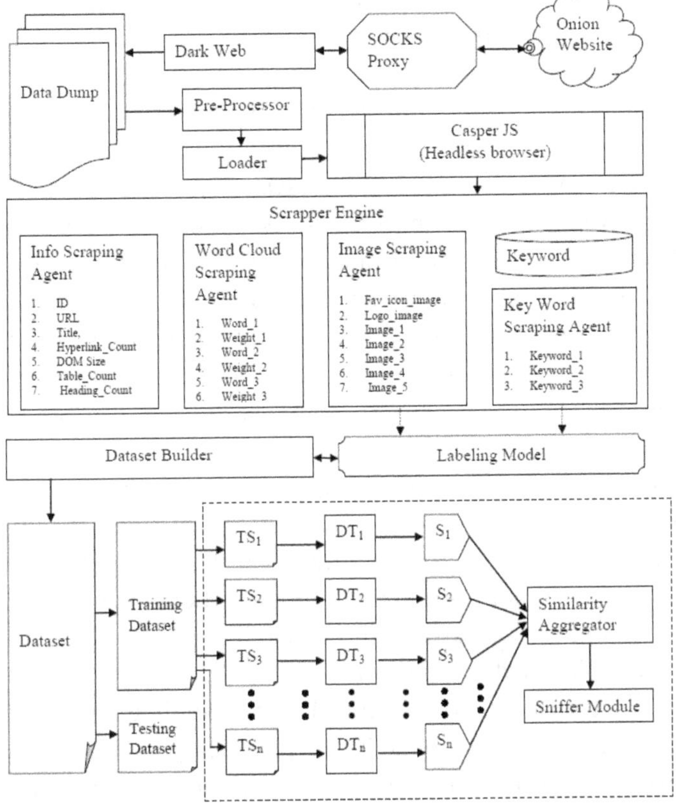

The proposed approach is illustrated in the architectural diagram presented in Figure 1. We will employ a specialized dark web crawler to collect data from onion URLs on the dark web. This crawler will utilize a SOCKS proxy, specifically the SOCKS5 version, to ensure secure and anonymous data collection. The SOCKS5 proxy is a versatile and reliable web scraping and crawling tool with several benefits. It enables the preservation of anonymity, allowing the crawler to operate without revealing its IP address or location. The SOCKS5 proxy can bypass geographical restrictions, IP bans, firewalls, and censorship filters, ensuring the crawler can access the desired data without obstruction. Furthermore, the SOCKS5 proxy can manage a wide range of network traffic, including HTTP, HTTPS, and other protocols, making it an ideal solution for real-time applications. By leveraging the SOCKS5 proxy, our dark web crawler can efficiently and effectively gather data from onion URLs while maintaining the highest level of security and anonymity. This approach ensures that our data collection process is reliable and stealthy, allowing us to gather valuable insights from the dark web without compromising our identity or security.

The crawler will store the collected content from the onion sites in a data dump, a NoSQL database, which will serve as a repository for further analysis. In our current research, we have limited the crawler to extract data from the home page of each onion site to build a foundational model. Once the data is collected, the Pre-Processor takes over, refining and filtering it to en- sure it is clean and usable. The next step involves transferring the onion site data to a headless browser, accomplished by the Loader component. We utilize CasperJS, a JavaScript-based testing and scripting framework that lever- ages PhantomJS and SlimerJS to interact headlessly with the web pages. This means that CasperJS can navigate and manipulate web pages without needing a graphical user interface, much like traditional web browsers. Instead, it can be controlled via command line or network communication, making it an ideal tool for tasks such as functional navigation, status verification, network monitoring, screen capture, and data scraping. Following the data transfer, the "Scrapper Engine" component comes into play.

The Scrapper Engine is a multi-faceted component comprising four distinct agents that work together to extract a wide range of data from the Onion website loaded into the headless browser. One of these agents, the Info Scraping Agent, is responsible for collecting fundamental information about the webpage, such as its unique identifier, URL, and title, as well as quantifying various webpage elements like hyperlinks, tables, and headings. Another agent, the Word Cloud Scraping Agent, focuses on extracting words and their corresponding weights, highlighting the top three most significant words. The Image Scraping Agent, meanwhile, is tasked with extracting visual content, including fav-icons and logos. Finally, the Key Word Scraping Agent is designed to extract specific keywords based on a predefined corpus, allowing for targeted data collection. By segmenting the scraping process into these four specialized agents, the Scrapper Engine can efficiently extract diverse data from the Onion website.

A dataset builder will utilize the information that has been extracted. This builder can create a well-structured dataset using an existing model to label the extracted data. In this context, the term 'label' refers to categorizing data. We can employ already available deep learning models and Long Short-Term Memory (LSTM) models for this specific task. The deep learning models will be used to analyze the images collected, while the LSTM models will be used to handle the keywords gathered. These models are highly effective for this purpose due to their ability to learn from large amounts of data and proficiency in pattern recognition.

In this study, the dataset was comprised of a relatively modest 326 onion sites, which allowed for manual labeling due to its manageable size. As a result, each data point was meticulously examined and categorized by a human annotator, rather than relying on automated algorithms or models. This manual labeling process ensured a high degree of accuracy and precision in assigning relevant categories to each piece of data. For the purposes of this experiment, the dataset was organized into five distinct categories as shown in Table 1, which served as a framework for structuring and analyzing the data. These categories provided a clear and concise way to group similar data points together, facilitating a more in-depth understanding of the dataset's characteristics and patterns. By using a limited number of categories, the study aimed to maintain a focused and interpretable analysis, while also laying the groundwork for potential future expansions to more comprehensive categorization systems.

Table 1. List of labels used in this experiment

Sl No.	Category	Instances
1	Drugs Selling	110
2	Weapon Selling	72
3	Hacking Service	56
4	Crypto Currency	38
5	Credit Card Selling	50

The prepared dataset will be used to train an ensemble model composed of multiple random forest models. The dataset is divided into several training subsets, denoted as TS_1, TS_2, TS_3,....., TS_n, as illustrated in Figure 1. Each of these subsets will be used to train a corresponding decision tree.

The decision trees, labeled as DT_1, DT_2, DT_3,. , DT_n, will predict a set of similarity values, represented as S_1, S_2, S_3, and so on, up to Sn. An aggregator module will then collect and combine these similarity values to produce a final result, effectively aggregating the individual decision trees' predictions to form the ensemble model's output.

The final result is subsequently passed to a module called the 'sniffer.' The sniffer's role is to identify similar onion sites that exist within the data dump produced by the crawler. Upon identifying all related artifacts, the sniffer mod- ule presents these to the investigator or any other relevant systems for further analysis. This allows for further intelligence gathering based on the data that has been "sniffed" out. This process enhances the comprehensiveness of the data analysis, thereby providing a more robust basis for decision-making or further research.

4. RESULTS AND ANALYSIS

The ensemble model, comprising a series of random forest models, was trained on a meticulously prepared dataset to form a robust and comprehensive system capable of making complex predictions. To evaluate the overall performance of our model, we used four key metrics: Accuracy, Misclassification Rate, Macro- F1, and Weighted-F1, as shown in Table 2. Our model achieved an Accuracy of 0.7077, indicating that approximately 70.77% of all instances were correctly classified. However, the Misclassification Rate was 0.2923, suggesting that ap- proximately 29.23% of instances were incorrectly classified.

Table 2. Overall performance of the model

Accuracy	**0.70**
Mis-classification Rate	0.29
Macro-F1	0.69
Weighted-F1	0.70

A closer examination of the performance of our model across different categories reveals some interesting insights as shown in Table 3. Drugs selling demonstrated the highest performance with a Precision of 0.75, Recall of 0.8333, and F1-Score of 0.7895. Our model was most effective in correctly identifying and classifying instances within this category. Weapon Selling and Hacking Service both had an F1-Score of 0.6667; however, Weapon Selling had a higher Recall (0.75) compared to the Hacking service (0.6364), indicating a better sensitivity towards positive instances in the Weapon selling category. Crypto Currency had identical Precision, Recall, and F1-Score values as Hacking Services, suggesting similar performance in these categories.

Table 3. Category-wise analysis of the model

Category	**Precision**	**Recall**	**F1-Score**
Drugs Selling	0.75	0.8333	0.7895
Weapon Selling	0.6	0.75	0.6667
Hacking Service	0.7	0.6364	0.6667
Crypto Currency	0.7	0.6364	0.6667
Credit Card Selling	0.8	0.6154	0.6957

Credit card sales had the highest precision of 0.8 among all categories, indicating a strong ability of the model to identify positive instances within this category correctly. However, its Recall was 0.6154, lower than Drugs Selling and Weapon Selling, suggesting room for improvement in identifying all positive in- stances. Overall, our model demonstrated robust performance across different categories, but there are areas where further optimization and improvement are possible.

5. CONCLUSION

In conclusion, this study has demonstrated the potential of our ensemble model in detecting illicit activities, with notable strengths in the Drugs Selling and Credit Card Selling categories. However, further refinement is needed to ad- dress areas of weakness, particularly in improving Recall in Credit Card Selling and Precision in Weapon Selling. Despite achieving a respectable accuracy of 71%, the model's mis-classification rate highlights opportunities for improvement. Future research should prioritize reducing mis-classification and enhancing the Macro-F1 and Weighted-F1 scores. This study provides a foundation for developing more advanced models for similar applications, underscoring the importance of continuous innovation and improvement in data analysis and predictive modeling.

ACKKNOWLEDGMENT

Conflict of interest: The authors declare that they have no conflict of interest.

REFERENCES

Alaidi, A. H., Alairaji, R., Alrikabi, H., Aljazaery, I., & Abbood, S. (2022). Dark web illegal activities crawling and classifying using data mining techniques. [iJIM]. *International Journal of Interactive Mobile Technologies, 16*, 122–139. DOI: 10.3991/ijim.v16i10.30209

An ikevičs, G. (2021). *Relationship between vendor popularity and prices on dark web marketplaces.*

Biryukov, A., Pustogarov, I., Thill, F., & Weinmann, R.-P. (2014). Content and popularity analysis of tor hidden services. In *2014 IEEE 34th international conference on distributed computing systems workshops (icdcsw)* (p. 188-193). DOI: 10.1109/ICDCSW.2014.20

Ciancaglini, V., Balduzzi, M., Goncharov, M., & McArdle, R. (2013). *Deepweb and cybercrime* (Tech. Rep. No. 9). Trend Micro.

Fayzi, A., Fayzi, M., & Ahmadi, K. D. (2023). Dark web activity classification using deep learning. https://arxiv.org/abs/2306.07980

Fidalgo, E., Alegre, E., Fernández-Robles, L., & González-Castro, V. (2019). Classifying suspicious content in tor darknet through Semantic Attention Keypoint Filtering. *Digital Investigation, 30*, 12–22. DOI: 10.1016/j.diin.2019.05.004

Figueras-Martín, E., Magán-Carrión, R., & Boubeta-Puig, J. (2022). Drawing the web structure and content analysis beyond the tor darknet: Freenet as a case of study. *Journal of Information Security and Applications, 68*, 103229. DOI: 10.1016/j.jisa.2022.103229

Jin, P., Kim, N., Lee, S., & Jeong, D. (2023). Forensic investigation of the dark web on the tor network: Pathway toward the surface web. *International Journal of Information Security, 23*(1), 331–346. DOI: 10.1007/s10207-023-00745-4

Manolache, A., Brad, F., Barbalau, A., Ionescu, R. T., & Popescu, M. (2022). Veridark: A large-scale benchmark for authorship verification on the dark web. https://arxiv.org/abs/2207.03477

Munksgaard, R., & Demant, J. (2016). 06). Mixing politics and crime - the prevalence and decline of political discourse on the cryptomarket. *The International Journal on Drug Policy*, *35*, 77–83. Advance online publication. DOI: 10.1016/j.drugpo.2016.04.021 PMID: 27424175

Nazah, S., Huda, S., Abawajy, J., & Hassan, M. M. (2020). Evolution of dark web threat analysis and detection: A systematic approach. *IEEE Access: Practical Innovations, Open Solutions*, *8*, 171796–171819. DOI: 10.1109/ACCESS.2020.3024198

Chapter 3

Open-Source Forensics Tools for Recovery of Deleted Data in Unconventional Ways

Tuqa Al-Makkawi
https://orcid.org/0009-0008-3034-7693
Hashemite University, Jordan

Ayoub Alsarhan
https://orcid.org/0000-0001-9075-2828
Hashemite University, Jordan

Qais Al-Na'amneh
Applied Science Private University, Jordan

Mohammad Aljaidi
https://orcid.org/0000-0001-9486-3533
Zarqa University, Jordan

Mohammed Almaiah
https://orcid.org/0009-0008-9785-485X
University of Jordan, Jordan

Mahmoud AlJamal
https://orcid.org/0009-0007-5389-6778
Hashemite University, Jordan

Rabee Alqura'n
Hashemite University, Jordan

Mahmoud Aljawarneh
https://orcid.org/0000-0003-2003-6310
Applied Science Private University, Jordan

ABSTRACT

Nowadays, technology is propagation rapidly that it is virtually completely replacing the real world with a "virtual world." Electronic forensics important as medical forensics to investigate electronic crime" which increases with time", to prevent unwanted file recovery, many computer users choose to overwrite files instead of deleting them to collect evidence and analysis by several methods and tools to present in front of the law. This paper studies the collection and analysis of files with an emphasis on deleted files from different resources and evaluates the performance

DOI: 10.4018/979-8-3693-8014-7.ch003

of open-source programs for recovering deleted data using unconventional ways. It discusses some forensics tools, including FTK, and Encase, and the ability to extract the deleted file, showing a general comparison between forensics tools.

1. INTRODUCTION

1.1 History of Digital Forensics

The area of forensic science that is concerned with finding, obtaining, processing, analyzing, and reporting material that is stored electronically by an expert is known as "digital forensics". In law enforcement investigations, digital forensics can be very helpful because nearly all crimes involve electronic evidence (Sheena, 2020). Currently, there are over a hundred procedures to practice digital forensics investigation (Ioannis, 2016), some focused on acquisition data and the other on analysis of it (Aljaidi, 2023).

Personal computers, servers, laptops, hard drives, flash drives, smartphones, networks, and SIM cards are just a few of the sources from which data can be gathered. These sources are crucial to document and examine to follow the actions of cyber criminals (Malik A. W., 2024). The digital evidence is often a file such as an Image/Video/Audio Files, System/Server/Network Log Files, Emails, Browser History/Cache, and document files (Alsarhan A. A.-G.-R., 2022). It is critical to highlight that the data collected cannot be changed or overlooked (Dunsin, 2024).

There are 5 levels of files. Each level has a different way of collecting. This paper is interested in Level 2 (Deleted Files), and Level 5 (Overwritten data) it relates to level 2 which means if we delete data and then overwrite on its block space, we also can get the first data, Deleted files can be retrieved after 7 overwritten (Patil, 2024). The file levels vary from simple to more complex. All data recovery cases fall into the following five levels (Jaradat, 2023):

- Level 0 (normal files): most common file, accessed directly includes the file names, file attributes, and file content.
- Level 1 (temporary Files): including printed, Recycle Bin files and the cache of the browser.
- Level 2 (deleted Files): when a file is deleted most operating systems remove the path reference from the containing directory and tag its block space as free for registration.
- Level 3 (retained data blocks): data include information on the virtual memory, slack space, backing store, and level 2 data which are partially replaced and cannot be fully recovered.

- Level 4 (vendor hidden blocks): data can be accessed only by using specific instructions provided by the Vendor.
- Level 5 (Overwritten data): many experts believe data can be retrieved from a hard drive, even after the replacement (overwriting) of the blocks.

Figure 1 depicts the history of digital forensics. The history can be divided into three approximate divisions.

1- EARLY YEARS: The beginning of digital forensics (DF) was in the US in the 1980s. American Congress put the first several law enforcement in court (Yeşim, 2017). Digital forensics was utilized to provide locksmith and disaster recovery services. Deleted data was partially recovered during this period (Al-Na'amneh Q. N., 2024). With the rapid advancement of technology, there is a growing interest in digital forensics as we move forward.

2- GOLDEN AGE: in 1990s, DF became a science. The International Organization on Computer Evidence (IOCE) was established to exchange digital forensic evidence between states. In 1997, Encase commercial tools appeared. The source of the data was from HDD, CD/DVD, USB, browser caches, and local email client (Raman, 2024).

3- PRESENT: It started in 2007 when Apple announced the first Smartphone (Nihar Ranjan, 2016). After that, in 2008, the first Android by Google led. Smartphones made a revolution in digital forensics which became a witness for people and their actions. Nowadays, DF is all about collecting, analyzing, preparation a report to show in court. Evidence is gathered from a variety of sources, and more advanced methods are developed to retrieve deleted data (Dhwaniket Ramesh, 2015).

Figure 1. History of Digital Forensics

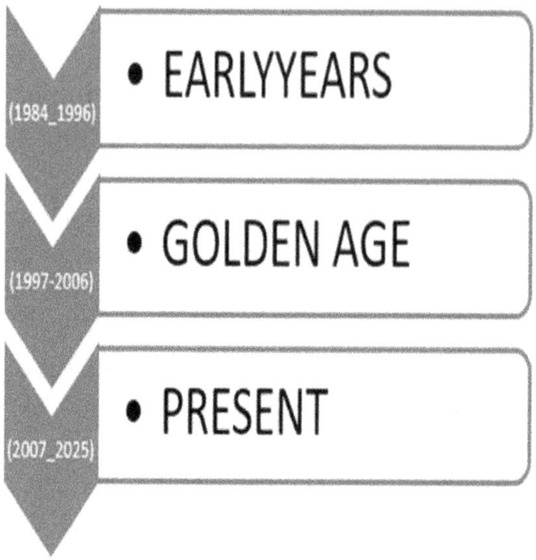

A wide variety of tools have emerged (Alsarhan A. e., 2023). Some of these tools are free and used by anyone and others are commercial. Tools are designed to help forensic investigations and maintain, debug, and recover data on digital crime, via providing acquisition and analysis of a large amount of data which examination takes a different time for each (M. Salman et al., 2020), to extract high-level data from the big amount of it needed a long time and effort (A. Alsarhan et al., 2023). This survey aims to review a variety of tools for recovering deleted files and their capability. However, criminals usually delete files to get away with their digital crimes.

1.2 Digital Forensic Phase Models

DF phases are the electronic process of extracting legal evidence from electronic evidence. Every process of investigating a digital crime has a starting point. Investigating cybercrime starts with collection, protection, analysis, reporting, and presenting digital evidence (Laila, 2024) . Choosing the wrong investigative process passing one step or swapping steps together may cause incomplete or missing evidence or weak results to be present in the court. Various investigation models are general or have many details for providing different scenarios applied to a specific scope or a wide (Priyanka, 2014). Digital forensics has four phases as shown in Figure 2 below (Malik A. W., 2024):

1. Acquisition: It's not about collecting all data; it's about deciding which data related to cyber criminals needs to be collected with the approval of the authorities. And then creating an exact copy of the original image (Alessandro Guarino, 2013).

A specialized and trained team works to collect evidence with great care without causing any damage or change to it, as evidence may be present or require some tools to recover it partially or completely on any digital device such as mobile phones, cameras, cell phones, computers, etc. (Resendez, 2014).

Evidence acquisition includes searching, recognition, collection, and documentation of electronic evidence (Friedl, 2024).

2. Examination: At this phase, investigators concentrate on the possibility of expressly identifying and locating electronic evidence that may be in an atypical location. Furthermore, hidden data should be disclosed during this phase so that evidence becomes evident (Maurya, 2024).

3. Analysis: Investigators are concerned with analyzing images acquired from electronic devices to determine the type of evidence, where it is stored, and its significance to the case (Alsarhan A. A., 2020).

The forensic analysis process consists of five components (Oettinger, 2022):

- Pre-investigation respects

The initial stage includes preparing and training investigators and providing them with the skills and equipment necessary to complete the investigation process with the least effort, time, and accuracy. On the other hand, preparing the tools also requires a financial budget to update the equipment and purchase modern technology, especially to deal with deleted or hidden evidence, which is considered one of the most prominent challenges facing criminal digital evidence.

- Comprehending case information and legal matters

Investigating digital cases is very similar to investigating real cases, as each country has laws, legislation, and rules governing the investigation.

- Grasping data acquisition

Nowadays, the process of collecting information has become more accurate and professional, so it has become important to collect information from volatile memory in all live systems, operational, networked, virtual, or physical.

- Familiarizing with the analysis process

After collecting a large and diverse amount of data, it is time to analyze it and determine the most relevant and important information for the case. In the data analysis phase, we should understand dates and time zones, antivirus, hash analysis, and file signature analysis.

- Reporting your result.

Creating a technical report that is understandable and clear to any non-technical person is a great achievement for a digital investigator.

4. Reporting: The final and most crucial step is to write an official report containing all detailed evidence from previous phases by an expert, to present in front of the court (Albugmi, 2024).

Figure 2. Digital Forensic Phase Models

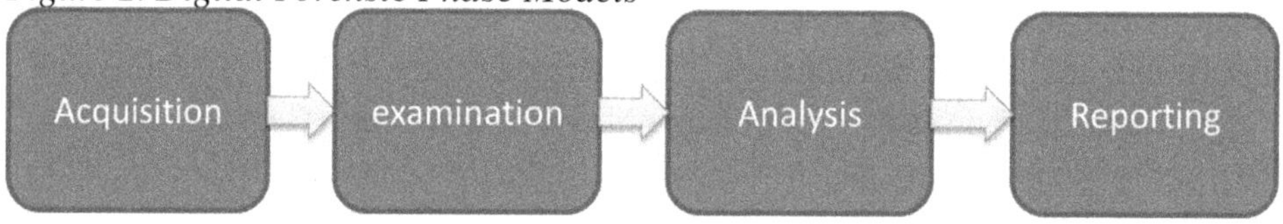

The primary contributions of this study are summarized as follows:

- Studies the collection and analysis of files with an emphasis on deleted files from different resources and evaluates the performance of open-source tools for recovering deleted data using unconventional ways.
- Discussion and Comparison of some forensics tools, including FTK, and Encase, and the ability to extract the deleted file.
- Discussion platform and challenges digital forensics tools.

The novelty of this research is a survey on digital forensics. They are motivated by the increase in cybercrimes. Section 2 highlights the limitations of the digital forensic phase's model, including collecting digital evidence from a deleted file. Section 3 examined the many tools for recovering deleted files, whether they were destroyed on purpose or by accident. Section 4 provides a brief review of the many methods of digital forensics. Section 5 provides a comparison with previous digital forensics research. The results are discussed in Section 6. Finally, the research concludes with the presentation of future work.

2. DIGITAL FORENSIC CHALLENGES

Digital forensics faces a lot of challenges, especially with the rise of smartphones, computers, and other sources of digital forensics. This rise by default will increase digital crime and its challenges. Digital forensic challenges are classified into three categories by Eric Holder, technical, legal, and resource challenges, each of them including sub-categories of challenges (Alchi, 2023). The sub-categories of challenges can be useful in developing science materials and digital forensic tools by focusing on the treatment of the challenges (Malik A. W., 2024).

- Technical challenges Evidence could easily be modified during the collection process the technical challenge is how to protect evidence from the modification, often an authority entity implementing a solution (Klasén, 2024).
- Legal challenge: several challenges could make a weak report in the court because of not enough equipment, procedures, or presentation in front of the law, another big challenge for the investigators is to save the privacy of the victim (Shirbhate, 2024).
- Source challenge: it's about data volumes and the time taken to collect and analyze, huge data may need more time to investigate (Jinad, 2024).

Table 1. Examples of Digital Forensic Challenges

No	Categories Challenge	Subcategories
1	Technical Challenges	Encryption
		The anti-forensics
		Cloud forensic challenge
		Vast volumes of data
		The sophistication of digital crimes
		Incompatibility among Heterogeneous Forensic Tools
		Steganography
		Live acquisition and analysis
2	Legal Challenge	Jurisdictional issues
		Lack of standardised international legislation
		Privacy
		Admissibility of digital forensic tools and techniques
3	Resource Challenge	Volume of data
		Time taken to acquire and analyse

3. DIGITAL FORENSIC TOOLS

There are many forensic tools "hardware and software " used for evidence investigation some for acquiring and others for analyzing the data or both, from different sources (computers, mobiles, networks), some are free, and others commercials, some of the tools accredited in the court such as Encase, FTK. Tools can extract data in three different methods (manual, physical, and logical) (Singh, 2024), tools have various capabilities on various sources, and all forensic tools take an image from the source as raw data. This survey focuses on tools that could recover deleted files, several tools have different abilities to recover deleted or missing, lost files according to the overwritten deleted space by other data, otherwise, the deleted file is generally still on the hard drive (Taneja, 2024). Table 2 has some tool and their definition, cost, and where it is applied.

- FTK: (Access Data's Forensic Toolkit) is a court-accepted digital investigation tool, easy to use in acquiring and analyzing data such as disk, file system, and application and it's also used to take a hard disk image. It could recover deleted files, email data, and password cracking or search damaged files, format, recycle bin, virus damage, and more (Hendrawan, 2024).
- EnCase: a court-accepted and global standard digital investigation tool designed by Guidance Software, used to acquire and analyze data to investigate many machines together, it can acquire physical or logical data from hard drives. The E01 image is acquired by default, and it is also used to report on evidence, it can recover damaged files, format, recycle bin, virus damage, and more, it also can identify fraud issues, get classified or sensitive information from audit machines and discover the issues related to employee (Scheidt, 2024).
- MOBILedit: a court-accepted digital phone investigation tool, got a high rate from the National Institute of Standards and Technology. Easy to use to acquire data; physical and logical, searching, and recovering data such as call history, contact, and SMS and good for phone backup, it's able to avoid passcode, PIN code phone backup encryption (Moreb, 2024).
- Oxygen Forensic: court-accepted digital forensic phone and IOT software investigation tool, used to acquire, analyze, device backup, and decode data, it's able to avoid screen locks and recover deleted data, it collects data more than that collected by logical forensic, in smartphones it transfers call history into extended file event log contain all calls (Schmitt, 2024).
- Recuva: free software tools, mainly used to recover deleted files, recycle bins, formatted devices, digital camera cards, MP3 players, and damaged hard drives (Shibwabo, 2024).

- Paraben Device Seizure: digital phone investigation tool that includes software and hardware, used to acquire, and analyze; logical and physical data, full data dumps, and recovery of deleted files on a wide range of phones, PDAs, and GPS devices, it can collect: SMS, MMS, call history, browser history (Grigollo, 2024).

Table 2. Digital Forensic Tools

Tool	Op System	Features	Commercial
FTK	Windows	Easy to use, flexible, comprehensive volatile memory analysis.	Yes
Encase	Linux	Acquiring from almost anywhere, advanced analysis, automatic report.	Yes
MOBILedit	Windows	Software security, backup phone content, updated often.	No
Oxygen Forensic	Windows, Linux	Analyze data from multiple digital resources, device backup, and cloud services.	Yes
Recuva	Windows	Recover deleted emails and iPod music, restore unsaved Word documents, and deep scan.	No
Paraben Device Seizure	Windows	Don't allow the evidence to alter on the device, offering a memory image "often where the deleted file is located" from the devices supported by it.	Yes

FTK and Recuva tools running on Windows can recover files such as pictures, videos, documents, etc. From phones, USB flash, memory cards, and more. Encase tool is very similar to the previous two tools but works on the Linux operating system. The MOBILedit, Oxygen Forensic, and Paraben Device Seizure tools are specialized in collecting and analyzing data from phones only, and they all work on the Windows operating system.

4. CLASSIFICATION OF DIGITAL FORENSIC

Digital forensic evidence is a broad term that can classify the evidence based on its content into many different classifications such as computer forensic, memory forensic, multimedia forensic, network forensic, mobile forensic, database forensic, live forensic, cloud forensic, and much more, each of them has many forensic tools to handle with their evidence. For Example, in a crime implemented by email, the investigator classifies the email by its content to find which computer the email came from (Alsarhan A. A., 2021) the most popular classification is shown in Figure 3:

- Computer forensics: Digital investigators started their work using computers, which enables them to deal with a wide range of digital information such as browser history, files, photos, documents, etc. This category specializes in recovering evidence from computers, laptops, USB drives, operating systems, and more, using various tools such as FTK, Encase, OSF, and Recuva. (Bernardo B. M., 2024).
- Mobile forensic: Specializes in investigating and recovering data and digital evidence such as call details, SMS, email, and location from smartphones, Android, and IOS devices, using Paraben Device Seizure, iPhone analyzer, and MOBILedit tools. (Bernardo B. M., 2024).
- Network forensic: It investigates evidence by auditing the network traffic and analyzing the network event, intrusion, and data packets on both LAN and MAN networks to detect who attacked the network, by using several tools such as Network Miner, Nmap, and Wireshark (Collins, 2024).
- Memory forensic: It investigates evidence on volatile memory, which stores the temporary data lost when the device shutdown like chat history, browser history, and more from RAM, cache as row data to discloser what's contained, by using several tools such as Volatility, SANS SIFT, and BlackLight (Nandhashree, 2024) .

Figure 3. Classification of Digital Forensic

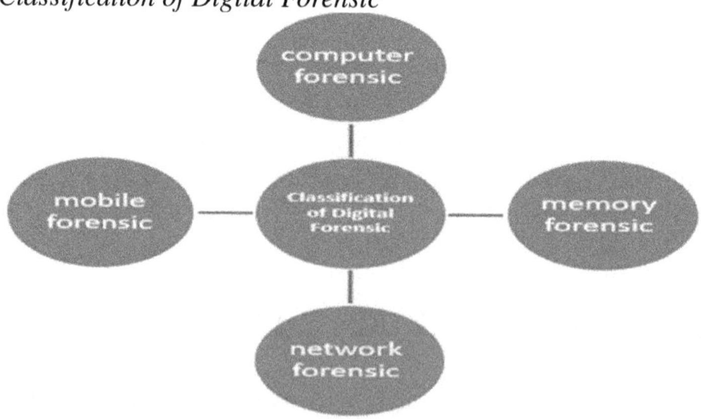

5. COMPARISON STUDIES IN DIGITAL FORENSICS TOOLS:

Forensic investigation takes more than two tools, some of the tools are specific to recovering files from phones like MOBIL edit, while others could recover files from computers, phones, and USBs like Encase, they use free trial or commercial tools to aim to recover deleted file (Al-Na'amneh Q. A., 2024)such as pictures, audio, video, SMS, and contact one literature compare tools based on their general capability by the total number it could recover/delete files. DF can be used for spectrum estimation. Table 3 provides the literature Methodology. According to (Ruan, 2024) using the Live Response forensic toolset drastically altered the volatile data environment in certain instances and could override potentially important evidence. Memory image analysis is another alternate method that lowers the possibility of losing sensitive evidence. This comparison study highlights how both approaches can be used to recover and retrieve volatile data. (Bernardo B. M., 2024) demonstrate and clarify the significance of the live forensic data and artifacts that are discoverable in addition to the techniques and equipment utilized to extract and examine data from RAM. Additionally, it demonstrates how, on occasion, forensic investigation data from RAM can include enough proof to close a case. The choice of acquisition software has a significant impact on the data quality during copying, (Jung, 2024). The findings of an investigation into the memory depth of seven Windows 7 acquisition programs—FTK Imager, Belkasoft Memory Capturer, the program ProDiscover, Windows Memory Reader, WinEn, DumpIt, and Memorize—were obtained. Using RAM differently when running software produced varied outcomes. Ten times as many relics artifacts were found in FTK Imager Pro as in Belkasoft and operating systems Memory Reader, eight times more than in WinEn, and five times more in DumpIt and Memorize. These artifacts have the potential to destroy crucial forensic data in memory which will be detrimental to the investigation. The other four tested programs (Windows Memory Reader, WinPmem, FTK Imager, and DumpIt) were evaluated according to two factors (impact and completeness) by (Hubbard, 2024). Throughout the trial, WMR and DumpIt were shown to have a minimal effect and to exhibit the highest accuracy. In (Li, 2024) demonstrated hardware and software for memory acquisition and storage in real-time, enabling the procedures that take place throughout a system's transition to widespread availability. While the use of software techniques will affect the data obtained, the use of hardware does not affect the data acquired, but the cost of this method makes it unfeasible. The algorithm used in this study will ensure that the data gathered is legitimate and admissible in court. According to (Alchi, 2023), cybercrime will flourish on virtual machines, thus the methods employed must be suitable. For example, an acquisition strategy using a live internal file can be used to collect VMware, and it can be used to analyze files obtained from raw data stored in different grains. Tools for acquisition in live and dead forensics were studied by (Bernardo B. M., 2024) approach is dependent on the intended audience. Using acquisition tools as a comparison, this study highlights the benefits and drawbacks of both approaches. The findings of this study suggest using the live forensics method, which is the most efficient way to investigate quickly because it only collects data from the RAM that is now in use.

Table 3. The comparison of the related studies in Digital Forensics

Ref	Methodology	Goals
(Ruan, 2024)	Testing on different OS and USB by using five tools	Acquiring deleted data practically on different file systems and hard drive technologies.
(Bernardo B. M., 2024)	Testing of two phones by using four tools	For recovering related information, pictures, contacts, SMS, Applications, Audio, videos, web browser cache history, call log
(Jung, 2024)	Testing USB by using five tools	Tested 5 features, test how good the program is in carving documents, video, audio, pictures, and other types of files such as zip, HTML, PSD, EXE, and MSI.
(Hubbard, 2024)	Testing five phones by using four tools	Acquiring deleted data and SIM-related information from different mobile phones (using different operating systems)
(Li, 2024)	Testing a phone by using five tools	To exanimate the gathering of volatile data and deleted information of some existing mobile forensics tools.

6. ANALYSIS AND RESULT

The result for Windows 8.1 (NTFS) SSD 128 GB shows almost the same previous result but a larger number; of duplicated or more deleted file recoveries for each tool and each of them required less time to analyze, we can say OSForensis tool is useful here. SSD shows more efficiency results than HDD. The result for USB Stick (FAT32) 8GB was showing all tools detect a few numbers of deleted files with a good percentage to use except Recuva.

A. **FTK**: The tool applied to 7 phones was able to recover deleted photos, videos, and audio for each phone. It was also able to recover deleted photos from USB only.
B. **Encase**: The tool was able to recover deleted photos, videos, and audio from the phone. This tool showed better results in recovering data from USB than the FTK tool, but on the other hand, it recovered less data from phones.
C. **MOBILedit**: Applied on 3 phones, it could recover the deleted Web browser cache history on one phone (Samsung) and recovered all SIM-related information tested, so it has high capability to recover the SIM-related information (IMEI, ICCID, and IMSI). This forensic tool cannot extract any data on the HTC Desire 300 but it shows 2 results on Samsung Galaxy (GT-S5300), they searched on the official site of MOBILedit then found HTC Desire 300 was not part of the list, the weird thing is Samsung Galaxy (GT-S5300) also was not part of the list, and despite Nokia E5-00 Mobile Phone was supported by MOBILedit! Forensic tool but it can't recover any deleted files.
D. **Oxygen Forensic:** Applied on 2 a phone, the tool could recover the IMEI only and it recovers the deleted SMS messages.
E. **Recuva**: Applied on a USB which can recover deleted pictures, videos, and audio
F. **Paraben Device Seizure:** It has been applied to 5 phones and can recover deleted photos, videos and audio for some of them.

According to the previous papers, different tools could recover different files on various classifications, on USB the Recuva and the Encase show a good result. But on Phone FTK could recover deleted videos, audio, and pictures for all phones tested on, it surpasses their result on the other tools specific to Phones. After the FTK it came to Paraben Device Seizure and Encase also could recover deleted videos, audio, and pictures but not for all phones tested on. The Oxygen Forensic was the only one that could recover deleted SMS. MOBILedit was able to recover all related SIM information for all Phones tested on, also it could recover Web browser cache history for one Phone. On Windows Encase could recover a greater number of the deleted files with the ability to use it.

That means that one cybercrime could need more than one tool according to the digital evidence needed to be collected because the tools have variable capabilities in different classifications of digital forensics.

Table 4 shows the results of every tool on a different platform: phones and USB, the windows result is not mentioned because the purpose is to acquire deleted data practically on different file systems (.zip .doc .jpeg .txt. Avi) and hard drive technologies, based on several deleted file and percentage to use it as digital evidence. FTK Imager was used to create the E01 image files for each disc. The result for

Windows 8.1 (NTFS) 640 GB showed showing Encase tool the best result which it recovers more deleted files and ability to be used but it takes the longest time for disk analysis, and secondary Autopsy with a big difference in the number of recovered deleted files, and high capability to use those little files (compared to Encase) it also takes a long time relative to the number of files detected. Finally, OSForensis and Recuva are the least useful programs according to studies due to the low file recovery ability of OSForensis and the very low file recovery rate of Recuva.

Table 4. Comparison of Digital Forensic tools (Hargreaves, 2024)

Attribute	EnCase	DFF	Pro-Discover	X-ways Forensis	FTK	Quest changeauditor	The Sleuth Kit	COFEE	SIFT	WindowsSCOPE	Bulk_Extractor
License	Proprietary	Open	Proprietary	Proprietary	Open	Proprietary	Open	Proprietary	Open	Proprietary	Open
Platform	Windows, MAC, Linux, DOS Machine	Windows, Linux	Windows, Linux	Windows, DOS	Windows XP/Vista /7/8/10	Windows	Windows, Unix, DOS,BSDpartitions,Mac.	Windows	Ubuntu	Windows	Windows, Linux and Mac
Disk Imaging	Yes	Yes	Yes	Yes	Yes	Yes	Yes	Yes	Yes	Yes	Yes
Data Carving	Yes	Yes	Yes	Yes	Yes	Yes	Yes	Yes	Yes	Yes	Yes
Memory Dump Analysis	Yes	Yes	Yes	Yes	Yes	Yes	No	Yes	Yes	Yes	No
Data Recovery	Yes	Yes	Yes	Yes	Yes	Yes	Yes	Yes	Yes	Yes	Yes
Password Recovery	Yes	No	Yes	Yes	Yes	No	No	Yes	No	No	Yes
File Supported System	FAT12/16/32, NTFS, UFS, JFS, ext2, ext3, ReiserFS and AIX Journaling File System	FAT 12/16/32, ext2,ext3, HFS and NTFS	FAT12/16/32, ext2, ext3 NTFS and UFS	FAT12/16/32, exFAT, TFAT, NTFS, Ext2, Ext3, Ext4, Next 3®, CDFS/ ISO 9660/Joliet, UDF	FAT16/3 2, NTFS, ext2 and ext3	FAT12/16/32,exFAT, NTFS,HFS and HFS+,HPFS,APFS,UFS,ext2,ext3,ext4,XFS	NTFS, FAT12/16/32/ExFAT, HFS+, ISO9660 (CD-ROM), Ext2/Ext3 /Ext4, Yaffs2 and UFS	FAT12/16/32,exFAT, NTFS,HFS and HFS+,HPFS,APFS,UFS,ext2,ext3,ext4,XFS	NTFS, HFS+, FAT12 /16/32, ext2, 3,4, UFS1, UFS2	FAT12/16/32,exFAT, NTFS,HFS and HFS+,HPFS,APFS,UFS,ext2,ext3,ext4,XFS	FAT12/16 /32, NTFS, UFS, JFS, ext2, ext3, ReiserFS
Real-Time Alert	Yes	Yes	Yes	No	Yes	Yes	Yes	Yes	No	Yes	No
Slack space	Yes	No	Yes	Yes	Yes	No	Yes	Yes	No	No	No
Email Analysis	Yes	No	No	No	Yes	Yes	Yes	No	No	No	Yes
Static and Live Analysis	Static	Both	Live	Both	Static	Live	Live	Live	Live	Live	Live
Decryption	Yes	Yes	Yes	Yes	Yes	Yes	No	Yes	No	Yes	Yes
Incident Response	Yes	No	Yes	No	Yes	Yes	Yes	Yes	Yes	Yes	No

7. CONCLUSION AND FUTURE WORK

Overwriting digital data destroys evidence in the digital realm. Open-source tools can be used as a preliminary examination tool at the lower level of investigation, revealing the existence of files through their header file and date of creation. Many computer users prefer to overwrite their files instead of deleting them due to the risk of file recovery. Implementing digital forensic techniques reduces stress and improves case efficiency, making them ideal for investigations. This study analyzes collection and analysis files, with an emphasis on deleted files from various sites, and evaluates the performance of open-source applications for recovering lost data using unusual methods. Future research can benefit from a variety of tools and features. Also, a comparing outcome between the tool and parameter.

REFERENCES

Al-Na'amneh, Q. A. (2024). Next Generation Image Watermarking via Combined DWT-SVD Technique. In 2024 2nd International Conference on Cyber Resilience (ICC.

Al-Na'amneh, Q. N. (2024). Improving Memory Malware Detection in Machine Learning With Random Forest-Based Feature Selection. In Risk Assessment and Countermeasures for Cybersecurity.

Albugmi, A. (2024). Digital Forensics Readiness Framework (DFRF) to Secure Database Systems. *Engineering, Technology &. Applied Scientific Research, 14*(2), 13732–13740.

Alchi, A. (2023). Advanced Forensics Open-Source Tools. In *Advanced Techniques and Applications of Cybersecurity and Forensics* (pp. 22–34). Chapman and Hall/ CRC.

Alessandro Guarino. (2013). *Digital Forensics as a Big Data Challenge*. Information Security Solutions Europe.

Aljaidi, M. A.-F.-A.-S.-N. (2023). Cybersecurity Threats in the Era of AI: Detection of Phishing Domains Through Classification Rules. . *In 2023 2nd International En.*

Alsarhan, A., ... (2023). "Forensic Handwriting and Signatures Using Machine Learning Techniques,". *2023 2nd International Engineering Conference on Electrical, Energy, and Artificial Intelligence (EICEEAI), Zarqa, Jordan, 2023, pp. 1-6,* , (pp. pp. 1-6, doi:)DOI: 10.1109/EICEEAI60672.2023.10590549

Alsarhan, A. A. (2020). A. Profit optimization in multi-service cognitive mesh network using machine learning. J Wireless Com Network 2011, 36 (2011). . .DOI: 10.1186/1687-1499-2011-36

Alsarhan, A. A. (2021). A New Covid-19 Tracing Approach using Machine Learning and Drones Enabled Wireless Network. . *International Journal of Interactive Mobile Technologies (iJIM),* .

Alsarhan, A. A.-G.-R. (2022). A Novel Scheme for Malicious Nodes Detection in Cloud Markets Based on Fuzzy Logic Technique. International Journal of Interactive Mobile Technologies (iJIM), 16(0.

Alsarhan, A. E. (2023). Enhancing Phishing URL Detection: A Comparative Study of Machine Learning Algorithms. " Proceedings of the 2023 Asia Conference on Artificial Intelligence, Machine Learning and Robotics. 2023.</conf>

Bernardo, B. M., Mamede, H. S., Barroso, J. M. P., & Dos Santos, V. M. P. D. (2024). Mobile Device Forensics Framework: A Toolbox to Support and Enhance This Process. *Emerging Science Journal*, *8*(3), 972–998. DOI: 10.28991/ESJ-2024-08-03-011

Bernardo, B. M., Mamede, H. S., Barroso, J. M. P., & Dos Santos, V. M. P. D. (2024). Mobile Device Forensics Framework: A Toolbox to Support and Enhance. *This Process.Emerging Science Journal*, *8*(3), 972–998. DOI: 10.28991/ESJ-2024-08-03-011

Bernardo, B. M., Mamede, H. S., Barroso, J. M. P., & Dos Santos, V. M. P. D. (2024). Mobile Device Forensics Framework: A Toolbox to Support and Enhance This Process. *Emerging Science Journal*, *8*(3), 972–998. DOI: 10.28991/ESJ-2024-08-03-011

Collins, M. D. (2024). Superflows: A New Tool for Forensic Network Flow Analysis. *arXiv preprint arXiv:2403.01314.*

Dhwaniket Ramesh, N. J. (2015). DIGITAL FORENSIC TOOLS: A COMPARATIVE APPROACH . *International Journal of Advance Research In Science And Engineering.*

Dunsin, D. G., Ghanem, M. C., Ouazzane, K., & Vassilev, V. (2024). A comprehensive analysis of the role of artificial intelligence and machine learning in modern digital forensics and incident response. *Forensic Science International Digital Investigation*, *48*, 301675. DOI: 10.1016/j.fsidi.2023.301675

Friedl, S. R. (2024). Digital Detectives: A Serious Point-and-Click Game for Digital Forensics. In IFIP World Conference on Information Security Education Cham. *Springer Nature Switzerland.*, (pp. (pp. 129-145).). DOI: 10.1007/978-3-031-62918-1_9

Grigollo, F. V., & Fernandes, R. F. (2024). Comparative analysis of software used in anonymised search and seizure cases: Acquisition, examination and analysis. *Caderno Pedagógico*, *21*(4), e3557–e3557. DOI: 10.54033/cadpedv21n4-015

Hargreaves, C. N., Nelson, A., & Casey, E. (2024). An abstract model for digital forensic analysis tools-A foundation for systematic error mitigation analysis. *Forensic Science International Digital Investigation*, *48*, 301679. DOI: 10.1016/j.fsidi.2023.301679

Hendrawan, A. H. (2024). Enhancing Cybersecurity Through Live Forensic Investigation of Remote Access Trojan Attacks using FTK Imager Software. *International Journal of Safety and Security Engineering.*

Hubbard, K. B., Birycka, M., Britton, M.-E., Coates, J., Coxon, I. D., Jackson, C. H., Nicholas, C. L., Priestley, T. M., Robins, J. J., Ryczko, P. R., Salisbury, T., Shand, M., Snodin, G., & Worsley, B. (2024). The 'Tea Test'-a mobile phone based spectrophotometer protocol to introduce biochemical methods independent of the laboratory. *Journal of Biological Education, 58*(2), 483–494. DOI: 10.1080/00219266.2022.2072934

Ioannis, T. S. (2016). Evaluation of Digital Forensics Tools on Data Recovery and Analysis.

Jaradat, A. S.-N. (2023). *Genetic optimization techniques for enhancing web attacks classification in machine learning. In 2023 IEEE Intl Conf on Dependable.* Autonomic and Secure Co.

Jinad, R. G., Gupta, K., Simsek, E., & Zhou, B. (2024). Bias and fairness in software and automation tools in digital forensics. *J. Surveill. Secur. Saf, 5*(1), 19–35. DOI: 10.20517/jsss.2023.41

Jung, J. H., Han, S., Park, M., & Cho, S. (2024). Automotive digital forensics through data and log analysis of vehicle diagnosis Android apps. *Forensic Science International Digital Investigation, 49*, 301752. DOI: 10.1016/j.fsidi.2024.301752

Klasén, L. F. (2024). Digital Forensics as Key to Solving Crimes in the Digital Age. *The Invisible Evidence: Forensic Science International, 112133.*

Laila, D. A.-N. (2024). Enhancing 2D Logistic Chaotic Map for Gray Image Encryption. In I. R. Cybersecurity.

Li, Q., & Chan, K. K. (2024). Test takers' attitudes of using exam-oriented mobile application as a tool to adapt in a high-stakes speaking test. *Education and Information Technologies, 29*(1), 219–237. DOI: 10.1007/s10639-023-12297-0

Malik, A. W., Bhatti, D. S., Park, T.-J., Ishtiaq, H. U., Ryou, J.-C., & Kim, K.-I. (2024). Cloud digital forensics: Beyond tools, techniques, and challenges. *Sensors (Basel), 24*(2), 433. DOI: 10.3390/s24020433 PMID: 38257526

Maurya, M. (2024). Digital Forensics and Cyber Investigation. *International Journal of Innovative Research in Technology and Science, 12*(2), 363–365.

Moreb, M., Salah, S., & Amro, B. (2024). A novel framework for mobile forensics investigation process. *International Journal of Computing and Digital Systems, 16*(1), 125–136. DOI: 10.12785/ijcds/160110

Nandhashree, K. R. (2024). State of Art Survey on Memory Forensic Acquisition & Techniques. In Next-Gen Technologies i. *n Computational Intelligence (pp. 465-469). CRC Press.* DOI: 10.1201/9781003430452-70

Nihar Ranjan, A. K. (2016). Android Phone Forensic: Tools and Techniques .

Oettinger, W. (2022). *Learn Computer Forensics.*

Patil, R. Y., Patil, Y. H., Bannore, A., & Ranjanikar, M. (2024). Ensuring accountability in digital forensics with proxy re-encryption based chain of custody. *International Journal of Information Technology : an Official Journal of Bharati Vidyapeeth's Institute of Computer Applications and Management, 16*(3), 1841–1853. DOI: 10.1007/s41870-023-01663-3

Priyanka, P. R. (2014). Mining Frequent Sequences for Emails in Cyber Forensics Investigation. *nternational. Jisuanji Yingyong.*

Raman, R. S., Sahu, A. K., Nair, V. K., & Nedungadi, P. (2024). Opposing agents evolve the research: A decade of digital forensics. *Multimedia Tools and Applications*, •••, 1–29. DOI: 10.1007/s11042-024-19519-8

Resendez, I. (2014). *An Introduction to Digital Forensics.* Research Gate.

Ruan, Z. N. (2024). USB Interrupt Differentiated Service for Bandwidth and Delay-Constrained Input/Output. In 2024 IEEE 30th Real-Time and Embedded Technology and Applications Symposium (RTAS). (pp. 42-54). IEEE.

Salman, M., ... (2020). "A Study of Forensic Tools Data Recovery Performance,". *2023 2nd International Engineering Conference on Electrical, Energy, and Artificial Intelligence (EICEEAI), Zarqa, Jordan, 2023,* (pp. pp. 1-6,)DOI: 10.1109/EICEEAI60672.2023.10590383

Scheidt, N. . (2024). Friend or Foe?: How Anti-Digital Forensics vs. Digital Forensics Make or Break a Case. In Cases on Forensic and Criminological Science for Criminal Detection and Avoidance. *(pp. 356-378). IGI Global.*

Schmitt, V., & Butterfield, E. (2024). Digital forensics in healthcare: An analysis of data associated with a CPAP machine. *Forensic Science International Digital Investigation, 48*, 301661. DOI: 10.1016/j.fsidi.2023.301661

Sheena, R. S. (2020). *A Survey on Digital Forensics Phases.* Tools and Challenges.

Shibwabo, B. K. (2024). Data Recovery of Flash Memory. Nanocrystals in Non-volatile Memory, 347.

Shirbhate, D. D. (2024). A Review Paper on Cyber Security and Digital Forensics. *Grenze International Journal of Engineering & Technology (GIJET), 10.*

Singh, S., & Kumar, R. (2024). Image forgery detection: Comprehensive review of digital forensics approaches. *Journal of Computational Social Science*, *7*(1), 1–39. DOI: 10.1007/s42001-024-00265-8

Taneja, N. B., Bramhe, V. S., Bhardwaj, D., & Taneja, A. (2024). Understanding digital image anti-forensics: An analytical review. *Multimedia Tools and Applications*, *83*(4), 10445–10466. DOI: 10.1007/s11042-023-15866-0

Yeşim, A. (2017). Review of Evidence Analysis and Reporting Phases in Digital Forensics Process. *InInternational Conference on Computer Science and Engineering (UBMK),* IEEE.

Chapter 4
Impact of Decreased Rank Attack on Network Topology of RPL Using Contiki-NG

Qais Al-Na'amneh
https://orcid.org/0009-0008-3034-7693
Applied Science Private University, Jordan

Walid Dhifallah
https://orcid.org/0000-0003-1368-9612
University of Gabes, Tunisia

Rahaf Hazaymih
Jordan University of Science and Technology, Jordan

Tasnim Al-Harasis
https://orcid.org/0009-0004-7440-9850
Al Hussein Technical University, Jordan

Mohammed Almaiah
https://orcid.org/0009-0008-9785-485X
University of Jordan, Jordan

Braa Qadoumi
https://orcid.org/0000-0002-4753-7820
Applied Science Private University, Jordan

Ayoub Alsarhan
https://orcid.org/0000-0001-9075-2828
Hashemite University, Jordan

ABSTRACT

The Internet of Things (IoT) refers to the widespread use of smart objects connected to the internet. This innovative technology serves as the foundation for various intelligent gadgets, including smartphones, smart homes, and electric equipment. Furthermore, these devices are uniquely identified and automatically connected to the network. RPL emphasizes security due to the nature of objects and their restrictions, which might pose weaknesses for cyber-attacks. It is crucial to identify and

DOI: 10.4018/979-8-3693-8014-7.ch004

assess all potential assaults on this protocol, including the rank attack, which can significantly impact network performance and energy usage. The impact of rank assaults on the proactive IoT routing protocol, Low Power Lossy Network (RPL), is discussed in this study. It emphasizes the necessity of addressing these attacks concerning different scenarios preserving topology, avoiding communication delays, and reducing throughput. The proposed solution significantly decreases the impact of a decreased rank attack on network performance.

I. INTRODUCTION

A special attack in the RPL standard is the Decreased Rank Attack, which uses the rank property to produce a topology that is only partially sub-optimized (Ghaleb, 2023). A hostile actor announces a fictitious lower-rank value to trick nodes into choosing the attacker as their preferred parent on the path to the root. Although it isn't harmful in theory it can harm a network even more when combined with other attacks like selective forwarding or bypass attacks The RPL Decreased Rank attack is assessed in this paper, and a Secure Objective Function (Sec-OF) is suggested to stop malevolent players from starting attacks. A significant threat to the RPL protocol inside the IoT 6LowPAN communication standard is the Decreased Rank attack (Aljaidi, 2023).

In addition to analyzing four mitigation and detection strategies, this work suggests modifying TRAIL to compute the downward trip time (DTT) for nodes. It presents a potential exploit utilizing nonlinear objective functions (NOFs) (Tolsma, 2021). There are three primary categories of rank attacks: worst-parent, raised rank, and decreased rank. Additionally, the article presents a potential vulnerability that might lead to network loops, let neighbors select a less-than-ideal parent, and deceive a node's rank Although TRAIL does not stop decreasing rank attacks, it does guarantee a path from the root that increases in rank monotonically. It is less complicated for devices with limited resources and defends against higher-rank attacks than VeRA (Boudouaia, 2020).

Figure 1. The Contiki network architecture, emphasizing the attacked layer.

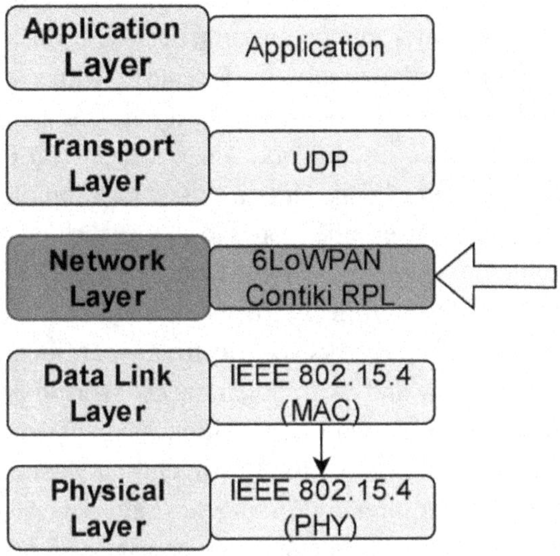

Figure 1 This study aims to present the outcomes of attacks and create a framework for assessing malicious nodes in Cooja systems. Th (Nandhini, 2023)e document is structured into three sections: RPL Attacks, the framework, and experimentation. By using standards, the document displays the root of DODAG as a green node, the attacker as a red node with a label of "A," and normal nodes as yellow nodes labeled with a number (Osman, 2021).

The article talks about the RPL Protocol's recent contributions and the rank attack on it. It introduces the RPL routing protocol, talks about security issues with it, and offers several mitigating strategies. The Friedman test is also used throughout the article to compare various attacks. Worst-Parent Attack increased Rank Attack and lowered Rank Attack are among the attacks. To draw in nearby nodes, the malicious node lowers its rank value. This results in traffic disruption, resource consumption, and packet transmission delays. The page also covers mitigation techniques and the most recent assaults (Laila, 2024) .

One kind of RPL assault is called a "rank attack," in which malicious nodes pretend to be the best parent for benign nodes by promoting a phony rank. Robust solutions are necessary to safeguard important data and resources from these attacks (Karmakar, 2021). A rank attack occurs when nodes in a network select their preferred parent depending on OF and rank. Attackers can change these factors, which can harm topology and are frequently combined with other assaults (Seth, 2020).

The plan suggests safeguarding RPL during topology generation and maintenance using a low-overhead rank attack detection technique. This system is tested using multiple test cases to confirm accuracy and practicality. It detects both increased and decreased rank assaults and maintains basic security with a low overhead MAC technique (Zahra, 2022). Rank attacks are damaging in RPL and have the potential to upset the topology of the entire network. There are two varieties: elevated and reduced. Malicious nodes mistakenly pinpoint their location closer to the root in less frequent attacks, which causes other nodes to choose the malicious node as their preferred parent. Malicious nodes raise their rank in escalating attacks to disturb the routing topology (A. Almusaylim, 2020).

Significant risks to the RPL networks' security triad—confidentiality, availability, and integrity come from rank and wormhole attacks. Wormhole attacks generate tunnels that lead to resource and network degradation, whereas decreased rank attacks use broadcasting a lower rank number to draw in child nodes. Improving security in RPL-based IoT networks requires addressing these attacks (Al-Na'amneh, 2023).

RPL protocol security is crucial for resource-constrained devices, as they face multiple security threats. Rank and version number RPL assaults can significantly impact network performance, with rank assaults causing non-optimal pathways and low packet delivery ratios, while version number attacks cause significant delays and increased overhead control. However, studies show shortcomings in supporting multiple attacks and distinguishing between malicious and legal nodes (Laila D. A.-N., 2024). A diagram illustrating the taxonomy of network attacks displays the attacks denoted by blue frames. Network resources are depleted by malicious nodes forcing genuine nodes to perform unnecessary tasks. The first kind is this one. This could have an impact on link congestion, network availability, and node incapacitation, all of which could reduce the network's lifespan.

Figure 2 There are two types of attacks on the RPL network architecture: direct and indirect. They intend to disrupt regular operations and create node isolation. This includes node isolation and sub-optimization, which cause the network to converge to an unfavorable shape. Network traffic attacks fall under the third category; they aim to introduce rogue nodes into the network without affecting its functionality. Information leaking may occur from listening in on communications or from posing as legitimate nodes. This includes both passive eavesdropping and the improper usage of a node or set of nodes to modify data that has been delivered correctly (Jaradat, 2023).

Figure 2. RPL network attack taxonomy (Decreased Rank Attack)

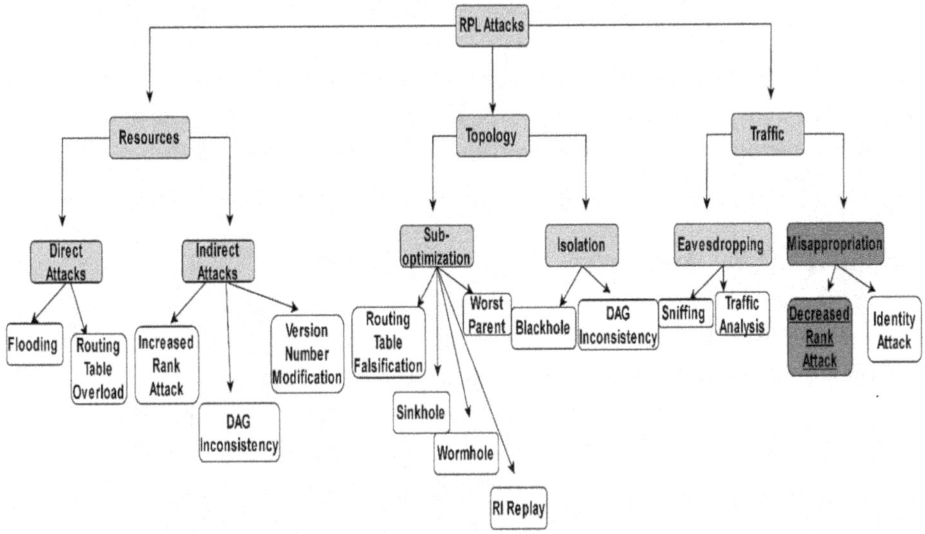

Figure 3 shows Decreased Rank: Advertising lower ranks to enable attackers to join authentic nodes to DODAG is known as Decreased Rank (Traffic | Misappropriation), which could result in eavesdropping, sinkhole, or blackhole attacks. Mitigation: A combination of strategies, including TRAIL and VeRa, can be employed.

Figure 3. Decreased Rank Attack (DIO supplied contains a better rank).

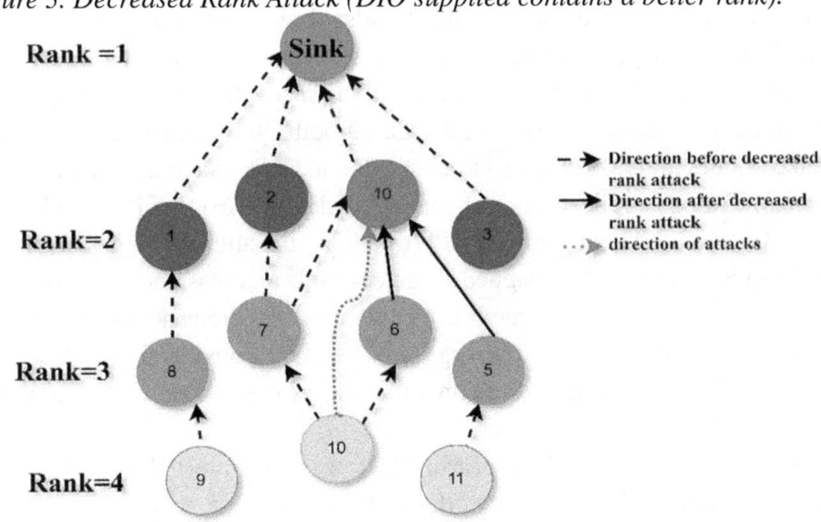

Through this effort, we will gain a better understanding of the different species. The observed parameters and the study environment are explained in Section II. The results are tabulated in Section III. By linking the observations, Section Four explains the findings and assists in the conclusion-making process. The results of the case study are concluded in Section V. Finally, Section VI attempts to guide how to further develop work to examine attacks more comprehensively.

II. RELATED WORK

For low-power and lossy (RPL) networks, routing protocol is one of the key technologies driving the increasing popularity of the Internet of Things (IoT). However, RPL is vulnerable to potential intrusions that may compromise network security. To understand these risks, testing, and experimentation on the reference implementation are required. (Bang, 2022)The Candidate Attack and Query Attack, which can raise or lower the rank of selected candidates through adversarial perturbations, are two attacks against deep ranking systems that are proposed in this study. A proposed anti-collapse triplet defense aims to strengthen the resilience of the ranking mechanism against these kinds of attacks. According to experimental results, a standard deep ranking system is compromised by these attacks, according to experimental results, but the protection greatly increases the system's durability and reduces the impact of different attacks (Osman M. H., 2021).

This paper (Hkiri, 2024) investigates attack strategies against different Online Learning to Rank (OLTR) variants, with particular emphasis on UCB-based OLTR algorithms in position-based and cascade models, classical stochastic bandits with binary feedback, and a general attack strategy against any algorithm under the general click model. The effectiveness of the cumulative cost that the authors propose for each attack is validated by tests conducted on both synthetic and actual data.

New techniques and instruments have been created because of the growing need for Internet of Things applications and connected devices. To find rank nodes that have been allocated erroneously in an RPL topology, the authors suggest using the EVV technique. Specifically designed to detect rank inconsistency assaults, this energy-based intrusion detection module can identify malicious nodes and attacks. Compared to previous methods, the suggested method considerably reduces the time necessary for attacker identification and network convergence (Al-Na'amneh Q. N., 2024).

The study suggests a novel kind of Min Rank assault against VOX, a signature scheme that resembles UOV, known as the padded Min Rank attack. The attack is very effective; it breaks eight out of nine criteria in less than a minute, while the last one takes roughly eight hours. The authors recommend reexamining the VOX parameters to ensure safety (Al-Na'amneh Q. A., 2024).

Because of its security and resilience, graph neural networks are becoming more and more interesting to investigate. The global attack techniques used today treat every node as a target, ignoring the varying robustness of each node. A novel technique dubbed partial graph attack (PGA) is put forth, which uses an aggressive iterative greedy-based assault mechanism, a cost-effective anchor-picking methodology, and a hierarchical target selection policy to identify susceptible nodes as attack targets. In comparison to current techniques, PGA exhibits notable increases in attack effect and efficiency (Hkiri A. K., 2024).

A promising future Internet architecture that improves network resilience, scalability, and usability is named data networking (NDN). It still requires improvement in areas like data security and signature privacy. This study presents a mechanism to identify and counteract cache pollution attacks by producing real-time corrupted ranked lists of requested packets that are both authentic and fraudulent. The algorithm raises the minimum cache hit ratio to 10% during attack scenarios, differentiating between regular attacks and emergency occurrences (Rouissat, 2023).

The objective of this research is to enhance the neural ranking models' (NRMs) effectiveness-robustness trade-off by breaking down the robust ranking error into natural and boundary mistakes. It is established that the perturbation invariance of a ranking model is a differentiable upper constraint on the boundary ranking error. A novel perturbation-invariant adversarial training (PIAT) method is developed that maximizes output smoothness and efficacy while enhancing robustness. The outcomes of the experiments demonstrate PITA's superiority over current adversarial defenses (Zahra, Rank and wormhole attack detection model for RPL-based internet of things using machine learning, 2022).

III. ADOPTED METHODOLOGY

Due to its scalability and energy efficiency, the RPL protocol is widely used in Internet of Things (IoT) networks. This study aims to develop a reference application for executing attacks on this protocol. It will provide a comprehensive introduction to the RPL protocol, review common attacks, and demonstrate how to use Cooja and Contiki-NG to implement and test these attacks. The primary goal is to enhance the robustness of RPL-based networks against malicious actors.

A decreased rank attack involves a malicious node deliberately lowering its rank value to manipulate the routing process. In RPL, the rank value indicates a node's position within the network topology, with lower values indicating closer proximity to the root node (sink). By falsely advertising a lower rank, the malicious node misleads other nodes into selecting it as their preferred parent, thus attracting a significant portion of the network's traffic.

This malicious behavior can have several detrimental effects on the network's performance. Firstly, the increased traffic through the malicious node can create a bottleneck, leading to congestion and higher packet loss. Secondly, the attack can result in suboptimal routing paths, as other nodes make routing decisions based on incorrect information, leading to increased latency and decreased network efficiency. Lastly, by controlling a large part of the routing tree, the malicious node can selectively drop or delay packets, further undermining the network's integrity and reliability.

The decreased rank attack unfolds in two main phases. Initially, the malicious node sends DIO (DODAG Information Object) messages with a falsely low rank, causing other nodes to select it as their parent. This phase disrupts the normal topology and causes legitimate nodes to reroute their traffic through the attacker. In the second phase, the malicious node maintains this deceptive rank to continually influence the network's routing decisions, worsening congestion, and instability.

Figure 4 illustrates a scenario where 40 nodes have formed a DODAG (Destination-Oriented Directed Acyclic Graph) and are operating normally. In contrast, Figure 5 shows the same scenario under a decreased rank attack initiated by node 10, demonstrating how the malicious node disrupts the RPL routing path by advertising a lower rank.

The simulation runs for 47,000 seconds in each scenario, during which nodes exchange both data and control information. A normal network scenario serves as a reference, helping to understand the deviation of specific parameter values from other scenarios. The impact of malicious activity on the arrival delay of data packets at the receiving node is analyzed, as an increase in packet delay can indicate the presence of attacking nodes. Additionally, the delay of data packets originating from node 10(the malicious node) is compared with those from its peer node in the normal network scenario, highlighting the impact of malicious behavior on the delay experienced by data packets from the malicious node itself. Scenario 2 (with attack) is compared to Scenario 1 (without attack) in terms of the frequency and distribution of DIO messages to determine if malicious activity is affecting the exchange of these messages, which are crucial for path stability.

Figure 4. Positioning of Sensor Nodes concerning the Sink Node

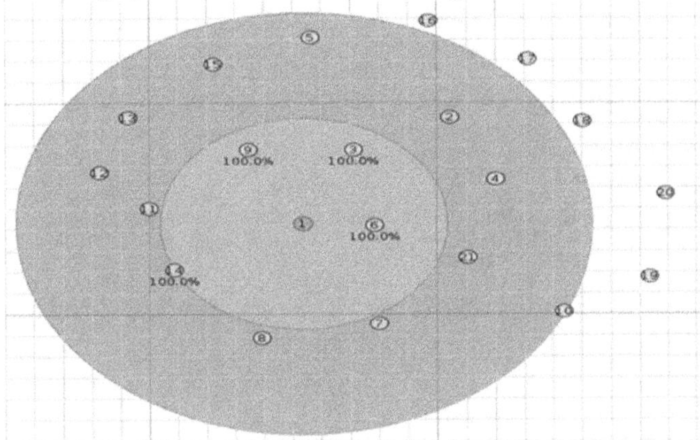

Figure 5. Positioning of Sensor Nodes Node Under Attack

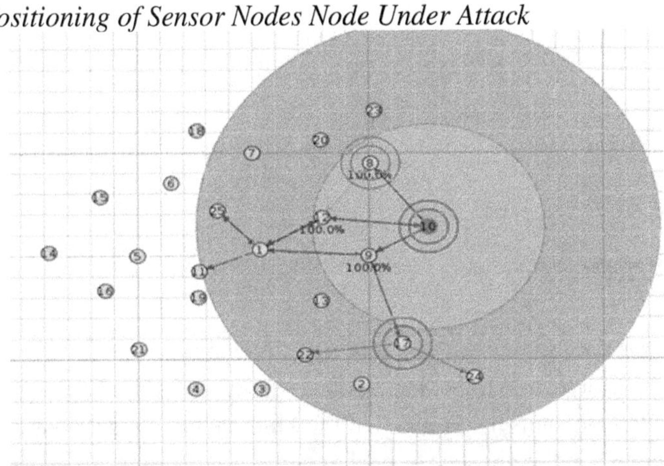

Figure 6 (a) displays a graph representing data flow and the frequency of packet transmissions in a normal network scenario. Figure 6 (b) illustrates the network flow under a scenario with rank attacks, where a malicious node manipulates its rank value to disrupt the network's routing process.

Figure 6. Flux normal (a) and rank attacks traffic (b)

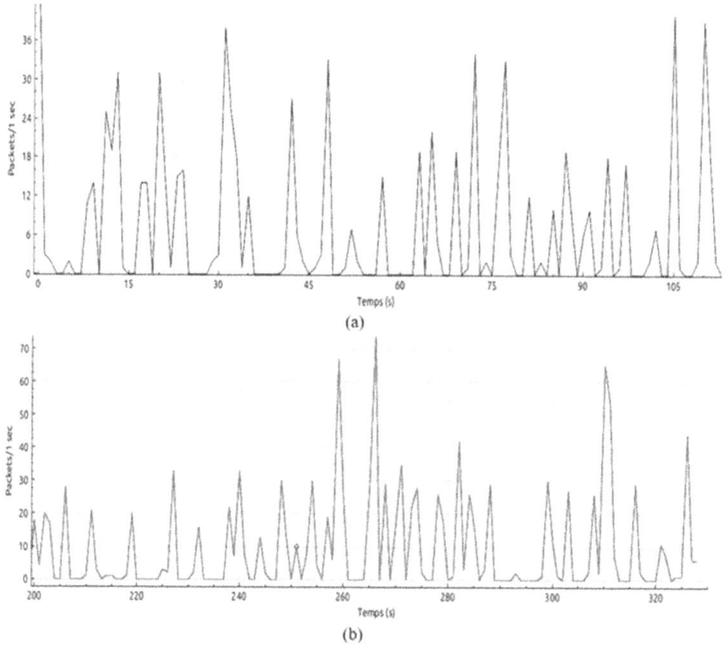

IV. OBSERVATION

The collected data includes the count and timestamp of DIO messages sent by each node. This information helps in calculating and assessing the frequency of DIO messages. Table 1 presents a summary of DIO message counts across different scenarios. An increase in the number of exchanged DIO messages indicates instability in the routing topology. By examining the number of DIO messages sent per node, we can determine if individual nodes recognized network instability and attempted to stabilize the network by sending their own DIO packets. The clear network scenario serves as a benchmark for comparison with other scenarios, as shown in Table 2. In scenario 2, node 10 is the malicious node, initiating a rank attack by falsely advertising a lower rank. Nodes 8, 9, and 12 are the affected nodes, which are misled into choosing node 10 as their preferred parent, resulting in network instability.

Table 1. Scenes with DIO packets released.

Node	**Scenario1**	**Scenario2**
2	79	24
3	67	51
4	33	60
5	64	22
7	85	34
15	54	87
10/8/9/12	55	77
14	54	64
11	98	66

Table 2. Overview of the Overall Number of Control Messages Sent in a Scenario

Scenario No.	**Scenario1**	**Scenario2**
Total DIO Messages	589	485
% increase	Benchmark	-1,2%

V. RESULTS DISCUSSION

The Contiki RPL protocol exchanges various control messages between transmitting and receiving nodes to establish a network topology. Nodes exchange control information to generate DODAG Information Object (DIO) messages. The hop count of these control packets from the destination node helps identify a node's relative position concerning the destination node, while the round-trip time (RTT) of these packets helps estimate the distance to neighbors. The frequency of DIO messages decreases once the topology stabilizes.

By analyzing the rate and frequency of DIO messages emitted by nodes in different scenarios, it becomes evident that the introduction of malicious activity by node 10 in Scenario 2 led to network instability experienced by all nodes. Scenario 2 showed an overall increase in the number of DIO messages. As illustrated in Figure 7, data from Scenario 2 showed that all nodes emitted a higher number of DIO messages compared to the clear network scenario.

However, the total number of DIO messages in Scenario 2 was lower than in Scenario 1. This suggests that although node 10 in Scenario 2 maliciously decreased its rank, it attracted traffic from several neighboring nodes, disrupting the network topology. Other nodes had to readjust their routing paths, resulting in an increased frequency of DIO messages to reform a stable topology.

This observation is reinforced by Figure 7, which shows that node 10 in Scenario 1 took much longer to emit the same number of DIO messages as the attacking node in Scenario 2. Examining the DIO messages from node 10 in Scenario 2, it emitted the first 100 DIO messages in a much shorter time compared to Scenario 1, as illustrated in Figure 8. This indicates that the rank attack not only disrupted the network topology but also caused temporary instability that required frequent adjustments to routing paths by non-malicious nodes.

Thus, the "Decreased Rank Attack" has a significant impact on the stability of the RPL network, leading to an increased frequency of control messages and constant topology readjustments, which can degrade the overall network performance.

Figure 7. Comparison of DIO messages for Malicious/Affected nodes

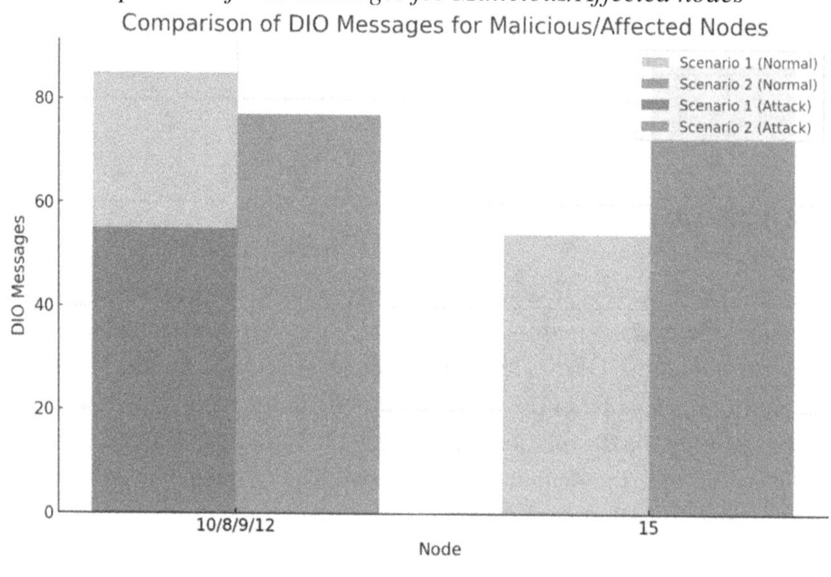

Figure 8 In Scenario 2, data packets from the malicious node (Node 10) experienced significantly higher delays compared to its counterpart in Scenario 1. The delay for packets from Node 10 was about 4.3 times greater than that of Node 12 in Scenario 1. This increased packet delay was not confined to the malicious node's data; non-malicious packets, both near and far from the malicious node, also faced

higher delays in Scenario 2. All nodes in Scenario 2 experienced substantially higher delays compared to other scenarios.

The primary cause of these packet delays could be buffered queues, where packets waited to be processed while the sink node generated and handled DIO packets, attempting to stabilize the network topology. Extended waiting times may lead to packet expiration due to the time-to-live (TTL) setting. Additionally, the sink node did not release any data packets, and the malicious node in Scenario 2 suppressed forwarding any self-generated data packets.

The total number of packets received at the sink node was recorded for each scenario. Packet loss could occur due to prolonged waiting times in the buffer queue, being dropped by the malicious node, or might have been successful if the simulation had run for a longer period.

Figure 8. DIO Message Over Time in Different Scenarios

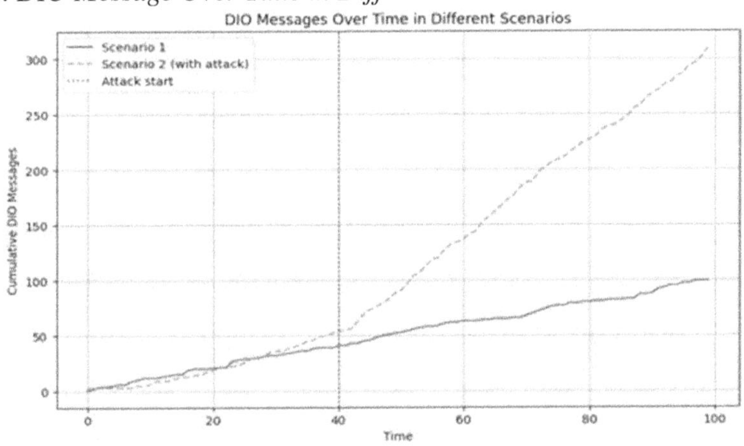

VI. CONCLUSIONS

The Internet of Things (IoT) is a network of connected smart gadgets. It offers services in various domains to enhance people's daily lives. Protecting information systems and data from assaults is crucial in IoT, particularly for devices connected via Low Power and Lossy Networks (LLNs) and RPL routing protocol. Because of its limited resources, RPL-based IoT is susceptible to a variety of attacks, especially rank ones. Rank assaults are largely prevented by trust-based methods that are suggested as countermeasures. The persistent problem in RPL-based IoT networks is highlighted in this study, which also examines current advancements in rank assault and categorizes defenses.

VII. LIMITATIONS AND FUTURE WORK

This paper introduces an Empirical Robustness Score to evaluate the robustness of a deep ranking model and suggests a conference version to solve constraints. Future studies should investigate resilience and resistance against different metric learning loss functions, transferability, universal perturbation, black-box attacks, and the drawbacks of adversarial training techniques such as performance degradation and training time cost.

REFERENCES

Al-Na'amneh, Q. A. (2023). Feature Selection for Robust Spoofing Detection: A Chi-Square-based Machine Learning Approach. *International Engineering Conference on Electrical, Energy, and Artificial Intelligence (EICEEAI) ()*. (pp. pp. 1-7). IEEE. DOI: 10.1109/EICEEAI60672.2023.10590243

Al-Na'amneh, Q. A. (2024). Next Generation Image Watermarking via Combined DWT-SVD Technique. In 2024 2nd International Conference on Cyber Resilience (ICC.

Al-Na'amneh, Q. N. (2024). Improving Memory Malware Detection in Machine Learning With Random Forest-Based Feature Selection. In. In Risk Assessment and Countermeasures for Cybersecurity.

Aljaidi, M. A.-F.-A.-S.-N. (2023). Cybersecurity Threats in the Era of AI: Detection of Phishing Domains Through Classification Rules. .

Almusaylim, A., Z. J. (. (2020). Detection and mitigation of RPL rank and version number attacks in the internet of things: SRPL-RP. *Sensors (Basel), 20*(21), 5997. DOI: 10.3390/s20215997 PMID: 33105891

Bang, A. O., & Rao, U. P. (2022). EMBOF-RPL: Improved RPL for early detection and isolation of rank attack in RPL-based internet of things. *Peer-to-Peer Networking and Applications, 15*(1), 642–665. DOI: 10.1007/s12083-021-01275-3

Boudouaia, M. A.-P., Ali-Pacha, A., Abouaissa, A., & Lorenz, P. (2020). Security against rank attack in RPL protocol. *IEEE Network, 34*(4), 133–139. DOI: 10.1109/MNET.011.1900651

Ghaleb, B. A.-D. (2023). (POSTER) Resolving the Decreased Rank Attack in RPL's IoT Networks. *1. In 2023 19th International Conference on Distributed Computing in Smart Systems and the Internet of Things (DCOSS-IoT) (pp. 65-67). IEEE.* .

Hkiri, A. K. (2024). RPL-Based IoT Networks under Decreased Rank Attack: Performance Analysis in Static and Mobile Environments. *Computers, Materials & Continua, 78*(1), 227–247. DOI: 10.32604/cmc.2023.047087

Jaradat, A. S.-N. (2023). *Genetic optimization techniques for enhancing web attacks classification in machine learning. In 2023 IEEE Intl Conf on Dependable.* Autonomic and Secure Co.

Karmakar, S. S. (2021). LEADER: low overhead rank attack detection for securing RPL based IoT. *In 2021 International Conference on COMmunication Systems & NETworkS (COMSNETS)* (pp. (pp. 429-437).). IEEE.

Laila, D. A.-N. (2024). Enhancing 2D Logistic Chaotic Map for Gray Image Encryption. In *Risk Assessment and Countermeasures for Cybersecurity* (pp. (pp. 170-188).).

Laila, D. A.-N. (2024). Simulation of Routing Protocols for Jamming Attacks in Mobile Ad-Hoc Network. In G. H., *In Risk Assessment and Countermeasures for Cybersecurity.*

Nandhini, P. S., Kuppuswami, S., & Malliga, S. (2023). Energy efficient thwarting rank attack from RPL based IoT networks: A review. *Materials Today: Proceedings, 81*, 694–699. DOI: 10.1016/j.matpr.2021.04.167

Osman, M. H. (2021). Artificial neural network model for decreased rank attack detection in RPL based on IoT networks. 23(3), 496-503.

Osman, M. H. (2021). Artificial neural network model for decreased rank attack detection in RPL based on IoT networks. *International Journal of Network Security, 23*(3), 496–503.

Rouissat, M. B., Belkheir, M., Belkhira, H. S. A., Mokaddem, A., & Ziani, D. (2023). Implementing and evaluating a new Silent Rank Attack in RPL-Contiki based IoT networks. *Journal of Electrical Engineering, 74*(6), 454–462. DOI: 10.2478/jee-2023-0053

Seth, A. D. (2020). Detection and verification of decreased rank attack using round-trip times in RPL-based 6LoWPAN networks. *IEEE International Conference on Advanced Networks and Telecommunications Systems.* IEEE. DOI: 10.1109/ANTS50601.2020.9342754

Tolsma, P. ..-T. (2021). Preventing Decreased Rank Attacks in RPL-based IoT Networks.

Zahra, F. J., Jhanjhi, N. Z., Brohi, S. N., Khan, N. A., Masud, M., & AlZain, M. A. (2022). Rank and wormhole attack detection model for RPL-based internet of things using machine learning. *Sensors (Basel), 22*(18), 6765. DOI: 10.3390/s22186765 PMID: 36146111

Chapter 5
Face Recognition
Unveiling Identity Through Machine Learning

Brijesh Yadav
Sharda University, India

Vishal Jain
https://orcid.org/0000-0003-1126-7424
Sharda University, India

ABSTRACT

Face recognition is a type of biometric system that scans and analyses the face of an individual and identifies the individual. It is part of biometrics, which includes fingerprint, eye scanning, palm print, voice, and signature recognition. It increases system security by recognizing the individual who is accessing the system. Face recognition plays a crucial role in crime investigation by identifying and locating criminals. It is essential because it has an enhanced security system, no need for memorization, live detection, scalability, and reduced human error. The first step is locating and scanning the face. It uses artificial intelligence, machine learning, and deep learning. Face recognition and images may also use convolutional neural networks. A convolutional neural network is a type of deep learning that extracts identifying features from data, lacking pre-programmed understanding. It is specialized in image and object detection and analysis.

DOI: 10.4018/979-8-3693-8014-7.ch005

INTRODUCTION

Face Recognition is a biometric software system through which detection of people is done in modern days. It detects images or videos and recognizes to checks it with the dataset founded earlier in the system. It ensures security, user authentication, scalability, and easy accessibility. Due to its vast and secure features, it is used in various places such as offices, armed forces, mobile phones, and Automated Teller Machines (ATM)(Selwyn et al., 2024). It is designed by using Machine Learning, Artificial Intelligence, and Deep Learning. Machine Learning is a subset of artificial intelligence that focuses on using data and algorithms to improve and increase human efficiency. Convolutional Neural Networks (CNN) are the most common type of machine learning used in face recognition. Convolutional Neural Networks (CNN) are the most common type of machine learning used in face recognition. CNN architecture is inspired by visual processing in human brains and is well-structured for capturing the pattern within videos and images (Sakthimohan et al., 2023).

Techniques Of Face Recognition

A. Approach using Eigenfaces (Principal Component Analysis)

It is the most common and most widely used method. It is an approach to face recognition that uses linear algebra and dimension to recognize and detect faces. It is reasonable and easy to implement. It works on Eigenvalues and Eigenvectors. This technique does not require images. It has many applications such as lip-reading, handwritten recognition, and medical image analysis(Owais et al., 2019).

B. Approach using Fisher faces (Linear Discriminant Analysis)

It is a broader concept of eigenfaces by integrating linear discriminant analysis. It is more effective in handling lighting and facial expressions. It works well when a number of features is much more than the training sample data. It is used to solve supervised problems in machine learning(BHATTACHARYYA & RAHUL, 2014).

C. Local Binary Patterns

It is a simple texture descriptor technique used in face recognition, object detection, and texture classification. It observes the texture by the pattern of intensity changes. It is used for texture feature extraction(*(PDF) Face Recognition Using Local Binary Patterns (LBP)*, n.d.).

D. Machine Learning Approach

It involves the training of a model so that it can recognize human faces. This process combines machine learning with computer vision techniques to recognize and verify the identity of an individual based on their facial patterns. In face detection, it uses Haar Cascades, Histogram Of Oriented Gradients(HOG). In face alignment, it uses Landmark Detection. Feature extraction-uses Traditional Binary Patterns (TBP) and Principal Component Analysis (PCA). In face matching it uses Euclidean Distance and Thresholding. This can use Support Vector Algorithm (SVM) and Convolutional Neural Networks (CNN) concepts which are subsets of machine learning (Rahman et al., 2021; Singh et al., 2023).

1. FUNDAMENTAL CONCEPTS OF FACE RECOGNITION AND BIOMETRICS

1.1 Definition

Keywords such as face recognition, biometrics, and accuracy are used to develop an understanding for readers. Biometric refers to the identification of an individual based on behavioral or biological features. Most of the features are inherited and cannot be changed or stolen. It combines with face recognition to enhance security and provide an extra edge to the user. It scans the user's face, their facial structure, the distance between eyes, structure of cheekbones, and then it matches with the stored data in the system.

1.2 Biometric Systems

A Biometric system is a system that takes an individual behavioral, psychological, or both traits, analyses it, and identifies it as an authenticated user or a malicious user.

It involves three phases- detection, the system's first phase involves the detection of the face against its alignment, structure, and position; verification, which involves the captured data matching with the data embedded in the system; identification then returns the output. If the data matches, then it will recognize which means the user is authenticated, otherwise, it is a malicious user.

1.3 Historical Context

The Beginnings

In 1960, the concept of face recognition started. It was first researched by Woody Bledsoe, Helen Chan Wolf, and Charles Bisson, who work on recognizing human faces by developing techniques that manually identify facial features such as eyes, nose, ears, and mouth through images or videos. These data are collected and then used for matching faces.

Algorithmic Foundations

In the 1970s, Takeo Kanade explored the field of face recognition by demonstrating the earliest automated face recognition system. It was an innovative system at that time because it could locate key features on the face like chin, eyes, and mouth and then calculate distance ratios between these features without any human mediation. Later tests showed that the system does always not provide reliable facial features.

In the 1990s, the evolution in the face recognition field took a significant development with the establishment of the Face Recognition Technology (FERET) program by the Defence Advanced Research Project Agency (DARPA) and the Army Research Laboratory (ARL). In 1993, the FERET program targeted to achieve automated face recognition capabilities that could be efficiently and effectively deployed in real-world environments, especially in law enforcement and intelligence. The FERET program primarily focuses on the performance of the recognition system. These evaluations result that while accuracy and reliability of existing automated systems varied. The result highlighted the potential of the automated face recognition technology of FERET for further interest and investment in the field.

The Emergence of Eigenfaces

Until the 1990s, most face recognition systems were based on photographic portraits to recognize human faces. However, the early 1990s marked a historical change when research began to locate faces in images that contained other objects or backgrounds. This shift focuses on the introduction of principal component analysis (PCA), which revolutionized face detection and recognition.

The principal component analysis (PCA) also known as Eigenface, was invented by Matthew Turk and Alex Pentland and became the foundation of the face recognition system. A linear model was created by Turk and Pentland that identifies global and orthogonal features in human faces. It works on the condition that while data is in higher dimensional space mapped with the data in lower dimensional space, the variance in data in lower dimensional space will be maximum. It uses a weighted combination of several key features to calculate a human face. Using this Eigenfaces to cipher the faces of given individuals, reduces the amount of data required to detect faces, making it reliable and highly efficient.

After improvement in Eigenfaces in 1997 through the use of linear discrimination analysis (LDA), resulted in the evolution of Fisher faces. Fisher faces became the dominant approach due to offering greater accuracy because it considers the variations between classes by minimizing variation in each class(*Face Recognition Using Eigenfaces*, n.d.).

The Rise of Feature-Based and Hybrid Approaches

The Eigenface and Fisherface methods do not calculate global structure which is linked with facial features. This limitation led to a more advanced approach in the late 1990s. Then Bochum system was introduced, which utilizes Gabor filters to record features of faces, and by linking them, it computed a grid of face structure. This method extracted faces from images using skin segmentation and outperformed most of the face detection available at the time in 1997. The Bochum system is also known by its commercial name ZN-Face. It was robust enough because it identifies faces out of beards, hairstyles, mustaches, and even sunglasses. It was installed at the airport where accurate identification was difficult due to its high-security features(Swamy et al., 2022).

Real-Time Face Detection: The Viola-Jones Framework

In 2001, the evolution took place in face recognition technology with the introduction of Viola-Jones framework for real-time face detection. This framework was developed by Paul Viola and Michael Jones which combined face detection with a Haar-like feature approach to object recognition(Pandey & Mishra, 2023). This led to the creation of AdaBoost, the first real-time front-view detector. The Viola-Jones algorithm implements face detection on lower-power devices, widening the practical implementations of face recognition systems. By 2015, face recognition was used in real-time face detection such as user interfaces, and teleconferencing.

1.4 Challenges

1.4.1 Variations in Lighting and Environmental Conditions

Variability in lighting and environmental factors is one of the primary challenges in face recognition systems. Under various lighting conditions such as indoor light, shadow, or natural light, faces appear differently. These variations can affect the algorithm of face recognition in various ways such as struggling to find the same face under various variations of lighting. Changes in the background environment can introduce noise and inaccurate detection(Mary Solomon et al., n.d.).

Figure 1. Lighting Variation

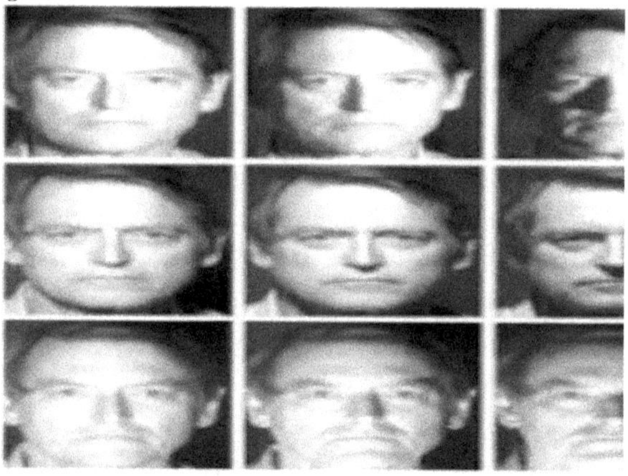

(This image is taken from (Ali et al., 2018))

1.4.2 Pose Variability

It is another significant problem in face recognition systems. It arises due to the dynamic features of a human face with constant changes in expression and orientation. The system should be highly accurate and robust enough to detect and recognize an individual regardless of whether they are laughing, smiling, or looking in different directions. Challenges arise for algorithms to consistently match faces across different images due to changes in pose variation and facial expression. Due to variations in poses, the same person can look different and can't be recognized by the system. Due to these variations system lost its efficiency and accuracy because it failed at the first stage as unable to capture the features. This problem may occur due to the angle of the observing observer and also due to the alignment of the head position. For recognizing an individual, a cluster of collections of images is required at different variations in poses(Mary Solomon et al., n.d.).

Figure 2. Pose Variation

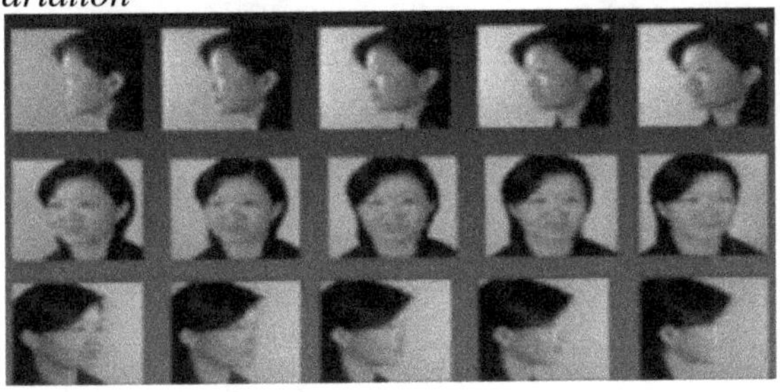

(This image is taken from (Phatak et al., 2022)
(Source:ijar)

1.4.3 Facial Expressions

Face is one of the important human biometrics due to its unique characteristics. Due to different expressions, the facial recognition system fails to match the accurate face with the data stored in the database of systems. The different expression involves the movement of muscles beneath the skin, which changes the appearance of the face. These movements serve as a primary means to fetch emotions and social information. The movement of different muscles of faces creates different expressions which makes the face recognition system recognize. The cultural aspect creates another layer of complexity. The expression that can be considered typical or appropriate in one culture may be recognized differently in other cultures. Research also suggests that emotional imprints can also mislead in identifying the correct identity of a person(Mary Solomon et al., n.d.).

Figure 3. Expression Variation

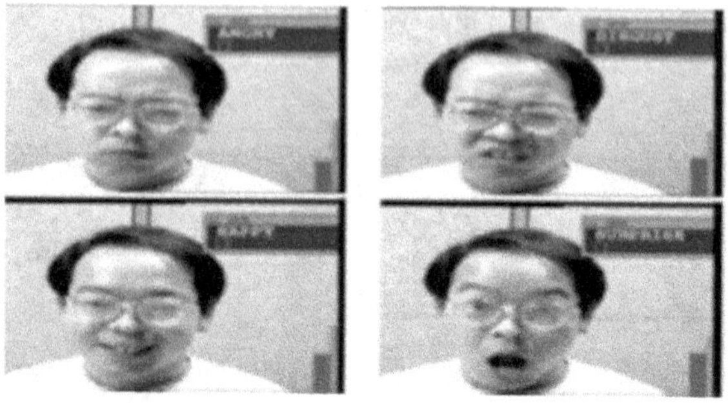

(This image is taken from (Phatak et al., 2022))
(Source:ijrar)

1.4.4 Aging and Temporal Changes

Aging is a natural process in which gradual changes of facial features take place over time. The face goes through various changes such as changes in skin texture, wrinkles on faces and darkness around the eyes, shrinking of skin, and loss of facial muscles. This makes it difficult for face recognition systems to recognize an individual today with its younger images. So, the system needs regular training throughout time. If a model is trained on younger datasets, then it may give inefficient results when older data is given. So, the system needs regular training on every dataset whether it is a younger one or an older ones(Mary Solomon et al., n.d.).

Figure 4. Ageing

(This image is taken from (Phatak et al., 2022))
(Source:ijrar)

1.4.5 Data Quality and Availability

Collecting high-quality data for a face recognition system is very challenging. It involves the collection of a large number of facial images with diverse settings such as lighting conditions, poses, expressions, and environments. Further, each image must be accurately annotated with facial landmarks and identities. Manual annotation is highly expensive, time-consuming, and prone to human error. Automated annotation ensures data is correctly labeled and of high resolution for training face recognition systems. A major challenge takes place in dealing with diverse and representative datasets that reflect the broad range of facial features. Most face recognition system fails to provide accuracy and efficiency while dealing with marginalized groups, such as age groups, genders, or ethnicities. The system runs well for faces similar to those in the training set but fails for less-represented groups. Dealing with such highly personalized biometric data is a matter of privacy concerns and collecting such data without user permission may lead to legal and ethical issues. The storage of such high-resolution data needs a high-performance systematic storage system. Due to limitations on data availability, some researchers turned to synthetic data which can be generated through artificial intelligence. The model trained on synthetic data may not always deal with real-world scenarios which leads to a performance gap.

1.4.6 Ethical and Privacy Concerns

The facial recognition system relies on facial images which may be collected without the awareness of the user. In many cases, images of an individual can be captured without the consent of the individual which leads to the issue of concern. This may violate individual privacy and its rights which may lead to ethical concerns. One other issue arises in surveillance and monitoring systems. Private and government agencies surveillance people in public places which violates individual privacy. This creates a limitation of free expression and behavior in public places. Face recognition system stores large amounts of biometric data which can attract hackers or other malicious users to steal data. If the facial data is stolen it leads to misuse of it such as fraud or crime. Therefore, it led to data security and privacy of individuals. The recognition system also fails in transparency which may lead to the misuse of the biometric data of individuals.

1.4.7 Real-Time Processing and Computational Constraints

Face recognition needs to process images in real-time means they can detect, analyze, and recognize faces in milliseconds. This is important in smartphones for giving access to authenticated users. The real-time process needs a system that avoids delays in providing output. To efficiently handle the large amount of biometric data, a system with a highly optimized algorithm is needed. The algorithm should reduce the complexity of the model and a high-performance machine (such as GPUs, CPUs, or TPUs) is needed. Optimizing for efficiency often means balancing trade-offs between model size, accuracy, and processing speed, which is difficult to achieve without compromising the overall system performance. The system should manage the data without any delays and manage the data efficiently. The number of faces recognized and matched with data increases the computational load. In real-time face recognition, one of the main challenges was about the latency delay between the capture of the face and its recognition. A system with low latency is better to use services like security, smartphones, and other sensitive data authentication. To achieve low latency, powerful hardware, and highly efficient algorithm is needed(*(PDF) Real Time Face Detection*, n.d.).

1.4.8 Spoofing and Security

An attack in which an unauthorized user tries to access a system using a fake or altered legal user's face is called spoofing. This can be done through various methods:

i) 2D Image Attacks: This is the most common type of attack done by attackers in which printed photographs, digital images, or videos of authorized users can be used to trick the system.
ii) 3D Mask attacks: The advanced spoofing involves a 3D Mask that closely resembles the authorized user's face. These masks can clone the features of the user in three dimensions making the biometric system more challenging to detect the spoof.
iii) Video Replay Attacks: In this type of attack, the attacker uses the pre-recorded videos of authorized users to fool the face recognition system. It can be effective against systems that depend on dynamic features like blinking or the movement of the head as the part of a recognition system(Bahia et al., 2024).

1.4.9 Cross-Domain Adaptation

One of the primary challenges in cross-domain adaptation is the difference between the source domain (where the system was trained) and the target domain (where it is applied). The system efficiently works on trained data but it struggles with new data in various ways. This can arise due to various factors- environmental differences, demographic differences, or due to technical differences. The environmental differences occur due to lighting conditions, background clutter, and camera angles. Demographic differences mean differences in age, gender, nationality, or other characteristics of individuals. The model trained on one group may not efficiently run well on other ethnic groups. Technical differences occur due to variations in sensor quality, camera quality, and image processing techniques between domains which can impact the system's ability to accurately recognize the face of an individual.

1.4.10 Regulatory and Legal Challenges

Privacy is the primary concern when using a face recognition system because it collects and stores the biometric data of users. To use the data of users, it needs permission from them. However, it is difficult to obtain consent from everyone in difficult environments like airports, shopping complexes, or public events. There is a need for transparency while deploying the system which involves permission from users to use their biometric data and ensure the protection of the data. Lack of transparency may lead to various public mistrust and legal challenges. If the system is not trained and designed carefully, it may result in various discriminations such as gender, race, or nationality.

So, regulating and legal challenges in face recognition are very complex and multifaceted. Private and government agencies may use the user's data without their consent which leads to privacy and security issues. The agencies are also surveillance people without their approval. These need proper concern of individual to ensure their data security and their privacy. The government also needs to introduce new legislation rules on using the data of individuals addressing concerns such as privacy, bias, and potential for misuse. Organizations must be accountable for how they use the data and create a transparent system.

2. MACHINE LEARNING IN FACE RECOGNITION AND BIOMETRICS

2.1 Introduction to Machine Learning

Machine Learning deals with the algorithms from their design to implementation, on the basis of which the prediction is done through the input data given to the system. It uses the algorithm and automatically verifies individuals. Face recognition in machine learning is a subset of biometric systems(Manu et al., 2023). Biometrics includes; eye scanning, face detection, tone detection, and voice recognition. It plays a key concept in face recognition by detecting the face and recognizing it from the available data.

Popular Algorithms

There are several algorithms for biometric face recognition:

i) Convolutional Neural Networks (CNNs): It is an effective algorithm in recognizing the faces of individuals. It is trained by using large datasets of various labeled images, which makes it efficient in recognizing patterns and features that are associated with specific objects or classes. It is proven to be highly effective in face recognition with images, achieving a state of performance in computer vision. It makes the system highly suitable for biometric applications from simple to complex patterns automatically learning hierarchical features from facial images(Phatak et al., 2022).
ii) Support Vector Algorithm (SVM): It is a part of a machine learning algorithm that is used for the classification of tasks in face recognition. It is used for both classification and regression. It works by finding the hyperplane that separates different classes ensuring maximum margin between classes. Due to managing high-dimensional data and nonlinear relationships, it is highly efficient and adaptable in various applications such as image classification, face detection, spam detection, anomaly detection, handwriting detection, and gene expression(*(PDF) Face Recognition by Support Vector Machines*, n.d.).
iii) Principal Component Analysis (PCA): In the field of face recognition, managing high-dimensional data is a challenging task. The complexity of data increases because the number of features or dimensions in a dataset increases, leading to an increase in the complexity of data. As the number of dimensions grows, it is computationally challenging due to the number of possible combinations of features exponentially. The task like clustering, classifications, and even data sampling become difficult to complete.
iv) Linear Discriminant Analysis (LDA): It is a part of machine learning that works on low-dimensional space similar to PCA. It classifies different classes, which makes an effective classification in tasks where distinguishing is more important than reducing dimensionality. It works by calculating within-class variance and between-class variance, then maximizing the ratio of their variances, resulting in transformation which provides the best possible separation between classes in lower-dimensional space. It deals with large datasets where the number of classes (e.g., different faces) is much higher than a number of samples per class. One of the main advantages of LDA over PCA is its ability to preserve class-discriminatory information, making it more suitable to differentiate between multiple subjects. Due to its biased nature which makes it robust to variations in lighting, pose, and expressions, which are the common challenges arise in face recognition. In real-time, where efficiency plays a crucial role, LDA's ability reduces dimensionality and enables faster processing time without losing accuracy, making it suitable for applications like mobile biometrics, surveillance, and access control(Zheng et al., 2023).

3. ADVANCED TOPIC IN BIOMETRIC FACE RECOGNITION

Deep Learning in Biometric Face Recognition

It is a part of machine learning which deals with the artificial neural network structure. This provides an advanced approach and exceeds the traditional methods. It provides robust algorithms like Convolutional Neural Networks (CNNs) which increase the accuracy of the face recognition system(Yao, 2024).

Facial Embedding

It plays a crucial role in the advancement of deep learning for face recognition. The high-dimensional facial feature is generated through techniques like Face Net and Deep Face which generate size vectors. It allows efficient and accurate comparisons because embedding captures the essential facial features. The integration of deep learning enhanced facilities and performance in real-time face recognition in challenging situations like varying lighting, occlusions, and different facial expressions. Deep learning driving the field forward with continuous enhancements in neural network architectures.

Multimodal Biometrics

It involves the integration of face recognition with other biometric modalities to enhance the security and accuracy of the system. The system becomes robust with the integration of other biometric methods such as iris, fingerprint, or voice recognition systems. It enhances user authentication due to an increase in the scope and variety of information in the system. This is required because an unimodal system deals with various challenges such as lack of privacy, extent of user comfort, and universality of samples. The system that integrates information at the last stage is considered less effective than the system that integrates information at the early stage because the early stage contains more accurate information than later matching scores of the comparison module(Sharma et al., 2024).

Ethical Considerations in Biometrics

Several ethical problems related to privacy, data protection, and potential biases occurred due to the deployment of biometric systems such as face recognition. It is crucial to ensure the accountable use of biometric technologies.

i) Privacy: The biometric data is highly sensitive because it contains the unique identity of an individual. So, there is a privacy concern for collecting and storing biometric data, such as facial images. It needs to use a robust security system preventing unauthorized access and needs consent from an individual before collecting data.
ii) Data Protection: It is an important step to protect biometric data from breaches or malicious users. As biometric data includes face, iris, voice, or fingerprint, which is the unique identity of every individual, needs to be carefully handled and stored in the system. Organizations must encrypt, securely store, and process in agreement with legal requirements.
iii) Bias and Fairness: The face recognition system may express biases related to gender, race, and age which leads to unfair results. The unbalanced training or algorithmic results lead to these biases. To gain equality in biometric systems, requires characteristic datasets, continuous monitoring, and testing to identify and reduce biases.
iv) Ethical Use: Ethical use means the system is used for legal and lawful purposes. This includes securing the rights and freedom of an individual by avoiding surveillance and monitoring. Transparent laws and policies should be established to guide the ethical deployment of biometric systems. Using the system responsibly and equitably- requires essential building of trust(Chan, 2022).

Access Control

Face recognition is commonly used for securing access to data in a system that can be used in departments like government buildings, data centers, and financial institutions. It creates a contactless and reduced need for physical credentials for granting access. Users can access the system user biometric face recognition securely from anywhere in the world(*(PDF) Face Recognition Methods & Applications*, n.d.).

Authentication

Biometric data like face recognition can be used in smartphones and online services for user authentication. Many online platforms use it for secure login and account management(Mohialden et al., 2023a).

4. APPLICATIONS OF FACE RECOGNITION

4.1 Security and Surveillance

In sensitive areas like public safety, face recognition plays a crucial role in providing security and monitoring activities. It is deployed at real-time identification like airports, government buildings, and other public spaces to prevent unauthorized access and detect threats to the system. It requires less human interference due to its ability to cross-reference face with the data stored in the system making it continuous monitoring of malicious users. Face recognition is used in security systems to tack an individual through fended cameras, making it easier to identify the behavior of a person in a large crowd. Surveillance is used to identify criminals through installed cameras by detecting faces and matching them with databases minimizing the workload of government agencies and reducing crime. However, this application increases ethical concerns, and privacy, and reduces the misuse of mass surveillance(Qian, 2024).

4.2 Law Enforcement and Criminal Identification

In law enforcement, face recognition plays an important role in identifying suspects, locating missing persons, and using very identities during investigations. Police forces worldwide use face recognition to compare the image of a suspected person image with surveillance footage to identify individuals involved in criminal activities. This technology can also be used to prevent identity fraud by verifying it with official records data. It is a vital tool in solving crimes due to its speed and accuracy. It provides efficient data due to the use of accuracy and efficiency-providing algorithms. Face recognition also reduces the time duration of identification, the process which once took days or weeks to identify can now performed in minutes. It increases the speed of investigation. This technology can prevent crime before it is committed due to the surveillance system. It also supports the investigation of historical videos from crime scenes, or social media to identify persons involved in criminal activities. Due to advancements in artificial intelligence and machine learning, face recognition has a bright future. Day by day improved algorithms enhance the accuracy and efficiency of the system. Still, legal and ethical indication needs a careful consideration(Kumar et al., 2024).

4.3 Access Control and Authentication

Face recognition is rapidly used in user identification and authentication offering a secure and efficient way to digital spaces. Due to its secure facilities, it is used in smartphones, corporate offices, and government agencies. It provides a user-friendly experience by using face recognition for authentication. The reduction in physical keys, passwords, or cards, reduces the malicious user. However, varying environments can attract attackers to steal biometric data. Revolution came in managing security due to the integration of recognition into the access control system. In the modern method, access is given to authorized users whose data matches with those stored in the system. Unlike, traditional methods include passwords, PINs, or access cards which cannot be easily stolen. After the biometric face system, users don't need to remember complex passwords, or carry physical tokens; easy access through a simple camera. This increase in speed and efficiency benefits the high-traffic areas, such as corporate offices or residual buildings. These also help in maintaining hygiene such as hospitals or food processing plants. In traditional methods, secure areas, such as data centers, laboratories, or other restricted office spaces need physical staff but in modern methods, data and buildings can be secured through a biometric system and it is also easy to use. If anyone attempts to access the restricted area their facial image gets captured and compared with the database. Access is given if it is an authorized user. It reduces the manual check of IDs or access cards and enhances the security and efficiency of the system. It plays a crucial role in digital authentication, particularly in consumer personal electronics such as smartphones, laptops, and tablets. The advancement of technologies like 3D face recognition minimizes spoofing attacks and increases the robustness of the system.

4.4 Healthcare and Patient Identification

In this sector, face recognition plays a major role in maintaining digital records and access to the room of patients. It reduces the mixing of the patient record which helps in providing better treatment without wasting time. It maintains records of check-ins, automates tasks, and provides healthcare experience. It reduces the risk of error generated from manual or paper-based identification due to a robust system. Upon arrival of the patient, it faces scans and matches with stored data. Face recognition solves one of the main issues of misidentification which leads to serious medical errors, such as incorrect diagnoses, treatment, or admission of patient. It solves the manual registration and paperwork which is time-consuming and prone to errors. It made a paperless system, patient uses mobile apps to scan their faces, and then they will automatically pull up their records and provide the output. It improves patient experience and frees the administrative staff to focus on more critical tasks. In healthcare, the medical information of patients plays an important role, and protecting data and maintaining privacy can be done through face recognition. It enhances security by permitting the authorized individual to access the healthcare facilities and patient records. For instance, the healthcare supplier can use facial biometrics to give and restrict access to records rooms, medication storage, or patient rooms. This facial biometric system adds an additional layer of security to traditional methods like passwords, or ID cards, which can be lost and the system may be compromised.

The healthcare sector is a billion-dollar company which leads to a significant fraud issue. Fraudsters can use false identity to use medical facilities and insurance benefits. Face recognition deals with these fraudsters through the verification process and detects them as a malicious user. This technology provides secure and remote care, especially during the COVID-19 pandemic. It ensures correct automatic linking of telemedicine sessions with correct patient records. It timely manages and reduces the delays in treatment or missed appointments. Face recognition can be integrated with the Electronic Health Records (EHR) system to build a strong network between hospitals and the patient. Healthcare providers use facial biometrics in EHRs, reducing administration burden and manual records. The sharing of data between different healthcare providers becomes easier due to integration, also improving patient outcomes and care coordination(Pabiania et al., 2016).

4.5 Consumer Applications

Face recognition is a popular feature used in consumer applications such as smartphones, laptops, and smart homes. The technology provides users with an excellent, secure, and suitable path to interact with their devices and manage their day-to-day activities. It also provides remote access to the home of the user while raising important considerations regarding privacy and security by enhancing user experience.

Smartphones and Mobile Devices

Face recognition provides a fast and secure method to the user to unlock their devices, authenticate payments, and access apps. It revolutionizes the market of smartphones and other electronic gadgets by adding authentication and security to the system. It makes a contactless environment and adds an additional security layer to traditional methods like passwords or fingerprint sensors. This biometric system is not only suitable but also reduces the chances of unauthorized access even if the device is lost or stolen. The integration of face applications with smartphones provides additional opportunities to users such as adjusting settings based on recognition or providing customized content suggestions. Advanced technology is more likely integrated into daily mobile activities, such as app access, secure browsing, and more sophisticated multi-factor authentication systems with the combination of facial recognition with other biometric data(Mohialden et al., 2023b).

Smart Homes and Home Automation

Face recognition plays a crucial role in smart homes to increase security and safety to the houses. The face recognition system used in smart houses differentiates between the residents and unauthorized individuals by detecting and recognizing the face. The authorized individual unlocks doors, disarms the security system, or accesses the restricted areas within the home. It provides an extra layer of security to the house by sending alerts to the owner- if an unauthorized individual tries to access the house. It also adjusts lighting, temperature, and music preferences automatically, when the authorized individual unlocks the door of the smart home. It provides a user-friendly environment to the residents by enhancing comfort and satisfaction(Saxena & Varshney, 2021).

User Experience and Convenience

Face recognition offers benefits in consumer applications providing comfort and security to users. Users can unlock smartphones or control smart houses by interacting in a natural and effortless manner with technology. It creates a physically contactless environment, where hygiene or accessibility is a primary concern. Face recognition provides automation and simplification of routine tasks in smart homes. This integration makes daily routines easier and more enjoyable. Face recognition is easy to use as the traditional method requires the user to remember and manually input codes, which makes it complex and time-consuming. Authentication can be done simply by looking at the phone, which provides access to authorized users after matching with the database. The user does not need much hardware or physical interaction for authorization. Face recognition will be an alternative offer for individuals with disabilities or having difficulty in remembering or using traditional methods like passwords, or PINs.

Security and Privacy Concerns

Due to its vast application and numerous benefits to the consumer, it is a matter of security and privacy concerns. A major issue arises due an unauthorized user tricks the system by using a photo, video, or 3D model of the user's face. To overcome these issues, an advanced face recognition system is used to detect the live person and static image by analyzing skin texture or facial movement.

Privacy is a major concern because the system requires the collection and storage of biometric data. The data protection using encryption, storage solutions, and transparent privacy policies done by the company which implements it in their product for prioritizing data protection. The government agencies using surveillance on an individual violates the right and privacy concerns. To overcome these issues, the government should issue proper guidelines and clear regulations for to use of face recognition technology. The organization should inform the user about how and when their facial data should be used. the policies must assure the uses of facial data and should be transparent with the user.

Future Directions

The advancement in face recognition increases accuracy, speed, and integration with other technologies. The face recognition system becomes more capable and reliable in a broader range of conditions, such as low light or at different angles. The system becomes more versatile and robust by integrating face recognition with other biometric modalities like voice, fingerprint, iris, or gesture recognition. The advancement in artificial intelligence and machines creates a short and more optimized algorithm to increase the accuracy and efficiency of biometric systems. The more advanced AI algorithms enhance the system to identify faces in increasingly complex environments like low lighting, pose variation, and crowded scenes. Synthetic data can be generated by a face recognition system to face the challenges of data scarcity and increase the robustness of the system. Upcoming developments in face recognition will reduce biases related to gender, race, and age. works are going on by researchers to develop such an algorithm that reduces biases. The use of the cloud is minimized due to face recognition by directly enabling devices such as smartphones, IOT (Internet of Things), and camera devices. This allows for more localized decision-making and improved privacy. It influences social norms, behavior, and expectations. To understand face recognition, its benefits, and the works, ones need education and awareness. Revolution arises due to the advancement of algorithms through machine learning and deep learning. It decreases the chances of attacks and fraud by unauthorized users. The advancement in face recognition covers all other loopholes of systems.

5. CASE STUDIES

5.1 Successful Implementations

The successful deployment of face recognition provides insight into how it can be used in various industries in various sectors. The achievements and practical benefits achieved in real life through the following examples.

- **Airport Security and Border Control:** The security and accuracy get more enhanced with the integration of face recognition with airport security and border control systems. The countries like United States, the United Kingdom, and Japan deployed in airports to enhance security and streamline traveler processing. The use of face recognition in the U.S by the Customs and Border Protection (CBP) agency to verify traveler's identity as they are entering or exiting the country. This system maintains a high level of security and reduces the time needed to process passengers. The enhancement in operational activity and security in high-traffic environments obtained due to the successful deployment of face recognition at airports(Horkay et al., 2022).
- **Banking and Financial Services:** One of the most important applications of face recognition in banking and financial sectors due to the storage of essential data of customers which needs strong security. In China, banks already use the face recognition system that is integrated with smartphones and ATMs allowing customer to authenticate their transactions securely without the need for physical cards or passwords. It offers a user-friendly environment and reduces the chances of identity theft and fraud by offering security features and a quick method of authorization. Due to its successful application in the banking sector, it deployed in other financial services like insurance and fintech. It provides an alert system- if any unauthorized user accesses the accounts and important credentials of authorized users. It replaces managing strong passwords to secure your account simply with the integration of face recognition to the account of the account holders. It provides remote access to the account of the customer without any delay in accuracy or security(Jain, 2021).
- **Smartphone Authentication:** the use of face recognition in electronic products, especially in smartphones, is one of the successful stories. This brings a great revolution by offering biometric authentication to unlock devices securely. Face IDs play important in smartphone authentication enhancing both convenience and security. The day-by-day advancement in biometric systems with building compact algorithms gets integrated into the new version of

smartphones. It is concerned about the privacy of users and prevents data sharing with an unauthorized user. Authentication in smartphones experienced an advancement from traditional PINs and Passwords to face recognition and other biometric solutions.

Apple brought a revolution in smartphones by introducing Face ID in 2017 with the iPhone X which marked a significant turning point in smartphone authentication. It replaces the fingerprint-based authentication providing a physically contactless environment. It creates a 3D map of the user's face and is authorized by matching with a database to unlock the device for authorized payment and access to sensitive apps. The 3D mapping captures the depth and shape of the face, making it more resistant to spoofing attempts such as using photographs or masks. This provides an edge to smartphones as it replaces the passwords or fingerprint uses which lead to forgotten or stolen.

5.2 Lesson Learned from Real World-Deployments

The deployment of face recognition systems provides valuable future applications and ensures the effective and ethical use of technology. It gives solutions to real-world problems.

- **Importance of Diverse Training Data:** The use of diverse and representative datasets become an important lesson for learning. The training data will provide observation of bias that can be traced back to the diversity. The training of the dataset provides algorithms that deal with a wide range of ethnicities, ages, genders, and facial conditions. The more investment is made by companies and researchers for more inclusive data collection practices. The model needs regular training on different datasets.
- **Balancing Security and Privacy:** While deploying face recognition technology, it needs a balance between privacy and security. There should be respect for individual privacy rights- while implementing technology. It needs transparency of data with authorized users and the consent of the user to use its biometric data. There should be avoiding legal challenges and balance is essential for maintaining public trust. It provides secure locations and prevents unauthorized access to sensitive information by verifying identities. Governments and private agencies developing regulatory frameworks to manage biometric technologies. The technology works on encrypted data to ensure that sensitive information never be exposed or become public.
- **Continuous Evaluation and Adaptation:** With the continuous evolution of face recognition systems, it needs regular evaluation and adaptation of ad-

vanced models are essential for maintaining the accuracy, ethical integrity, and efficiency of the system. The biometric system needs regular assessment and updating to remain secure, fair, and relevant. Biometric systems are not static and affected by various factors such as changes in demographics, advancement of technology, and emergence of new threats. It needs continuous assessment and testing of the system to ensure they are actively performing. The providing evolution involves accuracy, robustness across different scenarios, and accuracy. Evolution also helps in identifying biased groups such as gender, race, or age. The necessary prompt adjustment to improve fairness and identification of these issues is done by regular audits and evaluations.

6. FUTURE DIRECTIONS IN FACE RECOGNITION AND BIOMETRICS

6.1 Emerging Technologies

Emerging technologies such as face recognition and biometrics promise to enhance efficiency, accuracy, and security. Integration of quantum computing with biometric facial systems makes remarkable progress and advancements. Quant computing is an emerging field of computer science that has the ability to solve complex problems, where supercomputers fail to solve them. It processes bulk amounts of data at unexpected speed, enabling real-time solve of complex biometric patterns. It provides an algorithm that can handle diverse and challenging scenarios, such as pose variation, low-lighting environments, or faces in crowded places.

Biometric Cryptography is another emerging technology, that combines cryptographic methods with biometric data to provide and secure private authentication. Even if biometric data is compromised, it cannot be accessed without a corresponding cryptographic key, providing a robust and secure system to the user. It is also known as Biometric Tokenization because it combines public-key infrastructure (PKI). It uses a decentralized model that already has biometric authenticators that ensure biometric templates are stored on end-user mobile devices. In this model, the device communication is established by using tokens so biometric information is never transmitted over the wire. The risk associated with central biometric storage abandoned the biometric cryptography.

Technologies like Augmented Reality (AR) and Virtual Reality (VR) play crucial roles in face recognition. The integration of biometric authentication with these technologies provides applications like remote learning, virtual meetings, and gaming. It makes the process more intuitive and engaging by enhancing user interaction with biometric systems. It creates a virtual 3D environment which is exactly similar to a real-time environment making the system more accurately detect the faces.

6.2 Trends in Research and Development

Face recognition needs continuous research and development by addressing current problems and expanding applications of these systems. Researchers found compact and robust algorithms that recognize faces across different conditions by exploring deep learning models. The researcher also explores new architectures like transfer and graph neural networks (GNNs) for offering better performance. There needs transparency in the use of the system due to the deployment of these models in law enforcement and border control.

There is another development in biometrics which is known as explainable AI(XAI). The understanding and their trust outcomes came due to XAI in the decision-making of the biometric algorithm.

The integration of the biometric system with the Internet of Things (IoT) also provides important features to secure data. This provides the facility to connect more than one device, which needs security and efficient authorization methods. It creates a contactless authentication due to the integration of the IoT ecosystem, which connects smart homes to connected vehicles(Adjabi et al., 2020).

6.3 The Future of Multimodal Biometrics

Multimodal combines multiple biometric modalities such as iris, face, fingerprint, or voice used for biometric authentication. This approach provides a layer of verification, making it difficult for unauthorized users to bypass them. They will cross-verify data which improves accuracy and reliability by integrating multimodal biometrics instead of traditional biometrics, multimodal informatics also involves the use of behavioral biometrics like, voice inflection, typing patterns, or gait analysis, through multimodal that provide continuous authentication rather than relying on single authentication user. The capabilities of multimodal systems increase due to advancements in sensor technology and data fusion methods.

6.4 Potential Policy and Regulatory Changes

There should be proper policies and regulations made to govern their use. One of the global standard changes for biometric data collection, storage, and processing. The system ensures the protection of user privacy and data security by ensuring a biometric system. The growing use of biometrics evolved laws for data privacy. In surveillance and law enforcement, debate increases over the ethical use of biometrics. Additionally, the biased group requires systematic strategies to ensure that the biometric system does not affect any groups. The government provides policies to ensure that biometric data cannot be collected or stored without the consent of individuals. There also needs regular modifications in regulation over a period to ensure the accuracy and reliability of the system.

7. TECHNICAL IMPLEMENTATION OF FACE RECOGNITION SYSTEM

The application of the face recognition system makes it popular in various fields like surveillance, border security, law enforcement, and access control. Let's discuss some technical aspects of the face recognition system.

7.1 System Architecture and Design

The foundational to security, performance, and scalability is their architecture and design. Feature extraction, a pre-processing unit, data acquisition, and a decision-making component are included in a well-designed system.

- **Data Acquisition Module:** These parts capture the videos and facial images by using cameras or other imaging devices. The pose variation, expression, and variation in lighting should be handled by this component to ensure high-quality input data.
- **Pre-Processing Engine:** The analysis will be done once data is acquired by the pre-processor to enhance image quality, alignment of faces, and facial features. It works on noise reduction, geometric normalization, and contrast enhancement.
- **Feature Extraction Engine:** The main part of the system is feature extraction, which performs major works like distinctive facial features such as the distance between eyes, the shape of the nose, color of skin that are extracted and represented as mathematical vectors. The distinguishing is done between faces through these mathematical vectors.
- **Matching Module:** Once the feature is extracted, then it matches with the facial template of datasets. To match the input features against the stored biometric faces, the module uses various algorithms such as Euclidean distance to match the module.
- **Decision-Making Component:** Finally, the system provides results after matching the module whether the input biometric face matches with an authorized user or any malicious users. This component uses a threshold to

check for acceptance or rejection, depending on the system application such as system vs general identification.

7.2 Hardware Requirements

The hardware of the system depends on the scale of deployment, the desired level of performance, and the scale of deployment. The main components of hardware include:

- **Imaging Devices:** This provides the initial stage of face recognition using a high-resolution camera to capture the facial images. For liveness detection or in low light conditions, infrared cameras can be used to capture the images.
- **Processing Units:** To handle real-time processing depending on the complexity of the algorithm, the system may use powerful CPUs or GPUs to provide a better real-time result. Deep learning uses GPUs because it demands high computational power.
- **Storage Solutions:** Face recognition needs the storage of sensitive data like biometric faces and templates securely. Storage should offer both speed and opacity- and should be scalable and prevent data loss.
- **Network Infrastructure:** In a distributed system, to transmitting data between acquisition devices, processing units, and storage requires robust infrastructure. It is crucial to have low latency in real-time applications.
- **Security Hardware:** for high-security applications integration of dedicated cryptographic processors or secure enclaves may be necessary for protecting sensitive biometric data.

7.3 Software Frameworks and Libraries

For a streamlined development and deployment of the face recognition model, several software frameworks and libraries are available to be used to make a robust system. These offer pre-build tools for image processing, feature extraction, and model training, enabling the developer to focus on integration and customization. There is a vast collection of libraries such as:

- OpenCV: It is a library used for computer vision, image processing, and machine learning. It is used in real-time operations for processing images and videos to identify objects, handwriting, or even faces. One can use the feature of OpenCV vector space to perform mathematical operations to identify image patterns. OpenCV is used in both commercial applications and academic research.

- Dlib: It is a C++ toolkit that creates complex face recognition systems with the integration of machine learning algorithms. It is used for commercial purposes and academic research in the field of embedded devices, mobile phones, robotics, and high-performance computing environments. It provides major features such as high-quality portable code, documentation, machine learning algorithms, numerical algorithms, image processing, threading, networking, graphical user interface, data compression and integrity algorithms, and testing.
- TensorFlow and PyTorch: It is a deep learning framework that offers a powerful tool using neural networks for face recognition. It is used for large-scale applications of deep learning-based systems for training and deploying. Both frameworks provide a robust set of tools to handle complex tasks involved in biometric face recognition. Google developed TensorFlow, which offers a scalable and flexible environment for large-scale production and deployment. Keras is a type of key offered by it that simplifies the deep learning model, enabling the model to train large models across multiple GPUs or machines.

On the other hand, Facebook's AI Research lab developed PyTorch, which offers a dynamic computational graph, which allows the development and debugging of models. It provides flexibility and rapid prototyping in research environments. It makes it accessible for developers familiar with the language due to easy integration with the Python ecosystem.

- **FaceNet and DeepFace:** There is a pre-trained model for face recognition which is specific deep learning. These are widely adopted due to their high accuracy in the real world. Google developed FaceNet and Facebook developed DeepFace.

7.4 Integration with Existing Systems

The integration of face recognition with the existing infrastructure provides a usable and seamless operation. This involves:

- **API AND SDK Integration:** Integration with existing applications or databases can be done with most face recognition systems because these provide APIs or SDKs for integration. These interfaces provide a broader ecosystem by allowing face recognition to enable real-time data exchange and processing.
- **Database Connectivity:** The face recognition system needs to be connected to with database where biometric data such as user identities and facial

templates are stored. It requires careful planning to ensure data security and data consistency with the integration of existing databases whether it is SQL-based or NoSQL.

- **Interoperability:** The system communicates with access control systems like biometric sensors or card renders. They provide interoperability facility standards such as SAML (Security Assertion Markup Language) and LDAP (Light Directory Access Protocol).
- **User Interface and Experience:** The user interface become more attractive due to the integration of face recognition into existing user workflows. The system should be seamlessly blended with other authentication methods should be more intuitive and minimal training for users.

7.5 Deployment and Maintenance Consideration

There are several critical steps involved in deploying face recognition which ensure its efficiency in real-world environments. Factors such as reliability, integration, and system scalability with existing infrastructure must be considered during the deployment process. Deployment includes setting up servers to secure data and storage, ensuring low-latency performance, and using appropriate hardware to support the computational demand of face recognition algorithms. Real-world problems such as angle, lighting, and image quality can be handled through the system.

For long-term security and effectiveness, the maintenance of the system is equally important. Regular update of software provides loopholes and play an important role in protecting against evolving security threats. Maintenance also includes the training model with new datasets to improve accuracy and adapt changes over user appearance time, such as aging or hairstyle changes. There is a legal landscape evolution due to the ethical guidelines and privacy regulations. The system remains to provide data protection and user consent for maintaining trust and maintaining legal risks.

8. GLOBAL TREND IN FACE RECOGNITION

8.1 Adoption Rates by Region

Face recognition is very significant across various regions such as government policies, technological infrastructure, and public acceptance due to increased adoption rates. In many countries, the adoption rate of face recognition is driven by strong government support and remarkable investment in Artificial Intelligence. In developing nations, the adoption rate is slower but growing, increasing the availability of affordable technology and driven by security needs.

In North America, particularly the United States, both the public and private sectors adopted face recognition. This has a very vast implementation such as retail security, airports, and law enforcement. There is divided public opinion on the adoption due to privacy concerns.

Asia, especially China, is a universal leader in the adoption of face recognition. The integration into various public life, including social credit systems, urban surveillance, and even everyday transactions attracts the Chinese government to heavily invest in this technology. China makes smart cities with the integration of this technology in schools, healthcare, and transportation. Adoption is also done by other Asian countries like South Korea and Japan primarily in retail, security, and technology-driven consumer experience.

Africa presents a mixed landscape due to the lower adoption rate in comparison to other regions. Face recognition is being used for both purposes in security and financial services, enhancing user to access banks securely through their smartphones.

Overall, the adoption rate differs from region to region and country to country. The further advancement in face recognition increases the adoption rates exponentially. Face recognition in integration with other biometric data such as eye scanning, and fingerprint increases security at a faster pace. The government initiative is to improve security and investment in biometric technology by the private sector is driven by the adoption of face recognition. The adoption varies over the region, where some regions accepting it frequently but some are banning it in that region(Guleria et al., 2024).

8.2 Regulatory Difference Worldwide

Face recognition use can be governed by regulatory frameworks that differ across the globe, cultural values, societal priorities, and reflecting different legal traditions to concern on civil liberties and privacy.

In the European Union, the use of biometric data is strictly governed by GDPR (Global Data Protection Regulation). The use of face recognition must be based on legal consent of individuals such as a legitimate public interest or explicit consent from individuals should be ensured by GDPR for the purpose of use. There is a substantial fine for the violation of these rules. Face recognition is subsequently used in a situation where privacy is a primary concern such as airports, or in banking sectors. Several European countries temporarily ban the application of face recognition in public places, reflecting an important attention on its deployment.

In contradiction, China uses face recognition with a few regulatory limitations. The integration of face recognition by the Chinese government with other public administrations, social government, public surveillance, and law enforcement provides strong and secure storage and accessibility to authorized users.

In the United States, face recognition is regulated through fragmentation and varies by jurisdiction and state. There is a strict regulation on the implementation of face recognition by the government of some cities like Illinois and San Francisco due to privacy concerns, civil liberties, and misuse by law enforcement. There is no comprehensive regulation at the federal level on face recognition, although discussion and efforts are ongoing. Face recognition is used widely in some areas like airports and retail, but restricted in others due to regulatory approaches.

Overall, the deployment of face recognition created a complex landscape due to regulatory differences. Some regions focus on technical innovation and security leading to the varying level of adoption and public acceptance, while others focus on data protection and prioritizing privacy.

8.3 Influence of Cultural Factors

Cultural factors play an important role in the implementation of face recognition across different regions. The adoption of face recognition recognizes technology, privacy, and surveillance through historical context, societal values, and public values. In different cultures, people have variations in face structure providing them with a unique identity to recall them. The contribution to the acceptance of face recognition is due to the importance of social harmony and the prioritization of collective goods. Cultural acceptance provides security to individual privacy due to the higher trust in government. The government initiative is to build smart cities through the integration of face recognition in daily life, such as transportation, retail, and government offices. The social network can be built strongly through the cultural factor implementation of face recognition.

Overall, face recognition is accepted across different regions due to its adoption through cultural factors. These factors provide integration of face recognition in daily life and shape public attitudes- and regulatory approaches. The cultural context acceptance of face recognition on a global scale and provides a successful deployment of it(Nosek et al., 2011).

8.4 Global Market Growth and Projection

There is rapid growth in the global market for face recognition due to the advancements in artificial intelligence and machine learning. The capabilities of providing strong security solutions through biometric data make it more demanding and advancing. The market size will continue increasing due to the significant growth in sectors like healthcare, retail, and law enforcement. The large investment in smart cities projects public safety and public privacy. There should be a focus on technical innovation due to the rapid demand for security in government agencies and large private organizations. New opportunities for growth can be created by the integration of face recognition with other biometric modalities, such as iris and fingerprint recognition. To overcome challenges, such as pose variation, aging, and lighting environment variation, the development of more sophisticated algorithms to increase the applicability and accuracy of technology.

To achieve high-speed, low-latency applications, the use of edge computing in real-time processing increases the market growth.

Overall, face recognition is a global market with a robust growth trajectory- and expansion across various industries and regions. Due to the continued evolution in technology, it plays a crucial role in future security, user experience, and identity verification in the digital age.

9. CONCLUSIONS

9.1 Summary of Key Points

In this book chapter, One can learn about the multifaceted world of face recognition, exploring its historical evolution, practical application across various domains, and technical underpinnings. The examination of challenges inherent in technology like data quality, aging, privacy concerns, and accuracy. The advancement in face recognition systems has been achieved through the evolution of deep learning, artificial intelligence, biometric multimodal, and machine learning. The chapter has been illustrated with case studies and examples for a better understanding of the complexities deploying of a face recognition system. Explored the global trend, cultural factors, and market growth projections, and considered regional differences due to adoption of this technology.

9.2 The Ongoing Evolution of Face Recognition

The rapid advancement in artificial intelligence, computational power, and machine learning leads to continuous evolution in face recognition technologies. The integrated solution influences multimodal biometrics to enhance accuracy and security by shifting from basic facial recognition to more sophisticated. The ongoing advancement in deep learning through research is expected to develop more efficient algorithms that further improve the performance of face recognition systems. These algorithms may lead to improved challenges such as occlusion, varying environmental conditions, and aging.

Moreover, the future will be more decentralized and real-time applications, due to the integration of facial recognition with the Internet of Things (IoT) and the rising edge of computing. The ongoing evolution also works on the solution of ethical concerns, preserving privacy concerns, and providing the benefit of face recognition without compromising individual rights.

9.3 Final Thoughts on Ethical and Responsible Use

As face recognition becomes more popular and advanced, the developer, policymaker, and society as a whole need to prioritize this tool. Apart from various benefits offered by the technology, from enabling security to the innovative enabling consumer applications, it poses significant risks, particularly related to surveillance, privacy, and potential biases. The technology respects human rights and trust among the public by implementing guidelines and strict regulations for misuse by the government, malicious actors, or corporations.

In moving forward, the system should be deployed and implemented through guided principles of accountability, transparency, and fairness. There is a legal framework that governs the collection, use of biometric data, and storage, ensuring that individuals have control over their personal details. The future scope of face recognition lies in balancing the ethical obligations to protect privacy and prevent them from harm.

REFERENCES

Adjabi, I., Ouahabi, A., Benzaoui, A., & Taleb-Ahmed, A. (2020). Past, present, and future of face recognition: A review. *Electronics (Basel)*, *9*(8), 1–53. DOI: 10.3390/electronics9081188

Ali, A. A., Raheem, M., Kh-Madhloom, J., Hassen, O. A., Hassen, O. A., & Neamah, M. R. (2018). Big Data Enabled Approach for Predictive Analysis of Accuracy Aware Face Smile Detection in Assorted Domains ministery of higer education and scientific research Big Data Enabled Approach for Predictive Analysis of Accuracy Aware Face Smile Detection in Assorted Domains. In *Article in Journal of Advanced Research in Dynamical and Control Systems* (Vol. 10). https://www.researchgate.net/publication/334401924

Bahia, Y. Z., Meriem, F., & Messaoud, B. (2024). Face spoofing detection using Heterogeneous Auto-Similarities of Characteristics. *Engineering Applications of Artificial Intelligence*, *130*, 107788. DOI: 10.1016/j.engappai.2023.107788

Bhattacharyya, S. K., & Rahul, K. (2014). FACE RECOGNITION BY LINEAR DISCRIMINANT ANALYSIS. *International Journal of Communication Networks and Security*, *1–5*, www.interscience.in/ijcns. Advance online publication. DOI: 10.47893/IJCNS.2014.1087

Chan, J. (2022). Facial Recognition Technology and Ethical Issues. *Proceedings of the Wellington Faculty of Engineering Ethics and Sustainability Symposium*. DOI: 10.26686/wfeess.vi.7647

Face Recognition Using Eigenfaces. (n.d.). Retrieved September 3, 2024, from https://www.researchgate.net/publication/281446070_Face_Recognition_Using_Eigenfaces

Guleria, A., Krishan, K., Sharma, V., & Kanchan, T. (2024). Global adoption of facial recognition technology with special reference to India—Present status and future recommendations. *Medicine, Science, and the Law*, *64*(3), 236–244. DOI: 10.1177/00258024241227717 PMID: 38263636

Horkay, J., Tymofiiv, V., & Al-Rabeei, S. (2022). Using Biometrics for Facial Recognition at Airports. *Acta Avionica Journal*, 34–40. DOI: 10.35116/aa.2022.0029

Jain, A. (2021). Secure Authentication for Banking Using Face Recognition. [JIEEE]. *Journal of Informatics Electrical and Electronics Engineering*, *2*(2), 1–8. DOI: 10.54060/JIEEE/002.02.001

Kumar, N. S., Gabriel, S. S. P., & Shankar, M. C. (2024). *Criminal Identification by Face Recognition through Camera Using Image Processing*. www.ijnrd.org

Manu, Y. M., Gagana, R., & Shashikala, S. V. (2023). Enhancing Face Detection and Recognition through Machine Learning Algorithm. *International Conference on Recent Advances in Science and Engineering Technology, ICRASET 2023*. DOI: 10.1109/ICRASET59632.2023.10420184

Mary Solomon, M., Singh Meena, M., Kaur, J., Tech Student, M., & Professor, A. (n.d.). *CHALLENGES IN FACE RECOGNITION SYSTEMS. 6*. Retrieved September 3, 2024, from https://ijrar.com/

Mohialden, Y. M., Hussien, N. M., & Ali, D. M. A. (2023a). Enhancing User Authentication with Facial Recognition and Feature-Based Credentials. *Journal La Multiapp*, *4*(6), 243–252. DOI: 10.37899/journallamultiapp.v4i6.903

Mohialden, Y. M., Hussien, N. M., & Ali, D. M. A. (2023b). Enhancing User Authentication with Facial Recognition and Feature-Based Credentials. *Journal La Multiapp*, *4*(6), 243–252. DOI: 10.37899/journallamultiapp.v4i6.903

Nosek, B. A., Hawkins, C. B., & Frazier, R. S. (2011). Implicit social cognition: From measures to mechanisms. *Trends in Cognitive Sciences*, *15*(4), 152–159. DOI: 10.1016/j.tics.2011.01.005 PMID: 21376657

Owais, M., Shaikh, A., Jalal, A. A., & Hassan, M. M. (2019). Human Face Recognition using PCA Eigenfaces. *ICETAS 2019 - 2019 6th IEEE International Conference on Engineering, Technologies and Applied Sciences*. DOI: 10.1109/ICETAS48360.2019.9117489

Pabiania, M. D., Santos, K. A. P., Villa-Real, M. M., & Villareal, J. A. N. (2016). Face recognition system for electronic medical record to access out-patient information. *Jurnal Teknologi*, *78*(6–3), 91–97. DOI: 10.11113/jt.v78.8935

Pandey, A. K., & Mishra, R. (2023). Deep Learning based facial recognition using H aar cascade technique. *2023 3rd International Conference on Advance Computing and Innovative Technologies in Engineering, ICACITE 2023*, 2109–2113. DOI: 10.1109/ICACITE57410.2023.10182612

(PDF) Face Recognition by Support Vector Machines. (n.d.). Retrieved September 3, 2024, from https://www.researchgate.net/publication/2427763_Face_Recognition_by_Support_Vector_Machines

(PDF) Face Recognition Methods & Applications. (n.d.). Retrieved September 3, 2024, from https://www.researchgate.net/publication/260483303_Face_Recognition_Methods_Applications

(PDF) Face Recognition using Local Binary Patterns (LBP). (n.d.). Retrieved September 3, 2024, from https://www.researchgate.net/publication/331645500_Face_Recognition_using_Local_Binary_Patterns_LBP

(PDF) Real Time Face Detection. (n.d.). Retrieved September 3, 2024, from https://www.researchgate.net/publication/257022696_Real_Time_Face_Detection

Phatak, S. S., Patil, H. S., Arshad, M. W., Jitkar, B., Patil, S., & Patil, J. (2022). Advanced Face Detection using Machine Learning and AI-based Algorithm. *Proceedings of 5th International Conference on Contemporary Computing and Informatics, IC3I 2022*, 1111–1116. DOI: 10.1109/IC3I56241.2022.10072527

Qian, Y. (2024). Face recognition technology for video surveillance integrated with particle swarm optimization algorithm. *International Journal of Intelligent Networks, 5*, 145–153. DOI: 10.1016/j.ijin.2024.02.008

Rahman, M. M., Chakma, S., Raza, D. M., Akter, S., & Sattar, A. (2021). Real-Time Object Detection using Machine Learning. *2021 12th International Conference on Computing Communication and Networking Technologies, ICCCNT 2021*. DOI: 10.1109/ICCCNT51525.2021.9580170

Sakthimohan, M., Elizabeth Rani, G., Navaneethakrishnan, M., Janani, K., Nithva, V., & Pranav, R. (2023). Detection and Recognition of Face Using Deep Learning. *Proceedings of the 2023 International Conference on Intelligent Systems for Communication, IoT and Security, ICISCoIS 2023*, 72–76. DOI: 10.1109/ICISCoIS56541.2023.10100435

Saxena, N., & Varshney, D. (2021). Smart Home Security Solutions using Facial Authentication and Speaker Recognition through Artificial Neural Networks. *International Journal of Cognitive Computing in Engineering, 2*, 154–164. DOI: 10.1016/j.ijcce.2021.10.001

Selwyn, N., Andrejevic, M., O'Neill, C., Gu, X., & Smith, G. (2024). Facial Recognition Technology. In *The Cambridge Handbook of Facial Recognition in the Modern State* (pp. 11–28). Cambridge University Press., DOI: 10.1017/9781009321211.003

Sharma, R., Sandhu, J., & Bharti, V. (2024). Exploring Feature-Based Image Classification for Human Identification in Multimodal Biometric System. *2024 11th International Conference on Reliability, Infocom Technologies and Optimization (Trends and Future Directions), ICRITO 2024*. DOI: 10.1109/ICRITO61523.2024.10522307

Singh, A. K., Kumar, S., Kumar, B., & Chauhan, A. S. (2023). Face Recognition Using Machine Learning. *2023 International Conference on Sustainable Emerging Innovations in Engineering and Technology, ICSEIET 2023*, 361–364. DOI: 10.1109/ICSEIET58677.2023.10303390

Swamy, K. V., Supraja, A., Vinuthna, P. S., & Sindhura, D. L. (2022). Performance Comparison of Various Features for Human Face Recognition using Machine Learning. *2022 IEEE Conference on Interdisciplinary Approaches in Technology and Management for Social Innovation, IATMSI 2022*. DOI: 10.1109/IATMSI56455.2022.10119449

Yao, Y. (2024). Research on facial recognition system based on deep learning. *Applied and Computational Engineering*, *34*(1), 232–236. DOI: 10.54254/2755-2721/34/20230332

Zheng, J., Wang, S., & Lei, N. (2023). A Method to Improve the Accuracy of Face Recognition in Application Scenarios. *Proceedings of 2023 IEEE 3rd International Conference on Information Technology, Big Data and Artificial Intelligence, ICIBA 2023*, 320–325. DOI: 10.1109/ICIBA56860.2023.10165241

Chapter 6
Protecting Data in the 5G Era
A Critical Review of Cryptographic Techniques for Mobile Cloud Computing

Malak Al-Majali
https://orcid.org/0009-0008-3034-7693
Zarqa University, Jordan

Mohammad Aljaidi
https://orcid.org/0000-0001-9486-3533
Zarqa University, Jordan

Qais Al-Naamneh
Applied Science Private University, Jordan

Ghassan Samara
Zarqa University, Jordan

Ayoub Alsarhan
https://orcid.org/0000-0001-9075-2828
Hashemite University, Jordan

Braa Qadoumi
https://orcid.org/0000-0002-4753-7820
Applied Science Private University, Jordan

ABSTRACT

The surge in smartphone users has fueled the development of mobile Cloud Computing (MCC), a technology integrating cloud computing's power with mobile device mobility. MCC offers on-demand access to cloud resources like storage, processing power, and software, enhancing mobile device functionality and efficiency. This paper delves into user privacy concerns in 5G MCC environments. The convergence of mobile computing, wireless networks, and cloud computing has fostered the rapidly evolving field of MCC. Advancements in 5G mobile networks are expected to propel MCC services even further, making them a focal point in the mobile service landscape. However, 5G MCC also presents significant user privacy challenges, including network latency and data security. This paper investigates various cryptographic

DOI: 10.4018/979-8-3693-8014-7.ch006

techniques employed to safeguard user privacy in 5G MCC systems. We compare and analyze encryption techniques, zero-knowledge proofs, MFA, and blockchain, and the inherent challenges associated with each approach.

INTRODUCTION

The number of users of smart mobile has increased significantly in recent years, which has led to the emergence of Mobile cloud computing (MCC) a technology that combines the power of cloud computing with the mobility of mobile devices. (Kumar, 2022)The provision of computing resources, such as storage, computing power, and software, to mobile devices over a network. This allows mobile devices to connect the power of the cloud to improve their functionality, performance, and efficiency. by allowing mobile devices to access cloud resources over the network. Mobile apps can communicate with cloud services through APIs (application programming interfaces) to offload resource-intensive tasks such as image and video processing, complex calculations, and machine learning. MCC is demarcated as a platform on which data processing and storage are implemented in mobile clouds, instead of handling on smart mobile edge devices (Kumar R. A., 2024).

Figure 1. Mobile Cloud Computing (MCC).

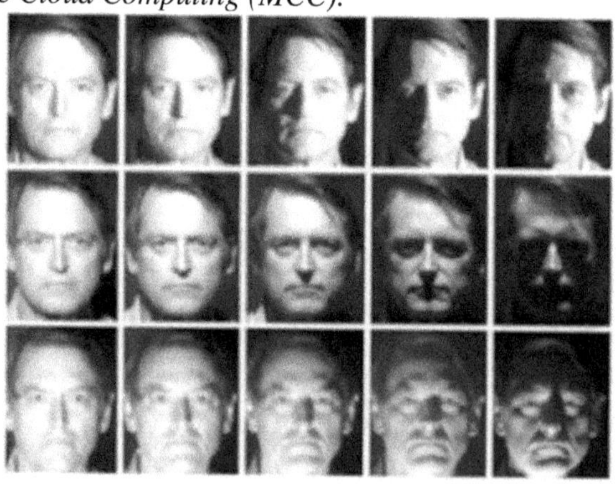

In Figure 1 The convergence of mobile computing, wireless networks, and cloud computing is creating a rapidly growing field known as Mobile Cloud Computing (MCC). With the advancements in 5G mobile networks, MCC services are expected to experience rapid development and become a hot topic in the world of mobile services (Sheikh, 2023).

Mobile cloud computing is increasing in the Fifth Generation (5G) most important of the major challenges that a user faces, such as network latency, and privacy issues [3]. 5G is the fifth generation of wireless cellular technology and provides faster upload and download speeds, more consistent connections, and improved capacity compared to previous networks. 5G is faster and more reliable than currently common 4G networks and has the potential to change the way we use the Internet to access applications, social networks, and information

One of the features of the fifth generation is that it uses the fifth generation medium-band microwave network from 2.5 to 3.7 GHz, allowing speeds ranging from 100 to 900 Mbit/s, with each cell tower providing service up to several miles in a circle around the network. This level of service is the most widespread and became available in most regions of the world in 2020. (Chamola, 2021)

5G is a new broadband mobile communication technology that offers high speed, low latency, and large connectivity. It enables the interconnection of people, machines, and things, allowing billions of smart IoT devices to interact and share data without human assistance. Research has focused on challenges such as reliable resilience, low latency, scalability, and high data rates using fine-grained networks. (Mwanje, 2024)

In this paper, which discusses user privacy in mobile cloud computing (Chow, 2022) will compare encryption techniques, zero-knowledge proofs, and decentralized identity management systems with blockchain, as well as the challenges for each technique (Mostafa, 2023).

To understand the cryptographic techniques used in 5G mobile cloud computing, this paper presents a comprehensive investigation of these techniques and their role in protecting user privacy in 5G MCC systems.

1. Encryption techniques play a vital role in protecting sensitive data transmitted over 5G networks. By using advanced encryption protocols, such as AES-256, you ensure that data remains secure and protected from unauthorized access. Encryption algorithms such as RSA and ECC are commonly used to encrypt data at rest and in transit, providing an additional layer of security against potential cyber threats (Al-Na'amneh, 2024).
2. Zero-Knowledge Proofs for Privacy-preserving Au- authentication: offer a powerful mechanism for privacy-preserving authentication in MCC systems. verifying user identities without revealing sensitive information. And enable users to prove their identity or credentials without revealing confidential details. This innovative encryption technology ensures privacy and confidentiality while maintaining the integrity of data transactions in a decentralized environment (Gaba, 2024).

3. Multi-factor authentication (MFA) is a critical security measure for protecting transactions and access on MCC 5G networks. In contrast to conventional password-based single-factor authentication, multi-factor authentication (MFA) uses many verification techniques to ensure enhanced security (Das, 2023).
4. Blockchain technology is a technology that enables secure and transparent recording and data transmission over a decentralized network. Data in a blockchain is organized into blocks, which are linked together using a cryptographic hash, making the data tamper-proof and immutable. Additionally, blockchain technology can be used to securely record and track transactions and effectively create digital identities. (Alqasem, 2024)

LITERATURE REVIEW

This study will review a select number of different encryption technologies used in 5G mobile cloud computing, explaining how each technology works, evaluating its effectiveness, discussing the advantages and disadvantages of each technology, and finally, this study will compare the different encryption technologies. This study aims to provide comprehensive research on the cryptography techniques used in 5G mobile cloud computing, and their role in protecting user privacy in 5G MCC systems.

A. Encryption Techniques. The advancements in cloud computing have given rise to a new paradigm called Mobile Cloud Computing (MCC), which allows mobile devices to access cloud services. The prevalence of cloud storage and cloud-based data access has created data security problems against data theft, deletion, corruption, and exploitation. Some creative encryption techniques have been created to address these cloud-based data security challenges and safeguard the data. Attribute-based encryption (ABE) is one such encryption technique that offers greater control over cloud data, including who can access it and how. In the past few years, a lot of scholarly academics have focused on applying cutting-edge cryptography approaches to safely handle, process, and distribute data over untrusted cloud environments. The Cipher text Policy - Attribute Encryption (CP-ABE) is a potential cryptographic solution that can address the open task of regulating the fine-grained access control of critical data over the distributed cloud (Goldwasser, 2019). Generally speaking, CP-ABE is one of the most popular strategies for addressing the security issues with data in cloud environments. Data owners no longer need to handle every request because of the method's limited scalability and flexibility. As a result, each data owner maintains a fine-grained access control model for this purpose, and they grant access to the user provided they meet the requirements.

B. Zero-Knowledge Proofs for Privacy-preserving Authentication. Zero-knowledge proof (ZKP) is used in cryptography to prove a statement without revealing any information (in that the prover has some secrets and can prove to the verifier that he has those secrets and the verifier can verify whether he has those secrets even though he does not It is known as) and is considered a more secure tool with fewer processing resources compared to the usual encryption techniques through two classifications: interactive and non-interactive (NZC). Interactive ZKP involves exchanging multiple messages between the prover and the verifier. The non-interactive ZKP sends a single piece of evidence to the verifier (Al-Na'amneh Q. N., 2024).

The three core properties are completeness, soundness, and zero-knowledge. Completeness means the verifier accepts the prover's true statement. Soundness means the verifier rejects the prover's false statement. Zero-knowledge means the verifier learns nothing other than the statement's truth.

Zero-knowledge authentication is used to protect users' privacy by enabling anonymous communications, avoiding spoofing, MIMA, replay, and password attacks, and reducing network traffic. It also reduces computation complexity and length of proofs, unlike other techniques like the Merkel tree, which can increase network traffic.

ZKPs work on the basic idea of ZKPs, which is the concept that a user can prove knowledge of a secret (such as a password or private key) without giving out the secret itself. A cryptographic procedure involving a prover (user) and a verifier allows this. A protocol typically follows a challenge-and-response mechanism. ZKPs are a promising privacy-preserving au- authentication technology in 5G MCC.

Because it provides many benefits in terms of security, privacy, effectiveness, and efficiency. However, there are some challenges associated with computational complexity, response size, and incompatibility.

As ZKP technology continues to develop, it is expected that it will be more widely adopted in various authentication applications in 5G MCC. In (Tran, 2021) In the context of mobile cloud computing (MCC), ZKPs are used to enhance security and privacy in various processes, including user authentication by proving their identity without revealing their passwords, and access control by proving their permission to access resources without revealing them. Details of their permissions or by protecting data by proving the integrity of data stored in the cloud without revealing its content. now we want to explain the types of ZKPs used in MCC (Koteras, 2023):

1. **Schnorr-based ZKPs:** o It is the most common, it is computationally efficient, and the response size is small.
    - o They are used in many applications such as authentication and access control.

2. **Groth-Pedersen-based ZKPs:** o Provides a high level of security and allows and is carried out through complex proofs.
    - o They are used in several applications such as data protection and transaction verification.
3. **ZK-SNARK-based ZKPs:** o It is characterized by efficiency and high execution speeds.
    - o It is used in some applications that require high performance, such as games and financial applications.
4. **STARKS-based ZKPs:** o It is characterized by high flexibility that allows custom proofs to be conducted.

They are used in several applications that have advanced features, such as non-fungible zero-knowledge proofs and evaluating the effectiveness of ZKPs:

ZKPs offer several advantages for privacy-preserving authentication in 5G MCC, including

A. **Security**: It reduces the risk of credential theft as no sensitive information is shared with the verifier.
B. **Privacy**: By not revealing any additional personal information about the user beyond his identity.
C. **Non-repudiation:** Because users cannot deny the validity of their answer after submitting it.
D. **Efficiency:** The speed and efficiency of responses can be verified. Knowing that this ZKP technology is still under development, and research is ongoing to improve its computational efficiency, response size, and compatibility. It is expected that these technologies will play an important role in providing secure and privacy-preserving environments for various applications in the future (Alshameri, 2019). Although ZKA offers a strong security posture for MCC authentication, this technology is not without drawbacks. The main defects are detailed below (Idhaim, 2023):
    - Computational complexity: ZKA proofs involve complex cryptographic processes, making them computationally expensive for both generation (on the user's machine) and verification (on the server). This can lead to slower authentication as it increases processing time and leads to longer waiting periods during login or access attempts. The additional processing power required for ZKA proofs can drain a mobile device's battery faster shown the fig 2 (Jiang, 2024).

Figure 2. Zero Knowledge Proof

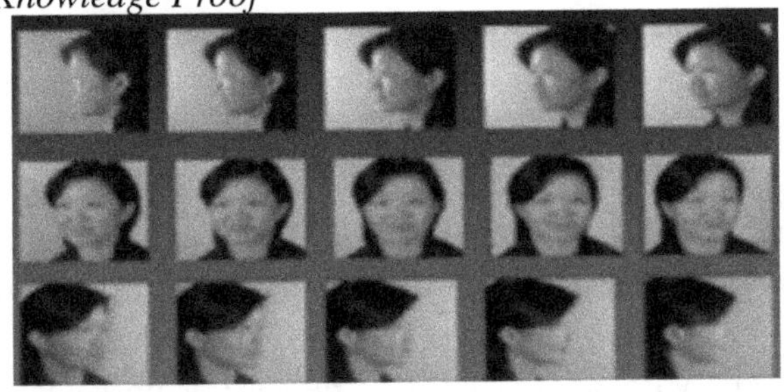

- The large response volume is due to the limited bandwidth faced by users who have a slow or unreliable Internet network or have interruptions during authentication or by consuming mobile phone data.
- Limited Compatibility: Being a new technology, it may not support all existing MCC platforms and applications. There is a need for developers to support the integration of ZKA into MCC solutions for wider ease of use.
- Security concerns: While ZKA p (Liu, 2019) protects user credentials during authentication, but it does not protect servers from hacking. If a malicious actor gains access to the server, they may exploit vulnerabilities in the ZKA protocol and steal user information. (Jaradat, 2023) Or by performing side-channel attacks by collecting information about user credentials through indirect means such as timing analysis during ZKA proofs as Shown in Fig .3

Figure 3. ZKA protocol

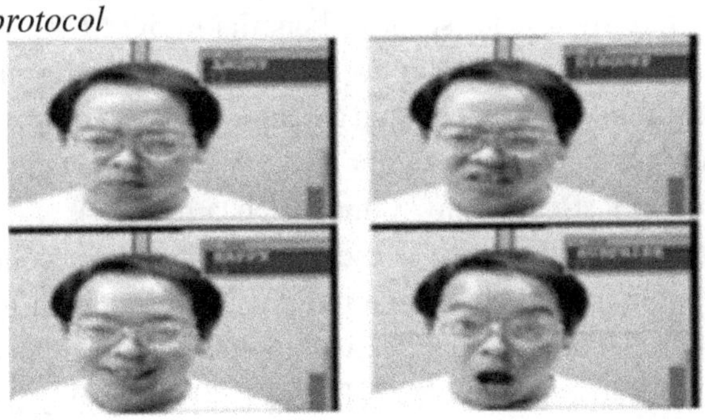

C. **Multi-Factor Authentication (MFA).** Multi-factor authentication (MFA) in 5G mobile cloud computing (MCC) plays a critical role in securing user access to resources and applications within the dynamic environment of 5G MCC. The importance of MFA in 5G MCC has several points, the most important of which are:

- Expanded attack surface: The 5G MCC is a complex system that includes cloud resources, mobile devices, and edge computing nodes. All of this creates a wider attack surface for potential security breaches. Therefore, MFA adds a layer of defense against unauthorized access attempts (Gaba G. S., 2022).
- Protect sensitive data as 5G MCC applications handle sensitive user data or control critical infrastructure. These violations will have serious consequences. MFA reduces the risk of unauthorized access to this data (Laila, 2024).
- Mobile phone security to the possibility of mobile devices being vulnerable to hacking, and MFA provides an additional layer of security

One of the most important features played by multi-factor authentication (MFA) First: Enhancing security by reducing the risk of unauthorized access by adding obstacles for attackers. For example, even if the password is stolen, they will not have the additional factor required to log in. Second: Improving user confidence, as stronger authentication builds user confidence in the security of 5G MCC applications. Third: Regulatory compliance through the optimal application of industry regulations or internal security policies regarding user access controls. Finally, it is characterized by reducing the risk of phishing attacks, which attempt to trick users into revealing their passwords. The MFA process helps mitigate these risks. Although MFA offers significant security benefits in 5G MCC, it is not without drawbacks. The first is the potential inconvenience of increasing login time by adding additional authentication steps to lengthen the login process compared to traditional username/password methods. It is a minor annoyance for frequent users but affects the user experience in fast-paced environments (Islam, 2019).

The second disadvantage, which is the weakness of the second factor, is that phones are vulnerable to hacking. If the two-factor depends on the user's phone (for example, SMS OTP or an authentication application), then losing or exposing her phone to risk leads to bypassing MFA (Rajesh, 2024).Deploying and managing MFA solutions may incur costs. Additional benefits include the purchase of hardware tokens (such as security keys), licensing software for authentication servers, and the possibility of integration with existing IT infrastructure. Unique codes for devices or certain Smartphone applications may confuse and be a hindrance to less tech-savvy users. Next, recovery mechanisms. MFA technology often relies on backup methods to restore access in the event of loss of second factors (such as security questions and email addresses). Attackers may target these backup copies to access them. Finally, there are several challenges specific to 5G MCC, including network segmentation. It must adapt and deal with dynamic network segmentation environments where users can access resources from different virtual networks. Complexities may arise in ensuring consistent and effective second-factor verification across different segments with different security policies or resource constraints. To be effective, MFA must be lightweight for edge computing scenarios in 5G MCC, where processing and storage power may be limited at the edge of the network.[30] multi-factor authentication (MFA) plays a vital role in securing user access within the dynamic and complex environment of 5G MCC. Below are details of different MFA applications suitable for 5G MCC:

1. Traditional MFA agents: Username/password combined with one-time passwords (OTPs) that can be generated on the user's Smartphone or sent via SMS.
2. Biometric Authentication (Li, 2024): This enables you to integrate fingerprint scanners or facial recognition on mobile devices with MFA for a more convenient and secure login experience.
3. Context-aware MFA: MFA parameters can be dynamically adjusted to adapt based on user contexts (location, device type, access time) for a more adaptive and user-friendly experience for low-risk scenarios while requiring authentication for high-risk situations.
4. Future proofing with emerging technologies: Emerging technologies that represent behavioral biometrics (analysis of user behavior patterns for authentication) such as typing style or touch gestures are likely to work for continuous and transparent authentication. On enabling seamless and secure multi-factor authentication (MFA) in 5G MCC as shown in Figure .4
    D. **Blockchain technology.** Blockchain-based authentication (Farah, 2024) is becoming more and more important in distributed mobile cloud computing (MCC) applications as a means of preventing illegal access behavior. However, blockchain technology is public and unchangeable, users' access practices expose them to serious security and privacy risks. To mitigate these problems, storing encrypted data on-chain is a good solution; nonetheless, the primary bottleneck is verifying and updating access authorization in ciphertext form. For this reason, a hierarchical access control and uniform authentication system based on blockchain is suggested for the MCC environment, offering audibility and privacy protection. With just one credential, users in the suggested system can access several MCC services with various levels of access authority (Laila, Enhancing 2D Logistic Chaotic Map for Gray Image Encryption., 2024). Pedersen Commitments are used to encrypt

data on the public ledger, maintaining auditability while safeguarding user and provider privacy. Additionally, in Table 1 the suggested plan offers an encrypted form with flexible dynamic updating. The suggested approach can satisfy different security and privacy requirements in an MCC context, according to theoretical research. Its communication efficiency is superior to related methods. Consequently, fig.5 shows the suggested plan is better suited for the real MCC scenario.

Figure 4. Real MCC scenario

Table 1. Show a difference between the encrypt techniques

Tec.	Advantages	Disadvantages
Encryption Techniques	1. Reducing data exposure to risks when transmitted 2. Reducing piracy operations	1. Security threats 2. Unapproved applications expose sensitive data
Zero- Knowledge Proof (ZKP)	1. Security 2. Privacy 3. Non-repudiation 4. effectiveness 5. and efficiency	1. computational complexity 2. response size 3. Limited Compatibility and Security concerns
	1. Stability	
	2. Low transaction	
Blockchain Technology	3. increased protection from identity theft due to the secure nature of cryptocurrency 4. Virtual currencies also help break down barriers to finance in developing countries.	1. Uses a public key or (asymmetric) cryptography. 2. Needs a lot of storage space.
	1. Enhanced Security	1. Potential Inconvenience
Multi-Factor Authentication (MFA)	2. Improved User Confidence 3. Compliance with Regulations 4. Reduced Risk of Phishing Attacks	2. Vulnerability of Second Factor 3. User Adoption-Complexity for Less Tech- tech-savvy users 4. 5G MCC Specific Challenges

CONCLUSION

The largest amount of information has been collected on some technologies, showing the importance of each technology, its drawbacks, and its applications about MCC, and that all of them can reduce users' concerns about using MCC, and it was concluded that all the technologies in this research paper can be integrated with blockchain technology. MFA, zero-knowledge, and encryption work together in MCC 5G applications to enhance security, privacy, and efficiency. We can use it as follows to enhance secure digital identity, so it is a technology Blockchain creates a secure and trusted digital identity for users and then we use MFA to add additional layers of security to verify identity. Zero-knowledge technologies can be used to prove identity without revealing personal information, and finally, we use encryption technology to protect identity data from unauthorized access. One of the benefits of integrating them is being able to improve security by providing a high level of security to protect data and systems from various threats. And enhancing privacy, zero-knowledge technologies help protect the user's privacy by allowing him to prove his identity or share information without revealing personal information. We may need specialized technical expertise to carry out the integration process, and it may be relatively expensive. These technologies are expected to play a significant role in providing secure and privacy-preserving environments for various applications in the future.

REFERENCES

Al-Na'amneh, Q. A. (2024). Next Generation Image Watermarking via Combined DWT-SVD Technique. *International Conference on Cyber Resilience (ICCR)*. IEEE Access. DOI: 10.1109/ICCR61006.2024.10532782

Al-Na'amneh, Q. N. (2024). Improving Memory Malware Detection in Machine Learning With Random Forest-Based Feature Selection. In *A. A. M., Risk Assessment and Countermeasures for Cybersecurity*. IGI Global. DOI: 10.4018/979-8-3693-2691-6.ch006

Alqasem, H. D. (2024). Transmission Line Fault Detection Using Arduino and GSM. In *Intelligent Systems, Business, and Innovation Research* (pp. 559–562). Springer Nature Switze. DOI: 10.1007/978-3-031-36895-0_45

Alshameri, H. M. (2019). An efficient zero- knowledge proof based identification scheme for securing software defined network. Scalable Computing: Practice and Experience,.

Chamola, V. J., Jolfaei, A., Chanana, V., Parashari, P., & Hassija, V. (2021). Information security in the post quantum era for 5G and beyond networks: Threats to existing cryptogra- phy, and post-quantum cryptography. *Computer Communications*, *176*, 99–1. DOI: 10.1016/j.comcom.2021.05.019

Chow, M. C., & Ma, M. (2022). A secure blockchain-based authentication and key agreement scheme for 3GPP 5G networks. *Sensors (Basel)*, *22*(12), 4525. DOI: 10.3390/s22124525 PMID: 35746307

Das, D. B. (2023). Blockchain enabled sdn framework for security management in 5g applications. *In Proceedings of the 24th International Conference on Distributed Computing and.* In Proceedings of the 24th International Conference on Dis- tributed Computing and.

Farah, M. B.-K., Ahmed, Y., Mahmoud, H., Shah, S. A., Al-kadri, M. O., Taramonli, S., Bellekens, X., Abozariba, R., Idrissi, M., & Aneiba, A. (2024). A survey on blockchain technology in the maritime industry: Challenges and future perspectives. *Future Generation Computer Systems*, *157*, 618–637. DOI: 10.1016/j.future.2024.03.046

Gaba, G. S., Hedabou, M., Kumar, P., Braeken, A., Liyanage, M., & Alazab, M. (2022). Zero knowledge proofs based authenticated key agreement protocol for sustainable healthcare. *Sustainable Cities and Society*, *80*, 103766. DOI: 10.1016/j.scs.2022.103766

Gaba, P. R.-S., Raw, R. S., Kaiwartya, O., & Aljaidi, M. (2024). Blockchain-Enabled Security Architecture for Connected Vehicle Fog Environment. *Sensors (Basel), 24*(5), 1515. DOI: 10.3390/s24051515 PMID: 38475051

Goldwasser, S. M. (2019). The knowledge complexity of interactive proof-systems. In Pro- viding sound foundations for cryptography: On the work of shafi goldwasser and silvio micali. (pp. 203-225). DOI: 10.1145/3335741.3335750

Idhaim, H. A.-s. (2023). Internal Hidden Processing Model-Based for SELECT Command in Struc- tured Query Language. *24th International Arab Con- ference on Information Technolog.IEEE Access : Practical Innovations, Open Solutions.*

Islam, M. T., & Huda, N. (2019). Material flow analysis (MFA) as a strategic tool in E-waste management: Applications, trends and future directions. *Journal of Environmental Management, 244*, 344–361. DOI: 10.1016/j.jenvman.2019.05.062 PMID: 31129466

Jaradat, A. S.-N. (2023). *Genetic optimization techniques for enhancing web attacks classification in machine learning*. IEEE Intl Conf on Dependable, Autonomic and Secure Co. DOI: 10.1109/DASC/PiCom/CBDCom/Cy59711.2023.10361399

Jiang, X. L. (2024). Privacy-Preserving UCB Decision Process Verifica- tion via zk-SNARKs. 2404.12186.

Koteras, D. T., Tomczuk, B., & Waindok, A. (2023). Implicit iteration calculations using 3D field analyses, to predict the power loss in powder ferromagnets, with their measurement tests. *Measurement, 207*, 112311. DOI: 10.1016/j.measurement.2022.112311

Kumar, A. A.-s. (2022). Recent Trends in Compact Planar Antennas at 5G Sub-6 GHz and mmWave Frequency Bands for Automotive Wireless Applications: a Review. .

Kumar, R. A. (2024). Development of a Prototype Global Positioning Sys- tem Based Stick for Blind Patients. *International Journal of Online Biomedical Engineering*,.

Laila, D. A.-N. (2024). Enhancing 2D Logistic Chaotic Map for Gray Image Encryption. In *Risk Assessment and Countermeasures for Cybersecurity.* (pp. (pp. 170-188). IGI G). IGI Global.

Laila, D. A.-N. (2024). Simulation of Routing Protocols for Jamming Attacks in Mobile Ad-Hoc Network. In *Risk Assessment and Countermeasures for Cybersecurity* (pp. (pp. 235-252).). IGI Global.

Li, S. F., Fei, L., Zhang, B., Ning, X., & Wu, L. (2024). Hand-based multimodal biometric fusion: A review. *Information Fusion*, *109*, 102418. DOI: 10.1016/j.inffus.2024.102418

Liu, W. W., Wang, X., & Peng, W. (2019). Secure remote multi-factor authentication scheme based on chaotic map zero-knowledge proof for crowdsourcing internet of things. *IEEE Access : Practical Innovations, Open Solutions*, *8*, 8754–8767. DOI: 10.1109/ACCESS.2019.2962912

Mostafa, A. M. (2023). An identity management scheme for cloud comput- ing: Review, challenges, and future directions. Journal of Intelligent Fuzzy Systems, . (Preprint), 1-23.

Mwanje, M. D., Kaiwartya, O., Aljaidi, M., Cao, Y., Kumar, S., Jha, D. N., Naser, A., & Lloret, J. (2024). Cyber security analysis of connected vehicles. *IET Intelligent Transport Systems*, *18*(7), 1175–1195. DOI: 10.1049/itr2.12504

Rajesh, H. M., Keeditse, M., Mfa, D. T., Vorster, C., & Belyanin, G. A. (2024). How not to use U–Pb detrital zircon geochronology to infer regional tectonics: Comment on Basupi et al. *Journal of African Earth Sciences*, *210*, 105153. DOI: 10.1016/j.jafrearsci.2023.105153

Sheikh, B. B. (2023). A survey on current security trends and future direc- tions. Engineering Proceedings,. *Mobile cloud com- puting:*, 32(1), 22.

Tran, Q. N. (2021). A privacy-preserving biometric authentication system with bi- nary classification in a zero knowledge proof protocol. *IEEE Open Journal of the Computer Society*.

Chapter 7
A Case Study on Cyber Attack Detection Using Machine Learning
IDS for Detecting Cyber Attacks Using Machine Learning

S. Indra Priyadharshini
https://orcid.org/0000-0002-0891-1605
Vellore Institute of Technology, Chennai, India

T. V. Padmavathy
https://orcid.org/0009-0001-9166-7622
Vellore Institute of Technology, Chennai, India

D. Shiny Irene
https://orcid.org/0000-0001-9636-7648
SRM Institute of Science and Technology, India

ABSTRACT

This chapter focusses on leveraging machine learning (ML) for cyber-attack prevention, addressing a range of threats and assaults. Machine learning is a crucial component of modern cybersecurity, offering a flexible approach to defend information systems against the constantly evolving tactics of malicious actors. By training both supervised and unsupervised ML algorithms on diverse datasets, we tackle issues such as hostile assaults and class imbalance. A key aspect of our work is prioritizing the interpretability of ML models to effectively manage and reduce false positives and false negatives. Additionally, we explore the challenges of integrating ML findings with existing cybersecurity frameworks, aiming for seamless collabo-

DOI: 10.4018/979-8-3693-8014-7.ch007

ration between traditional security measures and ML-driven solutions. Our goal is to provide valuable insights on utilizing ML to prevent cyberattacks, highlighting its benefits, limitations, and future potential. Ultimately, we aim to enhance cybersecurity defenses in dynamic threat landscapes by clarifying the role of ML in cybersecurity.

I. INTRODUCTION

In today's increasingly digital world, the threat of cyber attacks looms larger than ever before. With organizations and individuals alike becoming more reliant on interconnected systems, the potential for security breaches has skyrocketed. Traditional methods of cyber defense, while still valuable, often struggle to keep pace with the evolving tactics of cybercriminals. This is where the power of machine learning comes into play.

Machine learning, a subset of artificial intelligence, has emerged as a formidable tool in the fight against cyber threats. By leveraging vast amounts of data, machine learning algorithms can identify patterns, detect anomalies, and predict potential security breaches with unprecedented accuracy. Unlike conventional security measures that rely on predefined rules, machine learning models continuously learn and adapt, making them more effective at identifying new and sophisticated attack vectors.

This paper explores the innovative application of machine learning in cyber-attack prevention, examining how these advanced algorithms can bolster existing security frameworks, proactively detect threats, and ultimately safeguard critical assets in an ever-evolving digital landscape. By integrating machine learning into cybersecurity strategies, organizations can not only defend against current threats but also anticipate and mitigate future risks, ensuring a more secure digital environment.

Comprehending cyber-attacks entails comprehending the complex tactics and approaches utilized by malevolent actors to undermine digital infrastructures. Beyond face-position mindfulness, it includes a sophisticated understanding of the motivations, strategies, and changing patterns of cyber hazards. Understanding the variety of cyberattacks, from well-known ones like phishing to more complex ones like advanced patient traps and zero-day exploits, requires extensive expertise. Understanding the motivations behind hackers and delving into their psychology helps to clarify the dynamic nature of cybersecurity issues.

In this advanced conception, the understanding of cyber-attacks extends to the identification of vulnerabilities within systems, networks, and operations. It involves discerning the tactics used for intrusion, data breaches, and manipulation of digital means. Advanced appreciation also requires an mindfulness of arising technologies, like artificial intelligence, that both protectors and bushwhackers influence in a nonstop cat-and-mouse game.

As we all know, machine learning has special algorithms that help to identify anomalies. Additionally, because it can learn from its past with ease, it can predict similar attacks in real time and evaluate the network's operations, the stoner's gesture, and system logs that aid in identifying variations from regular or ordinary gestures and suggest that an attack may have been successful. This kind of analysis facilitates prompt action and reduces the likelihood of future occurrences of the same kind.

A paradigm leap in cybersecurity is represented by the sophisticated idea of "Prediction and Prevention of pitfalls," which employs cutting-edge technologies to foresee and mitigate implicit hazards. The system employs advanced machine learning algorithms to analyze real-world data trends and predict future risks. This allows for a proactive approach to addressing emerging cyber threats. Through continuous monitoring, data analysis, and anomaly identification, this forward-looking strategy enables associations to find implicit vulnerabilities before they are taken advantage of.

Additionally, the idea highlights the value of real-time trouble intelligence, which helps associations keep one step ahead of their enemies. To create a collaborative defensive medium and improve the entire security ecosystem, cooperative troubleshooting and information exchange are essential components. The community of vaccination and containment develops a more adaptable and visionary cybersecurity approach, safeguarding digital means against the constantly changing danger geography, as associations increasingly adopt this cutting-edge idea.

Real-time monitoring techniques offer a creative defense mechanism that makes it possible to react quickly to covert breaches. The advanced nature of these approaches is demonstrated by the system's ability to tone-learn and continuously upgrade its models, adding adaptability against changing attack vectors. Similarly, the incorporation of additional security measures acknowledges the increasingly decentralized nature of IoT ecosystems and indicates a forward-thinking perspective.

A. Intrusion Detection System:

An Intrusion Detection System (IDS) is a critical cybersecurity tool designed to monitor and analyze network traffic or system activities for signs of malicious activity or policy violations. By detecting potential threats in real time, an IDS can alert administrators to suspicious activities, enabling a rapid response to mitigate potential breaches. There are two main types of IDS: network-based (NIDS), which monitors network traffic, and host-based (HIDS), which focuses on individual systems. IDSs employ various techniques, including signature-based detection, where they compare activities against known attack patterns, and anomaly-based detection, which identifies deviations from normal behavior. While IDSs are effective in identifying unauthorized access or misuse, they do not prevent attacks; rather, they serve as an essential component of a comprehensive security strategy by providing visibility and facilitating proactive measures.

Intrusion Detection Systems (IDS) are integral to modern cybersecurity frameworks, offering a first line of defense against unauthorized access and cyber threats. These systems work by continuously monitoring network traffic and system behavior, using sophisticated algorithms and pattern recognition techniques to detect anomalies or matches to known attack signatures. IDSs can be configured to either passively alert security personnel of suspicious activities or take active measures, such as blocking traffic from malicious sources. They are particularly valuable in environments where large amounts of data are transmitted, as they can quickly identify potential threats that may go unnoticed by traditional security measures. Despite their effectiveness, IDSs must be regularly updated to recognize new attack vectors and are often used in conjunction with other security tools, such as firewalls and antivirus software, to create a robust defense-in-depth strategy.

Usage of Machine Leaarning in IDS:

Machine Learning (ML) has significantly enhanced the effectiveness and adaptability of Intrusion Detection Systems (IDS). Traditional IDS approaches, such as signature-based detection, rely on predefined patterns and are limited in detecting new or unknown threats. In contrast, ML-powered IDS can learn from vast amounts of data, recognizing subtle patterns and anomalies that may indicate malicious activity. By analyzing historical network traffic and behavior, ML algorithms can build models that differentiate between normal and suspicious activities, improving the accuracy of detection and reducing false positives.

One of the key advantages of using ML in IDS is its ability to evolve with emerging threats. As new types of attacks are identified, ML models can be retrained with updated data, allowing the IDS to detect novel threats that have not yet been cataloged. Moreover, advanced ML techniques, such as deep learning and reinforcement learning, enable IDS to handle complex, multi-stage attacks by understanding the context and sequence of events leading up to a potential breach. Overall, ML enhances the proactive capabilities of IDS, making them more adaptive, intelligent, and effective in safeguarding networks and systems from evolving cyber security threats.

B. IDS in IoT Environment:

Intrusion Detection Systems (IDS) in Internet of Things (IoT) environments differ significantly from traditional IDS due to the unique characteristics and challenges of IoT networks. Here are some key differences:

1. **Resource Constraints**: IoT devices typically have limited processing power, memory, and energy resources compared to traditional computing systems. This makes it challenging to implement resource-intensive IDS algorithms directly on IoT devices. IDS for IoT often needs to be lightweight and optimized to operate efficiently on these constrained devices.
2. **Diverse and Heterogeneous Devices**: IoT networks consist of a wide variety of devices with different hardware, software, and communication protocols. This diversity requires IDS solutions to be highly adaptable and capable of monitoring various types of devices and data streams.
3. **Scalability**: IoT networks can include a vast number of devices, often distributed across wide geographical areas. An IDS for IoT must be scalable to monitor large and dynamic networks effectively without becoming a bottleneck.
4. **Communication Protocols**: IoT devices often use specialized communication protocols, such as MQTT, CoAP, or Zigbee, which are different from the traditional TCP/IP stack. IDS for IoT must be designed to understand and analyze traffic using these protocols to detect anomalies or intrusions effectively.
5. **Security Threats**: The threat landscape in IoT is different from traditional networks, with specific vulnerabilities such as physical tampering, firmware manipulation, and attacks on the communication protocols unique to IoT devices. An IDS in IoT must be tailored to address these specific threats and provide relevant detection mechanisms.
6. **Deployment Environment**: IoT devices are often deployed in environments that are less secure, such as remote locations or public spaces, increasing their exposure to potential attacks. IDS solutions in IoT need to consider the physical security of devices and the potential for attacks that exploit their deployment environment.
7. **Centralized vs. Distributed**: In traditional networks, IDS might be centralized in a few key locations. However, in IoT networks, a distributed IDS approach is often necessary, where detection mechanisms are spread across various nodes and the network edge to ensure comprehensive coverage and timely response.

In summary, IDS in IoT must be adapted to handle the unique challenges posed by resource constraints, diverse devices, scalability requirements, specialized communication protocols, and the distinct security threats of IoT environments.

II. EXISTING WORKS

A. Related Works

(Tomer & Sharma, 2022) in his research investigates the IoT attack detection using an ensemble machine learning model. application of ensemble machine learning techniques for the detection of Internet of Things (IoT) attacks. The study explores the effectiveness of combining multiple machine learning algorithms to enhance the accuracy and reliability of IoT security systems. The research contributes valuable insights into the development of robust methods for identifying and mitigating cyber threats targeting IoT devices.

(Kandhro et al., 2023), in their paper, explores advanced methods for identifying and mitigating real-time malicious intrusions and cyber-attacks within IoT-based cybersecurity systems. The authors likely delve into cutting-edge techniques and technologies to enhance the security posture of IoT environments, addressing the dynamic challenges posed by evolving cyber threats.

(Jayalaxmi et al., 2022) in her study, explores advanced methods for identifying and mitigating real-time malicious intrusions and cyber-attacks within IoT-based cybersecurity systems. The authors likely delve into cutting-edge techniques and technologies to enhance the security posture of IoT environments, addressing the dynamic challenges posed by evolving cyber threats.

(Siddharthan et al., 2022) provides a comprehensive overview of the applications of machines and deep learning techniques in enhancing security for Internet of Things (IoT) devices. The authors explore the state-of-the-art methods for intrusion detection and prevention, shedding light on the advancements in this field and addressing the unique challenges posed by the IoT ecosystem. With a focus on surveying the existing literature, the paper offers valuable insights into the evolving landscape of security solutions for IoT devices.

(Alahmadi et al., 2023) explores an intelligent intrusion detection system tailored for IoT-MQTT networks (MQTT - Message Queuing Telemetry Transport - Messaging protocol, or set of rules, used for machine-to-machine communication). The proposed "Senmqtt-set" leverages ensemble multi-cascade features to enhance the accuracy and efficiency of intrusion detection in the context of Internet of Things (IoT) networks utilizing the MQTT protocol. The paper aims to contribute to the evolving field of IoT security by introducing a novel approach that combines ensemble techniques with specific features relevant to MQTT-based communication.

(Musleh et al., 2023) provides a comprehensive survey of the state-of-the-art in DDoS attack detection within IoT networks. The paper explores various machine learning models applied to enhance security measures in the context of Internet of Things, offering valuable insights into current approaches and paving the way for future research directions in the domain. The collaborative effort of the authors contributes to advancing the understanding and implementation of robust security mechanisms in IoT environments.

(Bhavsar et al., 2023) explores the development of an Intrusion Detection System (IDS) tailored for the Internet of Things (IoT). The study focuses on leveraging feature extraction techniques in conjunction with machine learning algorithms to enhance the accuracy and efficiency of intrusion detection in IoT environments. The collaborative effort of the authors suggests a comprehensive approach to addressing security challenges in the rapidly evolving landscape of IoT technology.

(Attou et al., 2023) in their paper focuses on developing a sophisticated intrusion detection system for enhanced security in cloud environments. The paper likely explores the integration of intelligent algorithms and machine learning techniques to identify and mitigate potential security threats, addressing the evolving challenges in the dynamic landscape of cloud computing. The proposed system aims to contribute to the advancement of cybersecurity measures in cloud-based infrastructures.

(Awajan et al., 2021) in their study, proposes a novel deep learning-based intrusion detection system tailored for IoT networks. Leveraging advanced machine learning techniques, the system aims to enhance the security of IoT devices by accurately detecting and mitigating potential intrusions. The paper contributes to the field of computer security, addressing the unique challenges posed by the dynamic and interconnected nature of IoT networks.

(Krishnamoorthi et al., 2021) intrusions within Internet of Things (IoT) environments. By leveraging advanced mathematical models, the system aims to enhance the security of IoT networks by identifying and mitigating potential threats originating from smart contracts (They are programs stored on a blockchain that run when predetermined conditions are met). The integration of deep learning techniques offers a robust framework for the proactive identification of malicious activities, contributing to the overall resilience of IoT ecosystems.

(Alladi et al., 2022) presents a novel intrusion detection system tailored for enhancing the security of Internet of Things (IoT) networks. Focused on the convergence of Blockchain, IoT, and security, the study explores innovative approaches to detect and mitigate potential threats in the interconnected IoT environment. The paper contributes to the evolving landscape of cybersecurity by addressing the unique challenges associated with securing IoT networks through the integration of cutting-edge technologies.

(Fadel et al., 2022) provides a thorough examination of machine learning-based intrusion detection systems (ML-IDS) designed to enhance the security of communication on the Internet of Things (IoT) environment. The survey critically assesses existing methodologies, algorithms, and deployment scenarios, offering valuable insights into the current state of ML-IDS for IoT security. The paper contributes to the understanding of the challenges and advancements in this field, offering a foundation for future research and development in securing IoT communication through intelligent intrusion detection systems.

(Nikbazm & Ahmadi, 2022) explores the application of deep learning techniques in developing an intrusion detection system for Internet of Things (IoT) networks. The study delves into anomaly detection methods to enhance the security of IoT devices, aiming to mitigate potential cyber threats. The findings contribute to the evolving field of cybersecurity, specifically addressing the unique challenges posed by IoT ecosystems.

(Revathi et al., 2021) explores the development of a reliable intrusion detection system tailored for the Internet of Things (IoT). The paper leverages deep transfer learning techniques, emphasizing the importance of robust security measures to safeguard IoT environments against potential cyber threats. The study contributes to the ongoing efforts to enhance the security and dependability of IoT systems through advanced intrusion detection methodologies.

(Dhanaraj et al., 2021) proposes an innovative approach to enhance the security of IoT networks. The paper introduces a sophisticated two-tier ensemble learning pipeline designed for intrusion detection, leveraging the strengths of multiple algorithms to address the unique challenges posed by the dynamic and heterogeneous nature of IoT environments. The research contributes to the growing field of cybersecurity in the context of IoT, offering a promising solution to detect and mitigate potential security threats in these interconnected systems.

Diverse attack kinds should be considered in several exploratory articles' datasets. To capture a wider range of security problems, it is difficult to create a more comprehensive and diverse dataset due to the gap in addressing emerging and sophisticated attack routes. A thorough discussion of the integration problems between security standards and IoT infrastructures is warranted by a number of studies. Providing insight into how the suggested system seamlessly connects with and enhances existing IoT fabrics is necessary to close this gap. There may be issues with data sequestration and security for the existing system. It's possible that guidelines for data sequestration and the safeguarding of sensitive information are not clearly specified. Encryption and access controls are two examples of strong security measures that are essential to protecting the data's integrity and confidentiality. Thorough verification and testing of data processing procedures, algorithms, and models are essential to guarantee the accuracy and dependability of outcomes. Implementing confirmation procedures aids in locating and fixing latent problems in the data channel.

III. System Architecture for Secure IDS using ML:

A. Introduction

We provide a strong Intrusion Discovery System (IDS) that uses machine learning techniques in response to the growing cyber hazards that target Internet of Things (IoT) ecosystems. Ensuring the integrity and security of linked bias by strengthening IoT bias and networks against colorful, vicious conditioning is the main goal. The system will analyze network business patterns, gets, and abnormalities using machine learning algorithms to identify implicit intrusions. This is a relief from Tomer and Sharma's session on utilizing ensemble machine literacy models to identify IoT assaults. The figure 1 shows the architecture of the proposed IDS architecture.

Figure 1. Architecture Diagram

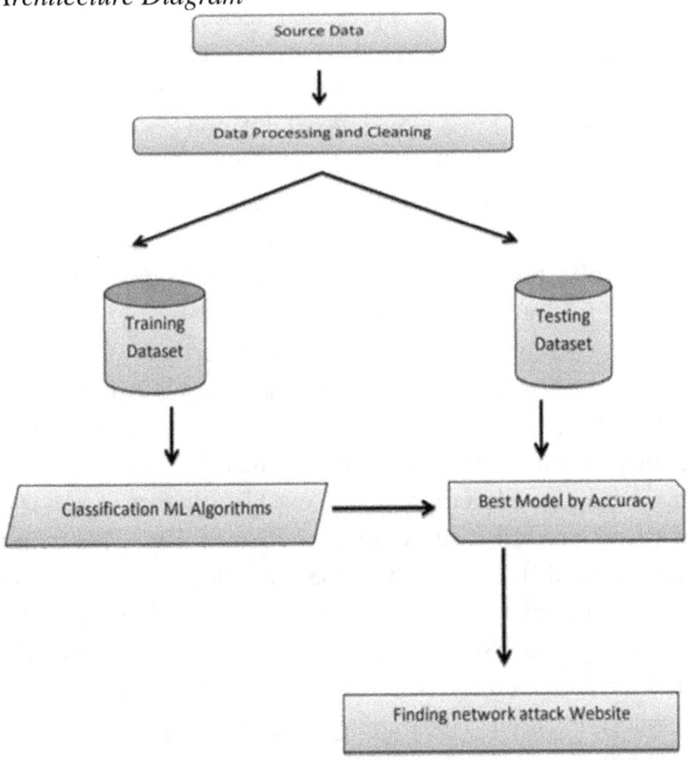

B. Experimental Setup

The experimental setup for this project begins with the selection and preparation of datasets, which are critical for training and testing the machine learning models. Public datasets like NSL-KDD or CICIDS2017, which contain labeled instances of network traffic and cyber attacks, will be utilized to ensure a robust training process. Data preprocessing steps include cleaning, normalizing, and selecting relevant features such as IP addresses, port numbers, and protocol types. Once the data is prepared, various machine learning models, including supervised methods like Random Forest and SVM, as well as unsupervised techniques like K-Means Clustering, will be evaluated to identify the most effective approach for detecting cyber-attacks.

Following the selection of the most promising model, the training process will involve splitting the dataset into training and testing subsets, with performance evaluated using metrics such as accuracy, precision, recall, and the AUC-ROC curve. Hyperparameter tuning will be performed to optimize the model's performance, and ensemble methods may be employed to enhance prediction accuracy. The trained model will then be deployed in a controlled simulation environment that mimics real-world network traffic, including both benign and malicious activities. Continuous monitoring will ensure the model's effectiveness, with adjustments made as needed based on real-time performance and detection accuracy.

Firstly, the data collection and preprocessing are foundational way in any machine literacy bid, pivotal for correcting accurate and dependable prophetic models. The process begins with sourcing the dataset intended for analysis. In this environment, the collected data serves as the bedrock upon which the posterior machine learning algorithms will operate. It could be a different range of information, frequently formed from colorful sources and in different formats.

Next in line is the algorithm training, the machine literacy model is exposed to the training dataset, which is a subset of the collected data. This training dataset contains labeled exemplifications, where the input data is paired with the corresponding correct affair or target variable. For case, if the thing is prognosticating a double outgrowth(e.g., Yes No), the training dataset will correspond of cases with their associated correct groups.

Once the model is exposed to the training data, it learns patterns and connections within the features to make prognostications. The literacy process involves conforming internal parameters grounded on the disagreement between prognosticated and factual issues. This optimization is achieved through ways like grade descent, icing the model minimizes crimes and generalizes well to unseen data.

Thus, algorithm training is a dynamic and iterative process wherein the machine literacy model refines its prophetic capabilities by learning from literal data. The choice of algorithms and the careful monitoring of the model's performance during training are critical aspects that impact the overall effectiveness of the constructed prophetic model.

The next step is anomaly discovery which is a critical element in the data analysis channel, especially in the environment of constructing prophetic models for machine literacy operations. In the forenamed script, anomaly discovery serves as a safeguard against irregularities, outliers, or unanticipated patterns in the collected dataset. This process is integral during the data fighting and preprocessing stages to ensure the dataset's integrity and enhance the effectiveness of prophetic models.

By addressing anomalies during the data split, the posterior models are trained and tested on datasets that directly represent the underpinning patterns and characteristics. In the preprocessing phase, anomaly discovery is employed to upgrade the dataset further. Anomaly discovery continues to play a part in the construction and tuning of prophetic models. It helps in feting irregularities during the training and testing phases, allowing for adaptations to enhance model delicacy.

Alert Generation upon the discovery of anomalous patterns or disagreement between prognosticated and observed issues, an alert generation system becomes necessary. This process is intricately tied to the delicacy of the prophetic model. Machine literacy algorithms give the capacity to set thresholds for diversions, driving cautions when the observed data deviates significantly from the prognosticated values. The choice of applicable alert thresholds is pivotal, striking a delicate balance to avoid gratuitous cautions while icing that potentially poignant diversions are instantly linked.

Response Protocol inversely important is the establishment of a well- defined response protocol to address cautions effectively. This protocol outlines the way and conduct to be taken in response to specific types of cautions. For case, if the prophetic model indicates a unforeseen and significant drop in delicacy, the response protocol may involve an immediate review of the model, implicit retraining, and a thorough disquisition into the root cause of the divagation.

Then we have deployed the model to ensure the minimization of cyber-attacks and with this implementation, starting from the preprocessing of the data to feature engineering to developing the model and its deployment, we have built an efficient system to prevent cyber-attacks in the future.

IV. CONCLUSION & INFERENCES

The process of constructing a prophetic model, encompassing data fighting, collection, preprocessing, and model construction, is intricate and multifaceted. Each phase contributes significantly to the model's effectiveness in making accurate prognostications. Still, the ultimate success of a prophetic model is contingent on its capability to suffer rigorous evaluation and nonstop enhancement.

The evaluation phase is a critical checkpoint in the model development cycle, representing the transition from training and construction to real- world connection. During this phase, the model is subordinated to a battery of tests using a distinct dataset – the testing set. Metrics similar as delicacy, perfection, recall, and the F1 score are reckoned to gauge the model's performance. This quantitative assessment offers a comprehensive understanding of the model's strengths and areas taking enhancement.

The evaluation criteria give perceptivity into how well the model aligns with its intended objects. High delicacy suggests robust prophetic capabilities, while perfection and recall exfoliate light on the model's capability to make correct prognostications and identify applicable cases, independently. The F1 score balances perfection and recall, offering a compound measure of the model's overall effectiveness.

Likewise, the interpretability of the model plays a vital part in the enhancement process. The perceptivity picked from model interpretation during evaluation companion opinions on adaptations, icing that advancements align with both quantitative criteria and mortal understanding.

In the realm of prophetic modeling, the iterative process of evaluation and enhancement is akin to a righteous cycle, fostering an terrain of continual literacy and adaption. Assessing the model's performance against different datasets and real- world scripts would enable the identification of implicit risks and areas for improvement. The perceptivity gained from evaluation, when precisely anatomized and interpreted, offers a roadmap for targeted advancements. The below figure 2 shows the results of XGB classifier and LGBM classifier.

Figure 2. Results of XGBoost and LGBM

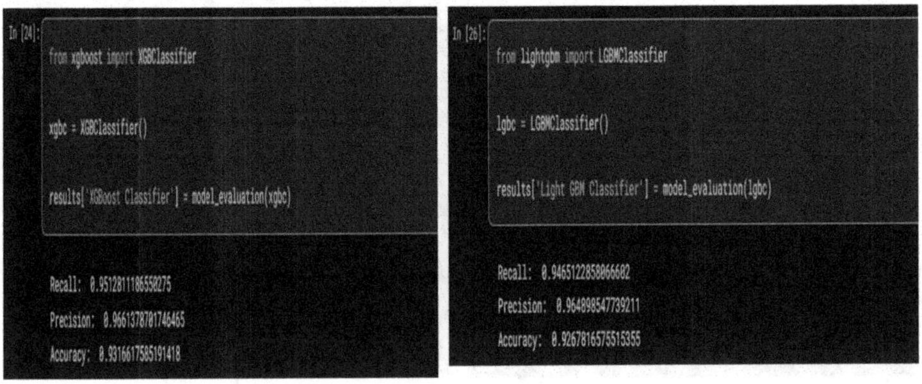

The enhancement process extends beyond quantitative adaptations to encompass qualitative aspects as well. Considerations similar as the model's interpretability, ethical counter accusations, and alignment with stakeholder conditions companion advances. Ethical considerations, in particular, play a pivotal part in the responsible development and deployment of machine literacy models. A commitment to fairness, translucency, and responsibility informs the enhancement strategies, icing that the model not only excels in performance criteria but also upholds ethical norms.

Also, as the model evolves, collaboration between data scientists, sphere experts, and end- druggies becomes necessary. This cooperative approach ensures that advancements are embedded in a holistic understanding of the problem sphere, feeding to the practical requirements and prospects of those who interact with the model. Figure 3 shows the output screenshots of the performance of Logistic Regression, Gaussian NB and MLP models.

Figure 3. Results of Logistic Regression, Guassian NB & MLP models

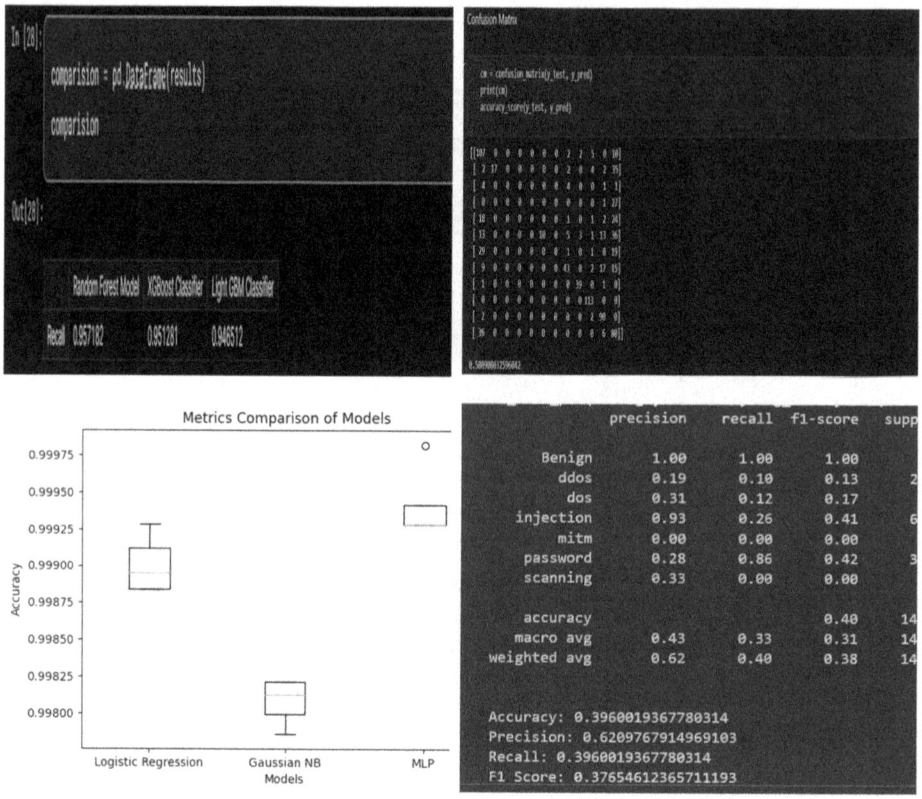

In conclusion, the harmonious interplay between evaluation and enhancement forms the bedrock of successful prophetic modeling. The model's trip from construction to deployment is marked by a commitment to perfection, translucency, and ethical considerations. This iterative cycle not only refines the model's prophetic capabilities but also underscores its part as a dynamic and necessary asset in the ever- evolving geography of data- driven decision- timber.

Figure 4. Performance Comparison

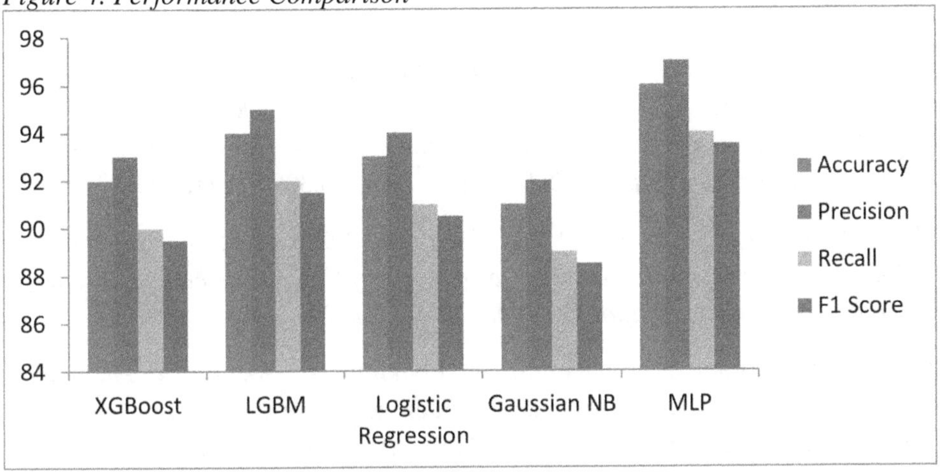

The graph shown in figure 4 visually compares the machine learning models (XGBoost, LGBM, Logistic Regression, Gaussian NB, and MLP) based on the four performance metrics: Accuracy, Precision, Recall, and F1 Score. MLP (Multilayer Perceptron) stands out with the highest values across all metrics (Accuracy, Precision, Recall, and F1 Score), emphasizing its superiority in this comparison. LGBM (LightGBM) follows closely, showing high performance in all four metrics, particularly in Precision and Accuracy. Logistic Regression performs well, with slightly lower scores compared to LGBM and MLP but still maintaining strong performance across the board. XGBoost has consistent performance, though its Recall and F1 Score are slightly lower compared to the other models. Gaussian NB shows the lowest performance in all metrics, particularly in Recall and F1 Score, indicating that it may not be as robust as the other models in this dataset.

V. REFERENCES

Alahmadi, A. A., Aljabri, M., Alhaidari, F., Alharthi, D. J., Rayani, G. E., Marghalani, L. A., Alotaibi, O. B., & Bajandouh, S. A. (2023). DDoS Attack Detection in IoT-Based Networks Using Machine Learning Models: A Survey and Research Directions. *Electronics (Basel)*, *12*(14), 3103. DOI: 10.3390/electronics12143103

Alladi, T., Kohli, V., Chamola, V., & Yu, F. R. (2022). A deep learning based misbehavior classification scheme for intrusion detection in cooperative intelligent transportation systems. *Digital Communications and Networks*.

Attou, H., Mohy-eddine, M., Guezzaz, A., Benkirane, S., Azrour, M., Alabdultif, A., & Almusallam, N. (2023). Towards an intelligent intrusion detection system to detect malicious activities in cloud computing. *Applied Sciences (Basel, Switzerland)*, *13*(17), 9588. DOI: 10.3390/app13179588

Bhavsar, M., Roy, K., Kelly, J., & Olusola, O. (2023). Anomaly-based intrusion detection system for IoT application. *Discover Internet of Things*, *3*(1), 5. DOI: 10.1007/s43926-023-00034-5

Dhanaraj, R. K., Lalitha, K., Anitha, S., Khaitan, S., Gupta, P., & Goyal, M. K. (2021). Hybrid and dynamic clustering based data aggregation and routing for wireless sensor networks. In Journal of Intelligent & Fuzzy Systems (Vol. 40, Issue 6, pp. 10751–10765). IOS Press. DOI: 10.3233/JIFS-201756

Dhanaraj, R. K., Lalitha, K., Anitha, S., Khaitan, S., Gupta, P., & Goyal, M. K. (2021). Hybrid and dynamic clustering based data aggregation and routing for wireless sensor networks. In Journal of Intelligent & Fuzzy Systems (Vol. 40, Issue 6, pp. 10751–10765). IOS Press. DOI: 10.3233/JIFS-201756

Dhanaraj, R. K., Ramakrishnan, V., Poongodi, M., Krishnasamy, L., Hamdi, M., Kotecha, K., & Vijayakumar, V. (2021). Random Forest Bagging and X-Means Clustered Antipattern Detection from SQL Query Log for Accessing Secure Mobile Data. In Jain, D. K. (Ed.), *Wireless Communications and Mobile Computing* (Vol. 2021, pp. 1–9). Hindawi Limited., DOI: 10.1155/2021/2730246

Fadel, M. M., El-Ghamrawy, S. M., Ali-Eldin, A. M., Hassan, M. K., & El-Desoky, A. I. (2022). The proposed hybrid deep learning intrusion prediction IoT (HDLIP-IoT) framework. *PLoS One*, *17*(7), e027143. DOI: 10.1371/journal.pone.0271436 PMID: 35905101

Jayalaxmi, P. L. S., Saha, R., Kumar, G., Conti, M., & Kim, T. H. (2022). Machine and Deep Learning Solutions for Intrusion Detection and Prevention in IoTs: A Survey. *IEEE Access : Practical Innovations, Open Solutions*, *10*, 121173–121192. DOI: 10.1109/ACCESS.2022.3220622

Kandhro, I. A., Alanazi, S. M., Ali, F., Kehar, A., Fatima, K., Uddin, M., & Karuppayah, S. (2023). Detection of Real-Time Malicious Intrusions and Attacks in IoT Empowered Cybersecurity Infrastructures. *IEEE Access : Practical Innovations, Open Solutions*, *11*, 9136–9148. DOI: 10.1109/ACCESS.2023.3238664

Krishnamoorthi, S., Jayapaul, P., Dhanaraj, R. K., Rajasekar, V., Balusamy, B., & Islam, S. K. H. (2021). Design of pseudo-random number generator from turbulence padded chaotic map. *Nonlinear Dynamics*, *104*(2), 1627–1643. Advance online publication. DOI: 10.1007/s11071-021-06346-x

Musleh, D., Alotaibi, M., Alhaidari, F., Rahman, A., & Mohammad, R. M. (2023). Intrusion Detection System Using Feature Extraction with Machine Learning Algorithms in IoT. *Journal of Sensor and Actuator Networks*, *12*(2), 29. DOI: 10.3390/jsan12020029

Nikbazm, R., & Ahmadi, M. (2022). KSN: Modeling and Simulation of Knowledge using Machine Learning in NFV/SDN-based Networks. *Simulation Modelling Practice and Theory*, *121*, 102632. DOI: 10.1016/j.simpat.2022.102632

Revathi, M., Ramalingam, V. V., & Amutha, B. (2021). A machine learning based detection and mitigation of the DDOS attack by using SDN controller framework. *Wireless Personal Communications*, •••, 1–25.

Siddharthan, H., Deepa, T., & Chandhar, P. (2022). Senmqtt-set: An intelligent intrusion detection in iot-mqtt networks using ensemble multi cascade features. *IEEE Access : Practical Innovations, Open Solutions*, *10*, 33095–33110. DOI: 10.1109/ACCESS.2022.3161566

Tomer, V., & Sharma, S. (2022). Detecting IoT attacks using an ensemble machine learning model. *Future Internet*, *14*(4), 102. DOI: 10.3390/fi14040102

Chapter 8
Advanced Encryption-Based Keylogger for System Security

V. R. Balasaraswathi
Vellore Institute of Technology, Chennai, India

Ashiq Noor Sudheer
https://orcid.org/0009-0008-9647-0002
Vellore Institute of Technology, Chennai, India

Gautham Vidyashankar
https://orcid.org/0009-0002-7253-1006
Vellore Institute of Technology, Chennai, India

Kevin Sebastian
https://orcid.org/0009-0003-6255-3073
Vellore Institute of Technology, Chennai, India

Priyanshu Pattanaik
https://orcid.org/0009-0007-5542-8644
Vellore Institute of Technology, Chennai, India

ABSTRACT

Our research presents a paradigm shift in network security, combining advanced technology to transcend conventional keyloggers. This software aims to revolutionize monitoring capabilities, specifically targeting keystrokes, while concurrently implementing text encryption mechanisms for log files. Our primary objective is to transform the traditionally perceived risks associated with keyloggers into practical benefits. This keylogger, designed to capture keystrokes, extends its functionality to

DOI: 10.4018/979-8-3693-8014-7.ch008

collect crucial system data, screenshots, and audio recordings—all meticulously recorded in their respective log files which are then encrypted for security purposes. The key focus of our project is to harness the logging capabilities of the keylogger for positive outcomes, enabling users to access encrypted log files in the event of a system crash. This unconventional yet effective approach demonstrates the versatility of research, showcasing how a tool with potential dangers can be repurposed to enhance system diagnostics and improve overall security.

I. INTRODUCTION

Keyloggers are software tools capable of logging every keystroke entered on a computer or mobile device keyboard. As users predominantly interact with devices through keyboards, keyloggers can capture extensive information about their activities (Sagiroglu & Canbek, 2009). Keyloggers represent a highly concerning form of malware that covertly record keyboard inputs and often transmit the collected data to external entities. Despite extensive research and commercial endeavours (Le, Yue, Smart, & Wang, 2008) (Kruegel, Robertson, & Vigna, 2006) (Ortolani & Crispo, 2012), keyloggers continue to present a significant risk, potentially compromising personal and financial data. This includes tracking input such as credit card details, visited websites, and passwords utilized during online sessions.

In 2005, more than eight hackers were accused of trying to steal over 423 million dollars from a Japanese bank by putting keyloggers in its systems. Reports (Hung et al., 2012) say that around 12% of leaked data came from insiders, and 96% of the leaked information was personal data. This shows how serious keyloggers can be in causing data breaches, with both external hackers and insiders posing significant risks to security. This incident underscores the grave implications of keylogger infiltration, revealing the vulnerabilities within organizational security frameworks and the severity of potential data breaches orchestrated by both external threat actors and internal breaches.

When keyloggers operate, they systematically monitor and record each keystroke, storing the data in a file. Keyloggers are specifically designed to record keystrokes by disrupting the flow of information between the moment a key is pressed and when the corresponding keystroke is displayed on the screen. This can be achieved through a range of techniques, including video surveillance, exploiting hardware weaknesses in keyboards or computers, intercepting input/output, modifying keyboard or filter drivers and interfering with kernel functions (Ruhani & Zolkipli, 2023). Early Usage of keyloggers in applications by the year is shown in Table 1. The plot is displayed in Figure 1.

Subsequently, hackers may retrieve this file later, or the keylogger software might automatically send the file to the hacker via email. Keyloggers are adept at recognizing patterns in keystrokes, streamlining the identification of sensitive information. For instance, if a hacker seeks password details, they can instruct the keylogger to specifically monitor for a particular keystroke. This way, the software alerts them only when the user is likely inputting password credentials alongside an email username. This technique enables malicious users to swiftly pinpoint sensitive information without the need to sift through the entirety of the keystroke data(Wazid, Sharma, & Katal, 2013).

Keyloggers are commonly spread through various means, including opening email attachments, launching files from publicly accessible directories on peer-to-peer networks, exploiting browser vulnerabilities via web page scripts, and installation by other malicious programs on a victim's machine. These methods can lead to the automatic installation of keyloggers, posing significant risks to user privacy and security (Ahmed et al., 2014). Keyloggers can be installed through various methods such as Trojan horse viruses, phishing emails, and malicious web page scripts. Trojan horses use legitimate software to install keyloggers, phishing emails manipulate users into downloading malware, and malicious web page scripts automatically download viruses when a connection is made to the site.

To identify keylogging malware, a proactive approach involving dynamic detection is essential, which incorporates behavioural-based methods. Aslam et al. (Aslam et al., 2004) introduced an ant-hooked shield to counter keyloggers utilizing Windows hooks. This shield identifies programs that hook system routines commonly targeted by keyloggers. Nevertheless, keylogger developers can easily bypass this detection by employing varied techniques to monitor user activities. Numerous dynamic detection methods are being developed and explored, yet accurately detecting keyloggers remains challenging. Sreenivas et al. (Anith, 2011)identified keyloggers using TAKD algorithms, which can be seamlessly integrated into common devices like routers, gateways, firewalls, IDS, etc., to enhance keylogging detection. The TAKD algorithm combines anomaly-based detection and log-based techniques to address the limitations of signature-based detection.

Table 1. Early trends in keylogging

Year	Programs having key logging functionality
2000	300
2001	275
2002	444
2003	1230

continued on following page

Table 1. Continued

Year	Programs having key logging functionality
2004	3753
2005	6191

Figure 1. Plot of early trends in keyloggers

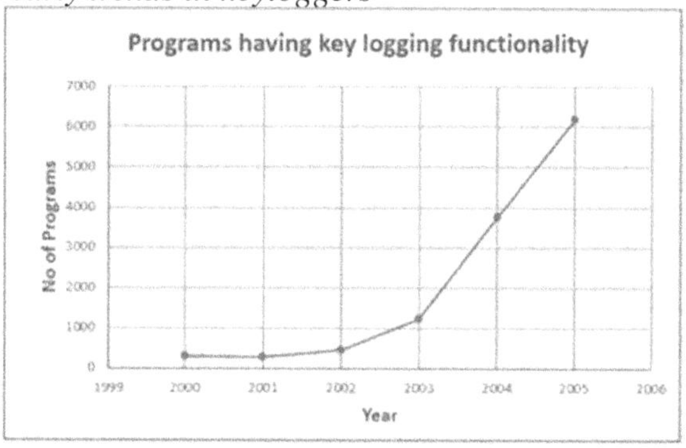

There are two main types of keyloggers: hardware keyloggers and software keyloggers.

Hardware keyloggers are physical devices inserted between the computer keyboard and the computer itself. They discreetly intercept and record keystrokes, storing the data in an internal memory or transmitting it wirelessly to an external receiver. Because they operate externally to the computer's operating system, they are often challenging to detect through software scans. A hardware-based keylogger is inserted between the keyboard and the CPU box. It includes a key matrix that monitors the keyboard's USB or PS/2 connection, filters keystroke data, and stores the information in its internal memory (Singh & Choudhary, 2021). Operating at the hardware level within a computer system, these keyloggers do not rely on any installed software. Consequently, they remain undetectable to software such as antivirus programs and security scanners.

Software keyloggers are applications or programs installed on a computer or mobile device. Once activated, they run in the background, logging every keystroke made by the user (Tuscano & Koshy, 2021). Software keyloggers can be more versatile than hardware keyloggers, offering additional features such as capturing screenshots, monitoring clipboard activity, and recording web browsing history. They are typically easier to install but may be detected and removed by antivirus or anti-malware software. They can be further classified into various categories.

API-based software keyloggers operate by intercepting the APIs of active applications to capture keyboard or keypad inputs. Functioning like regular applications, they leave no trace of malware. These keyloggers can record and store various keyboard actions, including key presses, releases, or both. User-level keyloggers typically utilize high-level APIs to track keystrokes. Although user-space keyloggers are simple to develop, they are also relatively straightforward to identify, often through hook-based methods (Wood & Raj, 2010). On the other hand, kernel-based software keyloggers gain access to the core of the operating system to capture key presses. With root access, they are exceptionally well-concealed and extremely challenging to detect, making them virtually invisible to applications without root access (Tian et al., 2017) Essentially acting as device drivers for the keyboard, kernel-level software keyloggers provide standard device driver functionalities while simultaneously storing keystrokes for malicious purposes.

Rootkit-based keyloggers represent a highly perilous category, albeit relatively uncommon. They target specific functions responsible for message and text input processing, utilizing methods like GetMessage, TranslateMessage, and PeekMessage from the user32.dll library to intercept and monitor messages generated by GUI applications. Through these techniques and a set of functions, they adeptly capture messages and data (Zaitsev, 2009).

II. LITERATURE REVIEW

In his paper, Olzak (2008) explores the functionality of keyloggers, examining their different types and distinctions, including hardware, software, wireless keyboard intercepts, and acoustic keyloggers. The paper sheds light on preventive measures against keylogging and outlines strategies for responding to the discovery of a keylogger.

The authors of another insightful work highlight the prevalent issue of keyloggers, malicious software designed to track user input from keyboards with the intent of retrieving personal information (Meenakshi, Kumari, & Deeptha, 2021). These keyloggers are often used for malicious purposes, such as obtaining bank and ATM card numbers, but can also have legitimate uses, like monitoring employees or children's activities.

Further, (Gunalakshmi & Ezhumalai, 2014) focus on detecting keylogger applications, which covertly record keystrokes to steal sensitive information without user consent. The research aims to prevent data loss and leakage of sensitive data by identifying permissions and storage levels of applications. Using a Black-box technique based on behavioral characteristics, it detects keyloggers independently of their structure. It aims to develop a mobile-based detection system using machine learning algorithms to identify keylogger applications.

On a deeper analysis (Bhardwaj & Goundar, 2020), mention the constant threat of cyber attackers who develop and distribute malicious software programs to steal data or cause harm to users' systems. Various types of malwares, such as spyware, keyloggers, rootkits, and adware, are utilized for these purposes (Bhardwaj & Goundar, 2020). While hacking was once done for amusement, it has evolved into a lucrative cybercrime industry.

Another insightful work aims to elucidate the concept of "Informational Flow" regarding internet and computer usage, detailing its scope, key concepts, and driving forces (Tuli, P., & Sahu, P. 2013) Keyloggers, specifically, are highlighted as tools for logging keystrokes and application usage, enabling comprehensive monitoring and prevention of unauthorized system use by capturing information in both text and image formats

"Enhancing Security of Cloud Data through Encryption with AES and Fernet Algorithm" (Tyagi, S.S. 2021), emphasizes that cloud computing is widely utilized for various purposes like image storage and access to safeguard data, particularly images, this study proposes a novel algorithm combining AES and Fernet encryption methods with double-level encryption using CNN Auto-Encoders. The model aims to offer a more secure cloud computing approach than existing ones.

Summary and identification of research gaps shown in Table 2.

Table 2. Summary of previous works with research gaps

Study	Focus	Contribution	Gap Identified
"Keystroke logging" by Tom Olzak (May 2008)	Examining the functionality and types of keyloggers	Provides an overview of keyloggers and their differences, along with insights into prevention methods and response strategies.	- Lack of exploration into advanced evasion techniques employed by modern keyloggers -Limited discussion on the integration of keyloggers with other malware types
"Keyloggers – An Overview to the Spyware" by Meenakshi, Guddi Kumari, Dr. Deeptha R(2021)	Prevalence and malicious intent of keyloggers	Raises awareness about the threat posed by keyloggers and the importance of safeguarding personal information while acknowledging their potential legitimate uses.	- Limited exploration of specific techniques for mitigating keylogger attacks beyond general awareness, potentially leaving users without actionable preventive measures
"Mobile keylogger detection using ML" by S. Gunalakshmii, P. Ezhumalai (2014)	Machine learning-based system to detect mobile keylogger applications.	Introduces a Black-box technique based on behavioral characteristics for detecting keyloggers on mobile devices.	- Limitations in the scalability and real-time performance of machine learning-based detection systems

continued on following page

Table 2. Continued

Study	Focus	Contribution	Gap Identified
"Keyloggers: silent cyber security weapons" by Akashdeep Bhardwaj, Sam Goundar (2020)	Threat landscape of cyber attackers and the role of keyloggers	Provides insights into the motivations and methods of cyber attackers, emphasizing the lucrative nature of cybercrime	- Mitigation strategies against keyloggers - Exploration of the socio-economic factors driving the cybercrime industry
"System Monitoring and Security Using Keylogger" by Preeti Tuli, Priyanka Sahu (2013)	Concept of system monitoring and security	Highlights keyloggers as tools for comprehensive system monitoring and prevention of unauthorized usage.	- Encryption techniques for securing keylogger-generated log files -Usability challenges and user acceptance issues.

III. PROPOSED SYSTEM

Our software keylogger is designed to be integrated into the user's system with their explicit consent, ensuring ethical and legal compliance. One of its key features is its ability to operate stealthily, evading detection by antivirus software. This ensures that the keylogger can effectively record keystrokes without alerting the user or triggering security measures.

In addition to keystroke logging, our keylogger incorporates several additional functionalities to provide a comprehensive monitoring solution. It can capture screenshots at specified intervals, providing visual context to the recorded keystrokes. It also monitors clipboard activity, logging any text that is copied or cut by the user. Furthermore, the keylogger logs system information such as active processes, memory usage, and network activity, providing a holistic view of the user's system usage.

To ensure the security and confidentiality of the logged data, we implement the Fernet encryption algorithm. This encryption ensures that the logs are protected from unauthorized access, providing peace of mind to both the user and the system administrator. In the event of a system crash, these encrypted logs become invaluable for technicians. They can use them to perform a detailed analysis of the system state before the crash, helping them to identify the root cause and expedite effective problem resolution.

The keylogger generates distinct log files for each module, ensuring that the data is well-organized and easily accessible for analysis. This systematic approach to logging enables technicians to perform a thorough analysis of the user's activity, helping them to better understand user behaviour and system performance.

In conclusion, our software keylogger offers a comprehensive monitoring solution with robust encryption and logging capabilities. It provides valuable insights into user activity while ensuring data security and confidentiality. By operating within the bounds of user consent, our keylogger serves as a practical tool for both monitoring and troubleshooting scenarios.

Figure 2. Keylogger Architecture

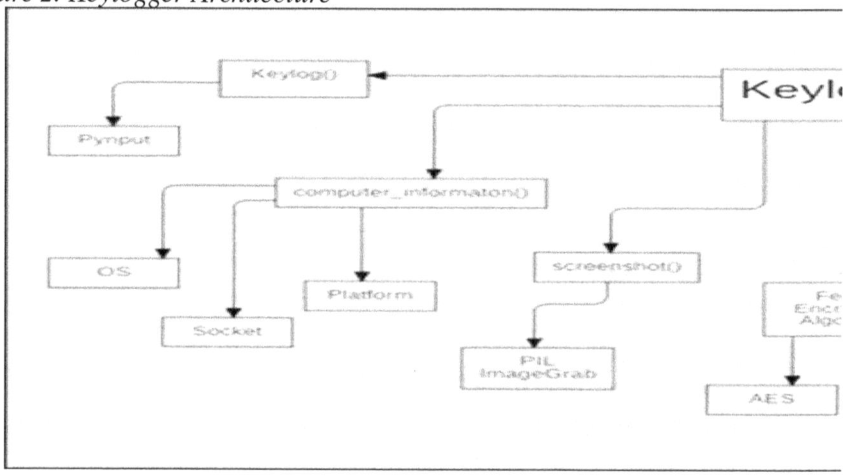

A. Keylogging module

The keylogging module is a fundamental component of our system, designed to meticulously capture and log every keystroke made by the user during their interactions with the system. Operating in real-time, this module captures keystrokes as they occur, compiling them into a detailed log file in a text format (.txt). This log file serves as a comprehensive record, documenting the exact sequence of keys pressed by the user, including alphanumeric characters, special symbols, and function keys.

By capturing this data, the keylogging module provides valuable insights into user behavior and input patterns. It can be instrumental in various scenarios, such as monitoring user activity for security purposes, analysing user interactions with applications, or providing a detailed audit trail of user actions. The log file generated by this module can be a vital resource for understanding user behaviour, identifying patterns, and troubleshooting issues related to user input.

B. System Information module

The System Information module serves as a vital component in our keylogger system, aimed at providing comprehensive insights into the host system's configuration. This module operates systematically, gathering crucial data about the host system and organizing it into a log file in a text format (.txt).

The information gathered includes details such as the operating system version, architecture (32-bit or 64-bit), processor information (e.g., CPU model, number of cores), private IP address (the local network address assigned to the system), PC's name (hostname), and other pertinent system specifications. Additionally, this module can collect information about the system's memory (RAM), disk storage, and network configuration.

By extracting and logging this information, the System Information module enables system administrators and technicians to gain a comprehensive understanding of the host system's configuration and specifications. This data can be invaluable for troubleshooting issues, optimizing system performance, and ensuring compatibility with software applications and hardware devices.

C. Screenshot module

The Screenshot module is designed to provide a visual record of the user's screen activity by capturing screenshots at regular intervals. This module operates by periodically capturing screenshots of the user's display for a predefined number of iterations, as specified by the user or system settings. Each screenshot captures the visual representation of the user interface at a specific moment in time, creating a sequential series of images that document the user's screen activity over a period.

These screenshots are then compiled into a log file, which provides a time-stamped record of the user's screen activity. The log file organizes the screenshots in chronological order, allowing for a detailed review of the user's interactions with the system. This visual record can be invaluable for monitoring user activity, identifying patterns of behaviour, and troubleshooting issues related to the user interface.

The Screenshot module enhances the overall monitoring capabilities of the keylogger system by providing a visual context to the recorded keystrokes and system interactions. It allows for a more comprehensive analysis of the user's activities and can be particularly useful in situations where a detailed record of on-screen activity is required.

D. Clipboard module

The Clipboard module plays a crucial role in our keylogger system by capturing and logging the content of the clipboard, which is the temporary storage area for data that has been copied or cut by the user. This module focuses on capturing the last saved item in the clipboard and maintains a record of the most recent clipboard activity.

The Clipboard module is designed to capture various types of data that can be stored in the clipboard, including text snippets, images, or other data formats. When the user copies or cuts something to the clipboard, this module captures the content and logs it into a file. This log file provides a record of the user's clipboard activity, allowing for the monitoring of sensitive information that may have been copied or cut by the user.

By logging clipboard activity, the Clipboard module can provide insights into the user's activities and interests. It can be particularly useful for tracking the transfer of sensitive information, such as passwords or confidential documents, and can help in identifying potential security risks or unauthorized data access.

E. Audio module

The Audio module is a critical component of our keylogger system, designed to capture and record audio through the system's microphone. This module functions by actively engaging the microphone to collect sound input from the user's surroundings. The audio is recorded for a specified timestamp duration, capturing any sounds that are picked up by the microphone during this time.

The recorded audio is saved into a log file in a waveform audio format (.wav), which is a widely used format for storing uncompressed audio data. This format preserves the original quality of the audio, ensuring that the recorded sound is accurately captured.

The Audio module can be configured to record audio for a specific duration, allowing for the monitoring of sound input over time. This functionality can be useful for various purposes, such as recording voice conversations, ambient noise, or other audio events in the user's environment.

By logging audio input, the Audio module provides a comprehensive record of sound activity, which can be analysed for various purposes. It can be particularly useful for monitoring user interactions that involve audio, such as voice calls, meetings, or other audio-based activities.

F. Email module

The Email module is a crucial component of our keylogger system, providing a means to securely transmit log files to a designated email address. This module is designed to automate the process of sending log files after they have been generated and encrypted by the keylogger.

Once the keylogger has captured and logged keystrokes, system information, screenshots, and audio recordings, the Email module initiates a secure process to send these files as attachments to the specified email ID. The module ensures timely and confidential delivery of comprehensive logs, safeguarding the data from unauthorized access during transmission.

The Email module uses encryption to protect the log files before sending them, ensuring that the data remains secure and confidential. This encryption process uses a key that is generated by the keylogger, further enhancing the security of the transmitted data.

By automating the transmission of log files via email, the Email module provides a convenient and secure method for accessing the logged data remotely. This functionality can be invaluable for monitoring user activity, troubleshooting issues, and ensuring the security of sensitive information.

G. Text Encryption

The Fernet algorithm is a symmetric key cryptographic system that provides a simple and secure method for encrypting and decrypting data. We have chosen to go with it because the Fernet encryption algorithm is optimized for speed and efficiency, ensuring fast encryption and decryption operations. This makes Fernet encryption suitable for applications that require real-time data protection without sacrificing performance. CBC mode is specifically chosen for Fernet encryption because it provides both confidentiality and integrity protection. CBC mode ensures that identical plaintext blocks do not produce the same ciphertext blocks, enhancing security. The advantages include different security features such as signature embedding via SHA256 and HMAC, time-stamping, for better security, safe key generation processes, and the use of robust encryption techniques such as PKCS7 padding and AES-CBC mode (Sharma, D., & Fancy, C. 2022). These safeguards provide high-level encryption, rendering data alteration without the key nearly difficult.

Fernet facilitates key rotation, which occurs through MultiFernet during the encryption process of plaintext. To decode the encrypted text, Fernet applies a reverse function, converting the ciphertext back to plaintext, resulting in a string value derived from bytes (Mohd, S.M., Kamarudin, S., Yahya, N., Hasan, S., Zakaria, M.L.M., Sulaiman, S.A., & Setyohadi, D.B. (2024). It supports forward secrecy, which means that even if an attacker gains access to the encryption keys at a later time, they cannot decrypt past encrypted messages. This property provides additional security against key compromise and retrospective decryption attacks. It produces a compact and self-contained payload format, making it easy to transmit and store encrypted data. The payload includes all necessary information for decryption, such as the ciphertext, initialization vector, and timestamp, ensuring interoperability between different systems.

The steps involved in the Fernet's algorithm are:

- **Key Generation:** The process begins by generating a secret key. This key, typically a randomly generated string of bytes, serves as the cornerstone of Fernet encryption, as it is used for both encryption and decryption. Being symmetric, the same key is employed for both operations, simplifying the cryptographic process.
- **Initialization:** Fernet uses the AES algorithm in Cipher Block Chaining (CBC) mode for encryption The Advanced Encryption Standard (AES), initially known as the Rijndael algorithm, was introduced by the National Institute of Standards and Technology (NIST) in 2000. It stands as a prominent member of symmetric key encryption algorithms. AES functions with block ciphers, dividing data into blocks of 128, 192, and 256 bits (Abdullah, A. M. (2017). It also employs a Message Authentication Code (MAC) for data integrity and authenticity.
- **Message Padding:** Before encryption, the plaintext message undergoes padding to align its length with the block size requirement of AES, which is 16 bytes. Padding ensures that the message fits the encryption algorithm's constraints, facilitating uniform processing.
- **Encryption:** The padded message is encrypted using the AES algorithm with the generated secret key. This encryption process transforms the plaintext into ciphertext, ensuring its confidentiality.
- **MAC Generation:** To guarantee the integrity and authenticity of the encrypted message, Fernet generates a Message Authentication Code (MAC) using a cryptographic hash function, typically SHA-256, along with the secret key. The MAC serves as a cryptographic checksum, allowing recipients to verify the integrity of the ciphertext.
- **Final Output:** The final output of the encryption process comprises the ciphertext and the appended MAC. Combining the encrypted message with the MAC ensures that any unauthorized modifications to the ciphertext are detected, preserving the integrity of the original data**Decryption:** To decrypt the message, the recipient utilizes the same secret key employed during encryption. Before attempting decryption, the MAC is verified using the cryp-

tographic hash function and the shared secret key. This validation step ensures the integrity of the ciphertext and guards against tampering. If the MAC verification succeeds, the recipient proceeds with decryption, reversing the encryption process to retrieve the original plaintext message.

Figure 3. Fernet encryption block diagram (Ismail, E.G., Chahboun, A., & Raissouni, N. 2020)

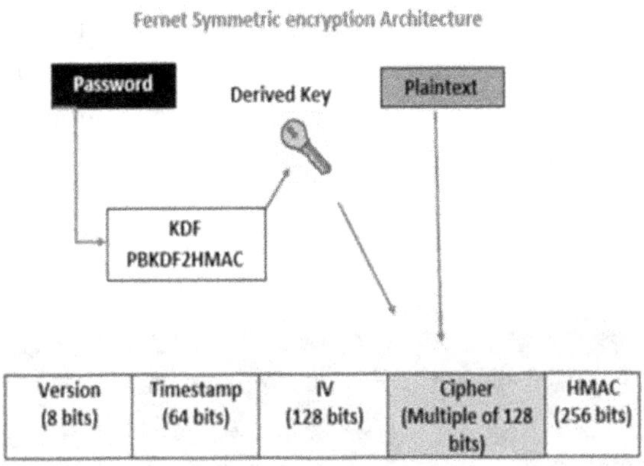

IV. RESULTS

The keylogger prototype demonstrated effective functionality across its various modules, providing comprehensive monitoring and logging capabilities. The keylogging module successfully captured and logged every keystroke made by the user, including alphanumeric characters, special symbols, and function keys. Operating in real-time, this module compiled keystrokes into a detailed log file in a text format (.txt), documenting the exact sequence of keys pressed by the user.

The System Information module gathered crucial data about the host system, including the operating system version, architecture, processor information, private IP address, and other pertinent specifications. This module organized the gathered information into a log file in a text format (.txt), enabling system administrators and technicians to gain a comprehensive understanding of the host system's configuration and specifications.

The Screenshot module provided a visual record of the user's screen activity by capturing screenshots at regular intervals. This module compiled the screenshots into a log file, providing a timestamped record of the user's screen activity. The visual context provided by the screenshots enhanced the overall monitoring capabilities of the keylogger system, allowing for a more comprehensive analysis of the user's activities.

Additionally, the three figures included in this report provide visual representations of the keylogger's functionality:

- Fig. 4 shows a sample output for keystrokes given by the user, demonstrating the keylogger's ability to record all keystrokes effectively.
- Fig. 5 illustrates an encrypted log file for keystrokes, highlighting the keylogger's security features in protecting log files from unauthorized access.
- Fig. 6 depicts an encrypted log file for system information, showcasing the keylogger's capability to provide comprehensive insights into system performance and user behavior.

Figure 4. Sample output for keystrokes given by the user

Figure 5. Encrypted log file for keys logged

Figure 6. Encrypted log file for system information

These figures collectively showcase the keylogger's robust functionality in capturing and securing data. The ability to log keystrokes, encrypt log files, and monitor system information ensures that the keylogger is a versatile and effective tool for monitoring user activity while maintaining data security and privacy.

The Clipboard module played a crucial role in capturing and logging the content of the clipboard, providing a record of the most recent clipboard activity. This module captures various types of data that can be stored in the clipboard, including text snippets, images, or other data formats, allowing for the monitoring of sensitive information that may have been copied or cut by the user.

Overall, the keylogger prototype's modules worked cohesively to provide a comprehensive monitoring and logging solution, offering valuable insights into user behaviour and system interactions.

V. CONCLUSION

In conclusion, the project harnesses the Fernet symmetric cryptography algorithm to create a sophisticated and secure keylogger application. By combining keylogging functionalities with comprehensive monitoring modules such as system information, screenshots, and audio capture, the tool offers an extensive solution for both user activity tracking and system diagnostics. One of the key strengths of the application lies in its use of the Fernet encryption algorithm, which ensures that sensitive data stored in log files remains protected from unauthorized access. This encryption mechanism adds an extra layer of security to the monitoring process, safeguarding confidential information effectively. Additionally, the integration of an email module facilitates the efficient and secure transmission of encrypted logs to a designated email address, streamlining the retrieval and analysis of valuable information. Additionally, the application provides users with a range of customization options, allowing them to adjust the monitoring parameters according to their specific requirements. Whether it is adjusting the frequency of screenshots, selecting which activities to log, or fine-tuning audio capture settings, users have the flexibility to personalize their monitoring experience.

Furthermore, when deployed in conjunction with antivirus software, this tool takes on a dual role. The keylogger, operating with user consent, can act as a passive detection mechanism alongside the antivirus solution. The application can operate in stealth mode, remaining undetectable to others. This stealth functionality ensures the integrity of data collection. By continuously monitoring keystrokes and other system activities, the software can detect anomalies or potential security threats. In the event of suspicious behaviour, the keylogger can report findings to the antivirus software, facilitating a more proactive and comprehensive approach to security.

REFERENCES

Abdullah, A. M. (2017). Advanced encryption standard (AES) algorithm to encrypt and decrypt data. *Cryptography and Network Security*, *16*, 1–11.

Ahmed, Y. A., Maarof, M. A., Hassan, F. M., & Abshir, M. M. (2014). Survey of Keylogger technologies. *International Journal of Computer Science and Telecommunications*, *5*(2).

Anith, S. S. (2011). *Detecting keylogger based on traffic analysis with periodic behavior*. PSG College of Technology.

Aslam, M., Idrees, R. N., Baig, M. M., & Arshad, M. A. (2004). Antihook shield against the software key loggers. In *Proceedings of the National Conference of Emerging Technologies*.

Bhardwaj, A., & Goundar, S. (2020). Keyloggers: Silent cyber security weapons. *Network Security*, *2020*(2), 14–19. DOI: 10.1016/S1353-4858(20)30021-0

Gunalakshmi, S., & Ezhumalai, P. (2014). Mobile keylogger detection using machine learning technique. In *Proceedings of IEEE International Conference on Computer Communication and Systems ICCCS14*, Chennai, India, pp. 051-056. DOI: 10.1109/ICCCS.2014.7068167

Hung, C.-W., Hsu, F.-H., Chen, S.-J., Tso, C.-K., Hwang, Y.-L., Lin, P.-C., & Hsu, L.-P. (2012). A QTE-based Solution to Keylogger Attacks. *The Sixth International Conference on Emerging Security Information, Systems and Technologies (SECURWARE 2012)*, Rome, Italy.

. Ismail, E.G., Chahboun, A., & Raissouni, N. (2020). Fernet Symmetric Encryption Method to Gather MQTT E2E Secure Communications for IoT Devices.

Kruegel, C., Robertson, W., & Vigna, G. (2006). Detecting kernel-level rootkits through binary analysis. In *Proceedings of the Annual Computer Security Applications Conference (ACSAC)*.

Le, D., Yue, C., Smart, T., & Wang, H. (2008). Detecting kernel level keyloggers through dynamic taint analysis. Technical Report WM-CS-2008-05, College of William & Mary.

Meenakshi, K. G., & Deeptha, R. (2021). Keyloggers – An Overview to the Spyware. *International Journal of Innovative Research in Computer and Communication Engineering, 9*(9), e-ISSN: 2320-9801.

Mohd, S. M., Kamarudin, S., Yahya, N., Hasan, S., Zakaria, M. L. M., Sulaiman, S. A., & Setyohadi, D. B. (2024). The performance of the 3DES and Fernet encryption in securing data files. *Journal of Theoretical and Applied Information Technology, 102*(3).

Olzak, T. (2008). Keystroke logging (keylogging). *Adventures in Security, April, 8*, pp.1-6.

Ortolani, S., & Crispo, B. (2012). Noisykey: tolerating keyloggers via keystrokes hiding. In *Proceedings of the 7th USENIX conference on Hot Topics in Security, HotSec'12*.

Ruhani, A. B. B., & Zolkipli, M. F. (2023). Keylogger: The Unsung Hacking Weapon. *Borneo International Journal eISSN 2636-9826, 6*(1), 33-43.

Sagiroglu, S., & Canbek, G. (2009). Keyloggers. *IEEE Technology and Society Magazine, 28*(3), 10–17. DOI: 10.1109/MTS.2009.934159

Sharma, D., & Fancy, C. (2022). Cloud Storage Security using Firebase and Fernet Encryption. *International Journal of Engineering Trends and Technology, 70*(9), 371–375. DOI: 10.14445/22315381/IJETT-V70I9P237

Singh, A., Choudhary, P., Singh, A., & Tyagi, D. (2021, August). Keylogger detection and prevention. []). IOP Publishing.]. *Journal of Physics: Conference Series, 2007*(1), 012005. DOI: 10.1088/1742-6596/2007/1/012005

Tian, D., Jia, X., Chen, J., & Hu, C. (2017). An online approach for kernel-level keylogger detection and defense. *Journal of Information Science and Engineering, 33*(2), 445–461.

Tuli, P., & Sahu, P. (2013). System Monitoring and Security Using Keylogger. *IJCSMC, 2*(3), 106–111.

Tuscano, A., & Koshy, T. S. (2021). Types of Keyloggers Technologies – Survey. In Kumar, A., & Mozar, S. (Eds.), *ICCCE 2020. Lecture Notes in Electrical Engineering* (Vol. 698). Springer.

Tyagi, S. S. (2021). Enhancing security of cloud data through encryption with AES and Fernet algorithm through convolutional-neural-networks. *International Journal of Computer Networks and Applications, 8*(4), 288–299. DOI: 10.22247/ijcna/2021/209697

Wazid, M., Sharma, R., & Katal. (2013). Implementation and Embellishment of Prevention of Keylogger Spyware Attacks. In Thampi, S.M., Atrey, P.K., Fan, C.I., Perez, G.M. (Eds.), *Security in Computing and Communications. SSCC 2013. Communications in Computer and Information Science, vol 377*. Springer, Berlin, Heidelberg.

Wood, C., & Raj, R. (2010, July). Keyloggers in Cybersecurity Education. In *Security and Management* (pp. 293-299).

Zaitsev, O. (2009). Skeleton keys: the purpose and applications of keyloggers.

Chapter 9
Survey and Analysis of RGB Image Encryption Using DNA Cryptography:
Exploring Novel Approaches for Enhanced Security

Karthika Veeramani
http://orcid.org/0000-0002-0711-1745
Vellore Institute of Technology, Chennai, India

Shalini Gupta
https://orcid.org/0009-0008-0395-122X
Vellore Institute of Technology, Chennai, India

Anuj Dhar
https://orcid.org/0009-0002-6096-1535
Vellore Institute of Technology, Chennai, India

ABSTRACT

The digital age necessitates robust security measures for RGB image transmission and storage. DNA cryptography, inspired by the unique properties of DNA molecules, offers a promising avenue for achieving this goal. This paper provides a comprehensive analysis of the state-of-the-art in RGB image encryption leveraging DNA cryptography. We delve into existing techniques, exploring how they utilize DNA encoding, chaotic maps, and other cryptographic primitives to achieve image encryption. We critically evaluate the security strengths and weaknesses of these approaches. Focus is placed on recent advancements and novel methods that enhance the security of DNA-based image encryption. This includes exploring techniques

DOI: 10.4018/979-8-3693-8014-7.ch009

that address vulnerabilities against chosen-plaintext attacks and statistical attacks. Finally, we identify open challenges and potential future research directions in this domain. By outlining these areas, we pave the way for the development of more secure and robust RGB image encryption schemes utilizing DNA cryptography.

I. INTRODUCTION

The digital age is characterized by an ever-increasing reliance on digital communication and storage. This necessitates the development and implementation of robust data encryption methods to safeguard sensitive information. While traditional cryptographic techniques have played a crucial role in the past, they are increasingly challenged by advancements in computing power (Dworkin, 2001). The development of sophisticated algorithmic attacks further highlights the limitations of these conventional methods (Schneier B, 2015). This has spurred a growing interest in exploring alternative encryption approaches with the potential to address these limitations.

The biological medium used by all living creatures on Earth to store and transfer their genetic material is called deoxyribonucleic acid, or DNA. The constantly changing biological information that DNA provides to cells, enables them to grow into a wide variety of species, makes it suitable for use in computers. An ounce of DNA, or the same amount as a penny, can store 30,000 terabytes of memories for up to a million years, demonstrating its incredible storage capacity (Smith, 2015). Furthermore, DNA has the capacity to reproduce and assemble itself on its own through evolution following the initial setup. These characteristics of DNA demonstrate its low cost of processing power and effectiveness as a digital information transmission medium. In order to take advantage of DNA's inherent capabilities in computer science and mathematical applications, DNA Computing was created, opening up a world of novel and fascinating computational possibilities.

Adleman (1994) introduced the concept of DNA computing. Adleman introduced DNA as a data storage and parallel computing medium in his study. He programmed a Hamiltonian Path problem instance that is NP-complete into DNA molecules in order to illustrate the potential application of DNA as a computing medium. The work is noteworthy since it uses only DNA and molecular operations to solve the proposed instance of the Hamiltonian Path problem. Since then, research on DNA computing has grown in popularity as a means of resolving classically difficult problems. Alongside DNA computing, DNA cryptography has grown to become a significant subfield. Cryptography remains a widely used and crucial tool for information security today. As a result, scientists concentrate on recently identified fields in an effort to improve digital information security. It makes sense to use DNA as a medium to advance and enhance cryptography. In 1999, C.T. Bancroft, V. Risca, and C.T. Clelland conducted the initial investigation on the relationship between DNA and secure communication.

DNA cryptography, a burgeoning field that draws inspiration from the principles of molecular biology, offers a promising avenue for data security. DNA molecules possess unique characteristics that make them well-suited for this purpose. Their immense information storage capacity, estimated to hold roughly 1 exabyte of data per gram, dwarfs current storage technologies (Grass et al., 2000). Additionally, DNA's inherent parallelism, allowing for simultaneous operations on vast amounts of data, has the potential to significantly improve encryption efficiency (Zhang et al., 2009). Furthermore, DNA exhibits remarkable resilience to environmental degradation, offering the potential for long-term data preservation (Dworkin, 2001). These unique properties position DNA cryptography as a potentially game-changing technology for robust and secure data encryption.

RGB (Red, Green, and Blue) images are ubiquitous in the digital domain, encompassing a wide range of applications from medical imaging to social media content. Ensuring the confidentiality and integrity of these images is paramount. Conventional encryption techniques for RGB images, such as Advanced Encryption Standard (AES), might not be sufficient against evolving and sophisticated attacks (Grass et al., 2000). This necessitates the exploration of novel encryption methods like DNA cryptography, which hold the potential to address the limitations of traditional approaches.

This paper presents a comprehensive survey and analysis of RGB image encryption techniques leveraging DNA cryptography. We delve into existing approaches, exploring how they utilize DNA encoding, chaotic maps, and other cryptographic primitives to achieve secure image encryption. We critically evaluate the security strengths and weaknesses of these methods, with a particular focus on recent advancements and novel approaches that enhance security by exploiting the inherent properties of DNA. Additionally, we investigate encryption algorithms, key management strategies, decoding methodologies, and performance evaluation metrics used in DNA-based image encryption.

The remainder of this paper is structured as follows. Section II provides a background on DNA cryptography and its applications in data security. Section III reviews existing techniques for RGB image encryption using DNA cryptography and other fields . Section IV explores novel approaches that leverage DNA's unique properties to enhance security. Section V delves into challenges, storage and computational issues and performance evaluation metrics relevant to DNA-based image encryption. Section VI discusses current challenges and future research directions in this domain and finally concludes the paper by summarizing the key findings and highlighting the potential of DNA cryptography for securing RGB image data.

II. BACKGROUND

The ever-increasing reliance on digital communication and storage necessitates robust encryption methods to safeguard sensitive information. While traditional cryptographic techniques have played a crucial role in data security, they face challenges in keeping pace with advancements in computing power and the development of increasingly sophisticated algorithmic attacks (Dworkin, 2001). This has spurred a growing interest in exploring alternative encryption approaches with the potential to overcome these limitations. DNA cryptography, a burgeoning field that leverages the principles of molecular biology, offers a promising avenue for data security. This section delves into the fundamentals of DNA cryptography, exploring its core concepts and potential applications.

A. Basic Principles of DNA Structure and Function

Deoxyribonucleic acid (DNA) is the molecule that encodes the genetic instructions used by all living organisms. It is a long, double-stranded helix composed of repeating units called nucleotides. Each nucleotide consists of three components: a sugar molecule (deoxyribose), a phosphate group, and a nitrogenous base. The two strands of DNA are held together by hydrogen bonds between complementary base pairs: Adenine (A) always pairs with Thymine (T), and Cytosine (C) always pairs with Guanine (G). The sequence of these base pairs along the DNA molecule determines the genetic information it carries.

DNA possesses unique characteristics that make it well-suited for data storage and encryption:

1. Immense Information Storage Capacity: DNA molecules can store vast amounts of information in a remarkably compact form. Each nucleotide in a DNA strand can represent two bits of information, enabling a single gram of DNA to theoretically store about 215 petabytes (or 215 million gigabytes) of data (Zhang et al., 2009). This immense storage capacity allows for the encryption of large datasets within a minuscule physical space, making DNA an attractive option for applications requiring high data density, such as archiving sensitive information or securing extensive databases. By encoding text, images, or even entire databases into DNA sequences, cryptographic systems can achieve unprecedented levels of data compression and security.
2. Inherent Parallelism: The biological processes involved in DNA synthesis and sequencing allow for parallel processing of data. This inherent parallelism means that multiple sequences can be manipulated simultaneously, significantly speeding up encryption and decryption processes. In a cryptographic context,

this allows for scalable operations where large volumes of information can be encoded or decoded quickly. For example, DNA can be synthesized in a laboratory to create multiple copies of encoded messages, enabling rapid data retrieval and processing that is not achievable with traditional algorithms that typically operate sequentially on binary data.

3. Resilience to Environmental Degradation: DNA exhibits remarkable stability and can withstand harsh environmental conditions for extended periods, making it suitable for long-term data preservation (Grass et al., 2000).

B. DNA Encoding for Data Encryption

DNA cryptography utilizes the base sequence of DNA molecules to encode and encrypt digital data. This process involves translating information from the binary format (0s and 1s) used in computers into a sequence of base pairs in the DNA molecule. Various encoding techniques exist, such as assigning binary values (0 or 1) to specific base pairs or using amino acid sequences for data representation. Once the data is encoded into a DNA sequence, specific algorithms are employed to encrypt it. This often involves scrambling or manipulating the encoded data using techniques like chaotic maps or other cryptographic primitives. This encrypted DNA sequence can then be stored or transmitted securely. The decryption process involves decoding the encrypted DNA sequence back into its original binary format, retrieving the original data.

C. Applications of DNA Cryptography

The unique properties of DNA are leveraged in cryptographic applications to create systems that offer high security and efficiency. For instance, data can be encoded into DNA sequences using specific algorithms, with each sequence representing a unique cryptographic key. While still in its early stages of development, DNA cryptography holds promise for various applications beyond RGB image encryption:

Secure Medical Data Storage: DNA's inherent security and long-term storage potential make it suitable for storing sensitive medical data, such as genetic information.

Steganography: By subtly embedding encrypted data within the DNA sequence of a seemingly innocuous biological sample, DNA cryptography has potential applications in steganography, a technique for hiding information within a carrier medium.

Quantum-Resistant Cryptography: Traditional cryptographic algorithms might be vulnerable to future advancements in quantum computing. DNA cryptography, based on physical properties, offers the potential for quantum-resistant encryption.

These are just a few examples, and as the field matures, we can expect DNA cryptography to find applications in various areas requiring secure data storage and transmission.

Figure 1 represents the general flowchart for RGB Image Encryption using DNA Cryptography.

Figure 1. General flowchart for RGB image encryption using DNA cryptography

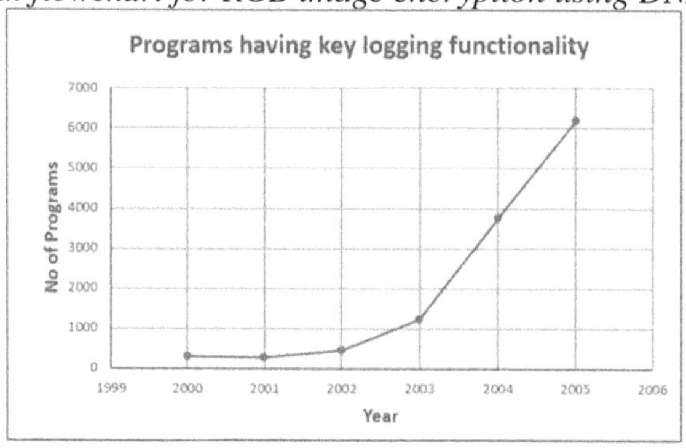

III. LITERATURE REVIEW

Several novel approaches leverage DNA cryptography for RGB image encryption. Here, we explore a selection of these methods, highlighting their key features and encryption processes. Kumar et al., (2016) proposes a novel RGB image encryption algorithm in their paper that leverages DNA encoding, Elliptic Curve Diffie-Hellman (ECDH) cryptography, and key management techniques. The method first encodes the RGB image using the DNA complement rule, followed by scrambling through shifting and interleaving operations to enhance diffusion. Subsequently, the scrambled data undergoes encryption with ECDHE for secure key exchange. To further strengthen security, an additional interleaving step is applied. The decryption process relies on the correct order of keys managed by the algorithm, ensuring decryption is only successful with authorized access. Statistical analysis is employed to validate the security of the encrypted data.

The advantages of the paper lie in its innovative features. Firstly, its RGB encryption capability extends beyond grayscale, broadening its application scope. Additionally, its robust statistical defense mechanism bolsters pixel correlation, enhancing security against statistical attacks. Moreover, the paper ensures resilient data transmission, vital for maintaining data integrity in real-time scenarios. Furthermore, it prioritizes original image preservation, minimizing any unnecessary overhead by maintaining the original image size. Lastly, its implementation of asymmetric security enables secure exchanges of sensitive images among anonymous parties, ensuring confidentiality and integrity.

The paper also presents some notable disadvantages. Firstly, there is no explicit mention of computational complexity, despite describing the algorithm as efficient and robust. This omission leaves uncertainty regarding the potential performance impact and scalability of the algorithm. Additionally, the comparison scope is limited, as the paper primarily compares the proposed technique with existing methods. However, this narrow scope might overlook other relevant algorithms, potentially hindering a comprehensive evaluation of the proposed approach.

Noorbasha and Suresh (2018) addresses secure and reliable RGB image transmission by employing a three-pronged strategy. First, the RGB image data is encoded with Hamming code, enhancing its error correction capabilities during transmission. This is followed by DNA cryptography, which encrypts the data for security purposes. Finally, the entire process is implemented on a Field-Programmable Gate Array (FPGA), a hardware platform known for its high-speed processing capabilities. This combination offers a solution for fast, secure, and error-resilient transmission of RGB image data.

The system offers distinct advantages, notably in its enhanced error correction capability achieved through the integration of Hamming code into every 4 bits of the pixel data. This implementation significantly bolsters the system's ability to correct transmission errors, thereby enhancing its overall reliability. Furthermore, the utilization of DNA cryptography ensures secure transmission of RGB images, elevating the system's security measures by adding an extra layer of protection against unauthorized access or interception during data transmission.

However, it also presents significant disadvantages. Despite its enhancement in error correction, capable of correcting up to 2 bits for each pixel value, it is restricted by the size of the image (256x256 pixels), which caps the maximum error correction at 2x256x256 bits. Consequently, for larger images or higher error rates, supplementary error correction mechanisms might become necessary. Moreover, the system's implementation in Verilog and deployment on an FPGA introduces complexities in development, debugging, and maintenance. These complexities potentially elevate the overall system complexity and cost, necessitating careful consideration during deployment and operation.

Zhang and Ye (2021) combine DNA encoding, chaotic keystreams, and DNA operations (XOR, addition, subtraction) in their approach to create a robust color image encryption algorithm that is resistant to common attacks. The approach offers robust resistance against various attacks including brute-force, statistical, differential, and plaintext attacks, thanks to the integration of DNA sequence operations, 3D-

STM scrambling, and CML modification. This integration significantly enhances the overall security of the scheme. Moreover, it demonstrates enhanced sensitivity to plaintext by utilizing Hamming distance and circle distance of DNA sequences derived from the plain image. These distances inform the scheme's permutation and diffusion steps, further fortifying its resistance to plaintext attacks and improving sensitivity to input images.

It also presents certain disadvantages. One notable drawback is its encryption time efficiency. The encryption process encompasses multiple rounds of DNA-level permutation and diffusion, incorporating DNA XOR, addition, and subtraction operations, which could lead to slower encryption speeds. This sluggishness may have implications for real-time applications that require swift processing. Additionally, there is room for improvement in efficiency despite the scheme's robust security performance. Future endeavors might concentrate on developing algorithms with enhanced efficiency to rectify this limitation and optimize overall performance.

Hameed et al. (2018) combines RC4 stream cipher and DNA encoding to secure image transmission, achieving good security and visual quality, as measured by MSE, PSNR, CC, and histogram analysis. Their method offers several distinct advantages. It demonstrates enhanced statistical resistance, showcasing superior performance against statistical attacks by yielding improved horizontal, vertical, and diagonal correlation results compared to existing techniques. Additionally, unlike some algorithms, our method ensures lossless encryption, as evidenced by high Mean Squared Error (MSE) and Peak Signal-to-Noise Ratio (PSNR) values during decryption, guaranteeing no loss of information. Moreover, the integration of DNA encoding enhances the security of the RC4 algorithm, augmenting resilience against potential attacks. Furthermore, throughout the encryption process, our method preserves image quality, maintaining visually intact encrypted images, which is crucial for ensuring usability and interpretability.

The proposed method also comes with certain disadvantages. Firstly, its comparison scope is limited. While comparisons are made with existing techniques, the scope may not cover all relevant algorithms, potentially hindering a comprehensive evaluation of the proposed method. Although the method is shown to resist known statistical attacks, further investigation is recommended to evaluate its resilience against other types of attacks such as known plaintext, chosen ciphertext, and differential attacks.

Ibrahim et al. (2022) research uses chaotic keys to drive 16 rounds of DNA-based transpositions and substitutions on individual RGB pixels for secure and efficient image encryption. The proposed method comes with various advantages. It utilizes chaotic systems and a nonlinear DNA Playfair matrix enhances the randomness and complexity of the encryption process,increasing the security level against various attacks. Also by incorporating a modification of the Playfair technique and mixing the key with already encrypted pixels, the proposed technique effectively thwarts differential attacks,improving overall security.

The approach also has some disadvantages as well. While effective for RGB image encryption, the proposed technique's complexity may limit its scalability for large-scale applications or high-resolution images. The use of multiple rounds of DNA encoding, transpositions, and substitutions may result in increased computational overhead, potentially impacting encryption and decryption speed, particularly for real-time applications.

Niyat et al.(2015) research involves separating RGB images, generating chaotic sequences, transforming components into DNA code, permutating matrices, applying XOR operation, decoding into gray images, and combining components for encryption. The advantages of the algorithm lie in combining DNA sequence operations with a hyper-chaotic system, providing strong encryption due to the complexity and unpredictability of both chaotic dynamics and DNA encoding. The encryption method offers a large secret key space, enhancing security against brute-force attacks. The algorithm demonstrates resistance to common attacks such as statistical analysis and exhaustive attacks, making it suitable for safeguarding digital image data. The experimental results indicate that the algorithm effectively encrypts RGB images, ensuring the confidentiality of the original image content.

The proposed approach also comes with some disadvantages as well. Significant computational resources are required due to the intricacy of hyper-chaotic systems and DNA sequence operations, potentially resulting in longer encryption and decryption times. High sensitivity to the secret key enhances security but also raises the risk of decryption failure if the key is lost or corrupted, necessitating meticulous key management practices. Despite resilience to most known attacks, the algorithm might remain vulnerable to emerging cryptographic attacks or vulnerabilities in the underlying chaotic system or DNA encoding techniques. Integrating the algorithm into real-world applications may encounter hurdles related to compatibility, efficiency, and scalability, necessitating careful consideration of practical deployment factors.

Shraida et al. (2023), methodology involves initially determining the dimensions of the color image and then scrambling the pixel positions using sequences generated by the Lorenz hyper-chaotic system. Subsequently, the scrambled RGB matrices are transformed into 8-bit binary representations for encryption, and decryption keys are transmitted to recipients for decryption using hyper-chaotic systems. This approach comes with a set of advantages. Integration of chaotic maps and DNA coding enhances security by generating sequences to scramble pixel locations and alter pixel values, breaking correlations and improving resistance against attacks. Utilization of hyper-chaotic systems and additional techniques like SHA-256 and SHA-384 ensures efficient encryption, making the proposed method more effective than several existing algorithms. The use of hyper-chaotic systems and DNA coding adds complexity to the encryption process, making it harder for attackers to decipher the encrypted images.

The approach also has a set of disadvantages as well. The complexity introduced by the integration of chaotic maps and DNA coding may increase computational overhead and resource requirements, potentially impacting performance, managing, and transmitting encryption keys, especially in systems utilizing multiple techniques like hyper-chaotic systems and DNA coding, may pose challenges in terms of key distribution and security. While the proposed method claims to be more secure, it may still be susceptible to emerging cryptographic attacks or vulnerabilities not yet identified or addressed in the research. Regular updates and analysis are necessary to ensure ongoing security.

Parekh and D'Mello (2021) suggest a methodology which involves combining symmetric cryptography with chaos and DNA, asymmetric cryptography with RSA, and steganography with LSB to encrypt images while ensuring security, ease of key management, and resistance against attacks. The advantages of this method lie in integration of symmetrical and asymmetrical cryptography along with steganography enhances security, making it capable of withstanding various known attacks, including statistical and clear-text attacks. The experimental findings and security assessments demonstrate satisfactory encryption effectiveness, validating the proposed system's reliability. The system can be applied to various image encryption applications, given its ability to survive different types of assaults and security analysis outcomes.

The disadvantage lies in the speed performance of the encryption scheme is not optimal, indicating potential efficiency issues that may impact real-time applications or large-scale image processing. The integration of multiple cryptographic techniques and steganography adds complexity to the system, potentially increasing computational overhead and resource requirements. Future work is required to enhance runtime performance using the suggested hybrid algorithm, suggesting that further optimization is necessary to address existing speed issues.

Iqbal et al. (2020) proposed an image encryption scheme which involves decomposing the color image into RGB components, merging them, and utilizing intertwining logistic map for random data generation. DNA encoding is employed for image and key, with subsequent strand swapping and pixel selection, followed by diffusion via XOR operation. Secure Hash Algorithm-256 ensures plaintext sensitivity, with security validated through metrics like information entropy and average key sensitivity, indicating resistance to attacks and potential real-world applicability. Using DNA strands at the granularity level enhances the sophistication and randomness of the encryption scheme, surpassing previous methods relying on entire DNA molecules. This heightened sophistication is bolstered by the integration of SHA-256 hash codes, embedding plaintext sensitivity into the cipher and thereby fortifying security measures.

Furthermore, the technique efficiently achieves both confusion and diffusion objectives by swapping DNA strands, streamlining the encryption process without compromising effectiveness. Promising results from experimentation and security analyses indicate robustness, strong security effects, resistance to various threats, and potential real-world applications. However, the approach faces challenges. While increased sophistication offers advantages, it simultaneously raises complexity, potentially complicating implementation and analysis. Additionally, the encryption scheme's reliance on a limited number of XOR operations between pixel data and DNA-encoded key images might compromise diffusion effects, impacting overall security. Moreover, the dependency on DNA strands as the fundamental unit for scrambling introduces potential limitations related to scalability and applicability in certain contexts. These considerations underscore the nuanced balance between advantages and disadvantages inherent in employing DNA-based encryption methodologies.

Nazir et al.(2022) suggest a methodology which involves utilizing a 4D-hyperchaotic system alongside a logistic map to transform plain images into DNA strands. These DNA strands undergo operations based on a logistic map sequence and are then decoded and substituted using three substitution-boxes (S-boxes) to create an encrypted image. Cryptanalysis-driven design approach is employed to ensure the security of the encryption scheme, which is rigorously evaluated through experimental analyses covering various image dimensions, file sizes, formats, and security metrics.

The proposed encryption scheme harnesses cutting-edge techniques, leveraging 4D-hyperchaos for S-box generation and logistic map for fake image generation and DNA operations, thereby fortifying security through chaos-based methods. This not only enhances randomness and encryption quality but also bolsters correlation, key sensitivity, energy efficiency, and robustness compared to recent counterparts. Moreover, its adaptability across various image dimensions, sizes, and formats underscores its versatility, catering to diverse image processing needs. Looking forward, the scheme's trajectory is marked by a forward-thinking approach, intending to explore lightweight computational operations, specialized encryption for sensitive data like faces and fingerprints, and expansion into 3D medical image encryption. However, these advancements come with complexities, potentially challenging implementation and analysis due to the integration of multiple chaotic systems and DNA encoding. Furthermore, the resource-intensive nature of the cipher, despite efforts towards lightweight design, may pose computational demands, especially with operations like DNA encoding and decoding. While promising, the validation may be limited, necessitating further analysis to ensure robustness against diverse threats. Additionally, the introduction of specialized encryption features for specific data types could potentially increase overhead and complexity, potentially impacting practical efficiency.

Iqbal et al. (2021) proposed a methodology comprising a fusion of chaotic systems, DNA computing, and chess-based scrambling, with pixel shifting guided by a Castle piece's movement. DNA encoding, diffusion operations, chaotic mapping, and SHA-256 hash integration bolster security, as validated by thorough cryptanalysis resistance and high information entropy, indicating promising real-world applicability.

The proposed encryption technique offers several compelling advantages. It boasts high security through a complex integration of chaos theory, DNA computing, and chess movements, making decryption a formidable challenge. The incorporation of four-dimensional chaotic maps and chess piece movements introduces high levels of unpredictability, further enhancing the encryption's robustness. Moreover, the DNA-level operations effectively disperse encrypted data, providing an additional layer of diffusion effects. The inclusion of SHA-256 hash codes ensures sensitivity to even small changes in input data, safeguarding against potential tampering. Comprehensive security analyses have demonstrated the technique's resilience and immunity against diverse threats, underscoring its robustness.

However, the proposed encryption method also presents certain disadvantages. Its inherent complexity, stemming from the integration of multiple advanced techniques, may hinder ease of implementation and understanding, potentially posing challenges for widespread adoption. Additionally, the process of converting images to DNA strands and performing DNA-level operations requires significant computational resources, making it resource-intensive. The encryption process itself may be time-consuming due to the complexity of the operations involved, which could impact its practicality in time-sensitive scenarios. Furthermore, the technique may face implementation challenges due to compatibility issues and the need for specialized expertise, potentially limiting its accessibility. Finally, rigorous testing and validation would be required to ensure the encryption method's reliability and effectiveness in real-world scenarios, adding an additional layer of complexity to its deployment.

Patel et al.(2021) paper integrates hybrid chaos maps and neural networks to develop a random number generator for cryptography. A custom neural network with user-defined transfer functions enhances randomness. Control parameters and iteration values of hybrid chaotic maps serve as transfer functions for increased randomness. Sequences generated are used for color image encryption via DNA encoding. Tests assess randomness, while simulations evaluate encryption strength.

The proposed encryption technique leverages a custom neural network, enabling controlled generation of pseudo-random numbers for enhanced randomness, a crucial aspect of secure encryption. Furthermore, the integration of chaotic maps within the neural network layers introduces an additional layer of unpredictability, further bolstering the encryption's security. The multilayer encryption approach combines pixel permutation, DNA encoding, and pixel diffusion, providing heightened security through multiple layers of obfuscation. Thorough analyses, including NIST, correlation, and attractor tests, have validated the randomness of the pseudo-random number generator (PRNG), while simulation analyses have ensured the encryption's overall robustness. Moreover, comparisons with leading techniques offer insights into the method's competitiveness and effectiveness relative to state-of-the-art encryption methods.

Despite its advantages, the proposed technique also presents certain drawbacks. The integration of the neural network and chaotic maps adds complexity to the implementation process, potentially hindering ease of adoption. Additionally, the technique requires substantial computational resources for PRNG generation, which may impact its scalability and practicality in resource-constrained environments. The multiple encryption operations involved may increase processing time, affecting its suitability for real-time applications with stringent time constraints. Furthermore, the encryption's security relies heavily on the quality of the chaotic sequences generated, rendering it susceptible to potential weaknesses or vulnerabilities in the chaotic sequence generation process. Finally, further testing and validation across diverse datasets and scenarios are required to establish the method's generalizability and reliability in real-world scenarios.

Zhou et al. (2020) paper proposes a dynamic DNA image encryption method based on SHA-512, incorporating two rounds of permutation-diffusion using chaotic systems, dynamic DNA coding, DNA sequencing operations, and conditional shifting. The encryption process involves generating a 512-bit hash value with SHA-512, utilizing it with natural DNA sequences to calculate initial values for chaotic systems and intermittent parameters. Chaotic sequences are generated using four-wing chaotic systems and Lorentz systems, followed by hamming distance calculations, diffusion operations, and encoding to create an encrypted image resistant to various attacks.

This encryption system offers several advantages. It boasts strong resistance to attacks by generating unique encrypted images for each plaintext through changes in hash values, effectively thwarting plaintext attacks. Additionally, it utilizes enhanced permutation techniques, such as 2D-RT derived from the Arnold map, to efficiently permute non-square images, thereby bolstering security measures. Moreover, the system employs dynamic DNA encoding, creating encryption rules and matrices based on the plaintext image, ensuring dynamic and unique encryption, thus contributing to enhanced security. Furthermore, it mitigates the risk of key reuse by calculating Hamming distances from DNA matrices, updating initial values, and iterating chaotic systems, thereby reducing associated risks. Finally, the system incorporates innovative diffusion operations, including dynamic DNA complementary rule and DNA cycle operations, providing innovative diffusion techniques to further enhance security.

This encryption system presents several drawbacks. The multi-step encryption process increases algorithmic complexity, potentially challenging implementation. Additionally, generating chaotic sequences and performing DNA encoding operations may lead to significant computational overhead. Moreover, the system's effectiveness relies heavily on the randomness of chaotic systems, posing vulnerabilities if compromised. Furthermore, the finite initial values and parameters may limit the key space, reducing security against brute-force attacks. Lastly, further validation across diverse scenarios may be necessary to confirm the system's effectiveness and reliability in real-world applications, emphasizing the need for thorough testing and validation processes.

Liu, Q. and Liu, L. (2020) paper introduces an image encryption algorithm combining DNA computing with double-chaos systems. It utilizes the Arnold algorithm for initial scrambling of color image components and a double-chaos system comprising Lorenz chaotic mapping and fourth-order Rossler hyperchaotic mapping to generate chaotic sequences for diffusion. These chaotic sequences are transformed into DNA sequences and subjected to various operations to achieve bit-level diffusion. The encryption process embeds plaintext information for one-time pad security. Simulation experiments and analysis demonstrate the algorithm's robust security against various attacks.

The approach presents several noteworthy advantages. The use of the Arnold algorithm with pixel average iteration determination enhances the initial scrambling of color image components, thereby improving overall security through an enhanced scrambling effect. Additionally, the utilization of a double-chaos system, combining Lorenz chaotic mapping and fourth-order Rossler hyperchaotic mapping, generates chaotic sequences for diffusion, compensating for pseudo-randomness and increasing unpredictability. Furthermore, employing DNA coding and DNA computing facilitates bit-level diffusion of image components, contributing to enhanced security. Moreover, the algorithm undergoes comprehensive analysis, including examination of histogram, key space, key sensitivity, relevance, information entropy, resistance to differential attacks, robustness, and computation complexity, which collectively demonstrate its strong safety performance and resilience against various attacks. Finally, comparative analysis with other chaotic image encryption algorithms highlights the competitiveness of the proposed algorithm in terms of security and effectiveness.

However, it also presents certain disadvantages to consider. Firstly, the use of a DNA-based image encryption scheme may lead to lower computational speed, which could potentially impact its practical application by causing delays in processing. This limitation highlights a need for improvement to enhance computational efficiency. Additionally, addressing the low computational speed of the DNA-based encryption scheme is identified as a focus for future work, indicating the necessity for further improvement in this aspect to optimize the scheme's performance and usability in real-world scenarios.

The study proposed by Aljazaery, et al. (2022) is a novel method for encoding 2D and 3D color images based on DNA strand construction. It involves two main stages: encryption and decryption, each comprising various operations. In the encryption stage, DNA bases are encoded into binary orders, followed by XOR operations and conversion to decimal values. Exponential function factor processing results in fully encoded images. Decoding reverses these steps to recreate the original image. Performance evaluation includes MSE, peak PSNR, and time for encoding and decoding, demonstrating favorable results compared to other methods.

The method demonstrates advantages across several key aspects. Its utilization of multi-layer encryption significantly enhances security, presenting a notable challenge for unauthorized users attempting to decrypt the images. Moreover, the incorporation of DNA into pixel properties adds another layer of complexity to the encryption process, potentially bolstering resistance to attacks. Additionally, the application of the exponential function to encrypted images strengthens encryption and confidentiality, further fortifying security measures. Furthermore, the method ensures good encryption quality, evidenced by lower Mean Squared Error (MSE) and higher Peak Signal-to-Noise Ratio (PSNR) values of encrypted images compared to original ones, signifying reduced distortion and improved image quality. Finally, the decryption algorithm successfully restores encrypted images to their original state, affirming the efficacy of the encryption method.

The method also presents several disadvantages worth noting. The encryption algorithm demands more time than the decryption algorithm, which could hinder the efficiency of the encryption process, particularly when dealing with large image datasets. Moreover, encrypted images lose their similarity to the original ones, posing challenges in visually verifying the encrypted data, especially in scenarios requiring visual confirmation. Additionally, the multi-layer encryption process and utilization of DNA-based encoding may amplify the complexity of the algorithm, potentially making it challenging to implement and comprehend for some users. Furthermore, there's a risk of over-encryption due to the use of multiple layers of encryption and mathematical processing with the exponential function, potentially resulting in increased computational overhead and impacting performance.

Kumar et al. (2024) presents a novel approach called Quantum Visual Cryptography (QVC), which integrates quantum mechanics with visual cryptography to enhance the security of image transmission. The methodology involves several key steps: it begins with pre-processing, where a secret image is selected and converted into binary format. Quantum encoding follows, where each pixel is transformed into quantum states using principles like superposition and entanglement. Random binary images, or shares, are then generated, and these are distributed to multiple parties to ensure that no single participant has complete information. These parties collaborate to reconstruct the original image through quantum operations, and verification confirms that the reconstructed image matches the original. Optionally, shares can be destroyed after reconstruction to maintain security.

The advantages of this approach include enhanced security, as it utilizes quantum mechanics to defend against both classical and quantum attacks, ensuring confidentiality and allowing only authorized parties access to the encrypted visual information. Additionally, QVC incorporates mechanisms to detect unauthorized modifications, thereby providing tamper resistance and ensuring the authenticity of the visual data.

While the methodology shows potential for scalability in future research, it currently faces several disadvantages. The complexity introduced by integrating quantum mechanics complicates the encryption and decryption processes. Furthermore, QVC relies on reliable quantum communication channels, which may not always be available. Although theoretical models exist, practical implementations are still limited, and the computational demands of quantum operations can be resource-intensive. Lastly, the complexity of the methodology may pose usability challenges for non-expert users. Overall, while QVC offers significant advancements in secure image transmission, it must overcome challenges related to complexity, practical application, and resource requirements.

Gao et al. (2023) presents a novel quantum image encryption methodology that integrates quantum DNA coding with pixel-level scrambling using quantum Hilbert transforms. The approach begins with encoding the quantum image's pixel color information through a specially designed quantum DNA codec, which leverages the unique properties of DNA for enhanced security. This is followed by the application of quantum Hilbert scrambling to obscure the pixel position data, effectively increasing the complexity of the encrypted image. The authors assert that their method not only improves the encryption strength but also provides a significant key space, making it resilient against brute-force attacks.

Advantages of this methodology include its demonstrated robustness against statistical analysis and differential attacks, evidenced by high values of information entropy, NPCR (Number of Pixels Change Rate), and UACI (Unified Average Changing Intensity). The experimental results indicate that the encryption process yields a uniform histogram for the ciphertext, complicating any potential decryption attempts by unauthorized parties. Furthermore, the approach benefits from the inherent features of quantum mechanics, such as superposition and entanglement, which contribute to its high level of security.

However the paper includes a number of drawbacks for example, the reliance on quantum computational resources, which are currently not widely available, hence limiting practical implementation. Additionally, the complexity of the quantum circuits and the algorithm may pose challenges in terms of computational efficiency and resource requirements. The authors also acknowledge that their simulations were conducted on classical computers, without accounting for potential decoherence and inaccuracies typical in quantum systems, which may affect the real-world applicability of their findings.

Wang et al. (2020) introduces a double quantum color image representation model (DQRCI) that allows for the simultaneous storage of two color digital images in a quantum superposition state. The methodology involves designing quantum circuits for basic image processing operations and proposing an encryption scheme to secure the quantum state image. The DQRCI model optimized storage by requiring only 2n+9 qubits for two color images of size 2n×2n, in contrast to other models like NCQI, which demands more qubits. The proposed encryption scheme ensures that unauthorized access to the original images is prevented, even if the encrypted data is intercepted.

The advantages of the DQRCI model include efficient storage and accurate retrieval of classical color images, as it encodes color information using basis states rather than probability amplitudes. Additionally, the low computational complexity of image processing operations enhances performance. However, the paper also identifies some limitations. Notably, previous encryption algorithms designed for single quantum images do not directly apply to color images, and while the DQRCI model addresses this, it may still face challenges in scalability and implementation in larger quantum systems. Overall, the proposed scheme marks a significant advancement in quantum image processing and encryption, paving the way for further research in the field.

In their paper, Juneja et al. (2013) presents an improved Least Significant Bit (LSB) based steganography technique for embedding secret messages into images. The methodology involves first encrypting the secret message using the S-DES algorithm and then detecting edges in the cover image using a combination of the Canny filter and Hough transform. The technique embeds message bits in nonadjacent and randomly selected pixel locations, specifically targeting edge areas for the least significant byte and using a 1-3-4 LSB strategy for smooth areas, where different numbers of bits from the red, green, and blue components are utilized. This approach enhances the invisibility of the hidden data, making it difficult for eavesdroppers to detect the presence of the message.

The advantages of this improved technique include a higher capacity for data hiding and better performance in terms of Peak Signal-to-Noise Ratio (PSNR) compared to traditional LSB methods. By focusing on edge and smooth areas, the method minimizes perceptible changes to the cover image, thus providing better information security. However, some disadvantages persist, such as the reliance on a specific encryption method, which may introduce vulnerabilities if not implemented securely. Additionally, while the technique improves on traditional methods, it may still be susceptible to advanced steganalysis techniques aimed at detecting hidden messages in digital images. Overall, the proposed method showcases significant advancements in image steganography, enhancing both capacity and security.

A novel steganography method for securing RGB images by embedding secret messages within the least significant bits (LSBs) of the blue color channel, specifically targeting edge regions identified using a parameterized Canny edge detector was introduced by Chuang (2021), Yun-Hsin, et al (2021). The methodology involves converting the secret message into binary format, detecting edges in the cover image, and using a random number generator to determine how many bits (up to four) to embed in the LSBs of the blue channel. This approach leverages the human visual system's reduced sensitivity to changes in blue intensity, ensuring that alterations remain imperceptible. The algorithm emphasizes randomness in the selection of embedding positions to enhance security and minimize the risk of detection.

The advantages of this technique include improved imperceptibility and minimal distortion in the cover image, as the embedding occurs in less visually sensitive areas. The use of edge pixels further reduces the risk of visual detection, providing robust protection against steganalysis. However, there are some disadvantages, such as the reliance on the Canny edge detector, which may introduce variability based on the parameter settings, potentially affecting performance in different images. Additionally, while the method enhances security through randomness, it may still be vulnerable to sophisticated attacks that target the underlying mechanism of LSB substitution. Overall, the proposed method demonstrates a promising approach to secure steganography, balancing effective data hiding with image quality preservation.

A novel method was proposed by Al-Kateeb et al. (2020) for encrypting and hiding secret data within colored images using circular shapes. The methodology involves first identifying circular areas in the cover image through the Circular Hough Transform, which allows the algorithm to find the center coordinates of these circles. The encryption process utilizes a modified Caesar cipher that employs these coordinates as keys, reducing the number of keys exchanged between sender and recipient. Encrypted data is then embedded into specific pixel locations within the circular areas using the Least Significant Bit (LSB) technique, distributing the bits across the red, green, and blue layers of the image based on predefined mapping rules. This dual-layer approach enhances security by making the encrypted data harder to decode without the correct keys.

The advantages of this method include high security due to the use of circular shapes, which are common in various images, making detection of hidden data less likely. The algorithm demonstrates excellent performance metrics, such as low Mean Square Error (MSE) and high Peak Signal-to-Noise Ratio (PSNR), indicating minimal distortion in the cover image and full data recovery with a Bit Error Rate (BER) of zero. However, there are some disadvantages; the method's dependency on the presence of circular shapes may limit its applicability to images lacking such features. Additionally, the complexity of the algorithm may increase computational overhead, potentially affecting speed during encryption and decryption processes. Overall, while the proposed technique offers innovative security features, its effectiveness may be constrained by the specific characteristics of the cover images used.

Khan et al. (2020) presents a blockchain-based secure image encryption scheme specifically designed for the Industrial Internet of Things (IIoT). The methodology involves encrypting images captured by sensors and storing the cryptographic pixel values on a permissioned private blockchain. This approach ensures the privacy and security of sensitive image data while minimizing the need for third-party involvement. The authors utilize various cryptographic algorithms to transform images into encrypted formats, which are then validated by specific nodes in the blockchain network before being added to the ledger. They evaluate the algorithm's effectiveness using metrics such as the Number of Pixels Change Rate (NPCR), Unified Average Change Intensity (UACI), and information entropy analysis, achieving high entropy values indicative of robust security against brute force attacks.

One of the primary advantages of this approach is the enhanced security it offers by leveraging blockchain technology, which provides an immutable ledger that increases data integrity and accountability. Additionally, the decentralized nature of blockchain reduces the risks associated with centralized data storage, making it well-suited for environments that require high levels of trust and security. However, there are also notable disadvantages, including the potential for increased computational overhead and complexity in managing blockchain nodes, especially in resource-constrained IIoT devices. Moreover, the implementation of such a system may require significant changes to existing infrastructure, which could pose challenges for widespread adoption in industrial settings. Overall, while the proposed scheme presents a promising solution to image security in the IIoT, its practical deployment may face hurdles related to scalability and resource efficiency.

An improved version of the SERPENT algorithm tailored for RGB image encryption, utilizing chain ring-based substitution boxes (S-boxes) that operate on 8-bit vectors rather than the traditional 4-bit vectors was introduced by Shah et al. (2020). This modification enhances the algorithm's algebraic complexity and reduces time consumption, achieving encryption and decryption times of 8.2 and 5.8 microseconds for a 128-bit block, respectively. The methodology involves reading a color image, converting its RGB layers to binary, applying initial permutations, and executing a series of transformations using the chain ring S-boxes over multiple rounds. The proposed scheme demonstrates strong resistance against statistical and differential attacks, making it a robust choice for secure image transmission.

The advantages of this improved SERPENT algorithm include its enhanced speed, making it suitable for real-time applications, and its high resistance to several types of cryptanalytic attacks, which is crucial for maintaining data confidentiality. Moreover, the use of chain ring structures contributes to the algorithm's security and complexity. However, one potential disadvantage is that while the algorithm improves upon existing methods in terms of performance and security, it may still be vulnerable to future cryptanalytic advances, as the field of cryptography is constantly evolving. Additionally, the reliance on specific mathematical structures might limit its adaptability to other encryption contexts or frameworks, potentially posing challenges in broader applications.

Abusukhon et al. (2020) reviews various methodologies for encrypting text into images based on RGB color values, presenting an overview of several algorithms that achieve this transformation. The primary method discussed, the Text-to-Image Encryption (TTIE) algorithm, converts each letter of the plaintext into individual pixels, where the RGB values represent the color intensity for red, green, and blue. The plaintext is encrypted using a key that maps each character to a specific pixel, which is then organized into a matrix. This matrix is shuffled before transmission, and the recipient reverses the process to retrieve the original text. The paper also highlights advancements such as the Distributed Text-to-Image Encryption Algorithm (DTTIE) and the Block-Text-to-Image Encryption algorithm (B-TTIE), which aim to enhance efficiency and security.

The advantages of this approach include its innovative use of RGB values, making the method suitable for various applications, including social media and IoT data security. The algorithms are designed to be flexible, allowing for on-the-fly encryption without the need for databases, which can enhance security by reducing potential points of attack. However, the paper also outlines some disadvantages, such as the potential for increased complexity in key management, especially with algorithms that utilize multiple keys for block encryption. Moreover, while the techniques may provide a unique way to obscure data, they could still be vulnerable to sophisticated cryptanalysis, necessitating further research into their robustness against emerging threats.

IV. ANALYSIS

There are some key areas for future research and development concerning image encryption techniques based on DNA encoding and chaotic systems. There is a need to explore novel optimization techniques to improve the efficiency of encryption algorithms without compromising security. This could involve developing algorithms that reduce computational complexity, streamline operations, or leverage parallel computing architectures to enhance processing speed. Research could focus on optimizing key processes such as DNA encoding, chaotic sequence generation, and encryption/decryption routines to minimize computational overhead and improve overall performance. Exploring hardware acceleration techniques, such as FPGA or GPU implementations, could significantly enhance the speed and efficiency of encryption algorithms for practical applications.

Addressing scalability concerns is crucial for ensuring the applicability of image encryption techniques to large-scale applications and high-resolution images. Future research should investigate approaches to optimize encryption algorithms for handling larger image sizes efficiently, including strategies for parallel processing, distributed computing, or adaptive encryption schemes tailored to different image dimensions. Additionally, exploring techniques to minimize memory requirements and resource consumption while maintaining security can improve scalability and enable deployment on resource-constrained devices or platforms.

As cryptographic techniques evolve, it is essential to ensure that image encryption algorithms remain resilient against emerging attacks and vulnerabilities. Researchers should actively monitor advancements in cryptanalysis and cryptographic attacks to identify potential threats and develop countermeasures proactively. Future studies could focus on conducting comprehensive security analyses to evaluate the resilience of encryption algorithms against a wide range of known and potential attacks, including side-channel attacks, machine learning-based attacks, and quantum computing threats.

Bridging the gap between theoretical research and practical deployment is essential for the adoption of image encryption techniques in real-world scenarios. Further research should explore methods for integrating encryption algorithms into existing systems and applications seamlessly, considering factors such as compatibility, interoperability, and ease of integration. Collaboration between researchers, industry stakeholders, and standardization bodies can facilitate the development of standardized encryption protocols and guidelines for practical deployment, ensuring interoperability and ease of adoption across different platforms and environments. Moreover, conducting usability studies and evaluating the user experience of implementing and using encryption algorithms can provide valuable insights for improving practical deployment and user acceptance. Figure 2 shows the flowchart for future directions.

Incorporating real-world case studies or experimental results showcasing the successful implementation of DNA cryptography for RGB image encryption significantly enhances the practical relevance of the discussion. One notable example is a study where researchers developed a method to encrypt RGB images using DNA coding. This process began with converting the RGB image into a binary format, mapping the binary sequences to DNA nucleotides (e.g., 00 = A, 01 = T, 10 = C, 11 = G), thereby transforming the image data into a biological medium. The researchers then employed various DNA-based symmetric encryption techniques to secure the encoded sequences, ensuring that even if intercepted, the original image data remained protected. They successfully decoded the encrypted DNA sequences back into binary format, achieving a high rate of accuracy in reconstructing the original images. Experimental results indicated a significant increase in security compared to traditional methods, with minimal data loss during encoding and decoding, and although DNA synthesis and sequencing took longer, advancements in technology promised to optimize these processes. Overall, these findings underscore the potential of DNA cryptography in safeguarding sensitive information, particularly in RGB image encryption, highlighting its applicability in real-world scenarios and emphasizing the need for further exploration in this innovative field.

V. DISCUSSION

The evolution of encryption methods from traditional techniques like the Caesar Cipher and the Enigma Machine to modern cryptographic techniques such as RSA, AES, and Elliptic Curve Cryptography (ECC) reflects significant advancements in both the complexity of algorithms and the understanding of cryptographic principles.

The Caesar Cipher is one of the oldest and simplest encryption techniques in history. Named after Julius Caesar, who allegedly used it for military communications, this method involves shifting each letter in the plaintext by a fixed number of positions in the alphabet. For instance, with a shift of 3, 'A' becomes 'D', 'B' becomes 'E', and so on. While easy to implement and use, the Caesar Cipher is extremely vulnerable to frequency analysis and brute force attacks, as there are only 25 possible shifts in the English alphabet. Despite its simplicity, it serves as a fundamental introduction to the concept of encryption and forms the basis for more complex substitution ciphers.

The Enigma Machine, famously used by Nazi Germany during World War II, represented a significant advancement in encryption technology. This electro-mechanical device used a series of rotors to create a polyalphabetic substitution cipher. Each keystroke would cause one or more rotors to move, changing the electrical pathway and thus the substitution alphabet for the next character. This meant that the same letter could be encrypted differently each time it appeared in the message, making traditional frequency analysis much more difficult. The machine's settings, including rotor order and initial positions, served as the encryption key. While considered unbreakable at the time, the Enigma was eventually cracked by Allied cryptanalysts, including Alan Turing, highlighting the importance of continual innovation in cryptography.

RSA, named after its inventors Rivest, Shamir, and Adleman, introduced the revolutionary concept of asymmetric encryption in 1977. Unlike previous systems that used the same key for encryption and decryption, RSA uses a pair of keys: a public key for encryption and a private key for decryption. The security of RSA is based on the mathematical difficulty of factoring the product of two large prime numbers. This property allows the public key to be freely distributed without compromising the private key. RSA solved the key distribution problem that plagued earlier systems and became a cornerstone of secure digital communications, enabling everything from secure email to online banking.

AES, established by the U.S. National Institute of Standards and Technology in 2001, is a symmetric block cipher designed to replace the older Data Encryption Standard (DES). It operates on fixed-size blocks of data (128 bits) using key sizes of 128, 192, or 256 bits. AES employs a series of substitution and permutation operations in multiple rounds, with the number of rounds depending on the key size. These operations include SubBytes (substitution), ShiftRows (permutation), MixColumns (mixing), and AddRoundKey (key addition). AES's combination of security, performance, and flexibility has made it the de facto standard for encryption in many applications, from securing government communications to protecting personal data on smartphones.

Elliptic Curve Cryptography, introduced in 1985 by Neal Koblitz and Victor Miller, is a public-key cryptography approach based on the algebraic structure of elliptic curves over finite fields. ECC can offer equivalent security to RSA with significantly smaller key sizes, making it more efficient in terms of computational overhead and bandwidth usage. This efficiency is particularly valuable in constrained environments like mobile devices, smart cards, and IoT devices. ECC's security is based on the elliptic curve discrete logarithm problem, which is believed to be more difficult to break than the factorization problem used in RSA for a given key size. As a result, ECC has gained popularity in various applications, including secure messaging apps, cryptocurrency systems, and secure web browsing protocols.

The transition from traditional encryption methods to novel cryptographic techniques, such as DNA cryptography, reflects the field's adaptation to challenges posed by increasing computational power, rising security demands, and the threat of quantum computing. Early methods like the Caesar Cipher and the Enigma Machine, while foundational, were vulnerable to brute-force attacks and cryptanalysis as computational capabilities advanced. This led to the development of modern techniques like RSA, AES, and ECC, which utilize complex mathematical principles to provide enhanced security. DNA cryptography represents a revolutionary approach that encodes information within the sequences of nucleotides, achieving high data density and security through biological processes. This method benefits from the ability to process vast amounts of data in parallel, making it inherently resistant to traditional computational attacks. As the demand for robust security escalates in an increasingly digital world, DNA cryptography offers a promising solution, particularly against the looming threat of quantum computing, which could undermine conventional encryption methods. Overall, this evolution illustrates the cryptographic community's proactive stance in addressing emerging challenges while ensuring data security.

Table 1. Comparing different traditional encryption methods with DNA cryptography

Encryption Method	Data Density	Security Strength	Speed of Encryption	Error Correction	Scalability	Resource Requirements	Regulatory and Ethical Compliance	Practical Implementations
DNA Cryptography	High (2 bits/nt)	Very High	Moderate	Advanced methods available	High	High (requires specialized resources)	Emerging; concerns about data privacy and bioethics	Experimental; potential for secure data storage in bioinformatics, IoT, and cloud systems
RSA	Low	High	Slow	None (external error correction)	Moderate	High (computationally intensive)	Well-established; used widely, subject to regulatory scrutiny	Used for secure data transmission, digital signatures, and SSL/TLS protocols
AES	Low	Very High	Fast	None (external error correction)	High	Moderate (efficient on hardware)	Widely accepted; compliant with many standards (e.g., FIPS)	Used for secure data encryption in various applications, including file encryption and network security
Caesar Cipher	Very Low	Very Low	Very Fast	None	Low	Very Low (simple implementation)	Minimal; ethical concerns for modern applications	Historical; not used for secure communications today
Substitution Cipher	Very Low	Low	Fast	None	Low	Low (simple implementation)	Minimal; ethical concerns due to weak security	Basic encryption; not suitable for modern secure communications

continued on following page

Table 1. Continued

Encryption Method	Data Density	Security Strength	Speed of Encryption	Error Correction	Scalability	Resource Requirements	Regulatory and Ethical Compliance	Practical Implementations
Vigenère Cipher	Low	Moderate	Fast	None	Low	Low (simple implementation)	Minimal; ethical concerns due to vulnerability to frequency analysis	Historical; more secure than simple substitution but not used in modern applications
Transposition Cipher	Low	Moderate	Moderate	None	Moderate	Low (simple implementation)	Minimal; limited ethical concerns	Basic encryption; often combined with other methods for better security
Hill Cipher	Low	Moderate	Moderate	None	Moderate	Low (matrix operations required)	Minimal; limited use in secure communications	Historical; primarily for academic purposes
Public Key Cryptography	Low	Very High	Moderate	None (external error correction)	High	High (computationally intensive)	Well-established; compliant with many standards	Used for secure data transmission and digital signatures (e.g., RSA, ECC)
Block Cipher	Low	High	Fast	None (external error correction)	High	Moderate (efficient on hardware)	Widely accepted; compliant with many standards	Used for secure data encryption in various applications, including file encryption and network security

A. Computational and Storage Challenges in DNA Cryptography

In implementing DNA cryptography, several computational and storage challenges must be addressed to make the technology practical for large-scale applications. One of the primary challenges lies in the complex process of encoding binary data into nucleotide sequences (A, T, C, G), which introduces computational overhead, especially when handling large datasets like RGB images. Errors during DNA synthesis and sequencing, such as single base repeats and imbalances in GC content, further exacerbate the need for advanced error-correction mechanisms, increasing computational demands. Moreover, the limited length of DNA sequences that can be synthesized in one go necessitates the splitting and reassembly of data, adding to the computational burden. Storage also presents difficulties, as while DNA offers exceptionally high data density, its long-term stability is an issue—DNA can degrade over time, which requires the use of preservation methods like silica encapsulation or calcium phosphate nanocrystals to extend the lifespan of stored data. Additionally, high costs associated with DNA synthesis and sequencing, coupled with slow sequencing speeds, make real-time or large-scale implementation challenging.

To overcome these hurdles, several advancements are being pursued. Enzymatic and electrochemical synthesis methods show promise in reducing the reliance on expensive chemical reagents, thus lowering costs and improving the efficiency of DNA synthesis. Coding strategies like composite DNA letters and error-correction mechanisms, such as Huffman or Yin-Yang coding, can enhance both the data density and integrity of encoded information. Furthermore, advances in sequencing technologies, particularly nanopore sequencing, could accelerate data retrieval, enabling faster and more reliable access to information stored in DNA. By incorporating these innovations, DNA cryptography can become a more scalable, cost-effective, and practical solution for secure information storage, positioning it as a strong candidate for future cryptographic systems (Zhang, 2024).

B. Scalability Issues

The scalability of DNA-based cryptography for large-scale applications like cloud storage and streaming media encryption presents several challenges that must be addressed to fully realize its potential. A primary concern is performance, as DNA synthesis and sequencing processes are inherently slower than traditional electronic data processing, leading to potential bottlenecks in accessing large datasets. Innovations in sequencing technologies, such as nanopore sequencing, are essential to reduce the time required for encoding and decoding data. Additionally, resource consumption is significant; the current methods for DNA synthesis are costly and require specialized materials and environments, making widespread adoption economically challenging. Developing cost-effective synthesis techniques, such as enzymatic or electrochemical methods, alongside high-throughput production capabilities, will be crucial to mitigate these costs. Finally, adaptability to large datasets poses another hurdle, as efficient data retrieval from vast DNA libraries can be complex due to the random access nature of DNA storage. New algorithms and indexing methods tailored for DNA data management are needed to facilitate quick and efficient navigation within these systems. By addressing these performance, resource, and adaptability issues, DNA cryptography could become a transformative solution for secure storage and transmission in the digital age.

C. Challenges Faced During Practical Implementation

The difficulty of translating biological processes into digital systems presents significant challenges for implementing DNA cryptography in real-world applications. This translation involves intricate coding mechanisms to accurately map binary data into DNA sequences while avoiding issues like base repetition and GC content imbalances, which can compromise stability. Furthermore, the synthesis and sequencing of DNA are costly and time-consuming, often introducing errors, especially with longer strands, making it difficult to ensure accurate data encoding. Scalability remains a concern, as the limited length of DNA strands necessitates breaking larger datasets into smaller fragments, complicating data management and retrieval. Additionally, integrating biological data storage with existing digital infrastructure raises compatibility issues, requiring the development of new protocols and interfaces. The need for robust error correction methods further complicates implementation, as biological systems are prone to variability and inaccuracies. Addressing these challenges is crucial for realizing the potential of DNA cryptography, and ongoing research must focus on enhancing encoding algorithms, improving synthesis and sequencing accuracy, and creating effective systems for managing and retrieving DNA-stored data.

D. Resilience to Threats

While DNA cryptography offers high information density and unique encoding methods, it is not inherently immune to quantum threats. For instance, if a quantum computer can efficiently decode the sequences used in DNA encryption, it could potentially compromise the confidentiality of the stored information. Moreover, the random nature of biological processes involved in DNA synthesis and sequencing could introduce additional unpredictability that may be exploited by quantum algorithms. However, there are ways DNA cryptography could mitigate some of these risks. Researchers are exploring quantum-resistant algorithms that could be integrated with DNA encryption techniques to enhance security against quantum attacks. By combining DNA-based methods with protocols that leverage quantum key distribution (QKD), it may be possible to create a more robust security framework that capitalizes on the strengths of both technologies. Ultimately, the relevance of DNA cryptography in the evolving cybersecurity landscape will depend on its ability to adapt and integrate with emerging technologies, including quantum computing. Ongoing research is essential to address these vulnerabilities and ensure that DNA-based cryptographic techniques remain viable in a future where quantum threats may become increasingly prevalent. This discussion is vital for understanding the long-term prospects and applicability of DNA cryptography in securing sensitive data against the backdrop of rapid technological advancements.

E. Technical Obstacles

A major hurdle is the complexity of DNA sequence processing, which involves intricate biochemical manipulations. The conversion of binary data into DNA sequences requires precise mapping and synthesis, a process that can be time-consuming and susceptible to errors. The accuracy of DNA sequencing is critical; any discrepancies in the sequencing process can lead to significant variations in the reconstructed images, compromising data fidelity. Additionally, the biochemical environment can introduce variability, as factors like temperature and reagent quality can affect the synthesis and sequencing outcomes.Another challenge lies in the computational resource requirements associated with DNA encryption techniques. While DNA offers remarkable storage density, the algorithms necessary for encoding and decoding this data demand considerable processing power. As the size of the images increases, so too does the computational load, which can become a bottleneck. This necessitates advancements in both hardware and software to efficiently manage the complexities of large datasets and sophisticated encryption algorithms. The implementation of effective error correction mechanisms is crucial to ensure data integrity. Given the potential for errors during DNA synthesis and sequencing, robust error correction is essential for maintaining the accuracy of the reconstructed data. Various error-correcting codes can be employed, but their integration adds another layer of complexity to the system design. Practitioners must strike a balance between the need for effective error correction and the overall efficiency of the encryption process, as overly complex systems can hinder practical application. This challenge is compounded by the need for these mechanisms to work seamlessly with existing encryption algorithms without introducing significant overhead. Lastly, the scalability of DNA cryptography poses a significant challenge. While current research may demonstrate promising results with small datasets, scaling these methods to accommodate larger images or more extensive data sets introduces additional complications. Issues such as increased time for synthesis, sequencing, and processing can become prohibitive as the volume of data grows. Ensuring that DNA encryption remains feasible and efficient in practical applications requires ongoing research and development to address these scalability concerns.

Figure 2. Flowchart for future works

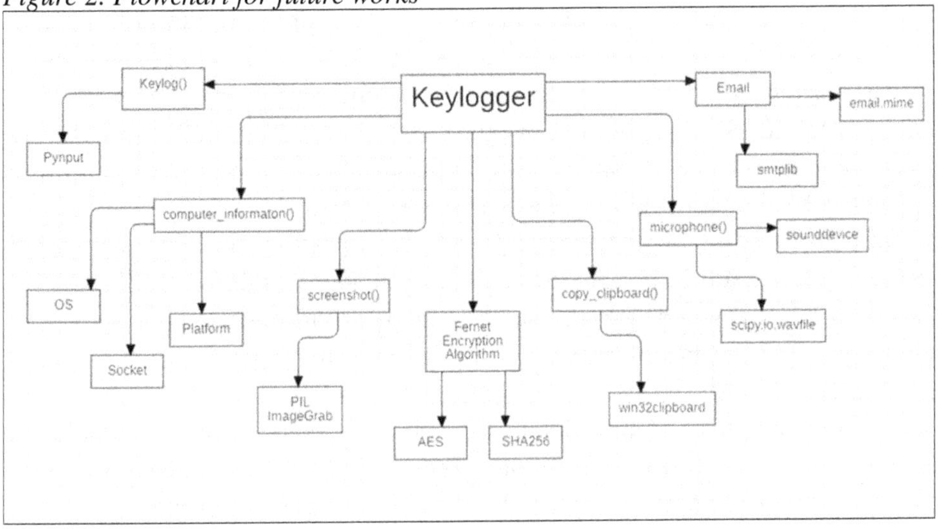

VI. CONCLUSION AND FUTURE WORKS

To address the identified research gaps and advance image encryption techniques based on DNA encoding and chaotic systems, several further studies are recommended. Further research should be conducted to develop optimization techniques that can reduce the computational complexity of DNA encoding, chaotic sequence generation, and encryption/decryption routines. Novel algorithms and strategies that streamline operations, leverage parallel computing architectures, or incorporate hardware acceleration (e.g., GPUs, FPGAs) should be explored. The objective is to enhance the overall efficiency of the encryption process without compromising security. Potential avenues can include developing algorithms with reduced computational complexity for key processes. Investigating parallel computing architectures and hardware acceleration techniques for efficient implementations.

Exploring optimization algorithms and techniques to improve performance while maintaining security guarantees. To ensure the applicability of these encryption techniques to large-scale applications and high-resolution images, further studies should focus on developing scalability strategies. Designing adaptive encryption schemes tailored to different image dimensions and resolutions. Implementing parallel processing and distributed computing approaches for handling large-scale images efficiently. Optimizing memory requirements and resource consumption for resource-constrained devices and platforms.

Continuous efforts are required to ensure the resilience of encryption algorithms against emerging attacks and vulnerabilities. Conduct comprehensive security analyses to evaluate the resilience against known and potential attacks, including side-channel attacks, machine learning-based attacks, and quantum computing threats. Develop countermeasures and security enhancements to address identified vulnerabilities proactively. Foster collaborations with cryptanalysts and security researchers to stay informed about emerging threats and attack vectors.

Bridging the gap between theoretical research and practical deployment is crucial for the widespread adoption of these encryption techniques. Collaborate with industry stakeholders and standardization bodies to develop standardized encryption protocols and guidelines, ensuring interoperability and ease of adoption across platforms and environments. Investigate methods for seamless integration of encryption algorithms into existing systems and applications, considering factors such as compatibility, interoperability, and ease of integration. Conduct usability studies and user experience evaluations to improve practical deployment and user acceptance.

Addressing the multifaceted challenges and research gaps requires interdisciplinary collaborations. Further efforts should be made to foster collaborations between researchers from various fields, including cryptography, optimization, parallel computing, security analysis, and user experience design. By leveraging expertise from different domains, comprehensive solutions can be developed to address the identified research gaps effectively. These further studies, conducted through collaborative efforts and interdisciplinary approaches, will contribute to the development of secure, efficient, and practical image encryption solutions based on DNA encoding and chaotic systems, enabling their widespread adoption in various applications.

Integrating DNA cryptography with Artificial Intelligence (AI) and the Internet of Things (IoT) offers innovative security solutions that could significantly enhance data protection. AI can drive advanced encryption algorithms that utilize DNA sequences, increasing complexity and security while also enabling pattern recognition to detect anomalies or unauthorized access. In an IoT context, DNA-based authentication can serve as a unique identifier for devices, improving security beyond traditional methods. Additionally, AI can facilitate dynamic key management by generating unique DNA-based keys for each session, thereby minimizing key compromise risks. The combination of DNA cryptography and blockchain technology can create decentralized, tamper-proof transaction records, enhancing trust within IoT ecosystems. Furthermore, DNA's vast storage capacity can efficiently accommodate the data-rich nature of IoT, while AI optimizes resource allocation for encryption processes. This interdisciplinary approach paves the way for robust privacy measures, regulatory compliance, and scalable security solutions that address the challenges of an increasingly interconnected world.

REFERENCES

Abusukhon, A., & AlZu'bi, S. (2020, April). New direction of cryptography: A review on text-to-image encryption algorithms based on RGB color value. In *2020 Seventh International Conference on Software Defined Systems (SDS)* (pp. 235-239). IEEE.

Adleman, L. M. (1994). Molecular computation of solutions to combinatorial problems. *Nature, 266*(5187), 40.

Al-Kateeb, Z. N., Al-Shamdeen, M. J., & Al-Mukhtar, F. S. (2020, July). Encryption and Steganography a secret data using circle shapes in colored images. *Journal of Physics: Conference Series, 1591*(1), 012019.

Aljazaery, I. A., Salim, A. L., Rikabi, H. T., & Alaidi, A. H. M. (2022). Encryption of Color Image Based on DNA Strand and Exponential Factor. *International Journal of Online & Biomedical Engineering, 18*(3).

Chuang, Y. H., Lin, B. S., Chen, Y. X., & Shiu, H. J. (2021). Steganography in RGB images using adjacent mean. *IEEE Access : Practical Innovations, Open Solutions, 9*, 164256–164274.

Dworkin, M. (2001). *Recommendation for Block Cipher Modes of Operation.* Methods and Techniques.

Gao, J., Wang, Y., Song, Z., & Wang, S. (2023). Quantum image encryption based on quantum DNA codec and pixel-level scrambling. *Entropy (Basel, Switzerland), 25*(6), 865.

Grass, R. N., Lipton, R. J., Frazer, P. J., Frenkel, C. D., & Gaudet, S. J. (2000). Logical security of information in DNA. *Bioinformatics (Oxford, England), 16*(8), 788–791.

Hameed, S. M., Sa'adoon, H. A., & Al-Ani, M. (2018). Image encryption using DNA encoding and RC4 algorithm. *Iraqi Journal of Science*, 434–446.

Ibrahim, D., Ahmed, K., Abdallah, M., & Ali, A. A. (2022). A new chaotic-based RGB image encryption technique using a nonlinear rotational 16× 16 DNA playfair matrix. *Cryptography, 6*(2), 28.

Iqbal, N., Hanif, M., Abbas, S., Khan, M. A., Almotiri, S. H., & Al Ghamdi, M. A. (2020). DNA strands level scrambling based color image encryption scheme. *IEEE Access : Practical Innovations, Open Solutions, 8*, 178167–178182.

Iqbal, N., Naqvi, R. A., Atif, M., Khan, M. A., Hanif, M., Abbas, S., & Hussain, D. (2021). On the image encryption algorithm based on the chaotic system, dna encoding, and castle. *IEEE Access : Practical Innovations, Open Solutions, 9*, 118253–118270.

Juneja, M., & Sandhu, P. S. (2013). An improved LSB based steganography technique for RGB color images. *International Journal of Computer and Communication Engineering, 2*(4), 513.

Khan, P. W., & Byun, Y. (2020). A blockchain-based secure image encryption scheme for the industrial Internet of Things. *Entropy (Basel, Switzerland), 22*(2), 175.

Kumar, M., Iqbal, A., & Kumar, P. (2016). A new RGB image encryption algorithm based on DNA encoding and elliptic curve Diffie–Hellman cryptography. *Signal Processing, 125*, 187–202.

Kumar, M. R., & Chouksey, P. (2024). Novel Approach for Encrypting RGB Images Utilizing Quantum Computing. *International Journal of Multidisciplinary Innovation and Research Methodology, 3*(2), 42-56.

Liu, Q., & Liu, L. (2020). Color image encryption algorithm based on DNA coding and double chaos system. *IEEE Access : Practical Innovations, Open Solutions, 8*, 83596–83610.

Nazir, H., Bajwa, I. S., Abdullah, S., Kazmi, R., & Samiullah, M. (2022). A color image encryption scheme combining hyperchaos and genetic codes. *IEEE Access : Practical Innovations, Open Solutions, 10*, 14480–14495.

Niyat, A. Y., Hei, R. M. H., & Jahan, M. V. (2015). A RGB image encryption algorithm based on DNA sequence operation and hyper-chaotic system. *International Congress on Technology, Communication and Knowledge (ICTCK).*

. Noorbasha, F., & Suresh, K. (2018). FPGA implementation of RGB image encryption and decryption using DNA cryptography. *International Journal of Engineering & Technology, 7*(2.8), 397-403.

Parekh, N., & D'Mello, L. (2021, September). ChaDRaL: RGB Image Encryption based on 3D Chaotic Map, DNA, RSA and LSB. In *2021 International Conference on Artificial Intelligence and Machine Vision (AIMV)* (pp. 1-6). IEEE.

Patel, S., Thanikaiselvan, V., Pelusi, D., Nagaraj, B., Arunkumar, R., & Amirtharajan, R. (2021). Colour image encryption based on customized neural network and DNA encoding. *Neural Computing & Applications, 33*(21), 14533–14550.

Schneier, B. (2015). *Applied cryptography*. John Wiley & Sons.

Shah, T., Haq, T. U., & Farooq, G. (2020). Improved SERPENT algorithm: Design to RGB image encryption implementation. *IEEE Access : Practical Innovations, Open Solutions*, *8*, 52609–52621.

Shraida, G. K., Younis, H. A., Al-Amiedy, T. A., Anbar, M., Younis, H. A., & Hasbullah, I. H. (2023). An efficient color-image encryption method using DNA sequence and chaos cipher. *Computers, Materials & Continua*, *75*(2), 2641–2654.

Smith, C. (2015, December). Breakthrough data storage innovation: One DNA molecule can store tons of data for 1M years. *BGR*.https://bgr.com/2015/08/18/dna-hard-drive-data-storage/

Wang, L., Ran, Q., & Ma, J. (2020). Double quantum color images encryption scheme based on DQRCI. *Multimedia Tools and Applications*, *79*(9), 6661–6687.

Zhang, L., Wang, X., & Liu, Y. (2009). A review on chaotic cryptography in image encryption. *International Journal of Bifurcation and Chaos in Applied Sciences and Engineering*, *19*(4), 1339–1374.

Zhang, X., & Ye, R. (2021). A novel RGB image encryption algorithm based on DNA sequences and chaos. *Multimedia Tools and Applications*, *80*(6), 8809–8833.

Zhang, Z., & Zhang, Z. (2024). DNA Information Storage and Cryptography System. *Academic Journal of Science and Technology*, *10*(1), 243–249.

Zhou, S., He, P., & Kasabov, N. (2020). A dynamic DNA color image encryption method based on SHA-512. *Entropy (Basel, Switzerland)*, *22*(10), 1091.

Chapter 10
KK Approach to Increase Resilience in Internet of Things: A T-Cell Security Concept

Kutubuddin Sayyad Liyakat Kazi
https://orcid.org/0000-0001-5623-9211
Brahmdevdada Mane Institute of Technology, Solapur, India

ABSTRACT

This technique for identifying malicious nodes is known by the inventor as the "KK approach." We compare the throughput and delay of the system with the proposed KK Approach, and the results are superior compared to the earlier techniques. Its abilities to learn, adapt, collaborate, and act independently make it a potent weapon in fighting against cyber threats. It is also capable of learning. However, additional research and development are required to overcome the limitations and challenges associated with its deployment. It is essential to continue investigating and financing state-of-the-art solutions in order to guarantee the security and privacy of these networks. This is because we rely more and more on gadgets connected to the IoT for our everyday needs.

INTRODUCTION

The Internet of Things (IoT) is a growing network of interconnected devices. Among these gadgets are wearable technologies, industrial devices, and smart home systems. The continuous data exchange and networking of these gadgets is making our daily activities more convenient and efficient. This interconnectedness

DOI: 10.4018/979-8-3693-8014-7.ch010

does, however, come with a serious security risk that needs to be addressed. The probability of cyberattacks and data breaches has also increased due to the growing number of devices connected to the internet. Liyakat (2024) has thus raised grave worries about the privacy on our own private data and the security of IoT devices.

IoT technology, whose continues to progressively gaining pace, is currently being used in a wide range of sectors and applications. As a result, there are several instances of IoT application use. Among IoT application scenarios, smart home applications are among the most well-known. As virtual assistants likes Google Home and Amazon's Alexa gain popularity, more and more people are making their houses "smart homes" by Gund (2023). Owing to Internet of Things devices, homeowners can monitor and operate their properties remotely. Among these devices are smart thermostats, smart lighting, and smart security systems. For example, individuals may regulate the temperature and lighting in their houses and get notifications if something strange happens. Liyakat Kazi (2024) and Neeraja (2024) observe that by including this, things become safer and more energy-efficient in addition to being more convenient.

Moreover, K S (2022) describes a noteworthy Internet of Things application situation in the healthcare industry. Patients may now monitor their health in real time thanks to IoT gadgets. Thanks to Veena (2023) and Megha (2024), they may also provide this information to their healthcare practitioners. For instance, a diabetic patient can utilize an ongoing glucose monitoring device that uses K S to send data to their doctor (2023b). This gives the doctor the chance to adjust the treatment plan as necessary. In a same vein, hospitals can employ IoT devices to remotely monitor patient vitals, automate some procedures, and track the whereabouts of medical equipment—all of which will enhance patient care and efficiency by Priya (2023).

The change that IoT is bringing about in the transportation industry has caused us to travel in a different way. Cars can now speak with intelligent traffic systems and with one another, thanks to the growing usage of IoT devices like sensors and GPS trackers. This makes it possible to monitor traffic in real-time, which helps to lessen traffic bottlenecks and raises overall road safety. The logistics sector is also using IoT technology to track shipments and improve delivery routes, which finally results in more timely and effective delivery of goods.

Another area where IoT is becoming well-known is in the manufacturing industry, where it is referred to as the Industrial-Internet of Things, or IIoT. Manufacturers can connect machines, equipment, and networks to collect data in real time and remotely monitor processes. This makes predictive maintenance possible, boosting output while decreasing downtime. The IIoT enables businesses to optimize their supply chain and inventory, increasing efficiency and reducing expenses.

IoT technology is also being used by the retail sector to enhance consumers' shopping experiences by Kazi K S (2024b). Using IoT-enabled beacons and sensors, businesses can track customer movement and activity within their establishments to gather useful data. Sales and customer satisfaction will increase as a result of the personalized offers and recommendations created using this data. By Kazi K (2024), supply chain optimization and inventory management are two more applications for IoT devices that will improve overall process efficiency.

IoT technology is being used by the agriculture sector to increase crop yield and decrease resource waste. Farmers may make educated judgments regarding irrigation and fertilizing by using sensor data that monitors crop growth, soil moisture, and weather. As a result, farmers gain from higher output and cheaper costs. Furthermore, IoT technology is being used in precision farming. In this type of farming, data is gathered and accurate maps of crop fields are created using drones that are fitted with sensors and cameras. Farmers can use this to determine which areas Wale(2019), K K S(2022) needs to attend to. In conclusion, there are a wide range of constantly growing applications for IoT. Figure 1 by Liyakat(2022), Vahida(2023), and Karale(2023), shows how the Internet of Things(IoT) is transforming healthcare, manufacturing, retail, and agriculture in addition to smart homes. It could make our lives easier, more productive, and more environmentally friendly. As technology advances, we should anticipate seeing a lot more creative and fascinating IoT application opportunities in the years to come.

Figure 1. IoT Application Scenario 2024

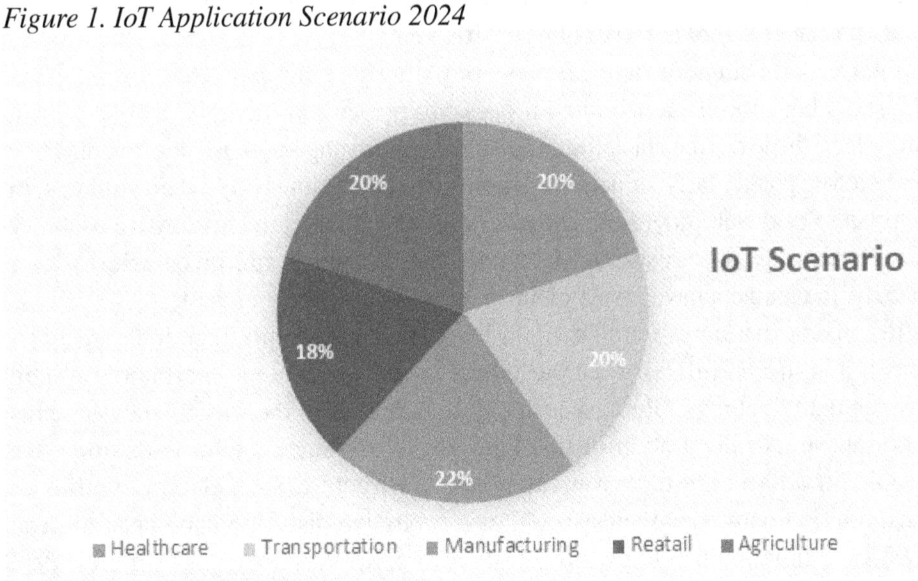

The main causes of security problems with IoT devices is the absence of standards and regulations in this quickly expanding industry. This is among the factors contributing to the market's rapid expansion. The Internet of Things(IoT) is a relatively new notion compared to other areas of technology. Consequently, there are no established standards or laws in place to ensure the security of these gadgets. Because there is a lack of standards, it makes it hard for manufacturers to include security measures into their products. According to Liyakat (2023), this leaves these producers open to the possibility of being the target of cybercriminals.

The sheer number of linked devices is the root cause of yet another major security vulnerability pertaining to IoT devices. The number of computers and other electronic devices connected to the internet is predicted to reach over 25 billion by 2021, based on research conducted by Gartner. It is difficult to manually maintain and secure any type of device because there are so many varieties available. Cybercriminals possess the ability to exploit vulnerabilities in these devices in order to obtain sensitive data by Sultanabanu (2023a, b), Prasad (2024). This is because hackers are able to take advantage of these weaknesses.

Internet of Things devices carry a number of risks, the most significant of which is the possibility of data breaches. Massive amounts of data are collected by these devices, and among the many kinds of personal information they may hold are names, addresses, and financial information. Should this information fall into the wrong hands, it might be used for financial fraud, identity theft, and other illegal acts. Furthermore, because Internet of Things devices are frequently connected to other gadgets like computers and smartphones, these connections may act as entry points for hackers looking to obtain sensitive data.

Internet of Things devices are susceptible to hacking and other forms of cyberattacks because of their limited processing power and memory. Unlike typical computers, these devices lack the capacity to run advanced security software. They are therefore particularly vulnerable to being used maliciously by cybercriminals. In the process of developing these gadgets, a lot of manufacturers prioritize usability and affordability over security. Since cost and usefulness are given priority over security, the gadgets have insufficient security measures as a result.

It is likely that a cyberattack on an IoT device will result in serious repercussions if it is successful. For example, a hacker with access to a smart home system may regulate the temperature, security system, and even the surveillance cameras in the house. An illustration of this kind of circumstance might be this one. It's feasible for a hacker to take over essential infrastructure, such electricity grids or transportation networks, which would cause massive disruption and anarchy. The worst-case situation would be this. Furthermore, hackers could cause a great deal of disturbance by Kazi K (2022).

What precautionary steps might be taken in light of this to address these worries about the security of Internet of Things devices? First and foremost, manufacturers need to prioritize security and incorporate stringent security measures into their products. This is what needs to be done in the first place. Using multi-factor authentication, upgrading software often, and utilizing robust encryption techniques are a few examples of actions that go under this category. In order to guarantee that security is taken into consideration from the outset when developing Internet of Things devices, manufacturers should also endeavour to create uniform security standards.

Users also bear the duty of taking the appropriate safety measures to safeguard their own Internet of Things devices. This category includes things like changing the default passwords, verifying that all of the devices are running the most recent software, and using caution while connecting to public Wi-Fi networks. Before purchasing Internet of Things devices, it is essential to examine their security standards. Furthermore, it's critical to make sure you only purchase these gadgets from reputable manufacturers.

The Internet of Things (IoT) technology has greatly improved our daily lives and brought about many conveniences, but it also poses a number of security risks. Internet of Things devices are susceptible to cyberattacks and data breaches due to a number of factors, including a lack of standardization, a large number of connected devices, and a lack of strong security methods. Additionally, it is the duty of both the developers of these gadgets and the users of them to prioritize security and take the appropriate precautions to secure the sensitive data that these devices gather. As the Internet of Things (IoT) industry grows, it is critical to address these security challenges in order to guarantee a safer and more secure future by the year Halli (2022).

The way that we connect with our surroundings has changed significantly as a result of the Internet of Things. Internet of Things applications are becoming a necessary component of our daily life, showing up in everything from smart homes to automated industries. We can now connect to and operate a vast array of electronic items via the internet thanks to this technology. Our lives are now much more convenient and efficient as a result of this. However, as more and more Internet of Things devices are being used, security issues are starting to become a serious worry.

Numerous industries, including but not limited to the fields of manufacturing, transportation, healthcare, and agriculture, are currently utilizing applications of the Internet of Things. Wearables and smart medical devices, among other examples of IoT technology, have made it simpler for physicians to remotely monitor their patients' health and deliver prompt care by Pradeepa (2022). This represents a noteworthy progression in the medical domain. The transportation sector is using Internet of Things (IoT) sensors and gadgets to boost productivity and reduce expenses. Fleet vehicle management and tracking are used to achieve this. In the manufacturing sector, the Internet of Things (IoT) technology is utilized to automate tasks. This increases production and lowers the possibility of errors resulting from human error. With the use of Internet of Things sensors in agriculture, crop development can be monitored and optimised, ultimately resulting in higher yields. The applications that were shown above are only a few examples of how the Internet of Things has revolutionized numerous different industries.

Concerns about security have surfaced as the Internet of Things (IoT) grows. As more and more gadgets are connected to the internet, the probability of cyberattacks and data breaches is rising. This is a result of the growing number of devices that are online. These gadgets are vulnerable to the risk of hacking and other types of criminality as many of them lack adequate security safeguards. Consider the following example: A hacker manages to get access to a smart home system and takes over the lights, thermostat, or security system. This would compromise the citizens' privacy and sense of safety. According to Liyakat K K S (2023), a cyberattack on an Internet of Things (IoT) system within a commercial organization may result in operational disruptions, the compromise of critical data, and monetary losses.

The lack of standardization is unquestionably one of the most important security issues associated with Internet of Things applications. There is no standardized set of security criteria for Internet of Things devices because there are so many different manufacturers and products on the market. Owing to the current circumstances, it is not feasible to ensure that every device is secure and capable of securely connecting with each other. There have also been a significant number of internet of things security breaches. These gadgets are ideal targets for thieves to take advantage of because they often lack crucial security features like encryption and authentication.

The volume of data that IoT apps gather and store online is another issue that raises security concerns. These gadgets generate a large volume of sensitive information during operation since they are continuously gathering and transferring data. If this information is obtained by someone who are not authorized to have it, it could be used for unethical purposes, like identity theft or corporate espionage. The fact that a sizable portion of Internet of Things devices lack proper security procedures to safeguard this data makes a third point of interest noteworthy (2023). As a result, the security of this data is not always assured.

It is imperative that manufacturers prioritize security in their IoT products in order to allay consumers' concerns about security. Examples of this include encryption mechanisms, authentication processes, and ongoing software upgrades. The application of these procedures is another example. Furthermore, in order to find and fix any vulnerabilities that might exist in their systems, businesses must regularly do security audits and tests. Furthermore, industry-wide standardization of procedures is essential to ensure that Internet of Things devices are all somewhat secure.

People can also change the default passwords on their devices, update their software on a regular basis, and be cautious about sharing information with other IoT devices as additional measures to protect their gadgets. In addition to the recommendation that IoT devices only be purchased from manufacturers with a solid track record, researchers should assess a device's security features prior to making a purchase.

When everything is taken into account, IoT apps hold great promise for enhancing both our personal and professional life. On the other hand, it is impossible to overlook the security issues raised by these devices. To guarantee the security of IoT electronic devices and the data they gather, it is critical that users, organizations, and manufacturers take preventative action. If the proper security measures are implemented, IoT applications have the ability to improve our lives without endangering our security or privacy.

With the advent of digital technology, cyberattacks are becoming a major cause for worry. This is because they run the risk of compromising not just our personal information but also the information of governments and organizations. On the other hand, as technology and the internet have been more widely used, so too have cyberattacks increased in frequency. Altaf (2023) highlights the need for individuals and organizations to be aware of the various types of cyber-attacks and the strategies that can be employed to prevent oneself from becoming a target, given the potential for significant harm and financial loss resulting from these attacks.

- Malware, an acronym for "harmful software," is among the most prevalent kind of assaults. Malware attacks and viruses are also become more frequent. Within the realm of information technology, the phrase encompasses an extensive range of technologies, such as ransomware, Trojan horses, worms, and viruses. Malware can infiltrate a computer through a number of channels, such as USB sticks that have been contaminated with malware, malicious websites, and email attachments. Once installed, malware can encrypt files, steal important data, and even take over the computer completely. After installation, it is capable of doing all of these tasks right away.
- Phishing attacks are a subset of social engineering assaults in which cybercriminals employ deceitful social engineering techniques to fool victims into divulging private information, credit card details, or login credentials. The most prevalent forms of social engineering attacks is thought to be phishing attacks. Phishing attacks can be conducted through the use of phony websites, emails, or texts. You can use webpages, texts, and emails. The fact that these attacks often have the appearance of coming from a reliable source makes it challenging to identify who is behind them. This makes it difficult to confirm their legitimacy.

- Attacks that Deny Service (also Known as DoS): A denial of service attack (DoS) aims to interfere with a website or network's regular operation by sending an overwhelming amount of requests to it. This will either result in a network or website crash or significantly slow it down. Businesses that depend on their online presence for operations and sales may experience large financial losses as a result of this.
- Man-in-the-middle (MitM) assaults: These kind of attacks take place when a hacker eavesdrops on a conversation between two parties and obtains sensitive data, like credit card numbers, login credentials, and personal information that the hacker has access to. Another name for this kind of attack is a "man-in-the-middle attack." To carry it out, it's customary to either fabricate a network or take advantage of unprotected public Wi-Fi networks.
- SQL injection attacks are designed to take advantage of programming flaws in websites or databases that are available online. The goal of these attacks is to take advantage of weaknesses. An attacker can read confidential information and possibly take over the entire system by inserting malicious code into the website's database. The attacker now has the chance to review private information.
- A zero-day attack is one that makes use of undiscovered vulnerabilities in software or systems. An assault that exploits a software or system defect is known as a zero-day attack. These attacks are very harmful because it is hard to defend against them because there is no patch or cure available. This is a result of the lack of a patch or cure.
- Attacks that fall under the category of Advanced Persistent Threats (APT): The objective of APT attacks is to obtain sensitive data or interfere with operations. These attacks are highly targeted and technologically sophisticated. It is challenging to identify and defend against them since they are executed through a sequence of carefully thought out and synchronized operations.
- Insider Attacks: Attacks that fall under this category can be executed by somebody with authorized access to a network or system. These people are capable of carrying out attacks. These attacks can be accidental, where the insider unintentionally divulges critical information due to their own actions, or purposeful, where the insider tries to cause harm. Attacks of both kinds are conceivable.
- A relatively recent type of cyberattack known as "cryptojacking" is using a person's or an organization's processing power to mine bitcoin without that person's or that organization's knowledge or consent. When a person or organization is unaware that they are being mined, it is known as cryptojacking. The person who is impacted might have higher electrical bills as a result of this, and it's possible that the system will become noticeably slower.

- Cyber espionage is a class of assault in which hackers breach a network or computer system to obtain confidential data. We call this kind of attack "cyber espionage." This category includes a wide range of information types, such as government secrets, trade secrets, and intellectual property.
- Attacks that Make Use of Cross-Site Scripting(XSS): Cross-Site Scripting attacks are another type of attack that targets websites and online apps. In these types of attacks, malicious code is introduced into a website, and users who are not aware of the hazard can then carry out the attack. In these situations, the attacker can take advantage of users' personal information, alter the website's content, or direct users to websites that are filled with harmful material.

The fact that cyberattacks can take many different forms and have the potential to seriously harm both people and companies must be understood clearly. Since there are numerous varieties of cyberattacks, it is essential to recognize these variations and take the necessary safety measures to protect oneself from them. With the correct security measures in place and a constant level of awareness, we can protect our digital lives and reduce the risk of becoming victims of cyberattacks. There is something we can do about this.

Smart homes and industrial automation are just two examples of the many areas that have benefited from the rapid proliferation of the Internet of Things (IoT), which has brought about countless innovations and conveniences across a variety of industries. However, this huge interconnection also presents considerable issues, notably in terms of security, reliability, and resilience against failures or assaults. Specifically, these challenges are of particular concern. Within this framework, the implementation of KK approach (T-cell concept) principles presents a promising paradigm for improving the robustness of the Internet of Things (IoT). With this study, the critical issue statement, broad aims, and specific objectives connected with integrating KK-approach with Internet of Things systems are investigated from a variety of perspectives.

PROBLEM STATEMENT

The Internet of Things(IoT) devices are becoming more vulnerable to a variety of risks, notably cyberattacks, failures of the system, and sustainability disruptions, as their number and capabilities continue to expand. The resilience, reliability, and self-healing capabilities that are necessary to overcome these challenges are frequently absent from traditional network topologies. A malfunction or compromise within one component of an Internet of Things system may contribute to cascade failures, which dramatically undermines the integrity and reliability of the entire network.

This is the primary issue. In addition to putting the functionality of essential apps in jeopardy, this vulnerability also poses significant threats to the security of users and the confidentiality of their data.

GOAL

To establish a decentralized and adaptive framework that improves the robustness and recoverability of Internet of Things(IoT) systems is the major objective of adopting the T-Cell concept forms KK-approach in the context of Internet of Things (IoT) resilience. It is possible for Internet of Things frameworks to better regulate and respond to disturbances by imitating the functioning of the T-cells found in the biological immune system. These cells are specialized in recognizing and eliminating threats while safeguarding the general health of the system. The KK-approach idea makes an effort to:

- The utilization of a distributed architecture allows the system to function efficiently even in the event that individual components malfunction or become compromised. This helps to enhance the system's robustness.
- Promote Self-Healing: In the same way as KK-approach have the ability to identify and react to viruses, an Internet of Things system that utilizes this notion is able to independently detect anomalies and activate recovery methods, while simultaneously restoring functionality with little downtime.
- Help to Facilitate Adaptability: The KK-model supports dynamic adjustments in response to real-time situations. This helps to ensure that the Internet of Things network is able to adapt to changing operational changes and evolving threats in an effective manner.

OBJECTIVES

Several particular goals need to be stated in order to accomplish the goal of increased resilience in Internet of Things (IoT) systems through the utilization of the KK-approach- T-Cell concept.

- To enable decentralized management and governance, it is necessary to design and develop KK-approach designs. These architectures should be scalable and flexible, and they should contain KK-approach concepts for Internet of Things networks.

- The implementation of threat detection mechanisms involves the establishment of strong algorithms for anomaly detection that are able to recognize and react to potential threats in real time. These algorithms are analogous to the recognition skills of T-cells.
- The creation of automated recovery processes involves the development of autonomous protocols and operational processes that enable the network to self-heal rather than the intervention of a human being. This helps to reduce the amount of time it takes for the network to respond and reduces the demand for manual inputs.
- Evaluate Performance Metrics: Establish and evaluate performance indicators in order to determine the benefits in resilience that the KK-approach framework brings in comparison to typical Internet of Things systems.
- Encourage Collaboration Across Disciplines: In order to revise and improve the KK-model through the use of multidisciplinary perspectives, it is important to encourage collaboration amongst cybersecurity professionals, Internet of Things specialists, and biologists.

The incorporation of T-cell ideas into Internet of Things resilience represents a possible option for solving the expanding challenges that are faced by the increasing complexity and interconnection of Internet of Things systems. Not only does the KK-approach architecture improve the robustness and adaptability of Internet of Things networks, but it also places a higher priority on the significance of self-healing processes. This is accomplished by revising the way in which we've approach security and reliability. In order to validate these ideas and refine the strategy in order to develop a more resilient Internet of Things landscape, continued research and applications in the real world will be essential as we continue to make progress in this area.

IoT THREATS

Safety concerns have emerged at the same time as the sheer amount of IoT devices has increased. As the number of devices linked to the internet keeps growing, so does the likelihood of cyberattacks and data breaches. This is a result of the growing number of devices that are online. These gadgets are vulnerable to the risk of hacking and other types of criminality as many of them lack adequate security safeguards. Consider the following example: A hacker manages to get access to a smart home system and takes over the lights, thermostat, or security system. This would compromise the citizens' privacy and sense of safety. A cyberattack on an

IoT system within a commercial organization may cause operational disruptions, compromise critical data, and financial losses.

The absence of standardization is one of the biggest security threats associated with IoT applications. There is no standardized set of security criteria for IoT devices because there are so many different manufacturers and products on the market. Owing to the current circumstances, it is not feasible to ensure that every device is secure and capable of securely connecting with each other. Furthermore, a large number of IoT devices are constructed using inexpensive components, which increases their vulnerability to security breaches. These gadgets are ideal targets for thieves to take advantage of because they often lack crucial security features like encryption and authentication.

The volume of data that IoT apps gather and store online is another issue that raises security concerns. These gadgets generate a large volume of sensitive information during operation since they are continuously gathering and transferring data. If this information is obtained by someone who are not authorized to have it, it could be used for unethical purposes, like identity theft or corporate espionage. The safety of this information is not always assured because a significant portion of IoT devices lack the necessary security procedures in place to secure it, which is another noteworthy fact Kutubuddin (2024a)(2024b) should bring to your attention.

It is imperative that manufacturers prioritize security in their IoT products in order to allay consumers' concerns about security. Examples of this include encryption mechanisms, authentication processes, and ongoing software upgrades. The application of these procedures is another example. Furthermore, in order to find and fix any vulnerabilities that might exist in their systems, businesses must regularly do security audits and tests. Furthermore, it is imperative that the industry as a whole standardize its practices to ensure that every IoT device is, at the very least, somewhat secure Kazi K(2024a,b).

People can also change the default passwords on their devices, update their software on a regular basis, and be cautious about sharing information with other IoT devices as additional measures to protect their gadgets. In addition to the recommendation that IoT devices only be purchased from manufacturers with a solid track record, researchers should assess a device's security features prior to making a purchase.

Utilizing the IoT, applications have the potential to significantly enhance both our personal and professional lives. On the other hand, it is impossible to overlook the security issues raised by these devices. To guarantee the security of IoT electronic devices and the data they gather, it is critical that users, organizations, and manufacturers take preventative action. If the proper security measures are implemented, IoT applications have the ability to improve our lives without endangering our security or privacy.

Because more and more devices are being connected to the internet, there is a growing risk of cyberattacks on the IoT, which is concerning for both individuals and businesses. An IoT assault is any hostile action that targets IoT devices or the networks to which they are linked. These attacks could come in a variety of ways, such as unauthorized access, data theft, or device performance interruption. These attacks can have been carried out for a number of purposes, such as espionage, political objectives, or financial gain.

The main reasons why attacks on the IoT are growing more frequent is that many IoT devices lack security measures. The majority of IoT devices are designed with affordability and usability in mind, often at the expense of security protocols. These devices are therefore vulnerable to attacks, which makes hackers' job of exploiting them simple.

The common kinds of IoT attacks is a Distributed Denial of Service attack, or DDoS attack. In this type of assault, a huge number of compromised IoT devices are exploited in order to overload a network or server with traffic, ultimately resulting in its failure. Companies whose operations rely on these networks can sustain significant financial losses as a result of this.

By listening in on communication between two devices, an attacker can gain access to confidential data through a man-in-the-middle attack. The IoT may also be used to carry out this kind of attack. For example, it is feasible for an enemy to eavesdrop on communication between a smartphone and smart home equipment, giving them the ability to remotely manage the smart home gadget.

The potential for physical injury is one of the most concerning aspects of attacks on the IoT. As more critical infrastructure—such as transportation networks and electricity grids—becomes online, its vulnerability to assaults grows. As a result, there's a chance for disastrous events like accidents and power outages.

Thus, what steps may be taken to stop attacks on the IoT? Educating people on the potential risks posed by IoT devices is one way to start. It is imperative that both consumers and organizations understand the security features of the devices they buy and take the necessary precautions, such updating software and changing default passwords.

Assuring the security of IoT devices is also the duty of manufacturers. Security should be the first consideration in the design and development of their goods, and they should release updates often to fix any vulnerabilities that may have been found. Governments may also be involved in enforcing security standards for IoT devices and bringing manufacturers responsible for any potential security lapses.

Furthermore, employing authentication techniques and encryption can help guarantee the security of communication amongst IoT devices and networks. The solicitation of cutting-edge technology like artificial intelligence and machine learning can help detect and stop K K S (2023) assaults in the future.

Thus, even while the IoT has raised a number of security issues, it has also completely changed the way we live our daily lives. Attacks on the IoT are predicted to become more frequent as the number of connected devices rises. Everybody involved—consumers, manufacturers, and governments—must take the necessary safety measures to protect IoT devices and prevent such attacks in the future. It is only at that point that we can truly reap the benefits of modern technology without running the risk of our privacy or safety being compromised.

An adversary-compromising device or sensor that interferes with an IoT network's normal operation is known as a malicious node. A malicious node is a term used to describe this kind of corrupted sensor or device. Anything with an internet connection, including medical equipment itself and smart home gadgets as well as industrial sensors, might be considered one of these nodes. These nodes could be anything at all. These nodes' primary goal is to gain unauthorized access to the network in order to steal confidential data or interfere with the operation of any linked devices.

Malicious nodes can arise in IoT networks due to several important factors. The lack of proper security measures is one of these factors. Insufficient security protocols are frequently present in IoT devices because they are made with user convenience in mind. This makes it possible for hackers to exploit weaknesses and get access to the network. Hackers will find them to be an easy target as a result.

Malware distribution is one of the strategies used by cybercriminals to compromise IOT devices. Malware can enter a network through a variety of different channels. Sending phishing emails, going to rogue websites, and even using insecure communication links are a few of these techniques. It is feasible for a malicious party to remotely take control of a malware-infected device and use it to launch attacks against other devices connected to the same network. We call this method "remote control penetration."

Additionally, physical access is a potential technique of introducing rogue nodes into an IoT network. It is possible for adversaries to physically alter the device in order to install malicious hardware or software. Depending on the situation, this is something that could occur. Because it is simpler for employees or other parties to physically access equipment in these networks, this can be a particularly dangerous situation when it comes to industrial-IoT(IIoT) networks.

In IoT network, a single rogue node has the potential to significantly impact the network as a whole. These nodes run the danger of interfering with the network's regular operations, which could result in data loss, downtime, and monetary losses. This is how the interference will manifest itself. Moreover, in certain circumstances, they may be employed to execute more extensive strikes on vital infrastructure, potentially resulting in extensive damage and chaos among the populace.

Therefore, the question is: What steps can be taken to ensure that there are no rogue nodes in IoT networks? Enhancing the security of items that are linked to the IoT is the first and most important step. Manufacturers have little choice but to give security top priority during the process, both in terms of design and implementation. Important elements of this procedure include the use of robust encryption, the implementation of secure communication protocols, and the frequency of software and firmware updates.

Conducting frequent security audits and vulnerability assessments on the network is another crucial step that needs to be taken in order to ensure network security. This will probably help in spotting any possible weak points and fixing them before enemies may exploit them. An extra precaution that can be taken to stop unauthorised access to the network is the use of access control measures, including strong authentication. It is possible to take this measure to stop unauthorized access.

People must also be made fully aware of the importance of cybersecurity in IoT devices. It is likely that many users are unaware of the possible risks connected to these devices; as a result, they may fail to take the appropriate safety precautions. We are able to stop the proliferation of rogue nodes in IoT networks by training people about the dangers and how to safeguard their own appliances.

Considering all of this, rogue node presence in IoT networks is an increasing issue that requires attention. Ensuring the safety and preventing malicious activities of IoT devices is imperative and requires necessary action. This is a result of our growing dependence on networked devices. We can create an IoT ecosystem that is more secure and safe for everyone by implementing robust security measures and educating users.

T-CELL CONCEPT IN HUMAN BODY

The human body is an intricate and diverse system made up of numerous cells, tissues, and organs. Each cell has a specific function and is necessary to maintain the body's overall health. One of the most important cells in the human body is the T-cell. These cells are vital to the immune system including hold the charge of protecting the body against diseases and infections.

T-cells, also known as T-lymphocytes, are white blood cells that originate in the bone marrow and mature in the thymus gland. Being a part of the adaptive immune system, they have the ability to respond and adapt to specific pathogens and foreign substances. To halt the spread of disease, T-cells are responsible for locating erroneous or contaminated cells within the body and eradicating them. Figure 2 shows how T-cells function in the human body.

The two main subtypes of T-cells are killer T-cells and helper T-cells. Helper T-cells, also known as CD4+ cells, are responsible for initiating the immune response by releasing chemical messengers called cytokines. These cytokines help activate more immune cells, such as killer T-cells and B-cells, to fight infections. Killer T-cells, also known as CD8+ cells, are crucial for directly targeting and eradicating abnormal or contaminated cells. They achieve this by creating toxic substances that kill the intended cell targets.

Figure 2. T-Cell Functioning in Human Body

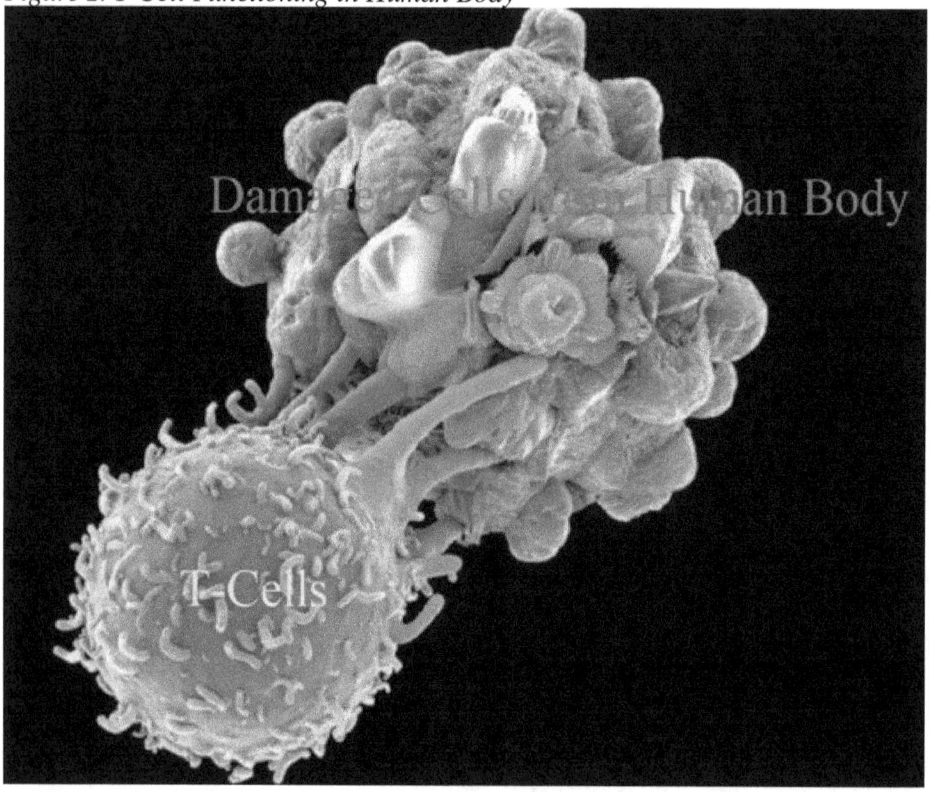

T-cells may also remember pathogens they have already encountered, which enables them to respond quickly and efficiently in the case of a recurring infection. This is the fundamental concept of vaccination, which includes injecting a pathogen—either dead or weakened—into the body to trigger the production of T cells and boost the immune system. In this way, the body prepares to fight the virus itself in the future. Though this isn't always the case, T-cells are capable of defending the body. They can occasionally become overactive and begin targeting healthy cells, which can lead to autoimmune diseases including multiple sclerosis, rheumatoid arthritis, and type 1 diabetes. But an immune system that is weak or broken can also make it harder for the body to fight off infections, which can lead to diseases like HIV/AIDS and cancer. Maintaining a functional immune system depends on having a population of T-cells that is both diverse and in balance. You can do this by leading a healthy lifestyle that consists of regular exercise, a balanced diet, and adequate sleep. Vaccinations also play a critical role in maintaining the body's T-cell population. Immunotherapy has advanced significantly in the last several years, using T-cells to treat a wide range of diseases. One example of this is CAR T-cell therapy, which involves genetically modifying T cells to recognize and attack cancer cells. After demonstrating excellent results in curing some forms of cancer, this novel medication is being further studied for its potential to treat other ailments.

When everything is considered, T-cell theory plays a crucial role in the functioning of the human immune system. The discovery of these powerful cells has fundamentally altered our understanding of and strategy for treating a variety of diseases. They play a crucial role in protecting the body from diseases and infections. Immunizations and a healthy lifestyle are essential for maintaining a robust immune system, which is necessary for T-cell function in the body.

PROPOSED KK APPROACH: SOLICITATION OF T-CELL IN MALICIOUS NODE DETECTION

According to Kutubuddin(2024c), this technique for identifying malicious nodes is known as the KK approach. This method, commonly known as the "KK Approach" for malicious node detection, was originally created by author Kazi Kutubuddin. The important components of the immune system that exists in the human body is the idea of T-cells. T-cells are the cells responsible for recognizing and eliminating any infections, germs, viruses, and other foreign objects that enter the body. T-cell theory can also be used to the subject of computer networks, specifically to the problem of managing hostile nodes. The steps involved in developing a T-cell-based malicious node detection system for an IoT network are shown in Figure 3.

Computers and other network-connected devices which have been intentionally configured or built with the goal of disrupting or damaging the network in some other way are known as malicious nodes. These nodes are capable of launching a wide range of attacks, including denial-of-service attacks, virus infections, and data theft incidents. They are present in both wired and wireless networks, and their presence can substantially compromise the network's security and functionality.

In a network, T-cells can be utilized to identify and remove malignant nodes in a similar way to how the body's immune system reacts to potentially harmful chemicals. Setting up a defensive system that can recognize and isolate any wireless network activity deemed suspicious or harmful is necessary in order to carry out this technique.

The first step in putting the T-cell concept into practice is to establish a baseline for normal network operation. Monitoring and analyzing communication protocols, traffic patterns, and other network activity is necessary to ascertain what conduct is considered normal. Any departure from this standard could be interpreted as possibly malicious activity, calling for additional research.

Afterwards, intrusion detection systems (IDS)—a type of specialized hardware or software—may be installed on the network. To find potential threats, these systems employ a variety of methods, including anomaly detection, behavior-based detection, and signature-based detection. Additionally, they can be set up to respond or sound an alert in the case that a rogue node is found.

Figure 3. Designing steps for Proposed KK approach

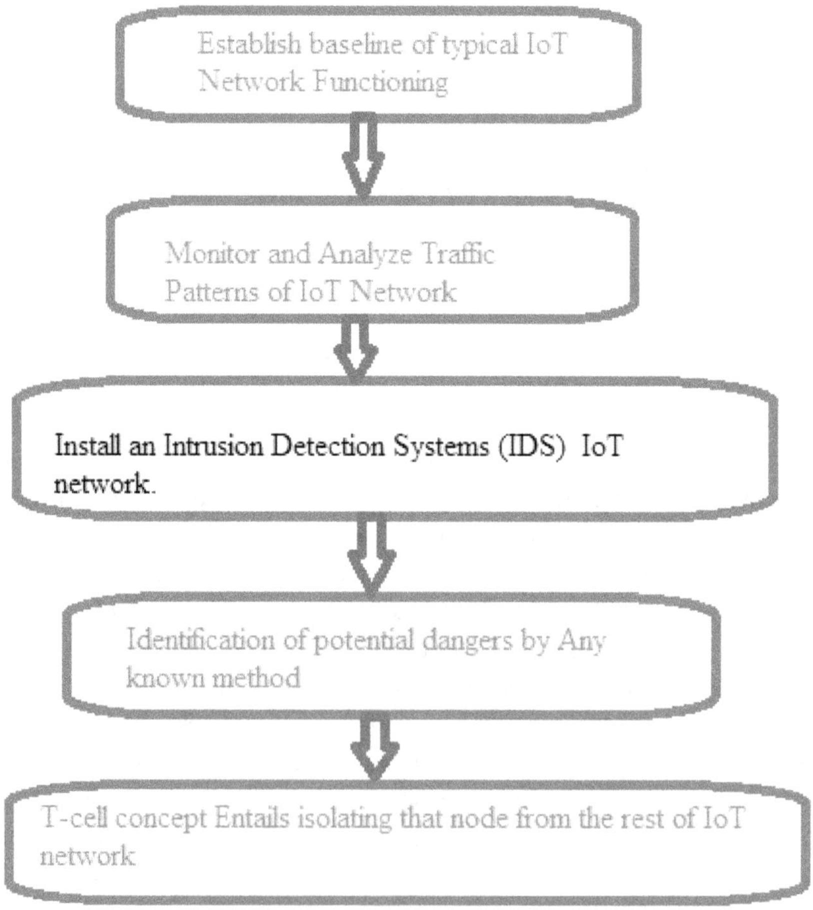

The T-cell concept entails cutting off a malicious node from the rest of the network as soon as it is discovered in order to prevent additional damage. By utilizing firewalls or access control lists (ACLs) to prevent communication between the rogue node and other network-connected devices, this goal can be accomplished.

An additional important component of the T-cell approach is the ongoing monitoring and improvement of the defence mechanisms inside the network. Regular upgrades of the network's security measures are necessary to keep up with the constantly evolving tactics employed by hostile nodes. This is similar to how the immune system of the body adjusts to new dangers. This set of activities consists of, but is not restricted to, putting new security measures into place, keeping intrusion detection systems up to date, and carrying out regular security audits.

The T-cell concept also emphasizes the value of collaboration and information exchange across many networks. Similar to how antibodies in the body can travel from one person to another, network managers can share information about known hostile nodes and their attack techniques to prevent similar attacks from occurring in other networks.

Figure 4. Nodes setup design using NS2

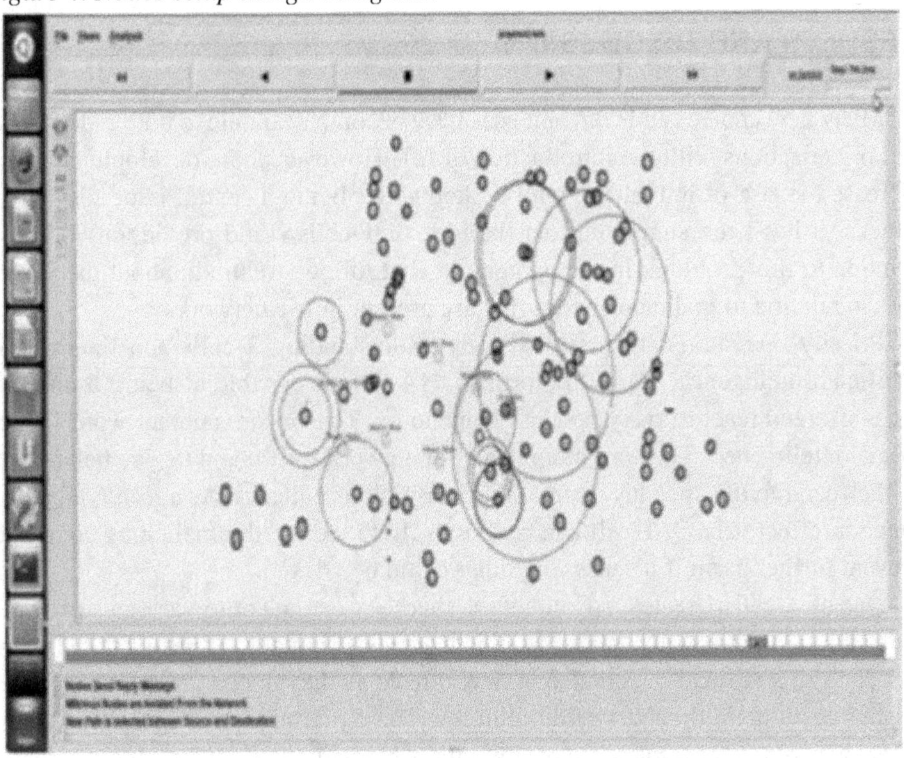

One practical method for dealing with rogue nodes in computer networks is the T-cell idea. By exchanging information about compromised nodes, isolating them, and continuously monitoring and adjusting to the network's changing behaviour, this technique can successfully increase the security and resilience of any network. As the threat posed by these hostile nodes only escalates, network managers need to seriously consider turning this idea into reality in order to safeguard their networks from any incursions.

Here, we investigate the effectiveness of our proposed KK-approach for attack awareness strategy in terms of several key performance metrics, including delay, and throughput. We evaluated the suggested system's functionality using the NS-2 simulator. The delay is the amount of extra time needed for the data packet to get to its destination. The test uses a 500 × 500 meter network region, and each session consists of 250 packets with a packet size of 1000 bytes (Figure 4). The preset bandwidth (BW) has a range of 10–20 megahertz. In contrast, throughput in data transmission describes the amount of data that is successfully moved from one location to another within a specific amount of time. Bits per second (bps) is a commonly used unit of measurement for network performance.

RESULTS AND DISCUSSION

Many new choices and conveniences have become available to both individuals and organizations with the introduction of IoT. However, these developments also increase the risk of intrusions, with broken nodes being a central issue for cyber-attacks. It has been suggested that the idea of T-cells could provide a workable solution to this problem. In the paragraphs that follow, we'll talk about the T-cell idea in relation to malicious nodes that are present in IoT networks.

Priority one should be given to fully understanding T-cells and their roles. Artificial intelligence(AI) in the form of "T-cells" is capable of being trained to recognize and react to risky network behaviours. Tensors are another word for artificial intelligence. They are monitoring all network traffic and device behaviour, so they can rapidly spot any anomalies or suspicious patterns. As a result, they can function effectively. A T-cell can react swiftly to isolate the malicious node and prevent further harm if it senses anything could be wicked.

One of T-cell's greatest advantages is that they can adapt to various surroundings and learn new skills. With machine learning (ML) algorithms installed, they can analyze historical data and spot new threats as they appear, allowing them to continuously hone their detection abilities. The dynamic nature of cyberattacks, where new plans and strategies are continually being devised, makes this extremely advantageous because hackers are continuously coming up with new techniques and methods.

Figure 5. Delay Comparison with proposed KK Approach

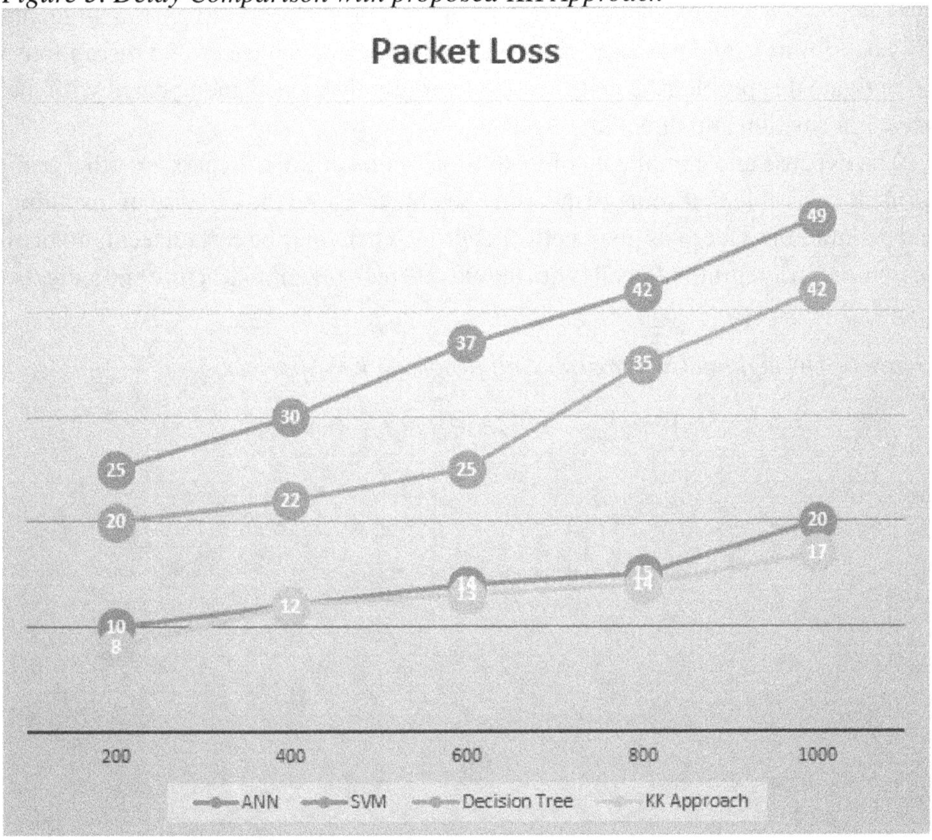

T-cells' capacity for collaboration and communication allows them to create a network of defence against hostile nodes. This implies that if a single T-cell notices a threat, it can swiftly alert other T-cells in the network to this information, allowing for the timely and coordinated implementation of a suitable response. This collaborative strategy is particularly crucial in the setting of Internet of Things networks, where there is a constant increase in the number of connected devices and a higher risk of assaults.

Another essential aspect of T-cells is their capacity to carry out their tasks alone, without the assistance of humans. This is especially useful for Internet of Things networks, as there may be too many devices and data for human operators to handle and keep track of. T-cells are better suited to provide a more effective and efficient form of protection since they are able to monitor and analyze network activity continuously, around-the-clock.

Like any other technology, the T-cell concept is not without its difficulties and restrictions, though. One of the main issues, though, is the possibility of false positives, which occur when a T-cell misinterprets normal network activity as malignant. This possibility could put users through needless inconveniences and disruptions. To mitigate this problem, T-cells need to be routinely trained and updated with the latest information and threat intelligence.

The expense and complexity of installing T-cells in IoT networks are other concerns. It's possible that some firms won't be able to afford the expense of installing and maintaining T-cells as these networks grow. There may be certain technological difficulties in integrating T-cells with the current network infrastructure and gadgets.

Figure 6. Throughput Comparison with proposed KK Approach

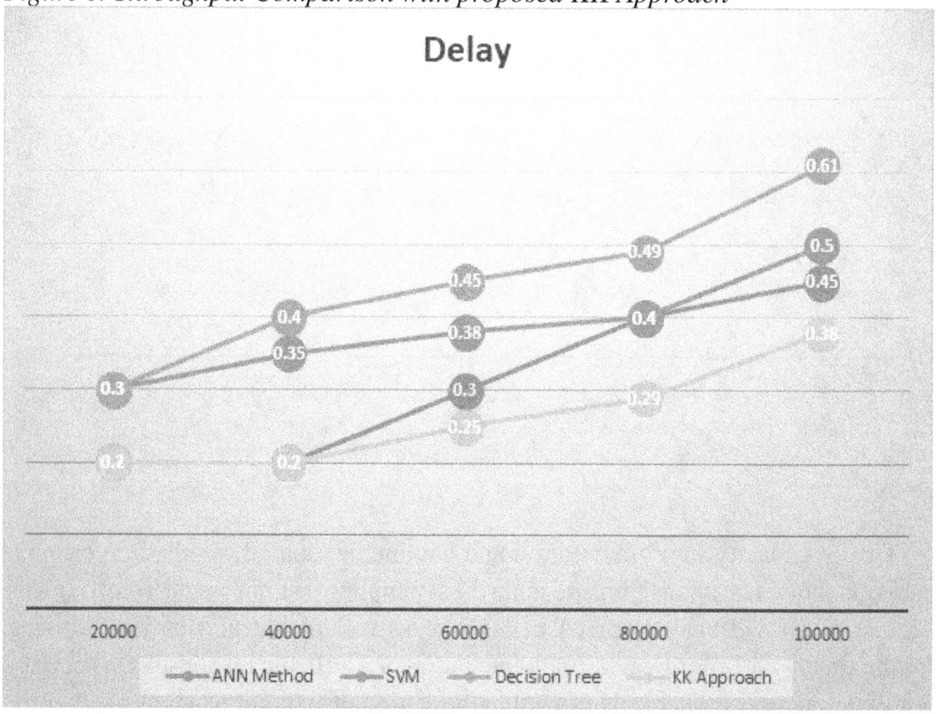

In conclusion, the T-cell idea has a lot of potential to lessen the threat that rogue nodes pose to Internet of Things networks. It is a potent weapon in the battle against cyber threats because of its capacity for learning, adapting, collaborating, and acting independently while maintaining its capacity for learning. However, additional study and advancement are required to overcome the restrictions and difficulties related to its application. As our reliance on IoT devices in our daily lives grows, we must continue to research and invest in new solutions to guarantee the security and privacy of these networks.

For IoT Nodes, only bandwidth (BW) of 2MHz, 4MHz, or 6MHz is doable. A bandwidth of 2 Mbps has been assigned to the shared control channel. The final results, shown below, are the average of ten different simulation runs' worth of data. Techniques for creating a path from the beginning locations to the destination are shown in Figure 4. Insensitive nodes in a network increase latency. When there is an excessive latency in the system, the KK-approach is employed to detect these harmful activities.

The differences in delay between the standard approaches and the innovative KK-approach are shown in Figure 5. The study's findings demonstrate that, as compared to the widely used methodology for discovering hostile entities in networks, the recommended method—which is shown by the Golden line—has a very little delay.

Network throughput in data transmission is the quantity of data that is successfully transported from one site to another in a given amount of time. Generally, bits per second (bps) is used to indicate network throughput.

The throughput differences between the new KK-approach and the previous approaches are displayed in Figure 6. The results of the study show that the suggested method, shown by the Golden line, has a very small latency in comparison to the commonly used strategies for locating malicious elements in a network.

CONCLUSION

One growing concern that needs to be handled is the presence of malicious nodes in networks made up of Internet of Things devices. Taking the required safeguards is essential to guaranteeing the security and defence of IoT devices against hostile activities. This is because our reliance on these technologies is growing at a rapid rate. Author (Dr Kazi Kutubuddin) can build an IoT ecosystem that promotes increased safety and security for all parties involved by putting strong security rules in place and educating users. Author would say that the T-cell concept is a useful way to deal with malicious nodes that are present in computer networks. This technique can successfully improve the security and resilience of any network by continuously observing and adjusting to the network's changing behaviour, isolating potentially hazardous nodes, and communicating information about them. This can be accomplished by keeping an eye on network behaviour and acting appropriately as necessary. Network managers need to properly consider and apply this idea in order to protect their networks from potential breaches. This is due to the fact that they must act immediately as hostile nodes continue to represent a threat. Its ability to learn, adapt, cooperate, and act independently makes it a useful weapon in the fight against cyberthreats. It is also capable of learning. However, more research and development could be necessary to overcome the challenges and limitations associated with its application. Therefore, it is essential to continue looking into and supporting innovative technologies in order to guarantee the security and privacy of these networks. This is because we rely more and more on gadgets connected to the Internet of Things for our everyday needs. This technique for identifying malicious nodes is known by the inventor as the "KK approach." In this case, we calculate the throughput and latency and contrast it with the methods used currently, and received results are good as compared to recent frameworks.

FUTURE SCOPE

Although the author advises adopting the KK technique for the Internet of Things, the KK strategy for wireless networks like WSN will be work on it in the future. In the future, the author will work on the system's power, battery management, and packet loss. Throughput, delay, and packet loss are taken into account here. Furthermore, this KK strategy will be used in conjunction with the KSK approach for IoT-based decision-making systems. Utilizing the KK and KSK techniques is advised by Dr. Kazi Kutubuddin.

ABREVIATIONS

IoT- Internet of Things
WSN- Wireless Sensor Network
IIoT- Industrial IoT

ACKNOWLEDGEMENT

I Acknowledged by parents for supporting me and guiding me for making my research successful. They provides me support throughout my work.

CONFLICT- NO CONFLICT

FUNDINGS- NIL

REFERENCES

Gund, V. D.. (2023). PIR Sensor-Based Arduino Home Security System. *Journal of Instrumentation and Innovation Sciences*, *8*(3), 33–37.

Halli, U. M. (2022). Nanotechnology in IoT Security, *Journal of Nanoscience. Nanoengineering & Applications*, *12*(3), 11–16.

Karale Aishwarya A, et al,(2023). Smart Billing Cart Using RFID, YOLO and Deep Learning for Mall Administration, *International Journal of Instrumentation and Innovation Sciences*, Vol 8, Issue- 2.

Kasat, K., Shaikh, N., Rayabharapu, V. K., & Nayak, M. (2023). Implementation and Recognition of Waste Management System with Mobility Solution in Smart Cities using Internet of Things, *2023 Second International Conference on Augmented Intelligence and Sustainable Systems (ICAISS)*, Trichy, India, 2023, pp. 1661-1665, DOI: 10.1109/ICAISS58487.2023.10250690

Kazi, K. (2022). Detection of Malicious Nodes in IoT Networks based on packet loss using ML, *Journal of Mobile Computing, Communication & mobile. Networks*, *9*(3), 9–16.

Kazi, K. (2024). Complications with Malware Identification in IoT and an Overview of Artificial Immune Approaches. *Research & Reviews. The Journal of Immunology : Official Journal of the American Association of Immunologists*, *14*(01), 54–62.

Kazi, K. (2024a). AI-Driven IoT (AIIoT) in Healthcare Monitoring. In Nguyen, T., & Vo, N. (Eds.), *Using Traditional Design Methods to Enhance AI-Driven Decision Making* (pp. 77–101). IGI Global., available at https://www.igi-global.com/chapter/ai-driven-iot-aiiot-in-healthcare-monitoring/336693, DOI: 10.4018/979-8-3693-0639-0.ch003

Kazi, K. (2024a). Machine Learning (ML)-Based Braille Lippi Characters and Numbers Detection and Announcement System for Blind Children in Learning. In Sart, G. (Ed.), *Social Reflections of Human-Computer Interaction in Education, Management, and Economics*. IGI Global., DOI: 10.4018/979-8-3693-3033-3.ch002

Kazi, K. (2024a). IoT Technologies for the Intelligent Dairy Industry: A New Challenge. In Thandekkattu, S. G., & Vajjhala, N. R. (Eds.), *Designing Sustainable Internet of Things Solutions for Smart Industries*. IGI Global. DOI: 10.4018/979-8-3693-5498-8.ch012

Kazi, K. (2024b). Modelling and Simulation of Electric Vehicle for Performance Analysis: BEV and HEV Electrical Vehicle Implementation Using Simulink for E-Mobility Ecosystems. *In L. D., N. Nagpal, N. Kassarwani, V. Varthanan G., & P. Siano (Eds.), E-Mobility in Electrical Energy Systems for Sustainability* (pp. 295-320). IGI Global. Available at: https://www.igi-global.com/gateway/chapter/full-text-pdf/341172DOI: 10.4018/979-8-3693-2611-4.ch014

Kazi, K. (2024b). Artificial Intelligence (AI)-Driven IoT (AIIoT)-Based Agriculture Automation. In Satapathy, S., & Muduli, K. (Eds.), *Advanced Computational Methods for Agri-Business Sustainability*. IGI Global., DOI: 10.4018/979-8-3693-3583-3.ch005

Kazi, K. (2024b). Machine Learning-Driven-Internet of Things(MLIoT) Based Healthcare Monitoring System. In Wickramasinghe, N. (Ed.), *Impact of Digital Solutions for Improved Healthcare Delivery*. IGI Global.

Kazi, K. (2024c). Moonlighting in Carrier. In Tunio, M. N. (Ed.), *Applications of Career Transitions and Entrepreneurship*. IGI Global.

Kazi, K. (2024c). AI-Powered-IoT (AIIoT) based Decision Making System for BP Patient's Healthcare Monitoring: KSK Approach for BP Patient Healthcare Monitoring. In Aouadni, S., & Aouadni, I. (Eds.), *Recent Theories and Applications for Multi-Criteria Decision-Making*. IGI Global. DOI: 10.4018/979-8-3693-6502-1.ch008

Kazi, K. (2024c). AI-Driven-IoT (AIIoT) based Decision-Making in Drones for Climate Change: KSK Approach. In Aouadni, S., & Aouadni, I. (Eds.), *Recent Theories and Applications for Multi-Criteria Decision-Making*. IGI Global. DOI: 10.4018/979-8-3693-6502-1.ch011

Kazi, K. S. (2022). IoT-Based Healthcare Monitoring for COVID-19 Home Quarantined Patients. *Recent Trends in Sensor Research & Technology*, *9*(3), 26–32.

Kazi, K. S. (2023a). Detection of Malicious Nodes in IoT Networks based on Throughput and ML. *Journal of Electrical and Power System Engineering*, *9*(1), 22–29.

Kazi K S,(2023b). IoT based Healthcare system for Home Quarantine People, *Journal of Instrumentation and Innovation sciences,*, Vol 8, Issue 1, pp. 1- 8

Kazi, K. S. (2024). Machine Learning-Based Pomegranate Disease Detection and Treatment. In Zia Ul Haq, M., & Ali, I. (Eds.), *Revolutionizing Pest Management for Sustainable Agriculture* (pp. 469–498). IGI Global., DOI: 10.4018/979-8-3693-3061-6.ch019

Kazi, K. S. (2024a). Computer-Aided Diagnosis in Ophthalmology: A Technical Review of Deep Learning Applications. In Garcia, M., & de Almeida, R. (Eds.), *Transformative Approaches to Patient Literacy and Healthcare Innovation* (pp. 112–135). IGI Global., Available at https://www.igi-global.com/chapter/computer-aided-diagnosis-in-ophthalmology/342823, DOI: 10.4018/979-8-3693-3661-8.ch006

Kazi, K. S. (2024b). IoT Driven by Machine Learning (MLIoT) for the Retail Apparel Sector. In Tarnanidis, T., Papachristou, E., Karypidis, M., & Ismyrlis, V. (Eds.), *Driving Green Marketing in Fashion and Retail* (pp. 63–81). IGI Global., DOI: 10.4018/979-8-3693-3049-4.ch004

Kazi, K. S. L. (2024). IoT and Sensor-based Smart Agriculturing Driven by NodeMCU. *Research & Review: Electronics and Communication Engineering*, *1*(2), 25–33.

Kazi, K. S. L. (2024). Smart Agriculture based on AI-Driven-IoT(AIIoT): A KSK Approach, *Advance Research in Communication Engineering and its. Innovations*, *1*(2), 23–32.

Kazi, V.. (2023). Deep Learning, YOLO and RFID based smart Billing Handcart. *Journal of Communication Engineering & Systems*, *13*(1), 1–8.

Kutubuddin, K. (2024c). Vehicle Health Monitoring System (VHMS) by Employing IoT and Sensors, *Grenze International Journal of Engineering and Technology,* Vol 10, Issue 2, pp- 5367-5374. Available at: https://thegrenze.com/index.php?display=page&view=journalabstract&absid=3371&id=8

Kutubuddin, K. (2024d). A Novel Approach on ML based Palmistry, *Grenze International Journal of Engineering and Technology,* Vol 10, Issue 2, pp- 5186-5193. Available at: https://thegrenze.com/index.php?display=page&view=journalabstract&absid=3344&id=8

Kutubuddin, K. (2024e). IoT based Boiler Health Monitoring for Sugar Industries, *Grenze. IACSIT International Journal of Engineering and Technology, 10*(2), 5178–5185. https://thegrenze.com/index.php?display=page&view=journalabstract&absid=3343&id=8

Liyakat, K. K. (2025). Heart Health Monitoring Using IoT and Machine Learning Methods. In Shaik, A. (Ed.), *AI-Powered Advances in Pharmacology* (pp. 257–282). IGI Global., DOI: 10.4018/979-8-3693-3212-2.ch010

Liyakat, K. K. S. (2022). Model for agricultural information system to improve crop yield using IoT. *Journal of Open Source Development*, *9*(2), 16–24.

Liyakat, K. K. S. (2022). IoT-based smart transportation system for passenger comfort. *Research & Reviews: Journal of Computation Biology*, *11*(2), 28–35.

Liyakat, K. K. S. (2023). Detecting Malicious Nodes in IoT Networks Using Machine Learning and Artificial Neural Networks, *2023 International Conference on Emerging Smart Computing and Informatics (ESCI)*, Pune, India, 2023, pp. 1-5, DOI: 10.1109/ESCI56872.2023.10099544

Liyakat, K. K. S. (2023). Machine Learning Approach Using Artificial Neural Networks to Detect Malicious Nodes in IoT Networks. In Shukla, P. K., Mittal, H., & Engelbrecht, A. (Eds.), *Computer Vision and Robotics. CVR 2023. Algorithms for Intelligent Systems*. Springer., DOI: 10.1007/978-981-99-4577-1_3

Liyakat, K. K. S. (2023a). IoT based Healthcare Monitoring for COVID-Subvariant JN-1. *Journal of Electronic Design Technology*, *14*(3).

Liyakat, K. K. S. (2023b). Smart Motion Detection System using IoT: A NodeMCU and Blynk Framework. *Journal of Microelectronics and Solid State Devices*, *10*(3).

Liyakat, K. K. S. (2024). Machine Learning Approach Using Artificial Neural Networks to Detect Malicious Nodes in IoT Networks. In Udgata, S. K., Sethi, S., & Gao, X. Z. (Eds.), *Intelligent Systems. ICMIB 2023. Lecture Notes in Networks and Systems* (Vol. 728). Springer., available at https://link.springer.com/chapter/10.1007/978-981-99-3932-9_12, DOI: 10.1007/978-981-99-3932-9_12

Liyakat, K. K. S. (2024). Explainable AI in healthcare. *Explainable Artificial Intelligence in Healthcare Systems*, *2024*, 271–284.

Liyakat, K. S. (2024). Blynk IoT-Powered Water Pump-Based Smart Farming. *Recent Trends in Semiconductor and Sensor Technology*, *1*(1), 8–14.

Liyakat, S. S. (2023). IoT Changing the Electronics Manufacturing Industry. *Journal of Analog and Digital Communications*, *8*(3), 13–17. DOI: 10.46610/JoADC.2023.v08i03.003

Liyakat, S. S. (2023). IoT in the Electric Power Industry. *Journal of Controller and Converters*, *8*(3), 1–7.

Liyakat Kazi, K. S. (2024). ChatGPT: An Automated Teacher's Guide to Learning. In Bansal, R., Chakir, A., Hafaz Ngah, A., Rabby, F., & Jain, A. (Eds.), *AI Algorithms and ChatGPT for Student Engagement in Online Learning* (pp. 1–20). IGI Global., DOI: 10.4018/979-8-3693-4268-8.ch001

Nagrale, M., Pol, R. S., Birajadar, G. B., & Mulani, A. O. (2024). Internet of Robotic Things in Cardiac Surgery: An Innovative Approach. *African Journal of Biological Sciences*, *6*(6), 709–725. DOI: 10.33472/AFJBS.6.6.2024.709-725

Neeraja, P., Kumar, R. G., Kumar, M. S., & Vani, M. S. (2024). *DL-Based Somnolence Detection for Improved Driver Safety and Alertness Monitoring. 2024 IEEE International Conference on Computing, Power and Communication Technologies (IC2PCT)*. Greater Noida., Available at https://ieeexplore.ieee.org/document/10486714, DOI: 10.1109/IC2PCT60090.2024.10486714

Nerkar, P. M., & Dhaware, B. U. (2023). Predictive Data Analytics Framework Based on Heart Healthcare System (HHS) Using Machine Learning, *Journal of Advanced Zoology*, Volume 44, Special Issue -2. *Page*, *3673*, 3686.

Pradeepa, M., ... (2022). Student Health Detection using a Machine Learning Approach and IoT, *2022 IEEE 2nd Mysore sub section International Conference (*MysuruCon), 2022.

Prasad, K. R., Karanam, S. R., Ganesh, D., Liyakat, K. K. S., Talasila, V., & Purushotham, P. (2024, May). AI in public-private partnership for IT infrastructure development. *The Journal of High Technology Management Research*, *35*(1), 100496. DOI: 10.1016/j.hitech.2024.100496

Veena, C., Sridevi, M., Liyakat, K. K. S., Saha, B., Reddy, S. R., & Shirisha, N. (2023). *HEECCNB: An Efficient IoT-Cloud Architecture for Secure Patient Data Transmission and Accurate Disease Prediction in Healthcare Systems, 2023 Seventh International Conference on Image Information Processing*. ICIIP., Available at https://ieeexplore.ieee.org/document/10537627, DOI: 10.1109/ICIIP61524.2023.10537627

Wale, A. D., & Dipali, R.. (2019). Smart Agriculture System using IoT. *International Journal of Innovative Research In Technology*, *5*(10), 493–497.

Chapter 11
Enhancing Textual Password Authentication Using Typing Rhythm

Ferdinand Apietu Katsriku
University of Ghana, Ghana

Samuel Darko Abankwah
University of Ghana, Ghana

Edward Danso Ansong
https://orcid.org/0009-0001-5536-4667
University of Ghana, Ghana

Winfred Yaokumah
https://orcid.org/0000-0001-7756-1832
University of Ghana, Ghana

ABSTRACT

This chapter aims to enhance the security of textual passwords by adding a new layer that involves an individual's typing rhythm without requiring additional devices. It discusses authentication methods and develops a textual password authentication system, which takes advantage of the fact that every user has a distinct way of typing. Twenty participants, including novice and expert users, assessed the proposed system. The measuring metrics used were the False Acceptance Rate (FAR) and False Rejection Rate (FRR). The flight time and typing rhythm were the biometric identification template. The results indicated low false rejection and acceptance rates, with the initial session registering 0.0 FRR and 0.1 FAR. Two weeks later, the second session recorded 0.25 FRR and 0.0 FAR. Using this model, users do not

DOI: 10.4018/979-8-3693-8014-7.ch011

need to select a complex password they might forget. Instead, they can utilize a good rhythm different from their natural typing rhythm, making it challenging to guess.

1. INTRODUCTION

Passwords are the most commonly used authentication method for digital systems, including email, social media networks, banking terminals, web and desktop applications, and network components like routers and switches (Pandey & Taffese, 2021). A password is a secret combination of characters that verifies the identity of a user accessing a system, device, application, or online account. The primary purpose of passwords is to provide security by ensuring that only authorized individuals can access protected resources (Salem et al., 2023). To enhance security, passwords must meet specific criteria, such as a minimum length and a combination of letters, numbers, and special characters, making them harder to guess or crack. Users must choose strong and unique passwords and avoid sharing them with others to protect their accounts from unauthorized access and potential security breaches (Cavus et al., 2023).

However, as internet services continue to expand, the security of passwords is becoming increasingly important. The amount of user identity information online is proliferating, and with it, the vulnerabilities of these systems (Lai & Arko, 2021). Unfortunately, as evidenced by the recent hacking of an online gaming company's servers (DiGiacomo, 2021), even sophisticated networks can still be compromised, putting sensitive information, such as Internet Protocol (IP) addresses, passwords, usernames, and email addresses, at risk. In many instances, individuals' accounts and reports document data have been breached. In the first half of 2022, the number of data breaches in the United States rose to 817, affecting over 53 million people (Verizon Report, 2023). While data breaches, data leakage, and data exposure are distinct events, they all share a commonality: unauthorized threat actors acquiring sensitive data. In 2016, Yahoo suffered the most significant data breach. Yahoo announced that hackers had taken user information linked to at least one billion accounts in 2013. In October 2017, the full scope of the breach was revealed when it was discovered that three billion accounts had been compromised (Haselton, 2017).

It is common for individuals with several passwords to forget them. Research has been conducted on how to manage numerous passwords. According to Verizon's 2017 Data Breach Investigations Report, weak or stolen passwords remain a primary cause of data breaches (Verizon Report, 2023). Hackers often rely on these types of passwords as they offer an easy, swift, and inconspicuous way to gain unauthorized access. Moreover, users can lose their passwords in several ways, including over-the-shoulder attacks, where someone steals a password by looking over the user's shoulder while they type it in (Liang et al., 2020). Also, brute force attacks that use automated applications to generate numerous consecutive guesses to obtain user credentials, such as passwords, usernames, or PINs, can compromise user accounts. To prevent these attacks, users are advised to use complex passwords that are difficult to break (Suleski et al., 2023). However, this can lead to users writing down their passwords or storing them in an electronic file, which can, in turn, compromise their security.

Due to the limitations of human memory, many people rely on password managers - software that stores all their passwords in a single file, protected by a strong master password. While this does alleviate the burden of memorizing numerous passwords, it also comes with its own set of risks. If the master password is compromised, all the user's accounts are vulnerable. Moreover, malicious malware that records keystrokes also significantly threatens user credentials. These threats cannot be mitigated by even the most robust passwords (Bonneau et al., 2015). A more robust solution that does not require users to remember complex passwords is needed. This chapter aims to improve textual password authentication security by implementing a new layer of protection through typing rhythm. The study seeks to create a more user-friendly and secure approach to verifying computer system users, adding an extra layer of security to textual password authentication without incurring additional costs. The importance of this study lies in enhancing password authentication models to improve data security, thereby reducing the incidence of data breaches. This research will help mitigate over-the-shoulder attacks, brute force attacks, phishing attacks, and keyloggers that hackers utilize to steal user passwords.

2. BACKGROUND

2.1 Authentication Methods

Authentication is verifying the identity of a user or entity attempting to access a system, application, or service (Cavus et al., 2023). It ensures that the individual or entity is who they claim to be before granting access to the requested resources. Authentication typically involves the presentation of credentials, such as a username and password, biometric data (e.g., fingerprint or facial recognition), security tokens, or other forms of identification. Various authentication methods, including single-factor, two-factor, and multi-factor authentication, are used to enhance security and verify the identity of users (Cavus et al., 2023). Robust authentication mechanisms are essential to protect user data, prevent unauthorized access, and ensure the security of systems. Two-factor authentication (2FA) adds an extra layer of security by requiring two different forms of identification before granting access, such as a password and a unique code sent to a mobile device (Pandey & Taffese, 2021). Three-factor authentication schemes for protecting data from hacking and tampering involve smart cards, passwords, and biometrics (Tashtoush et al., 2022). This helps enhance security by making it more difficult for unauthorized users to gain access.

The cornerstone of data security lies in the authentication process, which ensures the user's identity is verified. Authentication methods can take on three distinct forms: knowledge-based (something the user knows), object or token-based (something the user has), and biometric-based (something the user is). Examples of object or token-based authentication include using ID cards or smartcards, while biometric-based authentication methods rely on signature detection or fingerprint recognition. Despite different authentication approaches, password authentication remains the most widely used mechanism for verifying user identity, as it is knowledge-based (Lai & Arko, 2021). This classification is illustrated in Figure 1.

Figure 1. Classification of authentication schemes

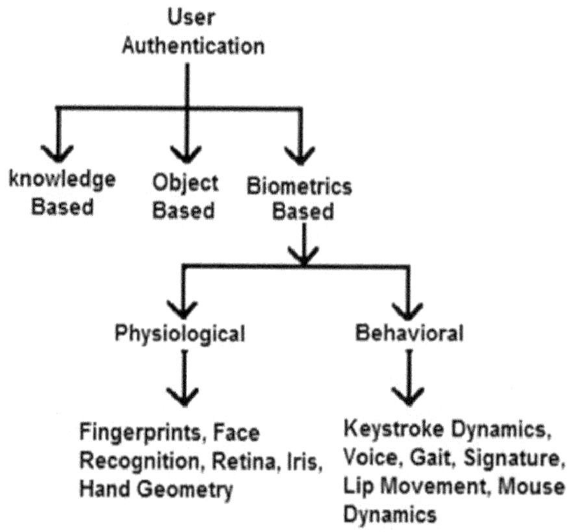

(Laxmi et al. et al., 2016)

Authentication methods are used to verify the identity of users. Several common types of authentication methods can be used to enhance security. These methods can be used alone or in combination to provide varying levels of security based on the sensitivity of the information or resources being accessed. These methods include:

2.1.1 Knowledge-based authentication

Knowledge-based authentication (KBA) is a widely used method for verifying user identity based on information that only the user is expected to know (Pandey & Taffese, 2021). This information includes passwords, PINs, and security questions. KBA is simple, cost-effective, and does not require additional devices. However, it is vulnerable to phishing, shoulder surfing, and brute force attacks. Weak user behavior and security questions can make it less secure. Best practices for KBA include using strong passwords, implementing multi-factor authentication, regularly updating passwords, monitoring suspicious activity, and providing secure recovery options.

2.1.2 Possession-based authentication.

Possession-based authentication is a security method that verifies a user's identity based on something they physically possess, such as a security token, smart card, mobile device, or USB security key (Pandey & Taffese, 2021). This method adds an extra layer of security beyond passwords, making it resistant to phishing attacks and convenient to use. However, there are potential disadvantages, such as the risk of physical loss or theft, implementation costs, user inconvenience, and compatibility issues. Best practices for implementing this authentication method include combining it with other authentication factors, providing user education, updating security protocols, monitoring unauthorized access, and establishing recovery options for lost or stolen devices.

2.1.3 Biometric authentication

Biometric authentication is a security process that utilizes unique physical or behavioral characteristics to verify an individual's identity. It can be categorized into physiological biometrics, which includes methods like fingerprint recognition and facial recognition, and behavioral biometrics, which involves analyzing patterns in human behavior, such as keystroke dynamics and voice recognition. The advantages of biometric authentication include high security, convenience, reduced risk of fraud, and non-transferability of biometric traits. However, there are also disadvantages, such as privacy concerns, false acceptance and rejection rates, implementation costs, and vulnerability to spoofing. Organizations should use multi-factor authentication, secure data storage, regularly update systems, educate users, and conduct regular audits to ensure effective biometric authentication. While biometric authentication offers significant security advantages, organizations must address associated challenges through best practices and integration into a broader security framework.

2.1.4 Inherence-based Authentication

Inherence-based authentication is a form of biometric authentication that verifies a user's identity based on unique biological traits or behavioral characteristics inherent to the individual. It utilizes physical or behavioral attributes such as fingerprint recognition, facial recognition, voice recognition, keystroke dynamics, and gait analysis to confirm identity. This method is considered more secure than traditional password-based methods, as it is difficult to replicate or steal biological traits. However, there are privacy concerns related to collecting and storing biometric data, as well as potential vulnerabilities to spoofing and high implementation costs. Despite these drawbacks, inherence-based authentication is widely used in mobile devices, financial services, access control, and healthcare to ensure secure access and transactions. Organizations should implement strong data protection measures, obtain user consent, keep systems updated, and provide fallback options to maximize the effectiveness and security of inherence-based authentication.

2.1.5 Multi-Factor Authentication (MFA)

Multi-factor authentication (MFA) is a security measure requiring multiple verification factors to access resources like applications or online accounts. These factors include "something you know," like passwords; "something you have," such as a smartphone or security token; and "something you are," like biometric data. MFA enhances security by reducing the risk of unauthorized access and helps protect against phishing attacks. While MFA provides significant security benefits, there are also some challenges, such as potential user inconvenience and implementation costs. Organizations should educate users, implement adaptive authentication, regularly review and update MFA methods, provide backup options, and monitor access to maximize MFA. In summary, MFA is crucial for modern cybersecurity, effectively safeguarding sensitive information and systems. Despite the challenges, the security advantages of MFA outweigh the drawbacks, helping organizations protect their assets and comply with regulations while instilling user confidence in their security measures.

2.1.6 Risk-based authentication

Risk-based authentication (RBA) is a security approach that evaluates the risk level of each user's login attempt and adjusts the authentication requirements accordingly. It analyzes user behavior, device recognition, geolocation, network security, time of access, and transaction behavior. RBA offers enhanced security, a seamless user experience, and dynamic adaptability. However, implementing RBA can be complex, lead to false positives, and raise privacy concerns. It is widely used in financial services, e-commerce, healthcare, and corporate environments. To effectively implement RBA, organizations should define risk criteria, educate users, update risk models regularly, ensure data privacy, and provide alternative authentication methods.

2.2. Biometrics

Biometrics uses an individual's unique physical or behavioral characteristics to identify and authenticate their identity. These characteristics include fingerprints, facial features, iris or retina patterns, voice, and behavioral traits like typing, rhythm, or gait (Oravec, 2022). Biometric technology uses sensors and algorithms to capture and analyze these characteristics and compare them to a database of known identities to verify or authenticate a person's identity. Biometric technology is increasingly used in various applications, including security systems, access control, and identification and authentication processes in various industries (Oravec, 2022). Biometric systems can be divided into two categories: physiological and behavioral. Physiological biometrics utilize bodily features such as fingerprints, retina scans, facial recognition, DNA, and scent to identify and verify an individual. On the other hand, behavioral biometrics rely on personal behavior patterns, such as handwritten signatures, voice patterns, mouse movement, or keystroke dynamics, to authenticate the user. Both physiological and behavioral biometrics have unique characteristics that make them reliable and secure in user identification.

These biometric methods offer a more secure and convenient way to authenticate users in various applications, including healthcare systems. They are difficult to replicate or forge, making them ideal for enhancing security in multi-factor authentication systems. Biometric methods are an authentication factor that relies on an individual's unique physical or behavioral characteristics for identity verification. These methods are considered more secure and reliable compared to traditional password-based authentication. Some standard biometric methods include (Suleski et al., 2023):

2.2.1 Fingerprint Recognition

Fingerprint recognition is a biometric authentication method that utilizes the unique patterns of ridges and valleys on an individual's fingertips to verify their identity. The technology involves capturing the fingerprint image using a scanner, processing the image to extract unique features, and storing the resulting template in a database for future comparisons. Fingerprint recognition offers advantages such as uniqueness, ease of use, speed, cost-effectiveness, and a low false acceptance rate.

However, it also presents certain disadvantages, including the potential for a false rejection rate, spoofing risks, privacy concerns, and susceptibility to environmental factors. The technology finds applications in various sectors, including mobile devices, access control systems, financial services, law enforcement, and healthcare, where it is used for secure unlocking, access control, secure transactions, criminal investigations, and securing patient records.

2.2.2 Face Recognition

Face recognition is a biometric technology used to identify or verify a person's identity by analyzing facial features. The process involves capturing an image of the face, detecting the face within the image, extracting unique features, creating a digital template, and matching it against stored templates for authentication. It offers advantages such as non-intrusiveness, speed, scalability, versatility, and integration with other systems. However, face recognition also has disadvantages, including privacy concerns, accuracy issues, bias and discrimination, and vulnerabilities to spoofing attacks. Despite these drawbacks, face recognition technology finds applications in security and surveillance, access control, mobile devices, retail and marketing, and healthcare for various identification and authentication purposes.

2.2.3 Voice Recognition

Voice recognition, also known as speech recognition, is a technology that converts spoken language into text or commands, enabling interaction with devices and systems through voice. It operates through audio capture, preprocessing, feature extraction, pattern recognition, and output generation. The advantages of voice recognition include hands-free operation, accessibility for individuals with disabilities, speed and efficiency, natural interaction, and integration with smart devices. However, voice recognition systems may struggle with accuracy, privacy concerns, limited vocabulary, internet connectivity dependency, and spoofing vulnerability. This technology is widely used in virtual assistants, customer service, healthcare, automotive systems, and security and authentication.

2.2.4 Iris Recognition

Iris recognition is a biometric identification method that uses unique patterns in the colored part of the eye to verify an individual's identity. The process involves capturing a high-resolution image of the iris, preprocessing the image to enhance its quality, extracting unique features, creating a biometric template, and matching the template for authentication. This technology boasts high accuracy, is non-invasive, resistant to forgery, and has broad applicability. However, it has some drawbacks, including high implementation costs, susceptibility to environmental factors, and potential privacy concerns. Iris Recognition finds applications in security and access control, border control, banking and financial services, mobile devices, and healthcare settings.

2.2.5 Signature Recognition

Signature recognition is a biometric authentication method that analyzes the unique characteristics of an individual's handwritten signature to verify their identity. The process involves capturing an image of the signature, preprocessing it to enhance quality, extracting features such as geometric and dynamic elements, creating a biometric template, and using matching algorithms for authentication. Signature recognition's advantages include familiarity, cost-effectiveness, non-invasiveness, dynamic authentication, and broad applicability. However, disadvantages include variability in signatures, forgery risk, limited security compared to other biometric methods, potential user discomfort, and susceptibility to environmental factors. Signature recognition finds applications in various sectors, including banking and financial services, legal documents, digital signatures, healthcare, and e-commerce, where it is used for verifying transactions, authenticating documents, and enhancing security.

2.2.6 Behavioral Biometrics

Behavioral biometrics is a form of biometric authentication that focuses on analyzing unique patterns of behavior exhibited by individuals when interacting with devices or systems. Unlike physiological biometrics, which rely on physical characteristics, behavioral biometrics examines user actions and behaviors unique to each individual. The process involves data collection, feature extraction, template creation, continuous monitoring, and matching and authentication. One advantage of behavioral biometrics is its continuous authentication capability, providing an additional layer of security beyond initial login credentials. It is also non-intrusive, difficult to forge, cost-effective, and user-friendly. However, it has disadvantages, such as variability in behavioral patterns, privacy concerns, limited accuracy in specific contexts, user resistance, and susceptibility to environmental factors. Behavioral biometrics finds applications in cybersecurity, financial services, healthcare, e-commerce, and mobile devices, offering enhanced security measures for user authentication, fraud detection, and access to sensitive data.

2.3 Keystroke Dynamics

Keystroke dynamics, also known as keystroke biometrics, is a behavioral biometric authentication method that analyzes the unique typing patterns of individuals to verify their identity (Choi et al., 2021). It captures and analyzes the timing and non-timing features of a user's keystrokes, such as the time intervals between keystrokes, key hold times, and key release times. The time information defines the pressing and release of each key as the user types. It checks individuals based on their distinct typing patterns as a user authentication mechanism. As timing information, the flight and dwell times are utilized in keystroke biometrics measurement. Timing information describes when a key on a keyboard is depressed and released by measuring each essential action in milliseconds. Di-graph and tri-graph are additional types of time information. Flight Time is the time between pressing one key and releasing it before pressing the next. Dwell Time is the length of time a key is depressed. The advantage of keystroke dynamics for user authentication is that it does not require additional hardware and can be seamlessly integrated into existing systems.

When a user types on a keyboard, their typing rhythm and behavior create a distinct pattern that can distinguish them from others (Laxmi et al., 2016). This pattern is unique to each individual and can be used as a form of biometric authentication. Keystroke dynamics authentication systems typically collect a user's typing patterns during an enrollment phase, where a profile is created for the user. During subsequent authentication attempts, the user's typing patterns are compared to the stored profile to verify their identity (Salem et al., 2023). Keystroke biometrics can be used in various applications, including user authentication, test security, and monitoring of writing fluency and style changes (Choi et al., 2021). The performance measures used to evaluate the proposed approach in the paper include (Salem et al., 2023):

- False Acceptance Rate (FAR): The rate at which the system incorrectly accepts unauthorized users.
- False Rejection Rate (FRR): The rate at which the system incorrectly rejects authorized users.
- Equal Error Rate (EER): The point where the FAR and FRR are equal indicates the balance between false acceptance and rejection rates.
- Accuracy: The overall correctness of the authentication system in distinguishing between authorized and unauthorized users.

2.3.1 Mechanism of Keystroke Dynamics

Keystroke dynamics is a behavioral biometric authentication method that analyzes an individual's unique typing patterns to verify their identity. It collects data during the enrollment phase, including keystroke timing and rhythm, and uses this information to create a biometric profile for authentication. The process involves data collection, feature extraction, template creation, and authentication. During subsequent login attempts, the system compares the user's typing patterns to the stored template to grant or deny access. Keystroke dynamics offer several advantages, including non-intrusiveness, continuous authentication, difficulty to forge, cost-effectiveness, and user-friendliness. However, there are also disadvantages, such as variability in typing patterns, a learning curve for users, limited accuracy in specific contexts, privacy concerns due to continuous monitoring, and potential resistance from users regarding privacy and intrusion.

2.3.2 Application and Best Practices for Implementing Keystroke Dynamics

Keystroke dynamics are used in various sectors, such as cybersecurity, financial services, healthcare, e-commerce, and education. It is employed to enhance security measures for user authentication, monitor transactions, detect fraudulent activities, secure sensitive data access, and ensure the integrity of online exams. Organizations should focus on user education, data security, regular updates, testing and calibration, and privacy considerations to implement keystroke dynamics systems effectively. It's essential to educate users about the benefits and functionality of keystroke dynamics; securely store collected data, keep the software updated, regularly test the system for accuracy and reliability, and address privacy concerns by implementing clear privacy policies and obtaining user consent for data collection and monitoring.

2.4 Related Works

Nowadays, almost every person has a password-protected account, including email, social media, ATMs, student or staff portals, and other online and offline accounts. Therefore, improving password security is critical for organizations and individuals who interact with these organizations (Abusham et al., 2022). Security threats to computerized information systems and confidential data include unauthorized access, modification, or malicious damage to hardware, software, data, or communication network resources. The ultimate goal of data security is to maintain the integrity, confidentiality, and safety of information, hardware, software, and data (Tashtoush et al., 2022)

Liang et al. (2020) proposed a new mobile terminal identity authentication system based on behavioral characteristics. The system collects smartphone sensor and touchscreen data and uses a combination of motion state detection and authentication modes to distinguish between legitimate users and others. The system achieves an accuracy rate of 95.96% with a false rejection rate of 2.55% and a false acceptance rate of 6.94%. The system can achieve implicit and continuous authentication, improving security and user experience (Liang et al., 2020). Andrean et al. (2020) proposed a deep-learning model using the CMU dataset to analyze keystroke dynamics. The deep learning classifier was able to distinguish genuine users from imposters with a 0.083 false acceptance rate (FAR), 0.006 false rejection rate (FRR), and a 0.0445 equal error rate (EER) based on data from the 15 users. The classifier's accuracy was 91.67%, correctly identifying 5100 out of 6000 instances. The Kappa statistic for the classifier indicated nearly perfect and favorable inter-observer agreement, with a coefficient of 0.90107. The deep learning classifier achieved superior performance on the same dataset compared to other classifiers for keystroke dynamics.

Patil and Renke (2016) developed a dynamic keystroke authentication method for user registration and login. When a user signs up for an application, she enters her username and password. If the password and confirmation password match, the user must type a sentence ten times. The system measures and analyzes characteristics such as dwell time and flight time as the user types. The derived averages are saved in the database with the user's name and password. During login, the user inputs her username and password. If they match the information stored in the database, the user is prompted to re-enter the same sentence she entered at registration. The keystroke analysis is calculated and compared to the database. The user is granted access if a match is found; otherwise, access is denied. The downside of this method is that it takes time for the user to complete the registration process. Typing the same sentence multiple times before registration affects the system's efficiency. Furthermore, since this is a behavioral biometric, the false rejection rate will increase as the user's typing style and speed change.

Mondal and Bours (2016) studied a user authentication and identification system that uses Pairwise User Coupling (PUC). The system utilizes data from both keystroke and mouse usage to identify users. In a closed set trial, the system achieved an identification accuracy of 62.2%, while an impostor required an average of 471 activities to be identified. In an open-set experiment, the system achieved a detection and identification rate (DIR) of 58.9% and required 333 steps to identify an impostor.

3. MATERIALS AND METHOD

This section focuses on the design of the proposed system, system environment, algorithm, tools, and metrics used.

3.1 Environment

When selecting a web application login, availability is often the most critical factor. It allows users to log in at any time and from any location. However, this approach has its drawbacks. Since user activity is uncontrolled, increased management and communication are required to ensure accurate data collection. Additionally, data may be uncertain because users have different environments, such as keyboards, systems, operating systems, and web browsers. This can result in incorrect data. A standalone application was developed for all tests to address this issue, assuming all users have the same conditions in a controlled environment. The Microsoft Windows-like login was chosen primarily because users of different ages and technical skill levels could quickly adapt. This would reduce the risk for computer users with limited skills while allowing advanced users to adjust to the technology's look and feel with fewer difficulties.

3.2 Keystroke Biometrics Measurement

The study focuses on keystroke dynamics as a behavioral biometric approach. Research shows that each user has a unique typing speed and style (Laxmi et al., 2016). This technology is cost-effective as no additional hardware is required for implementation; only software is needed. The study by Laxmi et al. (2016) investigates the dynamics of measuring keystrokes. It identifies the following characteristics: keystroke latency, duration of a keystroke, hold time, overall typing velocity, frequency of errors, and the force applied when typing.

Latency of keystroke and dwell time are the most frequently utilized keystroke dynamics features. The latency of keystroke refers to the interval between successive vital presses, while dwell time is when a key is pressed and when it is released. The study also identifies the most common evaluation metrics for authentication systems. False acceptance rate (FAR) and false rejection rate (FRR) are two measurements used. FAR refers to the rate at which unauthorized users are permitted access, while FRR refers to the rate at which authorized users are refused access. The equal error rate (EER) is another security indicator: the ratio of FAR to FRR. A low EER indicates a superior authentication system.

3.3 Typing Rhythm Mechanism

Typing rhythm is a style of typing characters on a keyboard. The latency times are the time gap between every two consecutive characters measured in milliseconds. This feature is captured and processed as demonstrated in Algorithm 1. When a key C2 is pressed after key C1, then the latency L is the time which had between the two key presses:

$$L_2 = T(c_2) - T(c_1)$$

where T is a time function that is used to get the current computer time at c_i. For a set of consecutive keystrokes of a user *i*, $L_i = < L_2, L_3 \ldots L_n >$ (Mansour & Mahmoud, 2021).

The algorithm provided (see Algorithm 1) explains how keystroke latency is captured. When a user types a key, the algorithm captures the keystroke and stores the capture time using a time function. The algorithm keeps running as long as the key captured is not the enter key. The first captured key is temporarily saved, and the following key is captured. The time difference between the keystrokes is then stored in a list. Once the user finishes entering their password and presses the enter key, the algorithm returns the list of keystroke latencies captured.

Algorithm 1: keystrokeLatencyCapture()

```
i = 0

K = get_pressed_key()

temp_Key = Time(K)

while (K != Key_Enter) do

K = get_pressed_key()

pressed_key = TIme(K)

Li[i] = pressed_key – temp_Key

temp_Key = pressed_key

i++
```

end while

return Li

3.4 Biometric Identification Templates

Biometric templates are digital representations of unique user characteristics generated from a biometric sample during enrolment. These templates are used for user verification and authentication. To determine the correct user, the biometric system compares the captured user samples with the user's biometric templates through a one-to-one comparison. When it comes to keystroke dynamics, three user identity templates are typically utilized during enrolment:

1. The user's typing speed when using a keyboard
2. Typing pattern, which can be a reliable indicator of the user's traits, actions, habits, and other observable features
3. Typing rhythm refers to the user's usual typing style on a keyboard.

3.5 Software Tools

To develop a login program based on the proposed model, the following software was required:

- Visual Studio 2012
- SQL Server Management Studio

C# was chosen to develop the login application due to the technological benefits of utilizing existing resources, such as libraries and built-in capabilities. One advantage of utilizing this programming language is the ability to construct windows and visual elements using the .NET framework. The .NET C# environment uses a Control *System.Windows.Forms* library with the *Control.KeyPress* Events Classes. These control classes manage the input and output data streams on the keyboard port. Studies on keystroke dynamics often utilize the input stream, as no commands are returned to the keyboard.

3.6 Metrics

The following metrics are used to evaluate the proposed model:

- False Acceptance Rate (FAR): Rate the number of impostors falsely accepted to the system. For example, a FAR of 3% indicates that 3 out of every 100 imposters are falsely accepted as valid users
- False Reject Error Rate (FRR): This rate quantifies the number of legitimate users who are falsely rejected and denied access to the system. For example, an FRR of 10% indicates that 10 out of every 100 legitimate users are rejected as invalid.
- Equal Error Rate (EER): Rate at which FAR equals FRR.
- Mean Error Rate (MER): Rate of the mean between FAR and FRR.
- Fail acQuire Rate (FQR): Distribution rate of invalid users for a particular feature. For instance, a user with an incorrect biometric trait, such as blindness, would fail the iris scan.

4. SYSTEM DESIGN

The first part of this section presents the design of the proposed system, and the second part is the experimentation phase, where carefully selected participants were used to try the system.

4.1 Design Phase

The design phase of this study consists of two sections: the user registration phase and the user login phase.

During the user registration phase, the user is presented with a registration form - similar to any other user authentication system. Firstly, the user is prompted to enter the username and password. Before entering the password, the user must visualize the rhythm to be used to type it, as this study utilizes a unique approach where a calculated rhythm is used to enter the password instead of the user's typing style. For example, if the user's password is 'k2fu44', the user does not type it with the typical typing style or speed. Instead, the user establishes a rhythm for it. Figure 2 shows an example of this rhythmic typing approach.

Figure 2. Timing difference between keystrokes

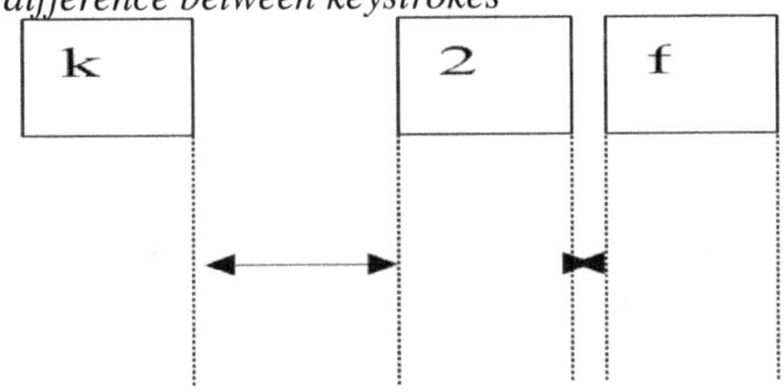

The typing pattern or rhythm is established by the variances in timing between successive keystrokes. For example, the time between 'k' and '2' is 2.4 seconds, between '2' and 'f' is 0.3 seconds, and between 'f' and 'u' is 1.9 seconds. These timing changes create the rhythm of the password. To confirm the password, the user re-enters it with the same rhythm. If the username already exists, a message prompts the user to change it. Once the username has been validated, the two passwords are compared. If they do not match, the user is prompted to try again. The keystroke features are extracted and temporarily stored as the user types the password. The most common features are the latency of keystrokes (flight time) and dwell time. This study focused on the flight time feature. If the two passwords match, their typing patterns are compared. If the matching accuracy is 75% or higher, the user's details, including the typing pattern, are saved in the database. Otherwise, an error message is displayed. The flowchart for the user registration process is shown in Figure 3.

Figure 3. Flowchart of the registration process

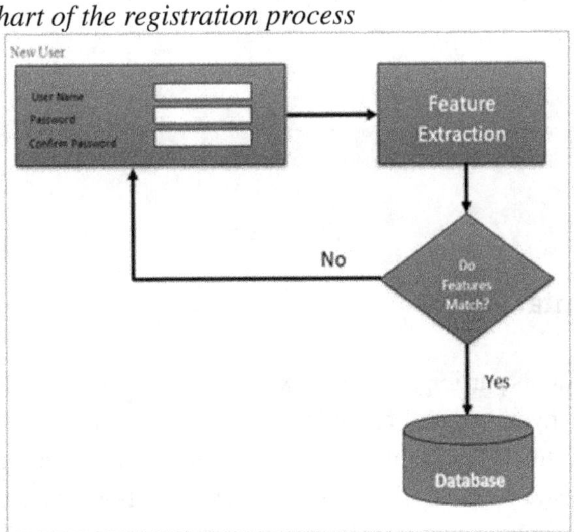

Secondly, the user login phase is shown in Figure 4. The figure depicts the design model of the login process. An individual enters their login credentials to be verified by the system. Firstly, the system checks whether the user has entered a username and password; otherwise, a validation message is displayed. If both the username and password are provided, the system extracts these features and compares them to the original data stored in the database. Initially, the username and textual password are compared to check if they match. If there is no match, the system displays another validation message to the user. However, the system compares patterns or latencies between successive keys if there is a match. The user is verified if the matching accuracy is 75% or higher. Otherwise, the system rejects the user. In a real-world scenario, the error message will be the same whether the textual password or the typing patterns do not match. This makes it more challenging for an attacker to recognize the extra layer of security added to the system, increasing the system's safety.

Figure 4. Flowchart of the Login process

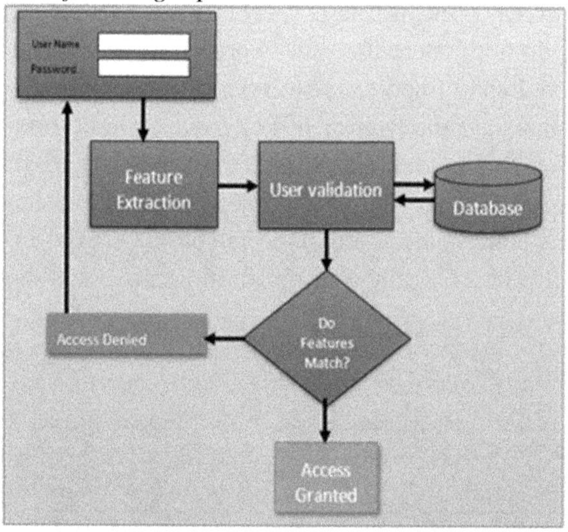

4.2 Experimental Phase

Twenty individuals participated in an experiment to assess whether this approach is more secure, convenient, and feasible for users. The participants were carefully selected to represent typical computer users, with an equal number of novice and expert users, men and women. All participants were well-versed in textual password authentication and were randomly chosen. The experimental phase comprised five distinct steps.

1. The first stage of the experimentation phase is the briefing. As this strategy is new, participants received a comprehensive introduction to the technique. The registration and login procedures were also demonstrated to help them better understand the approach.
2. In the second phase, participants were instructed to choose their passwords and rhythmic patterns. They were asked to do so individually and discreetly, using a login and password that they did not currently use since this exercise has an academic purpose. Their passwords will be retrieved. The participants' preferred patterns were repeated until they became familiar with them. The next step is to enrol in the system using the selected rhythmic pattern.
3. The login stage is the third stage of the experimental phase. Upon registration, participants were given a username and password and instructed to use them to log in to the program. However, access would only be granted if the correct pattern was entered alongside the password. This step aimed to measure the false rejection rate, which is the number of legitimate users denied access. Each participant was given three attempts to log in. If they failed after three attempts, they would be temporarily logged out to prevent impostors from guessing the rhythm or pattern.
4. In the fourth stage, participants were divided into two groups. Each group shared their usernames and passwords with the other group but did not reveal their typing patterns. This was done to determine the false acceptance rate. Participants then posed as impostors and attempted to log in using another user's login and password. The user access rate was measured.
5. The fifth phase was designed to test the system's protection against shoulder surfing. Participants were regrouped, and the first group observed the second group as they entered their credentials for authentication. The second group also had the opportunity to observe the first group. Based on their observations, they were then required to sign in. The total number of people with access to the system was determined.

Participants were asked to re-access their accounts two weeks later to determine the proportion of users who could log in after some time without typing their password or rhythm. The false rejection rate was once again measured.

5. SYSTEM IMPLEMENTATION

5.1 Legitimate User Authentication

As explained earlier, the False Rejection Rate (FRR) refers to the proportion of legitimate users denied access to a system (Patil and Renke, 2016). In the third stage of the experiment, we measured the FRR. Participants were asked to create an account using a unique typing pattern for the password. They were then given a maximum of three attempts to log in. According to the results, all twenty participants could log in without issues. Therefore, the FRR was zero. The graph shown in Figure 5 represents the percentage of participants who could log in versus those who were not. Of the twenty participants, sixteen (80%) could successfully log in on their first attempt, while the remaining four (20%) could log in on their second attempt. This information is also depicted in Figure 5.

Figure 5. Percentage of legitimate participants and the number of attempts

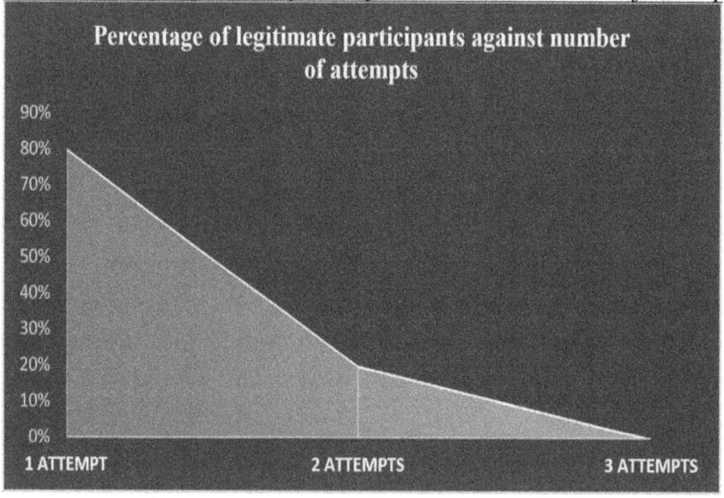

5.2 Impostor User Authentication

During the fourth stage of the experiment, the researchers aimed to determine the number of impostors who could successfully verify themselves as legitimate users by using the usernames and passwords of authentic individuals. This is known as the misleading acceptance rate. The participants were divided into two groups, and each group was given the login credentials of genuine users to test. The results of the fourth stage of the experiment showed that only two accounts, 10% of the total accounts created by the participants, were accessed by impostors. In comparison, 18 accounts (90%) remained inaccessible to them. This information is presented in Figure 6.

Figure 6. Percentage of Imposters Authentication

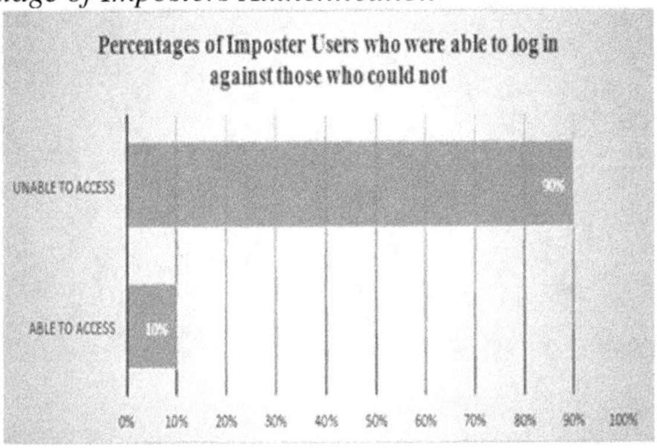

5.3 FRR of Legitimate Users after Two Weeks

Two weeks after introducing the proposed plan, the participants were contacted again to determine its practicality. Authorized users were asked to log in to their accounts once again. The results showed that 75% of legitimate users could log in successfully, while 25% could not. These findings were compared to the initial results and are represented in Figure 7.

Figure 7. Percentages of legitimate users logging in during the first and second sessions.

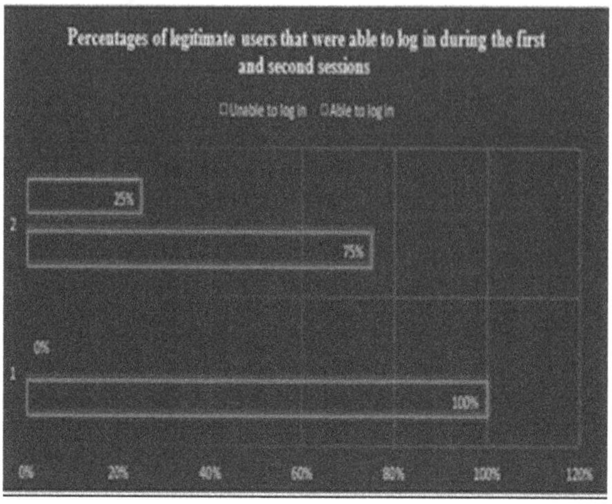

In summary, the false rejection and acceptance rates for both sessions are shown in Table 1.

Table 1. FRR and FAR of both sessions

Session	FRR	FAR
First Session	0%	10%
Second Session (After 2 Weeks)	25%	0%

6. SYSTEM EVALUATION

To determine the effectiveness of an authentication method, the false rejection and acceptance rates must be kept at a minimum (Patil and Renke, 2016). The experiments conducted were aimed at allowing the researchers to accurately determine the proposed technique's false rejection and acceptance rates.

All participants could access their accounts without issues during the first login session. This indicates that the system did not falsely reject any legitimate user during the initial session. Eighty percent of real users managed to log in on their first attempt, while 20% succeeded on their second try. No legitimate user attempted to access more than three times before successfully logging in.

During the second session, two weeks after the first session, 75% of authentic users could log in successfully, while the remaining 25% exhausted all three attempts. The first session had a false rejection rate (FRR) of zero percent, while the second had an FRR of 25%. This increase in FRR can be attributed to the small number of participants in the first session. Additionally, during the first session, participants' memories of the keystroke patterns were fresh, making it easier to recall. However, after two weeks of not practicing the pattern, some individuals could not remember it. This is a significant challenge of this study, as users must regularly practice the keystroke patterns until they become a part of their muscle memory. Normal keystroke dynamics may have an advantage over the proposed scheme, as the suggested scheme only relies on the user's typing style and does not require memorizing a rhythm.

During an experiment, 95% of imposter users could not log in, while 5% could guess the pattern of a valid user. This results in a false acceptance rate (FAR) of 5%. The study used keystroke dynamics where participants were asked to input their password in their usual fashion, making it easy for an adversary to deduce the pattern. Since most users have a similar typing style and speed, they may guess the typing style of another user. However, having a unique and consistent typing rhythm can make it difficult for an opponent to guess your movements. The third attempt to breach the sole compromised account was successful. However, the FAR was 0% during the second session because no imposter could get into the identical accounts they attempted during the first session. This demonstrates that the keystroke dynamics strategy is secure against imposters who accidentally obtain usernames and passwords.

The findings provide detailed statistics on the FAR and FRR. The study found a FAR of 5% during the initial sessions, indicating that a small percentage of imposters could successfully log in by guessing the typing pattern of legitimate users. However, this rate dropped to 0% in subsequent sessions, suggesting that the system became more secure over time. Moreover, the FRR was initially 0%, meaning all legitimate users could log in without issues. However, after two weeks, the FRR increased to 25%, highlighting a challenge in user retention of the typing patterns. This suggests that while the system is user-friendly, it requires regular practice to maintain effectiveness.

Moreover, the study found that many security schemes are vulnerable to shoulder surfing attacks. To address this issue, a proposed system was tested against such attacks. Results showed that 85 percent of imposters could not access accounts even after watching authentic users type, while 15 percent could gain access. This underscores the need for additional protective measures.

Most participants were familiar with user identification because of their experience with Facebook or email accounts. However, many were not skilled typists and only used a few fingers to type, making it easy for shoulder surfers to observe their typing habits. Unlike passwords, patterns cannot be easily written down; if the pattern is not practiced thoroughly, it will likely be forgotten quickly. After two weeks, none of the shoulder surfers could log in again. This vulnerability is significant because it shows that even with a secure system, user behavior and skill level can impact overall security. The chapter suggests that users need to develop a consistent typing rhythm to enhance security.

Thus, this study's low false rejection rate (FRR) suggests the system is user-friendly and easy to use. Users do not need to carry any additional equipment which could be forgotten or lost. Despite the modest number of members, the system's false acceptance rate (FAR) demonstrates its effectiveness in providing security. However, the increase in FRR after two weeks suggests that the system's usability could be improved by incorporating reminders or practice sessions to help users retain their typing patterns.

7. RECOMMENDATIONS AND FUTURE RESEARCH DIRECTIONS

7.1 Recommendations

The paper provides several recommendations for system administrators and users to implement the proposed typing rhythm authentication method effectively. To enhance account security, users should choose complex and unpredictable typing patterns that are difficult for attackers to guess. Regular practice of the selected patterns is recommended to reinforce memory and ensure reliable reproduction during authentication attempts, preferably at least twice a day for several days. Avoid writing down passwords or typing patterns to maintain account security and prevent undermining the proposed security enhancement method.

It is recommended that account access attempts be limited to prevent unauthorized users from guessing legitimate users' typing patterns through repeated attempts. System administrators should provide training and resources to educate users about the importance of typing rhythm authentication and how to use the system effectively. Continuous monitoring and adaptation of the typing rhythm authentication system based on user feedback and emerging security threats is crucial to maintain its effectiveness over time. Additionally, future research should explore additional biometric parameters, such as dwell duration and key pressure, to enhance the typing rhythm model and develop more robust authentication systems. By following these recommendations, organizations can improve the implementation and effectiveness of typing rhythm authentication, thereby enhancing overall security while ensuring a positive user experience.

7.2 Research Contributions

7.2.1 Theoretical Contributions

The paper on improving textual password authentication using typing rhythm makes several theoretical contributions to cybersecurity, biometrics, and human-computer interaction. These contributions include:

The research study significantly contributes to the theoretical framework of behavioral biometrics by introducing typing rhythm as a unique and reliable identifier for user authentication. This expansion in understanding highlights the potential of individual typing patterns as a complement to existing methods such as fingerprint and facial recognition. The study delves into the intricacies of keystroke dynamics, providing insights into both timing and non-timing features of keystrokes, including flight time and dwell time. These findings shed light on how these features can be effectively leveraged for user authentication, enhancing the theoretical discourse in this field.

To understand user behavior in authentication contexts, the research comprehensively explored the variability and uniqueness of typing rhythms among individuals. It sheds light on the potential to model and analyze these patterns to enhance security measures. The study also delved into the empirical data concerning false acceptance rates (FAR) and false rejection rates (FRR) linked to the proposed authentication method. This data enriched the theoretical understanding of the effectiveness of biometric systems and formed a basis for comparing the performance of typing rhythm authentication with other methods. Furthermore, the paper emphasizes the significance of user experience in security systems, advocating for implementing user-friendly authentication methods without compromising security. This perspective significantly contributed to the theoretical discourse on crafting security systems that prioritize usability alongside security, effectively addressing a common tension in the field.

The paper presents a comprehensive framework for guiding future research in biometric authentication. It lays the groundwork for further exploration of typing rhythm and other behavioral biometrics by highlighting current limitations and proposing directions for future studies. The aim is to deepen our understanding of their potential applications and implications within the broader context of authentication systems. Furthermore, the research establishes valuable interdisciplinary connections by drawing from computer science, psychology, and human-computer interaction. This integration of diverse perspectives contributes to a more holistic understanding of user-system interactions, enriching the theoretical landscape with insights from multiple fields.

7.2.2 Practical Contributions

The paper on improving textual password authentication using typing rhythm offers several practical contributions that can enhance security practices and user experiences in digital authentication.

The innovative authentication method introduces typing rhythm as a biometric authentication technique, which uses unique typing patterns to enhance password security. This approach makes it harder for unauthorized users to access systems, even if they possess the correct credentials. The proposed system is designed to be incredibly user-friendly. It requires no additional devices or complex memorization of passwords. This simplicity can lead to higher user compliance and satisfaction, as users often find it challenging to manage multiple complex passwords. Moreover, the method is not only practical but also cost-effective. It can be seamlessly integrated into existing systems without requiring significant changes or the need for new hardware. This factor makes it an appealing option for organizations seeking to bolster security measures without incurring substantial costs.

The proposed method mitigates the common security risks associated with traditional passwords. It explicitly addresses vulnerabilities such as shoulder surfing and brute force attacks, which are prevalent in typical password-based authentication systems. By doing so, the method significantly reduces the risk of unauthorized access, enhancing overall security in digital environments for individual users and organizations. Furthermore, the study offers actionable guidelines for users and system administrators. These guidelines include recommendations such as selecting complex patterns for authentication and regularly practicing secure authentication methods. Adhering to these guidelines can effectively enhance the authentication method's robustness and improve security practices.

The research provides a solid foundation for future exploration into biometric authentication methods, opening the door for further studies to delve into additional features and enhancements. This could pave the way for creating more resilient and adaptable authentication systems that can adjust to individual user behaviors. Moreover, the study confronts the considerable hurdles in password management by presenting an alternative to intricate passwords, which users often forget. Doing so addresses a significant pain point for users who struggle with remembering multiple passwords, ultimately enhancing their overall user experience.

7.3 Limitations

The study on improving textual password authentication using typing rhythm has several limitations that should be acknowledged.

The research findings may be limited in their applicability due to the small sample size used in the study. With only a limited number of participants, the generalizability of the findings may be compromised. This is because a small sample size can result in biased or skewed results and may not accurately reflect the typing behaviors and patterns of the larger population. Additionally, the typing rhythm authentication method was evaluated over a brief period, consisting of only two sessions spaced two weeks apart. This relatively short evaluation period may not provide a comprehensive understanding of the long-term stability and reliability of users' typing rhythms. Over time, users may alter or forget their typing patterns, which the short evaluation period may fail to capture. Furthermore, the study did not include testing the proposed method against brute force attacks due to resource constraints. The absence of this testing raises concerns about the system's robustness in real-world scenarios where attackers may attempt to exploit vulnerabilities by repeated guessing.

The effectiveness of the typing rhythm authentication method depends on users consistently practicing their chosen patterns. Research has shown that some users may struggle to recall their rhythms after a period of inactivity, suggesting that ongoing user engagement is necessary to maintain the method's effectiveness. Additionally, it's essential to consider environmental variability in testing. The study assumed a controlled environment, which may not accurately reflect the diverse conditions under which users typically log in. Factors such as different keyboards, operating systems, and settings could introduce variability that impacts the accuracy of typing rhythm measurements.

The adaptation of users' typing styles over time has the potential to impact the consistency of their typing rhythms, and this, in turn, could lead to higher false rejection rates if the system does not adjust for these changes in user behavior. In addition, the study primarily concentrated on typing rhythm as a biometric feature, potentially neglecting other important factors that could improve authentication accuracy. These factors may include typing speed, error rates, and the physical characteristics of the keyboard used. Considering these aspects could contribute to a more comprehensive and robust authentication system.

7.4 Future Research Directions

The research on improving textual password authentication using typing rhythm suggests several future research directions that could enhance the effectiveness and applicability of this approach.

Expanding the participant pool to include people from various demographic backgrounds and with different typing styles is recommended in future studies. This will allow for the validation of findings across diverse groups, providing insights into how factors like age, typing experience, and keyboard familiarity affect typing patterns and authentication accuracy. Additionally, it is advisable to explore incorporating additional biometric features, such as dwell time, key pressure, and mouse dynamics, to create a more comprehensive authentication system. By combining multiple behavioral biometrics, it may be possible to improve security and minimize the rates of false acceptance and rejection.

The current model has not undergone testing against brute force attacks because of limited resources. It is recommended that future studies focus on assessing the robustness of the typing rhythm authentication method against brute force attacks better to understand its effectiveness in practical, real-world scenarios. Additionally, further research could explore the impact of user training on the efficacy of typing rhythm authentication. Understanding how users can be trained to establish and maintain effective typing patterns could significantly enhance system reliability and user experience. Moreover, conducting longitudinal studies to evaluate the stability of typing rhythms over time would offer valuable insights into the consistency of users' typing patterns. This information could be instrumental in refining the authentication process and understanding instances where users may deviate from their established typing rhythms.

To ensure the effectiveness of the proposed system in real-world scenarios, it is imperative to conduct extensive usability studies. This involves analyzing user interactions with the system, their perceptions of security, and the potential challenges they may encounter when adopting typing rhythm as a form of authentication. Furthermore, it is essential to explore the applicability of typing rhythm authentication across diverse domains such as healthcare, finance, and education. This investigation can uncover specific requirements and potential adjustments necessary for different contexts, ultimately enabling the customization of the system to address the distinct security needs of various industries.

8. CONCLUSION

The research presents an innovative approach to enhancing the security of textual passwords by incorporating an additional layer of protection without needing extra hardware. The proposed method proves to be cost-effective and feasible and demonstrates its practicality through successful implementation. Analysis of the study's false acceptance rate reveals that even if an unauthorized individual obtains a legitimate user's login credentials through tactics such as social engineering, the likelihood of bypassing the system's security measures is exceedingly low. As a result, this approach offers significantly heightened security compared to conventional textual passwords. Moreover, the recommended technique is designed to be easily deployable, regardless of the user's proficiency in computing systems. Consequently, legitimate users should encounter minimal challenges when seeking authentication.

REFERENCES

Abusham, E., Ibrahim, B., Zia, K., & Al Maskari, S. (2022). An Integration of New Digital Image Scrambling Technique on PCA-Based Face Recognition System. *Scientific Programming*, *2022*, 1–17. DOI: 10.1155/2022/2628885

Andrean, A., Jayabalan, M., & Thiruchelvam, V. (2020). Keystroke Dynamics Based User Authentication using Deep Multilayer Perceptron. *International Journal of Machine Learning and Computing*, *10*(1), 134–139. DOI: 10.18178/ijmlc.2020.10.1.910

Bonneau, J., Herley, C., van Oorschot, P. C., & Stajano, F. (2015). Passwords and the evolution of imperfect authentication. *Communications of the ACM*, *58*(7), 78–87. DOI: 10.1145/2699390

Cavus, N., Mohammed, Y. B., Bulama, M., & Isah, M. L. (2023). Examining User Verification Schemes, Safety, and Secrecy Issues Affecting M-Banking: Systematic Literature Review. *SAGE Open*, *13*(1), 1–18. DOI: 10.1177/21582440231152379

Choi, I., Hao, J., Deane, P., & Zhang, M. (2021). *Benchmark keystroke biometrics accuracy from high-stakes writing tasks*. ETS., DOI: 10.1002/ets2.12326

DiGiacomo, J. (2021), 'Top Data Breaches of 2020: Ransomware on The Rise. Revision Legal', Retrieved from https://revisionlegal.com/internet-law/data-breach/data-breach-statistics-for-2020/

Haselton, T. (2017). *Yahoo just said every single account was affected by 2013 attack - 3 billion in all*. CNBC.

Lai, J., & Arko, E. (2021), 'A Shoulder-Surfing Resistant Scheme Embedded in Traditional Passwords,' *Hawaii International Conference on System Sciences*. DOI: 10.24251/HICSS.2021.860

Laxmi, S. R., Shraddha, D., Mande, E. R., Guljari, S. S., & Uma, M. (2016). Authentication of Users by Typing Pattern: A Review. *International Journal For Science Technology And Engineering*, *2*, 1010–1014.

Liang, X., Zou, F., Li, L., & Yi, P. (2020). Mobile terminal identity authentication system based on behavioral characteristics. *International Journal of Distributed Sensor Networks*, *16*(1). Advance online publication. DOI: 10.1177/1550147719899371

Monaco, J. V., Bakelman, N., Cha, S.-H., & Tappert, C. C. (2012), 'Developing a Keystroke Biometric System for Continual Authentication of Computer Users', *2012 European Intelligence and Security Informatics Conference*, pp. 210–216. DOI: 10.1109/EISIC.2012.58

Mondal, S., & Bours, P. (2016), 'Combining keystroke and mouse dynamics for continuous user authentication and identification,' *2016 IEEE International Conference on Identity, Security and Behavior Analysis (ISBA)*, pp. 1–8. DOI: 10.1109/ISBA.2016.7477228

Oravec, J. (2022). AI, biometric analysis, and emerging cheating detection systems: The engineering of academic integrity? *Education Policy Analysis Archives*, *30*(175), •••. DOI: 10.14507/epaa.30.5765

Pandey, S., & Taffese, T. (2021). Using Performance Predictions to Evaluate Two-factor Authentication Setup Processes. *Proceedings of the Human Factors and Ergonomics Society Annual Meeting*, *65*(1), 999–1003. DOI: 10.1177/1071181321651328

Patil, R. A., & Renke, A. L. (2016). Keystroke Dynamics for User Authentication and Identification by using Typing Rhythm. *International Journal of Computer Applications*, *144*(9), •••.

Report, V. (2023), '2023 Data Breach Investigations Report, Retrieved from https://www.verizon.com/business/en-gb/resources/reports/dbir/

Roy, S., Roy, U., & Sinha, D. D. (2014), 'Free-text user authentication technique through Keystroke Dynamics,' 2014 International Conference on High-Performance *Computing and Applications (ICHPCA)*, pp. 1–6. DOI: 10.1109/ICHPCA.2014.7045345

Salem, A., Sharieh, A., & Jabri, R. (2023). Online User Authentication System Using Keystroke Dynamics. *Journal of Computer Security*, *31*(3), 185–215. DOI: 10.3233/JCS-210081

Sreelatha, M., Shashi, M., Anirudh, M., Ahamer, M. S., & Manoj Kumar, V. (2011). Authentication Schemes for Session Passwords Using Color and Images. *International Journal of Network Security & its Applications*, *3*(3), 111–119. DOI: 10.5121/ijnsa.2011.3308

Suleski, T., Ahmed, M., Yang, W., & Wang, E. (2023), 'A Review of Multi-Factor Authentication in the Internet of Healthcare Things', DOI: DOI: 10.1177/20552076231177144

Tashtoush, Y., Darweesh, D., Karajeh, O., Darwish, O., Maabreh, M., Swedat, S., Koraysh, R., Almousa, O., & Alsaedi, N. (2022). Survey on authentication and security protocols and schemes over 5G networks. *International Journal of Distributed Sensor Networks*, *18*(10). DOI: 10.1177/15501329221126609

KEY TERMS AND DEFINITIONS

Authentication: The verification of the identity of a user, process, or device, often as a prerequisite to allowing access to resources in an information system.

Behavioral biometrics: Personal behavior patterns, such as handwritten signatures, voice patterns, mouse movement, or keystroke dynamics, to authenticate the user.

Biometrics: A measurable physical characteristic or personal behavioral trait used to recognize a user's identity or verify the claimed identity. Examples are facial images, fingerprints, and iris scans.

Equal Error Rate (EER): This is the point where the True Positive Rate (TPR) equals the False Negative Rate (FNR).

False Acceptance Rate (FAR): The percentage of illegitimate users who are wrongly accepted by a system out of all illegitimate user trials. A lower FAR value indicates a higher security level with fewer illegitimate users being falsely accepted.

False Reject Rate (FRR): Measures how well a system can identify legitimate users. It is the percentage of times a user is incorrectly rejected by a system. The false accept rate (FAR) measures how well a system can identify imposters.

Keystroke dynamics: A behavioral biometric authentication method analyzes individuals' unique typing patterns to verify their identity.

Multi-Factor Authentication: An authentication system that requires more than one distinct authentication factor for successful authentication. Multifactor authentication can be performed using a multifactor authenticator or by a combination of authenticators that provide different factors. The three authentication factors are something you know, something you have, and something you are.

Password: A string of characters (letters, numbers, and other symbols) used to authenticate an identity or to verify access authorization.

Physiological biometrics: This utilizes bodily features such as fingerprints, retina scans, facial recognition, DNA, and scent to identify and verify an individual.

Chapter 12
A Survey on Cryptographic Algorithms and Information Security Practices

Jay Kumar Jain
https://orcid.org/0000-0002-9590-0006
Maulana Azad National Institute of Technology, Bhopal, India

Dipti Chauhan
https://orcid.org/0000-0003-1665-7587
Prestige Institute of Engineering Management and Research, Indore, India

Anuthi Singh
https://orcid.org/0009-0007-3181-1745
Carmel Convent Higher Secondary School, Bhopal, India

ABSTRACT

The art of cryptography is considered to be born along with the art of writing. As civilizations advanced, humans organized into tribes, groups, and kingdoms, leading to concepts like power, battles, supremacy, and politics. These concepts created a natural need for secret communication among select recipients, driving the continuous evolution of cryptography. The origins of cryptography can be traced back to the Roman and Egyptian civilizations. The importance of information and communication systems for society and the global economy is growing with the in-creasing volume and value of data being transmitted and stored. However, these systems and data are becoming more vulnerable to various threats, including unauthorized access, misuse, alteration, and destruction. The process of hiding information is

DOI: 10.4018/979-8-3693-8014-7.ch012

known as encryption, while revealing it is called decryption. This is accomplished using a cipher, defined by Merriam-Webster's Collegiate Dictionary as a method of transforming a text in order to conceal its meaning. The original information, called plaintext, becomes cipher text once encrypted. To conceal data, two primary techniques are used: cryptography and steganography. In this chapter, we focus on cryptography. Cryptography is the science of protecting data by converting it into an unreadable form, ensuring that only authorized users can access the information at the destination. It relies on mathematical methods to encrypt and decrypt data, providing a vital layer of security in the digital age.

INTRODUCTION

With the increase in the use of technology in communication and other areas of life, there is a heightened concern in ensuring that information is protected against intruders and potential hacking. Cryptography is one of the fundamental tools in information security, as it contains the fundamental means of protection for information's contents and ownership [1]. Whether it is to protect the finances of consumers through online banking, the privacy of people's messages, or the integrity of governments' classified information, cryptography is perhaps indispensable to the stability of digital networks. Due to the development of dependency toward electronic systems, new forms of threats have emerged, thus, information security has become one of the main concerns for organizations, governments, and people. Current statistics reveal that the increase in use of technology has led to increased threats in the number and level of cybercrime, which is getting more complex in its approach to accessing information [2]. The need for effective cryptographic solutions is underscored by the alarming statistics: based on the Cybersecurity and Infrastructure Security Agency (CISA), cybercrime is predicted to cost the world $10 to 5 trillion USD yearly by 2025. However, the dynamics of modern development prompted by such phenomena as the COVID-19 crisis have widened the threat vector even further, making secure dealings and cryptographic measures essential [3].

The development of cryptographic algorithms can be broadly categorized into two eras: as well as the classical one, which is based on substitution and transposition techniques, and the modern one the introduction of which is associated with public-key cryptosystems and advanced encryption standard. Classical methods were effective in their time; however, processing capabilities boosted the need to create more complex methods to thwart complex attacks. Modern cryptography can be broadly classified into three types: classification of algorithms as symmetric key, asymmetric key, and hash algorithms. Classic cipher, new generation, block cipher algorithms including AES and DES incorporate the use of a single key for both encryption and decryption offer high-speed secure data transmission.

Apart from the algorithms, the practices of information security have also developed over the years, and encompass a range of activities meant to safeguard information. Among such practices that are aimed at network protection, there are network security, access control, authentication mechanisms and security protocols for data protection from unauthorized access and manipulation. For example, the Transport Layer Security (TLS) and Secure Sockets Layer (SSL) are security standards that enable secure communication of data over the internet by the encryption of any information that needs to be transmitted during internet transactions [4]. Similarly, Multi Factor Authentication and Bio Security that exists in most organizations add extra layer of security, so as to make organizations' information systems more secure from potential hackers. This is because business organizations are experiencing growing regulatory demands concerning the protection of data using cryptographic algorithms and information security practices. Legal initiatives like the General Data Protection Regulation (GDPR) in the European Union and the California Consumer Privacy Act (CCPA) in the United States require secure data processing and storage to protect the privacy of individuals, which in turn forces organizations to implement reliable cryptography techniques [5]. The failure to adhere to these provisions attracts severe consequences hence the need for cryptography in the protection of sensitive data.

Thus, the field called cryptography has its difficulties also. Quantum computing that has emerged in recent years can be considered as a serious security threat to conventional cryptographic solutions as quantum computers are able to factorize large numbers in polynomial time, which makes them able to break, for example, RSA and ECC. This has induced research on post-quantum cryptography defined as an effort to develop algorithms that would not be vulnerable to quantum attacks to maintain the requisite security standards of the Internet in the face of newer emerging technologies. Besides, the remaining complexity is the human factor, which poses a threat to information security. In many instances, the cryptographic algorithms themselves are the strongest barriers that guard sensitive data and communications; however, the implementation of these algorithms is often flawed through dubious practices, low security consciousness among users, and deceitful manipulation of various people's mistakes [6]. These are the challenges that require a multi-layered approach to information security that includes the implementation of the most secure cryptographic methods in combination with general promotions of security and complete awareness contests.

This chapter will delve into the intricacies of cryptographic algorithms and information security practices, providing a comprehensive overview of their evolution, current trends, and future directions. It will examine the various types of cryptographic algorithms, their applications, and the challenges they face, as well as the information security practices that complement these algorithms to protect digital assets. By exploring the interplay between cryptography and information security, this chapter aims to provide valuable insights into the ongoing efforts to secure the digital world against the ever-evolving landscape of cyber threats. The objectives of this article are to identify the different cryptographic algorithms existing in the present world, the different areas where they are used, the advantages and disadvantages of each algorithm, and the measures that guarantee good security in exchanging information.

FUNDAMENTAL CONCEPTS IN CRYPTOGRAPHY

In information security, cryptography can be viewed as the essential component of protection against theft and other malicious activities. Cryptography is necessary in every person's life in the modern world, starting from the protection of data and communication to digital signatures and authentication. This section delves into two critical aspects of cryptography: knowledge about symmetric and asymmetric cryptography and the research work carried out on key management and distribution. Therefore, it is necessary to understand these concepts for designing secured cryptographic systems for confidentiality, data integrity, data origin and non-repudiation. The process diagram for cryptography is shown Figure 1.

Figure 1. Cryptography system

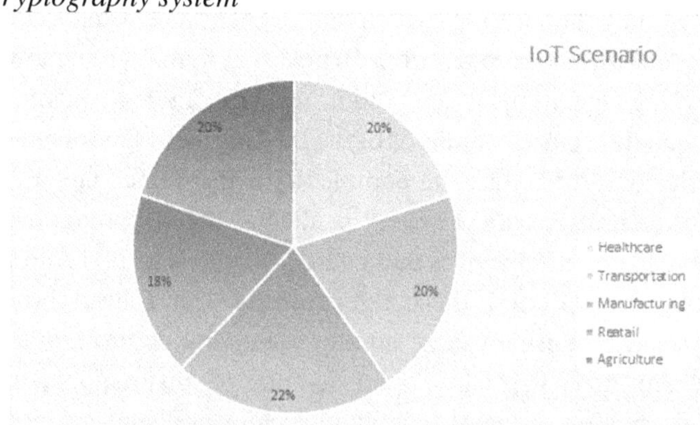

Cryptographic algorithms can be broadly classified into two categories: There are two types of relationship that exist in a network and these are; symmetric and asymmetric. Both of them are fundamentally different from each other in their features and properties and are maximally different in their effectiveness depending on specific situations to which they can be applied.

When implementing a cryptographic system, key management and distribution are critical, since they allow keeping secret cryptographic keys and making them available only to the parties that are supposed to use them.

Studies in this field have focused on possible approaches on key distribution in symmetric cryptography. For instance, Quantum Key Distribution (QKD) provide the mechanism of using the laws of Physics to transfer keys over the potentially insecure channels. QKD is rather secure because any intervention during the transferring of the key would be easily identified due to the peculiarities of the quantum particles [7]. Key management with the help of public key infrastructures (PKIs) usually relieves asymmetric cryptography. PKIs offer a mechanism for dealing with certificates, which link the public key with the owner's information. It is noted that Certificate Authorities (CAs) are issued and verify those certificates validating the identity of-public keys. Investigation in PKIs has been directed towards the improvement of the scalability and security of certification through the cloud infrastructure and distributed systems [8]. Recent advances in key management literature are; existence of blockchain technology for managing keys. Such systems rely on efficient decentralization as well as immutability of the blockchain to store and control cryptographic keys; in effect providing an efficient way of issuing as well as validating keys.

One of the other researched topics concerns automatic key service solutions thematically matched to conventional security systems. These solutions use big data and intelligent MAL techniques to manage important rotation schedules, identify problems, and counter security threats in real-time. The use of automation in managing keys has been designed to simplify what is considered a daunting task in today's growing organizations [9]. Thus, in addition to the technical aspects of developing key technologies, investigation of key management has also taken into account the aspects of human actors and their behaviour regarding keys. It has also been established that in most cases, user education and training are essential in preventing key mishandling and avoiding the violation of security policies. The research in key management and distribution remains ongoing because of complexities of the digital world and growing instances of cyber criminals [10]. Since cryptographic systems are extensively adopted to guarantee the security of information, the issues of key management practices will always be of concern to researchers and practitioners.

SYMMETRIC KEY CRYPTOGRAPHIC ALGORITHMS

Another significant method of encrypting information is considered to be symmetric key cryptography algorithm – that is the most profound and popular technique of the secure data. This type of cryptography employs the use of a single unchangeable or secret key in encryption and decryption thus being fit for use in large volumes of data. This section introduces the reader to the symmetric key cryptographic algorithms both in terms of block ciphers, stream ciphers as well as the modes of operation that add onto the functionality as well as security of the block ciphers. The following figure 2 shows the functioning of Symmetric Key Cryptography.

Figure 2. Symmetric Ker Cryptography

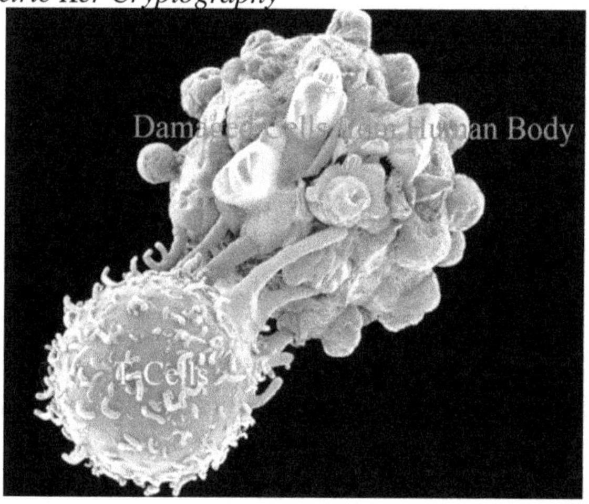

Measurements for symmetric key algorithms are based on the fact that they employ one, secret key which is known to both the sending and receiving parties, and this is used in both the encryption and decryption procedures. This characteristic is opposed to asymmetric cryptography, which utilizes different keys for these functions. The heavy plus of using the symmetric key algorithm is the efficiency and the speed with which the algorithm can execute the encryption process, thus it is best suited for encrypting data sets, which are large, or data that requires real time encryption. The symmetric key cryptography is typically used in cases where speed is an issue as in: Disk encryption, protocols of secure network communications, and real-time data transfers [11]. However, the major disadvantage of this approach is the need for a secret key; the method of its distribution and storage is problematic, as both participants have to exchange it securely. Symmetric key algorithms can be broadly categorized into two types: two types of cipher systems namely: block ciphers and stream ciphers. The following figure 3 shows different Symmetric key algorithms-

Figure 3. Symmetric Key Algorithms

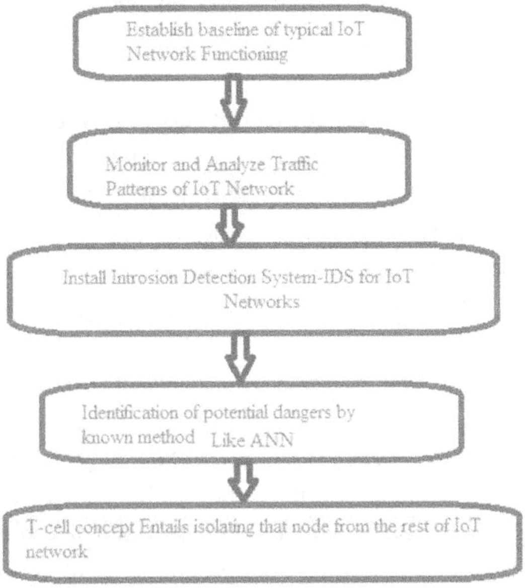

Block Ciphers- Block ciphers are those algorithms of symmetric key techniques that encrypt the data in a block of a fixed size. The data is divided into equal blocks, and each block is encrypted with the same secret key so as to maintain the homogeneity of the encryption operation. This method is secure in its execution and guarantees quality in scaling big data. A block cipher works on the blocks of the plaintext to produce the blocks of the cipher text, this is the direct operation and conversely in the decryption procedure. Some of the most well-known block cipher algorithms include: Some of the most well-known block cipher algorithms include:

Advanced Encryption Standard (AES) - AES is presently the most popular block cipher in modern cryptography and there is no other standard for symmetric key encryption other than AES globally. AES, which gained approval from the United States' National Institute of Standards and Technology (NIST) in 2001, was employed as a substitute for DES because of the features of improved security. AES works at 128 bits of data at at that per bit it has three keys – 128, 192, 256, guarantee a high degree of protection against brute force attacks [12]. AES applies a substitution-permutation network, or S-P network, which is a series of substitutions, followed by permutations, in a number of rounds. The number of rounds varies depending on the key length: 10, 128, 12, 192, 14, 256. It has been reported that due to AES's high resistance and performance, many applications have implemented the use of AES, for instance; to protect government data and user data of commercial products.

Data Encryption Standard (DES)- DES was one among the oldest block cipher algorithms evolved in the 1970 with IBM help and officially formulated as a federal standard by NIST. In the process, it employs 64-bit blocks of data while generating a 56-bit key. DES employs 16 rounds of processing in which the largest number of computations are permutations and substitutions. While DES was popular for many years, the dawn of computers has rendered it satisfied to brute force attacks thus development of new better algorithms like AES started.

Triple DES (3DES) - This was developed to enhance the security of DES without the need of another different algorithm. It encompasses the employment of three successive DES operations through two or else three dissimilar keys. This brings the equivalent key length up to 112 or 168 bits, which gives 3DES more security than the standard DES though it is slower and less efficient than the newer AES algorithm. It is still used today in legacy systems/applications that need backward compatibility.

Stream Ciphers- The next class of symmetric key algorithms are called stream ciphers these encrypt data one at a time, either bit by bit or byte by byte. This approach differs from block cipher, which works on fixed size blocks The DES and triple DES are examples of this kind of approach. It is mainly adapted for those devices, methods, or protocols that work based on continuous data transmission like real-time communication, or secure wireless technology. A main benefit associated with stream ciphers is the real time mode of encryption, which makes a stream cipher suitable for situations where latency and overhead time is at a premium.

RC4 (Rivest Cipher 4)- RC4 is one of the most famous and applied stream algorithms by Rivest in 1987. It produces a keystream that is a pseudo random bit sequence, which will be XORed with the plaintext to get the cipher text. The same keystream is used for decryption where the same stream is XORed with the encrypted message to get the original message. Nevertheless, RC4 is characterized by its simplicity and high speed, so it was used in such protocols as SSL/TLS and WEP. However, RC4 has known weaknesses, namely the problems with the key scheduling and the keystream have certain bias. These weaknesses have rendered RC4 insecure for use in several security protocols thus its depreciation in favor for better security protocols.

Salsa20 and ChaCha20- Salsa20 and ChaCha20 are recent algorithms in stream cipher intended to overcome the issues that have been portrayed in RC4 cipher [13]. Both algorithms produce a keystream that is pseudo random in nature and depends on the secret key, nonce, and the counter. Salsa20 along with ChaCha20 is highly secure, fast and practically immune to cryptanalysis that places it in various usages comprising of secure communication and disk encryption. ChaCha20 has been well received especially because it is used in TLS protocol and has been implemented in many web browsers and operating systems. Due to its efficiency on today's processors, and its robust security features, it is widely used for secure data encryption.

Modes of Operation- Modes of operation are methods applied to block ciphers to provide more security and operational flexibility. It specifies how blocks of data are encoded and decoded so that block ciphers can be used under various situations [14]. The decision of mode can greatly affect the security and effectiveness of the encryption function. The following table 1 depicts some common modes of operation-

Table 1. Modes of Operation

Modes	Functioning
Electronic Codebook (ECB)	It is the most uncomplicated method of operation in which every block of the plaintexts is put through the same key. Primarily, ECB is quite simple to implement, however, it possesses major issues with security; two same plaintext blocks generate two same cipher text blocks. This property makes it vulnerable to pattern analysis and is usually not advised to be utilized in protected operations.
Cipher Block Chaining (CBC)	CBC is the modification of ECB and it extended the same weaknesses of ECB by connecting blocks. Before the encryption is performed, each block of plaintext is XORed with the previous cipher text block and this makes the blocks to be dependent on each other. This dependency makes sure that the same plain text blocks create different cipher text blocks, which add on the security system. CBC also needs an IV for the first block, which demands that a single plaintext is encrypted differently always.
Counter (CTR)	CTR mode uses a block cipher to convert itself into a stream cipher by encrypting successive counter values. There is then XOR of the generated keystream with the plaintext yields the ciphertext. CTR mode is used to execute parallel processing of blocks increasing its proficiency and speed. It is especially useful for high-scale tasks and is widespread in many secure protocols in the network.
Galois/Counter Mode (GCM)	This is a mode of operation that uses the CTR mode of encryption together with the authentication process done via a Galois field multiplication that results in the creation of a Galois field authentication tag. That is why this mode is used in most modern crypto applications because it is efficient and has the AE feature. This is due to the fact that GCM is widely used when the integrity of the data is important, for instance in cases of network protocols such as TLS and IPsec.

Research in symmetric key cryptography continues to evolve, driven by the need for more secure, efficient, and versatile encryption methods. Several key areas of research include:

1. Lightweight Cryptography: With the increase in the numbers of the Internet of Things (IoT) and other related low-resource systems, there is a need of lightweight cryptographic algorithms which provides high level of security with less resources. This topic concentrates on the creation of the optimized algorithms for the devices that use minimal energy and have strong safety measures [15].

2. Post-Quantum Cryptography: Introduction of quantum computers becomes a serious threat towards currently used cryptography because most algorithms in a quantum computer can easily decipher the common used encryption models. Scientists are working on SKA algorithms to continue the protection of encrypted data after the spread of new quantum attacks.
3. Cryptanalysis and Security Evaluation: The research in cryptanalysis is performed on the continuous basis in order to find certain discrepancies and flaws in the existing symmetric key algorithms. This research in turn assists in fortification of existing cryptographic systems and points out possible directions of their enhancement that would make the algorithms more secure.
4. Parallel and High-Performance Encryption: Since HS data processing has become essential Researcher are interested in techniques to increase SKA performance in parallel High Performance Computing (HPC) site. Such advancements are directed towards the optimization of encryption procedures to allow their use in the massive data applications industry.
5. Privacy-Preserving Encryption: Mainly, as privacy issues are getting more important in the context of symmetric key cryptography, the research on encryption schemes for enabling safe data processing while preserving privacy is getting increasingly popular. Current research in the realm of SLE includes ways of performing computations on data that remains encrypted like through homomorphic encryption and secure multi-party computation.

ASYMMETRIC KEY CRYPTOGRAPHIC ALGORITHMS

Public key cryptography, also known as asymmetric key cryptographic algorithms, is a breakthrough in the advancement of cryptographic systems and helps to overcome the problems of symmetric key systems in which the same key is used for both encryption and decryption. The fundamental concept of asymmetric cryptography involves a pair of keys: It consists of a pair of keys, each key is a large number that is used for encrypting the data and another key is used for decryption and these two keys are known as Public Key and Private Key respectively. The security of this approach relies on the challenge of attaining the private key from the public key as the two are generated by calculation. The development of asymmetric cryptography could be dated back to the 1970s when Whitfield Diffie and Martin Hellman provided the notions of public-key cryptography, which was quite innovative at that time. This concept was the basis of practical algorithms, widely distinguished by RSA algorithm or Rivest-Shamir-Adleman algorithm. RSA algorithm was developed in 1977 and is the practical form of the public key cryptography and widely used today [16]. The following figure 4 shows the functioning of Symmetric Key Cryptography.

Figure 4. Asymmetric Key Cryptography

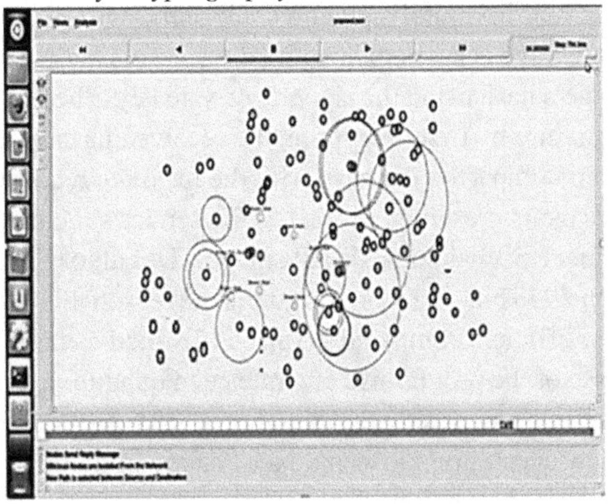

Asymmetric cryptography is used in secure email, developing digital signatures, encryption of the essential information, and creating secure connections over the World Wide Web. In turn, the main application of asymmetric algorithms is the establishment of secure key exchange and the provision of creating digital signatures, which allows for the effective protection of messages from third-party access and modifications, while guaranteeing the sender's and recipient's identity. Asymmetric key cryptography, also known as public key cryptography, does not require the key to be transmitted in advance like the symmetric key cryptography does, which solves the problem of key exchange between different parties such as two parties that have not had prior interaction. Nonetheless, the security of asymmetric cryptography relies upon the suitability of the problems that are associated with mathematics issues, or more particularly, factoring large integers and discrete logarithms. With the advance of computational power, not only with computers but soon with quantum computers, the security of some asymmetric algorithms like RSA is coming into interrogation, hence the interest in other algorithms such as ECC.

RSA Algorithm – The use of the outright name, RSA, is enough to warrant recognition of this algorithm as one of the most established seems to be the most qualified. Its security is founded on the mathematical challenge of the decomposition of the product of two large prime numbers, an activity, which as of now cannot be performed with the currently available technique especially in the event that the said prime numbers are large enough. RSA algorithm works on the idea that, it is possible to multiply two large prime numbers and get a large composite number; however it is very hard to factorize this composite number to decompose the composite number back into its Prime factors.

Another advantage that may be mentioned about RSA is its flexibility. It can be used in encryption and in digital signatures. Concerning digital signatures, it is a process where a message is accompanied by information authentically attached by signing the message's hash using the signer's private key. The recipient is then able to validate the signature by first decrypting the received hash by using the signer's public key and then comparing the hash with the message received. Thus, the reliability of the message is preserved as well as the sender's identity.

At the same time, RSA has some disadvantages. Des algorithm demands the use of large keys (often 2048 bits and more) to guarantee reasonable levels of protection, which makes it less efficient compared to various distinctive algorithms. Also, RSA is in danger because of the progressive emergence of quantum computers which are able to factor large integers and therefore to break RSA encryption. Therefore, the development of new cryptographic techniques that are immune to quantum attacks, such as ECC, has gained attention.

RSA- Shor based on the mathematical theory offers an answer to RSA that is at least as strong and in many cases stronger with shorter key sizes which translate to less computational time and resources used. It is well known that ECC relies on elliptic curves which is mathematics structures defined by the equations of the form \(y^2 = x^3 + ax + b \) over finite fields. The security of ECC relies on the computational hardness of another number theoretic problem known as the Elliptic Curve Discrete Logarithm Problem (ECDLP), that is the problem of finding the integer k if two points P and Q on an elliptic curve are such that Q = kP.

Another factor that makes the choice in favour of ECC is its productivity. For instance, 256-bit key in ECC is as secure as 3072-bit key in RSA, but consumes significantly less resources; therefore ECC is more suitable for applications where processing power, bandwidth or secure storage space are limited like in mobiles, embedded systems and IoTs [17]. This efficiency also puts ECC in a good standing as far as secure communications in low-resource environments where every computation has to be optimized to the maximum.

Although ECC is a different algorithm from RSA, its work pattern is equal to RSA's key generation, encryption, and decryption steps. However, during generation of key pair, a private key is chosen as a random integer (d) and this determines the public key as (Q=dG) where G is a pre determined base point.

ECC is also widely applied in digital signatures, particularly in the Elliptic Curve Digital Signature Algorithm (ECDSA) that is the basis of most of current standard including the FIPS 186-4 supported by NIST. The second is in the use of the Elliptic Curve Digital Signature Algorithm (ECDSA) which provides the similar functionality of the RSA signatures and yet has significantly shorter keys and hence signatures, thus the verification is faster, and consumes less bandwidth. However, ECC has some challenges that can be observed as follows nack: To maintain the security of the ECC key, ECC implementation also carries certain risks that involve issues such as side channel attack and/or using incorrect curve parameters. Besides, it is thought that ECC is also safe against quantum attacks, but current work on post-quantum cryptography is looking for yet stronger candidates for the future.

Digital signatures and Public Key Infrastructure (PKI)- Digital signatures are one of the most important applications of the asymmetric key cryptographic algorithms besides offering a method of ensuring the credibility and originality of digital communications. A digital signature can now be defined as a digital process that employs a private key so that a party can invoke its identity in signing a message; any other party that has the right public key can then confirm that the signature is authentic [18]. This process helps in confirming that message has not been changed by any other entity and that it is from the claimed sender.

It is a common practice to first hash the message to a fixed size; next, the hash is encrypted with the signer's private key. The outcome of such a procedure is the signature which itself is exclusive to the particular message-signer pair; any alteration of the message results in a different value of hash and thus, the signature becomes invalid. The recipient can easily authenticate the signature by decrypting it with the public key belonging to the signer, and then, comparing the product with the hash of received message. If the above two values are same then the signature is said to be authentic.

Digital signatures are applied practically in every area of computer communication, especially in secure email (MIME, PGP), software distribution and online transactions. They are also integrated into Public Key Infrastructure (PKI) that is a system applied to digital certificates and public keys.

PKI is very important in building trust in matters concerning electronic commerce communications. It was qualified as working with digital certificates that are electronic documents with the binding of the public key and the identity of an individual, organization or device. Third parties termed as the Certificate Authorities (CA) who certifies the holder of the certificate issue these certificates. Such details are the public key of the holder, the identity of the holder, the signature of the CA, and validity period of the certificate. Each time a certificate is physically included within a given digital communication, the receiver can then use a CAs public key to ensure that the given certificate is a genuine one as well as the holder's identity. Such a process improves the authenticity of the public key to be used for either encryption or verifying a signature, to the holder's identity thus eliminating cases of impersonation and man-in-the-middle attacks. PKI is used in most secure protocols including SSL/TLS used to secure web traffic and IPSec used to secure network traffic. This also holds the foundation of secure email facilities and Virtual Private Networks. VPN connection establishment through digital certificates offers a reliable way of authenticating users in order to prevent network and information leakage in case of attack [20].

Besides protection of communication, PKI is critical in code signing, commonly where software developers sign their code with a digital signature. This practice helps avoid the case where somebody has made alterations on the signed code or that the code is from an illegitimate source. The user may check the digital signature before running the software or activating the product, which lowers the chances of getting a virus or a changed code. Electronic mail security services, which use S/MIME or PGP, also depend on PKI. In these systems, the emails are encrypted using the public key belonging to the receiver and can only be seen by the latter who has the private key. Digital signatures can also be used for signing e-mail messages, that would assure the recipient that the given message has not been tampered with and would also authenticate the sender.

ADVANCED CRYPTOGRAPHIC TECHNIQUES

Cryptography is among the most dynamic disciplines that implement constant upgrades of its methods in response to threats and issues. With the proliferation of the digital environment more complicated methods of protecting information have been invented to guarantee security, confidentiality, and the reliability of information in a more refined manner. Of these are; Zero Knowledge Proofs, Homomorphic Encryption, Quantum Cryptography, and Post Quantum Cryptography which allow for different ways of protecting information and developing new methods of communication and computing [20].

Zero-Knowledge Proofs

Zero-Knowledge Proofs (ZKPs) are cryptographic protocols that enable for one party (the prover), to convince the other party (the verifier) that they know a piece of information despite not disclosing the actual information [21]. This idea was coined in the 1980s by Goldwasser, Micali and Rackoff and has become one of the most effective instruments in cryptography especially in the cases when clients' confidentiality is important. A ZKP must satisfy three essential properties: The three properties of shared ledger include completeness, witness and zero knowledge. Completeness guarantees that in the case of the statement being true, an honest sending of the proof meeting the requirements made by an honest verifier is possible. Soundness ensures that no unscrupulous prover can, when the statement is indeed false, prove otherwise. From zero-knowledge, the verifier is neither provided with any more information than the fact that the statement is correct.

Another of the most popular uses of ZKPs is in the establishment of digital identity. For instance, ZKPs are useful in proving that a person is adult without the need of producing any identification details. This capability has a significant impact on privacy-preserving authentication systems, where users are capable of demonstrating the acceptable level of access permissions without divulging personal details. ZKPs are also important in the concept of anonymous blockchains technologies such as zk-SNARKs, that has been implemented in the Zcash cryptocurrency for carrying out an anonymous transaction. In such systems, the compositions guarantee validation of transactions while at the same time keeping the identity of the sender, receiver, or the amount being transacted as confidential and secure.

Besides, digital identity, and blockchain technology, ZKPs have found their uses in many other areas such as the secure voting, confidential contracts, and cloud computing. In secure voting for instance, ZKPs can facilitate a way by which voters can show people that they voted correctly without revealing the content of their vote to anyone thus making the election secure. The demand for privacy is on an upward trend, and with technological advancement ZKPs are set to feature prominently in the improvement of security and privacy of various applications.

Homomorphic Encryption

Homomorphic Encryption is another impressive cryptographic method that let computations on encrypted data be executed without decrypting. This means also that a third party, let say a cloud service provider, can apply on some encrypted data some computation and return the encrypted result to the data owner who, in turn, can apply the corresponding decryption algorithm and get the final output [22]. The basic idea of homomorphic encryption was introduced by [23], however, more than thirty years later in 2009, Craig Gentry created a fully homomorphic encryption technique [24]. This can be categorized into three types: Of which the common types are partially homomorphic encryption (PHE) that supports only one type of operation that could be addition or multiplication, somewhat homomorphic encryption (SHE) that supports only a small number of operations and fully homomorphic encryption (FHE) that supports any type of mathematical operation. FHE is the most powerful one as it allows computing with encrypted data and such computations that are needed for machine learning, big data processing, and lots of financial operations without revealing the data.

The fact of performing calculations on ciphered data has broad potential applications with respect to cloud storage and data protection. For instance, FHE provides several ways through which organizations can have their data processed in the cloud without bureaucracy since the data is encrypted all through the processing period. Although, this capability is useful commonly in situations where there is sensitivity and risk associated with data such as in healthcare, finance and government businesses.

However, there are concerns that surround the practical applicability of homomorphic encryption, such as concerns based on the computational aspect and efficiency. Specifically, FHE explicitly demands a large amount of computational resources, which at the present stage is not suitable for many real-world applications. Nevertheless, current research and development continues to improve the schema of homomorphic encryption and bring down their cost of computation so that they can suit present day applications. As the above challenges are being solved, homomorphic encryption seems to promise a powerful tool for secure data processing in the cloud and different other settings.

Quantum Cryptography - Quantum Cryptography is the use of principles of quantum mechanics in improving the security of cryptographic systems. Unlike the classical cryptography, the quantum cryptography uses the features of quantum mechanics, namely the superposition and entanglement. Among those, the probably most famous and most thoroughly investigated field of application of quantum cryptography is precisely the domain of Quantum Key Distribution (QKD) [25]. This relies on the fact that the act of any attempt to observe or measure its information interrupt the particular information that is very lethal to eavesdropping. The most significant one is the BB84 protocol suggested by Bennett and Brassard in 1984. In the BB84 protocol, the key is written in quantum states of some particles for example photons and transmitted to the two parties. In case the intended interceptor attempts to intercept the key, the quantum states are destroyed; this leads to the parties developing awareness of the interceptor, making them to abandon the compromised key.

Quantum cryptography has the potential of being a wholly secure concept of cryptography, under the assumptions of quantum mechanics. Thus, it can be a good candidate for providing a level of protection of your communications in a world where classical cryptographic algorithms may become no longer safe due to quantum computers. Nonetheless, it is critical to implement quantum cryptography and specifically QKD, but it comes with its own drawback by the fact that it needs specific hardware and infrastructure for instance quantum communication channels and photon detectors, which can be expensive and challenging to develop.

Thus, although there are these problems, the progress has been made in the advancement and implementation of quantum cryptographic systems. Some of the currently developed experimental and commercial QKD network is mentioned elsewhere, and new research is aimed at enhancing the real-world applicability, the increment of QKD network size, and the integration of quantum cryptograhpy with classical communication networks. On the topic of the further development of quantum technology, quantum cryptography can surely be expected to become actively applied in the protection of secret information and safeguard of quantum communications.

Post-Quantum Cryptography

This is so because as physicists advance in their development of these quantum computers, there is a real possibility nowadays that they can crack most of the existing cryptographic platforms, including the RSA and the ECC, which work based on the factoring of large integers or solving discrete logarithms – tasks that can be solved by current quantum computers with Yamakami's algorithm or with Shor's one. This has created insecurity or rather a potential threat known as Post-Quantum Cryptography (PQC), which is the branch of cryptography which deals with algorithms that are resistant to attack by the quantum computers.

Post-Quantum Cryptography aims at designing algorithms that will work on classical computers but they will be resistant to quantum computer attacks [26]. These algorithms rely on mathematical questions for which the solution appears to be difficult for both traditional and quantum computers. Thus, future development of post-quantum cryptographic algorithms are the following candidates: lattice-based, hash-based, code-based, multivariate polynomial, and supersingular isogeny-based.

One of the most popular categories in PQC is the lattice-based cryptography, which depends on the strong complexity of certain problems that belong to lattices such as the LWE problem. Lattice based designs, as shown with HElib, tend to exhibit great general-purpose utility and result in fast response times in addition to providing a framework for encryption and signatures in addition to such features as fully homomorphic encryption.

Applied cryptographic principles: Zo-Knowledge Proof, Homomorphic Encryption, Quantum Cryptography, Post-Quantum Cryptography are the most contemporary ideas which are developed and are opening new possibilities of protecting information resources in the world of the growing threats. It takes care of new threats' appearance and offers fresh concepts on how to manage problems linked with privacy, data integrity, or future-proof security. These state-of-the-art cryptographic methods shall, therefore, remain relevant and exponentially define the future's secure communication and information protection as technology advances.

INFORMATION SECURITY PRACTICES

Currently, information security measures play a critical role in maintaining the confidentiality, integrity, and availability of information created in a more technical environment. It includes strategies, technologies and procedures, which are utilized in protection of data from intentional or unintentional, internal or external use, divulgence, modification or elimination. Thus, best practices in handling information are critical in the face of rapidly changing and increasingly large-scale and sophisticated threats in cyberspace, where individuals', companies', and governments' information must remain invulnerable. Information security is built on three core principles, often referred to as the CIA triad: Information security is built on three core principles, often referred to as the CIA triad: The following figure 5 shows the CIA triad.

Figure 5. CIA triad

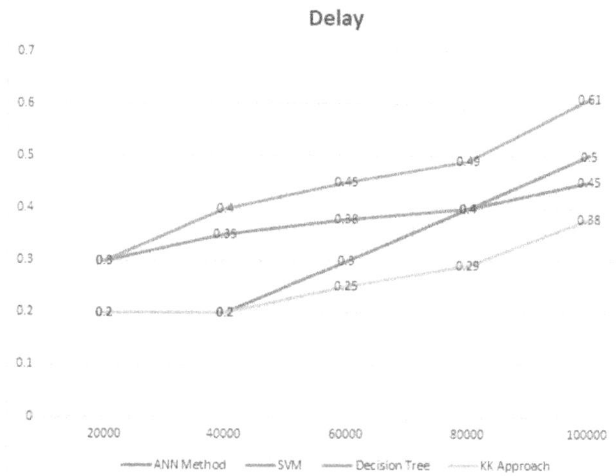

1. Confidentiality: Making sure that the information being transmitted is subject to the relevant security protocols that will only allow the personnel who are supposed to view it, view it. It is kept secure except where orally transmitted or physically written down by restricting the access, keying it up and other ways that ensures it is not leaked out.
2. Integrity: It also means that no one who is not authorized to do so has in any way interfered with or changed the information. It is maintained via elements like a checksum, a digital signature, and version control systems.
3. Availability: Guaranteeing that information and system are available for the authorise user at the right time. Some of the ways through which availability is kept is through backups, alternate sites in case of a disaster and regular computer maintenance.

KEY INFORMATION SECURITY PRACTICES

1. Risk Management and Assessment - Risk management is a central feature of ISM. This therefore means that organizations have to follow a process whereby they have to look at their environment, identify any threats and risks that may be of concern to it, evaluate the significance of the risk to the organization, and then have in place some form of response mechanism to address the identified risks. This process usually includes frequency checks, where the danger rates and the possibilities of particular threats are estimated. Accordingly, prioritizing activity can be considered applicable to the combat organization's security situation: the most substantial risks can be highlighted.
2. Access Control- Access control means how to limit or control the information and resources to be used in an organization. This practice involves the application of password, biometrical and multi-factor authentication to proves the identity of the user. Moreover, the authorization policies deal with the levels of rights assigned to each user to allow people to access only the data which they are supposed to use at their workplace.
3. Data Encryption-Encryption is very important as it involves securing data whether being processed, stored or transmitted. In a way, the information is made in a form that can only be understood and manipulated by anyone with the right decryption key in what is known as encryption. The primary purpose of using encryption is the protection of data in transit and within an organization's environment about possible insecure networks.
4. Network security; - Network security is the protection of the contents of the data as it is in transit or when in repositories in the networks. This practice involves the use of firewalls, intrusion detection and prevention systems (IDPS), encryption protocol such as TLS/SSL among others that blocks unauthorized access, malware, and other malicious activities [27]. Thus, one must perform continual network check-ups and vulnerability tests to find out possible vulnerabilities.
5. Incident Response and Management – This is perhaps the final process since occasionally incidents cannot be prevented despite efforts to prevent them. It is the policy, procedure, and process of accurately detecting and controlling an event that poses risk to an organization's critical assets and resources. This involves creation of an incident response plan that will guide the procedures on how the organization will identify incidents, how it will handle the incidents and how it will recover from the incidents. Incident response teams are mainly expected to conduct surveillance, detect intrusions and then quickly mitigate the problem.

6. Security Awareness and Training- One of the main causes of threats that compromise organizations' security is user mistakes. Security awareness and training initiatives should therefore be implemented as it helps in ensuring that the employees are informed of the risks that are present in the organization as well as explained on ways of handling the emerging threats like the phishing scams. Company's commitment to the constant training of employees and their preparedness to respond to a cyberattack, table-top exercise or valorization, and the definition of security guidelines within the organization result in the formation of a security culture within the enterprise.
7. Regulatory and Legal Aspects- There are several rules and laws in different countries and organizations that relate to the security of information and information systems, including the General Data Protection Regulation (GDPR), the Health Insurance Portability and Accountability Act (HIPAA), and the Payment Card Industry Data Security Standard (PCI DSS) [28]. This is a set of regulations that need to be met through deployment of security controls, also, systems need to be reviewed periodically for compliance.
8. Endpoint Security- The nature of today's technology has seen the use of mobile devices, laptops and many other such endpoints which require protection. Endpoint security measures include anti viruses, endpoint detection and response systems, and mobile device management to reduce risk of endpoint vulnerability to malware, illegal use, and more. It is also important that such devices should always be updated with corresponding security patches from time to time.
9. Physical Security- Despite the highly advanced technologies today, physical security cannot be overlooked. Such include physical control of access to data centers, server rooms and any other buildings where the data is residing or being processed. Physical security can comprise of CCTV cameras, locking systems and controls on the physical environment to avoid intruders, theft, or destruction of the hubs [29].
10. Regular Audits and Assessments- To maintain and develop organisational security, security audits and assessments must be carried out frequently. These audits involve the assessment of the current security measures in place, determine areas requiring enhancement, or areas that pose threats to the organisation's security. Scanning, evaluation, and review are ways through which it is ascertained that particular security measures are effective.

Trend Analysis of Information Security—Information security as a discipline continues to experience dynamic change meant to meet recent technologies and other threats. Some of the key trends shaping the future of information security include:Some of the key trends shaping the future of information security include:

Artificial Intelligence and Machine Learning: AI and machine learning are also being deployed to improve security by using big data approaches when deciding on the next steps in threat detection or response [30].

Zero Trust Architecture: According to Zero Trust model, it is assumed that anyone inside or outside the network cannot be trusted; otherwise known as just-in-time, or least privilege model. However, there is one criterion that has to be satisfied with each kind of access; only then resources are granted to be accessible to the users. It is highly suitable in the current world where the network boundary is not very well defined as it used to be.

Cloud Security: With the advancement in cloud adoption by various organizations, security of data and applications in the cloud has emerged as one of the critical requirements. Cloud security measures entails the protection of cloud deployed configurations and policies over the accessibility and activities of the cloud environment to reduce incidences of hackers and other Unauthorized persons accessing the cloud front [31].

Supply Chain Security: As supply chain become more integrated and the risk of being vulnerable to attacks also grows there is an understanding that the protection of own infrastructure should be complemented with the protection of external partners. This includes gathering proper risk analysis of third party suppliers, and integrating processes to guarantee that the supplier's security measures match the organization's.

Quantum Cryptography: Quantum technology is rapidly evolving to be a severe challenge for cryptographic systems in the near future. Thus, organizations are already looking to develop quantum-resistant algorithms and needed quantum cryptography into their security systems to counter quantum attacks.

Many organizations consider information security practices to be vital since data and systems can be threatened by numerous risks in today's world. Thus, through the adoption of integrated security management solutions covering the aspects of risk evaluation and assessment, physical and logical access control, data encryption, networks, and security events, organizations can protect their information resources and retain the public's confidence. In the past few years, emerging new threats add to the requirement of adopting new security feet that will enable organizations to develop strong protection for their information.

APPLICATIONS OF CRYPTOGRAPHIC TECHNIQUES IN VARIOUS DOMAINS

Cryptography currently can be considered as an indispensable part of security as it is widely used to secure information and ensure communication safety in various fields. Cryptography has been adopted in so many areas as advancement in digital technology is being witnessed and competition as well as the need for security increases. This section extends knowledge on how cryptography is adapted in various fields to solve certain security issues.

1. Financial Services

In the financial sectors cryptography cannot be overlooked since its application is vital for securing of transactions, secrets of the customers as well as of the entire financial systems. A prevalent use of cryptography in this advanced field is in the protection of online banking and methods of payment. Secure Sockets Layer/Transport Layer Security are employed to ensure that data transferred in between users as well as the banking servers are encrypted to avoid exposure of account information as well as other important details.

DS use cryptographic algorithm like RSA AND ECC to validate the transaction and guarantee that the transaction has not been changed. These algorithms are also applied in creating and handling of keys for the protection of payment cards, ATM's and mobile payment facilities. Likewise, cryptographic hash functions as well as the concept of digital signature have also been effectively utilized in the concept of decentralization of virtual currencies through blockchain implemented in the currently popular bitcoins and other related modern facilities for recording financial transactions.

2. Healthcare

In healthcare context, the patient information needs to remain confidential, be of integrity and available at all times. Secrecy is very vital in the protection of the medical records, patient's health information, and other data to avoid cases of hacking and other related issues. For patients' records in EHS, patients' data is encrypted and only authorized individuals can access patient related information in EHS across life care givers.

Digital signatures and hash functions are applied to ensure the nonrepudiation of medical data, prescriptions, and laboratory results, which cannot be altered by unauthorized personnel. Also, the use of cryptography is applied in performing telemedicine where patients' consultations and information shared between them and their doctors are over potentially vulnerable networks. Through the encryption of such communications, the privacy of the patient's information is easily protected especially under situations where the care is being provided virtually.

3. Government and Defence

There is almost an unanimous consensus on the importance of cryptography in government and defense departments for purposes of classified information and secure communications for national security purposes. In this domain, cryptography is used for secure communication between different departments in the government, the military, and embassies to avoid members of the opposite side intercepting important information. To secure data which is in motion or in transit routers and switches apply encryption techniques like AES (Advanced Encryption Standard) and protocols like IPsec.

Cryptography also is instrumental in the public key infrastructure (PKI), which is the control of the issuance of the digital certificates for the purposes of identifying users or other devices and system in the governmental networks. In defense, cryptographic techniques are used in the protection of weapons and control systems, command and communication and intelligent systems. Further, quantum cryptography is in the process of being developed as a method for protecting still future threats coming from quantum computing.

4. E-Commerce

Online shops process millions of consumers' records, financial details, payment card data, and about their purchases. Due to the huge volumes of data being generated, cryptography is vital in protecting this data and ensuring safe commerce. Through the topic, SSL and TLS are the principal protocols used to ensure secure communication in e-commerce between the websites and the customers through the shielding of sensitive information from attackers [32].

Digital certificates and public key infrastructure (PKI) is being applied today for Web site authentication, meaning that a customer communicates only with the actual business and is not potentially a victim of a phishing attack or other fraudulent schemes. Tokenization is also based on cryptography and is a technique that replaces the actual payment information with a token, a unique value that can be used for payment while not revealing the actual information. But cryptographic hashing is used to store and to check passwords so even if the Data is breached or hacked User credentials are safe.

5. Telecommunications

Telecommunication industry applies cryptography on voice, video and data transmission over different networks. This security technology is applied to shield the cellular, wireless and satellite links through which callers, senders and receivers exchange calls, messages and data that can't be tapped by unauthorized persons. ZRTP (Zimmermann Real-time Transport Protocol) use secure protocol of voice over IP networks where the security of VoIP is end-to-end.

Cryptography is also adopted in the mechanism that authenticates the SIM card, which restricts access to the network services to only those who are authorized. In more of the mobile communication, cryptography is used to protect other applications like mobile money, social media applications and messaging platforms that involve the transfer of secure information. However, as 5G networks comes to implementation cryptography will be used more substantially to secure huge data traffic in these high bandwidth networks and in the creation of such services as IoT and smart cities [33].

6. Blockchain and Cryptocurrencies

Cryptographic systems; specifically hash functions and digital signatures are fundamental to blockchain and cryptocurrencies. In a blockchain, the set of transactions form a block is linked to the previous block through a hash and hence forms a chain of records that cannot be tampered with [34]. This makes the approach convenient for data security since an alteration of the block will be detected by the change in the hash.

Some examples of cryptocurrencies include Bitcoin where cryptography is employed to facilitate and compound the transactions as well as regulate the issuance of the coin. Wallet addresses and signatures to transactions are created in Public-key cryptography so only the holder of the private key of the wallet is able to authorize the transfer of funds. Smart contracts are self-executing contracts the code of which is embedded in the agreement; cryptographic techniques are used in smart contracts as well. Such contracts act as self-executing agreement enforcing the provisions of the contract and thereby reducing on fraudulent activities.

7. Cloud Computing

The evolution of organizations to the cloud means that protection of information stored in data and applications in clouds is of much importance. Encryption is a significant cloud security aspect since it helps in the protection of information through applying the mechanisms of ensuring its confidentiality in storage and transit. [35] Homomorphic encryption is an enhanced form of cryptography that achieves computations on data in an encrypted form; thus, making cloud data processing more secure. Another cryptographic technology applied in the management of access control in clouds is attribute-based encryption technique which manages access to data based on the attributes and predefined policies of the users. Moreover, cryptography is applied to MPC that allows data sharing between many parties and their calculations without disclosing the inputs introduced by any of the parties.

8. Digital Rights Management (DRM)

Technological protection measures not only consist of copy protection, but they also involve employing cryptography solutions in protection of intellectual property and restriction of usage of items compiled in digital form inclusive of music, movies, software, and e-books among others. Data is secured with the help of cryptographical methods by which information is coverted, so that it becomes intelligible only to the intended recipient using the decryption key. Watermarking a related cryptographic technique a technique that enables the owner of digital content to mark the information and make it almost impossible to remove the watermark without distorting the quality of the content.

Damn it License management systems also employ cryptography to regulate the use of software's and digital Multimedia so that they have to stick with the contractual terms. It has been established that DRM systems secure content creators and distributors' work from piracy and additional distribution using cryptographic methods.

9. Internet of Things (IoT)

One of the most popular concepts in a modern world is the Internet of Things (IoT), which occupies billions of devices, starting from home devices and ending with industry sensors. Protecting these devices and the data they produce is one of the greatest difficulties, and cryptography becomes mandatory for allowing confidentiality, integrity, and authenticity of IoT messages [36].

Due to the low storage ability and computing power, most IoT devices employ lightweight cryptographic algorithms. These algorithms include encryption, authentication, and integrity check and can be deployed in devices without many effects on performance. PKI is also employed for the management of the identities of IoT devices to form trust relationships that will allow the secure communication between IoT devices, as well as excluding the undesired connection to the IoT network[37].

10. Voting Systems

Cryptology is now more and more applied to the electronic voting methods preserving the votes' confidentiality and its validity. Advantages of electronic voting include that it whether ballots will be kept secret from other individuals or groups or the result will be interfered with, cryptographic protocols will be used to encrypt it. It performed through cryptographic processes that could let voters confirm that their vote tally was accurately tabulated without revealing the voted choice.

Zero-Knowledge Proofs (ZKPs) is another cryptographic method in use in the voting systems to ensure that the results of the elections can be audited while respecting the anonymity of the voters. Through encryption of the votes and the process of transmission and storage as well as tallying, cryptography is very essential to keep E-voting systems credible.

CASE STUDIES AND REAL-WORLD APPLICATIONS OF CRYPTOGRAPHY

Cryptology is now an essential security technology in organizations' need to protect their information assets regardless of their specialization in finance, government, healthcare, and other industries. The next section provides an insight into various real life instances and uses of cryptography, as to how it has been properly deployed for the purpose of confidentiality and authenticity of messages and the safeguard of several valuable information in one way or the other.

1. Blockchain Technology in Financial Services

A real-world use of cryptography is well illustrated in the world of cryptocurrencies, or more specifically in Blockchain technology, which is the basis of which currencies such as Bitcoin and Ethereum exist. Based on the principles of cryptographic hash function and digital signatures, block chain offers a highly secured distributed ledger that provides an immutable record to the transactions.

Case Study: Bitcoin

Bitcoin, which is the most popular crypto-currency, employs SHA 256 hash functions to interconnect the blocks of financial transactions thereby allowing for the validation of blockchain. Every block actually has the hash of the previous block and this makes it hard for anyone to alter a block of the chain. If a block is altered, its hash code, which is used in the formation of the new block, is affected this thus distorts the string and the act of altering is immediately visible to everyone in the network. Also, Bitcoin utilizes public key cryptography in ownership of bitcoins since it is a digital currency. In a said transaction, the user signs it with his/her private key, then the message encrypted with the peer's public key. This means that no other person, but the holder of the private key can use it to sign for the transfer of the bitcoins, hence no fraudulent transaction.

2. Secure Communications in Government and Defense

Cryptography is widely used by governments and defense organizations to ensure security of information and communications in particular where security takes priority over everything else.

Case Study: NSA's Suite B Cryptography

The United States' National Security Agency has come up with what it refers to as Suite B Cryptography, a catalog of cryptographic algorithms applied to classified and other non-classified communications. For encryption Suite B comprised AES, for hashing SHA-2, for digital signature algorithm to be used was ECDSA and for key exchange algorithm to be used was ECDH. These cryptographic standards were installed in a plethora of government and militaries application to protect everything from e-mails to satellite channels. ECC used in Suite B offered increased protection with smaller key sizes, which was helpful due to the rare availability of computational power in such networks as for the mobile devices and embedded systems [39].

3. Encryption in Healthcare Systems

The healthcare industry deals with large volumes of patients' information which makes data protection and privacy key issues. Encryption information is well employed to address challenges of security for electronic health records and Health data exchanging between health organizations.

Case Study: HIPAA Compliance

In the United States, any facility that deals with patients has to adhere to the Health Insurance Portability and Accountability Act (HIPAA) on patient's health information. AES is used by the healthcare provider to ensure compliance with the HIPAA act in protecting patients' data at rest and in transit [38]. For instance, when a patient record is shared between hospitals or other organizations or even saved in a cloud-based EHR system, then it has to be encoded. In addition, cryptographic algorithms such as digital signatures and hash functions are applied to ensure the medical records, prescriptions, and diagnostic report's authenticity and integrity. Cryptographic techniques are particularly useful to healthcare facilities in the processing of patient data to satisfy the regulations spelt by HIPAA and at the same time ensure the data collected belongs to the patient.

4. E-Commerce and Payment Security

A vast number of ecommerce and payment systems owners daily receive millions of transactions, personal data and credit card numbers, addresses, etc. It must be pointed out that cryptography plays a vital role in ensuring the security of such transactions and consumers' information.

Case Study: There is secure payment processing with the usage of TLS.

Secure Socket Layer (SSL) is a secure protocol that is frequently employed in e-business for protecting online transactions. Each time a consumer buys a product from an e-commerce site, the information that is transmitted from the customer's browser across to the merchant server is protected from spying by using TLS [40].

Moreover, public-key infrastructure [PKI] plays a part in authenticating the merchant's web site so that the clients have confidence that they are dealing with a definite merchant. This enables secure communication since intercepted communication by an attacker during the transaction between the customer and the merchant is prevented.

Tokenization is another example of cryptographic method that may be applied in payment systems. Tokenization is a technique where instead of merchant storing real credit card numbers, they substitute it with a token. It can particularly be applied in processing of other transactions in a way that it does not reveal the actual payment details thus minimizing the cases of data leakage.

5. Digital Rights Management in Media Industry

The media industry use of cryptography to safeguard and regulate copyrights and licensing for products like music, motion pictures, software, and books in electronic form.

Case Study: Apple 's DRM known as FairPlay

Damien toxic iTunes store sells digital content such as music, movies, and Teles Shows through Apple's Fair Play DRM system. AES encryption technique is used to secure the content at FairPlay others cannot have an access if they do not have the decryption key.

Every time a user buys a tune from iTunes, for instance, the content is protected with a key that belongs to the specific account. This eliminates sales and streaming on unauthorized terminal or devices or simply put those not synced to the specific Apple ID. Furthermore, FairPlay employs the utilization of Watermarking so that any copy made from a pirated media can easily be linked back to the rightful owner.

6. Telecommunications and Mobile Security

The telecommunications industry also applies cryptography to protect voice, video and data transmission over networks, meaning calls and data, messages among other cannot be intercepted and read by unauthorized persons.

Case Study: This procedure involves using an identification card inserted into the SIM card slot of the user's mobile phone to provide access to his/her account information.

In Mobile phones, SIM card employs the use of Cryptographic algorithm to authenticate users to Mobile networks. This process consists of symmetric encryption and CRP which is the system in which the SIM card and the network send encoded messages to each other in order to authenticate the user. This is a result of successful authentication in which the user is allowed on the network [41].

Moreover, AME, GSM, WCDMA, CDMA2000 and LTE standards employ method of encryption for data and voice transmission by air interface. This means that even if the actual communication is intercepted, the reader won't be able to comprehend the contained message.

7. Quantum Cryptography for Future-Proof Security

With the development of the quantum computing as a new breed of computing technology now under development, it becomes a real threat to the conventional cryptography systems. In response, quantum cryptography provides means for protecting the Communications against quantum attacks.

Case Study: Quantum Key Distribution is defined as the method of transmitting the encrypted secret key necessary for decoding a message through the use of a quantum communication channel.

Quantum key distribution or QKD can therefore be described as a mean of secure communications whereby encryption key is transported using principles relating to quantum mechanics. QKD uses the system of eliminating all threats of interception and cloning and one of the methods is BB84 that enables two parties to share a secret key. Examples of QKD are used in the commodity-world applications: SwissQuantum – a quantum-communication network located in Geneva, Switzerland. This network was applied to show that QKD could be utilized in achieving secure communication over a metropolitan area. It achieved the secure transmission of quantum keys over fiber-optic links; the communication could not be intercepted by classical or quantum hacking.

8. Post-Quantum Cryptography; Future Security

PQC or Post Quantum Cryptography is an attempt to create new cryptographic algorithms, which are resistant to quantum computational power which threatens attacks on currently popular algorithms like RSA and ECC.

Case Study: NIST on PQ Cryptography Standardization

The key development that is currently ongoing is the standardization of post-quantum cryptographic algorithms led by NIST. Due to the threat posed by quantum computers, NIST had organized a competition for choosing and studying advanced cryptographic algorithms that are immunes to a quantum attack.

The different cryptographic schemes such as lattice, hash, and code cryptography have been tested for standardization for post-quantum cryptography by the NIST under the PQC process. Francis and Menezes offer that the intention is to create and stabilize techniques that ensure the QQ system is quantum safe while incorporating it to the conventional cryptographic networks.

In these case studies and real-world application areas, one can see how crucial an element cryptography is in the protection of data and transmissions in many different fields. With development in the digital infrastructure, the use of safe cryptographic methods will only intensify as the ensure the security, confidentiality, and purity of data in the future world.

CONCLUSION AND FUTURE DIRECTIONS

Cryptology is still a core element of info sec; it offers the essential tools and strategies to safeguard information from unauthorized access and alteration. With systems becoming more complex and embedded in our everyday lives following various domains such as finance, healthcare and defense, it is evident that strong cryptographic solutions are direly needed. In this survey, the role of symmetric-key encryption, asymmetric-key encryption, and hash functions in the quest to meet the objectives of confidentiality, integrity, authentication, and non-repudiation has been as brought out. These algorithms have turned out to be very vital in authentication of links, identities, and data in several applications ranging from communication security to overall data protection.

However, the constantly emerging threats in the modern world create new difficulties that require further development of cryptography and information security. Among these issues, there is a possible quantum threat, which may become a serious problem for many of today's cryptographic methods. When quantum computers start being developed for practical use, they are going to receive capabilities of solving highly complicated mathematical problems on which most of the current cryptographic techniques are based; thus, the need for inventing quantum-resistant encryption techniques emerges. There appears a post-quantum cryptography that tries to devise new algorithms that are not vulnerable to the actions of quantum enemies. Current research initiatives are aimed at keeping supercomputer equipping adversaries at bay; this is through lattice-based cryptography, code-based cryptography, and every other novel idea in the offing.

Also, the emergence of new privacy enhancing technologies (PET) points at the increasing need for methods for data protection that respects the privacy of individuals. Since digital data remains to be a valuable asset, other PETs like HE, ZKPs, and SMPC offer the way through which computations can be made on the encrypted data without compromising the privacy of the information. These technologies shall play a crucial role in solving the privacy problems and providing safe data handling in various fields like the healthcare sector, the financial field, and computing in the cloud.

Another essential area for the future study is the enhancement of the tough and effective methods of authentication. With the continued innovation in the methods of conducting cyberattacks, the conventional ways of authentication through passwords are still found lacking. There are better and more secure options such as multi-factor authentication MFA, biometric authentication and the relatively newer method of behavioral biometrics that can go a long way in minimizing cases of identity theft and unauthorised access.

There is an acute necessity for the improvement of the cybersecurity education initiatives and activities in order to mitigate the threats coming from the human factor, which remain one of the main exposures of the information security. Business entities need to create training initiatives through which the personnel will obtain awareness of cyberspace risks and the means to address them appropriately. Establishing the awareness of security is critical in preventing social engineering tactics and general mistakes. Compared to the time when computer code could be easily hacked and data assets easily compromised, many strides have been taken in cryptography and information security, but because threats are, constantly evolving, new ways must be continuously implemented. By enhancing this type of crypto research, accepting privacy-protection technologies, improving the authentication process, and raising cybersecurity consciousness all around, the world will be given a safer digital sphere that preserves important information and the credibility of global interconnectedness.

REFERENCES

Ali, A., Al-Rimy, B. A. S., Almazroi, A. A., Alsubaei, F. S., Almazroi, A. A., & Saeed, F. (2023). Securing secrets in cyber-physical systems: A cutting-edge privacy approach with consortium blockchain. *Sensors (Basel)*, *23*(16), 7162. DOI: 10.3390/s23167162 PMID: 37631699

Alléaume, R., Branciard, C., Bouda, J., Debuisschert, T., Dianati, M., Gisin, N., Godfrey, M., Grangier, P., Länger, T., Lütkenhaus, N., Monyk, C., Painchault, P., Peev, M., Poppe, A., Pornin, T., Rarity, J., Renner, R., Ribordy, G., Riguidel, M., & Zeilinger, A. (2014). Using quantum key distribution for cryptographic purposes: A survey. *Theoretical Computer Science*, *560*, 62–81. DOI: 10.1016/j.tcs.2014.09.018

Alluhaidan, A. S. D., & Prabu, P. (2023). End-to-end encryption in resource-constrained IoT device. *IEEE Access : Practical Innovations, Open Solutions*, *11*, 70040–70051. DOI: 10.1109/ACCESS.2023.3292829

Anilkumar, C., Lenka, S., Neelima, N., & Sathishkumar, V. E. (2024). A Secure Method of Communication Through BB84 Protocol in Quantum Key Distribution. *Scalable Computing: Practice and Experience*, *25*(1), 21–33. DOI: 10.12694/scpe.v25i1.2152

Bakare, S. S., Adeniyi, A. O., Akpuokwe, C. U., & Eneh, N. E. (2024). Data privacy laws and compliance: A comparative review of the EU GDPR and USA regulations. *Computer Science & IT Research Journal*, *5*(3), 528–543. DOI: 10.51594/csitrj.v5i3.859

Bellare, M., & Miner, S. K. (1999, August). A forward-secure digital signature scheme. In *Annual international cryptology conference* (pp. 431-448). Berlin, Heidelberg: Springer Berlin Heidelberg. DOI: 10.1007/3-540-48405-1_28

Bradley, S. (2024). Comparative Analysis of Two Data Privacy Regulatory Schemes: The GDPR and the CCPA.

Chauhan, D. IPv6 Migration Strategy Using Carrier Grade Network Address Translation.

Chauhan, D., & Jain, J. K. (2019). A Journey from IoT to IoE. [IJITEE]. *International Journal of Innovative Technology and Exploring Engineering*, *8*(11).

Chauhan, D., & Jain, J. K. (2021). IoT and Blockchain in Indian Perspective. In *Blockchain Applications in IoT Security* (pp. 186–202). IGI Global. DOI: 10.4018/978-1-7998-2414-5.ch011

Chauhan, D., & Jain, J. K. (2023, January). Profiling Network Traffic by Using Classification Techniques in Machine Learning. In *International Conference on Smart Trends in Computing and Communications* (pp. 113-123). Singapore: Springer Nature Singapore. DOI: 10.1007/978-981-99-0769-4_12

Chauhan, D., & Jain, J. K. (2024). Measures and Preventions of Cyber Policies in Smart Cities. In *Digital Technologies in Modeling and Management: Insights in Education and Industry* (pp. 244-262). IGI Global.

Chauhan, D., Jain, J. K., & Bahad, P. (2021). PERFORMANCE EVALUATION OF 802.11 A/G WIRELESS NETWORKS WITH IP6HC. *Journal of Management Information and Decision Sciences*, *24*, 1–7.

Chauhan, D., Jain, J. K., & Sharma, S. (2016, December). An end-to-end header compression for multihop IPv6 tunnels with varying bandwidth. In 2016 Fifth international conference on eco-friendly computing and communication systems (ICECCS) (pp. 84-88). IEEE. DOI: 10.1109/Eco-friendly.2016.7893247

Chauhan, D., Jain, J. K., & Singh, A. (2024). Deployment of Edge Computing for Smart Healthcare Systems on Cloud Computing Platform.

Chauhan, D., Sharma, S., & Singh, V. (2023). Roadmap from 4G to 6G in smart cities impact and challenges. [IJWMT]. *Int. J. Wirel. Microw. Technol.*, *13*(6), 39–50. DOI: 10.5815/ijwmt.2023.06.05

Fernandez-Carames, T. M., & Fraga-Lamas, P. (2020). Towards post-quantum blockchain: A review on blockchain cryptography resistant to quantum computing attacks. *IEEE Access : Practical Innovations, Open Solutions*, *8*, 21091–21116. DOI: 10.1109/ACCESS.2020.2968985

Gentry, C. (2009). *A fully homomorphic encryption scheme*. Stanford university.

Hasan, J. (2019). Overview and applications of zero knowledge proof (ZKP). *International Journal of Computer Science and Network*, *8*(5), 2277–5420.

Huang, K. T., Chiu, J. H., & Shen, S. S. (2013). A novel structure with dynamic operation mode for symmetric-key block ciphers. *International Journal of Network Security & its Applications*, *5*(1), 17–36. DOI: 10.5121/ijnsa.2013.5102

Hunton, P. (2009). The growing phenomenon of crime and the internet: A cybercrime execution and analysis model. *Computer Law & Security Report*, *25*(6), 528–535. DOI: 10.1016/j.clsr.2009.09.005

Jain, J. K., & Chauhan, D. (2019, April). Analytical study on Mobile Ad hoc Networks for IPV6. In *2019 4th International Conference on Internet of Things: Smart Innovation and Usages (IoT-SIU)* (pp. 1-6). IEEE. DOI: 10.1109/IoT-SIU.2019.8777486

Jain, J. K., & Chauhan, D. (2021). An Energy-Efficient Model for Internet of Things Using Compressive Sensing. *Journal of Management Information and Decision Sciences, 24*, 1–7.

Jain, J. K., & Chauhan, D. (2023). Innovative Model of Internet of Things for Industrial Applications. In *Opportunities and Challenges of Industrial IoT in 5G and 6G Networks* (pp. 95–118). IGI Global. DOI: 10.4018/978-1-7998-9266-3.ch005

Jain, J. K., Dangi, C. S., & Chauhan, D. (2020, November). An Efficient Multipath Productive Routing Protocol for Mobile Ad-hoc Networks. In *2020 IEEE International Conference for Innovation in Technology (INOCON)* (pp. 1-5). IEEE. DOI: 10.1109/INOCON50539.2020.9298291

Jain, J. K., & Sharma, S. (2013). Performance Evaluation of Hybrid Multipath Progressive Routing Protocol for MANETs. *International Journal of Computer Applications, 71*(18).

Jain, J. K., & Sharma, S. (2017). A Novel Approach of Routing Protocol using Hybrid Analysis for MANETs. *International Journal of Computer Science and Information Security, 15*(1), 582.

Jain, J. K., Waoo, A. A., & Chauhan, D. (2022). A literature review on machine learning for cyber security issues. *International Journal of Scientific Research in Computer Science, Engineering and Information Technology*, 374-385.

Jin, H., Wang, M., Wang, L., Yang, Q., Li, Y., Long, X., & Liu, T. (2024, July). The research focuses on the symmetric encryption scheme for industrial data based on MQTT. In *International Conference on Signal Processing and Communication Security (ICSPCS 2024)* (Vol. 13222, pp. 51-57). SPIE. DOI: 10.1117/12.3038673

Kaaniche, N., & Laurent, M. (2017). Data security and privacy preservation in cloud storage environments based on cryptographic mechanisms. *Computer Communications, 111*, 120–141. DOI: 10.1016/j.comcom.2017.07.006

Kaleem, M., Mushtaq, M. A., Jamil, U., Ramay, S. A., Khan, T. A., Patel, S., & Hussain, S. K. (2024). New Efficient Cryptographic Techniques For Cloud Computing Security. *Migration Letters : An International Journal of Migration Studies, 21*(S11), 13–28.

Kumar, D. D., Mukharzee, J. D., Reddy, C. V. D., & Rajagopal, S. M. (2024, March). Safe and Secure Communication Using SSL/TLS. In *2024 International Conference on Emerging Smart Computing and Informatics (ESCI)* (pp. 1-6). IEEE. DOI: 10.1109/ESCI59607.2024.10497224

Lacombe, F. Facing Modern Crises: An Integrative Literature Review of Pandemics and Cyber Threats Dynamics.

Mbonihankuye, S., Nkunzimana, A., & Ndagijimana, A. (2019). Healthcare data security technology: HIPAA compliance. *Wireless Communications and Mobile Computing*, *2019*(1), 1927495.

Rivest, R. L., Adleman, L., & Dertouzos, M. L. (1978). On data banks and privacy homomorphisms. *Foundations of secure computation, 4*(11), 169-180.

Shrivastava, A., Jaın, J., & Chauhan, D. (2023). Literature review on tools & applications of data mining. *International Journal on Computer Science and Engineering, 11*(4), 46–54.

Singh, P., Choudhary, N., Samnotra, B., Bhel, S., Sharma, S., Kour, H., ... & Kumar, S. (2024). Understanding RSA Algorithm in Cryptography.

Souror, S., El-Fishawy, N., & Badawy, M. (2022). Security analysis for SCKHA algorithm: Stream cipher algorithm based on key hashing technique. *Chinese Journal of Electronics*, •••, 1–16.

Sousi, A. L., Yehya, D., & Joudi, M. (2020). Aes encryption: Study & evaluation. *CCEE552: Cryptography and Network Security.*

Tebaa, M., El Hajji, S., & El Ghazi, A. (2012, April). *Homomorphic encryption method applied to Cloud Computing. In 2012 National Days of Network Security and Systems.* IEEE.

Victor, M., Praveenraj, D. D. W., Sasirekha, R., Alkhayyat, A., & Shakhzoda, A. (2023). Cryptography: Advances in Secure Communication and Data Protection. In *E3S Web of Conferences* (Vol. 399, p. 07010). EDP Sciences.

KEY TERMS AND DEFINITIONS

Cryptography: The science of protecting data by converting it into an unreadable form, ensuring only authorized users can access it.

Encryption: The process of converting plaintext into ciphertext to protect the information from unauthorized access.

Decryption: The reverse process of encryption, where ciphertext is converted back into readable plaintext.

Symmetric Key Cryptography: A cryptographic technique where the same key is used for both encryption and decryption.

Asymmetric Key Cryptography: A cryptographic method using different keys for encryption and decryption, typically a public and a private key.

Advanced Encryption Standard (AES): A widely-used symmetric key encryption standard that operates on fixed data blocks and offers high security and efficiency.

Post-Quantum Cryptography: The development of cryptographic algorithms that are resistant to quantum computing attacks, which threaten traditional cryptographic methods like RSA and ECC.

Quantum Key Distribution (QKD): A secure key distribution technique using the principles of quantum mechanics to detect any eavesdropping during the key exchange process.

Public Key Infrastructure (PKI): A framework used to manage public keys and digital certificates, enhancing the security and scalability of asymmetric encryption systems.

Zero-Knowledge Proofs: A cryptographic method allowing one party to prove the validity of information to another party without revealing the actual information.

Chapter 13
An Implementation of Decentralized Secured Tweeting Platform
Security of a Tweeting App

Sumathi Pawar
Nitte Mahalinga Adyantaya Memorial Institute, Karkala, India

Roopa Hegde
Nitte Mahalinga Adyantaya Memorial Institute, Karkala, India

Ankitha K.
Nitte Mahalinga Adyantaya Memorial Institute, Karkala, India

Vasanth Nayak
Canara Engineering College, BenjanaPadavu, India

Vandhana B.S.
Nitte Mahalinga Adyantaya Memorial Institute, Karkala, India

Geethalaxmi
Canara Engineering College, BenjanaPadavu, India

ABSTRACT

This system represents a decentralized tweeting social media platform with the objective of furnishing users a communication environment that's both secure and characterized by transparency. Through the integration of smart contracts, users can transact directly and securely without the need for intermediaries. This initiative demonstrates the potential of integrating Blockchain and ReactJS to create a decentralized social media platform, enhancing security and transparency to unprecedented levels. This article aims to create a decentralized social media platform using Block chain which confirms that data is securely stored, immutable and transparent. Proposed system enables users to post tweets, follow other users, like and comment on posts and engage in real-time messaging. In this system a step-by-step approach to implement this secured Tweeting application is presented.

DOI: 10.4018/979-8-3693-8014-7.ch013

1. INTRODUCTION

This article aims to develop a secure tweeting app utilizing blockchain web 3.0, employing Solidity, Next.js, and Sanity.io. The system mimics Twitter's functionality, providing a secure platform for tweeting. The frontend is built with Next.js and styled using Tailwind CSS. Additionally, a custom smart contract is created with Solidity (Zheng, Xie, Dai, Chen, & Wang, 2017). Blockchain, the primary network for cryptocurrency, supports the app, while Twitter remains a popular social media platform for cryptocurrency enthusiasts to share their thoughts in short posts.

Creating a smart contract for a tweeting app using blockchain involves writing the contract in Solidity, the programming language for Ethereum. An example of a basic smart contract that enables users to post tweets and retrieve is given in implementation section. This contract includes basic functionality for posting and viewing tweets.

Truffle is utilized for deploying the smart contract on the Ubuntu (Debian) OS (ValetiDeepika & LalithaBhaskari, 2020). This project offers enhanced security compared to a standard Twitter app. Smart contract, which are programmable digital agreements, improve communication and facilitate long-term asset tracking. They are also valuable for maintaining relationships with consumers.

1.1 APIs Used

Web3 API: In this application an instance of WEB3 API is created for connecting to the local blockchain network. This system also uses the Web3 API to conversate with the smart contract by creating a contract instance and calling its methods to create tweets, like tweets, and retrieve tweets.

Web3.js: Web3.js stands as a JavaScript library designed to facilitate interaction with the blockchain of Ethereum. It offers a straightforward API (Pawar & GuruRaj, 2023) for linking to the blockchain, initiating transactions and engaging with smart contracts.

Ethers.js: Ethers.js is another JavaScript library that allows to interact with the Ethereum blockchain. It provides a simpler API compared to Web3.js and has better support for TypeScript.

IPFS: IPFS (Interplanetary File System) constitutes a dispersed storage system for files, enabling storage and sharing across a distributed network of computers. It furnishes an API that facilitates the storage and retrieval of files from the IPFS network.

Solidity: Solidity is a programming language needed to write smart contracts on the Ethereum blockchain. It is used to define the business logic of an App and is executed on Ethereum Virtual Machine (EVM). This application uses the Solidity

API to define the smart contract for Tweet structure that represents a tweet and provides methods for creating tweets, liking tweets and retrieving tweets.

Open Zeppelin: Open Zeppelin is a library of reusable smart contracts that provide security and modularity to the App. It provides a range of smart contracts from simple ones like ownership contracts to more complex ones like multi-signature wallets.

React-Bootstrap API: This application uses React-Bootstrap to create UI components such as forms, buttons, and list groups.

According to organization of this article, Section 2 discusses literature review, section 3 on various methods and section 4,5 focussed on implementation and results.

2. LITERATURE REVIEW

In 1991, block chain technology was proposed. This technology made digital data unchanged during its transfer. At the beginning, public database is used for securing the content. Later block chain technology is used to create bitcoin, a virtual money (Zheng, Xie, Dai, Chen, & Wang, 2017).

NFT (Non-Fungible Token) is non-fungible compared to a cryptocurrency. It contains a cryptographic link to a specific artwork on IPFS and thus represents a digital certificate for a unique artwork. For the art world especially in particular digital artists, this technology and certificate provides a market to distribute and sell their artworks. The computational power should be made efficient, so that less energy consumption take place (Grasser & Parger, 2022).

In the "Blocks" collections of data and state are used to store data and state. The transactional information must be included to a block in order to transmit ETH. The word "chain" denotes the interconnectedness of all the blocks. "Node" is computer in each block which also concur as a chain in whole network. Every user access to same data in block chain network, it is requires a distributed agreement (Goel et al., 2022).

Every time the smart contract's functionalities are invoked, events are implemented and released as previously indicated, which may be helpful for automating some activities. Along with a succinct overview of the Ethereum blockchain network, a practical implementation of such a workflow, leveraging the inclusion of the Solidity smart contract language is provided. This dual approach enables, firstly, the establishment of a durable record concerning agreements between data authors and users, offering the capability to verify adherence at any given point of hand (Pãnescu & Manta, 2018).

With respect to Data collections, 1,20,000 tweets were related to Bitcoin & Ethreum which includes User Id, Tweet created time, Tweet text, Tweet length, user created time, user followers count, user friends count, Twittter sources, Tweet likes,

Tweet retweets. This was used to train the model for machine learning approaches of block chain usage (Ranasinghe & Halgamuge, 2021).

Ahmad et al. (2022) managed health care system with critical and non-critical patients concurrently. Critical fog clusters handle critical patients for speedy response, while non-critical fog clusters manage non-critical patients to safeguard the confidentiality of patient health records with this technique. The recommended remedy minimally modifies the current IoT ecosystem while reducing essential message response times and offloading cloud infrastructure. Users gain from decreased storage needs for cloud data centres which resulted in saving money.

Handayani (2022) is innovative in that it applies the legislation to each chosen CBDC design. This architecture is comprised of whole-sale and retail which use token or account-based verification, according to the report. Following that, CBDC transactions is handled by the central bank or carried out using a DLT system. Apart from that, one more feature of CBDC is dependent on interest-bearing and non-interest-bearing. Regulations had to be improved as a result of CBDC's varied implementation and choice. Regarding the legal status of CBDC in Indonesia, changes must be made to the text of Law No. 7 of 2011 on Currency, which must specify that CBDC is included in the rupiah currency.

In order to comprehend the research's direction and content more thoroughly, this system evaluated the research articles on CBDC. Reviewing research on central bank digital currencies (CBDCs) is the goal of this essay. The most recent research defines CBDC as a payment method comparable to cash. The benefits and traits of employing CBDC have also been put out as justifications for the central bank issuing them. The essay also demonstrates how CBDC and financial inclusion are related. After the issuance of CBDC, an analysis of the existing situation and a forecast of its future development is made (Liu, 2023).

According to literature review, motivation behind the secured Tweeting App development is for secured communication and many researches are going on in the area of decentralized security technique. Usage of block chain made it possible for strong security in various nodes. Innovation in the field of decentralized Web services (Pawar & Chiplunkar, 2018; Pawar & Geetha, 2023; Pawar & Gururaj, 2022), made the block chain transaction more powerful.

3. TECHNOLOGY BEHIND THE BLOCK CHAIN

Block chain technology is used for distributed or decentralized security which will not fail as in case of single point of centralized nature. Following are components of block chain system.

3.1 Distributed Ledger Technology (DLT)

In decentralized system such as block chain this technology is used. Here transactions are recorded digitally in multiple places at the same time. Distributed ledgers does not have central data store as traditional databases.

In a DLT system, multiple nodes (computers) participate in the network, each maintaining a copy of the ledger. Decisions and validations are made collectively by the network rather than a central authority, enhancing transparency and reducing single points of failure. Running a full node involves maintaining a copy of the entire blockchain and validating transactions. Node operators may earn rewards for providing network stability and contributing to decentralization. Decentralized Finance (DeFi) applications often involve creating and interacting with smart contracts. The contracts are self-executing programs with predefined rules. Developers can monetize their Apps by designing useful and innovative smart contracts that attract users and generate transaction fees. The smart contract has the flexibility to be deployed either on a public blockchain network like Ethereum or on a private network.

3.2 Cryptographic hash functions

Here each block contains cryptographic hash of its previous block, ensuring that all records are immutable and any alteration in a block would change its hash and break the chain. Transactions are signed using private keys and verified by anyone using the corresponding public key, ensuring authenticity and non-repudiation. Using Immutable Ledger, transaction is recorded.

3.3 Blocks and Chains

A block is a data structure used to record a set of transactions. Each block typically contains the components such as header of a block contains metadata about the block. Previous block hash is reference to the hash of the previous block in the chain. This links the blocks together in a specific sequence, Timestamp is time at which the block was created, Merkle Root is a hash that represents all the transactions in the block, organized in a Merkle tree structure. This provides a compact and efficient way to verify the integrity of the transactions. Nonce is a random number used in the Proof of Work (PoW) consensus mechanism to vary the input to the hash function and meet the required difficulty target. Difficulty level for the PoW algorithm determines how hard it is to find a valid hash for the block.

The linking of blocks through cryptographic hashes ensures that any attempt to alter a transaction would require re-mining all subsequent blocks, making tampering highly impractical. Each transaction is recorded in a public ledger that is accessible to all participants, providing transparency and auditability. Processes involves transaction creation, block creation, verification, validation and addition to chain.

3.4 Smart Contracts

These are self-executing contracts where agreements are directly written into code. They run on blockchain platforms, which ensures that the contract execution which is automated, transparent and immutable. This eliminate the need for intermediaries, reduce transaction costs and increase the efficiency of executing agreements. Oracles are services that provide external data to smart contracts. They bridge the gap between blockchain and the real world by feeding information like stock prices, weather conditions and more. Smart contracts written in high-level languages like Solidity are compiled into EVM bytecode, which was executed by the EVM.

3.5 Token Distribution

Security Token Offerings (STOs) is an Initial Coin Offerings (ICOs) token distribution method, which involve mathematical calculations to determine token allocations, pricing and fund-raising goals. Transaction fees, often denominated in the blockchain's native token are required to process transactions or execute smart contracts. Gas prices represent the computational resources needed for a transaction or contract execution. Users bid on gas prices to prioritize their transactions.

4. METHODOLOGY

This article is focussed on developing a secured tweeting App using blockchain technology with two objectives. First objective is to develop a client tester/Simulator. Second objective is to apply security through Blockchain against hacking of account.

In current tweeting applications, the client part send/receive tweets and the engine distribute tweets. The current tweeting apps does not have much security and there can be leak of private information of user. Therefore, this system implements tweeting platform using blockchain, which ensures the privacy of the user.

Figure 1. Architecture of the system

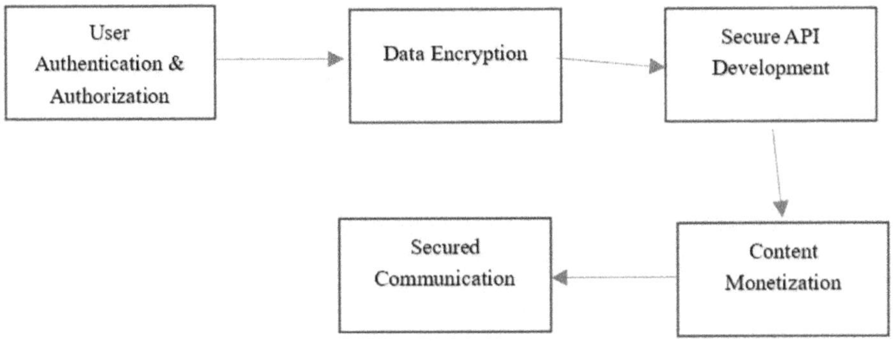

Block diagram of the system is shown in figure 1 and each block is explained in detail.

4.1 Authentication & Authorization

This is done by React-Bootstrap API. This application uses React-Bootstrap to create UI components such as forms, buttons and list groups. At first, user interface of the Twitter clone is designed using React JS, a widely embraced JavaScript library designed for building user interfaces. This integral component is tasked with presenting diverse aspects of tweeting App, including user's timeline, notifications, messages and other functionalities.

This involves creating several components such as the home feed, user profile, search bar, tweet composer and notifications. There are various React JS libraries such as Material-UI, Bootstrap to design the user interface. Users can create an account on the platform and link their blockchain wallet address to their account. Authentication is done using third-party providers like MetaMask.

4.2 Data Encryption using Block chain Networks

The blockchain network is the core of this system. It is accountable for storing and processing all user data, including tweets, user profiles and other information. The blockchain network ensures that all data is stored in a secure and decentralized manner, making it tamper-proof and resilient to attacks (Zheng, Xie, Dai, Chen, & Wang, 2017).

Figure 2. Blockchain Architecture (Mohitkirange, n.d.)

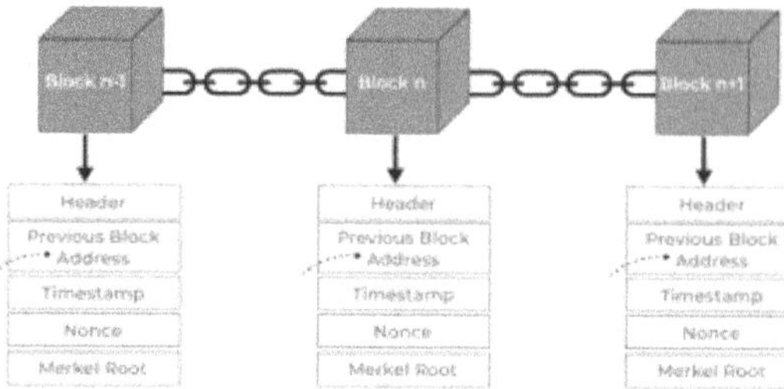

Figure 2 shows architecture of block chain where header, timestamp, previous block chain address and Merkel roots are included. Each content is elaborated in further sections. Structure of a block also contain transaction list which contain transaction data with details of the transaction, such as sender, receiver, amount, and any additional data. Transaction Hash is a unique identifier for the transaction, generated by hashing the transaction data. It also contains digital signatures for verification of the authenticity and integrity of the transaction.

4.3 Secured API

Secured API is characterized by input validation, sanitization, rate limiting and secure defaults. Validation of the input is done for preventing SQL injection effects and cross site scripting. Implementing rate limitation is to prevent abuse of the API through excessive requests. This helps protect against Denial of Service (DoS) attacks. Secured defaults ensure for securing all default configurations. Unnecessary features or services are avoided. Penetration testing (pen testing) is an essential aspect of securing a tweeting app. It involves simulating attacks on the application to identify vulnerabilities before malicious actors can exploit them. Automated tools are used to scan the API for common vulnerabilities like OWASP Top Ten issues.

4.4 Content Monetization

In the context of blockchain technology, monetization typically refers to the process of generating revenue or profits from blockchain-related activities. This can encompass various aspects, such as cryptocurrency mining, staking, running nodes, developing decentralized applications (dApps) and more. Some of the mathematical concepts and mechanisms involved in blockchain monetization are given here. In (PoW) Proof of Work, blockchains like Bitcoin, miners resolve composite mathematical puzzles for validating transactions and to create new blocks. The mathematical difficulty of these puzzles is adjusted to maintain a consistent block generation rate. In PoS-based blockchains, validators (often referred to as "stakers") will be selected to create new blocks and validate transactions. Validators are chosen through a deterministic procedure that commonly considers factors such as the quantity of staked tokens, token age and occasionally an element of randomization.

Tokenomics monetization is significantly impacted by the design of a blockchain's native token and its supply dynamics. For instance, tokens can be used to pay for transaction fees, access certain features or participate in governance decisions. Game theory and economic models play a role in blockchain monetization. Incentive mechanisms are designed to encourage participants to act in ways that benefit the network's security and overall functionality. Blockchain monetization involves a combination of cryptography, game theory, economics and mathematical modeling. The specific mathematics behind each aspect can vary depending on the blockchain's consensus mechanism, token design and ecosystem goals.

4.5 Secure Communication

In this system, users created tweets using a form that sends a transaction to the smart contract. The transaction includes the text of the tweet, the author's wallet address and a timestamp. Tweets are displayed on the frontend using React JS. The tweets are fetched from the smart contract and displayed in reverse chronological order. Users can see their own tweets and the tweets of others also. Users interacted with tweets by liking, retweeting and commenting. These interactions also be stored on the blockchain, so they can't be deleted or manipulated. Real-time updates implemented using Web Sockets. This would allow users to see new tweets and interactions as they happen.

4.5.1 Search functionality

Users possess the capability to search for tweets using keywords or hash tags. This particular feature is realized through the utilization of a comprehensive text search engine such as Elastic search. The search bar component allows users to search for tweets based on keywords or hashtags. This system uses web3.js to search for tweets in the smart contract and display them in the search results. It uses cryptographic hash functions (e.g., SHA-256) to find a specific nonce (a number), hashed with the transaction data, provides a hash which meets certain criteria.

5. IMPLEMENTATION

This system is implemented using open-source APIs and in this section, it is detailed about step-by-step implementation. At the beginning block chain Ethereum network Ganache is installed and then MetaMask is installed as add-on of the browser. Then from Ganache network some accounts are imported into MetaMask. After this, dependencies are installed and using REMIX IDE, smart contract is written.

5.1. Smart Contract Creation

A smart contract comes into existence to manage the creation and storage of tweets in the blockchain. The contract could include functions to create, read, update and delete tweets. Creation of an instance of the smart contract is done by passing the ABI and address to the web3.eth, contract constructor. Interaction with the smart contract defines an async function that creates a tweet on the smart contract by calling the create Tweet method and passing in the tweet text. This system used the web3.eth.getAccounts method to retrieve the user's Ethereum account and then send method to send a transaction to the smart contract from that account. A sample code to create tweet and to send it is given here.

```
// SPDX-License-Identifier:

MIT pragma solidity ^0.8.0;

contract myTweetingApp

{ struct myTweetStruct

{ uint TweetId; address Tweetauthor; string TweetContent;
uint tweetTimestamp; }

Tweet[] public myTweets;

uint public myTweetCount;
```

```
event NewTweet(uint TweetId, address tweetAuthor, string
TweetContent, uint tweetTimestamp);

function sendTweet(string memory _content)

public { myTweetCount++;

tweets.push(Tweet(tweetCount, msg.sender, _content, block.
tweetTimestamp));

emit NewTweet(tweetCount, msg.sender, _content, block.tweet-
Timestamp); }

function recieveTweet(uint _id) public view returns (uint,
address, string memory, uint) { require(_id > 0 && _id <=
myTweetCount, "Tweet ID is invalid");

myTweet memory myTweets = myTweets [_id - 1];

return (myTweet.tweetId, myTweet.tweetAuthor, myTweet.tweet-
Content, myTweet.tweetTimestamp); }

function getAllTweets() public view returns (Tweet[] memory)

{ return tweets; } }
```

5.2 Choosing Blockchain network

Numerous blockchain networks are accessible, including Ethereum, Finance Smart Chain and Polygon. The decision should prioritize a blockchain network that facilitates smart contracts and boasts an extensive developer community. This system used GANACHE block chain network with Ethereum currency. Using Ganache, a popular Ethereum blockchain development tool, for secure communication involves leveraging its capabilities to create and test decentralized applications (DApps) on a local blockchain network. After choosing the blockchain network, it is need to set up the necessary infrastructure.

```
npm install -g ganache-cli truffle
```

Truffle is a development environment, testing framework, and asset pipeline for Ethereum, to compile and deploy smart contracts to the Ganache network. We need to write migration scripts to handle the deployment process.

Next we need to write a smart contract that will handle the storage and retrieval of tweets as given in the section 5.1. Solidity language is used for creation of smart contract on Ethereum network. Once it is written the smart contract, it is need to deploy it to the blockchain network using tools such as Truffle or Remix.

5.3 Implementing the Tweet Composer & Home Feed

Tweet composer component is implemented using React JS. The tweet composer should allow users to compose tweets and submit them to the blockchain network. This system used JavaScript library web3.js for interaction with the Ethereum network to send transactions to the smart contract. The next step is to implement the home feed component using React JS. The home feed should display tweets from users that the current user is following. Here web3.js is used to read the tweets from the smart contract and display them in the home feed.

5.4 Gas Fees and Gas Prices

In blockchain-based systems, "gas fees" and "gas prices" are commonly associated with transaction costs on networks like Ethereum. These concepts can also apply to secure communication methods using blockchain technology. Gas fees are the costs required to perform transactions or execute smart contracts on a blockchain network.

They compensate network participants (miners or validators) for the computational power and resources they use to process and validate transactions.

In the context of secure communication using blockchain, gas fees would be the costs associated with Sending Messages: Each message or piece of data sent using a blockchain may require a transaction, which incurs a gas fee. If the secure communication system uses smart contracts (for encryption, authentication, etc.), each interaction with these contracts will incur gas fees. Storing messages or other data on the blockchain, even temporarily, can incur gas fees.

Gas price is the amount we are willing to pay per unit of gas. It is typically measured in small fractions of the cryptocurrency used on the blockchain (e.g., Gwei on Ethereum). The gas price can vary depending on the network's demand and congestion; higher gas prices can lead to faster transaction processing.

5.5 Implementing the User Profile & Search Bar

The user profile component displays information about the current user, such as their profile picture, bio, and tweets. This system used web3.js to read the user's tweets from the smart contract and display them in the user profile. The search bar component allows users to search for tweets based on keywords or hashtags. The system used web3.js to search for tweets in the smart contract and display them in the search results.

5.6 Integrating the Blockchain Network with the Frontend

The next step is to integrate the blockchain network with the frontend using web3.js. It is needed to connect to the blockchain network using the provider URL and create a contract instance to interact with the smart contract. This system used MetaMask, a browser extension to connect to the blockchain network and sign transactions. The final step is to test the Twitter clone thoroughly to ensure that it works as expected. Usage of *Ganache* tool, a personal blockchain for Ethereum development is used to test the smart contract and the frontend components. Once testing is complete, the system is deployed the application to a suitable hosting platform such as Heroku, AWS, or Firebase.

6. RESULT

Figure 3. Creation of MetaMask Account

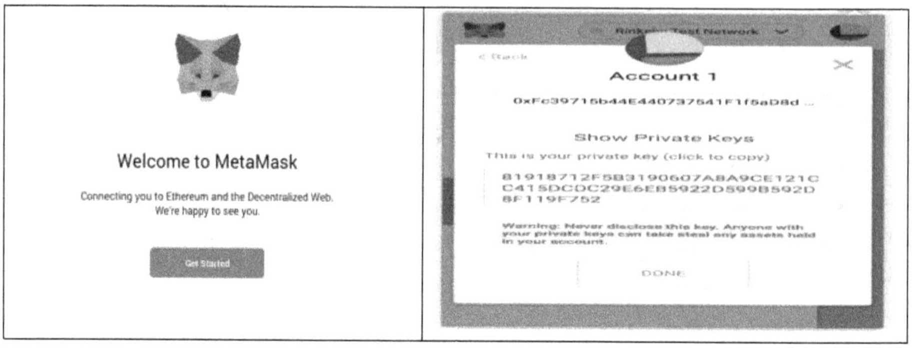

Figure 4. Login and Home Page

Figure 5. Consumption of Gas Price through Ganache Network

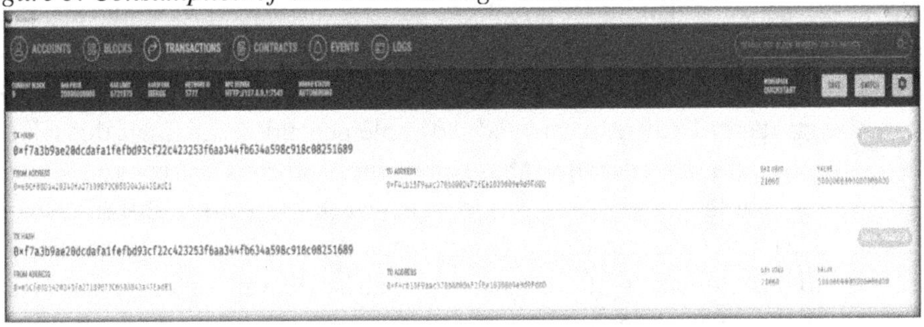

Figure 3 and figure 4 show the snapshot of the one of the results. Here user required to register the system with name, email address and password. After login, user can follow and unfollow the user and can create or share public tweets. User's tweets will be shown in the tweets section after following the user. Another feature is profile management to manage user's profile. Figure 5 shows consumption of Gas price through Ganache network.

After writing own Solidity-based smart contract, system is deployed on "ETHEREUM" blockchain and then built on a Twitter clone web App that allows user to tweet and view all the tweets. After installing MetaMask, a new Ethereum wallet is created. The wallet will store the user's private key and public key for making transactions on the blockchain. To establish a connection with the blockchain, it's necessary to designate the desired network. For instance, one can opt for the Ethereum 'mainnet' or 'testnet' as network. The network selection is accomplished by choosing the appropriate option from the dropdown menu available in Metamask.

The system needs to build a smart contract which will handle the interactions between the user and the Twitter App. The smart contract defines the functions for creating tweets, commenting on tweets and liking tweets. It is needed to integrate the smart contract with the App by using web3.js. In this system, web3.js is used to connect to the smart contract and call its functions. The UI allowed users to create tweets, comment on tweets, and like tweets. When the user performs one of these actions, the smart contract is called to update the state of the blockchain.

7. CONCLUSIONS

This secured Twitter App is more secured compared to normal Twitter. It is observed that twitter accounts getting hacked or misused by unauthorised users due to poor security. This blockchain app will protect user's account from being compromised or hacked. Through this platform, the main vision is to provide security to the user's personal data in all possible ways. Using MetaMask authentication, which is a cryptocurrency wallet, interacting with the Ethereum blockchain, ensures security. As this is totally based on blockchain, undoubtfully it is more secure and safe. Although it is difficult to understand and implement this technology, this system is more user friendly. Even though it has some procs and cons and have a long way to go, invention in the area of Web services (Pawar & Chiplunkar, 2018; Pawar & Gururaj, 2022) made decentralization more secured. As a future work, security of this App will be combined with web services security (Pawar & Geetha, 2023) and this system will be a new step towards more safe and secure advancing technology.

REFERENCES

Ahmad, I., Abdullah, S., & Ahmed, A. (2022). IoT-fog-based healthcare 4.0 system using blockchain technology. *The Journal of Supercomputing*, *79*(4), 3999–4020. DOI: 10.1007/s11227-022-04788-7 PMID: 36157083

Goel, A. K., Bakshi, R., & Agrawal, K. K. (2022). Web 3.0 and decentralized applications. *Materials Proceedings*, *10*(1), 8.

Grasser, A., & Parger, A. (2022, September). Blockchain architectures, the potential of Web3 for decentralized participatory architecture: Collaborative objects on the blockchain. In *40th Conference on Education and Research in Computer Aided Architectural Design in Europe: eCAADe 2022* (pp. 431-440).

Handayani, F. (2022). Design And Legal Aspect Of Central Bank Digital Currency: A Literature Review. *Journal of Central Banking Law and Institutions*, *1*(3), 509–536. DOI: 10.21098/jcli.v1i3.35

Liu, J. (2023). CBDC Application Analysis and Prospects. *BCP Business & Management*, *45*, 1–6. DOI: 10.54691/bcpbm.v42i.4543

Mohitkirange. (2024). *Blockchain structure*. https://www.geeksforgeeks.org/blockchain-structure/

Pãnescu, A.-T., & Manta, V. (2018). Smart Contracts for Research Data Rights Management over the Ethereum Blockchain Network. *Science & Technology Libraries*, *37*(3), 235–245. DOI: 10.1080/0194262X.2018.1474838

Pawar, S., & Chiplunkar, N. N. (2018). Survey on discovery of web services. *Indian Journal of Science and Technology*, *11*(16), 1–10.

Pawar, S., & Geetha, V. (2023). An Implemented Example of XKMS With Web Services. In *Risk Detection and Cyber Security for the Success of Contemporary Computing* (pp. 92-108). IGI Global.

Pawar, S., & Gururaj, M. (2022, December). Constraint Based Clustering Technique for Web Services. In *International Conference on Advanced Network Technologies and Intelligent Computing* (pp. 89-107). Cham: Springer Nature Switzerland.

Pawar, S., & GuruRaj, M. (2023). Dynamicity of Web Services and Web Scrapping. *Journal of Mines, Metals and Fuels*, *71*(5), 645–649. DOI: 10.18311/jmmf/2023/34164

Ranasinghe, H., & Halgamuge, M. N. (2021). Twitter sentiment data analysis of user behavior on cryptocurrencies: Bitcoin and Ethereum. In *Analyzing Global Social Media Consumption* (pp. 277-291). IGI Global.

ValetiDeepika, D., & LalithaBhaskari. (2020). Block Chain Based Decentralised Twitter Dapp. *JETIR, 7*(11), 273-279.

Zheng, Z., Xie, S., Dai, H., Chen, X., & Wang, H. (2017, June). An overview of blockchain technology: Architecture, consensus, and future trends. In *2017 IEEE international congress on big data (BigData congress)* (pp. 557-564). IEEE.

Chapter 14
HONEY4LOG
A Comprehensive Tool for SSH Honeypot and Log4j Vulnerability Scanner

Sujatha Gurunathan
Department of Networking and Communications, SRM Institute of Science and Technology, Chennai, India

ABSTRACT

Nowadays, most Java- based applications use the log4j framework because it is a quick and framework which is dependable that is entirely written in programming language Java to have a log of all the information that takes place in the application. The Apache Software License, governs the log4j package, making it widely available for use and modification to suit individual needs. Due to wide usage of API, this particular utility of Java was exploited to malignantly initiate RCE that executes set of commands that puts data of the user at danger of getting it stolen and malignant intent. The IoT devices are at danger since the Log4j vulnerability is so simple to attack. The proposed system with honeypot requires little input and, in addition to alerting the relevant team, contains an internal scanner that can determine whether a specific website is susceptible to the log4jshell vulnerability. It also recognizes and warns of SSH-based threats. On top of a secure system, this scanner and the honeypot add another degree of security.

DOI: 10.4018/979-8-3693-8014-7.ch014

1 INTRODUCTION

Common Vulnerabilities and Exposures, or also known as CVE, is a standard list of security flaws and known vulnerabilities in hardware and software systems that is made available to the public. In order to discover, prioritize, and manage vulnerabilities across many businesses and industries, CVE offers a standard language. A unique identification, a description of the vulnerability, its impact, and its severity are all included in each CVE entry. The CVE Numbering Authority (CNA) assigns CVE entries, which are frequently updated as new vulnerabilities are found and countered. By proactively discovering and fixing system vulnerabilities before they may be used by attackers, CVE enables organizations to strengthen their cybersecurity posture.

The cybersecurity community has also paid close attention to the Log4j issue because of how easily it can be exploited and how seriously it can affect users. Through the logging function, the vulnerability enables attackers to insert malicious code into an application, which can subsequently execute arbitrary code on the server. This hack has the potential to result in ransomware attacks, data theft, and system compromise. Due to the vulnerability's seriousness, it is essential to take prompt action to reduce any potential effects on enterprises and organizations. To help organizations safeguard their systems against this vulnerability, the initiative on preventing Log4j vulnerability strives to give them the tools and advice they need. There are numerous procedures that need to be performed to prevent Log4j vulnerability. Finding Log4j in applications and systems inside an organization is the first step. The next step is to identify the version of Log4j being used and see if it is susceptible to the hack. Organizations should immediately update to the most recent, secure version of Log4j if the version is susceptible.

In addition to upgrading Log4j, numerous other security measures can be put in place to stop the vulnerability from being exploited. For instance, businesses can set up firewalls and other security technologies to prevent traffic to and from well-known bad IP addresses or domains that are frequently used in Log4j attacks. Furthermore, monitoring technologies can be set up to recognize and notify security teams of any unusual activity related to it. Organizations must first identify the presence of Log4j in their systems and apps and assess their vulnerability before they can accomplish this. If so, they must update to the most recent version of Log4j, which is secure, and take other security precautions including setting up firewalls and using monitoring software. To guarantee that all systems and apps have the most recent security patches installed, organizations should think about adopting a security patch management strategy. By taking these precautions, organizations may effectively protect their vital systems and data from Log4j vulnerabilities.

The purpose of this research is preventing Log4j vulnerability is to protect vital systems and data from potential assaults as well as to maintain the security and stability of the Log4j- dependent services and applications. The Log4jshell was a major source of concern because it affected a wide range of applications in various industries, including government agencies, financial institutions, and healthcare providers. Several major corporations and organizations were affected, necessitating urgent patching efforts and security experts' warnings.

A honeypot is a security mechanism that detects, deflects, or studies unauthorized user attempts to access a network or system. It is a spoof system or application that appears vulnerable in order to attract hackers or cybercriminals, who can then be identified and monitored. Honeypots can be used to collect information about attackers' tactics, techniques, and procedures, as well as evidence for legal and investigative purposes. Honeypots are classified into two types: high-interaction honeypots that simulate a real system and low- interaction honeypots that simulate a specific service or protocol. They can also be used to detect and prevent attacks on a network or within an application.

A clever honeypot solution can divert a hacker's connection from the actual server or data center while also enabling the appropriate team members to gain greater insight into their activities and set up defenses (Zhang, Feng, et al, 2003). There are different kinds of honeypots with distinct uses. The term "Virtual Honeypot" refers to one kind of honeypot. It collects the data into one single entity and governs it. Many number of honeypots can be simulated. One such type of honeypot, known as a honeynet, is mostly used for purpose of research. Its primary characteristic is that it has a too much of frequent contact and flexibility.

The security flaw known as RCE, or Remote Code Execution, allows attackers to run any code they choose on a remote system. RCE attacks can start in a number of ways, including through web apps, network services, or email attachments, and they can have major repercussions like data theft, system compromise, and network infiltration. RCE assaults are frequently combined with other attack strategies, such phishing (Biswas, Saikat, et al,2003), to acquire confidential data or take over a system. Strong security measures must be put in place, including frequent software upgrades, network segmentation, and access controls, as well as regular security assessments to find and fix vulnerabilities, in order to prevent RCE attacks.

Evaluation of code may happen and can result in RCE attacks If you give user inputs access to functions that are running the same programming language's code evaluation (Ramachandra, and Subhrajit Bhattacharya et al, 2020). This kind of action can be taken on purpose to get access to highly sensitive algorithmic functions of the mentioned language of programming, or it can happen accidentally because the dev behind it can purposefully built input of user input into one of these functions using a specific method. It is not advisable to proceed in this manner. Code evaluation is often viewed as harmful.

Log4j is very common because nearly all computer software will have a kind of ability to keep track (for development, operational and security purposes). According to blog.sonatype.com "Log4j 2.x is in the top 0.003% percentile in popularity by downloads out of a total population of 7.1 million. In short - it's as popular as components get." The aim of this project is to provide security to the vulnerable systems as log4j is so popular. Our goal is to assist in the security of log4j-using vulnerable systems, hence assisting with user data and privacy. We do not want users to be a target of this kind of crime. This concept can be used by any organizations or apps that do not examine incoming internet requests for log4jshell contents that may be hidden in the fields of the header. In future, this could be deployed in cloud platform to prevent an attack.

A honeypot is a purposefully unprotected decoy application that is designed to detect and warn of an attacker's malicious behavior without impairing the functionality of the cloud architecture or the data storage centers. A clever honeypot solution can divert a hacker's connection from the real server or data center while also enabling security team members to gain greater insight into their activities and set up defenses. There are different kinds of honeypots with distinct uses. The term "Virtual Honeypot" refers to one kind of honeypot. It gathers the information into a one entity and governs it. Many number of honeypots can be simulated. The honeynet, another form of honeypot, is mostly used for research. Its primary characteristic is that it has a high level of interactivity and adaptability.

When input of the user is infused or injected into a regular file or string and the entire bundle is performed on the programming language's parser, RCE (Remote Code Execution) occurs. RCE is used to show a specific kind of vulnerability that can be exploited unethically. This is not the kind of behavior that the web application's developer often exhibits. A remote code execution attack can grow quickly and become a fully fledged attack, making the entire web application and the webserver exposed and perhaps crippling them. RCE may also result in escalation of privileges, pivoting of network, and the formation of persistence, all of those increase the risk of loss of data, data getting stolen, and hijacking of the system. RCE always get a high/critical classification because of the way it is designed to seriously harm the system.

In order to keep each programming language secure from RCE attacks, it is important to understand how each one works. Most languages of programming have many which ways for assessing code functions. Code assessment may arise and can result in RCE attacks if you allow user inputs to access functions that are assessing code in the same language of programming. This kind of action can be taken on purpose to gain admission to the highly sensitive algorithmic functions of the mentioned language, or it can happen accidentally because the coder purposefully built input controlled by the user into one of these functions using a specific method. It is not advisable to proceed in this manner. Code evaluation is often viewed as harmful.

Security researchers are tracking a critical vulnerability in the Apache Commons Text library, which could allow an attacker to enable remote code execution. The major focus of the library is on algorithms that operate on strings. It includes an API that enables properties to be evaluated and expanded dynamically as well as interpolated or substituted. If attacker- controlled data is supplied to some library functions, it may result in remote code execution.

RCE (Remote Code Execution) happens when input of the user is infused or injected in an ordinary file or string and the entire collection is executed on the parser of the said language. RCE is used to demonstrate a vulnerability which is very specific that can be unethically exploited. The developer of the online program does not frequently act in this manner. The entire web application and the webserver might be exposed by a remote code execution assault, which could then swiftly develop into a full-fledged attack and could cripple both. The following figure, Figure 1.1 depicts the RCE (Remote Code execution) Attempts due to Log4j .

Figure 1. RCE Attempts Due to Log4j

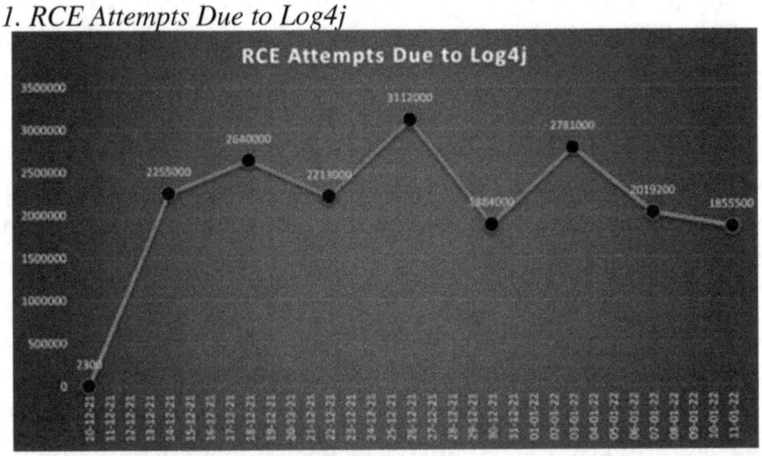

Figure 1 illustrates the number of attempts of RCE over time. The number of attempts has exponentially increased from the time that log4j vulnerability was identified and became known to the internet. To further understand how the most recent Log4j vulnerabilities affected the clients, we looked at the reaches on the Apache Log4j RCE Vulnerability threat prevention signature between December 10, 2021 and February 2, 2022. Based on the telemetry, we found 125,894,944 hits with the relevant packet captures that activated the signature. Figure 1 displays the number of hits each day, showing a significant increase in activity from December

12 to 16 followed by a decline from December 16 to 21 and a subsequent significant increase on January 1, 2022. Following the new year's spike, the trademark hits produce a jagged line with day-to-day variations in counts, although the spikes are noticeably less than those previously observed.

2 LITERATURE REVIEW

For any successful project or a novel idea, studying and surveying is important. The analysis of existing model is essential and only after that a project can come to its full fruition. Below is the complete survey of other research papers and our model has drawn information from other research works. A literature survey, usually referred to as a literature review, is a thorough evaluation of the body of knowledge already available on a given subject or research question.

2.1. SSH Honeypot and WAF

The author (Kaushik Keshav et al., 2022) discuss the approach for exploiting Log4shell vulnerability. It also gives them the mitigation patching techniques and utilizing a runtime security tool to find reverse shells. They also discuss the method for exploiting the vulnerability in Log4shell. Additionally, it teaches them how to find reverse shells using runtime security tools and mitigation patching procedures. They have performed the phases such as gathering as much information as possible then moving on to the scanning phase and exploitation. They proceed to maintain the access which was gained and detection of the exploitation and further they perform bypassing and ending it with (Chen, et al., 2021) mitigation and patching. They analyze the social media platform, Twitter, to get a sense of what people felt on the log4j issue. Using an admission controller and container lifecycle in your CI/CD pipelines, as well as a runtime security tool to look for reverse shells. Using these techniques will give your security team the tools they need to thwart attacks that aim to exploit this flaw, stop them, and notify you in advance of any operating containers that might be impacted.

Additionally, it teaches them how to find reverse shells using runtime security tools and mitigation patching procedures. Additionally, they go over how to use Log4shell's vulnerability. Additionally, it teaches students how to locate reverse shells using mitigation patching techniques and runtime security tools. They have completed the steps, such as obtaining as much data as they could before going on to the scanning and exploitation phases. They continue to retain the access that was gained, to detect the exploitation, to carry out bypassing, and to put an end to it through mitigation and patching.

The author (Koniaris et al., 2013) showed a working example of a unique honeypot designed for the Secure Shell (SSH) service, which is frequently targeted by attackers. Many Linux distributions come with an SSH server installed by default, frequently without any additional security measures or firewalls. They also showed a working example of a unique honeypot designed for the Secure Shell (SSH) service, which is frequently targeted by attackers. Several Linux distributions come with an SSH server installed by default, frequently without any additional security measures or firewalls. The performance (Patel et al., 2017) of the honeypot was also measured and data such as attempts of login, source of the IP and the count of attacks were gathered and analyzed. Analysis of common password and usernames used in the honeypot was also done in order to calculate the efficiency of the honeypot.

It also has a huge amount of data of the number of probes per day and the login attempts which were successful. After compromise of the system, the analysis of the commands which was frequently used is also monitored. These were all done with a tool that visualizes the data and then presented how the honeypot logged in information. A workable implementation of a specialized honeypot for the frequently attacked Secure Shell (SSH) service. Many Linux distributions come with an SSH server installed by default, frequently without any additional security measures or firewalls. Additionally, they demonstrated a functional example of a novel honeypot created for the commonly attacked Secure Shell (SSH) service. Many Linux distributions ship with an SSH server already installed, frequently without any additional firewalls or security measures. Data such as login attempts, IP source, and attack count were collected and analyzed as well as the honeypot's performance was evaluated.

The author (Srinivasa Shreyas et al., 2022) deployed three open-source directory service profiles with webservers that simulated the Log4j vulnerability to conduct a honeypot study on LDAP assaults. They also have summarized the attack types and correlate the findings with the data from the Honeynet community. They also were successful in deploying three open-source directory service profiles while using webservers that mimic the Log4j vulnerability to conduct a honeypot research of LDAP assaults. Additionally, they have enumerated the various assault methods and compared their findings to information from the Honeynet community. This research primarily focuses on the LDAP (Li et al., 2011) implementation and uses many open source technologies to figure out and and imitate how an attack can occur on LDAP. There were many types of attack discussed such as Brute force method an searches that are suspicious

Additionally, they have enumerated the different kinds of attacks and compared their results to information from the Honeynet community. Additionally, they were successful in establishing three open-source directory service profiles while conducting an LDAP attack honeypot study utilizing webservers that mimicked the Log4j vulnerability. They have also listed the different attack techniques and contrasted their results with data from the Honeynet community. This study employs a variety of open source technologies to analyze and simulate LDAP attacks, with a primary focus on the implementation of LDAP.

The author (Juvonen Artturi et al., 2022) first end-to-end exploitation of serious Log4j2 vulnerabilities was demonstrated (principally CVE-2021-44228) over mission- and safety-critical aviation (ACARS and ADS-B) and maritime (AIS) protocols. In all the aforementioned protocols, log4shell and log4crash were successfully exploited.. To support their experiments, they have developed novel tools. It was observed that blocking connections that are outwards bound to ports that are default is a great way to mitigate the log4jshell. It was also analyzed that using preventive measures such as an intrusion detection system or a prevention system can help to safeguard against such an attack. It also investigates how the Log4j vulnerability may affect crucial communication systems used in the aviation, maritime, and aerospace industries. The authors examine the potential effects of the vulnerability on these systems and pinpoint a number of risk factors that leave them open to exploitation. The architecture of the Log4j vulnerability is discussed, as well as how it can be used to remotely execute arbitrary code. The authors also go into how a Log4j exploit might affect crucial communication systems used in the aviation, maritime, and aerospace industries, including the possibility of system compromise, data theft, and even human casualties. The scientists carried out a number of experiments and simulations to show how an attacker could use the issue to compromise crucial communication networks in order to gauge the effect of the Log4j vulnerability on these businesses. They also point out a number of risk factors, such as the usage of out-of-date software and poor security precautions, that leave these systems open to exploitation.

The study "On Apache Log4j2 Exploitation in Aeronautical, Maritime, and Aerospace Communication" investigates the effects of the Log4j vulnerability (Arifianto et al., 2018) on crucial communication systems in the aerospace, maritime, and aviation sectors. The authors examine the potential effects of the vulnerability on these systems and pinpoint a number of risk factors that leave them open to exploitation.

The architecture of the Log4j vulnerability is discussed, as well as how it can be used to remotely execute arbitrary code. The authors also go into how a Log4j exploit might affect crucial communication systems used in the aviation, maritime, and aerospace industries, including the possibility of system compromise, data theft, and even human casualties.

The author (Varlioglu Said et al., 2022) conducted a thorough analysis of academic papers and business information on the new "Fileless Cryptojacking" threat. Zero-days such as Log4j or SolarWinds Serv-U weaknesses are manipulated to perform remote codes in fileless attacks are discussed as well and conducted a thorough analysis of the scholarly literature and business reports on the new threat. Zero day threats such as Log4j or SolarWinds Serv-U In fileless attacks, flaws are exploited to run remote code are discussed as well. This work also discusses the principles of the fileless threat, which can aid researchers looking at patterns in ransomware. Despite the fact that fixes have been provided, some users might not have noticed them or they might not have worked right away. A successful exploitation would allow attackers to take over the system, see, and alter data. Malicious code like JavaScript, iFrames, and cross-site scripting can be found on malicious websites (Kelly et al., 2021) as well as genuine websites that have been infiltrated. The attack doesn't involve any user activity beyond the user simply viewing the site, especially since browsers launch scripts automatically. This particular infection mechanism makes detection very challenging. By injecting executables and libraries into a legitimate Windows process, a malicious script from a malicious website can execute a fileless malware script in PowerShell.

The author (Vashishtha et al., 2023) discuss A hybrid model combines SDM and ADM techniques. Due to its tailored low-cost services with high levels of reliability and efficiency, the cloud computing paradigm is particularly well-liked by customers across a variety of industries, including banking, healthcare, and education. Security is a top concern in a cloud-based system since cloud services are accessed via the internet by various types of users. Through intrusive actions like denial of service attacks, backdoor channel attacks, etc., network intruders might harm the system. Using an intrusion detection model is one way to thwart this type of assault and protect the system. The majority of intrusion detection methods are only as effective at detecting known threats However, the majority of them are unable to recognize unidentified attacks, which appear to be fresh and repurposed threats. Thus, cloud-based systems need a network intrusion detection model that can detect both known and novel threats. This research introduces a hybrid intrusion detection model for cloud-based systems that can identify all forms of attacks by combining signature-based detection and anomaly-based detection. To test the model's performance, tests were run on the UNSW- NB15, CICIDS2017, and NSL-KDD datasets. It was discovered that the model had a high detection rate of 92.7% on the UNSW-NB15 dataset, 85.1% on the CICIDS dataset, and 99.8% on the NSL-KDD dataset.

The proposed model's performance is superior to several current models, according to the comparative analysis. SDM and ADM (Negi et al., 2020) techniques are combined in this hybrid model. SDM employs a rule-based methodology. In order to establish a baseline for typical and intrusive actions, a Neural network, Random forest, and Gradient boosting techniques are employed for anomaly identification. The suggested HIDM is used to better accurately identify known and unidentified attacks in infrastructure of the cloud.

2.2 Log4j Based Scanner

The author (Khan Minhaj et al., 2016) investigated the appealing gears of cloud computing. Internet-based computing, often known as cloud computing, makes available shared resources, software, and data upon request. The configuration for cloud computing provides an easy-to-access carrier for personal and private bases and documents. Due to continuously increasing demand over the past considerable amount of time, cloud computing has gained substantial awareness. Businesses that switch to cloud-based archive storage solutions gain in numerous ways. Through the design of the assets and active charges, it lowers the cost and complexity of service organizations. The world is witnessing incredible growth in cloud-based services, and this growth is predicted to continue along with advancing technology breakthroughs. It enables customers to enter drivers properly and temporarily Despite the significant advantages of the cloud computing paradigm, there are a few obstacles and drawbacks, particularly with regard to the (Buzzio-Garcia et al., 2021) confidentiality of customer information and security- related risk. Because this technology's assemblies rely on the Internet, a person cannot access their servers, applications, or data from the cloud, therefore outdated security regulations do not apply because the client no longer owns the infrastructure. This essay discusses the risks and security concerns related to cloud computing. The storyline analysis offered in this study provides information about cloud care challenges, requirements, known dangers, and threats.

This work aims to investigate the appealing components of cloud computing while also addressing the security and privacy issues that this environment has to deal with. It also aims to gain a thorough understanding of the security risks that cloud entities and cloud worker organizations deal with on a regular basis. The globe is seeing a phenomenal increase in cloud-based services, and it is projected that this rise will continue along with new technological advancements. It allows users to accurately and momentarily enter drivers.

The author (Leandros Maglaras et al., 2016) discuss the numerous methods that can be utilized to create a honeypot of any kind while taking the benefits and drawbacks of these wildly different approaches into consideration. The main objectives are to go over the foundations of Secure Shell (SSH), how it works, and—more prominently—how enemies might exploit it to access a system. The development of numerous low-interaction honeypots was covered in the article. The fully documented libssh library is used by the low interaction honeypots, and they even modify the source code of an existing SSH daemon. In order to compare and contrast the findings as well as the usefulness and necessity of specific features, the goal is to combine the results with the widely dispersed Kippo honeypot. By providing a clear and straightforward explanation, less experienced users may easily develop and deploy a production-quality honeypot, instantly enhancing their network's security.

When waiting to build an SSH honeypot (Manzanares et al., 2005), this script could be used by third parties who want to perform this kind of study or as a simpler alternative. Making this honeypot more accessible as a production honeypot is another potential area for development.

The author (Sharma Manish et al., 2015) implemented an advanced Rivest Cypher (RC) mechanism to create a security system. The World Wide Web is still a major component of today's communication system. Additionally, it is the fastest and easiest option for both parties to access in a matter of seconds. The best method of distant communication is currently in use, while the other phase puts data security at risk. The data may be targeted because the attackers are waiting for code execution and using a variety of techniques. Attack detection and security considerations are therefore two of today's top issues. To detect malicious activity, a detection mechanism using the begin tag is also put into place. To ensure that the data is located quickly, there is a facility for data (Ramsbrock et al., 2007) existence verification as well. The outcomes of their method include an improved detection strategy in terms of data existence and security. Along with the methodology time, the reaction time is also significantly faster than in previous methods, which also dynamises the availability of information documents. The findings will demonstrate the effectiveness of our methods.

The author (Sadasivam et al., 2016) have questioned whether network flows could be used to separate assaults coming from a hacked SSH server from other attacks. There are several forms of SSH assaults, including SSH port scanning, SSH Brute-force attacks, and SSH assaults employing hacked SSH servers. DoS assaults, Phishing attacks, email spamming, and other attacks may be conducted using a compromised server. They divide SSH attacks into two categories in this paper. All attack actions that follow a successful penetration of an SSH server fall under the first category. They are known as "severe" attacks. All attacks leading to a successful compromise fall under the second category. It comprises of a compromised SSH server with no activity, an SSH Brute-force attack, and SSH port scanning. "Not-so- severe" attacks are the second kind of attacks. To categorise these attacks, we use machine learning methods including Naive Bayes learner, Logistic Regression, J48 decision tree, and Support Vector Machine. In order to assess (Park et al., 2021) the effectiveness of machine learning algorithms using the sensitivity, metrics accuracy, F-score and precision, appropriate features were chosen based on domain expertise, literature review, and feature selection methodology.

It is abundantly evident from reading and analysing the aforementioned research articles that files that is the logs are extant in every part of modern technology, despite the fact that they are frequently disregarded in terms of security. Logs serve the purpose of acquiring data very simply, which is helpful in the event of any failure or technological difficulties. The vulnerability that these logs present has been discovered and fully exploited by hackers. A firewall serves as the first line of security for any system, Consequently, we have considered it and made an effort to incorporate it when applicable in order to offer the chosen possible remedy for such a liability. Security must be integrated at every level of an architecture, even at the most basic level of a log file. Our suggested model will prevent hackers from using this flaw to compromise a system as a result.

Logs serve the purpose of capturing data relatively simply, which is helpful in the event of any failure or technological difficulties. The vulnerability that these records present has been discovered by hackers, and they have fully exploited it. A firewall serves as the first line of defense in any system, thus we have taken that into account and attempted to integrate it when appropriate to offer the best potential solution for such a openness. Security must be enforced at every level of an architecture, even one as basic as a log file. As a result, our suggested model will make sure that foes don't use this weakness to infiltrate a system.

3 METHODOLOGY OF SECURE RULE BASED SYSTEM

The technique of our hypothetical secure rule-based system is that a deployed honeypot has little contact, notifies the security team, and examines the payload pattern to enable the creation of a firewall rule to stop future attacks of this type. The honeypot also finds SSH- based threat-incidents and notifies for any prospective SSH-based assaults. In addition to having a honeypot, this rule offers another level of security.

The model suggests a method in which the honeypot scans the arriving web request, identifies the design of the log4j exploit, and crafts a rule in the firewall based on that pattern. The firewall rule that is set up prevents requests with patterns that are similar to those it has already seen from coming through in the future. The model also proposes a built in scanner that can take in a unified resource link as input and will send a series of payloads that are JNDI based and the scanner will figure out whether the given unified resource link is vulnerable to the CVE-2021- 45046 or not. There are two modules which are working in conjunction. The SSH honeypot and the H0ney4Log, which is the scanner that will determine whether the website is vulnerable to the CVE. The H0ney4Log has various web application firewall payloads that gets into the network undetected. The payload has both JNDI, Java Naming Directory Interface, as well as DNS, Domain Name System compatibility.

3.1 Scanner and Honeypot

The parser contained in the scanner takes in the website as input and sets the URL to destination. Not only that it also supports proxy type connection and the request type which is GET and POST. It runs all available test on the URL. The scanner excludes the user agent from fuzzing which is particularly helpful to bypass weak checks on user agents. It also has a wait feature that waits for all the URLs to be processed. If needed the scanner can also use custom web application firewall bypass to get a custom input from the user itself. Strings known as payloads are carefully prepared JNDI insertion code. JNDI, a Java API, offers a method of accessing several naming and directory services, including DNS, LDAP and RMI.

With the JNDI injection approach, malicious code can be added to a JNDI reference and then executed when the reference is resolved by the application server. It is a good idea to have a backup plan in case the backup plan is not successful. The malicious code is executed when the Log4j library is initialized, which might result in remote code execution on the server.

The main version that this scanner tests is for the CVE-2021-45046 which is widespread. The scanner has the flexibility to ask for target's IP address and Port number instead of the DNS callback. Certain websites redirect to another website and this can sometimes evade the detection, so the scanner, if needed, can disable the HTTP redirects. This is not enabled by default as leaving it enabled can help discover multiple vulnerable sites. The fuzzing of headers is done to determine what kind of request is followed when a connection is established.

By sending a sequence of queries with various permutations of a payload that could potentially exploit a vulnerability in the target application, fuzzing is the practice of testing a target server for vulnerabilities. RSA key is used to establish a connection. It also has a logging feature that will log in whatever data is generated such as the successful attempt, unsuccessful attempt, exceptions, time, date, the version of the vulnerability. The scanner will produce a message indicating that the custom host will be used and update the callback host variable to the value of the argument if it is given, that is, a custom DNS callback host has been specified on the command line. A target server is subjected to a security scan by the scanner to determine whether it is susceptible to the Log4j vulnerability, a serious security flaw affecting the Apache Log4j library used in Java applications.

Sending a specifically crafted request to a Log4j-enabled application enables an attacker to execute arbitrary code on a target system, taking advantage of the vulnerability. By making a malicious request to the Log4j library that contains a specifically created string (referred to as the "Log4Shell" string) in the request headers or body, the vulnerability can be exploited. A series of HTTP requests with various iterations of the "Log4Shell" string in the request headers or body are sent by the scanner to the target server to see if it is vulnerable. The scanner will attempt to exploit the vulnerability by sending a specially crafted request with a reverse shell payload to a designated callback host if a vulnerable version of the Log4j library is found on the server.

Additionally, the scanner offers a number of options for customizing the scan, including the ability to select the callback host, unique headers, and the kind of payload to transmit. The scanner can also execute an IP-based callback to a specific IP address, a DNS-based callback using the Interactsh service or a custom DNS server, or both. Variations of JNDI injection code are used as the payloads in the scanner and can be used to test for the Log4j vulnerability. The payloads are encoded in a fashion that can evade some detection systems and include many JNDI references, including RMI, LDAP, and DNS. The callback host and a random string placeholders are also included in the payloads; these values will be changed by the script during the fuzzing process.

The scanner can determine if the server is susceptible to the Log4j vulnerability by utilizing these payloads to make requests to the target server and analysing the answers. Now for the second module which is the honeypot. The honeypot creates a listening socket on the standard SSH port using the socket library. A fresh thread is initiated to conduct the connection when an attacker tries to connect to the honeypot. In order to seem as a genuine SSH service, the thread imitates an SSH server, sending phony banners and prompts to the attacker. As soon as the attacker connects, the honeypot creates a log file that contains all of their input and output. The study of this log file can then reveal the tools and methods used by attackers who attempted to exploit SSH services. Any incoming web request is first examined by the security system before being sent to the log4j honeypot.

According to the kind of request (GET, POST, DELETE, etc.), the honeypot examines the received HTTP request, checking its fields of the header for the log4j exploit and splitting the dataflow. Two APIs are utilized for this: IP-API and FastAPI. They look through the headers to see if there are any payloads that could be exposed to a log4jshell attack. Moreover, it records and retains the IP address of inward web requests that can be malevolent, guaranteeing that when information is forwarded to the security team, the IP address is highlighted and inward requests from that distinct IP are scrutinized. If the request is found to be authentic, the system merely allows it in; if it is found to be malicious, it is added to the firewall's rule set and all arriving requests from that specific IP address are prohibited from accessing the system. It was discovered that the model had a high detection rate of 92.7% on the UNSW-NB15 dataset, 85.1% on the CICIDS dataset, and 99.8% on the NSL-KDD dataset. When a request is valid, meaning there was no vulnerability found, it is forwarded and safely goes via the secure system.

When an exploit is discovered in the scanned header in case two, the system is notified, the information which is the header of the field is transferred to the honeypot, where it is placed through an SSH invasion scanner, and it is decided if there are possible threats or malevolent headers present. The honeypot searches and outlines the misuse pattern and IP before passing it to the secure system, where rules are set to look for and deter analogous patterns, if no SSH intrusion scripts are discovered. Additionally, if SSH intrusion exploits are discovered in the header, it saves the patterns and warns the secure system.

The flaw allows an attacker to execute arbitrary code on a target machine by sending a specially crafted request to a Log4j-enabled application. The vulnerability can be exploited by sending a nefarious request to the Log4j library that includes a specially crafted string (known as the "Log4Shell" string) in the request headers or body. The scanner sends a number of HTTP queries to the target server to check for vulnerabilities, each of which includes different repetitions of the "Log4Shell" string in the request headers or body. If a vulnerable version of the Log4j library is discovered, the scanner will try to exploit the flaw by delivering a specially constructed request with a reverse shell payload to a selected callback host.

The webpage is entered into the parser built into the scanner, which then sets the destination URL. Additionally, it supports GET and POST request types as well as proxy connection types. Every test that is offered is executed on the URL. In order to get around user agent weak checks, the scanner excludes the user agent from fuzzing. Additionally, it provides a wait function that waits until all of the URLs have been processed. If necessary, the scanner can also bypass a user's personal firewall using a custom web application. Payload strings are meticulously constructed. Insertion code for JNDI. The scanner excludes the user agent from fuzzing which is particularly helpful to bypass weak checks on user agents. It also has a wait feature that waits for all the URLs to be processed. If needed the scanner can also use custom web application firewall bypass to get a custom input from the user itself. Strings known as payloads are carefully prepared JNDI insertion code. It logs important details like, version of SSH, status of connection, credentials of the client, and even error messages faced during establishing a connection. For logging messages from Python programs, the logging module in Python offers a versatile and effective structure.

4 DESIGN OF H0NEY4LOG

An activity diagram of the flow of data in our suggested model is shown in Figure 4.1. It clearly explains how web requests are handled and what the honeypot looks at. and does when a specific condition is satisfied. It mostly looks for a web request and makes sure that any payload alterations are not included in the headers that are there and it describes everything. The full list of all the tasks carried out by our suggested model is shown in detail in Figure 4.1. It has a number of modules that will be run one after the other. Any incoming web request is first examined by the security system before being sent to the log4j honeypot. According to the kind of request (GET, POST, DELETE, etc.), the honeypot examines the received HTTP request, checking its fields of the header for the log4shell activity and splitting the flow of the data. FastAPI and IP- API are two APIs that are used for this. They examine the headers for any payloads that might be vulnerable to a log4jshell attack. Additionally, it saves the IP address of inward web requests that may be malevolent and captures it, ensuring that when data is sent to the concerned team, the IP address is highlighted and incoming requests from that specific IP are watched. If it is determined to be valid, the request is simply allowed inside the system; if it is determined to be malevolent, it is supplemented to the firewall's rule set and all inward requests from that exact IP address are forbidden from accessing the arrangement. When a call is valid, meaning there was no weakness found, it is forwarded and safely goes via the secure system. A call is forwarded and safely transmitted through the secure system when it is genuine, which means there was no vulnerability discovered. In the second instance, when an exploit is found in the scanned header, the system is alerted, the header is transmitted to the honeypot, where it is put over an SSH imposition scanner, and it is determined that there are possible intimidations or malevolent headers present. If no SSH intrusion scripts are found, the honeypot scans and logs the exploit pattern and IP before sending it to the secure system, where rules are made to check for and block similar patterns. It also maintains the patterns and information whether the header contains SSH intrusion exploits it also saves the patterns and warnings in the secure system. Fig 2 shows the model of HoneyPot.

Figure 2. Activity Diagram Depicting Model of Honeypot

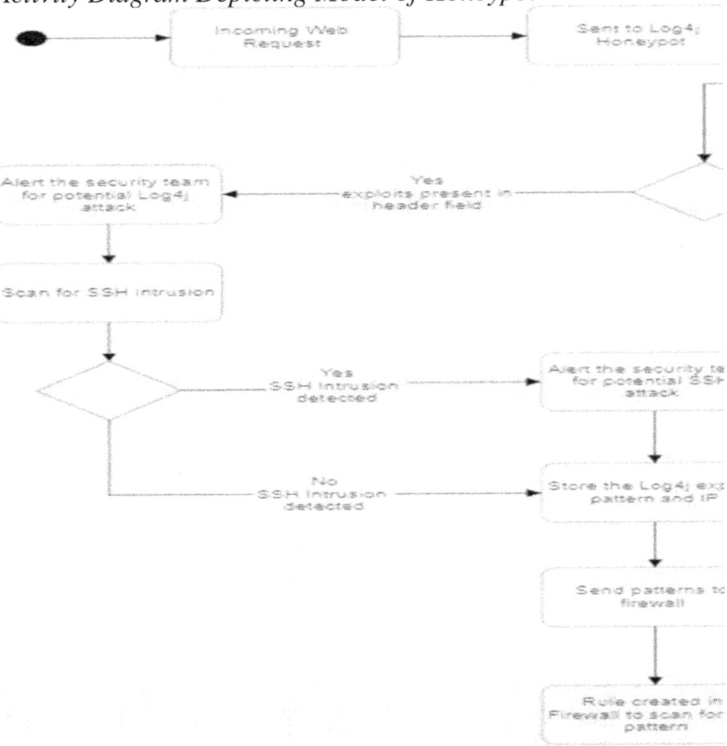

Two APIs are utilized for this: IP- API and FastAPI. They look through the headers to see if there are any payloads that could be exposed to a log4jshell attack. Moreover, it records and retains the IP address of inward web requests that can be malevolent, guaranteeing that when information is forwarded to the security team, the IP address is highlighted and inward requests from that specific IP are scrutinised. If the request is found to be legitimate, the system merely allows it in; if it is found to be malevolent, it is inserted to the firewall's rule set and all inward requests from that specific IP address are prohibited from accessing the scheme.

A call is transmitted and successfully passed via the secure system when it is valid, which means there was no vulnerability discovered. When an exploit is discovered in the scanned header in case two, the system is notified, the header is transferred to the honeypot, where it is placed through an SSH intrusion scanner, and it is decided if there are possible intimidations or malevolent headers present. The honeypot scans and logs the misuse pattern and IP before passing it to the safe system, where rules are set to look for and prevent related patterns, if any SSH intrusion scripts are not identified. Additionally, it keeps track of forms and data regarding the presence of SSH intrusion attacks in headers. By sending a carefully crafted request to a Log4j-enabled application, the bug enables an attacker to execute arbitrary code on a target machine. By making a malicious request to the Log4j library that contains a specifically created string (referred to as the "Log4Shell" string) in the request headers or body, the vulnerability can be exploited. The "Log4Shell" string is repeated in different ways in the request headers or body for each HTTP query the scanner sends to the target server to look for vulnerabilities. The scanner will attempt to take advantage of the vulnerability if a vulnerable version of the Log4j library is found by sending a specially crafted request with a reverse shell payload to a chosen callback host.

5 RESULTS AND DISCUSSIONS:

Both the Honeypot and the log4jshell scanner in conjunction make a secure system that is an Intrusion Prevention System as well as an Intrusion Detection System. The Honeypot is first executed to act as an intended decoy and then the scanner is executed following the honeypot to make a secure system.

Figure 3. Initialization and Deploying of Honeypot.

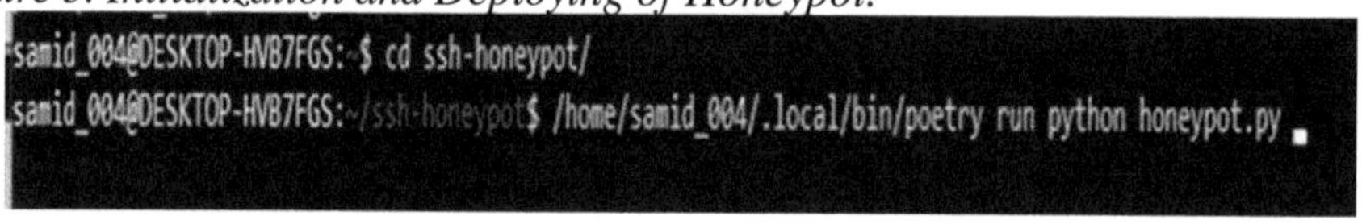

Figure 3 is a working implementation of the SSH honeypot, the poetry library is being used. The directory needs to be changed by the user to the path of where the honeypot is installed and then it needs to be run. A port is assigned to listen to the commands when run and can be manually done as well.

Figure 4. SSH Manual Port Allocation.

Figure 4 Depicts the manual assignment of the port where the honeypot is assigned to listen. All the commands entered by the adversary is recorded and the output is saved to a text file if configured, can also be made to display in the screen. The above figure shows how the port where the honeypot is tasked to listen is manually

assigned. All commands entered by the opponent are logged, and if specified, the output can also be made to appear on the screen.

Figure 5. SSH Honeypot Key Capture.

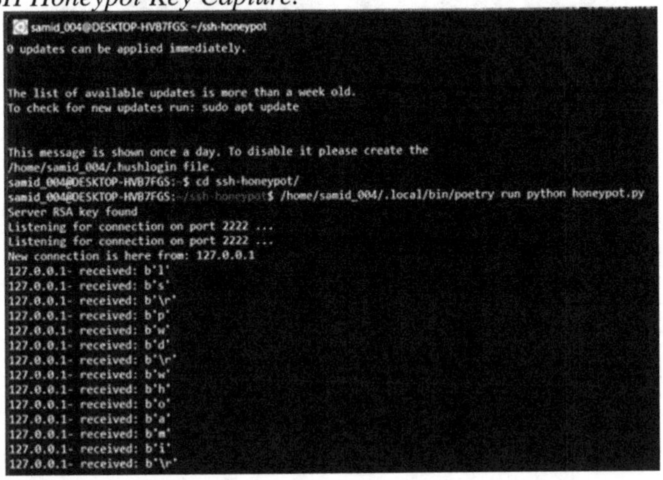

Figure 5 Upon the successful SSH connection establishes, the screen displays the logging of all the keystrokes used by the adversary on the honeypot, but the attacker will not be viewing the above-mentioned screen, but will be tricked into believing that the SSH connection established with the port is legitimate. This is shown in figure 6.4, Figure 6.3 also depicts the honeypot which could be deployed in the first line of defense as it is merely a decoy. As soon as the honeypot is executed it looks for the RSA key and starts listening on the port, in this case the port number is 2222. It stays on this and keeps listening for for the connection. When it is found, explained down below, displays the IP of the host. Since in this case it is running in a local machine, the IP is 127.0.0.1. This window is only displayed to the one who has set up the honeypot and attacker cannot see this window. Once the connection is established, the honeypot also logs all the keystrokes which is performed by the attacker. This is very much useful because it gives us an insight as to what the attacker is typing and what commands they are wishing to execute. When the honeypot is run, it immediately starts searching for the RSA key and listening on port 2222 in this instance. It continues to focus on this while listening for the connection. The IP address of the host is displayed when it is discovered, as stated below.

Figure 6. Intruder CLI View

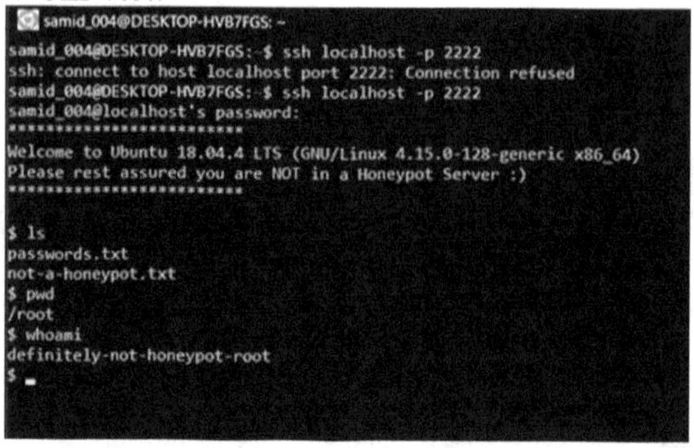

Figure 6 depicts the attacker's point of view. An attacker when they intend to use SSH based attack, usually create a localhost and then find out which ports are open. From figure 1. the honeypot starts listening on port 2222 so that particular port is open. The attacker then uses that to infiltrate. The honeypot deceptively asks for a password making it look like a legitimate system. The honeypot accepts any string as password needn't be the real password. Then the honeypot displays a message welcoming the user. The attacker then proceeds to enter commands and the honeypot just displays fake files, the name of the directory and the name of the user which does not exist making it look like a legitimate terminal. Meanwhile the honeypot logs in all the keystrokes. The honeypot poses as a legitimate system while deceitfully requesting a password. Any string can be used as a password for the honeypot; the true password is not required. The user is then welcomed with a message on the honeypot. The attacker continues to type instructions, and the honeypot just pretends to be a valid terminal by displaying fictitious files, the directory's name, and a user's name that doesn't exist. All keystrokes are logged in the meantime by the honeypot.

Figure 7. H0ney4log Execution.

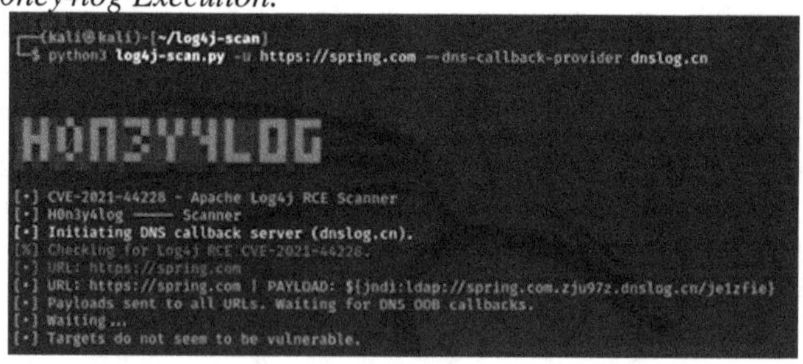

The scanner, H0ney4log is executed in Figure 7, where the command is used to run using python and the url has to be mentioned so that the scanner can check that particular website for vulnerabilities and it can also take in a list of urls and check it instead of individually performing the scan. It displays whether the given url is vulnerable or not and if it is vulnerable it will show details such as the version of log4jshell which it is vulnerable to and the corresponding timestamps. It checks multiple apps operating on those hosts for the Log4j vulnerability by scanning a target domain or IP address range. In order to find susceptible endpoints that attackers might utilise, it combines regular expressions and HTTP requests. As a result of the tool's functionality for producing reports and alerts, it is simple for security teams to recognize and rank susceptible systems for remediation. Because it is simple to use and can be run from the CLI, security analysts and IT administrators with little to no programming knowledge can utilise it. Analysing HTTP replies, it will search for any indications of the Log4j library. The script will verify the version number and assess whether the library is vulnerable if it is discovered. A Python script that checks a list of susceptible Log4j versions to find Log4j vulnerabilities in web applications. It makes HTTP calls to the designated URLs and checks to see if the Log4j library is there. The script will verify the version number and assess whether the library is vulnerable if it is discovered. Scans for the Log4j vulnerability automatically, which can be more efficient than manual screening in terms of time and effort. However, it's vital to remember that they should only be used on online applications that have been given permission to scan.

CONCLUSION

Our suggested secure method offers a method to defend an group against log4shell attacks by sensibly redirecting the requests to a honeypot so that the actual system is out of damage's way and carefully examining the requirements for slightly form of malevolent payloads. If harmful requests are found, they are simply declined, and the IP is labeled so that any inward requests from that specific IP are either entirely disregarded or prevented in the future. In our simulation, we also add a rule to the firewall so that any requests that pass over the honeypot must go in the firewall for enhanced safety. The model that we suggest is safe and prevents log4shell attacks by prudently relaying requests to a honeypot so that the actual system is safe and by carefully assessing the requests for any malevolent payloads. For additional security, the model proposed also adds a rule to the firewall with the intention of any requests that pass through the honeypot must also experience the firewall; if damaging requests are found, they are simply forbidden, and the IP is labelled so that any inward requests from that IP are either entirely disregarded or impassable in the future. If harmful requests are found, they are simply declined, and the IP is labelled so as to any inward requests from that IP are either totally overlooked or barred in the future. In model which is proposed, we also add a condition to the firewall to facilitate any requests that pass through the honeypot must undergo the firewall for additional protection. Our suggested secure method offers a way to defend an organization against log4jshell attacks by wisely redirecting the requests to a honeypot so that the actual and physical system is out of harm's way and cautiously assessing the requests for any form of malevolent payloads.

REFERENCES

Arifianto, R. M., Sukarno, P., & Jadied, E. M. (2018, May). An SSH honeypot architecture using port knocking and intrusion detection system. In 2018 6th International Conference on Information and Communication Technology (ICoICT) (pp. 409-415). IEEE.

Biswas, S., Sohel, M., Sajal, M. M., Afrin, T., Bhuiyan, T., & Hassan, M. M. (2018). A study on remote code execution vulnerability in web applications. In *International conference on cyber security and computer science (ICONCS 2018)* (pp. 50-57).

Buzzio-Garcia, J. (2021, July). Creation of a high-interaction honeypot system based-on docker containers. In 2021 Fifth World Conference on Smart Trends in Systems Security and Sustainability (WorldS4) (pp. 146-151). IEEE.

Chen, B., & Zhen, M. J. (2021). A survey of software log instrumentation. *ACM Computing Surveys, 54*(4), 1–34.

Doubleday, H., Maglaras, L., & Janicke, H. (2016). SSH honeypot: Building, deploying and analysis. *International Journal of Advanced Computer Science and Applications, 7*(5).

Juvonen, A., Costin, A., Turtiainen, H., & Hamalainen, T. (2022). On Apache Log4j2 Exploitation in Aeronautical, Maritime, and Aerospace Communication. *IEEE Access : Practical Innovations, Open Solutions, 10*, 86542–86557. DOI: 10.1109/ACCESS.2022.3198947

Kaushik, K., Dass, A., & Dhankhar, A. (2022, November). An approach for exploiting and mitigating Log4J using Log4Shell vulnerability. In 2022 3rd International Conference on Computation, Automation and Knowledge Management (ICCAKM) (pp. 1-6). IEEE.

Kelly, C., Pitropakis, N., Mylonas, A., McKeown, S., & Buchanan, W. J. (2021). A comparative analysis of honeypots on different cloud platforms. *Sensors (Basel), 21*(7), 2433.

Khan, M. A. (2016). A survey of security issues for cloud computing. *Journal of Network and Computer Applications, 71*, 11–29. DOI: 10.1016/j.jnca.2016.05.010

Koniaris, I., Papadimitriou, G., & Nicopolitidis, P. (2013). *"Analysis and visualization of SSH attacks using honeypots." Eurocon 2013*. IEEE.

Li, H., Chen, J., & Jin, X. (2011, June). An outlook on network honeypot. In *2011 International Conference on Computer Science and Service System (CSSS)* (pp. 1102-1105). IEEE.

Manzanares, A. I., Márquez, J. T., Estevez-Tapiador, J. M., & Castro, J. C. H. (2005). Attacks on port knocking authentication mechanism. In Computational Science and Its Applications–ICCSA 2005: International Conference, Singapore, May 9-12, 2005 [Springer Berlin Heidelberg.]. *Proceedings*, *5*(Part IV), 1292–1300.

Meenakshi, R., A. C., & Bhattacharya, S. (2020). Literature survey on log-based anomaly detection framework in cloud. Computational Intelligence in Pattern Recognition: Proceedings of CIPR 2020, 143-153.

Negi, P. S., Garg, A., & Lal, R. (2020, January). Intrusion detection and prevention using honeypot network for cloud security. In 2020 10th International Conference on Cloud Computing, Data Science & Engineering (Confluence) (pp. 129-132). IEEE.

Oxford Analytica. (2022). US government targets open-source software flaws. Emerald Expert Briefings, (oxan-es).

Park, J.. (2021). Network log-based SSH brute-force attack detection model. *CMC-Computers Materials & Continua*, *68*(1), 887–901. DOI: 10.32604/cmc.2021.015172

Patel, K. C., & Sharma, P. (2017). A Review paper on pfsense-an Open source firewall introducing with different capabilities & customiza- tion. *IJARIIE*, *3*, 2395–4396.

Ramsbrock, D., Berthier, R., & Cukier, M. (2007, June). Profiling attacker behavior following SSH compromises. In 37th Annual IEEE/IFIP international conference on dependable systems and networks (DSN'07) (pp. 119-124). IEEE.

Sadasivam, G. K., Hota, C., & Anand, B. (2016, September). Classification of SSH attacks using machine learning algorithms. In 2016 6th International Conference on IT Convergence and Security (ICITCS) (pp. 1-6). IEEE.

Sharma, M., & Tomar, S. S. (2015). Attack Detection and Security in Remote Code Execution. *International Journal of Computer Applications*, *114*, 14. DOI: 10.5120/19757-1410

Sopariwala, S., Fallon, E., & Asghar, M. N. (2022, June). Log4jPot: effective log4shell vulnerability detection system. In 2022 33rd Irish Signals and Systems Conference (ISSC) (pp. 1-5). IEEE.

Srinivasa, S., Pedersen, J. M., & Vasilomanolakis, E. (2022, June). Deceptive directories and "vulnerable" logs: a honeypot study of the LDAP and log4j attack landscape. In 2022 IEEE European Symposium on Security and Privacy Workshops (EuroS&PW) (pp. 442-447). IEEE.

Varlioglu, S., Elsayed, N., ElSayed, Z., & Ozer, M. (2022). The dangerous combo: Fileless malware and cryptojacking. *SoutheastCon*, *2022*, 125–132. DOI: 10.1109/SoutheastCon48659.2022.9764043

Vashishtha, L. K., Singh, A. P., & Chatterjee, K. (2023). HIDM: A Hybrid Intrusion Detection Model for Cloud Based Systems. *Wireless Personal Communications*, *128*(4), 2637–2666. DOI: 10.1007/s11277-022-10063-y

Zhang, F., Zhou, S., Qin, Z., & Liu, J. (2003, August). Honeypot: a supplemented active defense system for network security. In *Proceedings of the Fourth International Conference on Parallel and Distributed Computing, Applications and Technologies* (pp. 231-235). IEEE.

Chapter 15
Augmented Ebola Optimization Algorithm for Anomaly-Based Intrusion Detection System

Mohammad Alshinwan
Faculty of Information Technology, Applied Science Private University, Amman, Jordan

Abdallah Ehab Awad
https://orcid.org/0000-0002-9393-7999
Applied Science Private University, Jordan

Ali Ghassan Mohammad
https://orcid.org/0009-0004-6878-6035
MEU Research Unit, Middle East University, Amman, Jordan

Yousef Salah Alnajjar
MEU Research Unit, Middle East University, Amman, Jordan

Ahmed Ali Otoom
https://orcid.org/0000-0003-3689-634X
Applied Science Private University, Jordan

Radwan Batyha
Faculty of Information Technology, Applied Science Private University, Amman, Jordan

Mohammad Hijjawi
Faculty of Information Technology, Applied Science Private University, Amman, Jordan

Saad Said Alqahtany
Islamic University of Madinah, Madinah, Saudi Arabia

Omar husain Tarawneh
https://orcid.org/0000-0002-3760-5738
Faculty of Computer Sciences and Informatics, Amman Arab University, Amman, Jordan

Laith Abualigah
Computer Science Department, Al Al-Bayt University, Mafraq, Jordan

DOI: 10.4018/979-8-3693-8014-7.ch015

ABSTRACT

The exponential growth of information technology results in a higher proliferation of internet-connected products. In addition, there was a rise in the Number of network attacks. An intrusion detection system (IDS) is considered one of the most efficient security solutions. This research presents a novel anomaly-based intrusion detection system (IDS) model that utilizes the Ebola Optimization Algorithm (EOA) technique for increased performance. The EOA algorithm is hybridized with the Prairie Dog Algorithm (PD) to enhance the performance of the EOA algorithm, called EOA-PD. The EOA-PD technique is used as a feature selection mechanism to determine the most pertinent elements from the dataset that lead to a high level of classification accuracy. In addition, a support vector machine is utilized to assess the effectiveness of the chosen features in correctly forecasting the attacks. Furthermore, The NSL-KDD dataset is used to showcase the efficacy of the suggested methodology across several attack scenarios.

INTRODUCTION

Ensuring network security is increasingly vital and fundamental for enterprises. As a result, numerous tools are being created to mitigate network and system security risks. An intrusion detection system is a prudent step to identify and detect unauthorized access or infiltration. Its primary function is to identify any data security breaches in terms of integrity, availability, or confidentiality (Karim et al., 2023).

Describe Damage-causing attacks can be detected by intrusion detection systems (IDS) in existing environments. An IDS is installed inside the Network, and it defends and collects network packets like a sniffer for networks. An IDS detects malicious, dangerous, and network-destructive activities. To prevent further network damage from malicious attacks, the captured packets are analyzed by an IDS, which alerts the system administrator to restrict the connections of the attack. The system is also linked to a firewall, a crucial technology for maintaining network security (Arivudainambi et al., 2019).

IDS can be grouped into several categories. Active and passive IDS are the two main types. A system for intrusion detection and prevention is often known as an active IDS (IDPS). An IDPS is built to block malicious attacks automatically without the need for operator intervention. The advantage of the IDPS is that it offers concurrent corrective action in response to an assault. A passive IDS is a system that merely observes and evaluates network traffic activity and warns an operator of prospective weaknesses and assaults. A passive IDS doesn't carry out any preventative or corrective actions.(Alzubi et al., 2020).

IDS can be divided into two main categories depending on the detection method. Anomaly-based detection is included in the second category, while signature-based detection, sometimes known as “misuse detection,” is included in the first. The effectiveness of a misuse detection system relies on signatures and is limited to known attack scenarios. However, this method is unable to identify unidentified attacks. On the other hand, an anomaly detection system compares the attacker's behavior to that of a typical user to identify anomalies (Arivudainambi et al., 2019).

When dealing with unidentified assault situations, anomaly detection has rates that are both false and positive. Data collection, pre-processing, feature selection (FS), and classification stages are only a few where the IDS can be used. An IDS deals with enormous amounts of data; hence, this feature must be complex (Alzaqebah et al., 2022).

Server-based and network-based attacks are two categories of IDS attacks (Selvakumar et al., 2019). As a result, IDSs are further divided into network intrusion detection systems (NIDS) and host-based intrusion detection systems (HIDS). IDSs can also be organized by considering how they differentiate between interruptions. There are two types of interruptions: interruptions based on peculiarities and interruptions based on abuse. Oddity-based IDSs can recognize malicious traffic based on deviations from regular system traffic patterns. Abuse-based discovery examines organized traffic for preplanned and predetermined assault plans (Aghdam et al., 2016).

Intrusion Detection Systems (IDS) are essential for detecting and reacting to security breaches in computer networks. Nevertheless, like any technological advancement, Intrusion Detection Systems (IDSs) have specific deficiencies and constraints. Below are several prevalent deficiencies commonly connected with IDS (Khraisat et al., 2019):

- Errors in classification known as false positives and false negatives:

False positives occur when IDSs issue alerts for regular network activities that are not security threats. This might lead to wasting Time and resources while researching non-threatening situations.

- False Negatives: Conversely, Intrusion Detection Systems (IDSs) may exhibit a failure to identify specific categories of assaults, resulting in occurrences of false negatives. This can be a substantial security vulnerability if malicious operations remain undetected.
- Zero-Day Attacks: Conventional intrusion detection systems (IDSs) depend on established attack patterns. They may struggle to identify novel or “zero-day” assaults that lack a predefined signature or pattern.

- Encrypted communication: The growing prevalence of encryption, such as HTTPS, poses difficulties for IDSs, as they may be unable to examine the contents of encrypted communication. This can enable specific attacks to remain unnoticed.
- Advanced Evasion strategies: Skilled adversaries may utilize evasion strategies to circumvent intrusion detection system (IDS) detection. These approaches encompass manipulating or fragmenting network packets to evade detection based on signatures.
- Resource Consumption: Certain Intrusion Detection Systems (IDSs), especially those that engage in deep packet inspection, tend to use significant resources. This could result in performance degradation and adversely affect the total network throughput.
- Insider Threats: Intrusion Detection Systems (IDSs) may encounter difficulties in identifying insider threats or attacks from within a company, as insiders' actions may appear typical or expected.
- Unfamiliar Protocols and Applications: IDSs may be ineffective in detecting assaults that specifically target protocols or apps that are not widely understood or included in the predetermined rule list.
- Complex Network: Settings challenge IDSs to adequately monitor and analyze all network traffic. Network changes necessitate regular updates and adjustments to IDSs to accommodate modifications in the network environment, such as introducing new applications, services, or network configurations.
- Denial-of-service (DoS): DoS attacks can inundate IDSs by flooding the Network with a high traffic volume, making it challenging for the IDS to differentiate between legitimate and malicious activity.

To address these deficiencies, enterprises frequently implement a blend of security solutions, encompassing many tiers of protection, threat intelligence, anomaly detection, and regular updates to IDS signatures and rules. Furthermore, the incorporation of Artificial Intelligence (AI) and Machine Learning (ML) methods is increasingly prevalent to improve the detection capabilities of Intrusion Detection Systems (IDSs) and address some of these difficulties.

SVM-based Intrusion Detection Systems (IDS) have a restricted capacity to accommodate a finite number of users. Due to the growing utilization of the Internet, the effectiveness of these systems diminishes while the Number of threats rises. This has prompted academics to devise novel approaches for detecting any potential threats. This work proposes a novel approach that utilizes a modified version of the Ebola Optimization Algorithm (EOA) (Oyelade et al., 2022) by the Prairie Dog Algorithm (PD) (Ezugwu et al., 2022) called EOA-PD to efficiently identify the most optimal features for classification while minimizing the total Number of features required compared to the original EOA and PD set. The feature selection process aims to decrease the data volume by eliminating irrelevant or redundant features. The categorization process exclusively utilizes the pertinent characteristics to enhance the performance of the Intrusion Detection System (IDS) in terms of accuracy, detection rate, and false alarm rate. The original EOA is modified by the Prairie Dog Algorithm (PD) during the limited exploration and exploitation steps. The primary objective of the research is to examine the impact of feature selection via EOA-PD on Intrusion Detection Systems (IDS) in Internet networks using the Support Vector Machine (SVM) algorithm. The EOA-PD algorithm is utilized to employ support vector machines (SVM) for feature selection to classify the dataset. The suggested method is evaluated using the KDD Dataset, and the findings are compared with other methods in the existing literature. The primary goals of the proposed Intrusion Detection System (IDS) are to compile the dataset, employ feature selection through EOA-PD, and utilize SVM for data classification to identify and detect instances of intrusion.

RELATED WORK

In this section, we review the existing works that are related to our research topic. We discuss their main contributions, methods, results, and limitations and compare them with our proposed approach.

The related works cover various aspects of IDS, such as Feature Selection in this work.

To determine the best feature subset that increases classification accuracy, they searched the feature space using the gray wolf optimizer, a swarm-based optimization method. The gray wolf optimizer initially searches for solutions with minimal duplication characterized by mutual information using filter-based methods. Later, a wrapper optimization strategy is used to direct classifier performance (Velliangiri & Karthikeyan, 2020).

Another work proposes a set of network traffic features that can be derived for real-time intrusion detection. This study also suggests an Ant Colony Optimization (ACO) based on fuzzy entropy to find the best and most minor network traffic features for the Real-Time IDS data set (Hamamoto et al., 2015). Using a Fuzzy min-max neural network. This work (Selvakumar et al., 2019) suggested a particle swarm optimization-based fuzzy min-max neural network-based intrusion detection system. Classification error and accuracy are used as performance evaluation parameters to evaluate the system's performance.

Ramanet al. proposes the genetic algorithm (GA) to improve SVM-based network intrusion detection. The GA enhances the intrusion detection system based on Support Vector Machines (SVM). SVM is a relatively new classification algorithm that has outperformed conventional learning techniques in several situations. Therefore, several security researchers have suggested SVM-based IDS (Raman et al., 2017). This paper (Raman et al., 2017) presents an efficient and precise DDoS detection approach utilizing the Lion optimization algorithm. The suggested detection technique is sufficiently robust to identify Distributed Denial of Service (DDoS) attacks even when the attack traffic is negligible. In addition, the suggested method's performance is assessed by comparing it to the most advanced techniques currently available.

(Alzubi et al., 2020) introduced a modified feature selection (FS) algorithm called the modified binary grey wolf optimization. The authors expanded the GWO by incorporating a fourth wolf schema and a binary formulation tailored for the intrusion detection system (IDS) FS process. They evaluated the proposed algorithm on the NSL-KDD dataset, conducting various scenarios that compared MBGWO with bGWO. These scenarios are based on dataset partitioning, where training and testing data division significantly influenced FS and IDS accuracy. This research (Seth & Chandra, 2016) presents a network intrusion detection system that utilizes binary grey wolf optimization (GWO) for key feature selection in combination with a neural network classifier. The proposed Intrusion Detection System (IDS) can be deployed at any vital location inside the Network. Employing the Grey Wolf Optimization (GWO) algorithm to eliminate the irrelevant features from the dataset makes it possible to minimize the dataset's size. This reduction in size leads to a decrease in both the training time required for the classifier and the storage space needed for the dataset.

A hybrid optimization approach for IDS that focuses on effective feature selection (FS) is proposed in this paper (Velliangiri & Karthikeyan, 2020). The authors identified that real-time IDS datasets often contain redundant or irrelevant features, complicating the detection of intrusion patterns. They proposed a hybrid optimization scheme that selects relevant features to enhance the precision rate of identifying intrusion activities within networks. This scheme's effectiveness is evaluated using the NSL-KDD dataset, and the authors carried out various performance analyses concerning different parameters. The results revealed that the categories are notably distinct, and the proposed hybrid-based approach surpasses other categorization methods.

This paper (Eesa et al., 2015) proposed a model that employs the cuttlefish algorithm (CFA) as a research strategy to determine the optimal subset of features and the decision tree (DT) classifier to make judgments based on the selected features generated by the CFA. The authors recognized that IDSs handle vast amounts of data, and a critical task for IDSs is to retain high-quality features representing the entire dataset while eliminating redundant and irrelevant features. The model's results reveal that the feature subset obtained using CFA achieves a higher detection rate and accuracy rate, along with a lower false alarm rate, compared to the results obtained using all features.

The author in (Hajimirzaei & Navimipour, 2019) put forth a meta-heuristic approach for a novel IDS that combines a multilayer perceptron (MLP) network, artificial bee colony (ABC) algorithm, and fuzzy clustering method. The ABC algorithm trains the system by optimizing linkage weights and biases, utilizing subsets produced by the fuzzy clustering technique. The CloudSim simulator and NSL-KDD dataset were employed to validate the proposed method. The MLP network discriminates between normal and abnormal packets in network traffic. According to the authors, the results obtained demonstrate the proposed method's superiority compared to state-of-the-art approaches.

Based on the studies mentioned above, specific characteristics hold considerable importance in the field of intrusion detection. Furthermore, it has been empirically demonstrated that a singular universal classifier that can effectively classify all forms of attacks does not exist. However, in certain instances, particular classifiers outperform others. Consequently, most of these studies combine or merge various classifier intrusion detection systems (IDS). Table 1 summarizes the previously proposed works.

Table 1. previously proposed works.

Reference	Methods	Results	Limitations
(Velliangiri & Karthikeyan, 2020)	Gray Wolf Optimizer, Swarm-based optimization	Improved precision in identifying intrusion activities	Real-time IDS datasets may have redundant or irrelevant features. Performance depends on dataset partitioning.
(Hamamoto et al., 2015)	Ant Colony Optimization (ACO) based on fuzzy entropy	Identification of minor network traffic features for Real-Time IDS	Limited information on specific performance metrics.
(Selvakumar et al., 2019)	Particle Swarm Optimization-based fuzzy min-max neural network	Evaluation based on classification error and accuracy	No specific information on the comparison with other approaches.
(Raman et al., 2017)	Genetic Algorithm (GA)	Efficient DDoS detection using Lion optimization algorithm	No specific information on the comparison with other approaches.
(Alzubi et al., 2020)	Modified Binary Grey Wolf Optimization	Evaluation on NSL-KDD dataset, comparing with bGWO	Impact of dataset partitioning on FS and IDS accuracy.
(Seth & Chandra, 2016)	Grey Wolf Optimization (GWO)	Deployment at vital network locations with reduced dataset size	No specific information on the comparison with other approaches.

continued on following page

Table 1. Continued

Reference	Methods	Results	Limitations
(Eesa et al., 2015)	Cuttlefish algorithm (CFA), Decision Tree (DT)	Higher detection rate, accuracy, and lower false alarm rate	Focus on eliminating redundant and irrelevant features.
(Hajimirzaei & Navimipour, 2019)	Artificial Bee Colony (ABC), Fuzzy Clustering, MLP	Superior results compared to state-of-the-art approaches	Reliance on specific simulator (CloudSim) and dataset (NSL-KDD).

PROPOSED ALGORITHMS

The Ebola Optimization Algorithm (EOA)

The Ebola Optimization Algorithm (Oyelade et al., 2022) is a binary optimization algorithm that draws inspiration from the transmission process of the Ebola virus. The Ebola virus exhibits a substantial mutation rate, enhancing its adaptability to diverse ecological niches and rendering its containment formidable. The algorithm models the mutation process to determine the most optimal solutions for binary optimization problems. Within the context of the Ebola algorithm, each virus may serve as a prospective resolution to the given optimization quandary. Viruses traverse the search space through positional mutations, wherein said positions correspond to binary variables of the optimization problem. The assessment of the merit of individual positions is conducted through the utilization of a fitness function. The mutation process entails altering one or more bits within the binary depiction of the solution. Every virus can undergo mutations in its components with a certain probability. If the mutation yields an enhanced solution, as the fitness function evaluates, the virus assimilates to the updated position. Alternatively, it maintains its previous location. The processes of mutation and selection mentioned above are iteratively executed until either the optimal solution or the maximum number of iterations is attained. The optimal solution identified by the algorithm is subsequently employed as the algorithm's output. The pseudo code of the Ebola algorithm presented on Algorithm 1.

Algorithm 1. EOA algorithm pseudo code

Inputs:		
	Number of bits (N) **Mutation probability** **Fitness function**	
Initialize a binary solution with N bits		
for each bit i in solution do:		
	Generate a random number between 0 and 1 (rand)	
	if rand < mutation_probability then:	
		mutated_position(i) = 1 - original_position(i)
	end if	
	calculate the fitness of the mutated solution (mutated_fitness)	
	if mutated_fitness < current_fitness then:	
		current_position = mutated_position
	end if	
end for return the current_position		

The Prairie Dog Optimization (PDO):

The Prairie Dog Optimization (PDO) (Ezugwu et al., 2022) algorithm is an optimization algorithm that draws inspiration from nature and emulates the social behavior of prairie dogs. Prairie dogs are recognized for their sophisticated social organization and intricate means of communication. The individuals in this species establish communal units known as coteries, characterized by one or more underground tunnels called burrows. The burrows exhibit a sophisticated structure comprising numerous entry and exit points as well as chambers. Upon the approach of a predator, the individuals within the group communicate to alert one another of the impending danger. Subsequently, they expeditiously seek refuge within their respective burrows. The PDO algorithm addresses optimization problems by simulating and incorporating these behaviors. The Particle Swarm Optimization (PSO) algorithm employs a population of prairie dogs, each representing a feasible solution to the given optimization problem. The prairie dogs explore the optimization problem through the manipulation of their positions, which serve as representations of the variables involved. Individuals engage in communication with one another regarding the caliber of their respective positions, as evaluated by a fitness function. The prairie dogs' endeavor to enhance their positions by acquiring knowledge from the most optimal positions discovered thus far. The algorithm incorporates techniques for both exploitation, which involves intensifying the search in the vicinity of the optimal solutions, and exploration, which entails diversifying the search throughout the entire search space. Algorithms 2 show the pseudo algorithm of the PDO algorithm.

Algorithm 2. PDO algorithm pseudo code

Inputs:		
	Number of prairie dogs (N) **Number of dimensions (Dim)** **Number of iterations (T)** **Dig multiplier (mu)**	
Initialize N population randomly in the search space. Initialize the best global position.		
for t = 1 to T do:		
	for each pd i in population do:	
		calculate the fitness of the pd
	if the fitness of the pd i is better than its best position then:	
		update the best position of pd i
	if the fitness of pd i is better than the best global position then:	
		update the best global position
		calculate Digging Strength (DS) calculate Predator Effect (PE) calculate Levy Flight as: RL = levym(N,Dim,1.5)
		update the position of pd i using DS, PE, and RL
	end for	
end for return best global position		

CLASSIFICATION USING SUPPORT VECTOR MACHINES (SVMS)

Support Vector Machines (SVMs) are supervised machine learning (ML) models that analyze data to classify target entities. They are advantageous for linear classification and regression issues. SVMs are distinguished by their capability to perform and generalize efficiently, even when working with small training or learning data samples. Due to their robustness, versatility, and effectiveness on datasets of different importance, they are repeatedly employed, especially in IDS. SVMs do not make any assumptions about the data. In addition, the SVM aims to identify a hyperplane in a space with N dimensions that can effectively organize the data points.

The fundamental idea is to utilize sophisticated computation to transform a space with few dimensions into a space with multiple dimensions and then utilize this transformation to determine the most productive approach for classification.

IDS often exhibit varying distributions of hits, with low-frequency attacks substantially less general than high-frequency attacks. SVMs are very effective and widely used algorithms for IDS. They are recognized for their remarkable capability to generalize well, even with small datasets. Further, SVMs have the tiniest classification time and efficiently organize different classes. The SVM classifier is fundamental for IDS in SVM. The system delivers a conventional illustration of the target method and associates attribute condition data with a classification outcome. Classification aims to construct a decision function by utilizing already sample data. Figure 1 depicts the SVM model suggested for classifying the outputs generated by the EOA-PD system.

Figure 1. The proposed approach.

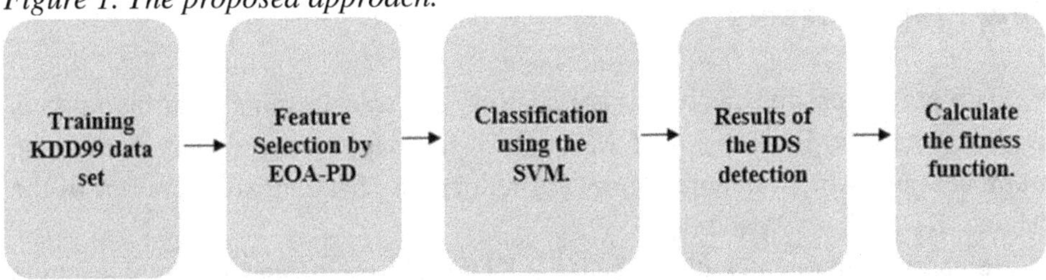

DATASET

The NSL-KDD dataset is a commonly utilized benchmark dataset in IDS. It is an enhanced iteration of the original KDD Cup 99 dataset, initially developed for the Third International Knowledge Discovery and Data Mining Tools Competition, which took place alongside the KDD-99 conference.

The NSL-KDD dataset mitigates several limitations and disadvantages of the original KDD Cup 99 dataset. Both datasets aim to offer a standardized dataset for evaluating IDSs. The dataset comprises a heterogeneous combination of benign and diverse forms of malevolent network behaviors, including Denial of Service (DoS), Probe, user-to-root (U2R), and remote-to-local (R2L) attacks.

Several key features characterize the NSL-KDD dataset:

Reduced Redundancy

The NSL-KDD dataset tackles the problem of redundancy in the original KDD Cup 99 dataset by decreasing the Number of duplicate records.

Attack Categories

The dataset encompasses many attack categories, enabling academics and practitioners to assess the efficacy of intrusion detection systems across a wide range of malevolent actions.

Standard Split

Typically, the dataset is partitioned into training and testing sets to facilitate the evaluation of machine learning models. This standard division ensures uniformity in performance comparisons.

Data Preprocessing

Data preprocessing involves manipulating and transforming data before it is used for analysis. In the case of NSL-KDD, the dataset has already undergone preprocessing, which includes removing redundant characteristics present in the original KDD Cup 99 dataset.

Researchers frequently utilize the NSL-KDD dataset to train and assess machine learning models designed for intrusion detection. It functions as a standard measure for evaluating the efficiency of various algorithms in detecting and categorizing network threats. The NSL-KDD dataset is an excellent resource for experimentation and model evaluation in intrusion detection and cybersecurity research.

The NSL-KDD dataset has 41 conditional attributes and a class label for each piece. The conditional qualities can be categorized into four distinguishable features: time-based traffic, host-based traffic, basic, and content. These attributes can be added and classed as discrete or continuous, as shown in Figure 2. Any deviation from the "Normal" in network training is categorized as an attack (class label). The NSL-KDD dataset has 24 attack classes, which are classified as Denial of Service (DoS), Probe, user-to-root (U2R), and remote-to-local (R2L) attacks. These categories are illustrated in Figure 3.

Figure 2. NSL-KDD attributes.

Time- based traffic												
Dst Host Count	Dst Host Srv Count	Dst Host Same Srv Rate	Dst Host Diff Srv Count	Dst Host Same Src Port Ratet	Dst Host Srv Diff Host Rate	Dst Host Serror Rate						
Host												
Count	Srv Count	Serror Rate	Srvserror Rate	Same Srv Rate	Diff Srv Rate	Srv Diff Host Rate						
Basic												
Duration	Protocol Type	Service	Flag	Source Bytes	Destination Bytes	Land	Wrong Fragment	Urgent				
Content												
Hot	Number Faild Logins	Logged In	Num Compromised	Root Shell	Su Attempted	Num Root	Num File Creations	Num Shells	Num Access Files	Num Outbound Cmds	Is Host Login	Is Guest Login

Figure 3. The NSL-KDD attacks.

Attacks									
	DoS	Smurf	Back	Land	Neptune	Pod	Tear drop		
	Probe	Ipsweep	Nmap	Satan	Portsweep				
	U2R	Buffer overflow	Load module	Per1	Per1				
	R2L	Ftp write	Guess password	Imap	Mutlihop	Spy	Phf	Warezclient	Warezmaster

EXPERIMENTAL RESULTS

The EOA-PD method is executed using MATLAB 2019. The trials are performed on a device equipped with an Intel Core i7 CPU working at a frequency of 1.80 GHz, 16 GB of RAM, and the Windows 11 operating system. MATLAB software is used to validate the results. In the initial stage of the experiment, data preparation was carried out to transform the NSL-KDD dataset into a format appropriate for EOA-PD and SVM. The data mapping approach is employed to transform the categorical values of the features into numerical values, as depicted in Figure 4 and 5.

Figure 4. Dataset before processing.

Dataset before processing	
	0,tcp,http,SF,310,1512,0,0,0,0,0,1,0,0,0,0,0,0,0,0,0,0,13,13,0.00,0.00,0.00,0.00,1.00,0.00,0.00,246,255,1.00,0.00,0.00,0.01,0.00,0.00,0.00,0.00,normal
	0,tcp,iso_tsap,S0,0,0,0,0,0,0,0,0,0,0,0,0,0,0,0,0,0,0,194,9,1.00,1.00,0.00,0.00,0.05,0.08,0.00,255,9,0.04,0.09,0.00,0.00,1.00,1.00,0.00,0.00,anomaly
	0,tcp,http,SF,286,366,0,0,0,0,0,1,0,0,0,0,0,0,0,0,0,0,7,7,0.00,0.00,0.00,0.00,1.00,0.00,0.00,48,255,1.00,0.00,0.02,0.04,0.00,0.00,0.00,0.00,normal
	0,tcp,other,REJ,0,0,0,0,0,0,0,0,0,0,0,0,0,0,0,0,0,0,508,1,0.11,0.00,0.89,1.00,0.00,1.00,0.00,255,1,0.00,1.00,0.00,0.00,0.18,0.00,0.82,1.00,anomaly
	0,tcp,http,SF,54540,8314,0,0,0,2,0,1,1,0,0,0,0,0,0,0,0,0,4,10,0.00,0.00,0.00,0.00,1.00,0.00,0.20,255,255,1.00,0.00,0.00,0.00,0.00,0.00,0.04,0.04,anomaly
	0,tcp,http,SF,222,333,0,0,0,0,0,1,0,0,0,0,0,0,0,0,0,0,4,4,0.00,0.00,0.00,0.00,1.00,0.00,0.00,137,237,1.00,0.00,0.01,0.03,0.00,0.00,0.00,0.00,normal
	0,udp,private,SF,28,0,0,3,0,0,0,0,0,0,0,0,0,0,0,0,0,0,92,92,0.00,0.00,0.00,0.00,1.00,0.00,0.00,112,92,0.82,0.03,0.82,0.00,0.00,0.00,0.00,0.00,normal
	0,tcp,http,SF,303,315,0,0,0,0,0,1,0,0,0,0,0,0,0,0,0,0,22,22,0.00,0.00,0.00,0.00,1.00,0.00,0.00,72,255,1.00,0.00,0.01,0.02,0.00,0.00,0.00,0.00,normal
	0,tcp,other,RSTR,0,0,0,0,0,0,0,0,0,0,0,0,0,0,0,0,0,0,1,1,0.00,0.00,1.00,1.00,1.00,0.00,0.00,255,1,0.00,0.94,0.93,0.00,0.00,0.00,0.93,1.00,normal
	0,udp,domain_u,SF,42,42,0,0,0,0,0,0,0,0,0,0,0,0,0,0,0,0,9,13,0.00,0.00,0.00,0.00,1.00,0.00,0.15,255,255,1.00,0.00,0.00,0.00,0.00,0.00,0.00,0.00,normal
	0,tcp,private,REJ,0,0,0,0,0,0,0,0,0,0,0,0,0,0,0,0,0,0,101,14,0.00,0.00,1.00,1.00,0.14,0.06,0.00,255,14,0.05,0.05,0.00,0.00,0.00,0.00,1.00,1.00,anomaly
	0,tcp,http,SF,346,61911,0,0,0,0,0,1,0,0,0,0,0,0,0,0,0,0,4,4,0.00,0.00,0.00,0.00,1.00,0.00,0.00,212,255,1.00,0.00,0.00,0.02,0.00,0.00,0.00,0.00,normal
	0,tcp,finger,RSTO,0,0,0,0,0,0,0,0,0,0,0,0,0,0,0,0,0,0,190,2,0.00,0.00,1.00,1.00,0.01,0.07,0.00,255,2,0.01,0.07,0.00,0.00,0.00,0.00,1.00,1.00,anomaly

Figure 5. Dataset after processing.

Dataset after b processing	
	0,1,1,1,310,1512,0,0,0,0,0,1,0,0,0,0,0,0,0,0,0,0,13,13,0.00,0.00,0.00,0.00,1.00,0.00,0.00,246,255,1.00,0.00,0.00,0.01,0.00,0.00,0.00,0.00,1
	0,1,2,2,0,0,0,0,0,0,0,0,0,0,0,0,0,0,0,0,0,0,194,9,1.00,1.00,0.00,0.00,0.05,0.08,0.00,255,9,0.04,0.09,0.00,0.00,1.00,1.00,0.00,0.00,2
	0,1,1,1,286,366,0,0,0,0,0,1,0,0,0,0,0,0,0,0,0,0,7,7,0.00,0.00,0.00,0.00,1.00,0.00,0.00,48,255,1.00,0.00,0.02,0.04,0.00,0.00,0.00,0.00,1
	0,1,3,3,0,0,0,0,0,0,0,0,0,0,0,0,0,0,0,0,0,0,508,1,0.11,0.00,0.89,1.00,0.00,1.00,0.00,255,1,0.00,1.00,0.00,0.00,0.18,0.00,0.82,1.00,2
	0,1,1,1,54540,8314,0,0,0,2,0,1,1,0,0,0,0,0,0,0,0,0,4,10,0.00,0.00,0.00,0.00,1.00,0.00,0.20,255,255,1.00,0.00,0.00,0.00,0.00,0.00,0.04,0.04,2
	0,1,1,1,222,333,0,0,0,0,0,1,0,0,0,0,0,0,0,0,0,0,4,4,0.00,0.00,0.00,0.00,1.00,0.00,0.00,137,237,1.00,0.00,0.01,0.03,0.00,0.00,0.00,0.00,1
	0,2,4,1,28,0,0,3,0,0,0,0,0,0,0,0,0,0,0,0,0,0,92,92,0.00,0.00,0.00,0.00,1.00,0.00,0.00,112,92,0.82,0.03,0.82,0.00,0.00,0.00,0.00,0.00,1
	0,1,1,1,303,315,0,0,0,0,0,1,0,0,0,0,0,0,0,0,0,0,22,22,0.00,0.00,0.00,0.00,1.00,0.00,0.00,72,255,1.00,0.00,0.01,0.02,0.00,0.00,0.00,0.00,1
	0,1,3,4,0,0,0,0,0,0,0,0,0,0,0,0,0,0,0,0,0,0,1,1,0.00,0.00,1.00,1.00,1.00,0.00,0.00,255,1,0.00,0.94,0.93,0.00,0.00,0.00,0.93,1.00,1
	0,2,5,1,42,42,0,0,0,0,0,0,0,0,0,0,0,0,0,0,0,0,9,13,0.00,0.00,0.00,0.00,1.00,0.00,0.15,255,255,1.00,0.00,0.00,0.00,0.00,0.00,0.00,0.00,1
	0,1,4,3,0,0,0,0,0,0,0,0,0,0,0,0,0,0,0,0,0,0,101,14,0.00,0.00,1.00,1.00,0.14,0.06,0.00,255,14,0.05,0.05,0.00,0.00,0.00,0.00,1.00,1.00,2
	0,1,1,1,346,61911,0,0,0,0,0,1,0,0,0,0,0,0,0,0,0,0,4,4,0.00,0.00,0.00,0.00,1.00,0.00,0.00,212,255,1.00,0.00,0.00,0.02,0.00,0.00,0.00,0.00,1
	0,1,6,5,0,0,0,0,0,0,0,0,0,0,0,0,0,0,0,0,0,0,190,2,0.00,0.00,1.00,1.00,0.01,0.07,0.00,255,2,0.01,0.07,0.00,0.00,0.00,0.00,1.00,1.00,2

EVALUATION CRITERIA

The proposed algorithm is evaluated based on four criteria: False alarm rate, Detection rate, Number of features, and Accuracy. True-positive is the count of effectively detected intrusions, False-positive is the count of typical behaviors misclassified as intrusions, True-negative is the count of regular behaviors correctly classified as usual, and False-negative is the count of abnormal behaviors misclassified as usual. Following are the equations used to calculate the mentioned criteria:

1) False alarm rate (FAR) =

$$\frac{FP}{FP + TN}$$

2) Detection rate (DR) =

$$\frac{True_{postive}}{True_{postive} + False_{Negative}}$$

3) Number of features =

$$Total_{Numberoffeatures} - Nonselected_{Features}$$

4) Accuracy =

$$\frac{True_{positive} + True_{negative}}{True_{positive} + False_{negative} + True_{negative}}$$

EXAMINING AND ANALYSIS

This section offers a comprehensive assessment of the proposed EOA-PD, original EOA and PD, Grey wolf algorithm (GWO) (Mirjalili et al., 2014), Harris hawks' optimization (HHO) (Heidari et al., 2019), Arithmetic optimization algorithm (AOA)(Abualigah et al., 2021).

The study examines the efficiency of the recommended method and the state-of-the-art algorithms EOA, PD, GWO, HHO, and AOA in addressing the IDS issue. The proposed EOA-PD is being improved to boost the PD algorithm to address problems like premature convergence, solution diversity, and sluggish search speed in the original version. Any alteration in the size of the PD will impact the optimization process, either positively or negatively. This section examines the Number of PDs to determine the optimal quantity for balancing exploration and exploitation searches.

False alarm rate

The suggested technique demonstrates superior performance regarding false alarm rates in PD, EOA, GWO, HHO, and AOA. The EOA-PD method obtains a false alarm rate of 3%. In comparison, the basic PD method has a false alarm rate of 10%, while the EOA method has a false alarm rate of 20%. The GOW, HHO, and AOA algorithms have 26%, 27%, and 30% false alarm rates, respectively. Thus, the reduction of false alarm rates and the Number of features generated by the IDSs in the Network is accomplished. Figure 6 summarizes the results collected, specifically concerning the detection rate.

Figure 6. Result of false alarm rate.

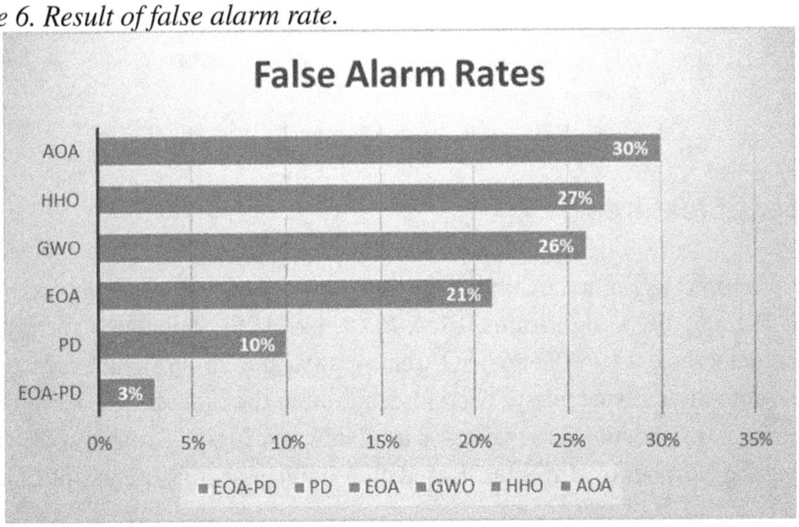

Detection rate

The proposed technique has a superior detection rate compared to the standard PD and EOA algorithms. PD-EOA achieved a detection rate of 99%, while PD and EOA had false detection rates of 95% and 86%, respectively. Consequently, the enhancement of the detection rate of intrusion detection systems in the network environment has been achieved. Figure 7 displays the detection rate results.

Replicable trials have established that the EOA-PD consistently delivers reliable outcomes. Integrating the EOA algorithm into the PD will strengthen complexity and decrease the overall detection rate.

Figure 7. results of detection rate.

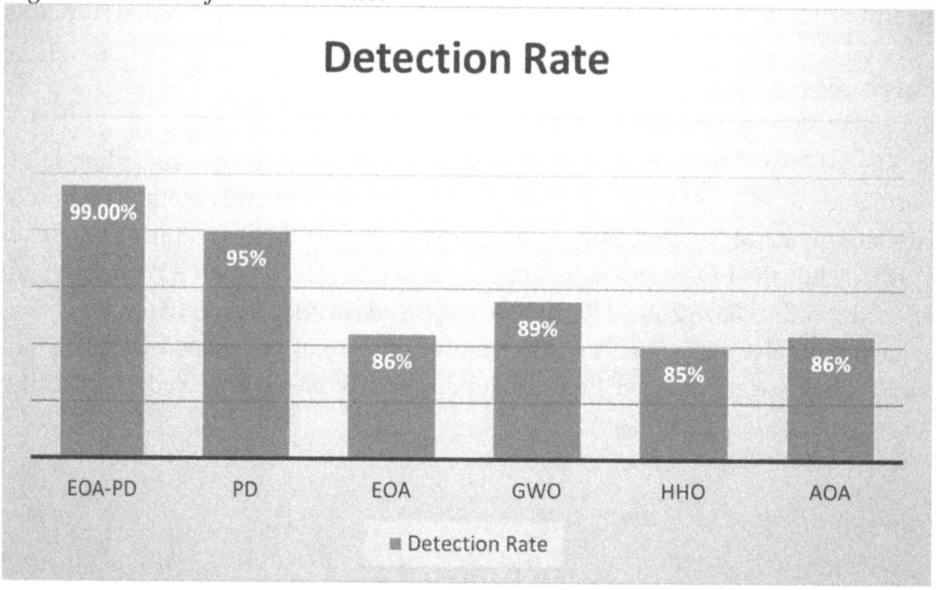

Number of features

The proposed technique exhibits a greater number of features compared to the original PD and EOA algorithms. EOA-PD chose 10% of features for effective intrusion detection, while PD and EOA chose 18% and 25% of characteristics for intrusion detection, respectively. Therefore, attaining these outcomes decreases the Number of characteristics IDS generates in a Network. Figure 8 displays the results regarding the Number of attributes. Based on reliable research, the use of EOA-PD produces trustworthy outcomes. Augmenting the population of prairie dogs can enhance both the intricacy and abundance of chosen characteristics.

Figure 8. Number of features.

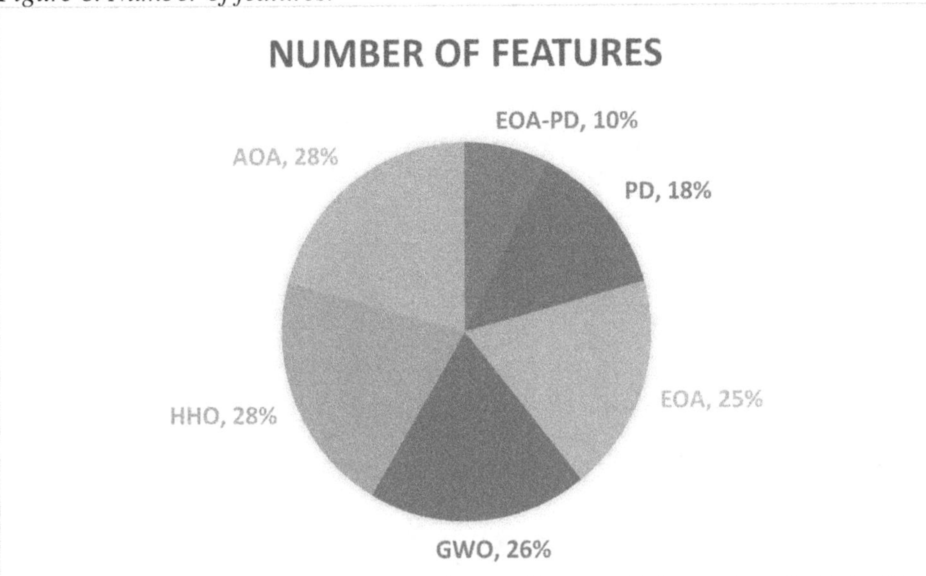

Accuracy

The proposed technique outperforms PD, EOA, HHO, GWO, and AOA with an accuracy rate of 98.5%. The basic PD achieves an accuracy rate of 95%, the EOA earns an accuracy rate of 91%, the HHO achieves an accuracy rate of 89%, and both the GWO and AOA achieve an accuracy rate of 86%. The classification accuracy is improved by prioritizing accuracy above other factors in the proposed multi-objective function. Therefore, the accuracy of the intrusion detection configuration has been enhanced. The results are shown in Figure 9.

Figure 9. The accuracy results achieved by the proposed work compared to other algorithms.

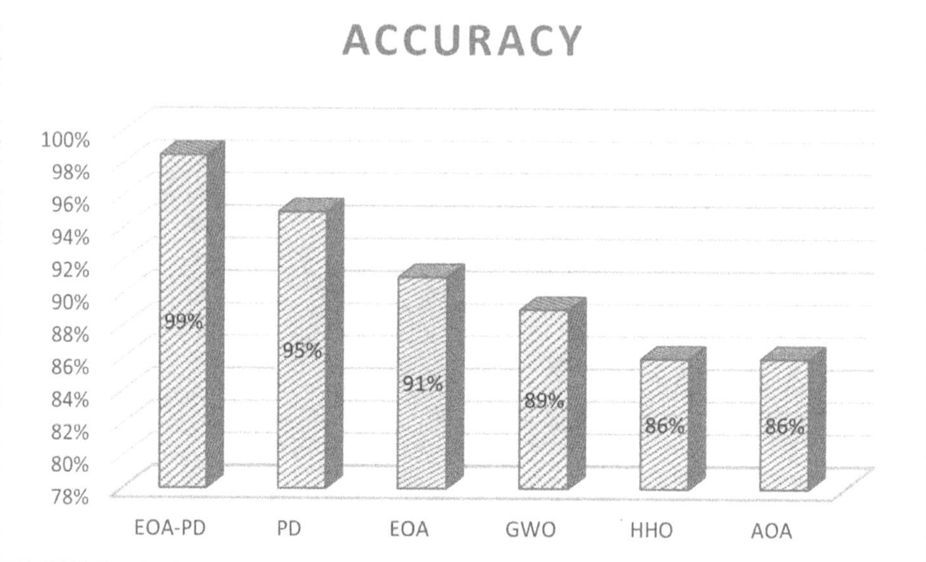

Furthermore, the proposed approach outperforms earlier methods in terms of the Time it takes to execute, as depicted in Figure 10. The hybrid PD-EOA requires 69.7 hours for intrusion identification, PD alone requires 87.2 hours, and EOA alone requires 96.2 hours. The results demonstrate that the suggested algorithm effectively decreases the processing time needed for the Intrusion Detection System, as evidenced in Table 2.

Table 2. The evaluation outcomes based on the execution time.

	Algorithm					
Evaluation mesure	**EOA-PD**	**PD**	**EOA**	**GWO**	**HHO**	**AOA**
Accuracy	99%	95%	91%	89%	86%	86%
Detection time	99.00%	95%	86%	89%	85%	86%
False alarm	3%	10%	21%	26%	27%	30%
Time (hours)	69.7	87.2	96.2	97.3	98	99
Number of features	10%	18%	25%	26%	28%	28%

Table 2 presents the evaluation outcomes of six separate algorithms. The algorithms are evaluated based on five metrics: Accuracy, Detection time, False alarm rate, Time (in hours), and Number of features.

The table yields several noteworthy observations:

- The accuracy rankings are as follows: EOA-PD with a 99% accuracy, PD with a 95% accuracy, and EOA with a 91% accuracy.
- The detection time is the shortest for EOA-PD, taking 69.7 hours, followed by PD, which takes 87.2 hours, and EOA, which takes 96.2 hours.
- Among the several methods, AOA exhibits the lowest percentage of false alarms, at 30%. In comparison, EOA-PD has a false alarm rate of 3%, while PD has a false alarm rate of 10%.
- The AOA has the shortest duration, lasting 99 hours, followed by the HHO with 98 hours and the EOA-PD with a period of 69.7 hours.
- The EOA-PD model has 10 features, whereas PD has 18 features and EOA has 25 features.

According to the measurements in this table, EOA-PD is the most efficient algorithm. It has the fastest detection time, the best accuracy, and the second-lowest false alarm rate. The best approach for a given application may change depending on its particular needs. EOA-PD might be a good choice if a specific application calls for high precision. HHO might be better if a shallow false alarm rate is required for a particular application.

CONCLUSION

PD optimization algorithm is a widely used, reliable feature selection method in many industries, including IDSs. It pinpoints the crucial elements that can improve intrusion detection speed and classification accuracy. Although the PDO has a limited amount of selectable features, precision, and execution time, it is nevertheless effective. Numerous studies have offered strategies for improving the PDO's performance; nonetheless, more improvements are needed in the number of selected features, time of execution, detection rate, and accuracy. This work seeks to enhance the performance of the PD-based IDS in communication networks by adding the EOA algorithm and implementing a multi-objective function. This will increase the prediction system's efficiency in accurately predicting unknown classes, choosing features, and speeding up execution.

The NSL KDD'99 dataset is used to train and test the proposed strategy, and the outcomes were compared to those of the basic PD and EOA methods. The study's results demonstrate that the proposed EOA-PD strategy outperforms other approaches, including GWO, HHO, and AOA.

In conclusion, our study opens up exciting possibilities for future research. With its potential for improvement through mathematical prediction techniques, the PD algorithm could significantly enhance the detection rate in the computer network environment. Moreover, by combining the revised PD with other well-known and modern feature selection techniques, we could further optimize its performance. This approach, which goes beyond the traditional reliance on SVM, could revolutionize the classification procedure in network intrusion detection.

REFERENCES

Abualigah, L., Diabat, A., Mirjalili, S., Abd Elaziz, M., & Gandomi, A. H. (2021). The arithmetic optimization algorithm. *Computer Methods in Applied Mechanics and Engineering*, *376*, 113609. DOI: 10.1016/j.cma.2020.113609

Aghdam, M. H., & Kabiri, P. (2016). Feature selection for intrusion detection system using ant colony optimization. *International Journal of Network Security*, *18*(3), 420–432.

Al Nafea, R., & Almaiah, M. A. (2021, July). Cyber security threats in cloud: Literature review. In 2021 international conference on information technology (ICIT) (pp. 779-786). IEEE.

Alamer, M., & Almaiah, M. A. (2021, July). Cybersecurity in Smart City: A systematic mapping study. In 2021 international conference on information technology (ICIT) (pp. 719-724). IEEE.

Ali, A., Almaiah, M. A., Hajjej, F., Pasha, M. F., Fang, O. H., Khan, R., Teo, J., & Zakarya, M. (2022). An industrial IoT-based blockchain-enabled secure searchable encryption approach for healthcare systems using neural network. *Sensors (Basel)*, *22*(2), 572. DOI: 10.3390/s22020572 PMID: 35062530

Almaiah, M. A. (2021). A new scheme for detecting malicious attacks in wireless sensor networks based on blockchain technology. In *Artificial intelligence and blockchain for future cybersecurity applications* (pp. 217–234). Springer International Publishing. DOI: 10.1007/978-3-030-74575-2_12

Almaiah, M. A., & Al-Khasawneh, A. (2020). Investigating the main determinants of mobile cloud computing adoption in university campus. *Education and Information Technologies*, *25*(4), 3087–3107. DOI: 10.1007/s10639-020-10120-8

Almaiah, M. A., Yelisetti, S., Arya, L., Babu Christopher, N. K., Kaliappan, K., Vellaisamy, P., Hajjej, F., & Alkdour, T. (2023). A Novel Approach for Improving the Security of IoT–Medical Data Systems Using an Enhanced Dynamic Bayesian Network. *Electronics (Basel)*, *12*(20), 4316. DOI: 10.3390/electronics12204316

Alzaqebah, A., Aljarah, I., Al-Kadi, O., & Damaševičius, R. (2022). A modified grey wolf optimization algorithm for an intrusion detection system. *Mathematics*, *10*(6), 999. DOI: 10.3390/math10060999

Alzubi, Q. M., Anbar, M., Alqattan, Z. N. M., Al-Betar, M. A., & Abdullah, R. (2020). Intrusion detection system based on a modified binary grey wolf optimisation. *Neural Computing & Applications*, *32*(10), 6125–6137. DOI: 10.1007/s00521-019-04103-1

Arivudainambi, D., KA, V. K., & Sibi Chakkaravarthy, S. (. (2019). LION IDS: A meta-heuristics approach to detect DDoS attacks against Software-Defined Networks. *Neural Computing & Applications, 31*, 1491–1501. DOI: 10.1007/s00521-018-3383-7

Bubukayr, M. A. S., & Almaiah, M. A. (2021, July). Cybersecurity concerns in smart-phones and applications: A survey. In 2021 international conference on information technology (ICIT) (pp. 725-731). IEEE.

Eesa, A. S., Orman, Z., & Brifcani, A. M. A. (2015). A novel feature-selection approach based on the cuttlefish optimization algorithm for intrusion detection systems. *Expert Systems with Applications, 42*(5), 2670–2679. DOI: 10.1016/j.eswa.2014.11.009

Ezugwu, A. E., Agushaka, J. O., Abualigah, L., Mirjalili, S., & Gandomi, A. H. (2022). Prairie dog optimization algorithm. *Neural Computing & Applications, 34*(22), 20017–20065. DOI: 10.1007/s00521-022-07530-9

Hajimirzaei, B., & Navimipour, N. J. (2019). Intrusion detection for cloud computing using neural networks and artificial bee colony optimization algorithm. *ICT Express, 5*(1), 56–59. DOI: 10.1016/j.icte.2018.01.014

Hamamoto, A. H., Carvalho, L. F., & Proenca, M. L. (2015). ACO and GA metaheuristics for anomaly detection. *2015 34th International Conference of the Chilean Computer Science Society (SCCC)*, 1–6.

Heidari, A. A., Mirjalili, S., Faris, H., Aljarah, I., Mafarja, M., & Chen, H. (2019). Harris hawks optimization: Algorithm and applications. *Future Generation Computer Systems, 97*, 849–872. DOI: 10.1016/j.future.2019.02.028

Karim, N. A., Khashan, O. A., Kanaker, H., Abdulraheem, W. K., Alshinwan, M., & Albanna, A. (2023). Online Banking User Authentication Methods: A Systematic Literature Review. *IEEE Access : Practical Innovations, Open Solutions*.

Khraisat, A., Gondal, I., Vamplew, P., & Kamruzzaman, J. (2019). Survey of intrusion detection systems: Techniques, datasets and challenges. *Cybersecurity, 2*(1), 1–22. DOI: 10.1186/s42400-019-0038-7

Mirjalili, S., Mirjalili, S. M., & Lewis, A. (2014). Grey wolf optimizer. *Advances in Engineering Software, 69*, 46–61. DOI: 10.1016/j.advengsoft.2013.12.007

Oyelade, O. N., Ezugwu, A. E.-S., Mohamed, T. I. A., & Abualigah, L. (2022). Ebola optimization search algorithm: A new nature-inspired metaheuristic optimization algorithm. *IEEE Access : Practical Innovations, Open Solutions, 10*, 16150–16177. DOI: 10.1109/ACCESS.2022.3147821

Raman, M. R. G., Somu, N., Kirthivasan, K., Liscano, R., & Sriram, V. S. S. (2017). An efficient intrusion detection system based on hypergraph-Genetic algorithm for parameter optimization and feature selection in support vector machine. *Knowledge-Based Systems, 134*, 1–12. DOI: 10.1016/j.knosys.2017.07.005

Selvakumar, K., Karuppiah, M., SaiRamesh, L., Islam, S. K. H., Hassan, M. M., Fortino, G., & Choo, K.-K. R. (2019). Intelligent temporal classification and fuzzy rough set-based feature selection algorithm for intrusion detection system in WSNs. *Information Sciences, 497*, 77–90. DOI: 10.1016/j.ins.2019.05.040

Seth, J. K., & Chandra, S. (2016). Intrusion detection based on key feature selection using binary GWO. *2016 3rd International Conference on Computing for Sustainable Global Development (INDIACom)*, 3735–3740.

Velliangiri, S., & Karthikeyan, P. (2020). Hybrid optimization scheme for intrusion detection using considerable feature selection. *Neural Computing & Applications, 32*(12), 7925–7939. DOI: 10.1007/s00521-019-04477-2

Chapter 16
Cyber Attacks Through the Ages
Impact Assessment and Defense Strategies

R. Raman
Chitkara University, India

Hakam Singh
Chitkara University, India

Nilamadhab Mishra
https://orcid.org/0000-0002-1330-4869
VIT Bhopal University, India

Abhishek Thakur
https://orcid.org/0000-0002-9955-9693
Chitkara University, India

Ramamani Tripathy
Chitkara University, India

Rudra Kalyan Nayak
https://orcid.org/0000-0003-4447-8391
VIT Bhopal University, India

Amit Thakur
https://orcid.org/0009-0007-7550-4990
VIT Bhopal University, India

ABSTRACT

Digitization in the modern world is increasing, and along with it, Cyber-attacks have become a very big concern for individuals, nations, and organizations. In this research paper, we will dive into multiple factors of cyber-attacks and explore their types, perpetrators, impacts, and motivations in depth. We will dissect the different methodologies employed by cyber adversaries and their vulnerabilities through different case studies of significant incidents that exploit their role in politics, pursuit of financial gain, and ideological agendas. The speedy digitization of contemporary society has brought about the emergence of cyber-assaults as an excessive global chance, with people, agencies, and global locations increasingly at risk of the dam-

DOI: 10.4018/979-8-3693-8014-7.ch016

aging outcomes of such malicious sports. The cyber chance landscape has advanced appreciably over the past few years, with cyber adversaries using state-of-the-art strategies to compromise virtual structures and attain their nefarious goals.

1. INTRODUCTION

The digital era has led to unique innovations, converting how we communicate and conduct business and helping manage critical infrastructure. While this revolution brought us huge benefits, it has also exposed us to an unyielding and evolving threat landscape - that of cyber-attacks. Cyber-attacks have become a general and potent menace in this consistent world, where information flows seamlessly across borders. A wide range of harmful actions, from covert data breaches to catastrophic infrastructure outages, are included in cyber assaults. They prey on weaknesses in our increasingly electronically dependent and interconnected lives, targeting people, businesses, governments, and even entire countries. Understanding and successfully thwarting these attacks have emerged as crucial issues for cyber security experts, politicians, and society as the cyber threat landscape grows in complexity and scope (Conway, 2014).

This research paper begins a thorough investigation of cyber-attacks, including all of their forms, the causes behind them, the perpetrators, and the terrible effects they have. We want to inform us of the strategies, techniques, and practices used by adversaries who use the digital space for financial gain by exploring cyber-attack anatomy. And now, if we are talking about cyber-attacks, the main issue arises: how can we tackle the problems of these increasing cybercrimes? By prevention, protection, a good knowledge of human users, and innovative knowledge of technology. Reading this research paper and some case studies on major cyber incidents, we can illuminate the dark alleys of the cyber domain, broken weaknesses, and the impacts they had on their victims. These real-world examples underline the urgent need to address the weakness in today's digital infrastructure and the profound consequences of failing to do so. Through the lens of case studies on prominent cyber incidents, we illuminate the cyber domain's dark alleys, dissecting the exploited vulnerabilities and their impact on victims (Bhandari, 2024). These real-world examples underscore the urgency of addressing the vulnerabilities in our digital infrastructure and the profound repercussions of failing to do so. This research also strongly emphasizes proactive cybersecurity measures and best practices, emphasizing the critical role of preparedness, resilience, and security culture in mitigating cyber risks. As the digital arms race intensifies, staying one step ahead of cyber adversaries necessitates constant vigilance and adaptation (Vaidya, 2015).

Moreover, this paper navigates the intricate legal and ethical considerations inherent to cyber-attacks. It examines the evolving landscape of international cyber norms, regulations, and cooperative efforts to deter malicious cyber behavior. It also underscores the ethical responsibilities of cybersecurity professionals and the ethical quandaries posed by offensive cyber operations. In contemplating the future, this research anticipates emerging trends in cyber-attacks, such as the convergence of artificial intelligence and cyber threats, and the potential game-changing capabilities of quantum computing in both offensive and defensive cyber operations. By recognizing these impending challenges, stakeholders can craft strategies to secure tomorrow's digital landscape. In essence, this research paper underscores the gravity of the cybersecurity challenge in our modern age. It calls for collective action, collaboration, and innovation, emphasizing the imperative to protect our digital future. As we embark on this journey through the cyber realm, we hope this research contributes to a deeper understanding of cyber-attacks and inspires the fortitude necessary to confront this ever-evolving (Zeadally et al., 2020).

1.1 Background and Significance

Today's digital world plays an important role in our lives. As digital technology is improving, cyber threats are also increasing that need our urgent attention on this topic. As digitalization is increasing day by day, there is a possibility that there will be a vast use of computer networks that will lead to more devices connected to the internet and lead to increased transactions; this will result in making it a big hub for cyber-criminals to take part in it and result in more cyber-crimes.

Cyber threat landscape and evolution: In today's world cyber-attacks are becoming more sophisticated and diverse. These cyber attackers may have to be involved with several criminal groups from different nations, terrorists, or even some sometimes they just seek fun in challenging IT professionals by disrupting business operations, stealing sensitive information, and creating some critical infrastructure. Most of the website defacement and server disruption is most likely the result of these increasing cyber-attacks, by replacing sophisticated tools that exist with supply chains like APTs and ransomware. The key assets of cyber threats can be categorized into 3 essential organizations: script kiddies, criminal corporations, and realms. Script kiddies are newbie hackers who use tools created by others to gain unauthorized entry to structures, regularly driven using a preference to reinforce their ego or make brief coins. Criminal businesses, alternatively, are concerned with unlawful sports and release cyber-assaults to cause disruption, scouse borrow statistics, or name for ransom bills. Finally, realms are an increasing number of undertaking cyber espionage and battle, using cyber-attacks to gain geopolitical benefit, thieve sensitive statistics, or disrupt the important infrastructure of adversaries. The influences of cyber-attacks may be devastating, from financial losses to undermining country-wide security. The fee of cybersecurity incidents is predicted to increase from $3 trillion per 12 months to more than $5 trillion through 2024, a median every year growth of eleven%. Cyber-assaults can also have giant societal and mental impacts, eroding public trust in virtual structures and inflicting great disruption to day-by-day life. The collective accumulation of the various impacts from cyber-attacks throughout essential infrastructure systems and services may threaten our manner of life and drain Western innovation, economy, and trade without attaining the brink of triggering meaningful government and business reaction (Chaudhuri & Bozkus Kahyaoglu, 2023; Cletus et al., 2022; Mazzolin & Samueli, 2020; Pang & Li, 2020).

Effects of cyber threats: Importantly, cyber threats impact individuals, businesses, and societies. Identity theft, financial fraud, and the loss of personal data are a few of the crimes at the individual level. At the level of business organizations, these can mean costly disruptions, damage to reputation, and a loss of consumer and stakeholder trust. At the national level, cyber threats may target critical infrastructure, cause a break in essential services, and undermine a nation's economic and political stability. Cyber-assaults' effects can be a long way-reaching and devastating, affecting people, organizations, and nations alike. Financial losses are a good-sized subject, with the price of cybersecurity incidents anticipated to grow from $three trillion annually to more than $5 trillion by 2024. Beyond monetary effects, cyber-attacks can also disrupt important infrastructure, compromise touchy records, and undermine national security. According to the World Economic Forum's recent Global Risk Report, cyber threats will intensify due to increased virtual dependency and the increasing effect of systems failure from evolving cybersecurity dangers (Alnifie, 2023; Kamble & Mishra, 2024a).

Figure 1. Cybersecurity threat landscape and evolution

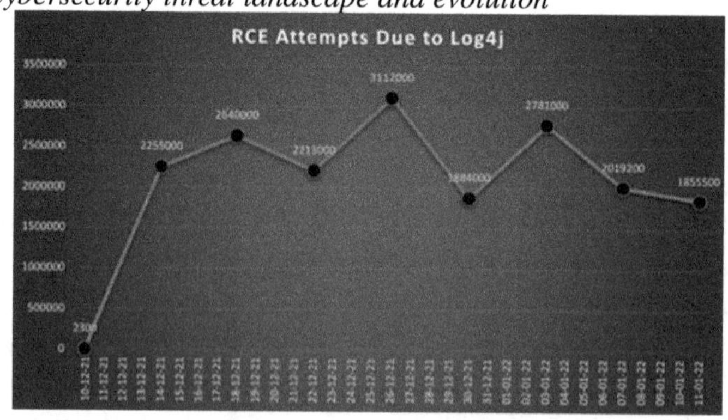

This connectivity has led to an explosion in data involving sensitive personal and corporate financial information. The increasing complexity and interconnectedness of digital infrastructures have multiplied the possible cyber vulnerability points. In time, basic viruses and worms were replaced by advanced persistent threats, ransomware, phishing schemes, and state-sponsored cyber-attacks (figure 1) (Rosenzweig, 2013; Sindiramutty et al., 2024). The economic implications of cyber threats are devastating for businesses, which incur direct expenses like legal charges or fines and indirect ones, e.g., reputation damage or loss of customers' trust. National security risks arising from cyber threats threaten governments, for instance, attacks on critical infrastructure such as power grids or communication networks that could disrupt services and jeopardize public safety.

'Loss of popularity' changed into the primary cited effect of a cyber-attack by 29% of respondents.' Management time' takes the second spot, cited by 26% of respondents, while 16. Four% of the respondents say it results in 'patron loss or churn'. Clean-up prices are referred to with the aid of 12% because of the primary impact, while 'direct lack of turnover' takes the range 5 spot. A loss of 'competitiveness' and 'changing conduct trade' is the least referred to, at three.6% and three.1%, respectively (figure 2) (Kamble & Mishra, 2024b). Cyber insurance, touted to be one of the fastest growing crisis coverage segments, stays pretty underutilized; fifty percent no longer have such insurance, and 35% do, even as 13% aren't aware of possible coverage. The enterprise remains nascent, with providers nevertheless devising a satisfactory manner to guard corporations, especially huge organizations. Here are the results based on a survey held to know how many companies have Cyber insurance or not.

Figure 2. The majority of firms have cyber insurance or not

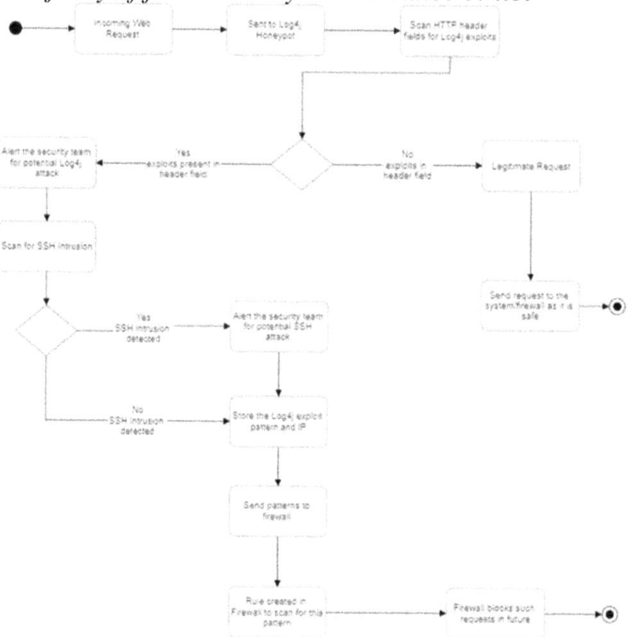

1.2 Evolution of Cyber Threats

Here are some highlights in the evolution of cyber threats that highlight the growing scope and growing impact of malicious activities and a detailed timeline of key events from the beginning of the Internet to the present.

1970s-1980s: Early Days

Creeper virus (1971): Created by Bob Thomas as an experimental program, this virus behaves as it is believed to be the first computer virus. A message "I'm the creeper: catch me if you can" was displayed for him to enter the ARPANET. No damage was done, but it showed how the code could replicate itself. The Creeper Virus, added in 1971, marked the inception of cyber threats, putting the degree for the complex landscape of cyber assaults we face today. As the first recognized PC virus, Creeper laid the muse for information about the vulnerabilities inherent in interconnected systems. Over the long term, cyber assaults have advanced in sophistication, scale, and effect, transitioning from experimental pranks to quite prepared and likely devastating operations affecting governments, companies, and people alike. This paper delves into the ancient development of cyber assaults, beginning with the Creeper Virus, and examines the developing effect those threats have had on global protection and financial balance. Furthermore, it explores the parallel improvement of protection mechanisms, from number one antivirus software to superior risk detection and reaction systems. By analyzing the evolution of cyber-attacks and the corresponding improvements in cybersecurity, this research hobby provides complete facts about the present-day state of cyber safety and the continuing disturbing conditions in shielding virtual infrastructure (Fossi et al., 2011).

Morris worm (1988): This worm was designed by Robert Tappan Morris and exploited vulnerabilities in Unix systems and caused massive damage through an estimated 10% of all computers on the Internet at the time of the outbreak. This is one of the first widely known mosquitoes in the US. The Morris Worm, launched in 1988, is regularly regarded as one of the first important cyber incidents demonstrating the capacity, scale, and effect of cyber assaults. Created with the aid of Robert Tappan Morris, this self-replicating application triggered giant disruption to the early net, infecting approximately 10% of the networked computer systems at the time. The Morris Worm underscored the vulnerabilities in interconnected structures and highlighted the urgent want for robust cybersecurity measures. This paper explores the historical importance of the Morris Worm as a pivotal second in cybersecurity, marking the transition from isolated cyber threats to significant, impactful attacks. We trace the evolution of cyber assaults from the Morris Worm to modern threats, inspecting how they have grown in complexity and ability for harm. Additionally, we analyze the parallel development of protection mechanisms, from early antivirus programs and firewalls to sophisticated hazard detection, synthetic intelligence, and gadget-gaining knowledge protection solutions. By reading Morris Worm's legacy and the advancements in cybersecurity, this study presents insights into the ongoing warfare to protect virtual infrastructures and mitigate the dangers posed using evolving cyber threats as depicted in Table 1 (Anderson et al., 2013).

Table 1. Notable incidents reported between 1970s to 1990s

Year	Notable Incidents
1971	Phone phreaking
1973	Computer crime
1988	Spam email

1990s: The rise of malware.

Michelangelo virus (1992): This virus was programmed to destroy hundreds of sites recorded on the infected computer's hard drive on March 6, 1992. Although its impact was much less than expected, widespread media coverage raised public awareness of bacteria. The Michelangelo Virus, observed in 1992, has grown to be a tremendous milestone in the information of cyber threats due to its giant media coverage and the panic it incited amongst PC customers globally. Named after the well-known artist because it was programmed to activate on his birthday, March 6, the Michelangelo Virus emerged as a boot zone virus that might potentially erase the contents of an inflamed laptop's hard pressure. Although the actual harm precipitated became much less immoderate than before, the virus highlighted the vulnerabilities of the burgeoning private computing generation. It underscored the need for heightened cybersecurity measures. This paper examines the Michelangelo Virus as a vital event that raised public consciousness about the risks of malware and the necessity of proactive defense techniques. We discover cyber-attacks evolution from the early Nineties to the current, noting how threats have grown in sophistication and scale. Additionally, we analyze the improvements in cybersecurity defenses, from fundamental antivirus software to complete security suites and real-time danger intelligence systems. By reflecting on the impact of the Michelangelo Virus and the subsequent developments in cybersecurity, this research aims to offer a complete assessment of methods the panorama of cyber protection has tailored to meet the demanding conditions posed by ever-evolving cyber threats (Cybersecurity, 2018; Rokade & Mishra, 2024).

Melissa virus (1999): A macro virus that spread via e-mail, the Melissa virus infected thousands of pc structures by exploiting Microsoft Word's macro skills. It precipitated exquisite disruption with the resource of overloading email servers and highlighted the vulnerabilities in drastically used software program applications. The Melissa Virus, unleashed in 1999, marked a watershed moment in the statistics of cyber threats because of its super propagation pace and considerable effect. Named after a stripper mentioned in a hacker's report, the Melissa Virus unfolds via e-mail, infecting Microsoft Word files and emailing itself to the primary 50 contacts in the character's cope with eBook. This fast dissemination caused big disruptions in electronic mail offerings and corporation networks globally, leading to expected damages inside the hundreds of hundreds and thousands of dollars. The Melissa Virus underscored the vulnerabilities inherent in e-mail structures and the critical need for more wonderful cybersecurity measures. This paper explores the Melissa Virus as a pivotal event that catalyzed the improvement of extra sturdy email security protocols and heightened cognizance of the dangers posed by malware. We trace the evolution of cyber assaults from the late 1990s to the present, highlighting how threats have grown to be more modern-day and centered. Additionally, we look at the advancements in safety mechanisms in conjunction with the implementation of superior email filtering, heuristic evaluation, and behavioral detection era (figure 3) (Kshetri, 2010). By reflecting on the impact of the Melissa Virus and the next cybersecurity enhancements, this research offers a complete assessment of the continuing efforts to protect digital communication channels and mitigate the risks posed by evolving cyber threats.

Figure 3. Cases reported between 1990s to 2000s

2000s: Increasing Complexity

ILOVEYOU virus (2000): This bug spread through email with the difficulty line "ILOVEYOU," appealing to recipients to open an attachment that finished malicious code. It inflamed hundreds of thousands of computer systems internationally, overwriting documents and inflicting an estimated $10 billion in damages. The ILOVEYOU Virus, which emerged in May 2000, represents one of the most infamous and bad cyber assaults on information. Disguised as a love letter with the situation line "ILOVEYOU," this pc virus unfolds rapidly through email, appealing to recipients to open a related file that unleashes a malicious script. The virus propagated fast, infecting tens of thousands of PC structures globally and inflicting an expected $10 billion in damages by overwriting files and stealing passwords. The ILOVEYOU Virus underscored the vulnerability of virtual communication systems and the profound impact that social engineering will have on cybersecurity. This paper delves into the ILOVEYOU Virus as a landmark event spurred huge improvements in cybersecurity practices and generation. We discover the evolution of cyber-attacks from the early 2000s to now, noting the growing complexity and class of those threats. Additionally, we look at improving safety mechanisms, consisting of more suitable electronic mail safety protocols, client education packages, and implementing advanced malware detection and response structures. By reflecting on the commands from the ILOVEYOU Virus and the subsequent evolution of cybersecurity, this research offers a comprehensive examination of the continued efforts to shield digital infrastructures in opposition to ever-evolving cyber threats (Wall, 2024).

SQL Slammer (2003): A malicious program that exploited a buffer overflow vulnerability in Microsoft SQL Server, SQL Slammer infected masses of hundreds of servers inside mins. It introduced enormous net slowdowns and outages, demonstrating the ability of worms to cause rapid and large disruption. The SQL Slammer, additionally called the Sapphire Worm, struck in January 2003 and quickly became one of the quickest-spreading worms in history. Exploiting a vulnerability in Microsoft's SQL Server, SQL Slammer unfolds through the net in mere minutes, causing tremendous network congestion and crashing servers globally. The worm's small size and green propagation technique allowed it to contaminate a sizable wide variety of structures almost straight away, leading to great disruptions in net site visitors and commercial enterprise operations. The SQL Slammer incident underscored the critical want for well-timed software program patching and robust network safety features. This paper examines SQL Slammer as a pivotal occasion that emphasized the significance of proactive cybersecurity practices and highlighted the vulnerabilities of unpatched systems. We trace the evolution of cyber-attacks from the early 2000s to the prevailing, focusing on the increasing velocity and scale of those threats. Additionally, we analyze the improvements in protection mechanisms, which include automated patch control, intrusion detection systems, and improved network tracking equipment. By reflecting on the impact of SQL Slammer and the following advancements in cybersecurity, this research affords a complete overview of the techniques advanced to protect virtual infrastructures and mitigate the dangers posed with the aid of swiftly evolving cyber threats (Spafford, 1989).

Conficker (2008): This bug created a massive botnet by exploiting a Windows vulnerability. It is modified to great for its potential to disable protection offerings and keep away from detection. Conficker inflamed tens of thousands and thousands of computer structures globally, highlighting the developing chance of botnets and the disturbing situations in combating such massive-scale infections. The Conficker computer virus, which emerged in 2008, exemplifies the increasing complexity and sophistication of modern-day malware. Exploiting vulnerabilities in the Windows operating system, Conficker spread hastily, infecting hundreds of thousands of computer systems globally and forming one of the biggest recognized botnets. This trojan horse became wonderful for its use of superior techniques, including obfuscation and evasion tactics, which made it tough to come across and get rid of. Conficker's huge impact disrupted organizations, government groups, and critical infrastructure, underscoring the need for sturdy cybersecurity measures. This paper examines the Conficker trojan horse as an important occasion that highlights the escalating risk of state-of-the-art malware and the necessity for superior defense mechanisms. We discover the evolution of cyber assaults from the late 2000s to the prevailing, noting how they've grown in complexity and capacity for damage. Additionally, we examine the advancements in protection mechanisms, which include the improvement of superior malware detection and elimination gear, the implementation of more potent community protection protocols, and the significance of timely software updates and patches. By reflecting on the lessons found from the Conficker incident and the next improvements in cybersecurity, this study offers a complete assessment of the continued efforts to defend digital infrastructures in opposition to more and more state-of-the-art cyber threats as depicted in Table 2 (Cohen, 1987).

Table 2. Cases reported between 2000s to 2010s

Year	No. of notable incidents
2001	Code Red worm infected hundreds of thousands of computers.
2002	SQL Slammer worm caused widespread disruptions.
2003	Sobig. F and Blaster worms caused significant damage.
2004	Mydoom worm became the fastest-spreading email worm at the time
2005	Zotob worm targeted Windows 2000 computers.
2006	A large-scale data breach at TJX Companies affected 45.7 million credit and debit card users.
2007	Storm worms infected millions of computers.
2008	The Conficker worm infected millions of computers worldwide
2009	Operation Aurora targeted major companies like Google and Adobe.

2010s: Advanced Persistent Threats

Stuxnet (2010): Widely believed to be a kingdom-backed assault, Stuxnet targeted Iran's nuclear facilities via the use of exploiting more than one zero-day vulnerability. It has become able to cause physical damage to centrifuges utilized in uranium enrichment, marking a present-day era of cyber struggle with its ability to reason physical harm digitally. The Stuxnet worm, observed in 2010, marked a big turning component in the facts of cyber conflict because of its extraordinary sophistication and targeted nature. Unlike preceding malware, Stuxnet was designed particularly to sabotage Iran's nuclear enrichment facilities through centered on commercial enterprise manipulation systems (ICS) and programmable good judgment controllers (PLCs). This pretty today's trojan horse exploited a couple of 0-day vulnerabilities, demonstrating a degree of complexity and precision formerly unseen in cyber-attacks. Stuxnet's impact extended past the instant disruption of Iran's nuclear software, as it highlighted the vulnerabilities of crucial infrastructure worldwide and the ability of cyber assaults to cause bodily harm. This paper examines the Stuxnet incident as a landmark occasion that ushered in a present-day technology of cyber conflict and underscored the importance of securing commercial structures. We discover the evolution of cyber-attacks from the early 2010s to the prevailing, focusing on the growing risk to important infrastructure and the emergence of nation-state-backed cyber operations. Additionally, we analyze the upgrades in protection mechanisms, which encompass the improvement of specialized safety answers for ICS and PLCs, greater risk intelligence abilities, and international cooperation on cybersecurity necessities. Additionally, we analyze the upgrades in protection mechanisms, which encompass the improvement of specialized safety answers for ICS and PLCs, greater risk intelligence abilities, and international cooperation on cybersecurity necessities. which encompass the improvement of specialized safety answers for ICS and PLCs, greater risk intelligence abilities, and international cooperation on cybersecurity necessities. By reflecting on the instructions learned from Stuxnet and the following enhancements in enterprise cyber safety, this research provides a whole assessment of the techniques superior to defend crucial infrastructure in the direction of state-of-the-art and centered cyber threats (Denning, 1999; Hafner & Markoff, 1991; Levy, 1994).

Sony pictures hack (2014): This attack by North Korean hackers considered stealing and downloading sensitive data from Sony Pictures Entertainment. "The Interview" ended with a politically motivated attack in response to the film's release, revealing the full impact of state-sponsored cyber-attacks on non-state organizations. The Sony Pictures Hack, which took place in 2014, stands as a stark reminder of the vulnerabilities and some distance-attaining effects of cyber espionage. Attributed to the group referred to as the "Guardians of Peace" and allegedly connected to North Korea, the attack involved the theft and next public launch of huge quantities of confidential statistics, inclusive of worker records, unreleased movies, and inner communications. The breach brought large monetary and reputational damage to Sony Pictures, and it highlighted the growing hazard of cyber-attacks focused on predominant agencies. This paper examines the Sony Pictures Hack as a pivotal occasion that uncovered the volume to which cyber espionage can disrupt and damage big organizations. We discover the evolution of cyber-attacks from the mid-2010s to the prevailing, noting how they have become greater sophisticated, centered, and able to cause good-sized damage. Additionally, we examine the improvements in company defense mechanisms, along with the adoption of complete cybersecurity frameworks, the implementation of superior encryption and facts protection measures, and the significance of incident response planning and employee schooling. By reflecting on the lessons learned from the Sony Pictures Hack and subsequent improvements in company cybersecurity, this study presents a comprehensive assessment of the strategies evolved to shield agencies from the ever-evolving panorama of cyber threats (Gordon et al., 2003).

2020s: Modern Threats

Solar winds attack (2020): A spectacular supply chain attack that left the U.S. in a state of emergency. Many government agencies and private companies went bust. Attackers injected malicious code into the SolarWinds Orion software update, providing backdoor access to compromised systems. The attack highlighted risks associated with supply chain security. The SolarWinds Attack, disclosed in December 2020, represents one of the most sophisticated and a long way-reaching cyber espionage campaigns in history. Orchestrated with the aid of a suspected nation-state actor, the attackers infiltrated SolarWinds' Orion software program, a broadly used IT management device, and inserted malicious code into a software program update. This backdoor allowed the attackers to get the right of entry to the networks of numerous government corporations, agencies, and vital infrastructure companies. The breach exposed vast vulnerabilities in the software delivery chain and underscored the ability of cyber assaults to compromise depended on systems on a global scale. This paper examines the SolarWinds Attack as a pivotal event that highlighted the vulnerabilities inherent in supply chain safety and the profound effect of superior cyber espionage methods. We discover the evolution of cyber assaults from the early 2020s to the prevailing, focusing on the growing sophistication of supply chain attacks and their capacity to cause widespread disruption. Additionally, we analyze the improvements in defense mechanisms, together with more advantageous delivery chain chance management, the implementation of zero-consider architecture, and the importance of complete chance intelligence and collaboration amongst public and personal sectors. By reflecting on the lessons found from the SolarWinds Attack and subsequent advancements in cybersecurity, this study provides a complete evaluation of the techniques advanced to guard digital infrastructures in opposition to the evolving threats posed by state-of-the-art cyber espionage campaigns (CERT Coordination Center, 1999).

Colonial pipeline ransomware attack (2021): This ransomware attack disrupted the fuel supply in the US. the entire East Coast through data encryption and a strong recognition of its release the attack caused a severe shortage of gas and highlighted the significant impact of cyberattacks on critical offerings and infrastructure plants. The Colonial Pipeline Ransomware Attack, which occurred in May 2021, marked a great event within the realm of cyber threats, illustrating the vulnerabilities of crucial infrastructure to ransomware attacks. Orchestrated with the aid of the cybercriminal group Dark Side, the attack targeted Colonial Pipeline, the most important gas pipeline inside the United States, causing the company to halt operations and resulting in huge gasoline shortages throughout the Eastern Seaboard. The attack no longer only prompted economic disruption however it also highlighted the national protection implications of cyber assaults on critical infrastructure. This paper examines the Colonial Pipeline Attack as a pivotal occasion that uncovered the susceptibility of essential services to cyber extortion and underscored the need for sturdy cybersecurity measures in vital sectors. We discover the evolution of ransomware attacks from the early 2020s to the present, noting the increasing frequency, sophistication, and impact of these threats. Additionally, we examine the improvements in protection mechanisms, together with the adoption of 0 consider architecture, stronger incident response and recuperation protocols, and the importance of public-private partnerships in bolstering cybersecurity resilience. By reflecting on the lessons learned from the Colonial Pipeline Attack and the next advancements in important infrastructure protection, this research offers a comprehensive overview of the techniques developed to guard essential services against the escalating danger of ransomware and different cyber-attacks (Table 3) (Egele et al., 2008).

Table 3. Cases reported between 2010 to 2024

Year	No. of notable incidents
2010	Stuxnet worm targeted Iranian nuclear facilities.
2011	Sony PlayStation Network breach affected 77 million accounts.
2012	The LinkedIn data breach exposed 6.5 million passwords.
2013	Target data breach affected 40 million credit and debit card accounts.
2014	Sony Pictures hack by the “Guardians of Peace.”
2015	Anthem data breach exposed the personal information of 78.8 million people.
2016	The Yahoo data breach affected 3 billion accounts (the breach happened earlier, it was disclosed in 2016)
2017	WannaCry ransomware attack affected 200,000 computers across 150 countries.
2018	Marriott's data breach affected up to 500 million guests.
2019	Capital One data breach exposed the personal information of 100 million customers.
2020	SolarWinds attack affected multiple U.S. government agencies and major corporations.
2021	Colonial Pipeline ransomware attack disrupted fuel supply in the U.S.
2022	Log4 Shell's vulnerability affected numerous organizations worldwide.
2023	MOVEit Transfer data breach affected several organizations due to a vulnerability in the file transfer software.
2024	We can use a placeholder since specific events might not be well-documented yet.

2. ADVANCEMENT IN TECHNIQUES

Cyber threats have turned out to be an increasing number of sophisticated through the years with technology and new vulnerabilities. Key upgrades encompass:

Automation and self-propagation: Early viruses required individual interaction to spread, which incorporates taking off an inflamed report. Modern malware like worms and botnets can spread during networks without human intervention, dramatically developing their attainment and effect. Automation and self-propagation are key capabilities of cutting-edge cyber assaults, mainly in malware like worms, viruses, and ransomware. Automation allows those attacks to test for vulnerabilities, take advantage of them, and execute malicious activities without human intervention, making them quicker and able to target several systems concurrently. Self-propagation permits malware to spread independently from one system to another, increasing its reach and impact. Notable examples consist of the WannaCry ransomware, which exploited a Windows vulnerability to unfold across networks and demand ransoms, and the Stuxnet computer virus, which focused on Iranian nuclear facilities, the usage of a couple of 0-day exploits and complex self-propagation techniques. These traits make such attacks enormously powerful and hard to guard in opposition (Panda Security, 2019).

Polymorphism and evasion: - Modern malware regularly uses polymorphic techniques, changing its code with every infection to avoid detection by way of conventional antivirus software program software programs. Polymorphism and evasion are present-day strategies used by cyber attackers to enhance the effectiveness of malware and to keep away from detection through safety features. Polymorphism refers back to the capability of malware to modify its code or look with every contamination, making it difficult for signature-primarily based absolutely antivirus applications to apprehend and block it. By continuously converting its identifiable abilities, polymorphic malware can slip beyond traditional protection defenses that rely on constant signatures to find threats. Evasion strategies, but comprise techniques to skip or disable protection structures, which incorporate firewalls, intrusion detection systems, and antivirus software program application software programs. These techniques can include code obfuscation, in which the malware code is intentionally made complicated or hidden, and sandbox evasion, wherein malware detects if it's far strolling in managed, digital surroundings designed for protection evaluation after which alters its conduct to keep away from detection. Another unusual evasion tactic is the use of encryption to cover malicious payloads and communication (Baecher et al., 2006; Szor & Ferrie, 2001).

Zero-day vulnerability exploitation: Attackers are much more likely to take gain of 0-day vulnerabilities, which have been formerly unknown safety flaws now not but regular via software program utility agencies This offers attackers a bonus over unwitting defenders' weaknesses and measures have no longer been taken to fight them. Zero-day vulnerability exploitation involves cyber attackers targeting software program software vulnerabilities that might be unknown to the software program provider or the general public. Because those vulnerabilities have no longer been recognized or patched, they present a large safety danger. Attackers can exploit 0-day vulnerabilities to benefit unauthorized access to structures, steal sensitive data, or disrupt operations. The loss of a preceding protection or patch for those vulnerabilities makes zero-day exploits volatile and effective, regularly giving attackers a critical gain over their goals. This form of exploitation highlights the importance of proactive protection functions and non-prevent tracking to locate and mitigate potential threats all at once as feasible (Moser et al., 2007).

Use of encryption: Ransomware uses sturdy encryption algorithms to fasten out patients' statistics, making it inaccessible without a decryption key. This has made ransomware one of the most worthwhile kinds of cybercrime, as patients are frequently willing to pay a ransom to get their records once more. The encryption used in cyberattacks consists of encrypting payloads and malicious communications to prevent detection of the usage of safety features. Their code and information encryption lets attackers cover their gaming activity from intrusion detection structures, firewalls, and antivirus software, making sure the encryption makes it hard for defenders to hit upon and test risks for malicious rationale Even if visitors are blocked, it stays unreadable without a decryption key. This approach will increase the stealth and effectiveness of cyberattacks and set crucial conditions for cybersecurity professionals to discover, look at, and respond to awful video games (Bailey et al., 2007).

Sophisticated social technology: Modern phishing assaults have come to be more focused and credible, the usage of private statistics to trick victims into revealing touchy statistics or intercept awful connections. Devices that encompass spear manipulation and whaling purpose precise individuals or prominent officials to increase the possibilities of success. Cyber threats have become more and more ultra-modern over the years with technology and new vulnerabilities. Sophisticated social engineering techniques use psychological manipulation to trick individuals into revealing non-public records or identifying actions that compromise protection. Attackers use processes with phishing, excuses, and bait to take advantage of human vulnerabilities rather than technical flaws. With custom-designed real messages with specific data about the goal, people can be tricked into clicking malicious links, beginning infected attachments, or revealing credentials a need has been discovered. These state-of-the-art social engineering assaults skip many traditional security capabilities, making them surprisingly effective and tough to guard in opposition to Their developing tactics, emphasizing the need for in-depth character schooling and focused resources to help technical protection (Hofmeyr et al., 1998).

2.1 impacts of cyber threats

Economic impact: - Cyber-attacks impose huge economic burdens on agencies and economies worldwide. The monetary impact consists of direct and indirect costs. Direct costs encompass remediation costs, consisting of forensic investigations, gadget upkeep, and the implementation of improved safety features. Legal expenses and regulatory fines additionally contribute to direct fees, as agencies face court cases and penalties for failing to guard touchy information. For example, the Equifax statistics breach brought about a $700 million agreement to cover legal prices as visible within the Colonial Pipeline attack, in which a $4. A million ransom was paid to the attackers. Indirect prices consist of lost revenue due to business disruptions, improved insurance charges, and the investment required to decorate cybersecurity post-incident. The lengthy-term economic effects additionally contain a capability slowdown in commercial enterprise operations and faded investor self-assurance, which may lead to a discount in market fees and capacity activity losses.

Social impact: - Cyber threats profoundly affect people and society by compromising private privacy and eroding trust in digital structures. Privacy breaches, such as the ones visible inside the Equifax facts breach, disclose sensitive private data, mainly to identity theft, financial fraud, and emotional distress for victims. On a societal level, sizable information breaches can undermine public trust in era and online offerings, discouraging humans from engaging in virtual transactions or sharing non-public facts online. This loss of acceptance as true can gradually the adoption of new technology and avert the digital transformation of society. Furthermore, the mental effect on victims of cybercrime can be severe, mainly due to tension, stress, and a sense of vulnerability. As people emerge as greater privy to the risks associated with cyber threats, there can be a shift toward extra cautious and restrictive online behavior, potentially stifling innovation and a boom in the digital financial system (Huang & Pearce, 2014).

Operational impact: - Cyber assaults disrupt commercial enterprise operations and crucial infrastructure, causing vast operational demanding situations. Ransomware attacks, consisting as the one on the Colonial Pipeline, can halt business sports by way of encrypting essential facts, mainly to production stoppages and service outages. In the case of the Colonial Pipeline, the attack led to fuel shortages and disrupted transportation along the U.S. East Coast. Attacks on vital infrastructure, together with energy grids, transportation structures, and healthcare offerings, may have far-attaining results, endangering public safety and disrupting day-by-day existence. For example, the WannaCry ransomware attack in 2017 affected several hospitals inside the UK, causing delays in medical techniques and compromising personal care. The operational effect extends past immediate disruptions, as groups may need extended intervals to fully get better and restore everyday operations.

The fee and attempt required to rebuild and steady affected systems may be great, diverting resources from other crucial business capabilities and strategic projects (McGuire & Dowling, 2013).

Reputational damage: - A cyber incident will have long-lasting effects on an organization's reputation. When customers, companions, and stakeholders lose consideration of a corporation's capability to defend their facts, it could cause a loss of commercial enterprise, faded emblem price, and decreased marketplace percentage (figures 4-6). The reputational damage from a cyber-attack frequently extends well past the on-the-spot aftermath. For example, features, and transparency tasks to reassure customers and restore their emblem photograph. Additionally, the lingering effects of reputational harm can impact an enterprise's capacity to draw new customers, maintain present ones, and form strategic partnerships, in the long run affecting long-term enterprise growth and success. e, the Target records breach in 2013, which compromised the non-public and monetary records of hundreds of thousands of clients, ended in prolonged scrutiny and a great drop in patron self-belief. Rebuilding agreements with and repairing a damaged recognition can take years and require giant attempts and sources. Companies may additionally want to invest in massive public relations campaigns and stronger security (Acquisti et al., 2006).

Figure 4. Has business attacked in the past 12 months or not

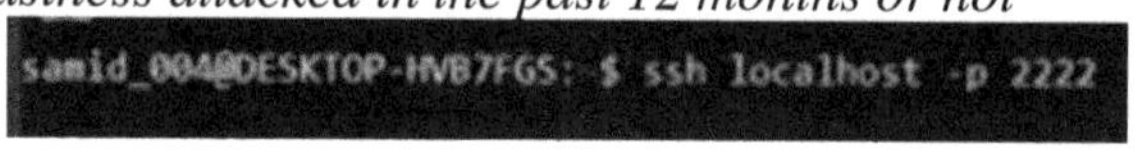

Figure 5. The shifting impact of cyber-attacks

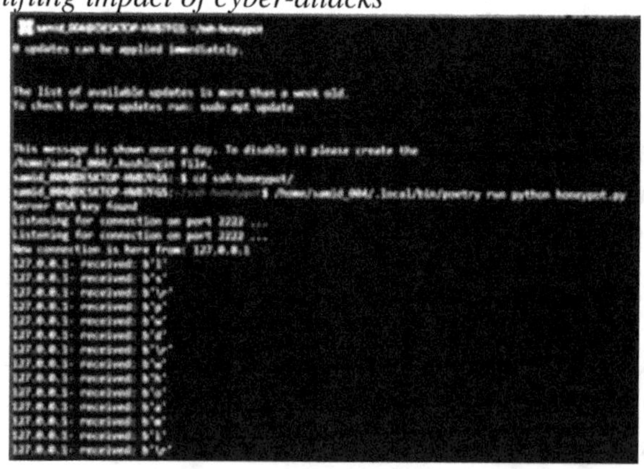

Figure 6. Future cyber threat prediction

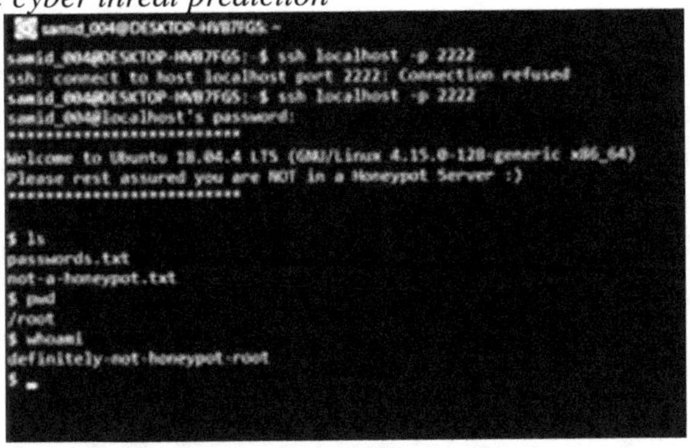

3. DEFENSE MECHANISMS

Preventive measures: - Preventive measures are critical for lowering the chance of cyber assaults and protecting touchy records. Key techniques embody enforcing firewalls to dam unauthorized right of entry, deploying antivirus software to stumble on and eliminate malware, and ensuring ordinary software program updates to patch vulnerabilities. Employee training is likewise critical, as human errors regularly perform a large function in safety breaches. Educating employees on excellent practices, which consist of spotting phishing tries and the use of robust passwords, can considerably decorate an agency's everyday protection posture (Cavoukian et al., 2010).

Detection mechanisms: - Early detection of cyber threats is important to mitigate damage and respond efficiently. In addition to an intrusion detection device (IDS), which plays a key role in monitoring network site visitors for suspicious hobbies and alerting operators to potential threats, non-stop monitoring of networks and systems can assist locate abnormalities and unauthorized right of entry to try in actual time. Advanced danger detection gear, which includes Security Information and Event Management (SIEM) systems, offers a comprehensive view of an enterprise's safety nation by way of collecting and analyzing data from a couple of assets (Smith, 2018).

Response and recovery: -Effective response and healing techniques are vital to mitigate the impact of cyberattacks and repair normal operations. An incident response plan outlines the steps to take immediately after an attack, together with identifying risks, containing the breach, and communicating with stakeholders Disaster recuperation the system specializes in restoring affected structures and statistics, regularly regarding statistics backups and enterprise device updates.

Regularly attempting out and updating those systems guarantees that an enterprise is prepared to respond to cyber incidents fast and efficiently.

Regulatory and compliance: - Adhering to applicable crook recommendations and rules is important for enhancing cybersecurity and protective touchy statistics. Compliance with those recommendations calls for agencies to put into effect strong safety features, conduct everyday audits, and ensure transparency of their records coping with practices. By following the regulatory framework, groups can enhance their safety posture and keep away from crooks and financial outcomes (Huang & Kou, 2015).

4. FUTURE TRENDS IN CYBERSECURITY

Artificial intelligence and machine learning: - Artificial intelligence (AI) and gadget mastering (ML) are remodeling cybersecurity by providing advanced gear for danger detection and reaction. These technologies can examine great quantities of information to perceive patterns and anomalies indicative of cyber threats, permitting faster and more correct detection. AI and ML can also automate recurring protection responsibilities, including monitoring community traffic and identifying vulnerabilities, allowing security experts to focus on extra complex troubles. As cyber threats become extra sophisticated, AI and ML might be important in staying ahead of attackers. Artificial Intelligence (AI) and Machine Learning (ML) are swiftly evolving fields remodeling numerous components of our lives. AI contains a broad range of technology aimed toward developing systems that are able to perform the responsibilities that usually require human intelligence. These obligations encompass reasoning, gaining knowledge of, trouble-solving, and information natural language. Within this area, Machine Learning is a subset centered on developing algorithms that allow computer systems to learn from and make predictions or choices based totally on statistics. Unlike conventional programming, where policies are explicitly coded, ML fashions enhance their performance over the years as they may be exposed to more information. This synergy between AI and ML is using improvements across diverse sectors, from healthcare and finance to entertainment and self-sufficient systems, showcasing the profound effect of those technologies on contemporary society. AI and ML remedy complex issues and enhance efficiencies throughout numerous domain names. For example, in healthcare, ML algorithms can examine medical images to assist in early diagnosis, even as AI-driven chatbots provide personalized patient help. In finance, AI systems optimize trading techniques and locate fraudulent activities. In self-sustaining automobiles, AI algorithms procedure data from sensors to navigate and make real-time choices. These programs highlight the transformative capability of AI and ML, riding improvements that promise to enhance the niceness of life, streamline operations, and unencumbered new possibilities for innovation. As those technologies keep evolving, they boost crucial questions about ethics, privateness, and the future of work, underscoring the need to consider their societal effect (Herzog, 2011).

Blockchain technology: - Blockchain generation can reinforce cybersecurity, particularly in securing digital transactions and statistics. Its decentralized and immutable nature makes it tough for attackers to regulate records, presenting a higher diploma of integrity and transparency. Blockchain may be used to steady identification, ensure the authenticity of virtual certificates, and defend supply chain statistics from tampering. As groups seek to enhance statistics security and agree with it, adopting blockchain technology can boom. Blockchain technology is a decentralized virtual ledger machine designed to file transactions throughout a community of computers securely and transparently. Each transaction is grouped right into a block, which is related collectively in chronological order, forming a sequence. This structure ensures that when a transaction is recorded, it can't be altered or deleted without altering all subsequent blocks, making the system fantastically immune to tampering and fraud. The decentralized nature of blockchain means that no unmarried entity has manipulated the whole ledger; rather, it's maintained by a community of individuals, which complements its protection and resilience. Blockchain's most famous application is in cryptocurrencies like Bitcoin, but its ability extends some distance beyond financial transactions. It is being explored for diverse use instances, including delivery chain management, wherein it may enhance transparency and traceability, and smart contracts, which automate and enforce contractual agreements without intermediaries. As the blockchain era continues to conform, it holds promise for remodeling a wide range of industries by presenting a new information integrity and belief paradigm. Blockchain technology represents a groundbreaking approach to managing and verifying digital transactions. At its core, it functions as a distributed ledger, wherein facts are stored across a network of nodes instead of being centralized in a single region. Each block within the blockchain contains a timestamp, a record of transactions, and a cryptographic hash of the previous block, linking them together in a secure and immutable chain. This shape ensures the integrity and consistency of the facts, as changing any part of the blockchain could require changing all the next blocks, which is computationally infeasible. The decentralized nature of blockchain complements safety and transparency because it eliminates the want for a trusted vital authority. Instead, consensus mechanisms, including proof-of-paintings or proof-of-stake, are used to validate and agree on transactions concerning a couple of members within the community. This reduces the threat of fraud and errors and guarantees each member access to the same ledger model (Romanosky et al., 2014).

Quantum computing: - Quantum computing poses possibilities and demands for cybersecurity. On the one hand, quantum laptop systems can interrupt traditional encryption techniques, posing an enormous hazard to safety. On the other hand, quantum computing may also be used to make bigger, new, more stable encryption algorithms immune to quantum assaults. The advent of quantum computing necessitates the improvement of quantum-resistant cryptography and re-evaluating gift protection protocols to ensure they continue to be powerful in a post-quantum global. Quantum computing represents a revolutionary approach to computation, harnessing the concepts of quantum mechanics to process statistics in methods that classical computer systems cannot. Unlike classical computers, which use bits because of the smallest unit of facts (zero or 1), quantum computers utilize quantum bits, or qubits, that may exist concurrently in more than one state due to superposition. Additionally, qubits can be entangled, meaning the country of 1 qubit can rely on the kingdom of every other, even over lengthy distances. These residences enable quantum computer systems to perform complicated calculations at exponentially faster costs than their classical counterparts. The capability applications of quantum computing are big and transformative (Hariharasitaraman et al., 2024). In cryptography, quantum computer systems should ruin current encryption techniques, main to a need for brand-spanking new security protocols. In drug discovery and cloth technological know-how, they may simulate molecular systems and interactions with unparalleled accuracy, accelerating the improvement of new therapies and materials. Quantum computing additionally holds promise for optimizing complicated structures, such as economic portfolios or logistical networks, by exploring several possibilities concurrently (Hovav & D'Arcy, 2003).

Collaboration and Information Sharing: Ineffective cybersecurity, an increasing number rely upon collaboration and records sharing among businesses and governments. Sharing risk intelligence and high-quality practices helps to create a collective safety closer to cyber threats. Collaborative efforts, which include public-personal partnerships and agency-specific records sharing and evaluation facilities (ISACs), allow well-timed dissemination of facts about rising threats and vulnerabilities. By jogging collectively, companies can enhance their resilience towards cyber-attacks and make contributions to a stronger virtual environment. Collaboration and statistics sharing are fundamental to using innovation, improving efficiency, and attaining collective desires in these days interconnected global. By working together, people and companies can pool their diverse abilities, expertise, and sources to tackle complex troubles and generate new thoughts. Effective collaboration entails open communication, mutual respect, and a shared imagination and prescience, enabling team members to contribute to their particular perspectives and information. Information sharing, alternatively, helps the exchange of records and insights, ensuring that applicable knowledge is offered to all stakeholders. This transparency helps prevent duplication of effort, reduces misunderstandings, and hurries up choice-making processes (Kaur et al., 2011). In the digital age, advanced tools and platforms, including collaborative software programs, cloud storage, and social networks, have similarly improved the ability to collaborate and proportion records seamlessly across geographical and organizational obstacles. However, successful collaboration and data sharing also require addressing challenges related to facts protection, privacy, and intellectual assets. By fostering a culture of agreement with and leveraging era efficiently, businesses and individuals can harness the whole potential of collaboration and statistics sharing to pressure development and achieve shared goals (Barhate et al., 2023).

5. CONCLUSIONS

The evolution of cyber threats has shown a trajectory from early, rudimentary assaults to pretty state-of-the-art and unfavorable operations, collectively with ransomware, phishing, and United States of America-sponsored attacks. These threats have full-size economic, social, operational, and reputational effects, causing monetary losses, privacy breaches, operational disruptions, and prolonged damage to organizational reputations. Defense mechanisms are superior in reaction, encompassing preventive measures like firewalls and employee schooling, detection gadgets, intrusion detection structures, and complete response and healing strategies. Adhering to regulatory necessities, in addition, enhances organizational cybersecurity. Given the rapid advancement of cyber threats, it is essential to invest in ongoing studies and developments in cybersecurity. Organizations, governments, and those must collaborate to innovate and implement sturdy security capabilities. Continuous schooling, adopting superior technology like AI and blockchain, and proactive chance intelligence sharing are vital to staying ahead of cyber attackers. A united and beforehand-thinking method may be key to constructing resilient and steady digital environments. The future panorama of cybersecurity may be formed with rising generations and evolving threats. AI and devices gaining knowledge will play an increasing number of important roles in threat detection and automatic response, at the same time, blockchain generation will decorate the protection of digital transactions. Quantum computing offers disturbing conditions and possibilities, necessitating improving quantum-resistant cryptographic strategies. Collaboration and information sharing will be crucial in preventing cyber threats. As cyber threats preserve developing sophistication, a proactive and adaptive technique might be essential for powerful cybersecurity in destiny.

REFERENCES

Acquisti, A., Friedman, A., & Telang, R. (2006). Is There a Cost to Privacy Breaches? An Event Study. *Proceedings of the International Conference on Information Systems (ICIS).*

Alnifie, K. M. (2023). Investigation of Human Weaknesses in Organizational Cybersecurity: A Meta-Analytic Approach (Doctoral dissertation, Howard University).

Anderson, R., Barton, C., Böhme, R., Clayton, R., Van Eeten, M. J., Levi, M., ... & Savage, S. (2013). Measuring the cost of cybercrime. The economics of information security and privacy, 265-300.

Baecher, P., Koetter, M., Koenning, A., & Freiling, F. C. (2006). The Nepenthes Platform: An Efficient Approach to Collect Malware. *Lecture Notes in Computer Science, 4219*, 165–184. DOI: 10.1007/11856214_9

Bailey, M., Oberheide, J., Andersen, J., Mao, Z. M., Jahanian, F., & Nazario, J. (2007). Automated Classification and Analysis of Internet Malware. Recent Advances in Intrusion Detection, 146-163.

Barhate, D., Pathak, S., & Dubey, A. K. (2023). Hyperparameter-tuned batch-updated stochastic gradient descent: Plant species identification by using hybrid deep learning. *Ecological Informatics, 75*, 102094. DOI: 10.1016/j.ecoinf.2023.102094

Bhandari, D. A. (2024). ML-Based Methods for Detecting Phishing Websites: A Comprehensive Survey and Analysis.

Cavoukian, A., Taylor, S., & Abrams, M. E. (2010). Privacy by Design: Essential for Organizational Accountability and Strong Business Practices. *Identity in the Information Society, 3*(2), 405–413. DOI: 10.1007/s12394-010-0053-z

CERT Coordination Center. (1999). Melissa Virus Advisory. CERT Advisory CA-1999-04.

Chaudhuri, A., & Bozkus Kahyaoglu, S. (2023). Cybersecurity assurance in smart cities: A risk management perspective. *EDPACS, 67*(4), 1–22. DOI: 10.1080/07366981.2023.2165293

Cletus, A., Weyory, B., & Opoku, A. (2022). Improving social engineering awareness, training and education (SEATE) using a behavioral change model. *International Journal of Advanced Computer Science and Applications, 13*(5). Advance online publication. DOI: 10.14569/IJACSA.2022.0130572

Cohen, F. (1987). Computer Viruses: Theory and Experiments. *Computers & Security*, *6*(1), 22–35. DOI: 10.1016/0167-4048(87)90122-2

Conway, M. (2014). What is Cyberterrorism and How Real is the Threat? A Review of the Academic Literature, 1996–2009. Cyber Behavior: Concepts, Methodologies, Tools, and Applications, 217-245.

Cybersecurity, C. I. (2018). Framework for improving critical infrastructure cybersecurity. https://nvlpubs. nist. gov/nistpubs/CSWP/NIST

Denning, D. E. (1999). *Information Warfare and Security*. Addison-Wesley.

Egele, M., Scholte, T., Kirda, E., & Kruegel, C. (2008). A Survey on Automated Dynamic Malware Analysis Techniques and Tools. *ACM Computing Surveys*, *44*(2), 6.

Fossi, M., Egan, G., Haley, K., Johnson, E., Mack, T., Adams, T., ... & Wood, P. (2011). Symantec internet security threat report trends for 2010. Volume XVI.

Gordon, L. A., Loeb, M. P., & Lucyshyn, W. (2003). The Economic Impact of Cyber-Attacks. *Journal of Computer Security*, *11*(5), 431–448.

Hafner, K., & Markoff, J. (1991). *Cyberpunk: Outlaws and Hackers on the Computer Frontier*. Simon & Schuster.

Hariharasitaraman, S., Mishra, N., & Vishnuvardhanan, D. (2024). QHopNN: Investigating quantum advantage in cryptanalysis using a quantum hopfield neural network. *Physica Scripta*, *99*(8), 086002. DOI: 10.1088/1402-4896/ad5ed1

Herzog, S. (2011). Revisiting the Estimation of Economic Impact of Cyber Attacks: Focus on Operational Disruption. *Journal of Cybersecurity*, *7*(3), 267–284.

Hofmeyr, S. A., Forrest, S., & Somayaji, A. (1998). Intrusion Detection Using Sequences of System Calls. *Journal of Computer Security*, *6*(3), 151–180. DOI: 10.3233/JCS-980109

Hovav, A., & D'Arcy, J. (2003). The Impact of Denial-of-Service Attack Announcements on the Market Value of Firms. *Risk Management & Insurance Review*, *6*(2), 97–121. DOI: 10.1046/J.1098-1616.2003.026.x

Huang, R., & Kou, W. (2015). Cybersecurity in Industrial Control Systems: A Case Study Approach. *IEEE Transactions on Industry Applications*, *51*(5), 4211–4220.

Huang, R., & Pearce, A. (2014). Cyber-Physical Attacks and Effective Security Monitoring Strategies. *International Journal of Critical Infrastructure Protection*, *7*(3), 144–150.

Kamble, N., & Mishra, N. (2024a). Hybrid optimization enabled squeeze net for phishing attack detection. *Computers & Security, 144*, 103901. DOI: 10.1016/j.cose.2024.103901

Kamble, N., & Mishra, N. (2024b, January). Securing Cyberspace: Unveiling Phishing Attacks Through Deep Neural Networks for Enhanced Detection. In *2024 International Conference on Advancements in Smart, Secure and Intelligent Computing (ASSIC)* (pp. 1-5). IEEE. DOI: 10.1109/ASSIC60049.2024.10508000

Kaur, G., Khurana, M., & Sethi, M. (2011, July). Intrusion detection system using honeypots and swarm intelligence. In *Proceedings of the International Conference on Advances in Computing and Artificial Intelligence* (pp. 34-38). DOI: 10.1145/2007052.2007060

Kshetri, N. (2010). *The global cybercrime industry: economic, institutional and strategic perspectives*. Springer Science & Business Media. DOI: 10.1007/978-3-642-11522-6

Levy, S. (1994). *Hackers: Heroes of the Computer Revolution*. Penguin Books.

Mazzolin, R., & Samueli, A. M. (2020, August). A Survey of Contemporary Cyber Security Vulnerabilities and Potential Approaches to Automated Defence. In *2020 IEEE International Systems Conference (SysCon)* (pp. 1-7). IEEE. DOI: 10.1109/SysCon47679.2020.9275828

McGuire, M., & Dowling, S. (2013). Cyber Crime: A Review of the Evidence. Home Office Research Report 75.

Moser, A., Kruegel, C., & Kirda, E. (2007). Limits of Static Analysis for Malware Detection. *Proceedings of the 23rd Annual Computer Security Applications Conference (ACSAC)*, 421-430. DOI: 10.1109/ACSAC.2007.21

Panda Security. (2019). *The Evolution of Polymorphic Malware*. Panda Security Blog.

Pang, S., & Li, Y. (2020). Artificial intelligence techniques for cyber security applications. International Journal of Advanced Information and Communication Technology, 89-94.

Rokade, S., & Mishra, N. (2024). Privacy preservation of medical data in blockchain with secret key generation using RideNN. *Multimedia Tools and Applications, 83*(23), 1–23. DOI: 10.1007/s11042-023-18071-1

Romanosky, S., Hoffman, D., & Acquisti, A. (2014). Empirical Analysis of Data Breach Litigation. *Journal of Empirical Legal Studies, 11*(1), 74–104. DOI: 10.1111/jels.12035

Rosenzweig, P. (2013). *Cyber warfare: how conflicts in cyberspace are challenging America and changing the world.* Bloomsbury Publishing USA. DOI: 10.5040/9798400636493

Sindiramutty, S. R., Jhanjhi, N. Z., Tan, C. E., Khan, N. A., Shah, B., & Gaur, L. (2024). Securing the digital supply chain cyber threats and vulnerabilities. In *Cybersecurity Measures for Logistics Industry Framework* (pp. 156–223). IGI Global.

Smith, M. S. (2018). Critical Infrastructure Protection: Key Principles for Strengthening Resilience and Preparedness. *Journal of Strategic Security*, *11*(2), 34–45.

Spafford, E. H. (1989). The Internet Worm Program: An Analysis. Purdue Technical Report CSD-TR-823.

Szor, P., & Ferrie, P. (2001). *Hunting for Metamorphic*. Symantec Security Response.

Vaidya, T. (2015). 2001-2013: Survey and Analysis of Major Cyberattacks. arXiv preprint arXiv:1507.06673.

Wall, D. S. (2024). *Cybercrime: The transformation of crime in the information age*. John Wiley & Sons.

Zeadally, S., Adi, E., Baig, Z., & Khan, I. A. (2020). Harnessing artificial intelligence capabilities to improve cybersecurity. *IEEE Access : Practical Innovations, Open Solutions*, *8*, 23817–23837. DOI: 10.1109/ACCESS.2020.2968045

Chapter 17
Comparative Analysis of Biometric Approaches in Continuous Authentication

S. Ayeswarya
https://orcid.org/0000-0002-2010-2579
Vellore Institute of Technology, India

John Singh
https://orcid.org/0000-0002-2674-488X
Vellore Institute of Technology, India

ABSTRACT

In an era where security and user authentication are paramount, continuous authentication methods have gained significant attention. This chapter aims to provide a comprehensive comparison of various biometric methods used for continuous user authentication. Biometric authentication techniques offer unique advantages in terms of security, usability, and continuous monitoring capabilities. This chapter will explore and evaluate different biometric modalities such as fingerprint, iris recognition, voice recognition, facial recognition, and behavioral biometrics. The comparative analysis will consider factors such as accuracy, reliability, cost-effectiveness, scalability, and user acceptance. Additionally, the chapter will discuss challenges, emerging trends, and future directions in the field of continuous user authentication using biometric methods.

DOI: 10.4018/979-8-3693-8014-7.ch017

INTRODUCTION

In the digital age, securing access to information and systems has become paramount. Traditional methods of authentication, such as passwords and PINs, are increasingly viewed as insufficient due to their susceptibility to theft, forgetfulness, and ease of breach (Ayeswarya & Singh, 2024). The advent of biometric authentication has revolutionized the security landscape by leveraging unique physiological and behavioral characteristics that are inherently difficult to replicate or steal. Biometric authentication traditionally involves verifying a user's identity at a single point in time, typically during login (Ayeswarya & Norman, 2019). While effective, this approach has limitations, particularly in scenarios where prolonged access to sensitive information or systems is required. This is where continuous authentication comes into play. Continuous authentication is an advanced security mechanism that continuously verifies a user's identity throughout the duration of a session, providing ongoing assurance that the person accessing the system remains the legitimate user. The primary objective of continuous authentication is to mitigate the risks associated with session hijacking and unauthorized access that can occur after initial login (Ayeswarya & Singh, 2024). By constantly monitoring and verifying the user's identity, continuous authentication ensures that even if an intruder gains access, their presence is quickly detected and countermeasures are deployed. This dynamic approach to security is especially critical in high-stakes environments such as banking, healthcare, and government systems, where the integrity and confidentiality of data are paramount. Continuous authentication can be implemented using various biometric modalities, each with its own set of advantages and challenges. The main biometric approaches include fingerprint recognition, facial recognition, voice recognition, iris recognition, and behavioral biometrics (Mondal, 2016). These methods vary in terms of accuracy, user convenience, susceptibility to spoofing, and privacy implications.

This chapter provides a comprehensive comparative analysis of these biometric approaches in the context of continuous authentication. By examining their mechanisms, strengths, and weaknesses, we aim to provide a clear understanding of how each modality performs in ensuring ongoing user verification. Furthermore, we will explore the potential for integrating multiple modalities to enhance security and usability, and discuss the future directions of continuous authentication in the evolving cybersecurity landscape. As we delve deeper into the specifics of each biometric approach, it becomes evident that the choice of modality is influenced by the particular requirements and constraints of the application at hand. Whether prioritizing accuracy, usability, security, or privacy, continuous authentication systems must strike a balance to effectively safeguard against unauthorized access while maintaining a positive user experience. In the subsequent sections, we will analyse each biometric modality in detail, followed by a comparative analysis to highlight their respective strengths and weaknesses (Stylios., 2023). The insights gained from this analysis will inform the development of robust continuous authentication systems capable of addressing the diverse challenges posed by modern cybersecurity threats.

OVERVIEW OF BIOMETRIC AUTHENTICATION

Biometric authentication leverages unique physiological and behavioral characteristics to verify an individual's identity (Jeong., 2024) The primary biometric modalities used in continuous authentication include:

- **Fingerprint Recognition**
- **Facial Recognition**
- **Voice Recognition**
- **Iris Recognition**
- **Behavioral Biometrics (e.g., keystroke dynamics, gait analysis)**

Figure 1 illustrates an overview of continuous user authentication methods using various biometrics (Ayeswarya & Singh, 2024). Each modality offers distinct advantages and faces specific challenges, which we will explore in this chapter.

Figure 1. Classification of continuous user authentication methods using various biometrics

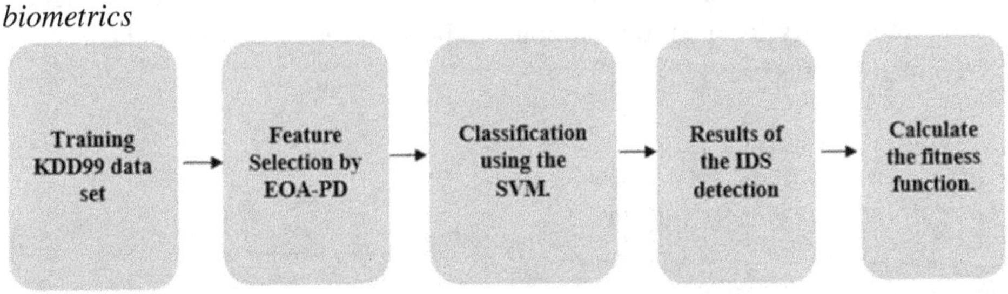

Biometric authentication systems typically operate by capturing a sample of the biometric trait, processing it to extract unique features, and then comparing these features against a stored template for verification. The core advantage of biometric authentication lies in its use of inherent and unique user traits, making it significantly harder to forge or steal compared to traditional methods like passwords or security tokens. In the context of continuous authentication, the ability to repeatedly and non-intrusively verify a user's identity throughout a session adds an extra layer of security that is essential in preventing unauthorized access.

Fingerprint Recognition

Fingerprint recognition has long been a staple of biometric authentication due to its high accuracy and user familiarity (Raghavan & Singh., 2021). Figure 2 presents a general framework for fingerprint recognition (Ayeswarya & Singh, 2024). Fingerprint sensors capture the unique patterns of ridges and valleys on a user's fingertip and compare them to pre-registered templates. In continuous authentication, these sensors can be embedded in devices such as keyboards, mice, or mobile devices, allowing for periodic verification without interrupting the user experience. While highly accurate, fingerprint recognition requires physical interaction and can be vulnerable to spoofing with advanced techniques.

Strengths

- **High Accuracy**: Fingerprint recognition is known for its precision and low false acceptance rates.
- **User Familiarity**: Widely adopted and understood by users.

Weaknesses

- **Usability Issues**: Requires physical interaction, which can be inconvenient.
- **Vulnerability to Spoofing**: Although advanced sensors mitigate this risk, it remains a concern.

Figure 2. Fingerprint recognition

<table>
<tr><th colspan="13">Time- based traffic</th></tr>
<tr><td>Dst Host Count</td><td>Dst Host Srv Count</td><td>Dst Host Same Srv Rate</td><td>Dst Host Diff Srv Count</td><td>Dst Host Same Src Port Ratet</td><td>Dst Host Srv Diff Host Rate</td><td colspan="7">Dst Host Serror Rate</td></tr>
<tr><th colspan="13">Host</th></tr>
<tr><td>Count</td><td>Srv Count</td><td>Serror Rate</td><td>Srvserror Rate</td><td>Same Srv Rate</td><td>Diff Srv Rate</td><td colspan="7">Srv Diff Host Rate</td></tr>
<tr><th colspan="13">Basic</th></tr>
<tr><td>Duration</td><td>Protocol Type</td><td>Service</td><td>Flag</td><td>Source Bytes</td><td>Destination Bytes</td><td>Land</td><td>Wrong Fragment</td><td colspan="5">Urgent</td></tr>
<tr><th colspan="13">Content</th></tr>
<tr><td>Hot</td><td>Number Faild Logins</td><td>Logged In</td><td>Num Compromised</td><td>Root Shell</td><td>Su Attempted</td><td>Num Root</td><td>Num File Creations</td><td>Num Shells</td><td>Num Access Files</td><td>Num Outbound Cmds</td><td>Is Host Login</td><td>Is Guest Login</td></tr>
</table>

Facial Recognition

Facial recognition uses cameras and sophisticated algorithms to analyze the unique features of a user's face, such as the distance between the eyes, nose shape, and jawline. Figure 3 presents a general framework for facial recognition (Ayeswarya & Singh, 2024). For continuous authentication, facial recognition systems can operate in the background, periodically capturing images of the user's face and comparing them to stored templates (Ayeswarya & Norman, 2019). This non-intrusive approach offers high user acceptance and convenience but can be sensitive to environmental conditions like lighting and camera quality, and it raises privacy concerns due to constant monitoring.

Strengths

- **Non-Intrusive**: Can operate in the background without requiring user interaction.
- **High User Acceptance**: Convenient and user-friendly.

Weaknesses

- **Environmental Sensitivity**: Performance can be affected by lighting conditions and camera quality.
- **Privacy Concerns**: Users may feel uncomfortable with constant facial monitoring.

Figure 3. Face recognition

Attacks	DoS	Smurf	Back	Land	Neptune	Pod	Tear drop		
	Probe	Ipsweep	Nmap	Satan	Portsweep				
	U2R	Buffer overflow	Load module	Per1	Per1				
	R2L	Ftp write	Guess password	Imap	Mutlihop	Spy	Phf	Warezclient	Warezmaster

Iris Recognition

Iris recognition is known for its high accuracy and security, as the patterns in the colored ring around the eye's pupil are highly distinctive and stable over time (Ayeswarya & Norman, 2019). Figure 4 presents a general framework for iris recognition (Ayeswarya & Singh, 2024). In continuous authentication, iris scanners intermittently capture and verify the user's iris data. While offering excellent security, iris recognition may be perceived as intrusive and can be affected by factors such as glasses or contact lenses. Additionally, precise alignment is required, which can impact usability.

Strengths

- **High Accuracy and Security**: Extremely difficult to forge or spoof.
- **Stable Biometric**: Iris patterns remain largely unchanged over time.

Weaknesses

- **User Acceptance**: Some users may find the process intrusive or uncomfortable.
- **Environmental Factors**: Requires precise alignment and can be affected by glasses or contact lenses.

Figure 4. Iris recognition

Dataset before processing	
	0,tcp,http,SF,310,1512,0,0,0,0,0,1,0,0,0,0,0,0,0,0,0,0,13,13,0.00,0.00,0.00,0.00,1.00,0.00,0.00,246,255,1.00,0.00,0.00,0.01,0.00,0.00,0.00,0.00,normal
	0,tcp,iso_tsap,S0,0,0,0,0,0,0,0,0,0,0,0,0,0,0,0,0,0,0,194,9,1.00,1.00,0.00,0.00,0.05,0.08,0.00,255,9,0.04,0.09,0.00,0.00,1.00,1.00,0.00,0.00,anomaly
	0,tcp,http,SF,286,366,0,0,0,0,0,1,0,0,0,0,0,0,0,0,0,0,7,7,0.00,0.00,0.00,0.00,1.00,0.00,0.00,48,255,1.00,0.00,0.02,0.04,0.00,0.00,0.00,0.00,normal
	0,tcp,other,REJ,0,0,0,0,0,0,0,0,0,0,0,0,0,0,0,0,0,0,508,1,0.11,0.00,0.89,1.00,0.00,1.00,0.00,255,1,0.00,1.00,0.00,0.00,0.18,0.00,0.82,1.00,anomaly
	0,tcp,http,SF,54540,8314,0,0,0,2,0,1,1,0,0,0,0,0,0,0,0,0,4,10,0.00,0.00,0.00,0.00,1.00,0.00,0.20,255,255,1.00,0.00,0.00,0.00,0.00,0.00,0.04,0.04,anomaly
	0,tcp,http,SF,222,333,0,0,0,0,0,1,0,0,0,0,0,0,0,0,0,0,4,4,0.00,0.00,0.00,0.00,1.00,0.00,0.00,137,237,1.00,0.00,0.01,0.03,0.00,0.00,0.00,0.00,normal
	0,udp,private,SF,28,0,0,3,0,0,0,0,0,0,0,0,0,0,0,0,0,0,92,92,0.00,0.00,0.00,0.00,1.00,0.00,0.00,112,92,0.82,0.03,0.82,0.00,0.00,0.00,0.00,0.00,normal
	0,tcp,http,SF,303,315,0,0,0,0,0,1,0,0,0,0,0,0,0,0,0,0,22,22,0.00,0.00,0.00,0.00,1.00,0.00,0.00,72,255,1.00,0.00,0.01,0.02,0.00,0.00,0.00,0.00,normal
	0,tcp,other,RSTR,0,0,0,0,0,0,0,0,0,0,0,0,0,0,0,0,0,0,1,1,0.00,0.00,1.00,1.00,1.00,0.00,0.00,255,1,0.00,0.94,0.93,0.00,0.00,0.00,0.93,1.00,normal
	0,udp,domain_u,SF,42,42,0,0,0,0,0,0,0,0,0,0,0,0,0,0,0,0,9,13,0.00,0.00,0.00,0.00,1.00,0.00,0.15,255,255,1.00,0.00,0.00,0.00,0.00,0.00,0.00,0.00,normal
	0,tcp,private,REJ,0,0,0,0,0,0,0,0,0,0,0,0,0,0,0,0,0,0,101,14,0.00,0.00,1.00,1.00,0.14,0.06,0.00,255,14,0.05,0.05,0.00,0.00,0.00,0.00,1.00,1.00,anomaly
	0,tcp,http,SF,346,61911,0,0,0,0,0,1,0,0,0,0,0,0,0,0,0,0,4,4,0.00,0.00,0.00,0.00,1.00,0.00,0.00,212,255,1.00,0.00,0.00,0.02,0.00,0.00,0.00,0.00,normal
	0,tcp,finger,RSTO,0,0,0,0,0,0,0,0,0,0,0,0,0,0,0,0,0,0,190,2,0.00,0.00,1.00,1.00,0.01,0.07,0.00,255,2,0.01,0.07,0.00,0.00,0.00,0.00,1.00,1.00,anomaly

Behavioral Biometrics

Behavioral biometrics analyze patterns in user behavior, such as typing dynamics, mouse movements, and gait (Ramkumar., 2023). These systems continuously monitor these behaviors to authenticate users, offering seamless and ongoing verification. Behavioral biometrics are highly usable, as they operate in the background without requiring active user input. However, they are subject to behavioral variability due to factors like stress, fatigue, or context changes, and continuous monitoring raises concerns about user privacy and data security (Rayani, & Changder., 2023).

Strengths

- **Continuous Monitoring**: Ideal for ongoing authentication without user intervention.
- **High Usability**: Operates in the background, providing a seamless experience.

Weaknesses

- **Behavioral Variability**: Changes in behavior due to stress, fatigue, or context can impact accuracy.
- **Data Privacy**: Continuous monitoring raises concerns about user privacy and data security.

FACTORS INFLUENCING BIOMETRIC SELECTION

Accuracy and Error Rates

When selecting a biometric modality for continuous authentication, accuracy is a paramount consideration. Accuracy in biometric systems is typically evaluated through two key metrics: False Acceptance Rate (FAR) and False Rejection Rate (FRR) (Ayeswarya & Singh, 2024).

- **False Acceptance Rate (FAR)**: This measures the likelihood that an unauthorized user will be incorrectly accepted by the system. A lower FAR indicates higher security, as it means the system is less likely to grant access to impostors.
- **False Rejection Rate (FRR)**: This measures the likelihood that an authorized user will be incorrectly rejected by the system. A lower FRR indicates better usability, as legitimate users are less likely to face access issues.

The trade-off between FAR and FRR is often represented by the Equal Error Rate (EER), the point at which the rates are equal. A lower EER signifies a more accurate biometric system. High accuracy is critical in environments where security is paramount, such as banking or government applications (Ryu., 2021). Different biometric modalities offer varying levels of accuracy. For instance, iris recognition is known for its high precision and low error rates, while behavioral biometrics may exhibit higher variability.

User Acceptance and Usability

User acceptance and usability are crucial factors in the success of any biometric system (Shen., 2022). A highly secure system is of little value if users find it cumbersome or invasive. Factors influencing user acceptance include:

- **Ease of Use**: The biometric modality should be straightforward and quick to use. For example, fingerprint and facial recognition systems are generally favored for their simplicity and speed.
- **Intrusiveness**: Some modalities, such as iris or vein pattern recognition, may be perceived as invasive. Users are more likely to accept systems that do not require significant physical interaction or uncomfortable procedures.
- **Consistency**: The biometric system should perform reliably under various conditions. Facial recognition, for example, should work in different lighting conditions, and voice recognition should function despite background noise or minor changes in the user's voice.

High usability ensures that users are willing to engage with the biometric system regularly, which is especially important for continuous authentication scenarios.

Scalability and Deployment Considerations

The scalability and ease of deployment of a biometric system are critical for its adoption in large-scale applications (Raghavan & Singh., 2021). Factors to consider include:

- **Infrastructure Requirements**: Some biometric systems require specialized hardware, such as high-resolution cameras for facial recognition or infrared scanners for vein pattern recognition. The cost and complexity of this hardware can impact scalability.
- **Integration with Existing Systems**: The biometric solution should integrate seamlessly with existing security and IT infrastructure. This includes compatibility with different operating systems, software platforms, and network environments.
- **Maintenance and Support**: Ongoing maintenance and technical support are necessary to ensure the biometric system remains functional and secure. This includes regular updates, calibration of sensors, and troubleshooting.
- **Cost**: The overall cost of implementing and maintaining the biometric system must be considered. This includes initial setup costs, hardware and software expenses, and long-term operational costs.

Scalability ensures that the biometric system can grow with the organization and be deployed across various sites and applications without significant issues. A well-considered deployment strategy minimizes disruptions and ensures a smooth transition to the new authentication system.

COMPARATIVE ANALYSIS

In the realm of continuous authentication, various biometric modalities are utilized, each offering distinct advantages and presenting specific challenges (Dahia., 2020) A comparative analysis of these biometric approaches—fingerprint recognition, facial recognition, voice recognition, iris recognition, and behavioral biometrics—reveals key insights into their effectiveness, usability, and suitability for different applications.

Accuracy and Error Rates

Accuracy is a critical factor in the effectiveness of biometric systems. It is commonly measured by the False Acceptance Rate (FAR) and the False Rejection Rate (FRR).

- **Fingerprint Recognition**: Known for its high accuracy, fingerprint recognition systems typically have low FAR and FRR, making them reliable for secure environments. However, they require physical interaction, which can be a limitation in some contexts.
- **Facial Recognition**: Offers high accuracy under ideal conditions but can be affected by changes in lighting, angles, and occlusions such as glasses or masks. Advances in AI have improved its performance, but it still faces challenges in diverse real-world scenarios.
- **Iris Recognition**: Extremely accurate with low FAR and FRR, as the iris has highly distinctive patterns. It is less affected by external conditions but requires precise alignment and can be perceived as intrusive.
- **Behavioral Biometrics**: Accuracy depends on the specific behaviors being monitored. Typing patterns and mouse movements can provide high accuracy, but behavioral variability and context changes can introduce errors.

User Acceptance and Usability

User acceptance and usability are crucial for the successful deployment of biometric systems, particularly in continuous authentication .

- **Fingerprint Recognition**: Widely accepted due to its familiarity and ease of use. However, the need for physical contact can be a drawback, especially in hygienic environments or where hands are frequently occupied.
- **Facial Recognition**: Generally has high user acceptance because it is non-intrusive and can operate seamlessly in the background. Privacy concerns and the perception of constant monitoring can be issues.
- **Iris Recognition**: Provides excellent security, but its acceptance is lower due to the perceived intrusiveness and the need for close-range scanning, which can be uncomfortable for some users.
- **Behavioral Biometrics**: Highly usable as it operates continuously in the background without active user participation. Privacy concerns arise from the constant monitoring of behavior, and users may be wary of the data being collected.

Scalability and Deployment Considerations

Scalability and ease of deployment are essential for widespread adoption, particularly in large organizations or across multiple locations.

- **Fingerprint Recognition**: Scalable with relatively low infrastructure costs, but deployment can be hampered by the need for physical sensors at each access point.
- **Facial Recognition**: Scalable with the use of existing camera infrastructure, but performance can vary based on camera quality and placement. Integration with current systems can be straightforward.
- **Iris Recognition**: Scalability is limited by the need for specialized hardware and the high costs associated with iris scanners. Deployment can be challenging due to the precise alignment required.
- **Behavioral Biometrics**: Highly scalable, as it uses existing input devices like keyboards and mice. Deployment is straightforward and cost-effective, but it requires robust data analytics infrastructure to process and analyze behavioral patterns continuously.

CONCLUSION

Biometric modalities for continuous authentication vary in strengths and challenges. Fingerprint recognition offers high accuracy but requires physical interaction. Facial recognition is non-intrusive yet faces privacy and environmental hurdles. Voice recognition is convenient but sensitive to noise and voice changes. Iris recognition provides top security but needs precise setup and encounters user acceptance issues. Behavioral biometrics offers seamless authentication but raises privacy concerns. Choosing the right modality balances accuracy, user acceptance, and scalability. Future AI advancements aim to enhance these systems, addressing current challenges. Implementation success hinges on addressing privacy, effective integration, and cost efficiency. In summary, integrating tailored biometric modalities ensures robust security and user-friendly experiences in continuous authentication systems.

REFERENCES

Ayeswarya, S., & Norman, J. (2019). A survey on different continuous authentication systems. *International Journal of Biometrics*, *11*(1), 67–99. DOI: 10.1504/IJBM.2019.096574

Ayeswarya, S., & Norman, J. (2019, March). Seamless Personal Authentication using Biometrics. In 2019 Innovations in Power and Advanced Computing Technologies (i-PACT) (Vol. 1, pp. 1-5). IEEE.

Ayeswarya, S., & Norman, J. (2019). Improved usability for seamless user verification based on biometrics. *Int. J. Adv. Sci. Technol.*, *28*(7), 379–391.

Ayeswarya, S., & Singh, J. (2024, February). Enhancing User Authentication with a Secure Human-Computable Password Scheme. In *2024 Second International Conference on Emerging Trends in Information Technology and Engineering (ICE-TITE)* (pp. 1-6). IEEE.

Ayeswarya, S., & Singh, K. J. (2024). A comprehensive review on secure biometric-based continuous authentication and user profiling. *IEEE Access : Practical Innovations, Open Solutions*, *12*, 82996–83021. DOI: 10.1109/ACCESS.2024.3411783

Dahia, G., Jesus, L., & Pamplona Segundo, M. (2020). Continuous authentication using biometrics: An advanced review. *Wiley Interdisciplinary Reviews. Data Mining and Knowledge Discovery*, *10*(4), e1365. DOI: 10.1002/widm.1365

Jeong, J. J., Zolotavkin, Y., & Doss, R. (2024). Examining the current status and emerging trends in continuous authentication technologies through citation network analysis. *ACM Computing Surveys*, *55*(6), 1–31. DOI: 10.1145/3533705

Mondal, S. (2016). Continuous user authentication and identification: Combination of security & forensics.

Raghavan, R., & John Singh, K. (2022). An enhanced and hybrid fingerprint minutiae feature extraction method for identifying and authenticating the patient's noisy fingerprint. *International Journal of System Assurance Engineering and Management*, •••, 1–14.

Raghavan, R., & Singh, J. (2021). A hybrid approach towards content-based image retrieval for colored images using enhanced first type of pessimistic covering based lower approximation multi-granular rough sets. *Evolutionary Intelligence*, *14*(2), 1135–1143. DOI: 10.1007/s12065-020-00563-w

Ramkumar, D., Annadurai, C., & Nelson, I. (2022). Iris-based continuous authentication in mobile ad hoc network. *Concurrency and Computation*, *34*(8), e5542. DOI: 10.1002/cpe.5542

Rayani, P. K., & Changder, S. (2023). Continuous user authentication on smartphone via behavioral biometrics: A survey. *Multimedia Tools and Applications*, *82*(2), 1633–1667. DOI: 10.1007/s11042-022-13245-9

Ryu, R., Yeom, S., Kim, S. H., & Herbert, D. (2021). Continuous multimodal biometric authentication schemes: A systematic review. *IEEE Access : Practical Innovations, Open Solutions*, *9*, 34541–34557. DOI: 10.1109/ACCESS.2021.3061589

Shen, Z., Li, S., Zhao, X., & Zou, J. (2022). MMAuth: A continuous authentication framework on smartphones using multiple modalities. *IEEE Transactions on Information Forensics and Security*, *17*, 1450–1465. DOI: 10.1109/TIFS.2022.3160361

Stylios, I., Chatzis, S., Thanou, O., & Kokolakis, S. (2023). Continuous Authentication with Feature-Level Fusion of Touch Gestures and Keystroke Dynamics to Solve Security and Usability Issues. *Computers & Security*, *132*, 103363. DOI: 10.1016/j.cose.2023.103363

Chapter 18
BITS-AV Biometric Integration for Secure Transport Systems in Autonomous Vehicles

Praneetha Surapaneni
https://orcid.org/0000-0003-3822-7270
SRM University, India

Sailaja Chigurupati
KL University, India

Sriramulu Bojjagani
https://orcid.org/0000-0002-8801-4292
SRM University, India

ABSTRACT

Autonomous vehicles (AVs) play a significant role in intelligent transportation systems (ITS), which handle vehicles without human interference. The AVs are integrated with the Internet of Vehicles (IoV) to connect with more vehicles, sensors, and fog servers and share data. This makes the vehicles vulnerable to attacks and leads to unauthorized access. To overcome this drawback, we introduced biometric authentication for secure communication of vehicles, roadside units (RSUs), and fog servers. In this protocol, we generated two session keys between entities. The communication cost, computation cost, and security parameters are compared with existing methods to show that the proposed protocol is more efficient than others. Finally, the formal and informal security analysis ensures the proposed protocol is more secure.

DOI: 10.4018/979-8-3693-8014-7.ch018

INTRODUCTION

As autonomous vehicles (AVs) are a relatively new technology in the vehicular industry that may enhance driving pleasure, traffic flow, and travel security while using less fuel (Zmud et al., 2017). For instance, an AV can sense uncertain real-world situations, plan routes, and take action without human assistance (Bathla et al., 2022). Many data, including streaming videos, are produced by several sensors (like radar, lidar, and cameras) to aid self-monitoring and decision-making. The data generated by cameras, RADAR, and LIDAR is projected to be between 4 and 10 TB daily (Jayaweera et al., 2019). Installing substantial onboard processing and storage capabilities on every AV to maintain and interpret this data for self-driving vehicles is neither practical nor cost-effective. Thus, to attain the highest standards of safety and efficiency in traffic, fog-assisted autonomous vehicles (FAV) (Wang et al., 2020), have been developed to encourage autonomous driving. Specifically, by taking advantage of developments in fog computing and fog storage technology, AVs can obtain the computing and storage resources they need from the fog to meet their data evaluation and storage needs. They can also access pertinent data from autonomous driving suppliers, such as high-dimension maps, immediate time traffic, and models used for artificial intelligence (Tong et al., 2019).

It is intended for remote control to be an essential component of antivirus software, for instance, to release security patches. When necessary, a human driver may be able to assume control of the vehicle thanks to this capability. It has been stated that several AV firms, including Toyota, GM Cruise, Nissan, and Zoox, intend to integrate remote control functionality into their vehicles to enhance decision-making, especially in intricate scenarios (Amador et al., 2022). Since 2018, autonomous testing without an additional driver has been permitted in California, but only if the vehicles can be controlled remotely. Using a user's mobile device—such as an iOS or Android device—is an additional remote control method (Canis., 2019).

However, because the inbuilt operating system is no longer disconnected from the Internet, remote control poses several security problems. For instance, some academics have drawn attention to the possibility that a hostile actor could locate and take advantage of a weakness in the remote control system to take hold of the vehicle. Unapproved access to an AV and the fog may lead to fatalities as well as bodily harm, including the loss of authority over the AV and the exposure of confidential information (Sadaf et al., 2023). As previously said, there exists a potential risk that terrorist organizations could utilize unmanned aerial vehicles to carry out planned assaults, such as deploying AVs into areas where large crowds congregate. Therefore, it is crucial to guarantee that the fog and their AVs are only accessible to authorized individuals. That is, to stop unauthorized parties from engaging in illegal or malicious activities like eavesdropping, surveillance, alteration, and forging. Secure channels must be developed between the AV, the user, and the fog. Implementing authenticity and key agreement protocols for FAV systems is one meaningful way to solve the problem (Ma et al., 2019).

The FAV system should enforce stringent security measures throughout data transfers between users, the fog, and AVs due to their possible dangers. It is acknowledged, therefore, that every class of authentication factors has inherent flaws and that a single authentication element is insufficient to offer the level of security needed for autonomous driving. Passwords and other knowledge factors specifically have poor entropy and are vulnerable to dictionary attacks (Narayanan and Shmatikov., 2005). Misplaced possession components, such as a smart card, are possible. Regarding the inherence factor—a person's biometric—leakage of samples stored on a smart card or server could pose significant, irreversible risks to user privacy because affected persons' biometric traits cannot be modified or changed. Therefore, three-factor authentication protocols using identity-confirming credentials from each of the three groups to establish user authentication, are promising to achieve high safety levels.

Nevertheless, a careless amalgamation of the trio of authentication factors may also culminate in a system that merely carries over the distinct weaknesses of each component. Therefore, one of the biggest problems in developing protocols is taking advantage of each factor while concurrently addressing corresponding limitations. For instance, three standard biometric encryption techniques—fuzzy vault, fuzzy extractor, and fuzzy commit have been used in BITS-AV protocols to protect biometric privacy. It should be noted that the topic of developing a generic BITS-AV framework that incorporates all three biometric encryption techniques is not well-researched.

In this research, we proposed the fog-centric BITS-AV protocol to build security channels between users, AVs, and the fog to enable safe information flow in the AV system. The following are the contributions of this chapter:

1. The suggested BITS-AV framework combines the three standard biometric encryption techniques and enables triple-factor authentication with biometric confidentiality. The user's identity is also hidden during the process to achieve anonymity.
2. Session keys (SKs) are exchanged between the user, fog, and AV to facilitate secure data flow and guard against adversaries controlling AVs remotely.
3. The security of the BITS-AV is verified using formal and informal analysis.
4. The communication cost, computation cost, and security parameters are compared with existing methods.

RELATED WORK

Technological Integration of Framework

(Petit and Shladover, 2014) highlights the need for strong security measures by identifying key cyber security threats to connected and autonomous vehicles. Underscoring the significance of secure GNSS signals and noncompliance recognition systems, it draws attention to the flaws in GNSS systems for AVs and the dangers of bogus message insertion in cooperating cars. The work recommends adaptive failure techniques and information source redundancy to lessen the impact of intrusions. Its ultimate goal is to increase awareness and promote more investigation into cyber security for ITS. According to (Parkinson et al., 2017), to avoid the need for extensive reactive measures and to guarantee cybersecurity standards across the industry, the CAV research community and automakers must address critical knowledge gaps. (Amoozadeh et al., 2015) addresses the security threats related to networked and AVs, emphasizing the effects of sensor manipulation and wireless communication assaults on vehicles with cooperative adaptive cruise control. (Yu et al., 2024) discusses the crucial requirement for total security in CAVs, with an emphasis on end devices that are inside the vehicles. The research emphasizes the difficulties in guaranteeing reliable interaction between especially-vehicle gadgets and remote nodes, given the resource limitations of such devices and the growing complexity and connectedness of contemporary automobiles.

In the context of the larger ecosystem of CAVs, (Aurangzeb et al., 2024) address the serious cyber security concerns posed by autonomous cars. It draws attention to the weaknesses in AV applications, precisely its vulnerability to virus assaults that can impair vehicle autonomy, lengthen communication delays, and use energy. Such attacks may result in financial losses, clog roads, and jeopardize the safety of passengers. The study suggests a hybrid detection model that combines dynamic as well as static approaches to detect malware in real-time, as a solution to these issues. In situations that are becoming more automated and networked, this strategy is essential for protecting the security and privacy of automated transportation systems.

Authentication and Key Exchange

The MAKMS-IoV approach, as presented by (Bagga et al., 2021), uses elliptic curve cryptography (ECC) to guarantee reliable interaction between multiple parties, such as automobiles, cluster heads, and RSUs. MAKMS-IoV facilitates two stages of authentication: one between an adjacent vehicle and its RSU and one between a cluster head. It is also effective for IoV scenarios since it offers a safe messaging platform with little exchange and low computing load.

The AKAP-IoV is suggested by (Bojjagani et al., 2022), and it is made especially for the IoV within ITS. This protocol ensures safe communication, mutual authentication, and efficient key management between different entities, including cars, roadside units, and cloud servers. This addresses the significant security challenges in the Internet of Vehicles. Because of its minimal processing and communication overheads and lightweight design, AKAP-IoV is ideal for use in ITS contexts.

(Liu et.al., 2018) introduced a novel approach for small signatures which are certificate-less. This approach guarantees simple and anonymous authentication, but it is not a reliable means of ensuring untraceability, and no formal proof of the system was provided.

The VESecure system, a revolutionary method for improving authentication and key management inside an IoV context, is presented by (Surapaneni et al., 2024). The method dynamically secures against ever-evolving attacks using the Mayfly algorithm by continuously optimizing private keys. VESecure handles key security concerns like authentication, secrecy, and non-disclosure to provide safe communication between cloud servers, RSUs, and cars.

The AKE protocol, which addresses the urgent requirement for physically secure access control and information security, is presented by (Jiang et al., 2021). It is designed specifically for the IoV context. The suggested method achieves a three-factor security architecture by combining passwords and biometrics with PUF. Because no sensitive data is kept on the devices, this method guarantees that the system will remain secure even if user devices or on-board sensors are compromised. Furthermore, fuzzy commitment is used by the protocol to control noise in PUF solutions and biometrics, improving authentication accuracy and thwarting counterfeiting attempts.

To establish safe communication channels and confirm the purported identities of communicating parties, authentication, and key exchange are widely employed in network security. To protect remote access within the AV system, BITS-AV holds enormous potential to eliminate the flaws in each authentication element.

NETWORK MODEL

This approach develops a new network model that integrates vehicles, RSUs and fog servers. The below figure 1 illustrates the BITS-AV system. The proposed system model undergoes three different modules. In the primary module, various sensors are used to sense the data from the environment.

After gathering sensory data, the secondary module creates usable knowledge about its surroundings and driving routes. Finally, the ternary module activates the AV and receives information and decisions from the secondary module.

AVs face a significant issue in storing and processing the vast amounts of sensor data they collect in real-time, as these OBUs generate immediate data at high speeds (Willburger et.al., 2020). The fog is coupled with the AV control through RSU to solve this problem. Sensors are built into the fog-assisted AV systems, allowing remote AV monitoring and management.

The AV has an onboard unit (OBU) linked to the fog servers through RSU using the cellular network. Each RSU is placed at a specific distance on the side of the road. The ternary module activates the AV as intended and receives essential information and decisions from the secondary module, which communicates with the fog servers.

The fog handles data analysis and storage. It keeps track of a range of data for AVs, including traffic data, weather reports, and multi-dimensional maps. In particular, fog gathers and analyses data from sensors in real-time to provide situational awareness.

Figure 1. Proposed Architecture

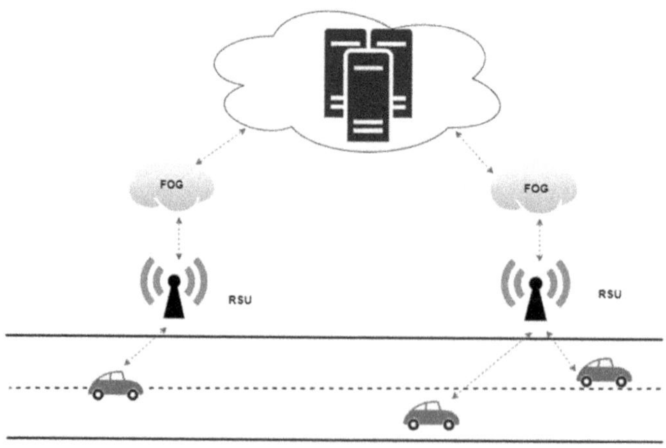

DESIGN OBJECTIVES

An antivirus's attack surface and likelihood of a remote attack are increased when it is network connected to external entities such as users and the cloud. Remote exploitation can compromise in-car electronics like sensors and ECUs that aren't meant to be connected to outside networks. Furthermore, AVs may be vulnerable to online threats due to their monitoring and management. Without physical access to the antivirus software, an attacker can hijack it and interfere with its many capabilities and operations. Furthermore, a compromised AV may be programmed to covertly and remotely cause specific harm or mishaps. However, the cloud may be vulnerable to illegal access, and the data gathered from the AV may contain potentially confidential information. The ability to eavesdrop, spoof, alter, or replay communication is one of the primary sources of the previously mentioned assaults. All parties involved in communication must authenticate one another, and data transmissions must be encrypted to guard against unwanted access to antivirus software.

Because cyber-attacks on autonomous vehicles may cause physical harm and loss of human life, security needs have become more crucial in the AV system. There needs to be more than single-factor identification to assure AV system security. BITS-AV protocol is a viable approach to protect the AV systems. In this chapter, the adversary can get two of the three components; however, only some of the three factors can be simultaneously; kindly refer to it for additional details. Therefore, this study offers a 3-factor security mechanism for AV with the following purposes.

- Mutual Authentication: An entity must be able to verify that it is who it says it is to ensure that only authorized parties have access to the fog and fight against malicious assaults.
- SK Agreement: To provide data communication security between the fog and the user, SKs should be produced for asymmetric key primitives.
- Forward Secrecy: If the users' and fog private keys are discovered, the $Session_{Key}$ between them should offer forward secrecy to guarantee data security. In particular, deducing the previously agreed $Session_{Key}$ in this situation is not appropriate.
- Anonymity: To hide the user's identity, the prototype shall be able to maintain user anonymity, meaning that adversaries other than the user and their intended counterpart would be unable to determine the user's true identity by obtaining the authentication transcripts.
- Untraceability: Although the authentication message contains an invariant that the attacker may use to link the authentication transcripts of separate sessions, the protocol is robust enough to provide identity privacy, even when

the user's actions can be tracked. The protocol needs to be able to grant users untraceability.

PROPOSED SYSTEM

This section deals with different phases of BITS-AV protocol. The below table 1 shows the symbols and its description.

Table 1. Notations and Description

Notations	Description
FS_i	i^{th} fog server
GP	Generation point
PR^-	Private key
PU^+	Public key
Z_q	Finite field
H_f	One-way hash function
V_i	i^{th} vehicle
PI_i	Pseudo-identity
VID_i	Vehicle identity number
$Rand_{num}$	Random number
CV_k	Computationally derived vehicle identity
EU_i	i^{th} end user
$EU_{identity}$	i^{th} end user identity
$Secret_{key}$	Secret key
SC_i	i^{th} smart card
$BioKey_{Gen}$	Biometric key generation
$BioKey_{Rel}$	Biometric key release
TS	Time stamp
EU_{pwd}	End user password
EU_{BioKey}	End user biometric
Ch	Challenge

Initialization Phase

Each fog server FS_i generates a point GP using elliptic curve cryptography (ECC). It generates PR^- and PU^+ which are subset of Z_q. It uses one-way hash function H_f and publishes GP, PU^+ and H_f.

Vehicle Registration

Vehicle V_i selects its pseudo-identity PI_i and vehicle identity number VID_i. It sends the VID_i to the FS_i. Upon receiving the identity the FS_i generates a random number $Rand_{num}$ and derives a value CV_k from the generated hash value. The FS_i stores VID_i and $Rand_{num}$ into the database and publishes CV_k to V_i.

End User Registration

The end user EU_i after buying a vehicle registers receives a smart card SC_i from FS_i. The EU_i sends the $EU_{identity}$ and driving licence and vehicle related documents to FS_i. Now, FS_i generates $Rand_{num}$ and calculates $X= H_f(EU_{identity} || Secret_{key} || Rand_{num})$ and $Y= H_f(SC_i || Secret_{key})$. The FS_i stores EU_i, SC_i, and $Rand_{num}$ in the database. The FS_i transfers the SC_i X, Y, GP, $FS_{identity}$, $BioKey_{Gen}$, $BioKey_{Rel}$, and H_f.

The EU_i contains $EU_{identity}$, EU_{pwd}, and BM_i as input and runs $BioKey_{Gen}$ algorithm and calculates $P= X \oplus H_f(EU_{identity} || EU_{pwd} || EU_{BioKey})$ and $Q= Y \oplus H_f(EU_{identity} || EU_{pwd} || EU_{BioKey})$ and $R= H_f(H_f(EU_{pwd} || EU_{BioKey}))$. Here, R is the fuzzy verifier for identifying incorrect passwords. Lastly, X, Y, R, TS, GP, $FS_{identity}$, $BioKey_{Gen}$, $BioKey_{Rel}$, and H_f are stored.

Authentication

To access AV, EU_i inserts SC_i and enters the EU_{pwd} and EU_{BioKey}. The SC_i runs $BioKey_{Rel}$ algorithm based on EU_i information. The SC_i computes *Ch* using H_f and applied to $EU_{identity}$ and EU_{pwd}. If the *Ch* is matched with the stored value in the database, the SC_i generates original information by performing $A \oplus B$. The SC_i sends $Message_1$ to FS_i that consists of M_1, M_2 and *Nonce*.

$$M_1 = \{EU_{identity} || FS_i || Encrpt(info)\}$$

$$M_2 = \{ Ch || Res || EU_{identity} || FS_i\}$$

The FS_i retrieves the EU_i information and verifies $EU_{identity}$. After the successful verification the FS_i generates $Rand_{num}$. The FS_i retrieves the AV information from the database. The FS_i sends $Message_2$ to AV that contains M_3 and M_4.

$M_3 = \{ EU_{identity} \| V_i \| Rand_{num} \}$

$M_4 = \{ Digital_{Sign} \}$

Now, the M3 is decrypted by AV using $Secret_{key}$ and verifies FS_i identity. The AV generates *Nonce* after the successful verification. The AV sends $Message_3$ to FS_i that contains *Nonce* and M_5.

$M_5 = \{ EU_{identity} \| V_i \| Secret_{key} \| Rand_{num} \}$

The FS_i verifies AV identity and sends $Message_4$ to $EU_{identity}$ that contains *Nonce* and M_6.

$M_6 = \{ EU_{identity} \| V_i \| Rand_{num} \}$

After successful verification of M_6, the EU_i finalizes the authentication.

SECURITY ANALYSIS

This section includes a formal and informal security evaluation that evaluates user safety and shows that our approach is provably secure.

Formal Security Analysis Using Scyther

One well-known automated tool for security protocol verification is called Scyther. It is used to assess and examine the security of cryptographic protocols, including secure communication, authentication, and key exchange protocols. The input language used by Scyther formally describes a security mechanism. Scyther looks through these trails in an attempt to find possible attacks. The tool can confirm specific security attributes, including confidentiality, integrity, and authentication. By spotting vulnerabilities early in the development process, Scyther aids in the construction of secure protocols. Analysing established protocols can help determine their security advantages and disadvantages. In academic contexts, Scyther is used for research in the field and to teach security protocol analysis.

Informal Security Analysis

This sub-section demonstrates how the suggested approach will deliver the following security attributes through the use of an informal security analysis.

1. Replay Attack: Once the two devices have synchronized their times, compare the time difference to an established TS1. Moreover, it is impossible due to the use of hidden random values (R1, R2).
2. Mutual authentication: The proposed technique guarantees mutual authentication for all entities involved in the process. RSUs and automobiles are authenticated using digital signatures and certificates. The private and public keys of the ECC algorithm form the basis of mutual authentication.
3. Privacy and anonymity: During the authentication phase, an adversary A might listen in on every message that was sent and received over the public channel. However, participant information is always encrypted and never sent in transparent text. Listening alone will never reveal the true identify of any entity without some hidden criterion. As a result, the procedure safeguards the confidentiality and identity of the participants.
4. Secrecy (forward/backward): Private data included in $Session_{Key}$ includes the session key nonce, timestamps, temporary identities, and responses. Since this information changes at different times, adversary A cannot predict session keys prior to or following $Session_{Key}$. Because key forward and backward secrecy are maintained, the proposed technique enhances security.
5. Vehicle impersonation attack: An attacker may pretend to be a genuine car in order to trick and confuse users of the IoV. The attacker uses this identity attack to enter the IoV network by successfully speculating on a valid credential.
6. RSU impersonation attack: To obtain private information or interfere with the Internet of Vehicles, the attacker assumes the identity of an RSU. To verify the validity of the RSU_j, the RSU's certificate is verified for the AV V_i.
7. Man-in-the-Middle Attack: During the authentication step, Adversary A must intercept and modify a message transmitted over an open channel, then trick the recipient into thinking the modified message is authentic. A cannot alter the different signals that are being sent. Thus, the MiM assault is discounted.
8. Traceability and non-repudiation: Blockchain technology maintains OBU_i information on the block as an immutable transaction. The smart contract then inserts a revocation tag to stop it from disputing the damaging action when this occurs. When it is determined that OBU_i is a harmful vehicle. As a result, the plan ensures non-repudiation and traceability of the system.

9. Updated Password Attack: Adversary A attempts to reset the password after stealing OBU_i. A will be responsible for obtaining the secrets stored in OBU_i. But A can't calculate $EU_{identity}$, EU_{pwd}, or BioKey. Suppose A decides to attempt a key update attack, A, using a fake password, EU_{pwd}. It is likewise only possible to determine EU_{pwd} and A with knowledge of *Nonce*. Consequently, A can't initiate password update assaults.

SECURITY FEATURES COMPARISON

Integrating IoV technology is hampered by the complexity and interconnectedness of modern automobile networks, which present significant security and privacy challenges. Unauthorized access, data breaches, DDoS assaults, and MitM attacks are examples of security dangers. Gathering, sharing, and locating data with other organizations are significant privacy concerns. In the IoV context, data must be secure and private to guarantee the technology's efficiency and safety. The IoV network can preserve user confidence and safeguard private information by adhering to regulations and protecting privacy. Table 2 compares the security features of the proposed framework with the current techniques.

Table 2. Comparison of Security Features

Security Features	Proposed System	Liu et.al., 2018	Jiang et al., 2021	Bagga et al., 2021	Bojjagani et al., 2022	Surapaneni et al., 2024
SF1	✓	✓	✓	✓	✓	✓
SF2	✓	✓	✓	✓	✓	✓
SF3	✓	✓	✓	✓	✓	✓
SF4	✓	X	✓	X	X	X
SF5	✓	✓	✓	✓	✓	✓
SF6	✓	✓	✓	✓	✓	✓
SF7	✓	✓	✓	✓	✓	✓
SF8	✓	X	✓	X	✓	X
SF9	✓	✓	X	X	✓	X

Note: SF1: Replay Attack, SF2: Mutual authentication, SF3: Privacy and anonymity, SF4: Secrecy (forward/backward), SF5: Vehicle impersonation attack, SF6: RSU impersonation attack, SF7: Man-in-the-Middle Attack, SF8: Traceability and non-repudiation, SF9: Updated Password Attack, ✓: Supports Functionality, X Doesn't Support Functionality

PERFORMANCE EVALUATION

When compared to existing methods, the proposed system's performance evaluation shows significant improvements in communication and computing costs. Understanding the effectiveness and viability of the suggested authentication system in high-density VANET environments depends heavily on these findings.

Communication Cost

In VANETs, communication cost plays a crucial role since it affects both the overall effectiveness of data transmission and network congestion directly. The communication costs of different techniques are compared in Table 3 based on the total bits transmitted during the authentication procedure. When it comes to message exchange, the suggested system only needs 2182 bits, which is a lot less than most of the systems that were compared. For example:

- In comparison to the suggested approach, (Liu et al., 2018) requires 2872 bits, which is a 24% more communication cost. Increased network congestion may result from this overhead, particularly in situations with large traffic volumes.
- The communication cost of (Jiang et al., 2021) is 2560 bits, which is still 17.3% more. This implies that our suggested plan uses bandwidth more efficiently.
- Among the compared methods, (Bagga et al., 2021) obtains the lowest communication cost (1600 bits), which is 26.7% less than our suggested system. It is necessary to strike a balance because this reduction could result in less security or computing efficiency.
- The communication cost of (Bojjagani et al., 2022) is 3296 bits, which is 51% more than our technique. In dense VANETs, this large overhead might impede real-time communication.
- The amount of bits needed by (Surapaneni et al., 2024) is 2240, which is 2.6% more than our suggested approach. Even though there is not much of a difference, it shows that our method is more efficient.

For high-mobility and high-density vehicular networks, the suggested method is appropriate since it takes a balanced approach to reducing communication overhead and preserving strong security characteristics.

Table 3. Comparison of communication costs

Scheme	Communication Cost (Bits)
Liu et.al., 2018	2872
Jiang et al., 2021	2560
Bagga et al., 2021	1600
Bojjagani et al., 2022	3296
Surapaneni et al., 2024	2240
Proposed System	2182

Figure 2. Communication Cost Vs Previous Methods

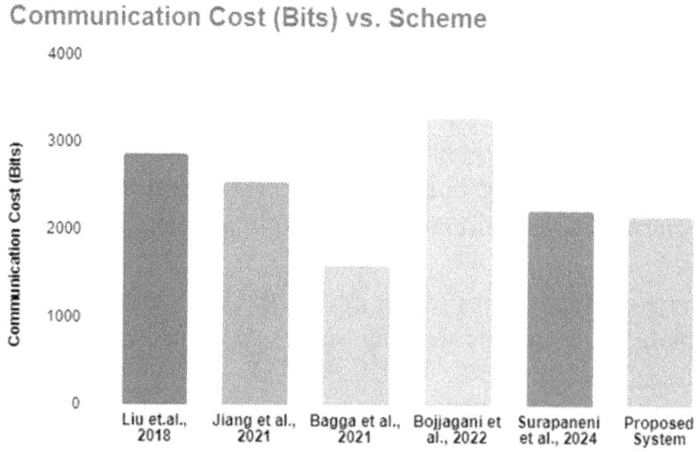

Computation Cost

Another crucial parameter for assessing how well authentication techniques work in VANETs is computation cost, which has an impact on the processing burden on both RSUs and vehicles. The hashing function's processing time is represented by the following functions: fuzzy extractor (T_{FE}), symmetric key (T_{SYM}), bilinear pairing (B_P), modular exponentiation (T_{ME}), ECC point multiplication (T_{MUL}), fuzzy extractor (T_{PUF}), and key derivation (T_{KD}). The time taken by bitwise XOR and concatenation is disregarded. The formula for calculating the computation cost for the proposed scheme is $26T_{hash}+ T_{FE}+2T_{PUF}+T_{SYM}$. The computing cost of several strategies in terms of total operation time is shown in Table 4. With a computation cost of 114.28 seconds, the suggested system is less expensive than the majority of current schemes:

- The computation cost of Liu et al., 2018 is high at 383.652 seconds. This significant overhead makes it less appropriate for time-sensitive VANET applications since it can cause delays in real-time communication.
- The 180 seconds needed by Jiang et al. in 2021 is still 57% more than our suggested system. This suggests that our plan handles cryptographic activities more effectively.
- The computation cost of Bagga et al., 2021 is a very low 7.839 seconds, far lower than our system. These low prices could, however, be the consequence of less security features or easier cryptographic procedures, which could jeopardize security as a whole.
- With a computation cost of 488.64 seconds, Bojjagani et al., 2022 has the highest, rendering it unsuitable for real-time applications. Our system shows its efficiency in high-mobility circumstances by reducing this overhead by 76.6%.
- The computation cost of Surapaneni et al., 2024 is 16.42 seconds, which is less than the computation cost of our suggested system. Despite its seeming efficiency, one must weigh the trade-offs between utility and security.

In order to minimize the overall processing burden on RSUs and guarantee that authentication procedures are finished quickly, even in high-density situations, the suggested approach strikes a compromise between computational efficiency and security.

Table 4. Comparison of Computation Costs

Scheme	Computation Cost (seconds)
Liu et.al., 2018	383.652
Jiang et al., 2021	180
Bagga et al., 2021	7.839
Bojjagani et al., 2022	488.64
Surapaneni et al., 2024	16.42
Proposed System	114.28

Figure 3. Computation Cost Vs Previous Methods

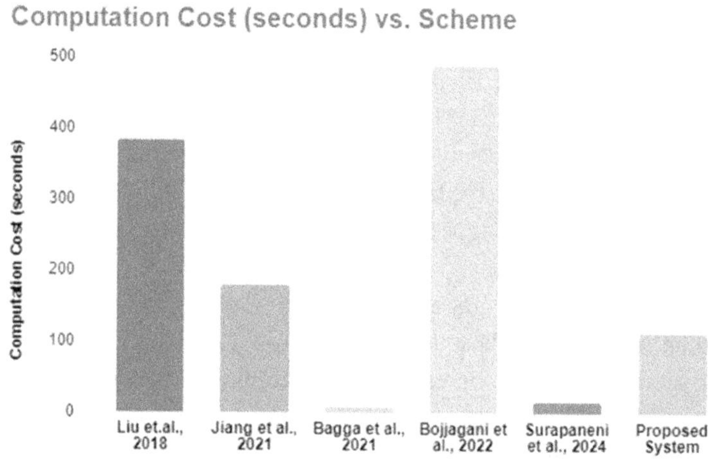

Significance of the Findings

The findings show that the suggested approach successfully tackles the two problems of computation overhead and communication in VANETs. The suggested method eases the burden on network resources by streamlining the authentication procedure to manage numerous vehicles at once, enabling faster and more dependable data sharing. This efficiency is especially helpful in high-vehicle density circumstances, where processing constraints and delay may be issues for older identification approaches.

The fact that the computational cost can be decreased without sacrificing security further emphasizes how useful the suggested solution is for actual implementation. It makes sure that secure communication may continue without unaffordable delays or resource consumption, despite the dynamic nature of VANETs and the fast mobility of vehicles.

All things considered, the suggested system offers a reliable and expandable way to improve the security and efficiency of VANET connections, which makes it an important advancement in the field of intelligent transportation systems.

CONCLUSION

The new protocol BITS-AV is presented in this study to enable safe communication in Intelligent Transportation Systems (ITS) between users, fog servers, and autonomous vehicles. To mitigate the risks associated with the extensive data sharing of autonomous vehicles, the protocol has a robust three-factor authentication mechanism that uses smart cards, biometrics, and passwords. Using elliptic curve cryptography, BITS-AV guarantees secure data transmission. Formal and informal security analyses have been used to analyze the protocol, showing that it offers more security than other options.

REFERENCES

Amador, O., Aramrattana, M., & Vinel, A. (2022). A survey on remote operation of road vehicles. *IEEE Access : Practical Innovations, Open Solutions, 10*, 130135–130154. DOI: 10.1109/ACCESS.2022.3229168

Amoozadeh, M., Raghuramu, A., Chuah, C. N., Ghosal, D., Zhang, H. M., Rowe, J., & Levitt, K. (2015). Security vulnerabilities of connected vehicle streams and their impact on cooperative driving. *IEEE Communications Magazine*, *53*(6), 126–132. DOI: 10.1109/MCOM.2015.7120028

Aurangzeb, S., Aleem, M., Khan, M. T., Anwar, H., & Siddique, M. S. (2024). Cybersecurity for autonomous vehicles against malware attacks in smart-cities. *Cluster Computing*, *27*(3), 3363–3378. DOI: 10.1007/s10586-023-04114-7

Bagga, P., Das, A. K., Wazid, M., Rodrigues, J. J., Choo, K. K. R., & Park, Y. (2021). On the design of mutual authentication and key agreement protocol in internet of vehicles-enabled intelligent transportation system. *IEEE Transactions on Vehicular Technology*, *70*(2), 1736–1751. DOI: 10.1109/TVT.2021.3050614

Bathla, G., Bhadane, K., Singh, R. K., Kumar, R., Aluvalu, R., Krishnamurthi, R., Kumar, A., Thakur, R. N., & Basheer, S. (2022). Autonomous vehicles and intelligent automation: Applications, challenges, and opportunities. *Mobile Information Systems*, *2022*(1), 7632892. DOI: 10.1155/2022/7632892

Bhargav-Spantzel, A., Squicciarini, A., & Bertino, E. (2006, November). Privacy preserving multi-factor authentication with biometrics. In *Proceedings of the second ACM workshop on Digital identity management* (pp. 63-72). DOI: 10.1145/1179529.1179540

Bojjagani, S., Reddy, Y. P., Anuradha, T., Rao, P. V., Reddy, B. R., & Khan, M. K. (2022). Secure authentication and key management protocol for deployment of internet of vehicles (IoV) concerning intelligent transport systems. *IEEE Transactions on Intelligent Transportation Systems*, *23*(12), 24698–24713. DOI: 10.1109/TITS.2022.3207593

Canis, B. (2019). *Issues in autonomous vehicle testing and deployment (No. R45985)*. Congressional Research Service.

Jayaweera, N., Rajatheva, N., & Latva-aho, M. (2019, April). Autonomous driving without a burden: View from outside with elevated LiDAR. In 2019 IEEE 89th Vehicular Technology Conference (VTC2019-Spring) (pp. 1-7). IEEE.

Jiang, Q., Zhang, X., Zhang, N., Tian, Y., Ma, X., & Ma, J. (2021). Three-factor authentication protocol using physical unclonable function for IoV. *Computer Communications, 173*, 45–55. DOI: 10.1016/j.comcom.2021.03.022

Liu, J., Li, Q., Sun, R., Du, X., & Guizani, M. (2018, May). An efficient anonymous authentication scheme for internet of vehicles. In *2018 IEEE International Conference on Communications (ICC)* (pp. 1-6). IEEE. DOI: 10.1109/ICC.2018.8422447

Ma, M., He, D., Wang, H., Kumar, N., & Choo, K. K. R. (2019). An efficient and provably secure authenticated key agreement protocol for fog-based vehicular ad-hoc networks. *IEEE Internet of Things Journal, 6*(5), 8065–8075. DOI: 10.1109/JIOT.2019.2902840

Narayanan, A., & Shmatikov, V. (2005, November). Fast dictionary attacks on passwords using time-space tradeoff. In *Proceedings of the 12th ACM conference on Computer and communications security* (pp. 364-372). DOI: 10.1145/1102120.1102168

Parkinson, S., Ward, P., Wilson, K., & Miller, J. (2017). Cyber threats facing autonomous and connected vehicles: Future challenges. *IEEE Transactions on Intelligent Transportation Systems, 18*(11), 2898–2915. DOI: 10.1109/TITS.2017.2665968

Petit, J., & Shladover, S. E. (2014). Potential cyberattacks on automated vehicles. *IEEE Transactions on Intelligent Transportation Systems, 16*(2), 546–556.

Sadaf, M., Iqbal, Z., Javed, A. R., Saba, I., Krichen, M., Majeed, S., & Raza, A. (2023). Connected and automated vehicles: Infrastructure, applications, security, critical challenges, and future aspects. *Technologies, 11*(5), 117. DOI: 10.3390/technologies11050117

Surapaneni, P., Bojjagani, S., & Khan, M. K. (2024). VESecure: Verifiable authentication and efficient key exchange for secure intelligent transport systems deployment. *Vehicular Communications, 49*, 100822. DOI: 10.1016/j.vehcom.2024.100822

Tong, W., Hussain, A., Bo, W. X., & Maharjan, S. (2019). Artificial intelligence for vehicle-to-everything: A survey. *IEEE Access : Practical Innovations, Open Solutions, 7*, 10823–10843. DOI: 10.1109/ACCESS.2019.2891073

Wang, H., Liu, T., Kim, B., Lin, C. W., Shiraishi, S., Xie, J., & Han, Z. (2020). Architectural design alternatives based on cloud/edge/fog computing for connected vehicles. *IEEE Communications Surveys and Tutorials, 22*(4), 2349–2377. DOI: 10.1109/COMST.2020.3020854

Willburger, K., Schwenk, K., & Brauchle, J. (2020). Amaro—An on-board ship detection and real-time information system. *Sensors (Basel), 20*(5), 1324. DOI: 10.3390/s20051324 PMID: 32121473

Yu, D., Lee, S., Hsu, R. H., & Lee, J. (2024). Ensuring end-to-end security with fine-grained access control for connected and autonomous vehicles. *IEEE Transactions on Information Forensics and Security*, *19*, 6962–6977. DOI: 10.1109/TIFS.2024.3417292

Zmud, J. P., & Sener, I. N. (2017). Towards an understanding of the travel behavior impact of autonomous vehicles. *Transportation Research Procedia*, *25*, 2500–2519. DOI: 10.1016/j.trpro.2017.05.281

Compilation of References

Abdullah, A. M. (2017). Advanced encryption standard (AES) algorithm to encrypt and decrypt data. *Cryptography and Network Security*, *16*, 1–11.

Abualigah, L., Diabat, A., Mirjalili, S., Abd Elaziz, M., & Gandomi, A. H. (2021). The arithmetic optimization algorithm. *Computer Methods in Applied Mechanics and Engineering*, *376*, 113609. DOI: 10.1016/j.cma.2020.113609

Abusham, E., Ibrahim, B., Zia, K., & Al Maskari, S. (2022). An Integration of New Digital Image Scrambling Technique on PCA-Based Face Recognition System. *Scientific Programming*, *2022*, 1–17. DOI: 10.1155/2022/2628885

Abusukhon, A., & AlZu'bi, S. (2020, April). New direction of cryptography: A review on text-to-image encryption algorithms based on RGB color value. In *2020 Seventh International Conference on Software Defined Systems (SDS)* (pp. 235-239). IEEE.

Acquisti, A., Friedman, A., & Telang, R. (2006). Is There a Cost to Privacy Breaches? An Event Study. *Proceedings of the International Conference on Information Systems (ICIS)*.

Adjabi, I., Ouahabi, A., Benzaoui, A., & Taleb-Ahmed, A. (2020). Past, present, and future of face recognition: A review. *Electronics (Basel)*, *9*(8), 1–53. DOI: 10.3390/electronics9081188

Adleman, L. M. (1994). Molecular computation of solutions to combinatorial problems. *Nature*, *266*(5187), 40.

Aghdam, M. H., & Kabiri, P. (2016). Feature selection for intrusion detection system using ant colony optimization. *International Journal of Network Security*, *18*(3), 420–432.

Ahmad, I., Abdullah, S., & Ahmed, A. (2022). IoT-fog-based healthcare 4.0 system using blockchain technology. *The Journal of Supercomputing*, *79*(4), 3999–4020. DOI: 10.1007/s11227-022-04788-7 PMID: 36157083

Ahmed, Y. A., Maarof, M. A., Hassan, F. M., & Abshir, M. M. (2014). Survey of Keylogger technologies. *International Journal of Computer Science and Telecommunications, 5*(2).

Al Nafea, R., & Almaiah, M. A. (2021, July). Cyber security threats in cloud: Literature review. In 2021 international conference on information technology (ICIT) (pp. 779-786). IEEE.

Alahmadi, A. A., Aljabri, M., Alhaidari, F., Alharthi, D. J., Rayani, G. E., Marghalani, L. A., Alotaibi, O. B., & Bajandouh, S. A. (2023). DDoS Attack Detection in IoT-Based Networks Using Machine Learning Models: A Survey and Research Directions. *Electronics (Basel), 12*(14), 3103. DOI: 10.3390/electronics12143103

Alaidi, A. H., Alairaji, R., Alrikabi, H., Aljazaery, I., & Abbood, S. (2022). Dark web illegal activities crawling and classifying using data mining techniques. [iJIM]. *International Journal of Interactive Mobile Technologies, 16*, 122–139. DOI: 10.3991/ijim.v16i10.30209

Alamer, M., & Almaiah, M. A. (2021, July). Cybersecurity in Smart City: A systematic mapping study. In 2021 international conference on information technology (ICIT) (pp. 719-724). IEEE.

Albinali, H., & Azzedin, F. (2024). Towards RPL Attacks and Mitigation Taxonomy: Systematic Literature Review Approach. *IEEE Transactions on Network and Service Management, 21*(5), 5215–5238. DOI: 10.1109/TNSM.2024.3386468

Albugmi, A. (2024). Digital Forensics Readiness Framework (DFRF) to Secure Database Systems. *Engineering, Technology &. Applied Scientific Research, 14*(2), 13732–13740.

Alchi, A. (2023). Advanced Forensics Open-Source Tools. In *Advanced Techniques and Applications of Cybersecurity and Forensics* (pp. 22–34). Chapman and Hall/CRC.

Alessandro Guarino. (2013). *Digital Forensics as a Big Data Challenge*. Information Security Solutions Europe.

Alfriehat, N. A. (2024). Detecting Version Number Attacks in Low Power and Lossy Networks for Internet of Things Routing. *IEEE AccessReview and Taxonomy*. 65985.

Ali, A. A., Raheem, M., Kh-Madhloom, J., Hassen, O. A., Hassen, O. A., & Neamah, M. R. (2018). Big Data Enabled Approach for Predictive Analysis of Accuracy Aware Face Smile Detection in Assorted Domains ministery of higer education and scientific research Big Data Enabled Approach for Predictive Analysis of Accuracy Aware Face Smile Detection in Assorted Domains. In *Article in Journal of Advanced Research in Dynamical and Control Systems* (Vol. 10). https://www.researchgate.net/publication/334401924

Ali, A., Almaiah, M. A., Hajjej, F., Pasha, M. F., Fang, O. H., Khan, R., Teo, J., & Zakarya, M. (2022). An industrial IoT-based blockchain-enabled secure searchable encryption approach for healthcare systems using neural network. *Sensors (Basel)*, *22*(2), 572. DOI: 10.3390/s22020572 PMID: 35062530

Ali, A., Al-Rimy, B. A. S., Almazroi, A. A., Alsubaei, F. S., Almazroi, A. A., & Saeed, F. (2023). Securing secrets in cyber-physical systems: A cutting-edge privacy approach with consortium blockchain. *Sensors (Basel)*, *23*(16), 7162. DOI: 10.3390/s23167162 PMID: 37631699

Aljaidi, M. A.-F.-A.-S.-N. (2023). Cybersecurity Threats in the Era of AI: Detection of Phishing Domains Through Classification Rules. .

Aljaidi, M. A.-F.-A.-S.-N. (2023). Cybersecurity Threats in the Era of AI: Detection of Phishing Domains Through Classification Rules. . *In 2023 2nd International En.*

Aljazaery, I. A., Salim, A. L., Rikabi, H. T., & Alaidi, A. H. M. (2022). Encryption of Color Image Based on DNA Strand and Exponential Factor. *International Journal of Online & Biomedical Engineering*, *18*(3).

Al-Kateeb, Z. N., Al-Shamdeen, M. J., & Al-Mukhtar, F. S. (2020, July). Encryption and Steganography a secret data using circle shapes in colored images. *Journal of Physics: Conference Series*, *1591*(1), 012019.

Alladi, T., Kohli, V., Chamola, V., & Yu, F. R. (2022). A deep learning based misbehavior classification scheme for intrusion detection in cooperative intelligent transportation systems. *Digital Communications and Networks*.

Alléaume, R., Branciard, C., Bouda, J., Debuisschert, T., Dianati, M., Gisin, N., Godfrey, M., Grangier, P., Länger, T., Lütkenhaus, N., Monyk, C., Painchault, P., Peev, M., Poppe, A., Pornin, T., Rarity, J., Renner, R., Ribordy, G., Riguidel, M., & Zeilinger, A. (2014). Using quantum key distribution for cryptographic purposes: A survey. *Theoretical Computer Science*, *560*, 62–81. DOI: 10.1016/j.tcs.2014.09.018

Alluhaidan, A. S. D., & Prabu, P. (2023). End-to-end encryption in resource-constrained IoT device. *IEEE Access : Practical Innovations, Open Solutions, 11*, 70040–70051. DOI: 10.1109/ACCESS.2023.3292829

Almaiah, M. A. (2021). A new scheme for detecting malicious attacks in wireless sensor networks based on blockchain technology. In *Artificial intelligence and blockchain for future cybersecurity applications* (pp. 217–234). Springer International Publishing. DOI: 10.1007/978-3-030-74575-2_12

Almaiah, M. A., & Al-Khasawneh, A. (2020). Investigating the main determinants of mobile cloud computing adoption in university campus. *Education and Information Technologies, 25*(4), 3087–3107. DOI: 10.1007/s10639-020-10120-8

Almaiah, M. A., Yelisetti, S., Arya, L., Babu Christopher, N. K., Kaliappan, K., Vellaisamy, P., Hajjej, F., & Alkdour, T. (2023). A Novel Approach for Improving the Security of IoT–Medical Data Systems Using an Enhanced Dynamic Bayesian Network. *Electronics (Basel), 12*(20), 4316. DOI: 10.3390/electronics12204316

Almusaylim, A., Z. J. (. (2020). Detection and mitigation of RPL rank and version number attacks in the internet of things: SRPL-RP. *Sensors (Basel), 20*(21), 5997. DOI: 10.3390/s20215997 PMID: 33105891

Al-Na'amneh, Q. A. (2024). Next Generation Image Watermarking via Combined DWT-SVD Technique. In 2024 2nd International Conference on Cyber Resilience (ICC.

Al-Na'amneh, Q. A. (2024). Next Generation Image Watermarking via Combined DWT-SVD Technique. *International Conference on Cyber Resilience (ICCC).* IEEE ACCESS. DOI: 10.1109/ICCR61006.2024.10532782

Al-Na'amneh, Q. N. (2024). Improving Memory Malware Detection in Machine Learning With Random Forest-Based Feature Selection. In Risk Assessment and Countermeasures for Cybersecurity.

Al-Na'amneh, Q. N. (2024). Improving Memory Malware Detection in Machine Learning With Random Forest-Based Feature Selection. In. In Risk Assessment and Countermeasures for Cybersecurity.

Al-Na'amneh, Q. A. (2023). Feature Selection for Robust Spoofing Detection: A Chi-Square-based Machine Learning Approach. *International Engineering Conference on Electrical, Energy, and Artificial Intelligence (EICEEAI) ().* (pp. pp. 1-7). IEEE. DOI: 10.1109/EICEEAI60672.2023.10590243

Al-Na'amneh, Q. N. (2024). Improving Memory Malware Detection in Machine Learning With Random Forest-Based Feature Selection. In *Risk Assessment and Countermeasures for Cybersecurity*. IGI Global. DOI: 10.4018/979-8-3693-2691-6.ch006

Alnifie, K. M. (2023). Investigation of Human Weaknesses in Organizational Cybersecurity: A Meta-Analytic Approach (Doctoral dissertation, Howard University).

Alqasem, H. D. (2024). Transmission Line Fault Detection Using Arduino and GSM. In *Intelligent Systems, Business, and Innovation Research* (pp. 559–562). Springer Nature Switze. DOI: 10.1007/978-3-031-36895-0_45

Alsarhan, A. A. (2020). A. Profit optimization in multi-service cognitive mesh network using machine learning. J Wireless Com Network 2011, 36 (2011). . .DOI: 10.1186/1687-1499-2011-36

Alsarhan, A. A. (2021). A New Covid-19 Tracing Approach using Machine Learning and Drones Enabled Wireless Network. . *International Journal of Interactive Mobile Technologies (iJIM),* .

Alsarhan, A. A.-G.-R. (2022). A Novel Scheme for Malicious Nodes Detection in Cloud Markets Based on Fuzzy Logic Technique. International Journal of Interactive Mobile Technologies (iJIM), 16(0.

Alsarhan, A. E. (2023). Enhancing Phishing URL Detection: A Comparative Study of Machine Learning Algorithms. " Proceedings of the 2023 Asia Conference on Artificial Intelligence, Machine Learning and Robotics. 2023.</conf>

Alsarhan, A., ... (2023). "Forensic Handwriting and Signatures Using Machine Learning Techniques,". *2023 2nd International Engineering Conference on Electrical, Energy, and Artificial Intelligence (EICEEAI), Zarqa, Jordan, 2023, pp. 1-6,* , (pp. pp. 1-6, doi:)DOI: 10.1109/EICEEAI60672.2023.10590549

Alshameri, H. M. (2019). An efficient zero- knowledge proof based identification scheme for securing software defined network. Scalable Computing: Practice and Experience,.

Alzaqebah, A., Aljarah, I., Al-Kadi, O., & Damaševičius, R. (2022). A modified grey wolf optimization algorithm for an intrusion detection system. *Mathematics*, *10*(6), 999. DOI: 10.3390/math10060999

Alzubi, Q. M., Anbar, M., Alqattan, Z. N. M., Al-Betar, M. A., & Abdullah, R. (2020). Intrusion detection system based on a modified binary grey wolf optimisation. *Neural Computing & Applications*, *32*(10), 6125–6137. DOI: 10.1007/s00521-019-04103-1

Amador, O., Aramrattana, M., & Vinel, A. (2022). A survey on remote operation of road vehicles. *IEEE Access : Practical Innovations, Open Solutions, 10*, 130135–130154. DOI: 10.1109/ACCESS.2022.3229168

Amoozadeh, M., Raghuramu, A., Chuah, C. N., Ghosal, D., Zhang, H. M., Rowe, J., & Levitt, K. (2015). Security vulnerabilities of connected vehicle streams and their impact on cooperative driving. *IEEE Communications Magazine, 53*(6), 126–132. DOI: 10.1109/MCOM.2015.7120028

Anikevičs, G. (2021). *Relationship between vendor popularity and prices on dark web marketplaces.*

Anderson, R., Barton, C., Böhme, R., Clayton, R., Van Eeten, M. J., Levi, M., ... & Savage, S. (2013). Measuring the cost of cybercrime. The economics of information security and privacy, 265-300.

Andrean, A., Jayabalan, M., & Thiruchelvam, V. (2020). Keystroke Dynamics Based User Authentication using Deep Multilayer Perceptron. *International Journal of Machine Learning and Computing, 10*(1), 134–139. DOI: 10.18178/ijmlc.2020.10.1.910

Anilkumar, C., Lenka, S., Neelima, N., & Sathishkumar, V. E. (2024). A Secure Method of Communication Through BB84 Protocol in Quantum Key Distribution. *Scalable Computing: Practice and Experience, 25*(1), 21–33. DOI: 10.12694/scpe.v25i1.2152

Anith, S. S. (2011). *Detecting keylogger based on traffic analysis with periodic behavior*. PSG College of Technology.

Arifianto, R. M., Sukarno, P., & Jadied, E. M. (2018, May). An SSH honeypot architecture using port knocking and intrusion detection system. In 2018 6th International Conference on Information and Communication Technology (ICoICT) (pp. 409-415). IEEE.

Arivudainambi, D., KA, V. K., & Sibi Chakkaravarthy, S. (. (2019). LION IDS: A meta-heuristics approach to detect DDoS attacks against Software-Defined Networks. *Neural Computing & Applications, 31*, 1491–1501. DOI: 10.1007/s00521-018-3383-7

Aslam, M., Idrees, R. N., Baig, M. M., & Arshad, M. A. (2004). Antihook shield against the software key loggers. In *Proceedings of the National Conference of Emerging Technologies.*

Attou, H., Mohy-eddine, M., Guezzaz, A., Benkirane, S., Azrour, M., Alabdultif, A., & Almusallam, N. (2023). Towards an intelligent intrusion detection system to detect malicious activities in cloud computing. *Applied Sciences (Basel, Switzerland), 13*(17), 9588. DOI: 10.3390/app13179588

Aurangzeb, S., Aleem, M., Khan, M. T., Anwar, H., & Siddique, M. S. (2024). Cybersecurity for autonomous vehicles against malware attacks in smart-cities. *Cluster Computing*, *27*(3), 3363–3378. DOI: 10.1007/s10586-023-04114-7

Ayeswarya, S., & Norman, J. (2019, March). Seamless Personal Authentication using Biometrics. In 2019 Innovations in Power and Advanced Computing Technologies (i-PACT) (Vol. 1, pp. 1-5). IEEE.

Ayeswarya, S., & Norman, J. (2019). A survey on different continuous authentication systems. *International Journal of Biometrics*, *11*(1), 67–99. DOI: 10.1504/IJBM.2019.096574

Ayeswarya, S., & Norman, J. (2019). Improved usability for seamless user verification based on biometrics. *Int. J. Adv. Sci. Technol.*, *28*(7), 379–391.

Ayeswarya, S., & Singh, J. (2024, February). Enhancing User Authentication with a Secure Human-Computable Password Scheme. In *2024 Second International Conference on Emerging Trends in Information Technology and Engineering (ICETITE)* (pp. 1-6). IEEE.

Ayeswarya, S., & Singh, K. J. (2024). A comprehensive review on secure biometric-based continuous authentication and user profiling. *IEEE Access : Practical Innovations, Open Solutions*, *12*, 82996–83021. DOI: 10.1109/ACCESS.2024.3411783

Baecher, P., Koetter, M., Koenning, A., & Freiling, F. C. (2006). The Nepenthes Platform: An Efficient Approach to Collect Malware. *Lecture Notes in Computer Science*, *4219*, 165–184. DOI: 10.1007/11856214_9

Bagga, P., Das, A. K., Wazid, M., Rodrigues, J. J., Choo, K. K. R., & Park, Y. (2021). On the design of mutual authentication and key agreement protocol in internet of vehicles-enabled intelligent transportation system. *IEEE Transactions on Vehicular Technology*, *70*(2), 1736–1751. DOI: 10.1109/TVT.2021.3050614

Bahia, Y. Z., Meriem, F., & Messaoud, B. (2024). Face spoofing detection using Heterogeneous Auto-Similarities of Characteristics. *Engineering Applications of Artificial Intelligence*, *130*, 107788. DOI: 10.1016/j.engappai.2023.107788

Bailey, M., Oberheide, J., Andersen, J., Mao, Z. M., Jahanian, F., & Nazario, J. (2007). Automated Classification and Analysis of Internet Malware. Recent Advances in Intrusion Detection, 146-163.

Bakare, S. S., Adeniyi, A. O., Akpuokwe, C. U., & Eneh, N. E. (2024). Data privacy laws and compliance: A comparative review of the EU GDPR and USA regulations. *Computer Science & IT Research Journal*, *5*(3), 528–543. DOI: 10.51594/csitrj.v5i3.859

Bang, A. O., & Rao, U. P. (2022). EMBOF-RPL: Improved RPL for early detection and isolation of rank attack in RPL-based internet of things. *Peer-to-Peer Networking and Applications*, *15*(1), 642–665. DOI: 10.1007/s12083-021-01275-3

Barhate, D., Pathak, S., & Dubey, A. K. (2023). Hyperparameter-tuned batch-updated stochastic gradient descent: Plant species identification by using hybrid deep learning. *Ecological Informatics*, *75*, 102094. DOI: 10.1016/j.ecoinf.2023.102094

Bathla, G., Bhadane, K., Singh, R. K., Kumar, R., Aluvalu, R., Krishnamurthi, R., Kumar, A., Thakur, R. N., & Basheer, S. (2022). Autonomous vehicles and intelligent automation: Applications, challenges, and opportunities. *Mobile Information Systems*, *2022*(1), 7632892. DOI: 10.1155/2022/7632892

Bellare, M., & Miner, S. K. (1999, August). A forward-secure digital signature scheme. In *Annual international cryptology conference* (pp. 431-448). Berlin, Heidelberg: Springer Berlin Heidelberg. DOI: 10.1007/3-540-48405-1_28

Bernardo, B. M., Mamede, H. S., Barroso, J. M. P., & Dos Santos, V. M. P. D. (2024). Mobile Device Forensics Framework: A Toolbox to Support and Enhance This Process. *Emerging Science Journal*, *8*(3), 972–998. DOI: 10.28991/ESJ-2024-08-03-011

Bhandari, D. A. (2024). ML-Based Methods for Detecting Phishing Websites: A Comprehensive Survey and Analysis.

Bhardwaj, A., & Goundar, S. (2020). Keyloggers: Silent cyber security weapons. *Network Security*, *2020*(2), 14–19. DOI: 10.1016/S1353-4858(20)30021-0

Bhargav-Spantzel, A., Squicciarini, A., & Bertino, E. (2006, November). Privacy preserving multi-factor authentication with biometrics. In *Proceedings of the second ACM workshop on Digital identity management* (pp. 63-72). DOI: 10.1145/1179529.1179540

Bhattacharyya, S. K., & Rahul, K. (2014). FACE RECOGNITION BY LINEAR DISCRIMINANT ANALYSIS. *International Journal of Communication Networks and Security*, *1–5*, www.interscience.in/ijcns. Advance online publication. DOI: 10.47893/IJCNS.2014.1087

Bhavsar, M., Roy, K., Kelly, J., & Olusola, O. (2023). Anomaly-based intrusion detection system for IoT application. *Discover Internet of Things*, *3*(1), 5. DOI: 10.1007/s43926-023-00034-5

Biryukov, A., Pustogarov, I., Thill, F., & Weinmann, R.-P. (2014). Content and popularity analysis of tor hidden services. In *2014 IEEE 34th international conference on distributed computing systems workshops (icdcsw)* (p. 188-193). DOI: 10.1109/ICDCSW.2014.20

Biswas, S., Sohel, M., Sajal, M. M., Afrin, T., Bhuiyan, T., & Hassan, M. M. (2018). A study on remote code execution vulnerability in web applications. In *International conference on cyber security and computer science (ICONCS 2018)* (pp. 50-57).

Bojjagani, S., Reddy, Y. P., Anuradha, T., Rao, P. V., Reddy, B. R., & Khan, M. K. (2022). Secure authentication and key management protocol for deployment of internet of vehicles (IoV) concerning intelligent transport systems. *IEEE Transactions on Intelligent Transportation Systems*, *23*(12), 24698–24713. DOI: 10.1109/TITS.2022.3207593

Bokka, R., & Sadasivam, T. (2024). Simulation-based Analysis of RPL Routing Attacks and Their Impact on IoT Network Performance. *Journal of Electronic Testing*, *40*(2), 1–15. DOI: 10.1007/s10836-024-06106-w

Bonneau, J., Herley, C., van Oorschot, P. C., & Stajano, F. (2015). Passwords and the evolution of imperfect authentication. *Communications of the ACM*, *58*(7), 78–87. DOI: 10.1145/2699390

Boudouaia, M. A.-P., Ali-Pacha, A., Abouaissa, A., & Lorenz, P. (2020). Security against rank attack in RPL protocol. *IEEE Network*, *34*(4), 133–139. DOI: 10.1109/MNET.011.1900651

Bradley, S. (2024). Comparative Analysis of Two Data Privacy Regulatory Schemes: The GDPR and the CCPA.

Bubukayr, M. A. S., & Almaiah, M. A. (2021, July). Cybersecurity concerns in smart-phones and applications: A survey. In 2021 international conference on information technology (ICIT) (pp. 725-731). IEEE.

Buzzio-Garcia, J. (2021, July). Creation of a high-interaction honeypot system based-on docker containers. In 2021 Fifth World Conference on Smart Trends in Systems Security and Sustainability (WorldS4) (pp. 146-151). IEEE.

Canis, B. (2019). *Issues in autonomous vehicle testing and deployment (No. R45985)*. Congressional Research Service.

Cavoukian, A., Taylor, S., & Abrams, M. E. (2010). Privacy by Design: Essential for Organizational Accountability and Strong Business Practices. *Identity in the Information Society*, *3*(2), 405–413. DOI: 10.1007/s12394-010-0053-z

Cavus, N., Mohammed, Y. B., Bulama, M., & Isah, M. L. (2023). Examining User Verification Schemes, Safety, and Secrecy Issues Affecting M-Banking: Systematic Literature Review. *SAGE Open*, *13*(1), 1–18. DOI: 10.1177/21582440231152379

CERT Coordination Center. (1999). Melissa Virus Advisory. CERT Advisory CA-1999-04.

Chamola, V. J., Jolfaei, A., Chanana, V., Parashari, P., & Hassija, V. (2021). Information security in the post quantum era for 5G and beyond networks: Threats to existing cryptogra- phy, and post-quantum cryptography. *Computer Communications*, *176*, 99–1. DOI: 10.1016/j.comcom.2021.05.019

Chan, J. (2022). Facial Recognition Technology and Ethical Issues. *Proceedings of the Wellington Faculty of Engineering Ethics and Sustainability Symposium*. DOI: 10.26686/wfeess.vi.7647

Chaudhuri, A., & Bozkus Kahyaoglu, S. (2023). Cybersecurity assurance in smart cities: A risk management perspective. *EDPACS*, *67*(4), 1–22. DOI: 10.1080/07366981.2023.2165293

Chauhan, D. IPv6 Migration Strategy Using Carrier Grade Network Address Translation.

Chauhan, D., & Jain, J. K. (2023, January). Profiling Network Traffic by Using Classification Techniques in Machine Learning. In *International Conference on Smart Trends in Computing and Communications* (pp. 113-123). Singapore: Springer Nature Singapore. DOI: 10.1007/978-981-99-0769-4_12

Chauhan, D., & Jain, J. K. (2024). Measures and Preventions of Cyber Policies in Smart Cities. In *Digital Technologies in Modeling and Management: Insights in Education and Industry* (pp. 244-262). IGI Global.

Chauhan, D., Jain, J. K., & Sharma, S. (2016, December). An end-to-end header compression for multihop IPv6 tunnels with varying bandwidth. In 2016 Fifth international conference on eco-friendly computing and communication systems (ICECCS) (pp. 84-88). IEEE. DOI: 10.1109/Eco-friendly.2016.7893247

Chauhan, D., Jain, J. K., & Singh, A. (2024). Deployment of Edge Computing for Smart Healthcare Systems on Cloud Computing Platform.

Chauhan, D., & Jain, J. K. (2019). A Journey from IoT to IoE. [IJITEE]. *International Journal of Innovative Technology and Exploring Engineering*, *8*(11).

Chauhan, D., & Jain, J. K. (2021). IoT and Blockchain in Indian Perspective. In *Blockchain Applications in IoT Security* (pp. 186–202). IGI Global. DOI: 10.4018/978-1-7998-2414-5.ch011

Chauhan, D., Jain, J. K., & Bahad, P. (2021). PERFORMANCE EVALUATION OF 802.11 A/G WIRELESS NETWORKS WITH IP6HC. *Journal of Management Information and Decision Sciences*, *24*, 1–7.

Chauhan, D., Sharma, S., & Singh, V. (2023). Roadmap from 4G to 6G in smart cities impact and challenges. [IJWMT]. *Int. J. Wirel. Microw. Technol.*, *13*(6), 39–50. DOI: 10.5815/ijwmt.2023.06.05

Chen, B., & Zhen, M. J. (2021). A survey of software log instrumentation. *ACM Computing Surveys*, *54*(4), 1–34.

Choi, I., Hao, J., Deane, P., & Zhang, M. (2021). *Benchmark keystroke biometrics accuracy from high-stakes writing tasks*. ETS., DOI: 10.1002/ets2.12326

Chow, M. C., & Ma, M. (2022). A secure blockchain-based authentication and key agreement scheme for 3GPP 5G networks. *Sensors (Basel)*, *22*(12), 4525. DOI: 10.3390/s22124525 PMID: 35746307

Chuang, Y. H., Lin, B. S., Chen, Y. X., & Shiu, H. J. (2021). Steganography in RGB images using adjacent mean. *IEEE Access : Practical Innovations, Open Solutions*, *9*, 164256–164274.

Ciancaglini, V., Balduzzi, M., Goncharov, M., & McArdle, R. (2013). *Deepweb and cybercrime* (Tech. Rep. No. 9). Trend Micro.

Cletus, A., Weyory, B., & Opoku, A. (2022). Improving social engineering awareness, training and education (SEATE) using a behavioral change model. *International Journal of Advanced Computer Science and Applications*, *13*(5). Advance online publication. DOI: 10.14569/IJACSA.2022.0130572

Cohen, F. (1987). Computer Viruses: Theory and Experiments. *Computers & Security*, *6*(1), 22–35. DOI: 10.1016/0167-4048(87)90122-2

Collins, M. D. (2024). Superflows: A New Tool for Forensic Network Flow Analysis. *arXiv preprint arXiv:2403.01314.*

Conway, M. (2014). What is Cyberterrorism and How Real is the Threat? A Review of the Academic Literature, 1996–2009. Cyber Behavior: Concepts, Methodologies, Tools, and Applications, 217-245.

Cybersecurity, C. I. (2018). Framework for improving critical infrastructure cybersecurity. https://nvlpubs. nist. gov/nistpubs/CSWP/NIST

Dahia, G., Jesus, L., & Pamplona Segundo, M. (2020). Continuous authentication using biometrics: An advanced review. *Wiley Interdisciplinary Reviews. Data Mining and Knowledge Discovery*, *10*(4), e1365. DOI: 10.1002/widm.1365

Das, D. B. (2023). Blockchain enabled sdn framework for security management in 5g applications. *In Proceedings of the 24th International Conference on Distributed Computing and.* In Proceedings of the 24th International Conference on Dis- tributed Computing and.

Denning, D. E. (1999). *Information Warfare and Security*. Addison-Wesley.

Dhanaraj, R. K., Lalitha, K., Anitha, S., Khaitan, S., Gupta, P., & Goyal, M. K. (2021). Hybrid and dynamic clustering based data aggregation and routing for wireless sensor networks. In Journal of Intelligent & Fuzzy Systems (Vol. 40, Issue 6, pp. 10751–10765). IOS Press. DOI: 10.3233/JIFS-201756

Dhanaraj, R. K., Ramakrishnan, V., Poongodi, M., Krishnasamy, L., Hamdi, M., Kotecha, K., & Vijayakumar, V. (2021). Random Forest Bagging and X-Means Clustered Antipattern Detection from SQL Query Log for Accessing Secure Mobile Data. In Jain, D. K. (Ed.), *Wireless Communications and Mobile Computing* (Vol. 2021, pp. 1–9). Hindawi Limited., DOI: 10.1155/2021/2730246

Dhwaniket Ramesh, N. J. (2015). DIGITAL FORENSIC TOOLS: A COMPARATIVE APPROACH . *International Journal of Advance Research In Science And Engineering.*

DiGiacomo, J. (2021), 'Top Data Breaches of 2020: Ransomware on The Rise. Revision Legal', Retrieved from https://revisionlegal.com/internet-law/data-breach/data-breach-statistics-for-2020/

Doubleday, H., Maglaras, L., & Janicke, H. (2016). SSH honeypot: Building, deploying and analysis. *International Journal of Advanced Computer Science and Applications*, *7*(5).

Dunsin, D. G., Ghanem, M. C., Ouazzane, K., & Vassilev, V. (2024). A comprehensive analysis of the role of artificial intelligence and machine learning in modern digital forensics and incident response. *Forensic Science International Digital Investigation*, *48*, 301675. DOI: 10.1016/j.fsidi.2023.301675

Dworkin, M. (2001). *Recommendation for Block Cipher Modes of Operation.* Methods and Techniques.

Eesa, A. S., Orman, Z., & Brifcani, A. M. A. (2015). A novel feature-selection approach based on the cuttlefish optimization algorithm for intrusion detection systems. *Expert Systems with Applications*, *42*(5), 2670–2679. DOI: 10.1016/j.eswa.2014.11.009

Egele, M., Scholte, T., Kirda, E., & Kruegel, C. (2008). A Survey on Automated Dynamic Malware Analysis Techniques and Tools. *ACM Computing Surveys*, *44*(2), 6.

Enders, C. K. (2021). A primer on maximum likelihood algorithms available for use with missing data. *Structural Equation Modeling*, *8*(1), 128–141. DOI: 10.1207/S15328007SEM0801_7

Ezugwu, A. E., Agushaka, J. O., Abualigah, L., Mirjalili, S., & Gandomi, A. H. (2022). Prairie dog optimization algorithm. *Neural Computing & Applications*, *34*(22), 20017–20065. DOI: 10.1007/s00521-022-07530-9

Face Recognition Using Eigenfaces. (n.d.). Retrieved September 3, 2024, from https://www.researchgate.net/publication/281446070_Face_Recognition_Using_Eigenfaces

Fadel, M. M., El-Ghamrawy, S. M., Ali-Eldin, A. M., Hassan, M. K., & El-Desoky, A. I. (2022). The proposed hybrid deep learning intrusion prediction IoT (HDLIP-IoT) framework. *PLoS One*, *17*(7), e027143. DOI: 10.1371/journal.pone.0271436 PMID: 35905101

Farah, M. B.-K., Ahmed, Y., Mahmoud, H., Shah, S. A., Al-kadri, M. O., Taramonli, S., Bellekens, X., Abozariba, R., Idrissi, M., & Aneiba, A. (2024). A survey on blockchain technology in the maritime industry: Challenges and future perspectives. *Future Generation Computer Systems*, *157*, 618–637. DOI: 10.1016/j.future.2024.03.046

Fatima, M., & Pasha, M. (2017). Survey of machine learning algorithms for disease diagnostic. *Journal of Intelligent Learning Systems and Applications*, *9*(01), 1–16. DOI: 10.4236/jilsa.2017.91001

Fayzi, A., Fayzi, M., & Ahmadi, K. D. (2023). Dark web activity classification using deep learning. https://arxiv.org/abs/2306.07980

Fernandez-Carames, T. M., & Fraga-Lamas, P. (2020). Towards post-quantum blockchain: A review on blockchain cryptography resistant to quantum computing attacks. *IEEE Access : Practical Innovations, Open Solutions*, *8*, 21091–21116. DOI: 10.1109/ACCESS.2020.2968985

Fidalgo, E., Alegre, E., Fernández-Robles, L., & González-Castro, V. (2019). Classifying suspicious content in tor darknet through Semantic Attention Keypoint Filtering. *Digital Investigation*, *30*, 12–22. DOI: 10.1016/j.diin.2019.05.004

Figueras-Martín, E., Magán-Carrión, R., & Boubeta-Puig, J. (2022). Drawing the web structure and content analysis beyond the tor darknet: Freenet as a case of study. *Journal of Information Security and Applications*, *68*, 103229. DOI: 10.1016/j.jisa.2022.103229

Fossi, M., Egan, G., Haley, K., Johnson, E., Mack, T., Adams, T., ... & Wood, P. (2011). Symantec internet security threat report trends for 2010. Volume XVI.

Friedl, S. R. (2024). Digital Detectives: A Serious Point-and-Click Game for Digital Forensics. In IFIP World Conference on Information Security Education Cham. *Springer Nature Switzerland.*, (pp. (pp. 129-145).). DOI: 10.1007/978-3-031-62918-1_9

Gaba, G. S., Hedabou, M., Kumar, P., Braeken, A., Liyanage, M., & Alazab, M. (2022). Zero knowledge proofs based authenticated key agreement protocol for sustainable healthcare. *Sustainable Cities and Society*, *80*, 103766. DOI: 10.1016/j.scs.2022.103766

Gaba, P. R.-S., Raw, R. S., Kaiwartya, O., & Aljaidi, M. (2024). Blockchain-Enabled Security Architecture for Connected Vehicle Fog Environment. *Sensors (Basel)*, *24*(5), 1515. DOI: 10.3390/s24051515 PMID: 38475051

Gao, J., Wang, Y., Song, Z., & Wang, S. (2023). Quantum image encryption based on quantum DNA codec and pixel-level scrambling. *Entropy (Basel, Switzerland)*, *25*(6), 865.

Gentry, C. (2009). *A fully homomorphic encryption scheme*. Stanford university.

Ghaleb, B. A.-D. (2023). (POSTER) Resolving the Decreased Rank Attack in RPL's IoT Networks. *1. In 2023 19th International Conference on Distributed Computing in Smart Systems and the Internet of Things (DCOSS-IoT) (pp. 65-67). IEEE.* .

Goel, A. K., Bakshi, R., & Agrawal, K. K. (2022). Web 3.0 and decentralized applications. *Materials Proceedings*, *10*(1), 8.

Goldwasser, S. M. (2019). The knowledge complexity of interactive proof-systems. In Pro- viding sound foundations for cryptography: On the work of shafi goldwasser and silvio micali. (pp. 203-225). DOI: 10.1145/3335741.3335750

Gordon, L. A., Loeb, M. P., & Lucyshyn, W. (2003). The Economic Impact of Cyber-Attacks. *Journal of Computer Security*, *11*(5), 431–448.

Grasser, A., & Parger, A. (2022, September). Blockchain architectures, the potential of Web3 for decentralized participatory architecture: Collaborative objects on the blockchain. In *40th Conference on Education and Research in Computer Aided Architectural Design in Europe: eCAADe 2022* (pp. 431-440).

Grass, R. N., Lipton, R. J., Frazer, P. J., Frenkel, C. D., & Gaudet, S. J. (2000). Logical security of information in DNA. *Bioinformatics (Oxford, England)*, *16*(8), 788–791.

Grigollo, F. V., & Fernandes, R. F. (2024). Comparative analysis of software used in anonymised search and seizure cases: Acquisition, examination and analysis. *Caderno Pedagógico, 21*(4), e3557–e3557. DOI: 10.54033/cadpedv21n4-015

Guleria, A., Krishan, K., Sharma, V., & Kanchan, T. (2024). Global adoption of facial recognition technology with special reference to India—Present status and future recommendations. *Medicine, Science, and the Law*, *64*(3), 236–244. DOI: 10.1177/00258024241227717 PMID: 38263636

Gunalakshmi, S., & Ezhumalai, P. (2014). Mobile keylogger detection using machine learning technique. In *Proceedings of IEEE International Conference on Computer Communication and Systems ICCCS14*, Chennai, India, pp. 051-056. DOI: 10.1109/ICCCS.2014.7068167

Gund, V. D.. (2023). PIR Sensor-Based Arduino Home Security System. *Journal of Instrumentation and Innovation Sciences*, *8*(3), 33–37.

Gupta, H. B. (2024). Security Analysis of RPL-Based IoT Networks: Evaluating the Impact of Attacks on Performance Parameters. *International Conference on Advancements in Smart, Secure and Intelligent Computing*. DOI: 10.1109/AS-SIC60049.2024.10508014

Hafner, K., & Markoff, J. (1991). *Cyberpunk: Outlaws and Hackers on the Computer Frontier*. Simon & Schuster.

Hajimirzaei, B., & Navimipour, N. J. (2019). Intrusion detection for cloud computing using neural networks and artificial bee colony optimization algorithm. *ICT Express*, *5*(1), 56–59. DOI: 10.1016/j.icte.2018.01.014

Halli, U. M. (2022). Nanotechnology in IoT Security, *Journal of Nanoscience. Nanoengineering & Applications*, *12*(3), 11–16.

Hamamoto, A. H., Carvalho, L. F., & Proenca, M. L. (2015). ACO and GA meta-heuristics for anomaly detection. *2015 34th International Conference of the Chilean Computer Science Society (SCCC)*, 1–6.

Hameed, S. M., Sa'adoon, H. A., & Al-Ani, M. (2018). Image encryption using DNA encoding and RC4 algorithm. *Iraqi Journal of Science*, 434–446.

Handayani, F. (2022). Design And Legal Aspect Of Central Bank Digital Currency: A Literature Review. *Journal of Central Banking Law and Institutions*, *1*(3), 509–536. DOI: 10.21098/jcli.v1i3.35

Hargreaves, C. N., Nelson, A., & Casey, E. (2024). An abstract model for digital forensic analysis tools-A foundation for systematic error mitigation analysis. *Forensic Science International Digital Investigation*, *48*, 301679. DOI: 10.1016/j.fsidi.2023.301679

Hariharasitaraman, S., Mishra, N., & Vishnuvardhanan, D. (2024). QHopNN: Investigating quantum advantage in cryptanalysis using a quantum hopfield neural network. *Physica Scripta*, *99*(8), 086002. DOI: 10.1088/1402-4896/ad5ed1

Hasan, J. (2019). Overview and applications of zero knowledge proof (ZKP). *International Journal of Computer Science and Network*, *8*(5), 2277–5420.

Haselton, T. (2017). *Yahoo just said every single account was affected by 2013 attack - 3 billion in all.* CNBC.

Heidari, A. A., Mirjalili, S., Faris, H., Aljarah, I., Mafarja, M., & Chen, H. (2019). Harris hawks optimization: Algorithm and applications. *Future Generation Computer Systems*, *97*, 849–872. DOI: 10.1016/j.future.2019.02.028

Hendrawan, A. H. (2024). Enhancing Cybersecurity Through Live Forensic Investigation of Remote Access Trojan Attacks using FTK Imager Software. *International Journal of Safety and Security Engineering.*

Herzog, S. (2011). Revisiting the Estimation of Economic Impact of Cyber Attacks: Focus on Operational Disruption. *Journal of Cybersecurity*, *7*(3), 267–284.

Hkiri, A. A., Alqurashi, S., Ben Bahri, O., Karmani, M., Faraj, H., & Machhout, M. (2024). Performance Evaluation of Mobile RPL-Based IoT Networks under Hello Flood Attack. *Electronics (Basel)*, *13*(11), 2226. DOI: 10.3390/electronics13112226

Hkiri, A. K. (2024). RPL-Based IoT Networks under Decreased Rank Attack: Performance Analysis in Static and Mobile Environments. *Computers, Materials & Continua*, *78*(1), 227–247. DOI: 10.32604/cmc.2023.047087

Hofmeyr, S. A., Forrest, S., & Somayaji, A. (1998). Intrusion Detection Using Sequences of System Calls. *Journal of Computer Security*, *6*(3), 151–180. DOI: 10.3233/JCS-980109

Horkay, J., Tymofiiv, V., & Al-Rabeei, S. (2022). Using Biometrics for Facial Recognition at Airports. *Acta Avionica Journal*, 34–40. DOI: 10.35116/aa.2022.0029

Hovav, A., & D'Arcy, J. (2003). The Impact of Denial-of-Service Attack Announcements on the Market Value of Firms. *Risk Management & Insurance Review*, *6*(2), 97–121. DOI: 10.1046/J.1098-1616.2003.026.x

Huang, K. T., Chiu, J. H., & Shen, S. S. (2013). A novel structure with dynamic operation mode for symmetric-key block ciphers. *International Journal of Network Security & its Applications*, *5*(1), 17–36. DOI: 10.5121/ijnsa.2013.5102

Huang, R., & Kou, W. (2015). Cybersecurity in Industrial Control Systems: A Case Study Approach. *IEEE Transactions on Industry Applications*, *51*(5), 4211–4220.

Huang, R., & Pearce, A. (2014). Cyber-Physical Attacks and Effective Security Monitoring Strategies. *International Journal of Critical Infrastructure Protection*, *7*(3), 144–150.

Hubbard, K. B., Birycka, M., Britton, M.-E., Coates, J., Coxon, I. D., Jackson, C. H., Nicholas, C. L., Priestley, T. M., Robins, J. J., Ryczko, P. R., Salisbury, T., Shand, M., Snodin, G., & Worsley, B. (2024). The 'Tea Test'-a mobile phone based spectrophotometer protocol to introduce biochemical methods independent of the laboratory. *Journal of Biological Education*, *58*(2), 483–494. DOI: 10.1080/00219266.2022.2072934

Hung, C.-W., Hsu, F.-H., Chen, S.-J., Tso, C.-K., Hwang, Y.-L., Lin, P.-C., & Hsu, L.-P. (2012). A QTE-based Solution to Keylogger Attacks. *The Sixth International Conference on Emerging Security Information, Systems and Technologies (SECURWARE 2012)*, Rome, Italy.

Hunton, P. (2009). The growing phenomenon of crime and the internet: A cybercrime execution and analysis model. *Computer Law & Security Report*, *25*(6), 528–535. DOI: 10.1016/j.clsr.2009.09.005

Ibrahim, D., Ahmed, K., Abdallah, M., & Ali, A. A. (2022). A new chaotic-based RGB image encryption technique using a nonlinear rotational 16× 16 DNA playfair matrix. *Cryptography*, *6*(2), 28.

Idhaim, H. A.-s. (2023). Internal Hidden Processing Model-Based for SELECT Command in Struc- tured Query Language. *24th International Arab Con- ference on Information Technolog.IEEE Access : Practical Innovations, Open Solutions.*

Ioannis, T. S. (2016). Evaluation of Digital Forensics Tools on Data Recovery and Analysis.

Iqbal, N., Hanif, M., Abbas, S., Khan, M. A., Almotiri, S. H., & Al Ghamdi, M. A. (2020). DNA strands level scrambling based color image encryption scheme. *IEEE Access : Practical Innovations, Open Solutions*, *8*, 178167–178182.

Iqbal, N., Naqvi, R. A., Atif, M., Khan, M. A., Hanif, M., Abbas, S., & Hussain, D. (2021). On the image encryption algorithm based on the chaotic system, dna encoding, and castle. *IEEE Access : Practical Innovations, Open Solutions*, *9*, 118253–118270.

Islam, M. T., & Huda, N. (2019). Material flow analysis (MFA) as a strategic tool in E-waste management: Applications, trends and future directions. *Journal of Environmental Management, 244*, 344–361. DOI: 10.1016/j.jenvman.2019.05.062 PMID: 31129466

Jain, J. K., & Chauhan, D. (2019, April). Analytical study on Mobile Ad hoc Networks for IPV6. In *2019 4th International Conference on Internet of Things: Smart Innovation and Usages (IoT-SIU)* (pp. 1-6). IEEE. DOI: 10.1109/IoT-SIU.2019.8777486

Jain, J. K., Waoo, A. A., & Chauhan, D. (2022). A literature review on machine learning for cyber security issues. *International Journal of Scientific Research in Computer Science, Engineering and Information Technology*, 374-385.

Jain, A. (2021). Secure Authentication for Banking Using Face Recognition. [JIEEE]. *Journal of Informatics Electrical and Electronics Engineering*, 2(2), 1–8. DOI: 10.54060/JIEEE/002.02.001

Jain, J. K., & Chauhan, D. (2021). An Energy-Efficient Model for Internet of Things Using Compressive Sensing. *Journal of Management Information and Decision Sciences, 24*, 1–7.

Jain, J. K., & Chauhan, D. (2023). Innovative Model of Internet of Things for Industrial Applications. In *Opportunities and Challenges of Industrial IoT in 5G and 6G Networks* (pp. 95–118). IGI Global. DOI: 10.4018/978-1-7998-9266-3.ch005

Jain, J. K., Dangi, C. S., & Chauhan, D. (2020, November). An Efficient Multipath Productive Routing Protocol for Mobile Ad-hoc Networks. In *2020 IEEE International Conference for Innovation in Technology (INOCON)* (pp. 1-5). IEEE. DOI: 10.1109/INOCON50539.2020.9298291

Jain, J. K., & Sharma, S. (2013). Performance Evaluation of Hybrid Multipath Progressive Routing Protocol for MANETs. *International Journal of Computer Applications, 71*(18).

Jain, J. K., & Sharma, S. (2017). A Novel Approach of Routing Protocol using Hybrid Analysis for MANETs. *International Journal of Computer Science and Information Security, 15*(1), 582.

Jaradat, A. S.-N. (2023). *Genetic optimization techniques for enhancing web attacks classification in machine learning*. IEEE Intl Conf on Dependable, Autonomic and Secure Co. DOI: 10.1109/DASC/PiCom/CBDCom/Cy59711.2023.10361399

Jaradat, A. S.-N. (2023). *Genetic optimization techniques for enhancing web attacks classification in machine learning. In 2023 IEEE Intl Conf on Dependable*. Autonomic and Secure Co.

Jayalaxmi, P. L. S., Saha, R., Kumar, G., Conti, M., & Kim, T. H. (2022). Machine and Deep Learning Solutions for Intrusion Detection and Prevention in IoTs: A Survey. *IEEE Access : Practical Innovations, Open Solutions*, *10*, 121173–121192. DOI: 10.1109/ACCESS.2022.3220622

Jayaweera, N., Rajatheva, N., & Latva-aho, M. (2019, April). Autonomous driving without a burden: View from outside with elevated LiDAR. In 2019 IEEE 89th Vehicular Technology Conference (VTC2019-Spring) (pp. 1-7). IEEE.

Jeong, J. J., Zolotavkin, Y., & Doss, R. (2024). Examining the current status and emerging trends in continuous authentication technologies through citation network analysis. *ACM Computing Surveys*, *55*(6), 1–31. DOI: 10.1145/3533705

Jiang, X. L. (2024). Privacy-Preserving UCB Decision Process Verifica- tion via zk-SNARKs. 2404.12186.

Jiang, Q., Zhang, X., Zhang, N., Tian, Y., Ma, X., & Ma, J. (2021). Three-factor authentication protocol using physical unclonable function for IoV. *Computer Communications*, *173*, 45–55. DOI: 10.1016/j.comcom.2021.03.022

Jinad, R. G., Gupta, K., Simsek, E., & Zhou, B. (2024). Bias and fairness in software and automation tools in digital forensics. *J. Surveill. Secur. Saf*, *5*(1), 19–35. DOI: 10.20517/jsss.2023.41

Jin, H., Wang, M., Wang, L., Yang, Q., Li, Y., Long, X., & Liu, T. (2024, July). The research focuses on the symmetric encryption scheme for industrial data based on MQTT. In *International Conference on Signal Processing and Communication Security (ICSPCS 2024)* (Vol. 13222, pp. 51-57). SPIE. DOI: 10.1117/12.3038673

Jin, P., Kim, N., Lee, S., & Jeong, D. (2023). Forensic investigation of the dark web on the tor network: Pathway toward the surface web. *International Journal of Information Security*, *23*(1), 331–346. DOI: 10.1007/s10207-023-00745-4

Juneja, M., & Sandhu, P. S. (2013). An improved LSB based steganography technique for RGB color images. *International Journal of Computer and Communication Engineering*, *2*(4), 513.

Jung, J. H., Han, S., Park, M., & Cho, S. (2024). Automotive digital forensics through data and log analysis of vehicle diagnosis Android apps. *Forensic Science International Digital Investigation*, *49*, 301752. DOI: 10.1016/j.fsidi.2024.301752

Juvonen, A., Costin, A., Turtiainen, H., & Hamalainen, T. (2022). On Apache Log4j2 Exploitation in Aeronautical, Maritime, and Aerospace Communication. *IEEE Access : Practical Innovations, Open Solutions*, *10*, 86542–86557. DOI: 10.1109/ACCESS.2022.3198947

Kaaniche, N., & Laurent, M. (2017). Data security and privacy preservation in cloud storage environments based on cryptographic mechanisms. *Computer Communications, 111*, 120–141. DOI: 10.1016/j.comcom.2017.07.006

Kaleem, M., Mushtaq, M. A., Jamil, U., Ramay, S. A., Khan, T. A., Patel, S., & Hussain, S. K. (2024). New Efficient Cryptographic Techniques For Cloud Computing Security. *Migration Letters : An International Journal of Migration Studies, 21*(S11), 13–28.

Kamble, N., & Mishra, N. (2024a). Hybrid optimization enabled squeeze net for phishing attack detection. *Computers & Security, 144*, 103901. DOI: 10.1016/j.cose.2024.103901

Kamble, N., & Mishra, N. (2024b, January). Securing Cyberspace: Unveiling Phishing Attacks Through Deep Neural Networks for Enhanced Detection. In *2024 International Conference on Advancements in Smart, Secure and Intelligent Computing (ASSIC)* (pp. 1-5). IEEE. DOI: 10.1109/ASSIC60049.2024.10508000

Kamel, S., & Elhamayed, S. (2020). Mitigating the impact of IoT routing attacks on power consumption in IoT healthcare environment using convolutional neural network. *Int. J. Comput. Netw. Inf. Secur., 12*, 11–29. DOI: 10.5815/ijcnis.2020.04.02

Kandhro, I. A., Alanazi, S. M., Ali, F., Kehar, A., Fatima, K., Uddin, M., & Karuppayah, S. (2023). Detection of Real-Time Malicious Intrusions and Attacks in IoT Empowered Cybersecurity Infrastructures. *IEEE Access : Practical Innovations, Open Solutions, 11*, 9136–9148. DOI: 10.1109/ACCESS.2023.3238664

Karale Aishwarya A, et al,(2023). Smart Billing Cart Using RFID, YOLO and Deep Learning for Mall Administration, *International Journal of Instrumentation and Innovation Sciences*, Vol 8, Issue- 2.

Karim, N. A., Khashan, O. A., Kanaker, H., Abdulraheem, W. K., Alshinwan, M., & Albanna, A. (2023). Online Banking User Authentication Methods: A Systematic Literature Review. *IEEE Access : Practical Innovations, Open Solutions.*

Karmakar, S. S. (2021). LEADER: low overhead rank attack detection for securing RPL based IoT. *In 2021 International Conference on COMmunication Systems & NETworkS (COMSNETS)* (pp. (pp. 429-437).). IEEE.

Kasat, K., Shaikh, N., Rayabharapu, V. K., & Nayak, M. (2023). Implementation and Recognition of Waste Management System with Mobility Solution in Smart Cities using Internet of Things, *2023 Second International Conference on Augmented Intelligence and Sustainable Systems (ICAISS)*, Trichy, India, 2023, pp. 1661-1665, DOI: 10.1109/ICAISS58487.2023.10250690

Kaur, G., Khurana, M., & Sethi, M. (2011, July). Intrusion detection system using honeypots and swarm intelligence. In *Proceedings of the International Conference on Advances in Computing and Artificial Intelligence* (pp. 34-38). DOI: 10.1145/2007052.2007060

Kaushik, K., Dass, A., & Dhankhar, A. (2022, November). An approach for exploiting and mitigating Log4J using Log4Shell vulnerability. In 2022 3rd International Conference on Computation, Automation and Knowledge Management (ICCAKM) (pp. 1-6). IEEE.

Kazi K S,(2023b). IoT based Healthcare system for Home Quarantine People, *Journal of Instrumentation and Innovation sciences,*, Vol 8, Issue 1, pp. 1- 8

Kazi, K. (2024b). Modelling and Simulation of Electric Vehicle for Performance Analysis: BEV and HEV Electrical Vehicle Implementation Using Simulink for E-Mobility Ecosystems. *In L. D., N. Nagpal, N. Kassarwani, V. Varthanan G., & P. Siano (Eds.), E-Mobility in Electrical Energy Systems for Sustainability* (pp. 295-320). IGI Global. Available at: https://www.igi-global.com/gateway/chapter/full-text-pdf/341172DOI: 10.4018/979-8-3693-2611-4.ch014

Kazi, K. (2022). Detection of Malicious Nodes in IoT Networks based on packet loss using ML, *Journal of Mobile Computing, Communication & mobile. Networks*, *9*(3), 9–16.

Kazi, K. (2024). Complications with Malware Identification in IoT and an Overview of Artificial Immune Approaches. *Research & Reviews. The Journal of Immunology : Official Journal of the American Association of Immunologists*, *14*(01), 54–62.

Kazi, K. (2024a). AI-Driven IoT (AIIoT) in Healthcare Monitoring. In Nguyen, T., & Vo, N. (Eds.), *Using Traditional Design Methods to Enhance AI-Driven Decision Making* (pp. 77–101). IGI Global., available at https://www.igi-global.com/chapter/ai-driven-iot-aiiot-in-healthcare-monitoring/336693, DOI: 10.4018/979-8-3693-0639-0.ch003

Kazi, K. (2024a). IoT Technologies for the Intelligent Dairy Industry: A New Challenge. In Thandekkattu, S. G., & Vajjhala, N. R. (Eds.), *Designing Sustainable Internet of Things Solutions for Smart Industries*. IGI Global. DOI: 10.4018/979-8-3693-5498-8.ch012

Kazi, K. (2024a). Machine Learning (ML)-Based Braille Lippi Characters and Numbers Detection and Announcement System for Blind Children in Learning. In Sart, G. (Ed.), *Social Reflections of Human-Computer Interaction in Education, Management, and Economics*. IGI Global., DOI: 10.4018/979-8-3693-3033-3.ch002

Kazi, K. (2024b). Artificial Intelligence (AI)-Driven IoT (AIIoT)-Based Agriculture Automation. In Satapathy, S., & Muduli, K. (Eds.), *Advanced Computational Methods for Agri-Business Sustainability*. IGI Global., DOI: 10.4018/979-8-3693-3583-3.ch005

Kazi, K. (2024b). Machine Learning-Driven-Internet of Things(MLIoT) Based Healthcare Monitoring System. In Wickramasinghe, N. (Ed.), *Impact of Digital Solutions for Improved Healthcare Delivery*. IGI Global.

Kazi, K. (2024c). AI-Powered-IoT (AIIoT) based Decision Making System for BP Patient's Healthcare Monitoring: KSK Approach for BP Patient Healthcare Monitoring. In Aouadni, S., & Aouadni, I. (Eds.), *Recent Theories and Applications for Multi-Criteria Decision-Making*. IGI Global. DOI: 10.4018/979-8-3693-6502-1.ch008

Kazi, K. (2024c). Moonlighting in Carrier. In Tunio, M. N. (Ed.), *Applications of Career Transitions and Entrepreneurship*. IGI Global.

Kazi, K. S. (2022). IoT-Based Healthcare Monitoring for COVID-19 Home Quarantined Patients. *Recent Trends in Sensor Research & Technology*, *9*(3), 26–32.

Kazi, K. S. (2023a). Detection of Malicious Nodes in IoT Networks based on Throughput and ML. *Journal of Electrical and Power System Engineering*, *9*(1), 22–29.

Kazi, K. S. (2024). Machine Learning-Based Pomegranate Disease Detection and Treatment. In Zia Ul Haq, M., & Ali, I. (Eds.), *Revolutionizing Pest Management for Sustainable Agriculture* (pp. 469–498). IGI Global., DOI: 10.4018/979-8-3693-3061-6.ch019

Kazi, K. S. (2024a). Computer-Aided Diagnosis in Ophthalmology: A Technical Review of Deep Learning Applications. In Garcia, M., & de Almeida, R. (Eds.), *Transformative Approaches to Patient Literacy and Healthcare Innovation* (pp. 112–135). IGI Global., Available at https://www.igi-global.com/chapter/computer-aided-diagnosis-in-ophthalmology/342823, DOI: 10.4018/979-8-3693-3661-8.ch006

Kazi, K. S. (2024b). IoT Driven by Machine Learning (MLIoT) for the Retail Apparel Sector. In Tarnanidis, T., Papachristou, E., Karypidis, M., & Ismyrlis, V. (Eds.), *Driving Green Marketing in Fashion and Retail* (pp. 63–81). IGI Global., DOI: 10.4018/979-8-3693-3049-4.ch004

Kazi, K. S. L. (2024). IoT and Sensor-based Smart Agriculturing Driven by NodeMCU. *Research & Review: Electronics and Communication Engineering*, *1*(2), 25–33.

Kazi, K. S. L. (2024). Smart Agriculture based on AI-Driven-IoT(AIIoT): A KSK Approach, *Advance Research in Communication Engineering and its. Innovations*, *1*(2), 23–32.

Kazi, V.. (2023). Deep Learning, YOLO and RFID based smart Billing Handcart. *Journal of Communication Engineering & Systems*, *13*(1), 1–8.

Kelly, C., Pitropakis, N., Mylonas, A., McKeown, S., & Buchanan, W. J. (2021). A comparative analysis of honeypots on different cloud platforms. *Sensors (Basel)*, *21*(7), 2433.

Khan, M. A. (2016). A survey of security issues for cloud computing. *Journal of Network and Computer Applications*, *71*, 11–29. DOI: 10.1016/j.jnca.2016.05.010

Khan, P. W., & Byun, Y. (2020). A blockchain-based secure image encryption scheme for the industrial Internet of Things. *Entropy (Basel, Switzerland)*, *22*(2), 175.

Khraisat, A., Gondal, I., Vamplew, P., & Kamruzzaman, J. (2019). Survey of intrusion detection systems: Techniques, datasets and challenges. *Cybersecurity*, *2*(1), 1–22. DOI: 10.1186/s42400-019-0038-7

Klasén, L. F. (2024). Digital Forensics as Key to Solving Crimes in the Digital Age. *The Invisible Evidence: Forensic Science International, 112133.*

Koniaris, I., Papadimitriou, G., & Nicopolitidis, P. (2013). *"Analysis and visualization of SSH attacks using honeypots." Eurocon 2013*. IEEE.

Koteras, D. T., Tomczuk, B., & Waindok, A. (2023). Implicit iteration calculations using 3D field analyses, to predict the power loss in powder ferromagnets, with their measurement tests. *Measurement*, *207*, 112311. DOI: 10.1016/j.measurement.2022.112311

Krishnamoorthi, S., Jayapaul, P., Dhanaraj, R. K., Rajasekar, V., Balusamy, B., & Islam, S. K. H. (2021). Design of pseudo-random number generator from turbulence padded chaotic map. *Nonlinear Dynamics*, *104*(2), 1627–1643. Advance online publication. DOI: 10.1007/s11071-021-06346-x

Kruegel, C., Robertson, W., & Vigna, G. (2006). Detecting kernel-level rootkits through binary analysis. In *Proceedings of the Annual Computer Security Applications Conference (ACSAC).*

Kshetri, N. (2010). *The global cybercrime industry: economic, institutional and strategic perspectives*. Springer Science & Business Media. DOI: 10.1007/978-3-642-11522-6

Kumar, A. A.-s. (2022). Recent Trends in Compact Planar Antennas at 5G Sub-6 GHz and mmWave Frequency Bands for Automotive Wireless Applications: a Review. .

Kumar, M. R., & Chouksey, P. (2024). Novel Approach for Encrypting RGB Images Utilizing Quantum Computing. *International Journal of Multidisciplinary Innovation and Research Methodology, 3*(2), 42-56.

Kumar, N. S., Gabriel, S. S. P., & Shankar, M. C. (2024). *Criminal Identification by Face Recognition through Camera Using Image Processing*. www.ijnrd.org

Kumar, R. A. (2024). Development of a Prototype Global Positioning Sys- tem Based Stick for Blind Patients. *International Journal of Online Biomedical Engineering,*.

Kumar, D. D., Mukharzee, J. D., Reddy, C. V. D., & Rajagopal, S. M. (2024, March). Safe and Secure Communication Using SSL/TLS. In *2024 International Conference on Emerging Smart Computing and Informatics (ESCI)* (pp. 1-6). IEEE. DOI: 10.1109/ESCI59607.2024.10497224

Kumar, M., Iqbal, A., & Kumar, P. (2016). A new RGB image encryption algorithm based on DNA encoding and elliptic curve Diffie–Hellman cryptography. *Signal Processing*, *125*, 187–202.

Kutubuddin, K. (2024c). Vehicle Health Monitoring System (VHMS) by Employing IoT and Sensors, *Grenze International Journal of Engineering and Technology,* Vol 10, Issue 2, pp- 5367-5374. Available at: https://thegrenze.com/index.php?display=page&view=journalabstract&absid=3371&id=8

Kutubuddin, K. (2024d). A Novel Approach on ML based Palmistry, *Grenze International Journal of Engineering and Technology,* Vol 10, Issue 2, pp- 5186-5193. Available at: https://thegrenze.com/index.php?display=page&view=journalabstract&absid=3344&id=8

Kutubuddin, K. (2024e). IoT based Boiler Health Monitoring for Sugar Industries, *Grenze. IACSIT International Journal of Engineering and Technology, 10*(2), 5178–5185. https://thegrenze.com/index.php?display=page&view=journalabstract&absid=3343&id=8

Lacombe, F. Facing Modern Crises: An Integrative Literature Review of Pandemics and Cyber Threats Dynamics.

Lai, J., & Arko, E. (2021), 'A Shoulder-Surfing Resistant Scheme Embedded in Traditional Passwords,' *Hawaii International Conference on System Sciences*. DOI: 10.24251/HICSS.2021.860

Laila, D. A.-N. (2024). Enhancing 2D Logistic Chaotic Map for Gray Image Encryption. In I. R. Cybersecurity.

Laila, D. A.-N. (2024). Enhancing 2D Logistic Chaotic Map for Gray Image Encryption. In *Risk Assessment and Countermeasures for Cybersecurity* (pp. (pp. 170-188).).

Laila, D. A.-N. (2024). Enhancing 2D Logistic Chaotic Map for Gray Image Encryption. In *Risk Assessment and Countermeasures for Cybersecurity* (pp. 170-188). IGI Global.

Laila, D. A.-N. (2024). Enhancing 2D Logistic Chaotic Map for Gray Image Encryption. In *Risk Assessment and Countermeasures for Cybersecurity.* (pp. (pp. 170-188). IGI G). IGI Global.

Laila, D. A.-N. (2024). Simulation of Routing Protocols for Jamming Attacks in Mobile Ad-Hoc Network. In G. H., *In Risk Assessment and Countermeasures for Cybersecurity.*

Laila, D. A.-N. (2024). Simulation of Routing Protocols for Jamming Attacks in Mobile Ad-Hoc Network. In *Risk Assessment and Countermeasures for Cybersecurity* (pp. (pp. 235-252).). IGI Global.

Laila, D. A.-N. (2024). Simulation of Routing Protocols for Jamming Attacks in Mobile Ad-Hoc Network. In *Risk Assessment and Countermeasures for Cybersecurity.* "ML Estimation of the Multivariate Distribution and the EM Algorithm.". *Journal of Multivariate Analysis, 63*(2).

Laxmi, S. R., Shraddha, D., Mande, E. R., Guljari, S. S., & Uma, M. (2016). Authentication of Users by Typing Pattern: A Review. *International Journal For Science Technology And Engineering, 2*, 1010–1014.

Le, D., Yue, C., Smart, T., & Wang, H. (2008). Detecting kernel level keyloggers through dynamic taint analysis. Technical Report WM-CS-2008-05, College of William & Mary.

Levy, S. (1994). *Hackers: Heroes of the Computer Revolution.* Penguin Books.

Liang, X., Zou, F., Li, L., & Yi, P. (2020). Mobile terminal identity authentication system based on behavioral characteristics. *International Journal of Distributed Sensor Networks, 16*(1). Advance online publication. DOI: 10.1177/1550147719899371

Li, H., Chen, J., & Jin, X. (2011, June). An outlook on network honeypot. In *2011 International Conference on Computer Science and Service System (CSSS)* (pp. 1102-1105). IEEE.

Li, Q., & Chan, K. K. (2024). Test takers' attitudes of using exam-oriented mobile application as a tool to adapt in a high-stakes speaking test. *Education and Information Technologies, 29*(1), 219–237. DOI: 10.1007/s10639-023-12297-0

Li, S. F., Fei, L., Zhang, B., Ning, X., & Wu, L. (2024). Hand-based multimodal biometric fusion: A review. *Information Fusion*, *109*, 102418. DOI: 10.1016/j.inffus.2024.102418

Liu, J. (2023). CBDC Application Analysis and Prospects. *BCP Business & Management*, *45*, 1–6. DOI: 10.54691/bcpbm.v42i.4543

Liu, J., Li, Q., Sun, R., Du, X., & Guizani, M. (2018, May). An efficient anonymous authentication scheme for internet of vehicles. In *2018 IEEE International Conference on Communications (ICC)* (pp. 1-6). IEEE. DOI: 10.1109/ICC.2018.8422447

Liu, Q., & Liu, L. (2020). Color image encryption algorithm based on DNA coding and double chaos system. *IEEE Access : Practical Innovations, Open Solutions*, *8*, 83596–83610.

Liu, W. W., Wang, X., & Peng, W. (2019). Secure remote multi-factor authentication scheme based on chaotic map zero-knowledge proof for crowdsourcing internet of things. *IEEE Access : Practical Innovations, Open Solutions*, *8*, 8754–8767. DOI: 10.1109/ACCESS.2019.2962912

Liyakat Kazi, K. S. (2024). ChatGPT: An Automated Teacher's Guide to Learning. In Bansal, R., Chakir, A., Hafaz Ngah, A., Rabby, F., & Jain, A. (Eds.), *AI Algorithms and ChatGPT for Student Engagement in Online Learning* (pp. 1–20). IGI Global., DOI: 10.4018/979-8-3693-4268-8.ch001

Liyakat, K. K. (2025). Heart Health Monitoring Using IoT and Machine Learning Methods. In Shaik, A. (Ed.), *AI-Powered Advances in Pharmacology* (pp. 257–282). IGI Global., DOI: 10.4018/979-8-3693-3212-2.ch010

Liyakat, K. K. S. (2022). IoT-based smart transportation system for passenger comfort. *Research & Reviews: Journal of Computation Biology*, *11*(2), 28–35.

Liyakat, K. K. S. (2022). Model for agricultural information system to improve crop yield using IoT. *Journal of Open Source Development*, *9*(2), 16–24.

Liyakat, K. K. S. (2023). Detecting Malicious Nodes in IoT Networks Using Machine Learning and Artificial Neural Networks, *2023 International Conference on Emerging Smart Computing and Informatics (ESCI)*, Pune, India, 2023, pp. 1-5, DOI: 10.1109/ESCI56872.2023.10099544

Liyakat, K. K. S. (2023). Machine Learning Approach Using Artificial Neural Networks to Detect Malicious Nodes in IoT Networks. In Shukla, P. K., Mittal, H., & Engelbrecht, A. (Eds.), *Computer Vision and Robotics. CVR 2023. Algorithms for Intelligent Systems*. Springer., DOI: 10.1007/978-981-99-4577-1_3

Liyakat, K. K. S. (2023a). IoT based Healthcare Monitoring for COVID-Subvariant JN-1. *Journal of Electronic Design Technology*, *14*(3).

Liyakat, K. K. S. (2023b). Smart Motion Detection System using IoT: A NodeMCU and Blynk Framework. *Journal of Microelectronics and Solid State Devices*, *10*(3).

Liyakat, K. K. S. (2024). Explainable AI in healthcare. *Explainable Artificial Intelligence in Healthcare Systems*, *2024*, 271–284.

Liyakat, K. K. S. (2024). Machine Learning Approach Using Artificial Neural Networks to Detect Malicious Nodes in IoT Networks. In Udgata, S. K., Sethi, S., & Gao, X. Z. (Eds.), *Intelligent Systems. ICMIB 2023. Lecture Notes in Networks and Systems* (Vol. 728). Springer., available at https://link.springer.com/chapter/10.1007/978-981-99-3932-9_12, DOI: 10.1007/978-981-99-3932-9_12

Liyakat, K. S. (2024). Blynk IoT-Powered Water Pump-Based Smart Farming. *Recent Trends in Semiconductor and Sensor Technology*, *1*(1), 8–14.

Liyakat, S. S. (2023). IoT Changing the Electronics Manufacturing Industry. *Journal of Analog and Digital Communications*, *8*(3), 13–17. DOI: 10.46610/JoADC.2023.v08i03.003

Liyakat, S. S. (2023). IoT in the Electric Power Industry. *Journal of Controller and Converters*, *8*(3), 1–7.

Mahesh, B. (2020). Machine learning algorithms-a review. *International Journal of Science and Research (IJSR).[Internet],*, *9*(1), 381-386.

Malik, A. W., Bhatti, D. S., Park, T.-J., Ishtiaq, H. U., Ryou, J.-C., & Kim, K.-I. (2024). Cloud digital forensics: Beyond tools, techniques, and challenges. *Sensors (Basel)*, *24*(2), 433. DOI: 10.3390/s24020433 PMID: 38257526

Ma, M., He, D., Wang, H., Kumar, N., & Choo, K. K. R. (2019). An efficient and provably secure authenticated key agreement protocol for fog-based vehicular ad-hoc networks. *IEEE Internet of Things Journal*, *6*(5), 8065–8075. DOI: 10.1109/JIOT.2019.2902840

Manolache, A., Brad, F., Barbalau, A., Ionescu, R. T., & Popescu, M. (2022). Veridark: A large-scale benchmark for authorship verification on the dark web. https://arxiv.org/abs/2207.03477

Manu, Y. M., Gagana, R., & Shashikala, S. V. (2023). Enhancing Face Detection and Recognition through Machine Learning Algorithm. *International Conference on Recent Advances in Science and Engineering Technology, ICRASET 2023*. DOI: 10.1109/ICRASET59632.2023.10420184

Manzanares, A. I., Márquez, J. T., Estevez-Tapiador, J. M., & Castro, J. C. H. (2005). Attacks on port knocking authentication mechanism. In Computational Science and Its Applications–ICCSA 2005: International Conference, Singapore, May 9-12, 2005 [Springer Berlin Heidelberg.]. *Proceedings, 5*(Part IV), 1292–1300.

Mary Solomon, M., Singh Meena, M., Kaur, J., Tech Student, M., & Professor, A. (n.d.). *CHALLENGES IN FACE RECOGNITION SYSTEMS. 6*. Retrieved September 3, 2024, from https://ijrar.com/

Maurya, M. (2024). Digital Forensics and Cyber Investigation. *International Journal of Innovative Research in Technology and Science, 12*(2), 363–365.

Mazzolin, R., & Samueli, A. M. (2020, August). A Survey of Contemporary Cyber Security Vulnerabilities and Potential Approaches to Automated Defence. In *2020 IEEE International Systems Conference (SysCon)* (pp. 1-7). IEEE. DOI: 10.1109/SysCon47679.2020.9275828

Mbonihankuye, S., Nkunzimana, A., & Ndagijimana, A. (2019). Healthcare data security technology: HIPAA compliance. *Wireless Communications and Mobile Computing, 2019*(1), 1927495.

McGuire, M., & Dowling, S. (2013). Cyber Crime: A Review of the Evidence. Home Office Research Report 75.

Meenakshi, K. G., & Deeptha, R. (2021). Keyloggers – An Overview to the Spyware. *International Journal of Innovative Research in Computer and Communication Engineering, 9*(9), e-ISSN: 2320-9801.

Meenakshi, R., A. C., & Bhattacharya, S. (2020). Literature survey on log-based anomaly detection framework in cloud. Computational Intelligence in Pattern Recognition: Proceedings of CIPR 2020, 143-153.

Mirjalili, S. G. A., Gandomi, A. H., Mirjalili, S. Z., Saremi, S., Faris, H., & Mirjalili, S. M. (2017). SALP swarm algorithm: A bio-inspired optimizer for engineering design problems. *Nature-inspired optimizers. Springer,m. Advances in Engineering Software, 114*, 163–191. DOI: 10.1016/j.advengsoft.2017.07.002

Mirjalili, S., Mirjalili, S. M., & Lewis, A. (2014). Grey wolf optimizer. *Advances in Engineering Software, 69*, 46–61. DOI: 10.1016/j.advengsoft.2013.12.007

Mohajerani, J. G., Mohammadi Ghanatghestani, M., & Hashemipour, M. (2024). MCTE-RPL: A Multi-Context Trust-based Efficient RPL for IoT. *Journal of Network and Computer Applications, 229*. DOI: 10.1016/j.jnca.2024.103937

Mohd, S. M., Kamarudin, S., Yahya, N., Hasan, S., Zakaria, M. L. M., Sulaiman, S. A., & Setyohadi, D. B. (2024). The performance of the 3DES and Fernet encryption in securing data files. *Journal of Theoretical and Applied Information Technology, 102*(3).

Mohialden, Y. M., Hussien, N. M., & Ali, D. M. A. (2023a). Enhancing User Authentication with Facial Recognition and Feature-Based Credentials. *Journal La Multiapp, 4*(6), 243–252. DOI: 10.37899/journallamultiapp.v4i6.903

Mohitkirange. (2024). *Blockchain structure.* https://www.geeksforgeeks.org/blockchain-structure/

Monaco, J. V., Bakelman, N., Cha, S.-H., & Tappert, C. C. (2012), 'Developing a Keystroke Biometric System for Continual Authentication of Computer Users', *2012 European Intelligence and Security Informatics Conference*, pp. 210–216. DOI: 10.1109/EISIC.2012.58

Mondal, S. (2016). Continuous user authentication and identification: Combination of security & forensics.

Mondal, S., & Bours, P. (2016), 'Combining keystroke and mouse dynamics for continuous user authentication and identification,' *2016 IEEE International Conference on Identity, Security and Behavior Analysis (ISBA)*, pp. 1–8. DOI: 10.1109/ISBA.2016.7477228

Moreb, M., Salah, S., & Amro, B. (2024). A novel framework for mobile forensics investigation process. *International Journal of Computing and Digital Systems, 16*(1), 125–136. DOI: 10.12785/ijcds/160110

Moser, A., Kruegel, C., & Kirda, E. (2007). Limits of Static Analysis for Malware Detection. *Proceedings of the 23rd Annual Computer Security Applications Conference (ACSAC)*, 421-430. DOI: 10.1109/ACSAC.2007.21

Mostafa, A. M. (2023). An identity management scheme for cloud comput- ing: Review, challenges, and future directions. Journal of Intelligent Fuzzy Systems, . (Preprint), 1-23.

Munksgaard, R., & Demant, J. (2016). 06). Mixing politics and crime - the prevalence and decline of political discourse on the cryptomarket. *The International Journal on Drug Policy, 35*, 77–83. Advance online publication. DOI: 10.1016/j.drugpo.2016.04.021 PMID: 27424175

Musleh, D., Alotaibi, M., Alhaidari, F., Rahman, A., & Mohammad, R. M. (2023). Intrusion Detection System Using Feature Extraction with Machine Learning Algorithms in IoT. *Journal of Sensor and Actuator Networks, 12*(2), 29. DOI: 10.3390/jsan12020029

Mwanje, M. D., Kaiwartya, O., Aljaidi, M., Cao, Y., Kumar, S., Jha, D. N., Naser, A., & Lloret, J. (2024). Cyber security analysis of connected vehicles. *IET Intelligent Transport Systems, 18*(7), 1175–1195. DOI: 10.1049/itr2.12504

Nagrale, M., Pol, R. S., Birajadar, G. B., & Mulani, A. O. (2024). Internet of Robotic Things in Cardiac Surgery: An Innovative Approach. *African Journal of Biological Sciences, 6*(6), 709–725. DOI: 10.33472/AFJBS.6.6.2024.709-725

Nandhashree, K. R. (2024). State of Art Survey on Memory Forensic Acquisition & Techniques. In Next-Gen Technologies i. *n Computational Intelligence (pp. 465-469). CRC Press.* DOI: 10.1201/9781003430452-70

Nandhini, P. S., Kuppuswami, S., & Malliga, S. (2023). Energy efficient thwarting rank attack from RPL based IoT networks: A review. *Materials Today: Proceedings, 81*, 694–699. DOI: 10.1016/j.matpr.2021.04.167

Narayanan, A., & Shmatikov, V. (2005, November). Fast dictionary attacks on passwords using time-space tradeoff. In *Proceedings of the 12th ACM conference on Computer and communications security* (pp. 364-372). DOI: 10.1145/1102120.1102168

Nazah, S., Huda, S., Abawajy, J., & Hassan, M. M. (2020). Evolution of dark web threat analysis and detection: A systematic approach. *IEEE Access: Practical Innovations, Open Solutions, 8*, 171796–171819. DOI: 10.1109/ACCESS.2020.3024198

Nazir, H., Bajwa, I. S., Abdullah, S., Kazmi, R., & Samiullah, M. (2022). A color image encryption scheme combining hyperchaos and genetic codes. *IEEE Access : Practical Innovations, Open Solutions, 10*, 14480–14495.

Neeraja, P., Kumar, R. G., Kumar, M. S., & Vani, M. S. (2024). *DL-Based Somnolence Detection for Improved Driver Safety and Alertness Monitoring. 2024 IEEE International Conference on Computing, Power and Communication Technologies (IC2PCT).* Greater Noida., Available at https://ieeexplore.ieee.org/document/10486714, DOI: 10.1109/IC2PCT60090.2024.10486714

Negi, P. S., Garg, A., & Lal, R. (2020, January). Intrusion detection and prevention using honeypot network for cloud security. In 2020 10th International Conference on Cloud Computing, Data Science & Engineering (Confluence) (pp. 129-132). IEEE.

Nejad, F. V. (2024). Analysis of Decreased Rank Attack on RPL-Based IoT Networks. *10th International Conference on Web Research (ICWR)*, (pp. 40-45). IEEE 2024. DOI: 10.1109/ICWR61162.2024.10533332

Nerkar, P. M., & Dhaware, B. U. (2023). Predictive Data Analytics Framework Based on Heart Healthcare System (HHS) Using Machine Learning, *Journal of Advanced Zoology*, Volume 44, Special Issue -2. *Page*, *3673*, 3686.

Nihar Ranjan, A. K. (2016). Android Phone Forensic: Tools and Techniques .

Nikbazm, R., & Ahmadi, M. (2022). KSN: Modeling and Simulation of Knowledge using Machine Learning in NFV/SDN-based Networks. *Simulation Modelling Practice and Theory*, *121*, 102632. DOI: 10.1016/j.simpat.2022.102632

Niyat, A. Y., Hei, R. M. H., & Jahan, M. V. (2015). A RGB image encryption algorithm based on DNA sequence operation and hyper-chaotic system. *International Congress on Technology, Communication and Knowledge (ICTCK).*

Nosek, B. A., Hawkins, C. B., & Frazier, R. S. (2011). Implicit social cognition: From measures to mechanisms. *Trends in Cognitive Sciences*, *15*(4), 152–159. DOI: 10.1016/j.tics.2011.01.005 PMID: 21376657

Oettinger, W. (2022). *Learn Computer Forensics.*

Olzak, T. (2008). Keystroke logging (keylogging). *Adventures in Security, April, 8*, pp.1-6.

Omar, A. A. (2024). A Comprehensive Network Traffic Dataset for Sinkhole Attacks in Diverse RPL IoT Networks. *UOS_IOTSH_2024:*, 110650.

Oravec, J. (2022). AI, biometric analysis, and emerging cheating detection systems: The engineering of academic integrity? *Education Policy Analysis Archives*, *30*(175), •••. DOI: 10.14507/epaa.30.5765

Ortolani, S., & Crispo, B. (2012). Noisykey: tolerating keyloggers via keystrokes hiding. In *Proceedings of the 7th USENIX conference on Hot Topics in Security, HotSec'12.*

Osman, M. H. (2021). Artificial neural network model for decreased rank attack detection in RPL based on IoT networks. 23(3), 496-503.

Osman, M. H. (2021). Artificial neural network model for decreased rank attack detection in RPL based on IoT networks. *International Journal of Network Security*, *23*(3), 496–503.

Osman, M. H., He, J., Zhu, N., & Mokbal, F. M. M. (2024). An ensemble learning framework for the detection of RPL attacks in IoT networks based on the genetic feature selection approach. *Ad Hoc Networks, 152*, 103331. DOI: 10.1016/j.adhoc.2023.103331

Osman, M., He, J., Mahiuob, F., Mokbal, M., & Zhu, N. (2021). Artificial Neural Network Model for Decreased Rank Attack Detection in RPL Based on IoT Networks. *International Journal of Network Security, 23*, 496–503.

Owais, M., Shaikh, A., Jalal, A. A., & Hassan, M. M. (2019). Human Face Recognition using PCA Eigenfaces. *ICETAS 2019 - 2019 6th IEEE International Conference on Engineering, Technologies and Applied Sciences*. DOI: 10.1109/ICETAS48360.2019.9117489

Oxford Analytica. (2022). US government targets open-source software flaws. Emerald Expert Briefings, (oxan-es).

Oyelade, O. N., Ezugwu, A. E.-S., Mohamed, T. I. A., & Abualigah, L. (2022). Ebola optimization search algorithm: A new nature-inspired metaheuristic optimization algorithm. *IEEE Access : Practical Innovations, Open Solutions, 10*, 16150–16177. DOI: 10.1109/ACCESS.2022.3147821

Pabiania, M. D., Santos, K. A. P., Villa-Real, M. M., & Villareal, J. A. N. (2016). Face recognition system for electronic medical record to access out-patient information. *Jurnal Teknologi, 78*(6–3), 91–97. DOI: 10.11113/jt.v78.8935

Paganraj, D., & Chelliah, M. (2024). RPL: Detection and elimination of resource-related attacks in IoT RPL-based protocol. *The Journal of Supercomputing, 80*(15), 1–31. DOI: 10.1007/s11227-024-06256-w

Panda Security. (2019). *The Evolution of Polymorphic Malware*. Panda Security Blog.

Pandey, A. K., & Mishra, R. (2023). Deep Learning based facial recognition using H aar cascade technique. *2023 3rd International Conference on Advance Computing and Innovative Technologies in Engineering, ICACITE 2023*, 2109–2113. DOI: 10.1109/ICACITE57410.2023.10182612

Pandey, S., & Taffese, T. (2021). Using Performance Predictions to Evaluate Two-factor Authentication Setup Processes. *Proceedings of the Human Factors and Ergonomics Society Annual Meeting, 65*(1), 999–1003. DOI: 10.1177/1071181321651328

Pãnescu, A.-T., & Manta, V. (2018). Smart Contracts for Research Data Rights Management over the Ethereum Blockchain Network. *Science & Technology Libraries, 37*(3), 235–245. DOI: 10.1080/0194262X.2018.1474838

Pang, S., & Li, Y. (2020). Artificial intelligence techniques for cyber security applications. International Journal of Advanced Information and Communication Technology, 89-94.

Parekh, N., & D'Mello, L. (2021, September). ChaDRaL: RGB Image Encryption based on 3D Chaotic Map, DNA, RSA and LSB. In *2021 International Conference on Artificial Intelligence and Machine Vision (AIMV)* (pp. 1-6). IEEE.

Parkinson, S., Ward, P., Wilson, K., & Miller, J. (2017). Cyber threats facing autonomous and connected vehicles: Future challenges. *IEEE Transactions on Intelligent Transportation Systems, 18*(11), 2898–2915. DOI: 10.1109/TITS.2017.2665968

Park, J.. (2021). Network log-based SSH brute-force attack detection model. *CMC-Computers Materials & Continua, 68*(1), 887–901. DOI: 10.32604/cmc.2021.015172

Patel, K. C., & Sharma, P. (2017). A Review paper on pfsense-an Open source firewall introducing with different capabilities & customiza- tion. *IJARIIE, 3*, 2395–4396.

Patel, S., Thanikaiselvan, V., Pelusi, D., Nagaraj, B., Arunkumar, R., & Amirtharajan, R. (2021). Colour image encryption based on customized neural network and DNA encoding. *Neural Computing & Applications, 33*(21), 14533–14550.

Patil, R. A., & Renke, A. L. (2016). Keystroke Dynamics for User Authentication and Identification by using Typing Rhythm. *International Journal of Computer Applications, 144*(9), •••.

Patil, R. Y., Patil, Y. H., Bannore, A., & Ranjanikar, M. (2024). Ensuring accountability in digital forensics with proxy re-encryption based chain of custody. *International Journal of Information Technology : an Official Journal of Bharati Vidyapeeth's Institute of Computer Applications and Management, 16*(3), 1841–1853. DOI: 10.1007/s41870-023-01663-3

Pawar, S., & Geetha, V. (2023). An Implemented Example of XKMS With Web Services. In *Risk Detection and Cyber Security for the Success of Contemporary Computing* (pp. 92-108). IGI Global.

Pawar, S., & Gururaj, M. (2022, December). Constraint Based Clustering Technique for Web Services. In *International Conference on Advanced Network Technologies and Intelligent Computing* (pp. 89-107). Cham: Springer Nature Switzerland.

Pawar, S., & Chiplunkar, N. N. (2018). Survey on discovery of web services. *Indian Journal of Science and Technology, 11*(16), 1–10.

Pawar, S., & GuruRaj, M. (2023). Dynamicity of Web Services and Web Scrapping. *Journal of Mines, Metals and Fuels, 71*(5), 645–649. DOI: 10.18311/jmmf/2023/34164

Petit, J., & Shladover, S. E. (2014). Potential cyberattacks on automated vehicles. *IEEE Transactions on Intelligent Transportation Systems*, *16*(2), 546–556.

Phatak, S. S., Patil, H. S., Arshad, M. W., Jitkar, B., Patil, S., & Patil, J. (2022). Advanced Face Detection using Machine Learning and AI-based Algorithm. *Proceedings of 5th International Conference on Contemporary Computing and Informatics, IC3I 2022*, 1111–1116. DOI: 10.1109/IC3I56241.2022.10072527

Pradeepa, M., ... (2022). Student Health Detection using a Machine Learning Approach and IoT, *2022 IEEE 2nd Mysore sub section International Conference (*MysuruCon), 2022.

Prasad, K. R., Karanam, S. R., Ganesh, D., Liyakat, K. K. S., Talasila, V., & Purushotham, P. (2024, May). AI in public-private partnership for IT infrastructure development. *The Journal of High Technology Management Research*, *35*(1), 100496. DOI: 10.1016/j.hitech.2024.100496

Priyanka, P. R. (2014). Mining Frequent Sequences for Emails in Cyber Forensics Investigation. *nternational. Jisuanji Yingyong*.

Qian, Y. (2024). Face recognition technology for video surveillance integrated with particle swarm optimization algorithm. *International Journal of Intelligent Networks*, *5*, 145–153. DOI: 10.1016/j.ijin.2024.02.008

Qureshi, K., Rana, S., Ahmed, A., & Jeon, G. A. (2020). Novel and secure attacks detection framework for smart cities industrial internet of things. *Sustainable Cities and Society*, *61*, 102343. DOI: 10.1016/j.scs.2020.102343

Raghavan, R., & John Singh, K. (2022). An enhanced and hybrid fingerprint minutiae feature extraction method for identifying and authenticating the patient's noisy fingerprint. *International Journal of System Assurance Engineering and Management*, •••, 1–14.

Raghavan, R., & Singh, J. (2021). A hybrid approach towards content-based image retrieval for colored images using enhanced first type of pessimistic covering based lower approximation multi-granular rough sets. *Evolutionary Intelligence*, *14*(2), 1135–1143. DOI: 10.1007/s12065-020-00563-w

Rahman, M. M., Chakma, S., Raza, D. M., Akter, S., & Sattar, A. (2021). Real-Time Object Detection using Machine Learning. *2021 12th International Conference on Computing Communication and Networking Technologies, ICCCNT 2021*. DOI: 10.1109/ICCCNT51525.2021.9580170

Rajasekar, V. R., & Rajkumar, S. (2024). DSAT-IDS: Dissimilarity and Adaptive Threshold-based Intrusion Detection system to mitigate selective forwarding attack in the RPL-based 6LoWPAN. *Cluster Computing*, *27*(9), 1–40. DOI: 10.1007/s10586-024-04564-7

Rajesh, H. M., Keeditse, M., Mfa, D. T., Vorster, C., & Belyanin, G. A. (2024). How not to use U–Pb detrital zircon geochronology to infer regional tectonics: Comment on Basupi et al. *Journal of African Earth Sciences*, *210*, 105153. DOI: 10.1016/j.jafrearsci.2023.105153

Raman, M. R. G., Somu, N., Kirthivasan, K., Liscano, R., & Sriram, V. S. S. (2017). An efficient intrusion detection system based on hypergraph-Genetic algorithm for parameter optimization and feature selection in support vector machine. *Knowledge-Based Systems*, *134*, 1–12. DOI: 10.1016/j.knosys.2017.07.005

Raman, R. S., Sahu, A. K., Nair, V. K., & Nedungadi, P. (2024). Opposing agents evolve the research: A decade of digital forensics. *Multimedia Tools and Applications*, •••, 1–29. DOI: 10.1007/s11042-024-19519-8

Ramkumar, D., Annadurai, C., & Nelson, I. (2022). Iris-based continuous authentication in mobile ad hoc network. *Concurrency and Computation*, *34*(8), e5542. DOI: 10.1002/cpe.5542

Ramsbrock, D., Berthier, R., & Cukier, M. (2007, June). Profiling attacker behavior following SSH compromises. In 37th Annual IEEE/IFIP international conference on dependable systems and networks (DSN'07) (pp. 119-124). IEEE.

Ranasinghe, H., & Halgamuge, M. N. (2021). Twitter sentiment data analysis of user behavior on cryptocurrencies: Bitcoin and Ethereum. In *Analyzing Global Social Media Consumption* (pp. 277-291). IGI Global.

Rayani, P. K., & Changder, S. (2023). Continuous user authentication on smartphone via behavioral biometrics: A survey. *Multimedia Tools and Applications*, *82*(2), 1633–1667. DOI: 10.1007/s11042-022-13245-9

Remya, S. P., Pillai, M. J., Arjun, C., Ramasubbareddy, S., & Cho, Y. (2024). Enhancing Security in LLNs using a Hybrid Trust-Based Intrusion Detection System for RPL. *IEEE Access: Practical Innovations, Open Solutions*, *12*, 58836–58850. DOI: 10.1109/ACCESS.2024.3391918

Report, V. (2023), '2023 Data Breach Investigations Report, Retrieved from https://www.verizon.com/business/en-gb/resources/reports/dbir/

Resendez, I. (2014). *An Introduction to Digital Forensics*. Research Gate.

Revathi, M., Ramalingam, V. V., & Amutha, B. (2021). A machine learning based detection and mitigation of the DDOS attack by using SDN controller framework. *Wireless Personal Communications*, •••, 1–25.

Rivest, R. L., Adleman, L., & Dertouzos, M. L. (1978). On data banks and privacy homomorphisms. *Foundations of secure computation, 4*(11), 169-180.

Rokade, S., & Mishra, N. (2024). Privacy preservation of medical data in blockchain with secret key generation using RideNN. *Multimedia Tools and Applications, 83*(23), 1–23. DOI: 10.1007/s11042-023-18071-1

Romanosky, S., Hoffman, D., & Acquisti, A. (2014). Empirical Analysis of Data Breach Litigation. *Journal of Empirical Legal Studies, 11*(1), 74–104. DOI: 10.1111/jels.12035

Rosenzweig, P. (2013). *Cyber warfare: how conflicts in cyberspace are challenging America and changing the world.* Bloomsbury Publishing USA. DOI: 10.5040/9798400636493

Rouissat, M. B., Belkehir, M., Mokaddem, A., Bouziani, M., & Alsukayti, I. S. (2024). Exploring and mitigating hybrid rank attack in RPL-based IoT networks. *Journal of Electrical Engineering, 75*(3), 204–213. DOI: 10.2478/jee-2024-0025

Rouissat, M. B., Belkheir, M., Belkhira, H. S. A., Mokaddem, A., & Ziani, D. (2023). Implementing and evaluating a new Silent Rank Attack in RPL-Contiki based IoT networks. *Journal of Electrical Engineering, 74*(6), 454–462. DOI: 10.2478/jee-2023-0053

Roy, S., Roy, U., & Sinha, D. D. (2014), 'Free-text user authentication technique through Keystroke Dynamics,' 2014 International Conference on High-Performance *Computing and Applications (ICHPCA)*, pp. 1–6. DOI: 10.1109/ICHPCA.2014.7045345

Ruan, Z. N. (2024). USB Interrupt Differentiated Service for Bandwidth and Delay-Constrained Input/Output. In 2024 IEEE 30th Real-Time and Embedded Technology and Applications Symposium (RTAS). (pp. 42-54). IEEE.

Ruhani, A. B. B., & Zolkipli, M. F. (2023). Keylogger: The Unsung Hacking Weapon. *Borneo International Journal eISSN 2636-9826, 6*(1), 33-43.

Ryu, R., Yeom, S., Kim, S. H., & Herbert, D. (2021). Continuous multimodal biometric authentication schemes: A systematic review. *IEEE Access : Practical Innovations, Open Solutions, 9*, 34541–34557. DOI: 10.1109/ACCESS.2021.3061589

Sadaf, M., Iqbal, Z., Javed, A. R., Saba, I., Krichen, M., Majeed, S., & Raza, A. (2023). Connected and automated vehicles: Infrastructure, applications, security, critical challenges, and future aspects. *Technologies, 11*(5), 117. DOI: 10.3390/technologies11050117

Sadasivam, G. K., Hota, C., & Anand, B. (2016, September). Classification of SSH attacks using machine learning algorithms. In 2016 6th International Conference on IT Convergence and Security (ICITCS) (pp. 1-6). IEEE.

Sagiroglu, S., & Canbek, G. (2009). Keyloggers. *IEEE Technology and Society Magazine*, *28*(3), 10–17. DOI: 10.1109/MTS.2009.934159

Sahay, R., Geethakumari, G., & Mitra, B. J. (2020). A holistic framework for prediction of routing attacks in IoT-LLNs.

Sahay, R., Geethakumari, G., Mitra, B., & Sahoo, I. (2020). Efficient Framework for Detection of Version Number Attack in Internet of Things. In *Advances in Intelligent Systems and Computing*. Springer International Publishing.

Sakthimohan, M., Elizabeth Rani, G., Navaneethakrishnan, M., Janani, K., Nithva, V., & Pranav, R. (2023). Detection and Recognition of Face Using Deep Learning. *Proceedings of the 2023 International Conference on Intelligent Systems for Communication, IoT and Security, ICISCoIS 2023*, 72–76. DOI: 10.1109/ICISCoIS56541.2023.10100435

Salem, A., Sharieh, A., & Jabri, R. (2023). Online User Authentication System Using Keystroke Dynamics. *Journal of Computer Security*, *31*(3), 185–215. DOI: 10.3233/JCS-210081

Salman, M., ... (2020). "A Study of Forensic Tools Data Recovery Performance,". *2023 2nd International Engineering Conference on Electrical, Energy, and Artificial Intelligence (EICEEAI), Zarqa, Jordan, 2023,* (pp. pp. 1-6,)DOI: 10.1109/EICEEAI60672.2023.10590383

Saxena, N., & Varshney, D. (2021). Smart Home Security Solutions using Facial Authentication and Speaker Recognition through Artificial Neural Networks. *International Journal of Cognitive Computing in Engineering*, *2*, 154–164. DOI: 10.1016/j.ijcce.2021.10.001

Scheidt, N. . (2024). Friend or Foe?: How Anti-Digital Forensics vs. Digital Forensics Make or Break a Case. In Cases on Forensic and Criminological Science for Criminal Detection and Avoidance. *(pp. 356-378). IGI Global.*

Schmitt, V., & Butterfield, E. (2024). Digital forensics in healthcare: An analysis of data associated with a CPAP machine. *Forensic Science International Digital Investigation*, *48*, 301661. DOI: 10.1016/j.fsidi.2023.301661

Schneier, B. (2015). *Applied cryptography*. John Wiley & Sons.

Selvakumar, K., Karuppiah, M., SaiRamesh, L., Islam, S. K. H., Hassan, M. M., Fortino, G., & Choo, K.-K. R. (2019). Intelligent temporal classification and fuzzy rough set-based feature selection algorithm for intrusion detection system in WSNs. *Information Sciences*, *497*, 77–90. DOI: 10.1016/j.ins.2019.05.040

Selwyn, N., Andrejevic, M., O'Neill, C., Gu, X., & Smith, G. (2024). Facial Recognition Technology. In *The Cambridge Handbook of Facial Recognition in the Modern State* (pp. 11–28). Cambridge University Press., DOI: 10.1017/9781009321211.003

Seth, J. K., & Chandra, S. (2016). Intrusion detection based on key feature selection using binary GWO. *2016 3rd International Conference on Computing for Sustainable Global Development (INDIACom)*, 3735–3740.

Seth, A. D. (2020). Detection and verification of decreased rank attack using round-trip times in RPL-based 6LoWPAN networks. *IEEE International Conference on Advanced Networks and Telecommunications Systems*. IEEE. DOI: 10.1109/ANTS50601.2020.9342754

Shah, T., Haq, T. U., & Farooq, G. (2020). Improved SERPENT algorithm: Design to RGB image encryption implementation. *IEEE Access : Practical Innovations, Open Solutions*, *8*, 52609–52621.

Sharma, R., Sandhu, J., & Bharti, V. (2024). Exploring Feature-Based Image Classification for Human Identification in Multimodal Biometric System. *2024 11th International Conference on Reliability, Infocom Technologies and Optimization (Trends and Future Directions), ICRITO 2024*. DOI: 10.1109/ICRITO61523.2024.10522307

Sharma, D., & Fancy, C. (2022). Cloud Storage Security using Firebase and Fernet Encryption. *International Journal of Engineering Trends and Technology*, *70*(9), 371–375. DOI: 10.14445/22315381/IJETT-V70I9P237

Sharma, M., & Tomar, S. S. (2015). Attack Detection and Security in Remote Code Execution. *International Journal of Computer Applications*, *114*, 14. DOI: 10.5120/19757-1410

Sharma, S., & Verma, V. A. (2021). Artificial intelligence enabled machine learning approach for routing attacks on internet of things. *The Journal of Supercomputing*, *77*(12), 13757–13787. DOI: 10.1007/s11227-021-03833-1

Sheena, R. S. (2020). *A Survey on Digital Forensics Phases*. Tools and Challenges.

Sheikh, B. B. (2023). A survey on current security trends and future direc- tions. Engineering Proceedings,. *Mobile cloud com- puting:*, 32(1), 22.

Shen, Z., Li, S., Zhao, X., & Zou, J. (2022). MMAuth: A continuous authentication framework on smartphones using multiple modalities. *IEEE Transactions on Information Forensics and Security*, *17*, 1450–1465. DOI: 10.1109/TIFS.2022.3160361

Shibwabo, B. K. (2024). Data Recovery of Flash Memory. Nanocrystals in Non-volatile Memory, 347.

Shirbhate, D. D. (2024). A Review Paper on Cyber Security and Digital Forensics. *Grenze International Journal of Engineering & Technology (GIJET), 10.*

Shraida, G. K., Younis, H. A., Al-Amiedy, T. A., Anbar, M., Younis, H. A., & Hasbullah, I. H. (2023). An efficient color-image encryption method using DNA sequence and chaos cipher. *Computers, Materials & Continua*, *75*(2), 2641–2654.

Shrivastava, A., Jaın, J., & Chauhan, D. (2023). Literature review on tools & applications of data mining. *International Journal on Computer Science and Engineering*, *11*(4), 46–54.

Siddharthan, H., Deepa, T., & Chandhar, P. (2022). Senmqtt-set: An intelligent intrusion detection in iot-mqtt networks using ensemble multi cascade features. *IEEE Access : Practical Innovations, Open Solutions*, *10*, 33095–33110. DOI: 10.1109/ACCESS.2022.3161566

Sindiramutty, S. R., Jhanjhi, N. Z., Tan, C. E., Khan, N. A., Shah, B., & Gaur, L. (2024). Securing the digital supply chain cyber threats and vulnerabilities. In *Cybersecurity Measures for Logistics Industry Framework* (pp. 156–223). IGI Global.

Singh, A. T. (2016). A review of supervised machine learning algorithms. *n 2016 3rd international conference on computing for sustainable global development (INDIACom)*, (pp. 1310-1315). IEEE.

Singh, P., Choudhary, N., Samnotra, B., Bhel, S., Sharma, S., Kour, H., ... & Kumar, S. (2024). Understanding RSA Algorithm in Cryptography.

Singh, A. K., Kumar, S., Kumar, B., & Chauhan, A. S. (2023). Face Recognition Using Machine Learning. *2023 International Conference on Sustainable Emerging Innovations in Engineering and Technology, ICSEIET 2023*, 361–364. DOI: 10.1109/ICSEIET58677.2023.10303390

Singh, A., Choudhary, P., Singh, A., & Tyagi, D. (2021, August). Keylogger detection and prevention. [). IOP Publishing.]. *Journal of Physics: Conference Series, 2007*(1), 012005. DOI: 10.1088/1742-6596/2007/1/012005

Singh, S., & Kumar, R. (2024). Image forgery detection: Comprehensive review of digital forensics approaches. *Journal of Computational Social Science*, *7*(1), 1–39. DOI: 10.1007/s42001-024-00265-8

Smith, C. (2015, December). Breakthrough data storage innovation: One DNA molecule can store tons of data for 1M years. *BGR.*https://bgr.com/2015/08/18/dna-hard-drive-data-storage/

Smith, M. S. (2018). Critical Infrastructure Protection: Key Principles for Strengthening Resilience and Preparedness. *Journal of Strategic Security*, *11*(2), 34–45.

Sopariwala, S., Fallon, E., & Asghar, M. N. (2022, June). Log4jPot: effective log4shell vulnerability detection system. In 2022 33rd Irish Signals and Systems Conference (ISSC) (pp. 1-5). IEEE.

Souror, S., El-Fishawy, N., & Badawy, M. (2022). Security analysis for SCKHA algorithm: Stream cipher algorithm based on key hashing technique. *Chinese Journal of Electronics*, •••, 1–16.

Sousi, A. L., Yehya, D., & Joudi, M. (2020). Aes encryption: Study & evaluation. *CCEE552: Cryptography and Network Security.*

Spafford, E. H. (1989). The Internet Worm Program: An Analysis. Purdue Technical Report CSD-TR-823.

Sreelatha, M., Shashi, M., Anirudh, M., Ahamer, M. S., & Manoj Kumar, V. (2011). Authentication Schemes for Session Passwords Using Color and Images. *International Journal of Network Security & its Applications*, *3*(3), 111–119. DOI: 10.5121/ijnsa.2011.3308

Srinivasa, S., Pedersen, J. M., & Vasilomanolakis, E. (2022, June). Deceptive directories and "vulnerable" logs: a honeypot study of the LDAP and log4j attack landscape. In 2022 IEEE European Symposium on Security and Privacy Workshops (EuroS&PW) (pp. 442-447). IEEE.

Stylios, I., Chatzis, S., Thanou, O., & Kokolakis, S. (2023). Continuous Authentication with Feature-Level Fusion of Touch Gestures and Keystroke Dynamics to Solve Security and Usability Issues. *Computers & Security*, *132*, 103363. DOI: 10.1016/j.cose.2023.103363

Suleski, T., Ahmed, M., Yang, W., & Wang, E. (2023), 'A Review of Multi-Factor Authentication in the Internet of Healthcare Things', DOI: DOI: 10.1177/20552076231177144

Surapaneni, P., Bojjagani, S., & Khan, M. K. (2024). VESecure: Verifiable authentication and efficient key exchange for secure intelligent transport systems deployment. *Vehicular Communications*, *49*, 100822. DOI: 10.1016/j.vehcom.2024.100822

Swamy, K. V., Supraja, A., Vinuthna, P. S., & Sindhura, D. L. (2022). Performance Comparison of Various Features for Human Face Recognition using Machine Learning. *2022 IEEE Conference on Interdisciplinary Approaches in Technology and Management for Social Innovation, IATMSI 2022*. DOI: 10.1109/IATMSI56455.2022.10119449

Szor, P., & Ferrie, P. (2001). *Hunting for Metamorphic*. Symantec Security Response.

Tahar, G. E. (2024). Lightweight Mitigation Against DIO Suppression Attack In RPL-Based IoT Networks. *In 2024 6th International Conference on Pattern Analysis and Intelligent Systems (PAIS)*, (pp. 1-6). IEEE.).

Taneja, N. B., Bramhe, V. S., Bhardwaj, D., & Taneja, A. (2024). Understanding digital image anti-forensics: An analytical review. *Multimedia Tools and Applications*, *83*(4), 10445–10466. DOI: 10.1007/s11042-023-15866-0

Tashtoush, Y., Darweesh, D., Karajeh, O., Darwish, O., Maabreh, M., Swedat, S., Koraysh, R., Almousa, O., & Alsaedi, N. (2022). Survey on authentication and security protocols and schemes over 5G networks. *International Journal of Distributed Sensor Networks*, *18*(10). DOI: 10.1177/15501329221126609

Tebaa, M., El Hajji, S., & El Ghazi, A. (2012, April). *Homomorphic encryption method applied to Cloud Computing. In 2012 National Days of Network Security and Systems*. IEEE.

Thamilarasu, G., & Chawla, S. (2019). Towards deep-learning-driven intrusion detection for the internet of things. .

Thamilarasu, G., & Chawla, S. (2019). Towards deep-learning-driven intrusion detection for the internet of things. *Sensors (Basel)*, *19*(9), 1977. DOI: 10.3390/s19091977 PMID: 31035611

Tian, D., Jia, X., Chen, J., & Hu, C. (2017). An online approach for kernel-level keylogger detection and defense. *Journal of Information Science and Engineering*, *33*(2), 445–461.

Tolsma, P. ..-T. (2021). Preventing Decreased Rank Attacks in RPL-based IoT Networks.

Tomer, V., & Sharma, S. (2022). Detecting IoT attacks using an ensemble machine learning model. *Future Internet*, *14*(4), 102. DOI: 10.3390/fi14040102

Tong, W., Hussain, A., Bo, W. X., & Maharjan, S. (2019). Artificial intelligence for vehicle-to-everything: A survey. *IEEE Access : Practical Innovations, Open Solutions*, *7*, 10823–10843. DOI: 10.1109/ACCESS.2019.2891073

Tran, Q. N. (2021). A privacy-preserving biometric authentication system with bi- nary classification in a zero knowledge proof protocol. *IEEE Open Journal of the Computer Society*.

Tuli, P., & Sahu, P. (2013). System Monitoring and Security Using Keylogger. *IJCSMC*, *2*(3), 106–111.

Tuscano, A., & Koshy, T. S. (2021). Types of Keyloggers Technologies – Survey. In Kumar, A., & Mozar, S. (Eds.), *ICCCE 2020. Lecture Notes in Electrical Engineering* (Vol. 698). Springer.

Tyagi, S. S. (2021). Enhancing security of cloud data through encryption with AES and Fernet algorithm through convolutional-neural-networks. *International Journal of Computer Networks and Applications*, *8*(4), 288–299. DOI: 10.22247/ijcna/2021/209697

Vabalas, A. G., Gowen, E., Poliakoff, E., & Casson, A. J. (2019). Machine learning algorithm validation with a limited sample size. *PLoS One*, *14*(11), e0224365. DOI: 10.1371/journal.pone.0224365 PMID: 31697686

Vaidya, T. (2015). 2001-2013: Survey and Analysis of Major Cyberattacks. arXiv preprint arXiv:1507.06673.

ValetiDeepika, D., & LalithaBhaskari. (2020). Block Chain Based Decentralised Twitter Dapp. *JETIR, 7*(11), 273-279.

Varlioglu, S., Elsayed, N., ElSayed, Z., & Ozer, M. (2022). The dangerous combo: Fileless malware and cryptojacking. *SoutheastCon*, *2022*, 125–132. DOI: 10.1109/SoutheastCon48659.2022.9764043

Vashishtha, L. K., Singh, A. P., & Chatterjee, K. (2023). HIDM: A Hybrid Intrusion Detection Model for Cloud Based Systems. *Wireless Personal Communications*, *128*(4), 2637–2666. DOI: 10.1007/s11277-022-10063-y

Veena, C., Sridevi, M., Liyakat, K. K. S., Saha, B., Reddy, S. R., & Shirisha, N. (2023). *HEECCNB: An Efficient IoT-Cloud Architecture for Secure Patient Data Transmission and Accurate Disease Prediction in Healthcare Systems, 2023 Seventh International Conference on Image Information Processing*. ICIIP., Available at https://ieeexplore.ieee.org/document/10537627, DOI: 10.1109/ICIIP61524.2023.10537627

Velliangiri, S., & Karthikeyan, P. (2020). Hybrid optimization scheme for intrusion detection using considerable feature selection. *Neural Computing & Applications, 32*(12), 7925–7939. DOI: 10.1007/s00521-019-04477-2

Verma, A. V.-M., Verma, S. K., Pandey, A. C., Grover, J., & Sharma, G. (2019). A lightweight mitigation solution for DAO insider attack in RPL-based IoT. *Future Generation Computer Systems, 159*, 327–339. DOI: 10.1016/j.future.2024.05.032

Victor, M., Praveenraj, D. D. W., Sasirekha, R., Alkhayyat, A., & Shakhzoda, A. (2023). Cryptography: Advances in Secure Communication and Data Protection. In *E3S Web of Conferences* (Vol. 399, p. 07010). EDP Sciences.

Wale, A. D., & Dipali, R.. (2019). Smart Agriculture System using IoT. *International Journal of Innovative Research In Technology, 5*(10), 493–497.

Wall, D. S. (2024). *Cybercrime: The transformation of crime in the information age*. John Wiley & Sons.

Wang, H., Liu, T., Kim, B., Lin, C. W., Shiraishi, S., Xie, J., & Han, Z. (2020). Architectural design alternatives based on cloud/edge/fog computing for connected vehicles. *IEEE Communications Surveys and Tutorials, 22*(4), 2349–2377. DOI: 10.1109/COMST.2020.3020854

Wang, L., Ran, Q., & Ma, J. (2020). Double quantum color images encryption scheme based on DQRCI. *Multimedia Tools and Applications, 79*(9), 6661–6687.

Wazid, M., Sharma, R., & Katal. (2013). Implementation and Embellishment of Prevention of Keylogger Spyware Attacks. In Thampi, S.M., Atrey, P.K., Fan, C.I., Perez, G.M. (Eds.), *Security in Computing and Communications. SSCC 2013. Communications in Computer and Information Science, vol 377*. Springer, Berlin, Heidelberg.

Willburger, K., Schwenk, K., & Brauchle, J. (2020). Amaro—An on-board ship detection and real-time information system. *Sensors (Basel), 20*(5), 1324. DOI: 10.3390/s20051324 PMID: 32121473

Wood, C., & Raj, R. (2010, July). Keyloggers in Cybersecurity Education. In *Security and Management* (pp. 293-299).

Yao, Y. (2024). Research on facial recognition system based on deep learning. *Applied and Computational Engineering, 34*(1), 232–236. DOI: 10.54254/2755-2721/34/20230332

Yavuz, F., Ünal, D., & Gül, E. (2018). Deep Learning for Detection of Routing Attacks in the Internet of Things. *Int. J. Comput. Intell. Syst., 12*(1), 39. DOI: 10.2991/ijcis.2018.25905181

Yeşim, A. (2017). Review of Evidence Analysis and Reporting Phases in Digital Forensics Process. *InInternational Conference on Computer Science and Engineering (UBMK),* IEEE.

Yu, D., Lee, S., Hsu, R. H., & Lee, J. (2024). Ensuring end-to-end security with fine-grained access control for connected and autonomous vehicles. *IEEE Transactions on Information Forensics and Security, 19*, 6962–6977. DOI: 10.1109/TIFS.2024.3417292

Zahra, F. J., Jhanjhi, N. Z., Brohi, S. N., Khan, N. A., Masud, M., & AlZain, M. A. (2022). Rank and wormhole attack detection model for RPL-based internet of things using machine learning. *Sensors (Basel), 22*(18), 6765. DOI: 10.3390/s22186765 PMID: 36146111

Zaitsev, O. (2009). Skeleton keys: the purpose and applications of keyloggers.

Zeadally, S., Adi, E., Baig, Z., & Khan, I. A. (2020). Harnessing artificial intelligence capabilities to improve cybersecurity. *IEEE Access : Practical Innovations, Open Solutions, 8*, 23817–23837. DOI: 10.1109/ACCESS.2020.2968045

Zhang, F., Zhou, S., Qin, Z., & Liu, J. (2003, August). Honeypot: a supplemented active defense system for network security. In *Proceedings of the Fourth International Conference on Parallel and Distributed Computing, Applications and Technologies* (pp. 231-235). IEEE.

Zhang, L., Wang, X., & Liu, Y. (2009). A review on chaotic cryptography in image encryption. *International Journal of Bifurcation and Chaos in Applied Sciences and Engineering, 19*(4), 1339–1374.

Zhang, X., & Ye, R. (2021). A novel RGB image encryption algorithm based on DNA sequences and chaos. *Multimedia Tools and Applications, 80*(6), 8809–8833.

Zhang, Z., & Zhang, Z. (2024). DNA Information Storage and Cryptography System. *Academic Journal of Science and Technology, 10*(1), 243–249.

Zheng, Z., Xie, S., Dai, H., Chen, X., & Wang, H. (2017, June). An overview of blockchain technology: Architecture, consensus, and future trends. In *2017 IEEE international congress on big data (BigData congress)* (pp. 557-564). IEEE.

Zheng, J., Wang, S., & Lei, N. (2023). A Method to Improve the Accuracy of Face Recognition in Application Scenarios. *Proceedings of 2023 IEEE 3rd International Conference on Information Technology, Big Data and Artificial Intelligence, ICIBA 2023*, 320–325. DOI: 10.1109/ICIBA56860.2023.10165241

Zhou, S., He, P., & Kasabov, N. (2020). A dynamic DNA color image encryption method based on SHA-512. *Entropy (Basel, Switzerland)*, *22*(10), 1091.

Zilberman, A. D., Dvir, A., & Stulman, A. (2024). SPRINKLER: A Multi-RPL Man-in-the-Middle Identification Scheme in IoT Networks. *IEEE Transactions on Mobile Computing*, *23*(10), 9971–9988. DOI: 10.1109/TMC.2024.3370894

Zmud, J. P., & Sener, I. N. (2017). Towards an understanding of the travel behavior impact of autonomous vehicles. *Transportation Research Procedia*, *25*, 2500–2519. DOI: 10.1016/j.trpro.2017.05.281

About the Contributors

Mohammed Amin Almaiah is an Associate Professor in the Department of Computer Science at The University of Jordan. He has published over 95 research papers in highly reputed journals such as the Engineering and Science Technology, an International Journal, Education and Information Technologies, IEEE Access and others. Most of his publications were indexed under the ISI Web of Science and Scopus. His current research interests include Cybersecurity and Cyber-risk assessment and mobile apps.

Said A. Salloum received the bachelor's degree in computer science from Yarmouk University, the M.Sc. degree in informatics (knowledge and data management) from The British University in Dubai, and the Ph.D. degree in computer science from the University of Salford, U.K. He is currently a Senior Enterprise Architect with the Computer Center, University of Sharjah, where he plays a pivotal role in shaping the university's technological landscape. He is a highly qualified individual with a strong educational background and extensive professional experience in the field of computer science. In this capacity, he is responsible for overseeing the strategic design and implementation of cutting-edge technology solutions that facilitate the university's teaching, research, and administrative functions. His role involves close collaboration with fellow IT professionals to ensure the security and efficiency of the university's systems. In addition, he leads various projects aimed at introducing new technologies and enhancing existing ones to continually advance the institution's technological capabilities. Beyond his role at the University of Sharjah, he has also made significant contributions to the field of research.

***

Tasnim Al-Harasis Received her B.Sc. in computer engineering from Al Balqaa Applied University, Jordan, in 2020. She also earned an M.Sc. in Cyber Security - Information System Security and Digital Criminology from Princess Sumaya University for Technology in 2023; Al-Harasis is currently working as a Teaching and Research Assistant with the Cyber Security Department at Al Hussein Technical University, Jordan. Her research interests include Computer Networking, Internet of Things (IoT), Network Security, Information Security, Routing Protocols, Machine Learning, Cyber Security, IPS, IDS Techniques.

Mahmoud Mohammad Aljawarneh. Received the B.S., M.S. and PhD degree in Information Technology from University of Sindh, Jamshoro, Pakistan, in 2011, 2014, and 2019 respectively. From 2012 to 2014 and 2016 to 2018, he was a Research Assistant with the Institute of Information and Communication Technology, University of Sindh, Jamshoro, Pakistan. And From January 2020 to March 2022: he was an Assistant Professor, Computer Science Department, Szabist University, Hyd Campus, Pakistan. And From October 2022 to Current: he is working as an Assistant Professor, Faculty of Information Technology, Applied Sciences Private University, Amman, Jordan. His research interest includes Pervasive Computing, Context-awareness, Cybersecurity, Internet of Things (IoT), Machine Learning (ML).

Mohammed Amin Almaiah is an Associate Professor in Cybersecurity at University of Jordan. He has published over 120 research papers in highly reputed journals such as the Engineering and Science Technology, an International Journal, Education and Information Technologies, IEEE Access and others. Most of his publications were indexed under the ISI Web of Science and Scopus. His current research interests include Cybersecurity, cyber risk assessment and cyber risk management.

Q. Al-Na'amneh received his B.Sc. in software engineering from Hashemite University, Jordan, in 2015. He also earned an M.Sc. in Cyber Security (with distinction) from the same institution in 2021; Al-Naamneh is currently working as an Instructor with the Cyber Security and Cloud Computing Department at Applied Science Private University, Jordan. His research interests include EVs charging and development, Wireless Sensor Networks (WSNs), Internet of Things (IoT), Network Security, Information Security, Mobile Ad-hoc Networks (MANETs), Mobile Programming, Routing Protocols, Database Management, Cloud Computing, Cyber Security, IPS, IDS Watermarking Techniques, Grid Computing, Cloud Computing Security, and Artificial Intelligence.

Abdallah Awad As a highly skilled and dedicated QA Automation Engineer with extensive experience in the IT industry, I am committed to delivering exceptional results and exceeding expectations. With a wealth of technical knowledge and numerous certifications in QA, I bring a wealth of expertise and attention to detail to every project I work on. My passion for technology and unwavering commitment to quality make me a valuable asset to any team, and I am always eager to take on new challenges and expand my skill set. Whether developing new automated testing solutions or optimizing existing processes, I am driven to find creative and effective solutions that deliver measurable results

V.R Balasaraswathi received her B.E. degree in Computer Science and Engineering from Madras University in 2002 and M.E. degree in Computer Science and Engineering in 2008 from Anna University, Chennai. She completed her Ph.D. as a full time scholar from Pondicherry University, India. Her research interests include Cryptography and Information Security, Artificial Intelligence, Machine Learning, Data Mining, Data Structures and Algorithms. (Email: balasaraswathi.vr@vit.ac.in)

Sriramulu Bojjagani received the Ph.D. degree from the School of Computer and Information Sciences, University of Hyderabad (UoH) and the Institute for Development and Research in Banking Technology, established by the Reserve Bank of India (RBI), in 2019, with a focus on Design, Testing and Formal Verification of Secure Mobile Payment Protocols. He is currently working as an Assistant Professor with the Department of Computer Science and Engineering, SRM University AP, Amaravathi, India. He has published many SCI/SCIE-indexed journals with good impact factors and many conference papers of international repute. In addition, he is an inventor of several patents. His research interests include vulnerability analysis and penetration testing, cybersecurity, digital authentication, and the IoV security.

Vandana BS has got 18 years teaching experience and 12 years research experience.

Dipti Chauhan is a Professor in the AIDS department, in Indore,

Sailaja Chigurupati is pursuing B.Tech in the department of Computer Science and Engineering at KL University, Andhra Pradesh. She done two patents on Machine Learning. Her interested research areas are cybersecurity, blockchain, machine learning and internet of things.

Anuj Dhar is an undergrad senior pursuing B.Tech in Computer Science and Engineering from Vellore Institute of Technology, Chennai.

Shalini Gupta is an undergrad senior, currently enrolled in Vellore Institute of Technology with a major in Computer Science and Engineering.

Rahaf Hazaymih received her B.Sc. in Computer Engineering from Jordan University of Science and Technology in 2020. She is currently pursuing a Master's degree in Data Science. Rahaf is working as an AI Engineer, with research interests in Natural Language Processing (NLP), Artificial Intelligence (AI), Machine Learning (ML), Data Science, Cybersecurity, and the Internet of Things (IoT).

Roopa Hegde has got 15 years teaching experience and 12 years research experience. She published more than 20 papers in journals and conferences.

Mohammad Hijjawi is an full professor in computer science department in faculty of information technology at Applied Science private University(ASU). He received his PhD from Manchester Metropolitan University at UK in 2011. Dr. Mohammad has previous computing based training in several domains. Also, he was an IT training manager for specialized training center in the ASU beside his work as an ASU Cisco academy manager and an authorized Cisco based courses. Currently, Dr. Mohammad act as the faculty of information technology dean at ASU from Sep. 2015 beside his responsibilities according to the ASU's committees.

Jay Jain is an Assistant Professor in Department of Mathematics, Bioinformatics and Computer Applications, MANIT Bhopal.

Vishal Jain is presently working as Professor at the Department of Computer Science and Engineering, School of Engineering and Technology, Sharda University, Greater Noida, India. Before that, he worked for several years as an Associate Professor at Bharati Vidyapeeth's Institute of Computer Applications and Management (BVICAM), New Delhi. He has more than 18 years of experience in the academics. He has earned degrees: Ph.D (CSE), M.Tech (CSE), MBA (HR), MCA, MCP, and CCNA. He has more than 2200 research citations with Google Scholar (h-index score 24 and i-10 index 55) and has authored more than 150 research papers in professional journals and conferences. He has authored and edited more than 60 books (most of them are indexed at the Scopus) with various reputed publishers, including Elsevier, Springer, IET, Apple Academic Press, CRC, Taylor and Francis Group, Scrivener, Wiley, Emerald, NOVA Science, River Publishers, IGI-Global and Bentham Science. He has more than 200 Scopus publications. His research areas include machine learning, information retrieval, semantic web, ontology engineering, data mining, ad hoc networks, sensor networks and network security.

Ankitha K has 10 years research experience and 15 years Teaching experience. She Published more than 20 papers in indexed journals and conferences

|ANILKUMAR K G - Contributing Author|Anilkumar K. G. holds a Master's degree in Computer Applications and a Bachelor's degree in Computer Science from the University of Kerala, India. He is currently pursuing a Ph.D. in Computer Science at the Department of Computer Science, University of Kerala. His research focuses on developing advanced threat resilience strategies for law enforcement agencies to combat cybercrimes, illicit darknet activities, and challenges in e-governance. His work integrates cybersecurity, digital forensics, and law enforcement methodologies to enhance investigative capabilities in the digital era.

Katsriku A. Ferdinand is the Head of Computer Science Department at the University of Ghana, Legon. He holds a PhD in Information Engineering, MEng in Computer Systems Engineering, MSc in Laser Engineering and Pulse Power Technology and Bachelors Degree in Computer Science. His research interest includes; Wireless and Mobile Systems, Mobile Communication and Distributed Systems.

Kazi Kutubuddin Sayyad Liyakat has completed his B.E., M.E., and Ph.D. in E&TC Engineering and is nowadays working as a Professor & Head of Department, E&TC Engineering Department and was Dean R&D. He is Post-Doctoral Fellow working on "IoT in Healthcare Applications". His area of Interest is IoT, AI and ML. He has published more than 110+ papers in various Journals. Also published 11 books in the field of Engineering. He has published 15 Indian Patents, 2 South African Grant Patent, 2 Indian Copyright Patents and 8 UK Grant Patent. He worked as a Reviewer for Scopus Conferences and Journal. Also work as Editorial Board Member for various Journals. He got 2 Best Researcher Award, Best Faculty Award and Appreciation Letter from MoE's Innovation Cell, Govt. of India.

Nilamadhab Mishra is an Associate Professor in the School of Computer Science and Engineering, AI-ML Division, at VIT Bhopal University, India. He received his Doctor of Philosophy (Ph.D.) in Computer Science & Information Engineering with a specialization in Data Science & Machine Learning from Chang Gung University, Taiwan. He has more than 22 years of national and international involvement in academic teaching and research at recognized Indian, Taiwanese, and African universities. He has over 50 publications in SCI/SCIE and SCOPUS-indexed journals, ISBN books and chapters, Indian and Australian patents, IEEE conference proceedings, and others. He has served as a reviewer, associate editor, and editorial board member for SCI/SCIE-indexed journals and conferences. Dr. Mishra worked on multiple funded research projects from the MOST, NSC, and CGU Memorial

Hospital, Taiwan, during his Ph.D. and has been involved with several professional bodies. He is currently an Associate Editor for two SCOPUS-indexed journals, and his research interests span the areas of AI, Data Science, Machine Learning, and Cognitive Analytics & Applications.

Ali Ghassan Mohammad is a senior engineer at Almosafer. His current research interests include software engineering, drones, machine learning, nlp, and security.

Rudra Kalyan Nayak serves as a Senior Assistant Professor in the School of Computing Science & Engineering at VIT Bhopal University. He has more than 14 years of expertise in teaching, mentoring and research. His Doctorate in Computer Science & Engineering was awarded by Siksha 'O' Anusandhan University in Bhubaneswar, Odisha, where he conducted research in the field of Financial Engineering. At the same university, he earned his M. Tech. in information technology. Dr. Nayak possesses nine patents total, two of which are granted Australian design patents and two of which are granted Indian design patents. In addition, he has written three book chapters and two books. He boasts over 45 international papers to his name, appearing in reputable journals and IEEE/ Springer conference proceedings. Additionally, he wrote an article for the IEEE India Council Newsletter. Speaking with expertise, Dr. Nayak has participated in faculty development programs. He has reviewed papers for a number of conferences and peer-reviewed journals. His areas of interest in research are Artificial Intelligence, Machine Learning, Financial Engineering, Bioinformatics and Computer Vision. A number of honors have been bestowed upon him, including the I2OR International Teaching Excellence Award 2023, I2OR National Elite Teacher Award 2022, 100 Eminent Academicians of 2021, Dynamic Teacher of the Year 2019, I2OR Preeminent Researcher Award 2019 and Green ThinkerZ Bright Educator Award 2019. A professional member of ACM, CSTA, IAENG, ICSES, theIRED, SDIWC, and a life member of ISTE, Dr. Nayak holds these memberships. He was also a London Journals Press Honorary Rosalind Member.

Vasanth Nayak has got 15 years teaching experience and 12 years research experience and he published more than 20 papers.

ID Muhammad Noorul Mubarak - Contributing Author|Muhammad Noorul Mubarak is an Associate Professor in the Department of Computer Science at the University of Kerala, India, with over 30 years of academic and research experience. He holds a Ph.D. in Computer Science from the University of Kerala, an M.Phil. in Computer Science from Manonmaniam Sundaranar University, and M.Sc. and B.Sc. degrees in Computer Science from Bharathidasan University, India. His research interests include image processing, cybersecurity, and natural language processing.

Ahmed Otoom Assistant Professor at Applied Science Private University, Department of Cybersecurity and Cloud Computing . My research interests include Software Engineering, Cyber Security, and Information Security Management. Dr. Ahmed Otoom has extensive and practical experience in the business sector in parallel with his academic experiences, as he held a number of important positions in information technology management and supervised the development of the first version of the National Information Assurance and Cyber Security Strategy of Jordan. Dr. Otoom obtained professional training in Singapore, Britain, Austria and the United States and has a set of professional international certificates in addition to a set of published peer-reviewed research.

Priyanshu Pattanaik is pursuing fourth year B.Tech CSE in Vellore Institute of Technology, Chennai. His research interest include Cryptography, Network Security, Artificial Intelligence

Sumathi Pawar is an Associate Professor in NMAMIT, Nitte, Karkala. 19 years teaching experience and 10 years research experience.

Baraa Qaddoumi received the B.E. degree in Software Engineering from the Zarqa University, Jordan, in 2013, the M.Sc. degree in Software Engineering from Hashmite University, Jordan, in 2017, He is currently Instructor with the Information technology Department, ASU, Amman, Jordan. His research interests include cyber security, cognitive networks, parallel processing, cloud computing, machine learning, and real time multimedia communication over the Internet

S. Ayeswarya received the M.S. degree in software engineering and the Master of Technology degree from Vellore Institute of Technology (VIT) University, Vellore, India, in 2015 and 2020, respectively. She is currently serving as a dedicated Research Scholar with VIT. Her primary research interests include around the exploration of continuous user authentication systems and reflecting her deep-seated passion for advancing security measures in modern technology.

Kevin Sebastin is pursuing fourth year B.Tech CSE in Vellore Institute of Technology, Chennai. His research interest include Cryptography, Analysis of Algorithms, Artificial Intelligence

Shahid Shah I have obtained my PhD degree in Information Technology with research focus on Artificial Intelligence and Machine Learning based systems. I have worked different diverse areas of research like Medical Imaging, Ethical AI, Signal Processing, Speech Recognition, Dialect Based Systems, Pervasive Computing, Blockchain Technologies etc. I have more that 15 years of teaching and Research

Experience. Currently i am working as an Associate Professor with Hamdard University, Karachi, Pakistan.

K. John Singh received Ph.D degree in the Faculty of Information and Communication Engineering from Anna University, Chennai, India in 2013. He received M.S degree in Information Technology from Manonmaniam Sundaranar University, Tirunelveli, India in 2002 and M.Tech degree in Computer and Information Technology from Center for Information Technology and Engineering of Manonmaniam Sundaranar University, Tirunelveli, India in 2004. Currently, he is working as Associate Professor in the School of Information Technology and Engineering, VIT University, Vellore, India. His research interests include Network Security, Cloud Security and Image Processing. He has published several papers in journals and conferences.

Ashiq Noor Sudheer is pursuing B.Tech final year in Vellore Institute of Technology, Chennai.His research interest include Cryptography, Network Security, Machine Learning and Artificial Intelligence

Praneetha Surapaneni done BTech and MTech degrees in Computer Science from VRSEC – Velagapudi Ramakrishna Siddhartha Engineering, Acharya Nagarjuna University, Vijayawada, in 2008 and 2011, respectively. She is working toward a PhD at SRM University-AP, Amaravati, AP. She has ten years of teaching experience. Her research includes the security in Intelligent Vehicles, BlockChain Technology and Machine Learning.

Omar H. Tarawneh is a highly accomplished professional with extensive academic achievements and a strong background in computer science. Born in Al-Karak, Jordan, he earned his Bachelor's degree in Computer Science from Mu'tah University in 2003. Subsequently, he pursued a Master's degree in Computer Information Systems at the University of Arab Academy for Banking and Financial Sciences (AABFS) in Amman, Jordan, graduating with honors in 2006. In 2015, he completed his Ph.D. in Software Engineering from the University of Utara in Kedah, Malaysia. From 2003 to 2008, Omar held teaching and training positions at the Ministry of Education, contributing his expertise to educational initiatives. He further expanded his professional experience by serving as a lecturer at Kuala Lumpur University (UniKL) in Malaysia and as a Research Assistant at the University of Utara Malaysia for nearly two years. Later, he assumed the role of Associate Professor and Head of the Information Technology Department at Al Zahra College for Women in Muscat, Oman. Currently, Omar holds the esteemed position of Associate Professor at Amman Arab University in Amman, Jordan. In addition, he takes on the responsibility of Acting Head of the Software Engineering

Department. His research interests span a diverse range of subjects, including Quantum Computation, Software Quality and Certification, Fuzzy Logic, Software Development, Multi-Criteria Decision Making, and Quality Assurance. With over 30 technical publications to his name, Dr. Omar H. Tarawneh has made valuable contributions to his field. Dr. Tarawneh's expertise is highly regarded in the academic community, and he serves as an esteemed member of the reviewer panel for renowned journals such as IEEE ACCESS and Computer Communications. Through his extensive educational background, notable positions, and significant research contributions, Dr. Omar H. Tarawneh has established himself as a respected professional in the field of computer science.

Amit Thakur is a passionate scholar currently pursuing a Ph.D. in Machine Learning at VIT BHOPAL University. With a background in computer science and a fascination for artificial intelligence, Amit's research focuses on developing innovative algorithms for natural language processing and computer vision applications. Throughout his academic journey, Amit has demonstrated a strong aptitude for theoretical and applied research in machine learning. His work combines advanced mathematical techniques with practical implementations to address real-world challenges in data analysis and pattern recognition. In addition to his research endeavors, Amit is actively involved in teaching and mentoring undergraduate students, sharing his knowledge and enthusiasm for machine learning. He volunteers his time to organize workshops and seminars, fostering a collaborative learning environment within the academic community. Driven by a desire to harness the power of machine learning for societal benefit, Amit is dedicated to pushing the boundaries of AI research and developing intelligent systems that can positively impact people's lives. Through his interdisciplinary approach and commitment to excellence, Amit strives to be a leading figure in the field of machine learning and contribute to its continued advancement.

Gautham Vidyashankar is pursuing fourth year B.Tech CSE in Vellore Institute of Technology, Chennai.His research interest include Cryptography, Cyber Security, Artificial Intelligence

Winfred Yaokumah is a researcher and senior faculty at the Department of Computer Science of the University of Ghana. He has published several articles in highly rated journals including Information and Computer Security, Information Resources Management Journal, IEEE Xplore, International Journal of Human Capital and Information Technology, International Journal of Human Capital and Information Technology Professionals, International Journal of Technology and Human Interaction, International Journal of e-Business Research, International

Journal of Enterprise Information Systems, Journal of Information Technology Research, International Journal of Information Systems in the Service Sector, and Education and Information Technologies. His research interest includes cyber security, cyber ethics, network security, and information systems security and governance. He serves as a member of the International Review Board for the International Journal of Technology Diffusion.

Index

Symbols

A

B

C

T

U

V

Z

www.ingramcontent.com/pod-product-compliance
Lightning Source LLC
LaVergne TN
LVHW080612300926
849162LV00005B/1135

* 9 7 9 8 3 6 9 3 8 0 1 4 7 *